THE TRUTH ABOUT WYATT EARP

by

Richard E. Erwin

SECOND EDITION

Manufactured in the United States of America

ISBN 0-9633930-2-2

Library of Congress 92-085048

Published by   THE O.K. PRESS
                 P.O. Box 203
                 Carpinteria, CA 93014

DEDICATION

This book is dedicated to my wife, Lyla B. Erwin, my daughter, Elizabeth Erwin Davison, and to my son, Richard E. Erwin, II.

ACKNOWLEDGEMENTS

I owe a lot of people a debt of gratitude for the assistance they gave me in ferreting out the truth about Wyatt Earp. Unfortunately space will not permit me to name all of them, but among those that have been most helpful and whose information I most appreciated are Carl Chafin of Culver City, California, who is probably the best informed person alive on the history of Tombstone. He provided me with priceless information, documents and records dealing with the history of Tombstone.

Glenn G. Boyer is one of the best researchers and an indefatigable writer on the Earps and their activities. He very generously supplied me with many of the articles he had written about the Earps and, of course, I relied heavily on his writings and research in preparing this book.

The history of the Kansas cow towns could not have been told with any degree of accuracy without relying on the writings of Nyle H. Miller and Joseph Snell of the Kansas State Historical Society, Topeka, Kansas.

Powell Greenland, author of A History of Port Hueneme, found the Clantons in Port Hueneme, California for me.

Robert K. DeArment's Bat Masterson, Dale T. Schoenberger's The Gunfighters and Paula Mitchell Marks' And Die in the West were all very helpful to me in sorting out and evaluating the conflicting stories told about Wyatt Earp.

I want to especially thank Lori Davisson, Research Assistant at the Arizona Historical Society, and Peter L. Steere, Manuscript Librarian at the University of Arizona Library, for their most helpful assistance in locating old documents, newspapers and manuscripts that were so helpful in putting this book together.

Finally, I must not overlook the contribution of Loren Nicholson of San Luis Obispo. He did a marvelous job of editing and revising my manuscript and putting it in shape for publication.

To all of them, I express my utmost thanks.

RICHARD E. ERWIN

TABLE OF CONTENTS

TABLE OF CONTENTS (Continued)

TABLE OF CONTENTS (Continued)

LIST OF EXHIBITS IN APPENDIX 1

Exhibit

1. Oath of office of U.S. Marshal executed by Virgil Earp at Tucson, Arizona.

2. Appointment of Wyatt Earp as Deputy Sheriff of Pima County.

3. Wyatt Earp's resignation as Deputy Sheriff of Pima County.

WYATT EARP Photo taken when he was in his 70's.
Autographed copy of this picture presented to
western movie star William S. Hart hangs in his
museum at Newhall, California
(Courtesy of Arizona Historical Society)

WYATT EARP and BAT MASTERSON
In their younger days at Dodge City
(Courtesy of Arizona Historical Society)

CHAPTER I

CREATORS AND DEBUNKERS OF THE WYATT EARP MYTH

WYATT Earp was born at Monmouth, Illinois on March 19, 1848. He died at Los Angeles, California on January 13, 1929. Between those two dates the American west was settled. The Indians were conquered and placed on reservations. The buffalo were exterminated. The California gold rush came and went, leaving California a populated and thriving state. The gold and silver mining rushes of the Northwest and the Southwest as well as Alaska ebbed and flowed and the phenomenon of the great cattle drives and rise and fall of the western cattle industry had their day.

Wyatt Earp lived through all of these exciting and historic times and had more than his share of personal experience in the winning and taming of the west. By the time he died in Los Angeles, the country was crisscrossed by railroads. America had fought and won the Spanish American War and World War I. Highways were becoming useable. The automobile had taken the place of the horse and carriage and many cities had public transportation systems. The telegraph, telephone and radio were in everyday use. Lindbergh had flown across the Atlantic. In short, the modern world was in the process of emerging.

In the 1920s, the public began to realize that the ranks of the old timers who had actively participated in the winning of the West and the establishment of modern civilization was rapidly thinning out, and there arose a great interest in recording the stories and recollections of those still surviving.

For many years, fiction writers had been creating western heroes and bad men out of pure or almost pure fiction. They sometimes had the names of some of the characters and possibly the occasions right, but in the main such writers as Ned Buntline thrived on writing stories about Buffalo Bill Cody, Wild Bill Hickock, Bat Masterson and Wyatt Earp that had no basis whatever in fact, but that were somehow accepted as history by much of the public.

Then, in 1931 a writer by the name of Stuart N. Lake created a whole new industry. He wrote what purported to be a true and authentic biography of Wyatt Earp entitled WYATT EARP, FRONTIER MARSHAL. The new industry was an attempt by various authors and researchers to prove either that Earp was the all-round greatest gunman and lawman the West ever produced, or that he was a crook, a thief, a liar and a murderer, and that his biographer had deliberately misrepresented the character and conduct of Wyatt Earp and had created a fictitious character out of the whole cloth.

In order to understand how Stuart Lake created the new industry, it is necessary to set out his Foreword to the Earp biography in full:

"Wyatt Earp was a man of action. He was born, reared, and lived in an environment which held words and theories of small account, in which sheer survival often, and eminence invariably, might be achieved through deeds alone. With all, Wyatt Earp was a thinking man, whose mental processes were as quick, as direct, as unflustered by circumstances and as effective as the actions they inspired.

"The man won from contemporaries who were his most competent judges - from intimates, from acquaintances, and from enemies alike - frontier-wide recognition as the most proficient peace officer, the greatest gun-fighting marshal that the Old West knew. He attained this eminence through the only method his time and place might comprehend. Wherefore, this narrative of Wyatt Earp's career, this account of his rise of forty-five-caliber dominance over cowtown and mining camp in the Red Decade of the Southwest, is set forth largely in terms of what Wyatt Earp did.

"To the lover of swift and decisive action, Wyatt Earp's achievements surely must be of interest in themselves. His taming of Mannen Clements and fifty cowboy killers in the streets of Wichita; his play against Clay Allison of the Washita in the Plaza at Dodge City; his protection of insignificant Johnny-Behind-the-Deuce against a Tombstone mob; the sanguinary battle of the O.K. Corral, possibly the most celebrated gun-fight in frontier history; or his sawed-off shotgun duel with Curly Bill - tales of these exploits could not fail, even were they meaningless, to stir a reader's blood. Through them Wyatt Earp moves steadily, surely, sagaciously, implacably on, guided by a philosophy fitted to his surroundings, to which he gave fullest expression in admonishment of Ike Clanton, braggart, outlaw, cow thief, and murderer.

"'Go on home, Ike,' Wyatt suggested in the face of Clanton's threats to gun the marshal; 'you talk too much for a fighting man.'

"In themselves, these things that Wyatt Earp did made him a myth of his own era, a legend while he lived, in mouth to mouth sagas of the West. But the judgement of the years has awarded a higher honor to the man. He no longer stands simply an unbelievable courageous figure distinguished by fabulous feats of arms and an extraordinary domination over men. In true perspective he is recognized as something more, as an epitomizing symbol of a powerful factor - an economic factor, if you will - all important in the history of the Western United States of America. The Old West cannot be understood unless Wyatt Earp also is understood. More than any other man of record in his time, possibly, he represents the exact combination of breeding and human experience which laid the foundations of Western empire. His genius is less an accident than an inevitable expression; Wyatt Earp is less an effect than a cause.

"Since Wyatt Earp has so long been a myth to lovers of the Old West, it is no more than fair to state definitely that this biography is in no part a mythic tale. It would be less than fair to subject and to reader if any least resource or effort had been spared in seeking the utmost accuracy of fact. Scores of eye-witnesses to the scenes portrayed have been interviewed to verify circumstantial details; thousands of miles have been traveled to unearth substantiating material; hundreds of time-worn documents and files of frontier newspapers have been examined for pertinent content; literally thousands of letters have been exchanged with competent old-timers in developing this work.

"The book had inception in an observation by Bat Masterson, more than twenty years ago.

"'The real story of the Old West can never be told,' Bat said, 'unless Wyatt Earp will tell what he knows; and Wyatt will not talk.'

"Happily, time and circumstances combined to bring Masterson's foreboding to naught, and Wyatt Earp was persuaded to devote the closing months of his long life to the narration of his full story, to a firsthand and factual account of his career. It is upon this account that the succeeding pages are entirely based.

"I make these statements, not in a spirit of pride, but in memory of that retiring, world-weary old gentleman with whom so many hours devoted to the work of compilation were spent. In view of the responsibility to him and to the reader which our association involves - a responsibility, I should add, which never was absent from his mind - my own feeling in offering the life-story of Wyatt Earp, Frontier Marshal, is one of notable inadequacy in the presence of the material of which this book is made."

STUART LAKE[1]

An examination of Mr. Lake's Forward might very well lead anyone of a suspicious frame of mind to suspect that he may be over-stating the qualities, character and conduct of his subject. In fact, several would-be historians have gone so far as to label Wyatt Earp and Stuart N. Lake fabricators and liars and, in the process of protesting the alleged good qualities of Wyatt Earp, have made charges and allegations of fraud and misconduct that are as far or farther off the mark than the writings of Mr. Lake.

I have divided these would-be historians into three categories.

---

[1]   Stuart N. Lake, <u>Wyatt Earp Frontier Marshal</u>, Forward p. vii-x.

ONE: The Myth makers.

TWO: The Earp bashers.

THREE: Those who told their story to the best of their ability.

CATEGORY ONE: THE MYTH MAKERS.

In this category I place Stuart N. Lake first and foremost. While not all he said about Wyatt Earp was false or fictitious, neither was it all true. The primary purpose of this book is to separate one from the other. In this category I would also have to place Walter Noble Burns whose book Tombstone pre-dated Lake's book by four years. Burns was a wonderful story teller, but not a very good historian. His stories went a long way toward fictionalizing Wyatt Earp's story and seem to have laid the groundwork for some of the stories told by Lake.

Also, in this category I would have to place John Myers, author of the books, The Last Chance and Doc Holliday. On first examination, Myers' books appear to be well researched and authenticated, but upon careful examination one finds that they are a re-hash of Walter Noble Burns and Stuart N. Lake. Almost nothing new is added, and there are some contradictions that will be explained later.

CATEGORY 2: THE EARP BASHERS.

There have been many authors who would fit into this category. Foremost among them, because his book appears to bear the stamp of authenticity, would have to be Frank Waters and his book The Earp Brothers of Tombstone.

Waters book is purportedly based on a long series of interviews with the widow of Wyatt's brother, Virgil Earp, known to him as Aunt Allie, plus substantial research supposed to verify the statements made to him by Mrs. Earp. In the introduction to his book, he tells how he met and dug the story out of Aunt Allie, and how after almost completing the book he was threatened with a lawsuit by Wyatt Earp's widow, and also ran into a lack of cooperation on the part of Aunt Allie. As a result, he decided against publishing the book and deposited the manuscript in the Arizona Pioneers' Historical Society in Tucson merely as a valuable record for its files. He cites The Arizona Pioneer Historical Society files more than 20 times in his book. Some of the citations refer to his own manuscript.

Glenn G. Boyer in the Editor's Epilogue to I Married Wyatt Earp, said of Waters' book: "Allie, who had adored her husband, repudiated the manuscript as a bunch of lies and threatened to sue if Waters published. Significantly, Waters' book did not appear until thirteen years after Allie had died and sixteen years after Josie had passed away."[1]

This is merely conjecture, but what I think really happened was this: Virgil's widow, Aunt Allie, entered into an agreement with Frank Waters to tell him of the exciting history of the Earp Brothers upon the assumption, if not on the express promise, that he would write the story in such a way as to show that her husband was the real hero and that Wyatt was always second fiddle, which was probably true in some cases. In writing the story Waters could not quite do that to her satisfaction, and, in fact, ended up making all of the Earps out as gunmen, desperados, robbers, crooks and lightweights. She balked. A short quote from Waters introduction will illustrate my point. Regarding the Earps, Waters said:

"Warren was a youth in his twenties when in Tombstone. He later became a stage driver, and was shot and killed during a drunken quarrel in a saloon."[2] The Coroner's Jury at Wilcox, Arizona called it self defense. Wyatt Earp called it murder.[3]

"Virgil was a wandering stage driver, ranch hand, prospector, and town marshal. In Tombstone he was ambushed at night outside a saloon, shot and maimed. Throughout the rest of his life he roamed the West, prospecting vainly for gold, and died unknown." (That was not a very flattering description of Virgil Earp, and certainly not one with which his widow would agree.)

"Wyatt was an itinerant saloon-keeper, card shark, gunman, bigamist, church deacon, policeman, bunco artist, and a supreme confidence man. A lifelong exhibitionist ridiculed alike by members of his own family, neighbors, contemporaries, and the public press, he lived his last years in poverty, still vainly trying to find someone to publicize his life, and died two years before his fictitious biography recast him in the role of America's most famous frontier marshal."[4]

It is obvious from reading Waters' book that he set out to prove the truth of the above statements. He very obviously had a point of view that he wanted to sell. Where two or more stories of any given event were available, he always chose to tell the one that reflected the most poorly on the Earps, and particularly on Wyatt Earp.

The second most prominent Earp Basher is Ed Bartholomew, an author from whom little has been heard. He wrote two books about Wyatt Earp, the first being <u>Wyatt Earp, The Untold Story, 1848 to</u>

---

[1]   Glen E. Boyer, <u>I Married Wyatt Earp</u>, P. 254.

[2]   <u>The Earp Brothers of Tombstone</u>, p. 7.

[3]   <u>I Married Wyatt Earp</u>, p. 196.

[4]   <u>The Earp Brothers of Tombstone</u>, p. 7

1880, published in 1963, and the second, Wyatt Earp, 1879 to 1882, The Man and the Myth, published in 1964. The inside cover of his first book pretty well tells what his objectives were when he set out to research the life of Wyatt Earp. It says:

"This book is the result of years of research in the early archives of the American West and for the first time the true story of the fabled Wyatt Earp is here told.

"This book, through the hundreds of documentary sources, brings about the unmasking of the much heralded legendary Western gunfighter. The author has spared not time and travel in his search for the documented facts; his travels over the West have been unrelenting; his patient study of hundreds of here-to-fore hidden archives and records has been done with the eye of the historian, the reporter. He has leveled his six-shooter at the Earp myth and has blasted it to shreds.

"Here is told 'The Untold Story,' told objectively, and unvarnished - the records of time have spoken."[1]

A cursory examination of his books might lead one to believe that here is the greatest researcher of all time. He has undoubtedly spent a great deal of time and effort in researching the records, but time and time again has come up with the wrong conclusion, or an unwarranted conclusion based on what he found. It's unfortunate too, because here is a man who really could have written a good, objective, factual book had he been willing to let the records speak for themselves, but he was apparently so determined to destroy what he considered to be the Earp myth that he put an adverse spin on almost every fact that turned up in his research. He engaged in adverse speculation and invariably sought to use the tactics of guilt by association in order to degrade Wyatt Earp.

It is little wonder that good, hard-working, legitimate authors who have tried to dig out the truth from the myths seldom, if ever, cite his books or research as authority for any fact that they purport to support. This is true even when he occasionally came up with some real pay dirt, such as the indictment of Wyatt Earp for horse stealing in the Western District of Arkansas on the 8th day of May 1871. Because of his obvious bias and prejudice, other authors have shied away from that story. I've checked it out and it may be true. More about it later.

Another Earp basher, Ramon F. Adams, whose book Burrs Under the Saddle is on par with Bartholomew, is responsible for disseminating many of the totally false stories that continue to find their way as facts into Earp literature. One example should be

---

[1]   Wyatt, Earp, The Untold Story 1848 to 1880, Inside Cover.

enough to alert the reader to view any purported factual statement by him with caution. Commenting on Lake's story of Earp's life, he said: "The trouble with these exploits is that none of them, except the O.K. Corral fight, took place, and this one was a case of murder, the shooting of men while their hands were up."

Odie B. Faulk has also written a couple of books and numerous articles about Tombstone and the Earps. None are well researched or well authenticated. Most of them are anti-Earp.

CATEGORY THREE: THOSE WHO TOLD THEIR STORY TO THE BEST OF THEIR ABILITY.

Another author, Glen G. Boyer, is hard to classify. He is an important researcher and writer and he mostly told the story to the best of his ability. Author of <u>The Suppressed Murder of Wyatt Earp</u>, published in 1967, he seemed to be anti-Earp, blaming him almost entirely for the death of his second wife, Mattie. He readily admits that he never could find a record of their marriage, although there is little question that she lived with Wyatt at Dodge City and came to Tombstone with him. She may have been one of the three women -- Sallie, Bessie and Eva Earp -- who were arrested and fined in 1874 at Wichita, Kansas, for operating or being in a bawdy house or brothel.[1] She was a known friend and associate of Big Nose Kate Fisher, a reputed prostitute and either wife or paramour of Doc Holliday.

Mattie left Tombstone with the exodus of most of the Earps when Virgil and his wife went by train to take the body of Morgan Earp to the Earp parents for burial at Colton California.[2] Her movements from that time until her death several years later near Globe, Arizona as a result of an accidental or intentional overdose of narcotics are shrouded in mystery. At a coroner's inquest, there was testimony that before she died she had made a statement blaming Wyatt Earp for her downfall and by implication for her death. In his book, Boyer takes the position that Wyatt Earp ruthlessly abandoned Mattie and took up with a young lady by the name of Josephine Sarah Marcus who at the time was the girl friend and paramour of Sheriff John Behan. This conduct on the part of Wyatt Earp, according to Boyer, was reprehensible, and rated being designated as murder, when she apparently took her own life. He doesn't seem to give Wyatt much credit for having married the Josephine Sarah Marcus girl and remaining devoted to her until his death on January 13, 1929.

Mr. Boyer wrote a number of articles for the Frontier Times and Real West in which he displayed unusual ability in digging a story out

---

[1]   <u>Great Gunfighters of the Kansas Cowtowns</u>, p. 79

[2]   <u>The Earp Brothers of Tombstone</u>, p. 194

of the past. In one, he shows the early relationship between Josephine Sarah Marcus and both John Behan and Wyatt Earp, which by implication set the stage for the Earp-Behan feud.[1] In those stories he appeared to be neither an Earp basher nor a Myth maker. He seems to have done an outstanding job of research and reporting. As collector and editor of the recollections of Josephine Sarah Marcus Earp in the book I Married Wyatt Earp, Glenn G. Boyer did a superb job of research and his Historical Notes and Editorial Comments at the end of each chapter are most informative and enlightening.

Many of the contemporaries of Wyatt Earp, both in the Kansas cowtowns and at Tombstone, wrote or dictated their memoirs which were later published. In order to make any realistic evaluation of the life and character of Wyatt Earp, it is necessary to study and consider these books along with the relationship of the writers to Wyatt Earp, and their possible bias, interest or prejudice for or against him.

Among the most prominent of these to be considered are:

Bat Masterson by **Richard O'Connor** (1957). Bat Masterson first met Wyatt Earp in the early 1870's when they were both engaged in buffalo hunting. They became fast friends and worked together in Dodge City. Afterward Masterson spent some time in Tombstone while Wyatt Earp was there. They remained friends and kept some contact with each other until Bat Masterson's death on October 25, 1921. Of course Bat Masterson only speaks highly of Wyatt Earp because that's the way he saw him, but many of the things in his book may be used to either verify or dispute some of the things said by other authors about Wyatt Earp.

George Whitwell Parsons. During Earp's stay at Tombstone one of the residents, George Whitwell Parsons, kept a fairly detailed journal of the events that occurred there. He later moved to Los Angeles, California, and engaged in business, becoming one of the organizers of the Los Angeles Chamber of Commerce and a member of it's board of directors for many years. His diary is considered by most authors and researchers to be one of the most honest and unbiased chronicles of the exciting events in Tombstone.

William M. Breakenridge, author of his autobiography entitled Helldorodo, (1928). Breakenridge was in and about Tombstone during the time the Earps were there. During a part of the time he was a deputy to Sheriff John Behan. Although some authors consider him to be an Earp basher, I don't consider him as such. It seems to me that considering his natural bias, interest and prejudice as a member of the Earp opposition and his natural desire to make himself look good, he told his story "perhaps to the best of his ability." Much

---

[1]   "Johnny Behan, Assistant Folk Hero, Real West, April 1881."

of what he wrote verifies to some degree the story told by the Earps and discloses the machinations of Sheriff Behan.

John P. Clum. He was Editor of the <u>Tombstone Epitaph</u>, and the third Mayor of Tombstone.[1] He was an Earp supporter all the way. He wrote a small book entitled, <u>It All Happened in Tombstone</u>, in which he detailed some of the controversial events that took place in Tombstone during the Earp period. Clum maintained a lifelong friendship with Wyatt Earp and had contacts with him in Alaska and California. He was one of the pallbearers at Earp's funeral in January 1929. Considering his personal friendship and the fact that they were on the same side of the Tombstone troubles, it can only be said that he told the story "perhaps to the best of his ability."

Fred Dodge. He shows up in the stories about Tombstone as the man about town, always present when anything untoward happened, always willing to lend a hand to law enforcement officers. He appeared to be making his living as a gambler and bartender. Years later, it turned out that all that time he was working as an undercover agent for Wells Fargo. As such an agent, it was his business to know what was going on and who was doing what. It is quite obvious that he told his story to the best of his ability, considering that he waited about 50 years to tell it. Dodge was in communication with Stuart N. Lake for a number of years before his death in 1938 at the age of 84. Lake had collected material on Fred Dodge for years with the intention of publishing a biography similar to the one he published on Wyatt Earp; however he never got around to it before he died in 1964. After his death his daughter, Carolyn, discovered her father's files on Fred Dodge. By that time she had become an accomplished author in her own right. She undertook to edit and publish the Dodge papers in a book entitled <u>Under Cover for Wells Fargo</u>, (1969). The book has to be a goldmine of first hand witness accounts of many of the controversial events that occurred in Tombstone. Since he remained friends with Wyatt Earp and stayed in communication with him right up to the time of his death, I suppose one could suspect a little prejudice in favor of Earp, but on the whole, his story seems to be honest and credible.

In addition to the books described above there have been several other books published that are extremely valuable to any researcher. When trying to unscramble the conflicting stories about various events, reference to these books is almost a must. They are:

<u>Tombstone's Epitaph</u> by Douglas D. Martin, published in 1951. This is an examination and reprinting with appropriate comments of some of the files of the Tombstone Epitaph. It solves some problems

---

[1]   After William A. Harwood and Alder Randall.

and creates others, but it serves to show how some of the conflicting stories came about.

Great Gunfighters of the Kansas Cowtowns, 1867-1886, by Nyle H. Miller and Joseph W. Snell, published in 1967. This book reprints most of the major news stories of the Kansas towns during the period that it covers. It is an excellent place to check up on the authenticity of other authors' stories.

The Earps Talk, edited by Alford E. Turner, published in 1980. Since the Earps are sometimes accused of being great liars and exaggerators, Mr. Turner has done historical researchers a great service by publishing everything that he could find that the Earps had said for publication. A study of The Earps Talk will sometimes tell you whether certain statements attributed to the Earps were actually made by them or were invented by someone else.

The O.K. Corral Inquest, also edited by Alford E. Turner, published in 1981, is a reprint of the records of the Coroner's Inquest held on the bodies of William Clanton, Frank McLaury and Thomas McLaury, killed in the so-called battle of the O.K. Corral, and of the testimony of the witnesses at the preliminary hearing of Wyatt Earp, Virgil Earp, Morgan Earp and Doc Holliday on the charge of murder committed in that shoot out.

And Die in the West, by Paula Mitchell Marks, published in 1989 is the best effort yet to examine the events surrounding the Earps and their activities in Tombstone.

She does not attempt to cover Wyatt Earp's life before or after Tombstone, but as to the Arizona phase of his life she has done a superb job of research. If there is any criticism of the book, it would be that she fails to give very good citations for the source of her information.

She has made the best analysis of the shoot-out at the O.K. Corral and the resultant court proceedings of any author that has attempted it and certainly better, and in more detail than this author expects to, except the reprinting of some of the transcript of the hearings.

Wyatt Earp, by John Henry Flood, an unpublished manuscript dated 1926 should be, but is not one of the best sources of information about Wyatt Earp. Flood was doubtless a personal friend and associate of Wyatt for many years. In the foreword of his manuscript he says that the story was dictated personally by Wyatt Earp and that "It is the only authoritative history that has been given to the world and turns at last the golden key of silence, and opens for all the story of Wyatt Earp."

Unfortunately, that is somewhat of an exaggeration. He misses completely many important events in Wyatt Earp's life and many of his stories are at odds with known and provable facts. He was never able to get his manuscript published and it remains today an unpublished manuscript. Nevertheless, because of his long friendship with Wyatt Earp and his claim that it was personally dictated by Wyatt, it remains an interesting source for anyone trying to search out the truth about Wyatt Earp.

In writing this book, it is my intention to examine the conflicting stories told by many of the authors and compare them, one to another and to any other records, such as court or official records or contemporary newspaper reports, and then comment on what I think the facts probably were. In order to do this, it will be necessary to provide a general outline of the lives of the Earp brothers.

CHAPTER II

FAMILY ORIGIN AND EARLY BEGINNINGS

THE roots of the Earp family run deep in the early American frontier. They were known to be in Virginia and the Carolinas at an early date, and then migrated to Texas, Arkansas, Missouri, Indiana and Illinois. The father of Wyatt, Nicholas Earp, was born in North Carolina on September 6, 1813. He was the son of Walter Earp and Martha Earp who had eight other children. Nicholas married Abigail Storm in 1836. There was one son of this marriage, Newton, born October 7, 1837. When he was about two years old his mother died. The following year, on July 30, 1840, Nicholas married Victoria Ann Cooksley. This marriage produced five sons who were destined to be known in the future as the fighting Earps. They were:

James C. Earp, born June 28, 1841 in Kentucky.
Virgil W. Earp born July 18, 1843 in Kentucky.
Wyatt Berry Stapp Earp, born March 19, 1848 in Illinois.
Morgan Earp, born April 24, 1851 in Marion County, Iowa.
Warren Earp, born March 9, 1855 at Pella, Iowa.

After James and Virgil were born, the family moved from Kentucky to Monmouth, Warren County, Illinois. Here, Nicholas worked a farm, opened a saloon, became popular with the locals and became a Justice of the Peace. It was also from here that he joined the Illinois Mounted Volunteers in 1847 to serve under his neighbor, Wyatt Berry Stapp. He went with his unit to Mexico and was injured and discharged from the service on December 24, 1847. Thereafter his movements are fairly traceable by his pension records.

He must have had a great admiration for his commanding officer, for when his wife gave birth to a boy on March 19, 1848, he gave him the full name of his former commander, Wyatt Berry Stapp.

The Earps, along with much of America, were always on the frontier. Soon after the close of the Mexican War, Nicholas and Victoria moved their ever growing brood farther west to Lake Prairie Township near Pella, Iowa. Here, Nicholas started a farm and opened a harness repair shop in Pella. Again, he soon became well acquainted with the populace and was appointed Justice of the Peace and a Notary Public. Here, also, his last two sons were born, Morgan on April 21, 1851, and Warren on March 9, 1855. One other child, a girl named Adelia, was born in 1861. She married a man by the name of Edwards.

In the late 1850s, Nicholas Earp succumbed to the urge to move farther west. He sold out his holdings in Lake Prairie Township, Iowa, and headed for Missouri where he made either an unsuccessful or unsatisfactory try at establishing another farming enterprise. At any rate, by early 1860, he and his family were back in Pella, Iowa.

It was here that in February 1860, Virgil Earp, then 17 years of age, created quite a stir by running away and marrying a neighbor girl named Ellen Rysdam. She was even younger than he. They supposedly kept the marriage secret until a daughter was born, but Virgil certainly was not welcomed back into the family and as one might imagine, he was in deep trouble. This situation may have had something to do with his joining the 83rd Illinois Infantry on August 21, 1862.

He stayed in the army until the end of the Civil War and was mustered out on June 26, 1865. In the meantime, his young wife, having heard that he had died, went west with her family where they settled in Washington Territory. Believing Virgil to be dead, she remarried and never saw him again. Many years later, the daughter got in touch with Virgil and they were reunited. She eventually claimed his body when he died in 1905 and had him buried in the Riverview cemetery at Portland, Oregon.

Other Earps fought in the Civil War. Newton, the eldest half brother, enlisted in the Fourth Cavalry, Iowa Volunteers on November 11, 1861. He was mustered out of the service at Louisville, Kentucky on June 26, 1865. James joined the 17th Illinois Infantry, Company F on May 18, 1861. He was discharged in 1863 for disability after having been wounded in battle. Like his father, his movements thereafter can be traced to some extent by his government pension records.

During the Civil War, while three of Nicholas Earp's sons fought for the North, he succeeded in getting appointed U.S. Provost Marshal at Pella, Iowa. In 1863, while the war still raged, he threw up his government job, pulled stakes and organized a wagon train for a trek to California. It has been said that this ox-drawn wagon train was comprised of about forty wagons and a hundred and fifty people. Wyatt Earp, then about sixteen years of age, his younger brothers and his older brother, James Earp, traveled with the train. The Earp train left Omaha, Nebraska in the spring of 1864. Wyatt fixed the date as May 12th.[1]

The trek across the plains to San Bernardino, California was hard, but exciting for a sixteen year old boy. Wyatt apparently assumed the burdens of a grown man -- driving the oxen, hunting game, fighting Indians and all the other responsibilities of such a

---

[1]   Wyatt Earp, Frontier Marshal, p. 19

journey. The trip was undoubtedly a good training ground for Wyatt, teaching him the ways and means for survival in those times and places. The journey ended on December 19, 1864 when they dropped down out of Cajon Pass and into San Bernardino, seven months and seven days from Council Bluffs, according to Stuart N. Lake.[1]

Nicholas Earp purchased land about twelve miles from San Bernardino which later became part of the city of Redlands. He also acquired acreage in what later became part of the city of San Bernardino. Although he left for a couple of years to dispose of his properties in the midwest, he always thereafter considered San Bernardino County to be his home. According to Wyatt, he headed the San Bernardino County Pioneer Society, was elected Justice of the Peace and served in that capacity for many years until his retirement.

According to Lake, the following year Wyatt got a job driving stage for General Phineas Banning between Los Angeles and San Bernardino, and afterward he worked for Frank Binkley driving a ten-animal team hauling freight between the port of San Pedro and Prescott, Arizona. This was a long, rough journey. The schedule allowed only twenty days for the trip of four hundred fifty miles. In this work, Wyatt undoubtedly continued improving his capacity to handle hardships and survive in the unfriendly world of the frontier country.

Of this work, Lake says: "Binkley, a noted frontier character, demanded just four qualities in a driver for each of the fifteen teams which ordinarily made up an Arizona train. First the ability to handle half-broken horses and mules well enough to make Prescott on schedule without injuring the animals; second, the physical strength and stamina to withstand great hardship; third, unerring skill with rifle and pistol; fourth, dauntless courage. As a rule, only drivers of seasoned maturity were hired for the Binkley trains."[2]

In the spring of 1866, Wyatt joined the freight outfit of Chris Taylor, a celebrated frontier wagonmaster driving a sixteen-animal outfit between San Bernardino and Salt Lake City. This was a rather hazardous route across burning deserts and through Indian country covering a distance of more than 700 miles.

According to Lake, when Wyatt returned from the Salt Lake trip he was chosen as one of a select group of freighters by San Bernardino County Sheriff, John King, to go to the rescue of a small detachment of U.S. Cavalry soldiers surrounded and trapped by

---

[1]   Ibid, p. 21

[2]   Wyatt Earp, Frontier Marshal, p. 23

several hundred Paiute Indians at Camp Cadiz. Bartholomew places Camp Cadiz in Nevada and makes fun of the whole episode, strongly implying that it never happened.[1]

Like so many of Lake's tales, there was just a bare modicum of fact on which to hang his story. In almost every respect, he was in error with this one. The criticism by Bartholomew wasn't based on a very good job of research either, since he didn't do anything but criticize the claim of Stuart N. Lake and Wyatt Earp about the story that Earp had assisted Sheriff John King in rescuing a regiment of soldiers from the Nevada desert.

The truth of the matter is that no such incident ever occurred in Camp Cadiz which Lake locates in California and Bartholomew located in Nevada. There was no Army outpost by the name of Camp Cadiz. However, there was a Camp Cady. There was an incident that occurred at Camp Cady in the later part of July, 1866 that supplied the fodder for Lake's story, but none of the reports substantiate any part of Lake's story. Dennis G. Casebier, who has done more research on the Mojave desert than almost any other living person, wrote a small book entitled The Battle at Camp Cady which was published in 1972. Casebier says there was a Camp Cady located on the banks of the Mojave River, far out in the Great Mojave Desert. On Sunday, June 29, 1866, the camp was commanded by a young second lieutenant by the name of James R. Hardenbergh. On that day, he led a platoon of six men in an attack on a band of Pah-Ute Indians who were passing the camp. His little group was soundly defeated. Three were killed outright and one was severely wounded and carried back to the fort. At the conclusion of the fight, there were only eight people left in the fort, including Hardenbergh, the camp doctor, a sergeant and three privates.

Hardenbergh prepared for an attack on the camp, but the Indians apparently had no such intentions. Nonetheless, the soldiers of the fort got little sleep that night or for the next few days, keeping watch for long hours at the walls and expecting an attack at any moment.

A few days later help arrived when some of Hardenbergh's soldiers, who had been on escort duty with the mail to Prescott, returned and a few citizens who were passing through arrived at the post. Later, a contingent of sixteen soldiers arrived under the command of John Crane, further relieving the occupants of the post from danger.

Casebier reported that the supposed battle at Cady created considerable excitement in San Bernardino and that preparations

---

[1]   Wyatt Earp, The Untold Story, p. 20

were made to raise a company of civilian volunteers to assist the military. It appears, however, that these plans never materialized and that no troops or relief party was ever organized in San Bernardino.[1]

Casebier's work is the only written reference this author located relating to an attempted rescue by a company of civilians from San Bernardino. However, I did locate some other material that makes Lake's story seem to be impossible. Lake says that in the spring of 1866, Wyatt joined John King, the sheriff of San Bernardino County to go to the rescue of a small detachment of U.S. Calvary soldiers surrounded and trapped by several hundred Paiute Indians at Camp Cadiz. Lake's story does not add up when these facts are considered.

"John C. King was born in Carrolton, Carol County Mississippi. He came to San Bernardino in the year 1868, arriving in September of that year. He worked in a harness shop for John M. Voy three years, then he and his brother, Robert, engaged in the same business until 1880. In 1879 he was elected Sheriff of San Bernardino County."[2]

Thus it is apparent that John C. King was not in San Bernardino County at all in 1866 when the supposed citizen's posse rescued the soldiers. Certainly he was not sheriff at that time since he was first elected in 1879, a good thirteen years after the event took place.

This is one of the best (or worst) examples of Lake's taking some obscure fact or event in history and changing it around and placing Wyatt Earp in the middle of it.

According to Earp (as he supposedly told Lake) in the spring of 1867, he accepted a partial interest in the freighting outfit of one Charles Chrisman who also ran freight to Salt Lake City, and afterward with Chrisman, he hauled freight from Julesberg, Colorado to Salt Lake. For such a youth, he supposedly accumulated a considerable stake for himself. If that is true, it would be consistent with his activities for the rest of his life, for it seems that he was always engaged in some kind of trade or business where he could make a small investment and turn it to a profit.

The following year, spring of 1868, Nicholas Earp decided to return east. Rather than traveling overland across the plains, the family went north east by wagon to the railhead of the Union Pacific that was then building west across Wyoming, where they boarded a train to take them back to Illinois. Apparently, at the rail head, Wyatt ran across his former employer and partner, Charles Chrisman who was engaged in railroad construction. Wyatt went to work for him.

---

[1]   Dennis G. Casebier, <u>The Battle at Camp Cady</u>, p. 1.

[2]   L.A. Ingersoll, Century Annals of San Bernardino County, Los Angeles, (1904), p. 776

Later, he acquired several teams of horses, hired drivers, and went into the railroad grading business.

During that summer, Wyatt got a good look at the rough and tumble element of society that he was to encounter thereafter. Although the worst of the inhabitants who followed the railroad construction crews stopped at the rail head, some few, at least the whiskey peddlers and some gamblers, pushed ahead of the construction project and supplied the needs of the rough and tumble laborers. This is where young Earp encountered them. Since there was little entertainment in the camps, boxing became one of the most popular sports. Wyatt, being young, husky and over six feet tall, participated in that sport with gusto, sometimes competing, sometimes refereeing and sometimes promoting bouts. His all-around experience in the sport was to serve him well in the future.[1]

---

[1]   Wyatt Earp, Frontier Marshal, pp. 25-27.

CHAPTER III

RETURN TO MONMOUTH, MARRIES AND HEADS WEST-ARRESTED

LATE that fall, when the railroad construction business was about finished, Wyatt sold his teams, and with a substantial stake set out to visit his grandfather, Walter Earp, at Monmouth, Illinois. His grandfather, according to Lake, was a Justice of the peace or a Judge. Here the grandfather attempted to get Wyatt interested in the study of Law, but it apparently was not for him.[1]

Like most everything else that Wyatt Earp purportedly said to Lake, Bartholomew insists this was lie. He says, "It could not have happened! If Wyatt Earp ever made this statement, he most certainly was deeply in error. The tombstone of Walter Earp, in the cemetery at Monmouth, states that he died in 1853! Then too, the files of the Monmouth Review Atlas, along with other sources of archival information, all further attest this simple fact! Wyatt Earp's grandfather had been dead for sixteen years when he claimed he had visited him in Monmouth, had a long talk with him, and was induced to try and make something of himself, but not to take up law."[2]

Lake says that soon after Wyatt arrived in Monmouth, Illinois he met and married the daughter of a family neighbor to his grandparents. According to Lake's chronology, this would probably have been early in 1869. Bartholomew again calls the story a lie. He says the marriage took place on January 10, 1870 at Lamar, Missouri, and that the marriage ceremony was performed by N.P. Earp, Wyatt's father.[3] This discrepancy of dates would be unimportant except for the fact that Lake goes on to tell how in December of 1869 Wyatt went to Springfield, Missouri where he joined a party of government surveyors as a hunter with the job of furnishing fresh meat for the men. He then says that in early January 1870 the surveying party left Baxter Springs, Kansas and drove south along the Neosha to the Creek Indian Agency, across the Arkansas from Fort Gibson.[2]

---

1   Wyatt Earp, Frontier Marshal, p. 29.

2   Wyatt Earp, The Untold Story, p. 21. Bartholomew was right - I checked it out.

3   Ibid, p. 24.

2   Wyatt Earp, Frontier Marshal, pp. 30-31.

About Wyatt's claim to have been with the Government Survey party, Bartholomew said, "If Wyatt was with a survey party early in January of 1870, he must have been married by proxy!"[1] A more serious discrepancy comes from the fact that Wyatt was elected town constable, having beat out his brother Newton for the job by 137 votes to 102.   It's difficult to determine the date of the election. Bartholomew says that it was after his marriage on January 10, 1870, but doesn't give any specific date.[2] Frank Waters doesn't give the date of the election, but says that in the same year, on January 10, 1870 Wyatt married a young girl by the name of Willa or Urilla Southerland and that she died a few months later.[3]   Dale T. Schoenberg fixes the date as about April 4, 1870[4] and cites Frank Waters as his source.

It seems quite certain that during the first part of the year 1870, Wyatt Earp was at Lamar, Missouri, either making love and getting married, or running for Town Constable and getting elected. The second of these events he apparently concealed from or failed to mention to Stuart N. Lake. Obviously he could not have joined a Government surveyors party at Springfield, Missouri in December 1869 as Lake reported, or left Baxter Springs, Kansas early in January 1870 and gone south along the Neosha to the Creek Indian Agency, across the Arkansas from Fort Gibson,[5] and at the same time get married and run for Constable in Lamar, Missouri.

However, I have not run across any other author who disputed the fact, as reported by Wyatt, that he joined a survey party and acted in the capacity of hunter, furnishing buffalo meat to the surveyors. He may have advanced the date of this activity by a year or two to cover the time he spent in Lamar, Missouri, wishing to conceal this information for some reason. No author or researcher seems to have uncovered a reason for concealing the fact that he was married at Lamar, Missouri and that about the time of the marriage he was elected Town Constable. Could it be that he was ashamed of the fact that he ran against and beat his older half-brother Newton? The Earps were always a close knit family with deep loyalties, and it seems completely out of character for one of them to run for a political office

[1]   Wyatt Earp, The Untold Story, p. 25.

[2]   Wyatt Earp The Untold Story, p. 26.

[3]   The Earp Brothers of Tombstone, p. 29.

[4]   The Gunfighters, p. 21.

[5]   Wyatt Earp, Frontier Marshal, p. 31.

against another. That is the only hint of family disloyalty that I have ever run across, and I suspect that Wyatt later became deeply ashamed of his conduct.

Further evidence that Lake's story was in error is as follows:

Lake reports that Wyatt stayed with the survey party during the winter of 1870-71 and that the party worked its way northward from the Red River, reaching the Kansas line in April, 1871 and then turned eastward to Arkansas City, where the men were paid off. He then tells how Wyatt, with a sum of $3,000.00 in his belt, made his way to Kansas City where he spent the summer loafing around and getting acquainted with buffalo hunters and westerners who were either famous, or would become famous in the future, and with whom he would come in contact many times later in his career. Lake quoted him as saying, "I met Wild Bill Hickock in Kansas City in 1871. Jack Gallagher, the celebrated scout, was there; and I remember Jack Martin, Billy Dixon, Jim Hanrahan, Tom O'Keefe, Cheyenne Jack, Billy Ogg, Bermuda Carlisle, Old Man Keeler, Kirk Jordan, and Andy Johnson." He went on to say that "Bill Hickock told me he'd made five thousand dollars between September 1 and April 1; as it turned out, he did not hunt that season of '71 and '72. Jack Gallagher expected his earnings to run even higher. So I decided to try my hand at the game." Earp claimed that he learned more about gun fighting from Wild Bill Hickock and Tom Speers than he had ever dreamed of, and that he had seen Wild Bill's demonstration of marksmanship and concluded that there was no man in the Kansas City group who was his equal with a six gun.[1]

The only problem is that Wild Bill Hickock did not spend the spring and summer of 1871 in Kansas City as Earp says. The evidence is found in the book, Great Gunfighters of the Kansas Cowtowns, 1867-1886, where Miller and Snell, writing about the city of Abilene said: "In April 1871, the newly elected city government, spurred by the approaching cattle season and its attendant increase in lawlessness appointed a city marshal within days of its election. The man chosen was Wild Bill Hickock, and on April 15 he was sworn into office."[2]

Thereafter, during the summer there are references to Bill Hickock's presence in Abilene. On May 8, 1871 his name was noted in the minute book of the meeting of the mayor and city councilmen.[3] On June 8, 1871 the Chronicle carried a story

---

[1]   Wyatt Earp, Frontier Marshal, pp. 33-37.

[2]   Great Gunfighters of the Kansas Cowtowns, p. 129.

[3]   Ibid, p. 129

reporting that Wild Bill had posted notices that the carrying of weapons in the city would be forbidden.[1] On June 28th the city council passed an ordinance authorizing the city treasurer to pay the marshal .50 cents for each unlicensed dog that he killed.[2] On July 31, 1871 the Hippo-Olympiad and Mammoth Circus owned by Mrs. Agnes Lake put on a show in Abilene. Wild Bill met the lady, and she later became his wife and widow.[3] In short, Wild Bill was working diligently during the summer of 1871 as Marshal of Abilene and from the reports, it appears that he was there most of the time. Certainly he had no time to lallygag around in Kansas City as purportedly described by Wyatt Earp.

Now this raises an interesting question, and I doubt that anyone can supply a solid answer. Did Wyatt Earp tell Lake about all his exploits in Kansas City, or did Lake dream them up in order to make the Earp story more interesting? If Earp did tell the story as written by Lake, was any part of it true? Were some of the characters that he mentioned there? Did he gratuitously bring in the name of Wild Bill Hickock so that he could bask in the shadow of his reputation? Or, since we have already determined that Wyatt could not have been the hunter for the survey party in the winter of 1870-71, could he have been telling the truth all along, but be a year off on his date? In researching history and even in trying to reconstruct past events of his own life, this author has found that a recounting of events is most apt to be in error when trying to recall the particular year that something happened than he is in recalling the day or month. Fixing the year of a long past event is very difficult and not always reliable.

Wild Bill's services as marshal of Abilene were terminated by action of the city council on December 13, 1871.[4] In the summer of 1872 he spent some time in Kansas City. On the 28th of September, 1872 it was reported in the Topeka Daily Commonwealth that "There were 30,000 people on the fair grounds yesterday, and to day [sic] the crowd was not lessened. Wild Bill made a big point at the fair grounds. A number of Texans prevailed upon the band to play Dixie, and then the Texans made demonstrations with the flourishing of pistols. Wild Bill stepped forward and stopped the music, and more than fifty pistols were presented at William's head, but he came away

---

[1]   Ibid, p. 130

[2]   Ibid, p. 131.

[3]   Ibid, p. 31.

[4]   Great Gunfighters of the Kansas Cowtowns, p. 134.

unscathed."[1]

An examination of Wild Bill's biography[2] reveals that during the summer of 1872 he could well have lounged around Kansas City and enjoyed the company of the others named by Wyatt Earp, and keeping in mind the impossibility of Wyatt's having been with the surveying party in '71, isn't it just possible that he was off by one year on his date and that the whole story could have been true if it were dated 1872 rather than 1871?

Although it is quite certain that Wyatt Earp did not spend the early spring of 1871 with a surveying party, he may have been present in the Indian Nations during the spring and summer of 1871. A goodly portion of that time may have been spent in jail there.

Ed Bartholomew almost gleefully describes his find of old court records in the National Archives showing that Wyatt Earp was once indicted for horse theft. He then embellishes the incident in his typical manner, thus making much more of it than the records justify. A quote from page 33 serves to illustrate the total bias and prejudice of Bartholomew and how he never hesitates to supply a little of his own imagination in order to cast the worst light possible on anything that he can dig up derogatory to Earp.

"The simple facts are that Wyatt Earp was arrested in the Indian Territory, now Oklahoma, late in March of 1871, and for horse theft! There is no doubt; the warrants and indictments clearly state, 'Wyatt S. Earp!!'"

Will the anguished cry's from the wounded television and armchair historians claim this an imposition? Will they loudly shout that everyone in those days was so charged, as they have so justified this man when he lived as a "sporting man," being fired from police jobs due to his evident connection with women of ill-fame. Perhaps. But Wyatt B. S. Earp could have named one deputy U.S. Marshal, for it was the real J. G. Owen who arrested him. Owen put him in chains and hauled him over the rough road from the prison stockade at Fort Gibson to face justice. The very document indicting Wyatt is on file in the United States Federal Records and has been examined by the author. It is given here verbatim:

"April 1, 1871, Bill of Information. U.S. vs. Wyatt S. Earp, Edward Kennedy, John Shown.

I, J.G. Owen, being duly sworn say that Wyatt S. Earp, Ed Kennedy, John Shown, white men and not Indians or members of any tribe of Indians by birth or marriage or adoption on the 28th day of

---

[1]   Ibid, p. 135.

[2]   They Called him Wild Bill, p. 226-227.

March AD 1871 in the Indian Country in said District did feloniously (did) willfully steal, take away, carry away two horses each of the value of one hundred dollars, the property goods and chattels of one William Keys and pray a writ. (signed) J.G. Owen."[1]

Owen says that "On the opposite side of this Bill of Information" it was subscribed and sworn to. The document is not labeled a Bill of Information, and it was subscribed and sworn to on the same side as the rest of the declaration in these words: "Sworn to and subscribed before me this 1st day of April, 1871, Jas. O. Churchill, U.S. Commissioner."

Maybe Bartholomew had a copy of a different document than I have. Mine came from the National Archives - Fort Worth Branch, Fort Worth, Texas 76115. They appear to be photocopies of original hand written documents.

Based on the sworn statement of Deputy United States Marshal, J.G. Owen, a document designated a "Writ" was issued by the U.S. Commissioner, Jas. O. Churchill in the following form:

"UNITED STATES OF AMERICA, Western District of Arkansas.

"THE PRESIDENT OF THE UNITED STATES OF AMERICA:

"To the Marshal of the Western District of Arkansas, - Greetings.

"WHEREAS, complaint on oath hath been made before me, charging that Wyatt S. Earp and Edward Kennedy did on or about the 28th day of March A.D. 1871, in the Western District of Arkansas feloniously steal and take away two horses from the lawful possession of James Keys, contrary to the form of the statute in such cases made and provided, and against the peace and dignity of the United States.

"NOW THEREFORE, You are hereby Commanded, in the name of the President of the United States to apprehend the said Wyatt S. Earp and Edward Kennedy and bring their bodies forthwith, before me, Jas. O. Churchill, a Commissioner appointed by the United States District court for said District, whenever they may be found, that they may then and there be dealt with according to law for said offense.

"Given under my hand this 1st day of April, A.D. 1871. in the 95th year of our Independence.

"Jas. O. Churchill

"U.S. Commissioner, Western Dist. Arks."

On the back of this document is a return of service filed at Van Buren, Arkansas on April 14, 1871 certifying that the Writ, or what would today be termed an Arrest Warrant was served on the named parties on the 6th day of April, 1871 at the Cherokee Nation. On the same sheet of paper was a list of the Marshal's costs for serving the

---

[1]   Wyatt Earp, The Untold Story, pp. 33-36.

Warrant. The writing is very difficult to read, but among other things there was a charge for 6 days of something for $12.00 and for 7 days of feeding for $31.00. The total bill was $121.50.

From this document one could conclude that it took the Marshal six or seven days to go wherever he had to go to serve the Warrant. Bartholomew says it was to Fort Gibson to get the prisoners and return them to court.

There is nothing in the records to indicate that they were transported in chains in either a wagon or stage as Bartholomew imagines. At any rate, the court records show that on April 14, 1871 three defendants, Wyatt Earp, Edward Kennedy and John Shown, were arraigned before the United States Commissioner and bail was set in the sum of $500.00 each. Nothing in the court file indicates that bail was posted, but subsequent events would lead to the conclusion that it must have been.

On the same day, Anna Shown, the wife of John Shown, gave a sworn statement to the U.S. Commissioner as follows:

"Sworn Statement made by Anna Shown before Jas. O. Churchill, U.S. Commissioner on the 13th day of April, A.D. 1871.

"I know Wyatt S. Earp and Ed Kennedy. They got my husband drunk near Ft. Gibson, I.T. about the 28th of March 1871. They went and got Mr. Jim Keys' horses, and put my husband on one and he led the other, and told him to ride 50 miles towards Kansas and then they would hitch the horses to a wagon, and he could ride. I went with these two men and met my husband 50 miles North of Fort Gibson, and rode with these two men (Earp and Kennedy) in a hack. On meeting my husband they took the two horses out of the hack and put in the two that he had. Earp drove on toward Kansas for three full nights (We laid over days). About 3 o'clock of the 3rd night James M. Keys overtook us. My husband John Shown said he could have the horses - the other left. Earp and Kennedy told Keys that my husband stole the horses. They also said that if Shown (my husband) turned states evidence then they would kill him.

"Anna (x) Shown   mark
"Witness: Jas. O. Churchill."

On the same day, April 1st, 1871, a subpoena was issued to James Keys and Anna Shown, commanding their appearance before the U.S. Commissioner in Van Buren Arkansas to give evidence in the case of United States vs. Wyatt S. Earp, Edward Kennedy and John Shown on April 1st 1871.

This must have been for some kind of a preliminary hearing, necessary under the rules of procedure in order to hold the defendants for the Grand Jury.

On November 10, another Subpoena was issued, this time adding the name of William Keys and commanding the witness' appearance at the court in Fort Smith, Arkansas.

The next document in the file indicated that they appeared before the Commissioner, waived examination, and bail was set in the sum of $500.00 each.

In 1871 the United States Congress passed legislation moving the United States Court for the Western District of Arkansas from Van Buren to Fort Smith.[1] Soon after, Wyatt Earp was arraigned and probably posted bail at Van Buren. The court at Fort Smith was soon to become the court of the famous hanging Judge, Isaac Charles Parker. On May 15, 1871, the Grand Jury at Fort Smith brought in their first indictments charging sixteen persons with major offenses.[2] Wyatt Earp was one of the persons named in that group of indictments. He, Edward Kennedy and John Shown were charged with stealing "Two horses, each horse of the value of one hundred dollars; two geldings, each of said geldings of the value of one hundred dollars; and two mares, each of said mares of the value of one hundred dollars; the property, goods and chattels of William Keys."   It's interesting to note that while the declarations of J.G. Owen and Anna Shown each mention specifically the theft of two horses, the Grand Jury Indictment accuses the defendants of the theft of six horses.   Why?   One possible explanation is super careful pleading by the prosecutor. He may not have known whether the stolen animals were horses, mares or geldings, and may not have believed that the word horse would cover either. Therefore, just to avoid any argument he pleaded the theft of horses, geldings and mares.   This isn't a very good or very logical explanation for the variance between the complaint and the indictment, and it may not be right, but I can't come up with a better one.

The next document in the file is an order directed to the Marshal of the Western District of Arkansas stating that on May 8, 1871 a true bill of Indictment had been brought into the court by the Grand Jury against Wyatt S. Earp and John Shown, that neither of them had appeared before the court, and ordering the Marshal to take them into custody and bring them before the court on November 13, 1871 to answer the Indictment. The date on this document May 8, 1871, has to be a clerical error, for the indictment was not issued until May 15th. Further, the notes on the front of the document state: "Issued June 8, 1871, Returnable November Term 1871." There is another notation dated November 21, 1871 on the front of the document certifying that Wyatt Earp and John Shown cannot be found in the

---

[1]   U.S. Statutes at Large, XVI, p. 47

[2]   Law West of Fort Smith, p. 5.

district.

There are no records showing that anything further happened in the case. Bartholomew says that "there is evidence that Kennedy himself was not found guilty of horse theft; he may have turned states evidence but he was actually and legally absolved of the charge, while Earp was to flee as a fugitive from Federal Justice."[1]

Again, Bartholomew's conclusions are not warranted by the record. There is nothing in the records to justify the conclusion that Kennedy turned state's evidence. If he had, he would in all probability have appeared as a witness before the Grand Jury as did James and William Keys and Anna Shown. He did not. A letter dated July 13, 1989 from National Archives - Fort Worth Branch, Fort Worth, Texas states: "In checking the Fort Smith court's index to sentences, 1866-1890 (entry 47), we found that Ed Kennedy was acquitted on June 5, 1871. There is no mention of the two other defendants."

Acquittal only occurs after a trial; therefore it can safely be assumed that Kennedy actually went to trial and was found not guilty by either a judge or a jury.

Possibly the reason that no further action was taken against Wyatt Earp and John Shown was that the evidence in the Kennedy case showed that no crime had been committed.

One possible explanation of the lack of records of the disposition of the case is the history of the court itself. According to Glenn Shirley,[2] on March 3, 1871, Congress passed an act moving the court from Van Buren, Arkansas to Fort Smith, and Henry J. Caldwell, then Judge of the Eastern District of Arkansas at Little Rock was appointed as first Judge of the Western District Court. He stayed only a short time and, according to Shirley, "In 1872 Caldwell was succeeded by an officious young lawyer named William Story. Story was a product of the "Carpetbag" rule of the Reconstruction Period of the Civil War, and a man of little character, who somehow wrangled the appointment from President Grant. He served less than fourteen months, and his tenure was attended by incompetency and corruption. Although court costs for the period ran into the fabulous sum of $400,000, few cases were ever tried, and Marshal Roots was removed from office. Marshal John Saber, who succeeded Roots, made little effort to improve conditions. Few arrests were made. Certificates issued witnesses and jurors for service went unpaid, and many who were subpoenaed from distant points on the frontier were forced to

---

[1]   Wyatt Earp, The Untold Story, p. 36.

[2]   Law West of Fort Smith, p. 16.

sell their personal effects to pay their expenses and walk home. A strong case of bribery, however, was made against Judge Story, and in June, 1874, he resigned to avoid impeachment proceedings."[1]

Thus it may well be, in view of the conditions prevailing in the court at the time, that the case of Wyatt Earp and his co-defendant just got lost in the shuffle. One thing is certain. Wyatt Earp was never convicted of the thefts charged and never thereafter conducted himself like a fugitive from Federal Justice as he is described by Bartholomew. He later held numerous jobs as policeman, City Marshal, Deputy Sheriff, Wells Fargo guard and detective and Deputy United States Marshal. He must have traveled on numerous occasions in the Indian Territory without fear of arrest, and he received national publicity on occasions that would have alerted any peace officers holding a warrant for his arrest. None of this case makes sense, and I can't find any records to explain it. Why did the Grand Jury charge the theft of six horses when the original declarations of Anne Shown and J.G. Owen specifically mentioned that only two horses were taken? Why don't the records show some ultimate disposition of the case?

Every book needs a mystery. This is a mystery that I have been unable to unravel. Hopefully some of my readers will.

---

[1]   Ibid, p. 17.

CHAPTER IV

THE KILLING OF
SHERIFF WHITNEY

WYATT Earp's movements for the next two or three years are hard to follow. Almost every writer tells a different story, but they all seem to agree that he spent this time in the buffalo country and at the end of the cattle driving trails, either hunting buffalo or gambling.

The summer of 1873 was a busy and exciting time for the small shipping town of Ellsworth, Kansas. At that time it was the end of the line for many Texas cattle drives, and the town was experiencing the same boom troubles that had previously prevailed in Abilene, and would later occur in Wichita and Dodge City. At Ellsworth on August 15, 1873, Sheriff Whitney was shot and killed by Bill Thompson, the brother of the notorious gunman and gambler, Ben Thompson. Bill rode out of town and was not apprehended for several years. Ben was disarmed and taken before the local judge, where he was either charged with disturbing the peace and paid a fine, or the case was dismissed, depending on whom you believe.

Stuart Lake used this incident to catapult Wyatt Earp into the ranks of super gunman, lawman, and all around hero. He used this event to create the Earp myth, and it was his recital of this incident more than anything else that caused most students of western history to view the balance of his book with suspicion, and created in the hearts and souls of many of them what seems to be a personal animosity toward Wyatt Earp, causing many of them to put an adverse twist on everything ever written, done or said by or about Earp thereafter.

In order to demonstrate how Lake went about creating the fictitious Wyatt Earp, it is necessary to quote at length from Lake's book in which he has Wyatt Earp single handedly backing down the notorious Ben Thompson and a whole army of blood thirsty Texans. First, he had to build up Ben Thompson as absolutely the most dangerous gunman in the west, thus making anyone who backed him down the top gun. To do this he wrote:

"Ben Thompson was leading spirit of the lawless; his right hand man was brother, Bill; as left bower, Ben and George Peshaur, another Texas killer, and as additional backing an army of cow-punchers who could be counted upon to the limit in any gunplay against Northern men. Of the cowboys, the ringleaders were Cad Pierce, John Good, and Neil Kane, notorious as trouble makers in every camp on the Texas trail.

"For two months of the summer of '73, Ben Thompson, from headquarters at the Grand Central, where he had opened his faro bank, defied the vaunted Ellsworth marshals with impunity, and the hundreds of cowboys in town did likewise. Citizenry, mayor, councilmen, and imported peace officers had been treed together and apparently did not intend to come down until the last Texas man had started South. Such was the status of Ellsworth's hope for law and order when Wyatt Earp reached the camp . . .

"Early in the afternoon of August 18, 1873, (he had the date wrong, it actually happened on August 15, 1873), Wyatt had the sun scorched plaza almost to himself as he lounged beneath the wooden awning which shaded Beebe's General Store and Brennan's Saloon, next door. At intervals someone passed on the walk, cowboys left one saloon for another, or a sweating horseman rode in from the prairie, hitched his cayuse and sought relief from the blazing heat at a favorite bar. For the most part, the dusty cowtown square was devoid of life, except the drooping horses tethered to the rails and their attendant swarms of flies. Sweltering wild and woolly, Ellsworth was as peaceful as a cool green-and-white New England village.

"In the saloon beyond Brennan's, Wyatt knew, an 'open' poker game was in progress, with stakes of unusual size. Play was so high that the Thompsons had left their faro bank to sit in. When informed of a table rule against guns, Ben and Bill had still been sufficiently intrigued by the size of the pots to send their weapons back to the Grand Central and draw cards. Wyatt had heard that the Thompsons were forcing the play, that Bill was drinking steadily and getting mean. Whereupon he was well satisfied to be out of the game. Wyatt had small fancy for the Thompsons in any case, less for Bill at a poker table with high stakes and drunk.

"From the saloon in which the Thompsons were gambling, a violent uproar was followed by the appearance of the brothers on the plaza. They came out of the door on the run, Bill cursing loudly and shouting threats over his shoulder as the pair made for the Grand Central. A moment later, they reappeared from the hotel and headed back toward the saloon, Ben carrying a double barreled shotgun and Bill, a rifle. At the rail in front of the saloon stood a pair of horses hitched to a hay wagon and behind this rack the Thompsons took their stand, Bill shouting threats and imprecations and Ben adding profanely insulting invitations to those inside the saloon to 'Come out and make your fight.'

"Wyatt stepped into Beebe's doorway, for cover from stray lead, as the racket of belligerent brothers drew several hundred persons from various establishments bordering the plaza as hopeful spectators. Sheriff Whitney hurried from his store, stopping at Beebe's doorway to ask Wyatt if he knew what started the row. The question was answered by a bystander at the poker game who had sensed that its immediate vicinity was not the safest place in Ellsworth. He had run from the saloon by the rear door and around to the plaza to view forthcoming festivities.

"'John Sterling slapped Bill Thompson's face,' this onlooker volunteered. 'Bill got nasty and John gave him the flat of his hand across the mouth. When Bill invited John to get a gun and meet him outside, John hit him again and knocked him out of his seat. Then Bill and Ben ran after their guns.'

"Sheriff Whitney was in his shirt sleeves and probably unarmed, yet without further hesitation he walked over to the hay wagon where the Thompsons stood with cocked weapons waiting for someone to come out of the saloon.

"'You keep out of this, Sheriff,' Ben warned him. 'We don't want to hurt you.'

"'Don't be foolish, Ben,' Whitney replied.

"Thompson's rejoinder was a torrent of profanity directed at Sterling and his friends, whereupon the sheriff went into the saloon. He returned to the walk with word that Sterling had been forcibly prevented from coming out to fight and had been taken by friends to his camp outside the town by way of the back door.

"Whitney feared that Sterling might be shot on sight by one of the Thompsons when he again came into Ellsworth, and to smooth over the quarrel, invited the Thompsons into Brennan's saloon for a drink and a talk. Cow-punchers and merchants went indoors, and as Wyatt moved back to his lounging place between Brennen's doorway and Beebe's entrance, he again had the plaza to himself. Fifteen minutes later, Whitney came out of the saloon, alone, and stopped to talk.

"'They've calmed down a bit,' the sheriff reported. 'They're inside with a bunch of Texas men.'

"'Did you take their guns aways from them?' Wyatt asked.

"'No,' Whitney replied, 'they wouldn't stand for that.'

"Before Wyatt had time to comment on this matter, Bill Thompson appeared in Brennan's doorway with Ben's shotgun.

"'I'll get a sheriff if I don't get anybody else,' he declared.

"Wyatt and Whitney turned to face him; Bill fired both barrels of the gun - eighteen buckshot - point-blank into the sheriff's breast, and ran back into the saloon.

"Wyatt caught Whitney in his arms.

"'I'm done,' the sheriff gasped. 'Get me home.'

"At the roar of gunfire, saloon, hotels, and stores spouted five hundred men into the Ellsworth plaza, nine tenths of them Texas gun-toters, an unarmed minority, local citizens. Ben and Bill Thompson walked deliberately out of Brennan's to a string of saddled cow-ponies at a nearby rail, Ben covering one flank with the rifle, Bill, the other with the shotgun. In front of the Grand Central, Thompson followers collected under George Peshaur, Cad Pierce, Neil Kane, and John Good, to forestall attack, and the brothers swung their gun muzzles back and forth to menace the store fronts as they argued over ensuing procedure.

"Friends of Sheriff Whitney volunteered to take the dying man home and Wyatt Earp turned his attention to the Thompsons. He stepped again into Beebe's entrance, and peered around the door facing into the plaza for sight of the Ellsworth peace officers. None was in view. Beebe's door opened, and there at Wyatt's shoulder was Happy Jack Morco, Indian fighter and six gun expert, two belts of ammunition around his waist and a forty-five-Colt at either hip. Wyatt gave way to let Morco reconnoiter.

"'For God's sake, get out of town.' Ben Thompson urged Bill. 'You shot Sheriff Whitney.'

"'I know it,' Bill replied. 'I'd have shot him if he'd been Jesus Christ.'

"Happy Jack peered cautiously around the door casing. Ben took a pot shot without sighting his rifle. The bullet struck half an inch above the deputy marshal's head and he ducked for cover.

"'Too high,' Ben informed Bill with an oath of regret. 'Get on that horse and get out of here before Whitney's friends get organized. Take this rifle and give me my shotgun. I'll cover your getaway.'

"Wyatt realized that the brothers were appropriating a cow-pony and exchanging weapons, as the rifle would be preferable for Bill on a long ride down the trail. Here was Happy Jack's opportunity.

"'Jump out and get 'em,' Wyatt suggested. 'Hurry, while they're switching guns.'

"'Not me,' Happy Jack replied. 'Those fellows across the street might get me.'

"'You'd get both Thompsons first,' Wyatt urged, but Morco refused to budge.

"Wyatt restrained an impulse to boot the deputy marshal onto the open walk and peered around the casing again. Bill was in the saddle with the Winchester in front of him; Ben, with the shotgun, backed into the road.

To quote the Ellsworth <u>Reporter</u>:

"He (Bill) then rode slowly out of town, cursing and inviting a fight.

"No one accepted the invitation.

"As Bill Thompson rode out of shooting range, Ben, still covering the assembled citizens with his shotgun, backed over to the Grand Central. A Texas man brought out his six-guns. With these favorites buckled in place and the shotgun in the crook of his arm, Ben paraded in front of the hotel shouting taunts and threats at the town of Ellsworth in general and at her peace officers in profane particular. At his back were a hundred Texas men, half of them man-killers of record, the rest more than willing to be. Peshaur, Pierce, Good, and Kane were slightly in advance of the crowd. In groups, around the plaza, three or four hundred more Texans were distributed. Every man-jack had six-guns at his hips and a gunhand itching for play. As Ben Thompson halted his tirade momentarily, Cad Pierce sought the limelight.

"'I'll give one thousand dollars to anybody who'll knock off another marshal!' he shouted.

"As the cowboys yelled appreciation of this offer, Deputy Marshal Brown appeared at the far end of a railroad building. A hundred forty five slugs screeched across the plaza, and Brown took cover.

To quote the Reporter again:

"Ben Thompson retained his arms for a full hour after this and no attempt was made to disarm him.   Mayor Miller was at his residence . . . During this long hour, where were the police? No arrest had been made and the street was full of armed men ready to defend Thompson. The police were arming themselves, and, as they claim, just ready to rally out and take alive or dead the violators of the law. They were loading their muskets (sic) just as the mayor, impatient at the delay in making arrests, came along and discharged the whole force. It would have been better to have increased the force and discharged or retained the old police after quiet had been restored. The mayor acted promptly and according to his judgement, but we certainly think it was a bad move. A poor police is better than none, and if, as they claim, they were just ready for work, they should have had a chance to redeem themselves and the honor of the city. Thus the city was left without a police, with no one but Deputy Sheriff Hogue to make arrests.' (Note: Here, Lake ceases to quote from the Reporter and inserts his own fictitious version of what happened. This, above all else, brands Lake's biography of Wyatt Earp as at least partly fictitious. He then proceeds with his own fictitious story as follows.)

"Hogue, . . . it chanced . . . was absent in the country. For some reason unexplained, beyond a statement that it was 'Not at liberty to do so,' the newspaper failed to publish later testimony before Coroner Duck and Police Judge Osbourne which furnished a detailed account of events precipitated by the belated appearance of Mayor Jim Miller on the side of the plaza farthest from Ben Thompson.

"Wyatt and Happy Jack were still in Beebe's doorway, and Ben Thompson was still strutting up and down before the hotel, when Mayor Miller edged around the corner to the store entrance. Brocky Jack Norton, the Marshal, came through Beebe's from the rear; he, too, wore a pair of forty-five-caliber Colt's. Deputy Marshal Brown, armed with a rifle and revolvers, was somewhere behind the railroad shacks. Deputy Marshal Crawford had not made the gesture of plaza appearance. The Mayor wasted ten minutes of time and breath in orders to his marshals for Ben Thompson's capture. Neither Brocky Jack nor Happy Jack relished obedience, and said so.

"Mayor Miller tried another tack. He shouted across the plaza to Thompson, ordering the gunman to lay down his arms and submit to arrest. Ben answered in raucous profanity, at which his followers whooped gleefully. Ellsworth was treed at the tip of the topmost limb.

"After urging Happy Jack to jump out and kill the Thompsons, Wyatt had kept silent. But the Mayor's plea to the Marshals and contempt for their discretion, abetted by reaction to the cold-blooded passion in which Sheriff Whitney had been shot down, moved him to comment.

"'Nice police force you have got,' Wyatt said to Miller.

"'Who are you?' the Mayor demanded.

"'Just a looker-on,' Wyatt replied.

"'Well, don't talk so much,' Miller snapped. 'You haven't even got a gun.'

"As Wyatt was in shirt-sleeves, it was evident that he was unarmed. He seldom carried weapons in the settlements and those he owned were in his hotel room.   "'It's none of my business,' Wyatt admitted, 'but if it was I'd get me a gun and arrest Ben Thompson or kill him.'

"Brocky Jack erred.

"'Don't pay any attention to that kid, Jim,' he interrupted. But Miller was desperate.

"'You're fired, Norton,' he said. 'You, too, Morco.'

"The Mayor snatched the Marshal's badge from Brocky Jack's shirt-front.

"'As soon as I can find Brown and Crawford, I'll fire them.'

"He turned to Wyatt Earp.

"'I'll make this your business. You're Marshal of Ellsworth. Here's your badge. Go into Beebe's and get some guns. I order you to arrest Ben Thompson.'

"To the best of Wyatt Earp's recollection, he voiced no formal acceptance of his impromptu appointment as an Ellsworth police officer. He turned and walked to Beebe's firearms counter and asked for a pair of second-hand forty-fives with holsters and cartridge belts.

"'New guns and holsters,' he explained in after years, 'might have slowed me down.'

"Selecting two six-shooters with trigger-dogs that some former gun wise owner had filed to split-second smoothness and a pair of well-worn holsters, Wyatt tested the weapons thoroughly, loaded five cylinders in each, spun them, filled the cartridge-loops, settled the guns on his hips, and walked out to the plaza. He said nothing to Mayor Miller or the two Jacks. Not one of the three offered company or suggestions. Beebe's clerk always asserted that the trio remained huddled in the doorway while the youthful Marshal, pro tem, walked out to face the deadliest gunman then alive.

"Wyatt Earp's short journey across the Ellsworth plaza under the muzzle of Ben Thompson's shotgun established for all time his preeminence among gun-fighters of the West, but the episode has been ignored in written tales. That the camp never shared popular recognition with Wichita and Dodge as a top notch cow town, that its glory was but a season long, may have been responsible for the oversight; in any event, narrators of Earp history seem unaware that Wyatt was Marshal of Ellsworth for one portentous hour. His appointment was not entered in the records, and he was never paid for the service; yet, the amazing single exploit of his brief incumbency was a word-of-mouth sensation in '73 from the Platte to the Rio Grande. From a number of onlookers who, all uncomprehendingly, were witnesses at the dawning of a new era in the Kansas cow towns and who later recounted what they saw, has come an authentic picture of high moment in Ellsworth's lurid heyday, and of Wyatt Earp as he appeared. As the young man stepped from the shelter of Beebe's door, he pulled at the brim of his black sombrero to set it firmly in place and started diagonally across the plaza toward the Grand Central. Ben Thompson squared around, shifting his shotgun to hold the weapon across his stomach, the four-end in his left hand, his right on grip and triggers. From that position a single motion would bring it into play.

"Ben Thompson was a squarely built, stocky fellow, about five feet eight inches in height. A bloated face, bushy brows above his wide blue eyes, and a sweeping mustache gave him an appearance of greater maturity than his thirty years would justify; and this, as well as his bulkiness, was accentuated as he squatted slightly for effective handling of his shotgun.

"Old timers have said that Wyatt Earp looked like a boy as he crossed the plaza. Six feet tall, weighing not more than one hundred fifty five pounds, he, too, was the owner of good blue eyes; but, in contrast to Thompson's red and puffy countenance, Wyatt's lean and muscular features were smooth-shaven and tanned brown, his slimness further set off by white shirt, black trousers, wide-brimmed black hat, and high-heeled horseman's boots. As he walked, his hands swung easily, conveniently close to his holsters, but making no overt moves.

"As Wyatt reached a point approximately fifty yards from Thompson, Cad Pierce said something to which Ben snarled over his shoulder in reply. Pierce subsided, and with the other Texas men waited for Ben to call the turn.

"Wyatt Earp had a definite course of action in mind as he advanced toward the hundred or more half-drunk cowboys, any and all of whom were keyed to cutting loose at him with twice that many guns for the mere satisfaction of seeing him die. He knew that to half the men in the crowd he was an utter stranger; the rest might know him by sight or name; he had no fear-inspiring record as a killer, and, so far as anyone in Ellsworth might know, had never used guns against a human adversary in all his life. He realized, too, that he was a target few men in the hundred could miss at fifty yards. That he was heeled with a pair of guns was evident to all; one false or hesitant gesture with either hand and he was fair game for the first to draw.

"'I knew what I would do before the Mayor pinned Brocky Jack's badge on my shirt,' Wyatt said in recalling the affair. 'I based my action on my knowledge of Ben Thompson's vanity and the Texas men in his crowd.'

"'In the first place, I knew better than to walk out of Beebe's with a gun in my hand. If I had, I would have been filled with lead before I reached the road but I also knew that, if I did not draw, the Texas men would leave it to Ben to make the play; he would have turned and shot down anyone who dared to cut loose before he opened the ball. Whatever happened must first be between him and me.

"'So, all I had to do was keep my eye on Ben's shotgun; not on the muzzle, but on his right hand at the grip and trigger-guard. That held my eye on the target I had picked, his stomach just back of his hand. I figured he'd wait for me to get within thirty or forty yards to make his weapon most effective and that he could not get the shotgun into action without "telegraphing the move" as a boxer would say, through his wrist. When I saw his wrist move to put his arm muscles into play, I'd go for my guns and I had enough confidence in myself to be certain that I could put at least one slug into his belly before he could pull a trigger.'

"'I realized that after I'd plugged Ben, some of his crowd might get me and I had some idea, I suppose of taking as many with me as I could. Beyond figuring to get Cad Pierce after I'd got Ben, if that was possible, I don't recall thinking much about that. All I really cared about was heading Thompson into his hole. I intended to arrest him if I could. But it was a moral certainty that he'd try to shoot. If he did, I'd kill him. I could hit a target the size of his stomach ten times out of ten shots with a forty-five at any range up to one hundred yards, and I had perfect confidence in my speed.'

"When Wyatt Earp was about forty yards distance, Ben Thompson called to him.

"'What do you want, Wyatt?' he shouted.

"'I want you, Ben,' Wyatt replied, walking steadily forward. Neither Ben Thompson nor any onlooker, and least of all Wyatt Earp, has offered a completely satisfactory explanation of what followed. Thompson made no move with his gun and did not speak again until Wyatt was less than thirty yards away.

"'I'd rather talk than fight,' the killer called.

"'I'll get you either way, Ben,' Wyatt assured him, without halting in his stride.

"'Wait a minute,' said Thompson. 'What do you want me to do?'

"'Throw your shotgun into the road, put up your hands, and tell your friends to stay out of this play,' Wyatt answered. Less than fifteen yards now separated the men.

"'Will you stop and let me talk to you?' Ben asked. Wyatt halted. He now knew positively that he could take Thompson, alive or dead, whichever way the gunman chose to turn events. He had Ben talking, which is the gravest error possible to a gun-thrower who has serious business at hand.

"'What are you going to do with me?' Thompson asked.

"'Kill you or take you to jail,' Wyatt informed him.

"'Brown's over there by the depot with a rifle,' Ben objected. 'The minute I give up my guns he'll cut loose on me.'

"'If he does,' Wyatt promised, 'I'll give you back your guns and we'll shoot it out with him. As long as you're my prisoner, the man that gets you will have to get me.'

"Thompson hesitated.

"'Come on,' Wyatt ordered; 'throw down your gun or make your fight.' Ben Thompson grinned.

"'You win,' he said, tossing his shotgun into the road and shoved both hands above his head.

"Wyatt Earp's guns were still in their holsters. Now for the first time his hand went to his right hip.

"'You fellows get back!' he ordered the Texas men. 'Move!'

"As they obeyed, Wyatt stepped up to Thompson and unbuckled his prisoner's gun belts.

"'Come on, Ben,' he said 'we'll go over to the calaboose!' With the famous Thompson six-guns dangling from their belts in his left hand, Wyatt marched his prisoner across the plaza to Judge V.B. Osbourne's court. Until he reached the entrance, no onlookers spoke to him, or moved to follow. Once Wyatt and Ben were inside, the Mayor and his erstwhile officers hurried after them. A moment later, five hundred milling men stormed at the narrow doorway, Thompson's friends leading the mob.

"Deputy Sheriff Hogue, who had just ridden into town, forced a way through the crowd as a messenger from the Whitney home arrived with the shouted news that the Sheriff was dead.   The announcement was premature - Whitney actually lived for several hours after the Thompson hearing - but to the mob that was final.

"There was talk of lynching, but Wyatt anticipated no serious trouble on that score; real danger would come with any attempt of the Texas men to rescue Ben from the law. The Thompson element dictated his next move. Peshaur, Pierce, Kane and Good shouldered into the front rank, each with his forty-fives belted to his waist and Pierce carrying the shotgun with which Whitney had been assassinated and which Ben had thrown into the road. Wyatt spoke to Hogue in an undertone, then turned to the gunman.

"'Get out of here!' he ordered. 'Pierce, Take your crowd outside and keep 'em there. They'll be no lynching and no rescue.'

"Pierce looked at Thompson.

"'Better go, Cad,' Ben suggested. 'He means what he says.' With the courtroom cleared, Thompson arraignment proceeded.

"'What's the charge?' asked Judge Osbourne.

"As no one else volunteered to reply, Wyatt suggested that Ben was probably an accessory to murder. The judge turned to Mayor Miller as the proper person to indicate the enormity of Thompson's offense. The Mayor hesitated, possibly in embarrassment under the keen blue eyes of his hastily selected peace officer, considered the economic importance of the Texas men to the community, then offered as an amendment his opinion that maybe Ben had disturbed the peace.

"'Guilty,' said the judge. 'Twenty-five dollar fine.'

"Thompson grinned as he peeled the assessment from a role of greenbacks.

"'Do I get my guns?' he inquired.

"'Certainly,' said the judge. 'You have paid your fine and the Marshal will restore your property that he may have taken from you.'

"As Thompson reached for his gun belt, Wyatt issued his last order as an Ellsworth police officer.

"'Ben,' he said, 'court or no court, don't you put those on here. You carry them straight to the Grand Central, and don't so much as hesitate on the way. I'll be watching you. Keep moving until you're out of my sight. After that, what you do will be none of my business.'

"Wyatt stood in the courtroom door with his eye on Thompson until the gunman reached his hotel, then turned to Mayor Miller.

"'Here,' he said, 'is your badge, and here are the guns I got at Beebe's. I don't need 'em any longer.'

"'Don't you want to be Marshal of Ellsworth?' Miller asked.

"'I do not,' Wyatt replied.

"'We'll pay you one hundred and twenty-five dollars a month,' the Mayor offered.

"'Ellsworth,' Wyatt answered sententiously, 'figures sheriffs at twenty-five dollars a head, I don't figure the town's my size.'"[1]

That's the story that, according to Stuart N. Lake made Wyatt Earp the greatest gunfighter of all time. Of course its not believed by anyone who has made a study of the event but if you want to check it out in Lake's own book, it's not to hard to do.

Just go back to page 86 where Lake was quoting from the Ellsworth Reporter, where he said. "Thus the City was left without police, with no one but Deputy Sheriff Edward O. Hogue to make the arrests." At that point he stopped quoting from the Reporter and injected his own statement that "Hogue, it chanced, was absent in the Country." What he did, and it had to be intentional, was to leave out the next sentence of the Reporter's story which was: 'Hogue received the arms of Ben Thompson on the agreement of Happy Jack to give up his arms!" Thus it is apparent that Lake substituted his own fictitious story for the true facts as reported in the newspaper that the arrest of Ben Thompson was made by Deputy Sheriff Edward O. Hogue.[2]

There was never any mention of Wyatt Earp being present or taking part in the arrest of Ben Thompson, either in the newspapers of the day or in any contemporary writings of any person claiming to have been present.

One of the premier researchers of the Kansas portion of the old west history was one Floyd B. Streeter. Mr. Streeter was head librarian at Kansas State College from 1926 until his retirement in 1953. He was situated in the heart of the fabled west, and he devoted much of his spare time and his vacations to research of old courthouse records, searching through newspaper files and conducting interviews with still living old timers. His analysis of the events surrounding the killing of Sheriff Whitney are probably as accurate as anyone who ever researched the subject. In his book, <u>Ben Thompson, Man With a Gun</u>, he recounted how Billy Thompson was eventually returned for trial and acquitted of the murder of Sheriff Whitney. He examined the court records of the trial and was able to glean from them a fairly accurate picture of what occurred. In his book he said:

"According to the biography of Wyatt Earp, which was published in early 1930s, Earp walked out from a group of lookers-on and offered to arrest Thompson; the mayor accepted the offer, and Earp made the arrest.

---

[1]   <u>Wyatt Earp, Frontier Marshal</u>, pp. 81-93.

[2]   <u>Wyatt Earp, Frontier Marshal</u>, p. 86.; "Ellsworth Reporter," August 21, (1883).; <u>Great Gunfighters of the Kansas Cowtowns</u>, p. 445.

"When this account appeared in print, the writer began a long and exhaustive search for all of the evidence on the subject. The investigation included interviews with five eye witnesses; and several old timers who had heard the story from eye witnesses; municipal, county, and state records; files of contemporaneous Kansas newspapers and out of state dailies; and printed reminiscences of the period. A study of the evidence has convinced the writer that Wyatt Earp did not arrest Ben Thompson and that the account in the local newspaper which closes with the following statement is correct: 'Thus, the city was left without a police force, with no one but Deputy Sheriff Hogue to make the arrest. He received the arms of Ben Thompson on the agreement of Happy Jack to give up his arms.'

"'After surrendering,' says Ben, 'I went with the mayor to his office, and it being too late to have an examining trial, . . .' (with some difficulty he was able to post a $10,000 bond to secure his appearance in court the next morning and was released.)

"The terms of the bond required Thompson to appear in court the following morning to answer the charge of shooting at Happy Jack Morco. He was in the court room at the appointed hour, but Happy Jack declined to appear against him so he was discharged and the case dismissed."[1]

No one else who has researched the event has found anything in print, any reminiscences by any old timer who happened to be there, no court records, nothing. The only statement that gives Wyatt Earp credit for arresting Ben Thompson in Ellsworth, Kansas on that day is the statement of Stewart N. Lake, his biographer, and his quotation of a purported statement by Bat Masterson:

"Some years after the Ellsworth episode, Bat Masterson asked Ben Thompson why he had so docilely submitted to arrest by Wyatt Earp. Thompson's reply is quoted for what it may be worth.

"'It was jus' a hunch,' Ben told Bat, 'a hunch that Wyatt would get me if I opened up. I wasn't afraid of him, but I didn't want to die just then, and I had a hunch I was slated to if Wyatt went after his guns. But that wasn't all. It took nerve to come after me the way he did. He was just a youngster, but I could tell he'd go through with his play. He wouldn't have stood a chance to live against my crowd, even if he had knocked me off. I didn't want to see a young fellow as game as Wyatt go out with no chance for an even break. Cad Pierce wanted me to cut loose when Wyatt was about halfway across the plaza. I didn't, and I've never regretted it; if I had, I wouldn't be

---

[1] <u>Ben Thompson, Man With a Gun</u>, p. 101-102.

here telling about it, either.'"[1]

I have read everything that I could find written by or about Bat Masterson and have never found such a quote in any of the material. I personally doubt that Bat Masterson ever made such a statement.

This is particularly true in view of the fact that the incident never occurred. Ben Thompson certainly knew it, and probably Bat Masterson did too.

It would seem unusual that someone would invent such a story out of the whole cloth. Most liars and inventors of tall tales have something on which to base their stories. It seems that, perhaps, Harry Sinclair Drago, a noted author and historian of the old west, may have discovered the basis for the story. In his book, Wild, Wooly and Wicked, he told of an event that occurred on July 6, 1874, in Wichita, Kansas. At that time, he says that Wyatt Earp was serving as a police officer of the city of Wichita and was apparently present when the event occurred. Drago said that police officer Botts attempted to disarm a man as he emerged from Friar Saloon. The man refused to give up his weapons and Drago thinks that it was an incident arranged to embarrass the Wichita police department. The next thing that officer Botts knew, Hurricane Bill Martin, who apparently held a position in Wichita similar to the position previously described to have been held by Ben Thompson in Ellsworth, and ten or twelve of his gang emerged onto the sidewalk with six-guns drawn. Botts apparently wanted no part of this group and turned around and walked away. At this time, there was a vigilante organization in Wichita, the chief organizer being one Sim Tucker, a lawyer. Tucker and the vigilantes were outspoken critics of Marshal Smith and his police force and had apparently determined to take the Law into their own hands. The alarm was sounded and within minutes, no less than half a hundred vigilantes armed with shotguns and rifles gathered to assist the Marshal and other officers in front of police headquarters. Drago tells the story this way:

"Smith spoke to Tucker and tried to get him to order the vigilantes to disburse, saying that this was a matter the police could handle.

"The lawyer refused to listen. Leading the way, the vigilantes marched up Douglas Avenue, with the police tagging along, and took a stand on the south side of the Avenue opposite Hurricane Bill and his men. As Streeter puts it, 'This array of men and guns looked like two armies facing each other.'

"Smith was still protesting that this war-like gathering was a mistake, that if a shot was fired it would be followed by a blast of

---

[1]   Wyatt Earp, Frontier Marshal, pp.93-94.

promiscuous shooting that would snuff out the life of scores of innocent citizens.

"Tucker expressed his contempt for the Marshal and the Police. He is reported to have said; 'This is the third time we've been called out like this without an arrest being made. We're not afraid of trouble; we're used to it. You walk over there and arrest Hurricane Bill or we will.'

"The feeling against Smith has been growing for weeks. This was the first time his hand had been called. Jimmy Cairens, the best man on the force, did not come to his rescue, nor did the others, including policeman Earp.

"Beside himself, the city marshal said, 'All right, Tucker, you arrest him.'

"Silence descended, so deep that when Tucker cocked one barrel of his shotgun, the sound of a hammer coming back could be heard coming across Douglas Avenue. Stepping out into the dusty street, he leveled the weapon. 'Bill you are under arrest,' he called out.

"The outlaws revolvers began an upward swing.

"'Drop those guns,' Tucker commanded without raising his voice. After an anxious moment's hesitation, Hurricane Bill said with a half smile; 'you can take me,' saying which, he tossed his revolvers into the street.

"Stunned by this action, his followers dropped their six-guns or tossed them into the weeds. Without the help of the officers, Hurricane Bill and his crowd were marched over to the police court, where Judge Jewett assessed fines totaling six hundred dollars.

"This episode ended the reign of the Texas gang. Fearful of the demonstrative power of the vigilantes, Hurricane Bill drifted out of Wichita, and most of his followers went with him. It also marked the town's loss of confidence and respect for city Marshal Smith. He was not dismissed, but even his staunchest supporters realized he was finished politically and could not be re-elected.

"There is another aspect to this incident that is worthy of examination. It lies in its amazing similarity to Wyatt Earp's account of what occurred in Ellsworth in '73. Substitute Ben Thompson for Hurricane Bill -- both noted gunman inexplicably throwing their guns away -- and Ellsworth for Wichita with Earp playing the part of Sim Tucker, and the two incidents are alike in every detail. There is one difference; the Wichita episode is fact, not fancy."[1]

It would be easy to site a half a dozen other well-respected authors who have researched the subject, all of whom assert that the incident of Wyatt Earp facing down Bill Thompson in Ellsworth,

---

[1]   Wild, Wooly & Wicked, pp. 204-206.

Kansas in 1873 never happened. Drago is wrong when he says Earp was a policeman in Wichita in 1874. He was not appointed to the Wichita Police Department until April 21, 1875 and he never served under William Smith, but he undoubtedly heard the story. Whether or not Wyatt Earp adopted this story as his own and gave it to Lake, or Lake invented it in order to expand the fictitious character that he was creating, it is hard to say.

The John Henry Flood manuscript previously referred to, and supposedly one of the documents that most likely came directly from Wyatt Earp, fails to mention the arrest of Ben Thompson in Ellsworth, Kansas. But, interestingly, he does mention in a story that will be reviewed later, an event that supposedly occurred in Wichita, Kansas in which Earp told of a crowd of Texans, who were harassing him and who had claimed that he had shot one of their friends in Abilene, to "go back uptown and ask Ben Thompson; he was in Abilene; he will tell you."

It seems unlikely that if at that time, Earp had been telling the story of his arrest of Ben Thompson in Ellsworth he would have told this gang of cowboys to check out his reputation with Ben Thompson the following year in Wichita. However, that does not answer the mystery of who invented the story about the arrest of Ben Thompson.

In the Lake collection at the Huntington Library there is a sheet of handwritten paper, apparently in the handwriting of Lake himself, which outlines the whole story of the Ellsworth, Kansas event in approximately the same way that it was printed in Lake's biography of Wyatt. Whether or not this was written by Lake at a time the story was being told to him by Wyatt Earp, or was hand written at some other time is impossible to say. I doubt that it was written at the time the story was being told because other notes made by Lake during interviews appear in very short statements of five or six words, or a line at most; merely ticklers or reminders of certain things for him to expand on when he started writing.

When Earp was interviewed by a reporter of the San Francisco Examiner on August 2, 1896,[1] he went into some detail about his past life and a lot of detail about the events of Tombstone. But significantly, he did not say anything about the arrest of Ben Thompson. If he were at that time, claiming the event to be true, it seems he missed an excellent opportunity to tell his story once again with some certainty that it would be published.

Lake says that Wyatt hunted buffalo again during the winter of 1873-74 but found it to be much less profitable than the previous years and that in the spring of '74 he decided he would not hunt

---

[1]   The San Francisco Examiner, August 2, 1896, p. 1.

buffalo commercially again. He squared his accounts and sold his outfit, declining an invitation from Bat Masterson, Billy Dixon, Jim Hanrahan and others to join a summer hunt in the Texas panhandle, and by so doing, missed participation in the famous Indian fight at Adobe Walls in June of '74.[1]

He supposedly had a hankering to go into the cattle business and struck out for Wichita, which was fast becoming the major shipping point for the Texas trail herds.

---

[1]   Wyatt Earp, Frontier Marshal, p. 94.

CHAPTER V

WYATT EARP, WICHITA POLICE OFFICER

EARP'S movements in 1873 and 1874 are hard to trace. There does not appear to be any paper trail that one can follow. Reading from various biographers doesn't solve the problem either. For instance, Schoenberg[1] states that Earp was in Hays City during the early days, "The father of a Hays City resident remembers Earp there as a gambler." As authority for this statement he cites in footnote 15, a letter from Benjamin Streeter to Frank Waters dated Jan. 4, 1938. Waters quotes Dr. Streeter's letter as follows:

"It also might interest you to know that Wyatt Earp drifted into Hays occasionally in the early days. The father of our Hays newspaperman was a pioneer businessman here and played cards a good deal, so was acquainted with members of the gambling fraternity. He says he never knew Wild Bill Hickock to cheat at cards, but said that he and his friends had little use for Earp because he was up to some dishonest tricks every time he played."[2]

I have read all the biographies and articles that I could find that were written about Wyatt Earp, and this is the only charge I have come across that he was a crooked gambler. It seems that if that were really true, it would have been mentioned by other authors.

Streeter's letter does not specify a date on which Wyatt Earp appeared in Hays, Kansas, but in view of the lack of solid evidence of what Earp was doing during the years of '73 and '74, I think it is probable that he spent those years buffalo hunting and generally wandering around in the booming cow towns of Kansas, engaged in gambling.

Lake has Wyatt Earp going to Wichita, Kansas in the spring of 1874 and by reason of the great reputation that he had made by arresting Ben Thompson in Ellsworth, an event that never occurred, he was hired as assistant Marshal in Wichita. In this case, Lake was completely mistaken since the journals of the city commission of Wichita show that Wyatt was not appointed to the Wichita police

---

[1]   The Gunfighters, p. 23.

[2]   The Earp Brothers of Tombstone, pp. 37-38.

department until April 21, 1875.[1]

However, there were Earps in Wichita in 1874 and 1875.

Miller and Snell state that "Bessy Earp, wife of James, Wyatt's brother, was fined in Wichita police court in May, 1874, for being a prostitute. So was Sally Earp, who apparently shared the same dwelling, but for whom no other identification has been found. Bessy and Sally were each fined $8 and $2 court costs. Sally's name appears regularly in the city's prostitute file list through February 1875 and Bessy's through March 1875."[2]

It seems that Miller and Snell were making an unwarranted assumption when they assumed that Bessie, the wife of James Earp was the Betsy arrested for prostitution. For they say:

"Sally and Bessie (or Betsy as she was named in the information) were arrested on the same day by Constable J.W. McCarthey, pleaded guilty and were remanded to the next term of the district court period. Unable to put up their bail of $250 each, they were assigned places in the county jail. Apparently, they eventually found the requisite sums, for the monthly city prostitute list testifies to their continued 'business' activity.

"The Earp girls came up before the district court on December 15, 1874 but upon motion of their attorney, William Baldwin, their case was dismissed."[3]

Miller and Snell also say that in August 1874 two other Earps (Earbs as they were sometimes listed) were fined as prostitutes; they were "Kate and Minnie." They do say that: "While the girls listed may not have been related to Wyatt's family, the surname is distinctive enough to warrant their inclusion in this sketch." Again, it seems that Miller and Snell are making rather precarious assumptions when they assume that Betsy was Bessie and that Earbs were Earps. They may be right, but again, they may be wrong. They demonstrate that when they say: "Only Bessie Earp has been definitely established as Wyatt's sister-in-law. The authoritative contemporary source is the 1880 United States census for Tombstone, Pima County, Arizona territory, which lists Bessie, then 36 years old, as James' wife."[4]

It should be noted that the census listed her as Bessie, not Betsy

---

[1]   Great Gunfighters of the Kansas Cowtowns, p. 80; Proceedings of the Governing Body, Records of the City of Wichita, Journal B pp. 44-53.

[2]   Great Gunfighters of Kansas Cowtowns, p. 79.

[3]   Great Gunfighters of the Kansas Cowtowns, p. 79.

[4]   Ibid, p. 79.

as the woman was named in the court records of Wichita.

As far as Wyatt is concerned, we do have some evidence that he was in Wichita in the summer of 1874 and did on at least one occasion, engaged in either private detective or collection agency work. The Wichita Eagle of October 29, 1874 printed the following story:

"The Higgenbottom outfit, who attempted to jump the country at an expense of twenty or thirty thousand dollars to Wichita, it appears among other games stuck M.R. Mosier for a new wagon, who instead of putting himself in communication by telegraph with the outside world just got two officers, John Behrens and Wyatt Earp, to light out upon the trail. These boys fear nothing and fear nobody. They made about seventy-five miles from sun to sun, across trackless prairies, striking the property and the thieves near the Indian line. To make a long and exciting story short, they just leveled a shotgun and a six shooter upon the scallywags as they lay concealed in some brush, and told then to 'dough over,' which they did to the amount of $146, one of them remarking that he was not going to die for the price of a wagon. It is amusing to hear Mosier tell how slick the boys did the work."[1]

There are two interesting facets to that news story. One is that it appears that Higgenbottom was about to leave the county "at an expense of twenty to thirty thousand dollars to Wichita" and later on in the story it appears that the account was settled for $146.00. There seems to be a lot of difference. The other is that the article says that Mr. Mosier got "two officers" thus listing Wyatt Earp as an officer, which he definitely was not at that time, although John Behrens was.

Miller and Snell state that "On April 21, 1875, Wyatt Earp was appointed policeman on the Wichita police force, and the appointment was entered on the records of the city. This was the first time that Earp's name appeared in the City's official records. Wichita's police force now consisted of Marshal Mike Megher, assistant Marshal John Behrens, and policemen James Cairns and Earp."[2]

Despite all the hair-raising events narrated by Lake and Flood which will be discussed hereafter, during Wyatt Earp's tour of duty on the Wichita police force, his name was mentioned in the newspapers only six times.

For instance, on May 12, 1875, the Weekly Beacon reported;

---

1   Wichita City Eagle, October 29, 1874; Great Gunfighters of the Kansas Cowtowns, p. 80.

2   Ibid, p. 80; "Proceedings of the Governing Body" Records of the city of Wichita, Journal B, pp. 44 - 53; Wichita Weekly Beacon, April 28, 1875.

"AN ARISTOCRATIC HORSE THIEF.

"On Tuesday evening of last week (May 4th), policeman Earp, in his rounds ran across a chap who's general appearance and get up answered to a description given of one W. W. Compton, who was said to have stolen two horses and a mule from the vicinity of Leroy, in Coffee county. Earp took him in tow, and inquired his name. He gave it as 'Jones'. This didn't satisfy the officer, who took Mr. Jones into the gold room on Douglas avenue in order that he might fully examine him by lamp light. Mr. Jones not liking the looks of things, lit out, running to the rear of Dennison's stables. Earp fired one shot across his poop deck to bring him to, to use a naughty-cal phrase and just as he did so, the man cast anchor near a clothes line, hauled down his colors and surrendered without firing a gun. The officer laid hold of him before he could recover his feet for another run, and taking him to jail placed him in the keeping of the Sheriff. On the way, 'Jones' acknowledged that he was the man wanted. The fact of the arrest was telegraphed to the Sheriff of Coffee County, who came down on Thursday night and removed Compton to the jail of that county. A black horse and buggy was found at one of the feed stables where Compton had left them. After stealing the stock from Coffee County, he went to Independence, where he traded them for a buggy, stole the black horse and came to this place. He will probably have an opportunity to do the state some service for a number of years, only to come out and go to horse stealing again, until a piece of twisted helm, or a stray bullet puts an end to his hankering after horse flesh."[1]

Again on November 10, 1875 the Weekly Beacon mentioned Wyatt Earp's name in connection with an arrest made by him and Marshal Meager. The newspaper story was as follows:

"THE TERRORS AND TEMPTATIONS OF BULL WHACKING.

"Last Friday [November 5], being hangman's day and generally regarded by the superstitious as the twenty-four hours in all the week, for all time, which the devil has reserved for himself against the holy Sabbath, appropriated by his enemies, it befell three turbulent twirlers of the long lash, stimulator's of the patient ox, to be wooed into ways that are dark and tricks that proved vain, and on the devil's own day. A bull train, consisting of two large wagons and eight yoke of oxen, had arrived at West Wichita, corralled and went into camp early that morning. There was nothing very remarkable in this fact, being of daily, almost hourly occurrence, but in the sequel, in the reproof of chance lay the proof of crime, with an apology, if it so please you, for spoiling one of Williams best and most quoted. Marshal Megher, as

[1]   Great Gunfighters of the Kansas Cowtowns, p. 81.

the wires and mails would so have it, had a description of this identical outfit in his pocket, with the names of the parties to it. The intelligence conveyed to him was that one Bill Potts, assisted by two gentlemen of color, had actually stolen these oxen and wagons, and stranger yet, under the very nose of their owner, and as slow as oxen travel, had most miraculously succeeded in eluding pursuit, evading highways and coming through the long prairie grass, reached Wichita, from Fort Sill, where this wholesale theft was committed. If nothing of reputation is left this little crowd of deprecators, one thing will ever remain tenaciously with their names, that they made the best bull time on record and are therefore entitled to the name of being the champion bull whackers of the Sill. We expect to see a dime edition out soon, with some such title and the usual daredevil wood cut, emblazoning in red, yellow and magenta this identical trio, whipping, goading and spurring amain the frantic longhorns.

"Be that as it may, Mike Megher soon spotted good M. Potts, the only white man in the crowd, who was threading his way through the busy throng on lower Main street making with all possible speed and with a business-like air, towards the individual whom he had put up to be the innocent purchaser. He sought out several buyers. In the meantime, Marshal Megher, having business always near by. At last Mr. Potts betook himself to Davidson's stables and securing a horse for himself, had old Mr. Davidson to mount another and together they crossed the long bridge, Mr. Davidson going to look at the cattle and make up his mind whether to buy or not. Mike Megher with Policeman Earp, also took an airing on horseback about the same time clattering the bridge with the music of their horses' hoofs in beautiful quartette with those that bore Mr. Potts and his victim, and so, until all the parties halted in the marauders' camp, when good Mr. Potts and his two able assistants were compelled to surrender at the point of the six shooter and were, when we saw them, marching up the center of Main street, three abreast, with the two mounted officers in the rear, herding them to jail. There they now are, waiting the certainty of that hour that will bring them to face offended law, and to go hence and be forgot, at least for a term of years. That is to say, and it is written with this express understanding, if they do not break jail."[1]

Miller and Snell state that on November 17, 1875, The <u>Beacon</u> changed its story giving credit for the arrest to Megher and Behrens, so that it may not have been true that Earp was involved in the arrest

---

[1]   <u>Great Gunfighters of the Kansas Cowtowns</u>, p. 81-82.

as originally reported.[1]

Again, on December 15, 1875 the Beacon mentioned Wyatt Earp in the following story:

"On last Wednesday (December 8), policeman Earp found a stranger lying near the bridge in a drunken stupor. He took him to the 'cooler' and on searching him found in the neighborhood of $500 on his person. He was taken next morning, before his honor, the police judge, paid his fine for his fun like a little man and went on his way rejoicing. He may congratulate himself that his lines, while he was drunk, were cast in such a pleasant place as Wichita as there are but few other places where that $500 roll would have been heard from. The integrity of our police force has never been seriously questioned."[2]

On January 12, 1876, the Wichita Beacon told a story of Wyatt Earp having a freak gun accident which resulted from his having all chambers of his six-shooter loaded in violation of what was then considered safety precautions. The story was as follows:

"Last Sunday night (January 9), while policeman Earp was sitting with two or three others in the back room of the Custom House Saloon, his revolver slipped from his holster, and falling to the floor, the hammer which was resting on the cap, is suppose to have struck the chair, causing a discharge of one of the barrels. The ball passed through his coat, struck the north wall then glanced off and passed out through the ceiling. It was a narrow escape and the occurrence got up a lively stampede from the room. One of the demoralized was under the impression that someone had fired through the window from the outside."[3]

In April of 1876, there was a local election, in which Mike Megher, City Marshal was pitted against one William Smith for the post. Wyatt Earp as a supporter of Mike Megher apparently created some ill will with candidate William Smith. He evidently got into a fight with Smith and it was reported in the Wichita Weekly Beacon on April the 5th as follows:

"On last Sunday night [April 2] a difficulty occurred between policeman Erp [sic] and Wm. Smith, candidate for city marshal. Erp [sic] was arrested for violation of the peace and order of the city and was fined on Monday afternoon by his honor Judge Atwood, $30 and cost, and was relieved from the police force. Occurring on the eve of

[1]   Great Gunfighters of the Kansas Cowtowns, p. 83.

[2]   Ibid, p. 83.

[3]   Great Gunfighters of the Kansas Cowtowns, p. 83.; Wichita Beacon, January 12, 1876.

the city election, and having its origin in the canvass, it aroused general partisan interest throughout the city. The rumors, freely circulated Monday morning, reflected very severely upon our city marshal. It was stated and quite generally credited that it was a put up job on the part of the city marshal and his assistant, to put the rival candidate for marshal hors de combat and thus remove an obstacle in the way of the re-election of the city marshal. These rumors, we say, were quietly largely credited, notwithstanding their essential improbability and their inconsistency with the well known character of Mike Megher, who is noted for his manly bearing and personal courage. The evidence before the court fully exonerated Megher from the charge of a cowardly conspiracy to mutilate and disable a rival candidate, but showed that he repeatedly ordered his subordinate to avoid any personal collision with Smith, and when the encounter took place, Mike used his utmost endeavor to separate the combatants. If there is any room to reflect on the marshal, it is that he did not order his subordinate out of Smith's room as soon as he entered, knowing as he did, that Erp [sic] had fight on the brain. It is well known that in periods of excitement people do not always act as they would when perfectly collected and unexcited. The remarks that Smith was said to have made in regard to the marshal sending for Erp's brothers to put them on the police force furnished no just grounds for an attack, and upon ordinary occasions we doubt if Erp [sic] would have given them a second thought. The good order of the city was properly vindicated in the fining and dismissal of Erp [sic]. It is but justice to Erp [sic] to say he has made an excellent officer, and hitherto his conduct has been unexceptionable."[1]

Miller and Snell report that the election was held on April 3rd, the day before the above article was printed in the Weekly Beacon, and that Megher won the Marshal election. They also reported that a new city counsel was elected on the same date and that it met on the 19th of April 1876 and among other business took up the matter of nominations for appointment to the police department. They quote the city clerk's minute book as follows:

"Numerous nominations were made for policeman, the vote on Mr. Wyatt Earp stood two for and six against.

"Mr. R.C. Richey was elected policeman, votes standing 6 for and two against. Mr. Dan Parks was also duly elected policeman. Votes standing five for and three against. On motion, the vote taken on Mr. Earp was reconsidered, the result of the ballots showing four for and

---

[1]   Great Gunfighters of the Kansas Cowtowns, p. 84.

four against."[1]

When the City Council met again on May 8, Wyatt Earp was allowed $40.00 for 20 days work in April. The counsel also ordered the committee on jail and police to investigate the matter relating to the collection of moneys due the city by persons not authorized to do so.[2]

On May 10, 1876 the police committee submitted its report as follows: "We the police Com. respectfully submit the following report. That policeman L (R.C.?) Richey be relieved from further duty and that the marshal enforce the vagrant act in the case of the 2 Earps, the long haired man, the man whose trial has been postponed, Sol Woodmancey and 'Red'. The script of W. Earp and John Behrns be withheld from payment until all moneys collected by them for the city be turned over to the city treasurer."[3]

On May 24, 1876, the Wichita Weekly Beacon reported that Wyatt Earp had been put on the police force at Dodge City.[4]

---

[1]   Ibid, p. 85.

[2]   Proceedings of the Governing Body, Records of the City of Wichita, Journal B, p. 103.

[3]   Misc. Papers, Records of the City of Wichita; Great Gunfighters of the Kansas Cowtowns, p. 85.

[4]   Ibid, p. 85.

CHAPTER VI

SOME FICTITIOUS EARP
EPISODES IN WICHITA

IN view of the fact that a study of the newspaper reports would indicate that the papers generally covered almost everything, even the most trivial, that appeared to be newsworthy in Wichita, one has to wonder about the stories told about the activities of Wyatt Earp in taming the town of Wichita.

For instance, Lake has Wyatt Earp appearing in Wichita in the spring of 1874 where he first looked up his brother Jim who had been in Wichita for several weeks and was apparently tending bar. He told what had to be a totally fictitious story because it was based somewhat on the fact that Wyatt had arrested Ben Thompson in Ellsworth, which of course never happened. The story went like this:

"Wyatt's first move was to hunt out his brother Jim, who had been in Wichita for several weeks. From him he had warning that Ben Thompson and George Peshaur were in town, making headquarters at the Keno House, then the most famous gambling-establishment in the prairie West, at the corner of Main Street and Douglas Avenue, and next door to which Jim had a job with one Pryor. Jim suggested that, as the Texas men were running wild in Wichita, it behooved Wyatt to watch for their attempt to even the Ellsworth score. Ben Thompson had little to say about the Whitney murder and its aftermath, but George Peshaur had boasted openly of what he would do to Wyatt Earp at the first opportunity; which those who knew the Texan took to mean the first time that Peshaur caught Wyatt short.

"On his second morning in town, Wyatt and several other men followed the noise of a ruction to the rear of Doc Black's corral, where they found the burly proprietor beating a small choreboy. In the struggle of prying Black's two hundred-odd pounds of fat and spleen away from his victim, Doc's rage carried him out of that discretion in matters of physical encounter for which he was noted and he swung wildly at those who interfered with discipline; by chance, he hit Wyatt in the face. Wyatt promptly blacked Doc's eyes and knocked him down. Upon regaining his feet, the corral proprietor hurried up Douglas Avenue, to return a few moments later with a deputy marshal.

"'I'm arresting you, Earp,' the deputy said. 'Black's charging you with assault.'

"'All right,' Wyatt answered. 'Let's see the judge and get it over.'

"Judge Ed Jewett was not in his court, the officer explained. Temporarily, the village was using a near-by shack as a jail, and if the prisoner would walk over to it and consider himself locked in, he could save trouble. Wyatt complied, and the deputy sat down in the doorway while the vindictively impatient Black waddled off to find the judge.

"All unwittingly, the deputy marshal had arrested Wyatt Earp at a time fixed by Texas gunmen for treeing Wichita. A few days earlier, two cowboys had run afoul of a giant negro hodcarrier, who had first drubbed the pair in a fist-fight, then added insult to their injuries by dragging them before Judge Jewett, who had fined them for assault. The cowboys and their friends decided to pay off the camp with an object lesson.

"Throughout the morning of the day appointed, Texas men had been drifting into town unostentatiously, and stationing themselves at strategic points, principally in saloons along Douglas Avenue. By the time of Wyatt's arrest, the earlier arrivals had absorbed enough whisky to wax impatient, and when Doc Black, in his search for Jewett, spread word that Wyatt Earp was under arrest, a dozen agreed that, while waiting to avenge the negro's insult, they might as well get the man who had discomfited their friends in Ellsworth.

"Wyatt and his guardian in the doorway of the shack saw the Texas crowd, on foot and patently very drunk, turn off Douglas Avenue in their direction.

"'I'll get some help,' the deputy marshal said, and started 'cross-lots.

"Wyatt slammed the flimsy door in the cowboys' faces.

"'Is Wyatt Earp in there?' a Texan demanded.

"'I'm Wyatt Earp. What do you want?'

"'We want you.'

"'What for?'

"'You killed a couple of our friends up in Ellsworth last Summer; that's what for,' someone answered.

"'You're wrong,' Wyatt parleyed. 'I didn't kill anyone in Ellsworth, but I'll kill the first man through this door. Before you start anything, go ask Ben Thompson what happened. He'll tell you, you don't want me.'

"The only weapon in Wyatt's possession was a stool with which he stood ready to bash in the first head that came in any rush through the doorway; he used Ben Thompson's name in the hope of diverting the maudlin gang long enough to let him reach more substantial cover. The Texans fell to arguing.

"'Come on,' Wyatt heard one suggest. 'We'll ask Ben if he wants us to knock this fellow off. We can get him any time. Let's get another drink, anyway.'

"The last argument prevailed, and the dozen or fifteen cowboys moved off toward the Douglas Avenue saloons. As they left, the deputy marshal returned.

"'Hell's going to pop some place,' he reported. 'Every joint in town is full of Texas men.'

"'Are they after me?' Wyatt asked.

"The deputy guessed they were, and that he'd better round up some assistance.

"'You expect me to stay here to be murdered by a bunch of drunks?' Wyatt inquired.

"'Well, I wouldn't want you to do that,' the deputy admitted. 'Haven't you got any guns?'

"'I checked 'em up at Pryor's,' Wyatt explained.

"'Take mine,' said the deputy. 'I'll get another pair uptown. If that mob comes after you, maybe you can stand 'em off. I'll get someone to come down here and help us.'

"Wyatt buckled on the gun belts and ran over to a stable, where he posted himself in a stall which commanded both street and rear entrance. He heard two pistol-shots in the distance, followed by the pound of hoofs down Douglas Avenue. A buckskin pony on the dead run, rider low in the saddle, sped past the doorway, over the toll bridge and on across the prairie. Behind him a mob of cowboys with drawn guns backed past the barn where Wyatt was concealed, and halted at the bridgehead.

"Wyatt was puzzled. The Texas men paid no attention to the shack in which he had been a prisoner, but held their eyes up Douglas Avenue. Borrowed pistols in hand, he peered around the corner of the stable doorway, and as he did so, Bill Smith, chief marshal of Wichita, sidled along the building directly in front of him.

"'Get out of the way,' Wyatt said. 'You're right in range.'

"Smith jumped.

"'Don't shoot,' he said; then looked around. 'Oh,' he added with apparent relief, 'you're Earp. They're not after you; they're covering Shorty's getaway.'

"'Who's Shorty?' Wyatt asked.

"'He's the fellow who crossed the bridge in a hurry. He killed a nigger up in Main Street. The nigger and some cowboys had trouble a few days ago, and the boys picked Shorty to pay the grudge. Shorty stood about fifty feet from where the nigger was working and waited until he got to the top of a ladder with a hod of bricks. Then he cut him down. The first shot drilled the nigger clean through the head, and while he and the bricks were in the air, Shorty put another slug through his belly. That nigger was dead before the first brick hit the ground. Then Shorty rode some.'

"'What are you going to do,' Wyatt asked, 'arrest them?'

"'Shorty's gone and there are too many to arrest,' the marshal replied. 'I'm going to see if I can keep them from hurrahing the whole town. You stay out of sight until I come for you!

"'Hey,' Smith called to the cowboys, 'I want to talk to you.'

"'Come on over,' one of the mob replied.

"The parley ended when the Texans agreed to put up their guns if they were not to be molested for the death of the hodcarrier. Wyatt waited in the barn while the marshal carried word of the compromise uptown. Twenty minutes later, Smith stuck his head in the door.

"'Come on,' he said, 'the mayor wants to see you.'

"At the entrance to the mayor's office, Wyatt met the deputy who had arrested him and returned the borrowed weapons. Inside, he found Jim Hope, mayor of Wichita, and two town councilmen.

"'Are you Wyatt Earp?' Hope asked.

"'That's my name.'

"'You the fellow that run it over Ben Thompson in Ellsworth last summer?'

"'I arrested him.'

"'How'd you like to be deputy marshal of Wichita?'

"Wyatt, who thought that he was on the carpet for punching Doc Black, was momentarily taken aback by the question. In after years he recalled clearly the rapid reasoning which followed surprise and determined his answer. There was a deal of egotism involved, he admitted; it had occurred to him before that he'd like to stack up against these men who terrorized the prairie towns and to try out certain theories concerning them. Briefly, he believed he was a better man than any braggart gun-thrower who rode the cattle-trail; there was considerable zest to be anticipated in this opportunity to justify that confidence.

"'We pay one hundred and twenty-five dollars a month and supply guns and ammunition,' Mayor Hope suggested.

"'I've got seventy-five hundred dollars in my clothes,' Wyatt replied, 'and the wages don't interest me.'

"Which remark, as Wyatt once commented, was bumptious, but honest. He was young, and seventy-five hundred dollars was a large sum of money in that time and country. Moreover, the last thing he foresaw was any extended career as a peace officer.

"'I was out to prove a little something,' he said; 'that accomplished, I'd be quitting.'

"In considering the manner in which the deputy's badge was tendered to Wyatt Earp, it should be recalled that in the seventies it often was difficult to obtain competent marshals for the frontier villages. The jobs were fraught with danger and applications for the positions were rarely made; in some instances the posts were filled by tempting able men with high wages; in many cases, the peace officers were youthful adventurers lured by promise of action; the roster of famous frontier peace officers reveals that a majority attained eminence well under the age of thirty.

"How far can I go in making your ordinances stick?' Wyatt asked.

"'The limit,' Mayor Hope answered.

"Jim Hope handed over a deputy marshal's badge.

"'Pin that on your shirt,' he said, 'and go down to the New York Store and get yourself some guns. Charge 'em to me. Then come back here.'

"Fifteen minutes later, Wyatt reentered Hope's office with a single-action Colt's forty-five at his right hip and a belt of cartridges around his waist. The mayor took one look at him.

"'Guns,' he snapped; 'not gun. You've got a two-gun job.'

"'Suits me,' Wyatt answered, and went back to add to his arsenal."[1]

Of course this story has to be fictional. In the first place Wyatt didn't join the Wichita police force until April, 1875, fully a year after the events described by Lake. Secondly, Wyatt Earp never worked for Marshal Bill Smith, who, incidentally was the person Wyatt was accused of slugging and the cause of his ultimate discharge from the Wichita police force. Mike Megher was the Marshal of Wichita at all times that Wyatt Earp was on the police force.

That Lake's story of Wyatt Earp in Wichita is simply fiction was further reinforced when he quoted a purported statement by Judge Patton who said; "I met Wyatt the day he joined the Marshal's force, I was told that he was the man who had arrested Ben Thompson in Ellsworth after the murder of Sheriff Whitney, and the rest of Wichita knew as much by nightfall. The Ellsworth exploit would have made him a marked man in any community, and when the town added to that, the evidence of capability which showed in every inch of him, we began to hope that at last we had a peace officer who could fill our sizable bill. Later, I saw Wyatt, single-handed go against some of the most desperate gunmen in the West -- I stood not 10 ft. away from him on two such occasions -- in action he bore out my highest expectations."[2]

Of course this quote cannot be accurate, since Wyatt Earp never arrested Ben Thompson in Ellsworth and his reputation could not be based on that event. And the quotation is also subject to some suspicion when he says that he stood not ten feet away from Wyatt

---

[1]   Wyatt Earp, Frontier Marshal, pp. 95-101.

[2]   Ibid, pp. 103-104.

Earp when on two occasions he went against some of the most desperate gunmen in the west. If that were true, one would think that he would tell the names of the desperate gunmen and the circumstances under which the events took place. None of that appears.

John Henry Flood's manuscript completely fails to mention the killing of Sheriff Whitney or the arrest of Ben Thompson that is supposed to have occurred in Ellsworth, but he does repeat the story just quoted from Lake's book about the run in with Doc Black. He adds an interesting factor to that story, however, that should be taken into consideration. He states that when the crowd gathered about the place where Wyatt Earp was confined the following conversation took place. After someone demanded to know if he was there he replied:

"'Yes I am here; what do you want?'

"'We want your hide,' a hoarse voice shouted.

"'It isn't worth much.'

"'We want it anyway; we're going to find out!' 'You shot one of our Texans at Abilene last summer!' and they milled around and around."[1]

Of course both stories, that is Lake's and Flood's, contain the statement that Wyatt Earp told the crowd to go ask Ben Thompson about what happened, except that Lake doesn't refer to Abilene as Flood does, but refers to Ellsworth. There's another facet to Lake's story that is questionable. That is the first part of his story where he said that "Temporarily, the village was using a near-by shack as a jail, and if a prisoner would walk over to it and consider himself locked in, he could save trouble."[2]

Miller and Snell, in their book Great Gunfighters of the Kansas Cow Towns, citing the proceedings of the governing body, records of the city of Wichita, Journal A, pp. 78-81, state that "the contract for building the city jail was let on June 1, 1871, early construction to be paid for by poll and dog taxes. So quickly was the work accomplished that by June 22, 1871, the Wichita Tribune was able to say, 'Our Saloon keepers sell the drinks, and next week Marshal Megher will be ready to cell the drinker. -- In the new calaboose.'"

At a meeting held June 28, the council authorized acceptance of the new jail provided the 'committee on calaboose' judged it satisfactory after a careful inspection."[3]

It seems peculiar, to say the least, that Wichita police would

---

[1]   Flood's Manuscript, p. 36.

[2]   Wyatt Earp, Frontier Marshal, p. 96.

[3]   Great Gunfighters of the Kansas Cowtowns, p. 345.

temporarily be using a near-by shack as a jail after the city had already built a permanent one in 1871. It doesn't make sense.

Another one of Lake's stories about Earp's activities in Wichita proves to be false.

He describes the killing of Red Redfern by Rowdy Joe Lowe as follows: "Just across the toll bridge and outside the municipality, Rowdy Joe Lowe and his wife, Rowdy Kate, ran a dance hall and saloon which they bragged was 'the swiftest joint in Kansas.' This claim was valiantly disputed by 'Red' and Mrs. 'Red' Redfern, who operated a similar establishment across the road along lines calculated to make idle their neighbors boasts of speed. Their rivalry continued until Rowdy Joe, armed with a shotgun, and Red, with a six-shooter, stepped into the road to settle the argument over pace in incontrovertible fashion. Rowdy Joe downed Red, but in the course of the killing a couple of stray buckshot took the eyes out of an innocent bystander. Sheriff Megher deputized Wyatt to arrest the dance hall proprietor which Wyatt did without difficulty, but Joe was promptly released when it was shown that the fight had been an even break. The bystander, it was held, could not prove legitimate business in the line of fire.[1]

Keep in mind that Wyatt Earp was appointed to the Wichita police force on April 21, 1875. Note the report of a fight between Rowdy Joe Lowe and Red Redfern reported in the Wichita Eagle on October 30, 1873:

"The dance houses on the west side of the river were again the scene of a terrible and fearful onset, on Monday night last. We have heard the versions of the principal actors, as also that of outsiders and the officers, with little satisfaction. Suffice it to say that the proprietors of the two dance houses in West Wichita, which stand in close proximity, 'Rowdy Joe' and 'Red', both being mad from the effects of distilled poison and armed with revolvers and shot guns, waltzed into a deadly melee. Rowdy Joe was shot in the back of the neck with a pistol ball. Wound is not dangerous. Red was wounded in the arm and hip by buck shot from a shot gun. The chances are that he will lose the lower part of his arm. A poor dance girl, Annie Franklin, sick at the time, received a shot in the abdomen, which the doctors think must prove fatal. Bill Anderson, who through mistake killed a man last spring, was shot in the head, the ball passing just back of the eyes. Was alive at last accounts. Rowdy Joe gave himself up, and now out on $2000. bail. No other arrests have been made, we believe.

---

[1]   Wyatt Earp, Frontier Marshal, p. 102.

Comment is unnecessary, and a further dilation worse than foolish."[1]

On November 13, 1873 the Wichita Eagle reported that Red had died on November 11th. Thereafter, the papers followed the case in great detail.

On November 20, 1873, the Eagle Reported that Joe Lowe, after an examination before Esquire Jewett had been bound over for appearance at the December term of the court for the murder of E.T. Beard.[2]

Again, on December 11, the Eagle reported that on December 9, a trial was commenced before Judge W.P. Campbell for the trial of Rowdy Joe Lowe on the charge of murder. The paper reported the proceedings of the trial in great detail for several days. The trial went to the jury on December 10, 1873 and the next morning Rowdy Joe was pronounced not guilty by the jury. The results of the trial were outlined in the Wichita Eagle of Dec. 18, 1873 as follows:

"In the culmination of the trial of Rowdy Joe on last Wednesday evening, for the killing of Red, more than ordinary interest was evinced by the people of the city. The judge charged the jury at great length on what constituted murder in the second degree, including five lesser crimes, either of which the prisoner might be found guilty under the charge. There were four speeches made by counsel, of the average duration of an hour each. H.C. Sluss, for the state, opened with a review of the entire testimony, giving his constructions and conclusions. After supper he was followed by S.M. Tucker for the defense, who not only in a clever but able manner reviewed the case in all its legal bearings. He in turn was followed by Smith Deveny, of Olathe, in an appeal to the jury, in which was recited the redeeming traits of Rowdy Joe, and in which was pictured in not very enviable colors the vagabond and desperado, Red. By this time the interest of the spectators was visible to court and jury.

"Mr. Sluss rose to close. His earnest manner told that he appreciated his surroundings. Embarrassed by his own witnesses, who were composed of men and women in full sympathy with the accused, whose sense of modesty and appreciation of right had long since been sacrificed with their virtue, and who cared little for the obligations of an oath, and less for the penalty that is attached to its violation, he had been conducting the case through almost hopeless surroundings. But unused by menaces and undismayed in the absence of sympathy, with all the earnestness of his nature, he stood up to defend the sacred right to life, and the majesty of the law.

---

[1]   Great Gunfighters of the Kansas Cowtowns, p. 157.

[2]   Ibid, p. 159.

"Despite the fact of being in a court of justice, upon closing his speech the spectators gave way to an uproarious applauding. It was a spontaneous acknowledgement by the better class of citizens of the able and conscientious manner in which the attorney for the people had discharged his duty. The jury retired at about 10 o'clock. A verdict of 'not guilty' was rendered next morning.

"Immediately, another writ was issued for his arrest for shooting Anderson; also, an action was commenced against him for damages. The pressure was too great, and Rowdy Joe came up missing last Sunday morning. He had eluded the vigilance of the officer, Mr. [John] Nugent, who had him in charge, and at this writing nothing has been heard of him. Sheriff [William] Smith with a posse followed all Saturday night, but returned disappointed. On Monday Smith had several parties arrested for participating or criminality in his escape, among them Rowdie Kate, the result of which we will inform our readers all in good season."[1]

Thereafter, the paper periodically wrote stories about the whereabouts of Rowdy Joe. In January of 1874 he was reported to have been arrested and released on a writ of habeas corpus by a judge in St. Louis, Missouri. After that he was again reported to be in various places and finally on November 29, 1874 the Wichita Eagle published a story stating that he had been murdered.[2]

At any rate, all of the proceedings had with, about or against Rowdy Joe Lowe occurred before Wyatt Earp joined the Wichita police force on April 21, 1875. This is a typical example of how Lake would use some real person's name, and a few events that may have occurred at some time to weave a story that would make his man a hero.

That there really was a Rowdy Joe Lowe and that his wife was either a prostitute or madam, sometimes known as Rowdy Kate and that they operated in Wichita, Kansas is not to be questioned. The real question is how much did Wyatt Earp know about this, and the answer is probably nothing.

Whether or not Earp ever arrested Rowdy Joe Lowe in Wichita, there is evidence that Joe's path and that of his wife, sometimes known as Rowdy Kate and sometimes as Nosy Kate Lowe, would cross that of Wyatt Earp again. Paula Mitchell Marks, in her book, And Die in the West, in listing the houses of prostitution and naming the "frail sisters" in Tombstone at its height, mentions the rough and tumble

---

[1]   Great Gunfighters of the Kansas Cowtowns, pp. 163-164.
       Wichita Eagle, December 18, 1873.

[2]   Great Gunfighters of the Kansas Cowtowns, pp. 163-167.

brothel of former Dodge City denizen Nosy Kate Lowe.[1]

Later, in 1883, when Wyatt Earp joined with Bat Masterson and others of the gambling fraternity in what was known as the Peace Commission and returned to Dodge City to protect the interests of one of their friends, Luke Short, he ran into Rowdy Joe Lowe. In telling about the affair, the Kansas City (Missouri) Journal of May 15, 1883 reported:

"Masterson precedes by twenty-four hours a few other pleasant gentlemen who are on their way to the tea party at Dodge. One of them is Wyatt Earp, the famous marshal of Dodge, another is Joe Lowe, otherwise known as 'Rowdy Joe;' and still another is 'Shotgun' Collins; but worse than all, is another ex-citizen and officer of Dodge, the famous Doc Holliday."[2]

---

[1]   And Die in the West, p. 49.

[2]   Great Gunfighters of the Kansas Cowtowns, p. 387.

CHAPTER VII

THE ARREST OF
SHANGHAI PEARCE

ANOTHER one of Lake's fictitious stories, probably designed to increase the stature of his fictitious marshal, was the arrest of Shanghai Pearce and his group of Texans. In this, he followed his usual pattern just as he did in telling the story of the arrest of Ben Thompson in Ellsworth. The story went like this:

"A CATTLE KING IS DEPOSED

"On a Saturday afternoon in early summer, a messenger dispatched by several Wichita merchants found Wyatt Earp on lower Douglas Avenue keeping tab on the cowboys streaming across the toll bridge for the Saturday carousal, which, in all well-regulated cowtowns, was several shades wilder and more widely inclusive than those of other days.

"'They want you up on Main Street,' the messenger told Wyatt. 'Shanghai Pearce is drunk and raising cain. Bill Potts [another deputy marshal] can't handle him. Shang says he'll kill the first man who lays hand on him.'

"Shanghai Pearce -- christened Abel, but better known to his friends as Colonel, or Shang -- was no gun-fighting desperado; although a hundred of the six-shooter gentry on the cowskin fed at his chuck-wagons and five times that number would rally to his call. But he was, perhaps, the most colorful character of all those romantic figures whom the Old West dubbed its cattle kings and, unquestionably, a prime factor in whatever prosperity Wichita anticipated for 1874.

"Sober, Abel Pearce was a jolly Connecticut Yankee transmogrified into a Texas beef baron, who, in personal appearance, mode of living, and domain governed, came closer to regal estate than any fellow sovereign who rode the Chisholm Trail. Six feet four he stood in his cow-puncher's boots, straight as an arrow with all his two hundred and twenty pounds, a fine full-bearded figure of a man. By his jovial personality and never-failing generosity he commanded a widespread loyalty and affection among cattlemen of the Southwest which no other of his time approached. Of him, George W. Saunders, president of the Old-Time Trail-Drivers' Association, has written, in 'The Trail-Drivers of Texas':

"'Shanghai Pearce has a record in the cattle industry never surpassed, and I doubt if ever equalled by any man. My first recollection of Mr. Pearce was just after the Civil War when he bought fat cattle all over South Texas. I remember seeing him many times come to our camp where he had contracts to receive beeves. He was a large, portly man, always rode a fine horse and would be accompanied by a negro who led a pack-horse loaded with gold and silver. When the cattle were classed and counted out to him, he would empty the money on a blanket and pay it out to the different stockmen. We all looked upon him as a redeemer, as money was scarce in those days. Colonel Pearce was a great talker and would keep the boys awake until midnight laughing at his stories. He was a loud talker and no man who ever heard him or saw him ever forgot his voice or appearance. His steers became known from the Rio Grande to the Canadian line as 'Shanghai Pearce's sea-lions.' He was a money-maker, an empire-builder, and a wonder to his friends, and I believe to himself.'

"It was this same Shanghai Pearce who introduced the walking-stick to Kansas, and who tickled the risibilities of the Young West with his offer to a financially embarrassed Nebraska of a ten thousand dollar annual payment for the exclusive right to deal monte on railway trains within the state's borders. When the Nebraska legislators hesitated over granting such a lucrative franchise to an individual, he further convoluted an appreciative frontier by offering the same money for the exclusive privilege of dealing the game against only such passengers as professed to be clergymen or missionaries.

"This second offer meeting legislative rebuff, Shanghai played upon the mingled emotions of admirers and acquaintances by spending his ten thousand dollars for a bronze statue of himself clad in all the cowboy trappings which he loved, a statue forty feet high which he had erected at his Rancho Grande headquarters, at Tres Palacios.

"'The statue was natural as life,' wrote Charlie Siringo, who rode with Shanghai's outfit in the early seventies, 'and when I looked at it, in imagination I could hear Shanghai's voice, which could be heard for half a mile, even when he whispered.'

"In a season when efforts to attract the cattle trade had started with open bribes to ranch foremen and trail-bosses, Shanghai Pearce's drive to Wichita was the crowning glory of that cowcamp's labors. Practically every cattle-owner of importance would follow Shanghai's lead in such matters. Wherefore, upon his arrival in Wichita with the first of his drives, for a stay which would terminate in September, Shanghai received whatever keys there were to the community. A redeemer for cash-shy cattle-owners in South Texas, in Wichita he was nothing short of a business savior, and the town accordingly kowtowed. If Shanghai had been somewhat careless with a running-iron in building his herds, so had others of his calling, and the

Wichita of '74 was no camp to get squeamish over such gossip; so she laid herself out in welcome. Then Shanghai got drunk, and the entertainment committee put in a hurry-call for the new deputy marshal.

"When Wyatt turned from Douglas Avenue into Main Street, he saw Shanghai Pearce sprawling on a chair in the middle of the walk outside of Billy Collins's saloon. At his right hip Shanghai wore the customary forty-five in an open holster, and as he roared defiance to anyone in Wichita who imagined that any such-and-such shorthorn village could tell the best so-and-so cattleman in Texas where to head in, he kept his hand on the gun butt. Particularly when Bill Potts presumed to request that he take himself indoors did Shanghai ascend to heights of noise and profanity that held Main Street's Saturday afternoon trade captivated to a standstill.

"Pearce was too drunk to be deadly; danger lay in the chance that some bystander might be injured by wild shooting. And Wyatt saw that Shanghai's gun was wedged beneath his thigh, held tightly in the holster against the chair by pressure of the man's whole weight, against which Shanghai was tugging vainly.

"With his fellow officer approaching, Potts grew bold enough to put a hand on the cowman's shoulder, a familiarity that Shanghai resented with a lurch that let his gun come free. Wyatt caught the cattle king's wrists.

"'Drop that gun,' he said.

"Shanghai's outburst changed to a roar of pain as Wyatt clamped the forearm back and down against the chair.

"The forty-five fell to the walk. Wyatt took the weapon inside to Collins's gun rack, and stepped back to the chair, where Shanghai was nursing an aching arm and cursing fluently.

"'Get up and get inside,' Wyatt ordered.

"Shanghai bellowed colorful defiance.

"'Hold the door open, Potts,' Wyatt directed, seized the cattle king by the shirt-collar with one hand, the belt with the other, yanked him from his seat, and hurled him halfway down the bar.

"'If Pearce has any friends in here,' Wyatt remarked to Collins's customers as a body, 'they'll ride herd on him. If I see him drunk on the street again today, I'll heave him into the calaboose, and he'll stay there until morning.'

"When Wyatt returned to lower Douglas Avenue, he dismissed the Pearce affair as a closed incident. An hour later, an intuitive impulse took him back to Main Street. Scores of cowboys had crossed the toll bridge since Shanghai's manhandling and, as Wyatt idled along Douglas Avenue, it struck him that thoroughfare was ominously quiet. Any lull in the uproar of a cowtown spree-day warranted investigation. Cairns was to come on duty in a few moments, and he started uptown to meet him.

"When Wyatt turned into Main Street, he did not know that word of his move had preceded him, or that he was under the eye of a lookout in Collin's doorway. When he was directly opposite the entrance through which he had hurled the cattle king, Collin's double-doors burst open and onto the walk surged a score of cowboys. In their midst towered Shanghai Pearce, still drunk and supported by two of his henchmen.

"'There he is!' a cow-puncher shouted. 'If he makes a move, let him have it.'

"Wyatt knew better than to go for his guns in the face of forty six-shooters ready for business. Ed Morrison, cowboy and professional fighting man, called the next turn.

"'If you think you can arrest Shang Pearce, try it!' he taunted. 'Come on! If you're so good with your guns, why don't you jerk 'em? We're taking Shang where he wants to go. Any move you make to touch him'll be your last one.'

"There followed a torrent of unprintable vituperation in which Morrison's followers joined, with Pearce in their midst they backed toward Douglas Avenue. Until they reached the corner, the cowboys held Wyatt motionless under their weapons, but as the gang disappeared around the turn, the deputy marshal darted into an alley at the rear of the buildings fronting Douglas Avenue and with an entrance on Main Street. As he ran parallel to the course the Texas men were taking, he heard them whooping derision and shouting threats, above the steady roar of gunfire. Certain of their supremacy over the local peace officers, they were shooting up Douglas Avenue in wholesale Texas fashion.

"From the northeast Wyatt heard, also, the resonant voice of the great iron triangle which hung before Judge Jewett's office and was sacred to the sole purpose of summoning Wichita citizens to a finish-fight with the cowmen. In all the cowcamp's history no one had cried 'Wolf!' with that triangle; the instrument had sounded the death-knell of many a Texas gun-thrower, not, however, without the sacrifice of numerous townsmen. Wyatt had hopes of getting into action on his own before any posse of citizens could reach Pearce and the cowboys. Not only was there a chance that he thus could save some needless killing; in his first big play as a Wichita peace officer, the Texas men now had him studded.

"Well in advance of the gang that was terrorizing Douglas Avenue, Wyatt ran by an alley entrance through a store to seize one of his cached shotguns. He jumped through the front doorway about fifty feet ahead of the Texans.

"'Throw up your hands!' he shouted. 'Throw 'em up or I'll blow hell out of you!'

"'You, Morrison!' -- the surprised cowboys, guns smoking but mostly empty, had halted in half-drunken confusion.

"'Throw up your hands or I'll kill you.'

"Ed Morrison, thus singled out, with Wyatt's eye focused on him above the barrels of a weapon ready to spray eighteen buckshot across the roadway, chose discretion. His six-guns dropped in the dirt as his hands went skyward.   Shanghai Pearce had been startled into something like sobriety and good sense.

"'Throw 'em up, boys!' he bellowed, as he obeyed Wyatt's order. Retinue followed the royal example in a body.

"Wyatt had the cowboys in line at the roadside when Marshal Smith and a citizen posse reached the scene. He held them that way while others took up their guns and gunbelts.

"'Now,' Wyatt said, 'we'll go see Judge Jewett. Walk ahead of me to Main Street, turn and head for the courtroom. Keep in the middle of the road and don't try any funny business. Get going.'

"As the procession of crestfallen gun-toters scuffed its spur jangling, high-heeled boots through the dust of Keno Corner under the muzzle of the double-barreled shotgun, a derisively raucous rebel yell served notice that Ben Thompson was viewing the parade from the balcony of Whitey Rupp's establishment.

"'Whoop-ee!' Ben jeered. 'Paint that one on your chuckwagons! I told you he was poison!'

"Judge Jewett fined each of the twenty-one Texas men whom Wyatt had arrested one hundred dollars, which Shanghai Pearce paid for all, with apologies to the municipality. As the culprits filed out, Wyatt turned to the judge.

"'There's one favor you can do for me,' he said. 'As long as I'm an officer in Wichita, don't ring that triangle again.'"[1]

Is the story true? A story of this kind, particularly if it was manufactured from a whole cloth, is more difficult to disprove than a story which is based on some facts. Note from the first, this story started on a "Saturday afternoon in early summer. . ." Question: what summer? '75, '76, or could it have been '73, '74? Lake gave no date. If we had a date, we might be able to prove that the story is either true or false. Fortunately, Flood, in his manuscript, gave us one. He says that at the time of the event the town was busy with the spring elections.[2] The elections were held on Tuesday, April 4th, 1876. The Saturday before the election would have been April 1, 1876.

---

[1]   Wyatt Earp Frontier Marshal, pp. 108-113.

[2]   Flood Manuscript, p. 48.

With the election of the incumbent Marshal being a hot public issue at the time, surely such a newsworthy event as the arrest of the biggest cattle dealer in town along with his crew of cowboys and taking them before the local Justice to be fined would have rated some notice in the local press. None has been found.

Miller and Snell in their <u>Great Gunfighters of Kansas Cowtowns</u> seem to have examined every newspaper article of that period in and around the cowtowns of Kansas, and they fail to find any story that even mentions the name of Shanghai Pearce. Sinclair Drago in his book, <u>Wild, Wooley and Wicked</u> seems to have carefully examined most of the events surrounding Wyatt Earps tenure in Wichita, and he fails to mention any such event. Frank Waters, and his book <u>The Earp Brothers of Tombstone</u> never let an opportunity to belittle Wyatt Earp pass, but he failed to mention any episode of Wyatt Earp arresting Shanghai Pearce. And the final clincher to me is that Ed Bartholomew in his book, <u>Wyatt Earp, the Untold Story</u> didn't even bother to call Earp a liar about this particular episode, although he rarely missed an opportunity to do so with respect to almost any event that Wyatt Earp had related.

An interesting fact that bears examination and some consideration is that in the Flood Manuscript substantially the same story is told except that Flood refers to Shanghai Pearce as Cad Pierce. It's very difficult to assess who invented this story, whether it was Earp or Flood, but it is unlikely that it was Lake. Flood wrote his manuscript several years before Earp ever met Lake, and it is quite certain that Lake had access to Flood's manuscript in writing his own book. At the end of the story in Flood's manuscript is another item of interest. He says:

"The town of Wichita was busy with its Spring elections and Earp occupied with other things. Mike Myer (his name was really Megher) was the people's choice for the job of marshal, and to show his appreciation, he made Earp his Chief Deputy. That was the beginning of his fame and he stuck with Wichita. He stuck until the conditions of Dodge became so bad that the mayor of that city wrote him a letter. It happened in the spring of 1876 supplemented with the plea of many friends of Earp who were living there. Earp listened and promised to investigate. On the 17th day of May, he made them a visit. That was what they wanted him to do, and they dept. him: they made it worth his while. And on the morning of the following day, Earp had a new charge, and Dodge had a new City Marshal."[1]

This statement of course, is purely fictional with no relationship to the facts whatsoever. Wyatt Earp never was Mike Megher's Chief

---

[1]   <u>Flood Manuscript</u>, pp. 42-48.

Deputy. Rather than being appointed Chief Deputy upon Megher's election, he was fired.

The <u>Weekly Beacon</u> of April 5, 1876 reported that Wyatt Earp was discharged from his job as a policeman because of a fight with William Smith, candidate against Mike Megher for city marshal.

Although Wyatt Earp did not perform the exciting exploits attributed to him by Lake and Flood, it seems apparent that he was a good and efficient police officer in performing the duties assigned to him while employed as a policeman in Wichita.

CHAPTER VIII

WYATT EARP MOVES TO DODGE CITY

THE Dodge City <u>Times</u> of September 1st, 1877 described Dodge City at that time in the following story:

". . . Dodge has many characteristics which prevent its being classed as a town of strictly moral ideas and principles, notwithstanding it is supplied with a church, a court-house, and a jail. Other institutions counterbalance the good works supposed to emanate from the first mentioned. Like all frontier towns of this modern day, fast men and fast women are around by the score, seeking whom they may devour, hunting for a soft snap, taking him in for cash, and many is the Texas cowboy who can testify as to their ability to follow up successfully the callings they have embraced in quest of money.

"Gambling ranges from a game of five-cent chuck-a-luck to a thousand dollar pocket-pot. Nothing is secret, but with open doors upon the main street the ball rolls on uninterruptedly. More than occasionally some dark-eyed virago or some brazen-faced blond, with a modern sun-down, will saunter in among the roughs of the gambling houses and saloons, entering with inexplicable zest into the disgusting sport, breathing the immoral atmosphere with a gusto which I defy modern writers to explain. Dance houses are ranged along at convenient distances and supplied abundantly with all the trappings and paraphernalia which go to complete institutions of that character. Here you see the greatest abandon. Men of every grade assemble to join in the dance. Nice men with white neck-ties, the cattle dealer with his good clothes, the sport with his well-turned fingers, smooth tongue and artistically twisted moustache, and last but not least, the cowboy, booted and spurred as he comes from the trail, his hard earnings in his pocket, all join in the wild revel; and yet with all this mixture of strange human nature a remarkable degree of order is preserved. Arms are not allowed to be worn, and any noisy whisky demonstrations are promptly checked by incarceration in the lock-up. Even the striations are promptly checked by incarceration in the lock-up. Even the Mayor of the city indulges in the giddy dance with the girls and with his cigar in one corner of his mouth and his hat tilted to one side, he makes a charming looking officer.

"Some things occur in Dodge that the world never knows of. Probably it is best so. Other things occur which leak out by degrees, notwithstanding the use of hush-money. That too is perhaps the best.

Men learn by such means.

"Most places are satisfied with one abode for the dead. In the grave there is no distinction. The rich are known from the poor only by their tombstones, so the sods upon the grave fail to reflect the characters buried beneath them; and yet Dodge boasts two burying spots, one for the tainted, whose very souls were steeped by immorality, and who have generally died with their boots on. 'Boot-hill' is the somewhat singular title applied to the burial place of the class just mentioned. The other is not designated by any particular title, but is supposed to contain the bodies of those who died with a clean sheet on their bed -- the soul in this case is a secondary consideration."[1]

This is the city that Wyatt Earp moved to in May of 1876. His reasons for going there are subject to dispute. Lake says that George Hoover who had only recently been selected Mayor of Dodge City had heard of Wyatt's reputation and had written him asking him to come to Dodge City. He said:

"Hoover wrote Wyatt and asked him to come to Dodge City; after a few more experiences with the Texas Men he took to Telegraphing.

"'You don't need me anymore,' Wyatt told Mike Megher, 'I don't blame you,' Mike answered somewhat enviously.

On May 16th, 1876 Wyatt started for Dodge City."[2]

The only other reference that I can find stating that Wyatt Earp went to Dodge City at the request of the Mayor or anyone else appears in the book Dodge City, Queen of Cowtowns, by Stanley Vestal. In his book he states:

"George M. Hoover was elected Mayor (1876). He ignored the pleas of those anxious not too disgruntle the Texans, and promptly brought in Jack Allen, a notorious gun-slinger, to serve as deputy under Marshal Larry Deger, Dodge City's Man-Mountain.

"Shortly after, a gang of cowboys ran Jack out of town. The mayor telegraphed offering the job to Wyatt Earp."[3]

A critical examination of Stanley Vestal's book indicates that he did considerable original research on this subject but also that he relied heavily on other western writers such as Stuart N. Lake. The story that Wyatt Earp came to Dodge City at the request of the Mayor, as far as I can determine, was first written by Flood,[4] was

---

[1]   Great Gunfighters of the Kansas Cowtowns, p. 5.

[2]   Wyatt Earp, Frontier Marshal, p. 135.

[3]   Stanley Vestal, Dodge City Queen of Cowtowns, p. 84.

[4]   Flood Manuscript, p. 48.

refined and retold by Lake[1] and was then picked up by Stanley Vestal. No other writers and no contemporary newspaper reports or documents of any kind have been found to substantiate the story. Vestal cites no authority for his statement. He probably got it from Lake.

It is highly unlikely that Earp went to Dodge at the request of a Mayor or anyone else. It appears that Earp was fired from his job as policeman in Wichita and went to Dodge looking for employment. It is apparent that he didn't waste a lot of time getting it, as it was reported in the <u>Wichita Weekly Beacon</u> of April 5, 1876 that Wyatt Earp was discharged from his job as a policeman, and it was reported in the same paper on May 24, 1876 that "Wyatt Earp has been put on the police force at Dodge City."[2]

Stanley Vestal reports that Wyatt Earp served as a police officer in Dodge during three periods: "May 17th through September 9th, 1876; July 6 to late November, 1877 and May 12th 1878 to September 8, 1879."[3]

Harry Sinclair Drago in his book <u>Wild, Wooley and Wicked</u> doubts that Wyatt Earp was a member of the Dodge City police force during the year of 1877. He says:

"Furthermore, what evidence is there that he was a member of the force at any time during the year of 1877? The answer is none. His name does not appear in Dodge City newspapers. Nor does it occur in the records of the police court, admitting that those records are not complete.

"This is where those that claimed he served only two hitches as assistant marshal part company with those commentators who insist that he wore a badge for three stretches. The latter have him on the force from July to September 1877. But they offer no evidence to support their contention. All they have for it is Earp's word."[4]

Miller and Snell in their <u>Great Gunfighters of the Kansas Cowtowns</u>, tried to establish the dates and times of Earp's service on the police force of Dodge City and came up with the following:

"Little is known about him in Dodge during 1876 and 1877. The only 1876 Dodge City newspaper in the files of the Kansas State Historical Society is a single issue of the <u>Times</u>, dated October 14th. On the first page, in a box labeled 'Official Directory,' Earp's name

---

[1]   <u>Wyatt Earp, Frontier Marshal</u>, p. 135.

[2]   <u>Great Gunfighters of the Kansas Cowtowns</u>, p. 85.

[3]   <u>Dodge City, Queen of Cowtowns</u>, p. 122.

[4]   Sinclair Drago, <u>Wild, Wooly and Wicked</u>, p. 294.

appeared as deputy city marshal. The next issue of this paper in this society's files is that of March 24, 1877. Earp was similarly listed in the directory of this issue as well as in that of March 31st. However, the Times of April 7th, 1877 in reporting the proceedings of the City Council meeting of April 4th, said the salary of Marshal Lawrence E. Deger was allowed for March, but no mention was made of Wyatt Earp."[1]

We know that Wyatt Earp was in Deadwood, Dakota territory in the spring of 1877, so the paper must have just failed to update its official directory box in 1877.

It should be noted that Vestal gave the date of Earp's 1877 service as commencing on July 6th, so that it does not prove anything that the meeting of April 4th, 1877 setting the salary for Lawrence E. Deger made no mention of Wyatt Earp. But there are other bits of evidence that make his service during the year of 1877 questionable. On July 7, 1877 the Dodge City Times noted: "Wyatt Earp, who was on our city police force last summer, is in town again. We hope he will accept a position on the force once more. He had a quiet way of taking the most desperate characters into custody which invariably gave one the impression that the city was able to enforce or mandate and preserve her dignity. It wasn't considered policy to draw a gun on Wyatt unless you got the drop and meant to burn powder without any preliminary talk."[2]

The July 7th Times report would not be too far from the July 6th date given by Vestal and that's probably where he got the date. However, a report from the Times of July 21, 1877 raises another question. In that report, the Times said: "Miss Franky Bell who wears the belt for superiority in point of muscular ability, heaped epithets upon the unoffending head of Mr. Earp to such an extent as to provoke a slap from the ex-officer, besides creating a disturbance of the quiet and dignity of the city, for which she received a night's lodging in the dog house and a reception at the police court the next morning, the expense of which was about $20.00. Wyatt Earp was assessed the lowest limit of the law, $1.00."[3]

I have little confidence in anything written by Frank Waters about the Earps. However, in his book, The Earp Brothers of Tombstone, he lends some support to the notion that Wyatt Earp acted as a policemen on three different occasions. He states: "Run out of Wichita, Wyatt turned up in Dodge City, where he

---

[1]   Great Gunfighters of the Kansas Cowtowns, pp. 85-86.

[2]   Great Gunfighters of the Kansas Cowtowns, p. 86.

[3]   Ibid, p. 86.

served two hitches as a policeman: from May 17, to September 9th, 1876, under Marshal Larry Deger and from July until November 1877 under Marshal Ed Masterson."[1]

In support of his statements he quotes the Dodge City <u>Times</u> story of July 21, 1877 to show that Wyatt Earp was acting as a policeman in Dodge City at that time but he failed to notice the part of the story that described Wyatt Earp as an ex-officer.

According to the <u>Times</u> story, on July 21, 1877 Earp was an ex-officer, not an officer. This is just another example of the sloppy research done by Frank Waters. He may have got the July to November, 1877 date from Stanley Vestal, whose book was published in 1952.

Although Ed Masterson was a Deputy Marshal in the summer of 1877, he was not appointed Marshal until December 4, 1877. His appointment was duly reported in the <u>Times</u>, on December 8, 1877. So, it is impossible that Wyatt served from July 1877 until November 1877 under Marshal Ed Masterson.[2]

Waters goes on to say:

"Wyatt then went to Texas. While there, in April, 1878, Marshal Ed Masterson of Dodge City was killed and Wyatt returned to Dodge. He was appointed assistant Marshal to Charles E. Bassett, the new Marshal, on May 12, 1878 and served until September 8, 1879 in that capacity-."[3]

At any rate, we know that Wyatt Earp became a deputy marshal in Dodge City in the Spring of 1876. His exploits there, as claimed by Lake, were heroic to say the least. Suffice to say that there is very little evidence extant to substantiate the truth of Lake's stories about Earp's activities. However, each one of his episodes should be examined to determine whether or not there is basis in fact at all for them.

Once again, in order to demonstrate the reason for the animosity of many historians towards Wyatt Earp, and particularly those from Kansas and environs, I will have to quote substantially from Stuart N. Lake's, <u>Wyatt Earp Frontier Marshal</u>. It was Lake's stories about Wyatt Earp's activities in Dodge City, added to the animosity towards him created by the fictitious Ben Thompson arrest in Ellsworth, that made many researchers and historians tab him as a liar and a braggart. Whether these stories were told to Lake by Wyatt Earp, or told to Flood and improved on by Lake, or whether Lake took a few

[1]   <u>The Earp Brothers of Tombstone</u>, p. 39.

[2]   <u>Great Gunfighters of the Kansas Cowtowns</u>, p. 175.

[3]   <u>The Earp Brothers of Tombstone</u>, p. 39.

notes from Wyatt Earp and then wrote the stories himself is hard to determine. At any rate, Lake's stories about Earp's conduct in Dodge City bare detailed examination. Lake quotes Earp as follows:

"The message that took me to Dodge had offered me the Marshal's job, Wyatt recalled, but Hoover told me that for political reasons he wanted Deger to complete his year in office. He would pay me more money as Chief Deputy than Deger was drawing. I would have power to hire and fire deputies, could follow my own ideas about my job and be Marshal in all but name. The Marshal's pay was $100 a month, but Mayor Hoover said they would pay me $250 a month, plus $2.50 for every arrest I made. Brown and Mason were discharged from the force, and I was to appoint three new deputies at wages of $75 a month, each, and make my own arrangements with them about the bonus.

"Bat Masterson's brother Jim was in Dodge, a good, game man who would handle himself in a fracas, and I picked him as one deputy, took Joe Mason back and was looking for the third when Bat himself came in from Sweetwater, Texas, still limping from the leg-wound he got when he killed Sergeant King. Bat's gun-hand was in working order, so I made him a deputy. He patrolled Front Street with a walking-stick for several weeks and used his cane to crack the heads of several wild men hunting trouble; even as a cripple he was a first-class peace officer.

"I told my deputies that all bounties would be pooled and shared, but would be paid only when prisoners were taken alive. Dead ones wouldn't count.   Each officer carried two six-guns and I placed shotguns at convenient points, as I had in Wichita, but killing was to be our last resort.

"I figured that if the cowboys were manhandled and heaved into the calaboose every time they showed in town with guns on, or cut loose in forbidden territory, they'd come to time quicker than if we kept them primed for gunplay. Hoover had hired me to cut down the killings in Dodge, not to increase them. As far as that went, any one of the deputies could give the average cowboy the best of a break, then kill him in a gunfight, but even when gunplay was necessary, we disabled men, rather than killed them.

"With this policy, we organized for a fairly peaceful summer. There were some killings in personal quarrels, but none by peace officers. We winged a few tough customers who insisted on shooting, but none of the victims died. On the other hand, we split seven or eight hundred dollars in bounties each month. That meant some three hundred arrests every thirty days, and as practically every prisoner heaved into the calaboose was thoroughly buffaloed in the process, we made quite a dent in cowboy conceit."[1]

There are a lot of things wrong with this statement. Remember, Wyatt was talking here about his first tour of duty in 1876. Miller and Snell citing Dodge City Times, July 6, 1878 as authority, state that:

"The younger Masterson (Jim) was hired as a policeman in early June 1878; his first salary payment indicating June 1, to be the exact date of his appointment. The local newspapers, however, did not report his employment until June 11, 1878 when the Ford County Globe stated that 'policeman Trask has resigned and Jim Masterson has taken his place on the force.' In any event, within two months of the death of Jim's brother Ed, city marshal of Dodge (April 9, 1878), another Masterson was wearing a badge."[2] (Note: This was 1878, not 1876).

Thus it is apparent that Earp/Lake's statement that Earp picked Jim Masterson as one of his deputies in 1876 has to be untrue.

The name of Joe Mason, another of his supposed deputies, shows up periodically in the newspaper reports during the year of 1876 and 1877 so it is probable that Joe Mason was actually on the police force at the same time that Wyatt Earp was in 1876. However, his statement that he: ". . . was looking for the third, when Bat himself came in from Sweetwater, Texas still limping from the leg-wound he got when he killed sergeant King. Bat's gun-hand was in working order so I made him a deputy,"[3] is doubtful.

If he did, it was for a very brief period, and there doesn't appear to be any reliable record of such service.

Miller and Snell say: "Contemporary records fail to indicate Bat's whereabouts between March 1875 and the spring of 1877."[4]

De Arment in his biography of Bat Masterson never tells of Bat joining the Marshal's office at Dodge City, but he does mention it in this statement: "News of gold strikes in the Black Hills of South Dakota swept Dodge in the summer of 1876. Gold fever burned through the town, and Texas cowboys and Kansas citizens caught the fever. In July, he resigned from the police force, his position being taken by Morgan Earp, Wyatt's younger brother, a new comer to

---

[1]   Wyatt Earp, Frontier Marshal, pp. 142-143.

[2]   Great Gunfighters of the Kansas Cowtowns, p. 186.

[3]   Wyatt Earp, Frontier Marshal, p. 142.

[4]   Great Gunfighters of the Kansas Cowtowns, p. 201.

Dodge."[1]

De Arment's statement, sounds suspiciously like it came from Lake.

Miller & Snell state that:

"The first definite identification of Bat Masterson in available local newspapers concerned some trouble he had with the Dodge City police force. On June 6, 1877, he tried to prevent the arrest of Bobby Gill (Robert Gilmore), a persistent and ubiquitous cowtown character. The Times, June 9, (1877) described Bat's attempt:

"THE GANG CORRALLED.

"The Opening of the Cattle Trade Celebrated in the Dog House.

"Bobby Gill done it again. Last Wednesday was a lively day for Dodge. Two hundred cattle men in the city; the gang in good shape for business; merchants happy, and money flooding the city, is a condition of affairs that could not continue in Dodge very long without an eruption, and that is the way it was last Wednesday. Robert Gilmore was making a talk for himself in a rather emphatic manner, to which Marshal Deger took exceptions, and started for the dog house with him. Bobby walked very leisurely -- so much so that Larry felt it necessary to administer a few paternal kicks in the rear. This act was soon interrupted by Bat Masterson, who wound his arm affectionately around the Marshal's neck and let the prisoner escape. Deger then grappled with Bat, at the same time calling upon the bystanders to take the offender's gun and assist in the arrest. Joe Mason appeared upon the scene at this critical moment and took the gun. But Masterson would not surrender yet, and came near getting hold of a pistol from among several which were strewed around over the sidewalk, but half a dozen Texas men came to the Marshal's aid and gave him a chance to draw his gun and beat Bat over the head until blood flew upon Joe Mason so that he kicked, and warded off the blows with his arm. Bat Masterson seemed possessed of extraordinary strength, and every inch of the way was closely contested, but the city dungeon was reached at last, and in he went. If he had got hold of his gun before going in there would have been a general killing. . .

"Ed Masterson accomplished his first official act in the arrest of Bobby Gilmore the same afternoon.

"Next day Judge [D.M.] Frost administered the penalty of the law by assessing twenty-five and costs to Bat . . . and five to Bobby.

"The boys are all at liberty now."[2]

It seems highly unlikely that if Bat Masterson had been working

---

[1]   Bat Masterson (De Arment), p. 74.

[2]   Great Gunfighters of The Kansas Cowtowns, pp. 202-203; The Times, June 9, 1877.

for Marshal Larry Deger in 1876, he would have interfered with his making an arrest, and engaged in a fight with him, resulting in his being thrown into jail in 1877. It also seems quite likely if such a thing had occurred, the newspaper in reporting it would have included the fact that Bat Masterson was a former Dodge City police officer working under Larry Deger, and that his brother Ed Masterson was Assistant Marshal at the time.

Dale T. Schoenberg seems to have done a credible job of researching the life of Bat Masterson, and in his book he says the whereabouts of Bat Masterson during the remainder of 1876 are difficult to pinpoint. He suggests that probably Masterson was often at Dodge City, where old-timers remembered him walking about with a cane as a result of the pelvic wound he had received in the fight with Sergeant King. Schoenberg says that other reports place him at Cheyenne, Wyoming, Denver, and Sydney, Nebraska at one time or another during 1876.[1]

The only logical conclusion is that Earp/Lake's statement that Earp hired Bat Masterson as his third deputy when he first became an officer at Dodge City is not true. Earp did not hire anybody, and Bat Masterson wasn't available.

Lake, in order to build up the prestige of Wyatt Earp, used Bat Masterson as a mouthpiece and quoted him extensively. It should be noted, however, that his quotations do not bear any reference to where they were made or to whom they were made, and it is impossible to verify whether or not Bat Masterson actually made these statements. It is known that when Masterson got old, he talked very glowingly about his adventures in the West, and everyone about whom he was asked was always declared to be the greatest, the biggest, the fastest and the meanest of any existing gunman. He may have engaged in such conversations about Wyatt Earp with tongue in cheek, or the reported quotes by Lake could have been strictly from his imagination. At any rate Lake said:

"As Bat spun his yarns of Wyatt Earp, no tales of gunplay offered such vivid pictures of prowess as the recollection of certain affrays in which Wyatt went against the hand-picked bullies of the cow outfits with no further weapons than his two fists.

"'Wyatt's speed and skill with a six-gun made almost any play against him with weapons no contest,' Bat once explained. 'Possibly there were more accomplished trick-shots than he, but in all my years in the West at its wildest, I never saw the man in action who could shade him in the prime essential of real gun-fighting -- the draw-and-shoot against something that could shoot back.'

---

[1]   The Gunfighters, p. 114.

"'In a day when almost every man possessed as a matter of course the ability to get a six-gun into action with a rapidity that a later generation simply will not credit, Wyatt's speed on the draw was considered phenomenal by those who literally were marvels at the same feat. His marksmanship at any range from four to four hundred yards was a perfect complement to his speed. On more than on occasion, I have seen him kill coyotes at the latter distance with his Colt's, and any man who ever has handled a six-gun will tell you that, while luck figures largely in such shooting, only a past-master of the weapon could do that.

"Most of the frontier gun-wielders practiced daily to keep their gun-hands in. I have known them to stand before mirrors, going through the motions of draw-and-shoot with empty guns for an hour at a time. Outdoors they were forever firing at tin cans, bottles, telegraph poles, or any targets that offered, and shooting-matches for prestige and money-stakes were daily events.

"I never knew Wyatt to practice the draw beyond trying his guns in the holsters when he first put them on for the day, or slipping them once to make sure they were free when he was heading into a possible argument. He seldom did any target work when there was no competition.

"Wyatt had a keen sense of humor, and one of his favorite amusements was to horn into target matches at which professional gunmen were engaged. The way he'd outdo the best the braggart gun-throwers had to offer fairly burned those fellows up, and the casual manner in which he did it was not calculated to soothe injured pride. But there was more than humor involved; it was Wyatt's quiet way of reminding the bad boys that against him they stood small chance. He was certain of that, and after he had made monkeys out of a few who went against him, others were willing to forego argument.

"Wyatt was the most perfect personification I ever saw of Western insistence that the true six-gun artist is born that way. A hundred men, more or less, with reputations as killers, whom I have known, have started gunplay against him only to look into the muzzle of Wyatt's Colt's before they could get their own guns half-drawn. In such a call, if a gunman thought particularly well of himself, or had any record as a fighting man, Wyatt would bend the long barrel of his Buntline Special around the gunman's head and lug him to the calaboose.

"In the old days, to buffalo a gun-toter was to inflict more than physical injury; it heaped upon him a greater calumny than any other form of insult could convey. A man for whom a camp had any respect whatsoever was entitled to be shot at; so Wyatt took particular delight in buffaloing the gunmen who set great store by themselves.

"When circumstances made it necessary for Wyatt to shoot, he preferred disabling men rather than killing them. Offhand, I could list fifty gun-fights in which Wyatt put a slug through the arm or the shoulder of some man who was shooting at him, when he might as certainly have shot him in the belly or through the heart. There were instances in which I thought Wyatt too lenient, when it would have been better for all concerned to have put some gunman completely out of business, then and there, and, what's more, I have told him so.

"'Didn't have to kill him,' Wyatt would answer, and that would be all he'd say.

"'Where human life was concerned, Wyatt was the softest-hearted gun-fighter I knew. Yet, if circumstances demanded, he could kill more swiftly and more surely than any other man of record in his time.'"[1]

Lake got it right when he said: "As Bat spun his yarns of Wyatt Earp." That's exactly what they were, yarns. Let's take a look at some of the statements attributed to Bat Masterson. For instance he is quoted as saying, "A hundred men, more or less with reputations as killers, whom I have known, have started gunplay against him only to look into the muzzle of Wyatt's Colt's before they could get their own guns half-drawn." In all of the writings about Wyatt Earp, I can discover none in which Wyatt Earp entered into a contest with another gunman and beat him to the draw. If there were over 100 of them, it would seem that Bat Masterson or someone could have named at least one. But the names of any of them are completely lacking in any literature.

Again, Masterson is quoted as saying, "When circumstances made it necessary for Wyatt to shoot, he preferred disabling men rather than killing them. Offhand, I could list fifty gun-fights in which Wyatt put a slug through the arm or the shoulder of some man who was shooting at him, when he might as certainly shot him in the belly or through the heart." Again it would seem that if Bat Masterson could list 50 gunfights in which Wyatt put a slug through the arm or shoulder of some gunman, he could have named at least one or two of them, but he failed to do so and no one else who has studied the history of Dodge City has been able to do so either.

Lake says that: ". . . late in July of '76, the excitement over gold discovery's at Deadwood, South Dakota, spread to Dodge. Cowboys up from Texas left their outfits to ride North as prospectors. Numerous Dodge residents started for the new diggings. Bat Masterson resigned as Wyatt's assistant and joined the rush. Wyatt

---

[1]   Wyatt Earp, Frontier Marshal, p. 146-148.

was deterred by a promise to Mayor Hoover that he would serve out the cattle-shipping Season as a marshal. Bat's place on the force was taken by Wyatt's younger brother, Morgan who had come to Dodge on his way to Deadwood."[1]

It is doubtful that Wyatt Earp's younger brother ever served as a police officer in Dodge City. Remember that Wyatt and Morgan left Dodge for Deadwood on September 9, 1876.[2] Harry Sinclair Drago mentions Morgan Earp in this brief paragraph:

"Charlie Bassett was serving by appointment as Sheriff of Ford County, with his deputies, Bill Tilghman and Morgan Earp. It was not part of their duty to assist in policing Dodge, but they were always available when City Marshal Degger requested their help."[3]

If Morgan Earp was serving as Deputy to Charlie Bassett, he had to do it before September 9, 1877 when he and Wyatt left for Dakota Territory. If he were a Deputy Sheriff then he was not a Deputy Marshal with Wyatt.

Another reference to Wyatt's brothers Morgan and Virgil being in law enforcement appears in The Earp Brothers of Tombstone. Waters repeats the story of Bat Masterson getting beat up by Marshal Larry Deger and being arrested and assessed a $25 fine, reported in the Times on June 6, 1877[4] and then proceeds as follows:

"Masterson then swung over to the side of the Law. Late that month he was appointed under sheriff of Ford County and in the November election beat out Larry Deger for sheriff by a narrow margin of three votes. While he was in office, Morgan Earp, who had failed to get a job as a policeman with Wyatt in Wichita, arrived in Dodge and finally secured an appointment as a deputy sheriff. Virgil, with the arrival of the Earp wagon train, was now appointed a deputy town policeman under Wyatt."[5]

Frank Waters quotation of Aunt Alley about Virgil Earp being appointed deputy town policeman under Wyatt Earp is not very reliable. As previously stated, the Earp party arrived by wagon at Dodge City in 1876, wintered at Peace, near Sterling and on May 8,

[1]   Wyatt Earp, Frontier Marshal, p. 154.

[2]   Ibid, p. 155.

[3]   Wild, Wooly and Wicked, p. 291.

[4]   Great Gunfighters of The Kansas Cow Towns, p. 202.

[5]   The Earp Brothers of Tombstone, p. 42.

1877 departed for San Bernardino, California.[1] Virgil Earp was in
that wagon train, so if Virgil Earp served as a deputy-town policemen
either under Wyatt or with Wyatt, it would have to have happened in
the summer of 1876. Remember, Wyatt Earp left for Deadwood on
September 9, 1876 taking brother Morgan with him.[2] It is difficult
to rely on Frank Waters for anything that has to do with dates. For
instance, note that right after he reported that Morgan had become
a deputy sheriff and Virgil a deputy town policemen, he launched into
a report on the difficulties encountered by Luke Short as proprietor
of the Long Branch Saloon and his rescue by what was afterwards
known as the peace commission. He said:

"The difficulty was soon solved. Wyatt rounded up Bat
Masterson and some other gun-tooting cronies and embarked on a
short shake down cruise. Under the fanciful and official name of the
Dodge City Peace Commission, they persuaded Mayor Webster to
revoke the ordinance and to allow Luke Short to run his Long-
Branch Saloon as he pleased."[3]

The only trouble with that story is that while something like that
did occur, it occurred in 1883, not in 1876.[4]

In summary, all that we can say with any certainty is that Wyatt
was a deputy marshal during the summer and fall of 1876. He was
neither marshal or assistant marshal. If his brothers, Virgil or
Morgan, or Bat Masterson served with him, it can not be proven by
any existing records.

---

[1]   The Earp Brothers of Tombstone, p. 46.

[2]   Wyatt Earp, Frontier Marshal, p. 155.

[3]   The Earp Brothers of Tombstone, p. 43.

[4]   Great Gunfighters of The Kansas Cowtowns, p. 293.

CHAPTER IX

WINTER IN THE
DAKOTA TERRITORY

LAKE says that,

"On September 9th (1876), Wyatt and Morgan left Dodge for Deadwood in a wagon drawn by the best four-horse hitch that money could buy. Behind him, Wyatt left an enviable record as a fighting man, a peace officer who's specialty was taming wild towns and wilder humans, a business of which he swore he had washed his hands. Ahead was adventure, and prospector's fortune."[1]

All of the writers and researchers about Wyatt Earp, except Stuart N. Lake, seem to give Wyatt's stay in Deadwood, Dakota Territory a short shift. For instance, Schoenberg's only reference to it is as follows:

"After resigning as Deputy Marshal at Dodge City, Wyatt had sojourned into the Black Hills in what is now the State of South Dakota. He returned to Dodge City by July 1, 1877."[2]

Lake tells quite a detailed story of Wyatt Earp's winter in Deadwood. He states that when he got there he found the town wide open to gambling and was very much interested in that since he customarily was a winning gambler and the camp was rich and running high, wide and handsome with play as big and continuous as any frontier town he had known. However, as winter approached it was apparent that there was very little wood for heating in the town and that it would be closed in by winter. Wyatt had a good team of horses and he went into the wood hauling business. Wyatt said:

"I didn't gamble much that winter, I delivered wood seven days a week and when night came I wanted to sleep. But I was young and tough, so were my horses, and we came through into spring in fine shape physically, with a profit of about $5,000."[3]

Here, Lake relates another one of those amazing incidents in the life of Wyatt Earp that deserves close scrutiny. In order to explain it fully, it is necessary to quote Lake's story rather fully. He said:

"In June, Wells, Fargo and Company faced the responsibility of

---

[1]   Wyatt Earp, Frontier Marshal, p. 155.

[2]   The Gunfighters, p. 33.

[3]   Wyatt Earp, Frontier Marshal, p. 157.

transporting the spring clean-up of the Deadwood mines -- a bulk shipment of more than $200,000 in bullion -- to Cheyenne by stage-coach. Ordinarily, this task might have involved risk, to lives of Wells-Fargo employees as well as to the shipment itself, by virtue of the highwaymanly propensities of numerous Deadwood citizens. On this occasion, it was rendered extraordinarily hazardous by the presence of the Dunc Blackburn gang of stage-robbers in the hills just outside the village limits.

"Blackburn and seven companions, all notorious outlaws with prices on their heads in a number of Western communities, had shown full appreciation of opportunities for their kind in the richness of the Deadwood diggings, an in the spring of '77 had set up camp in the near-by hills, whence they could maintain surveillance over all stage-lines. They had spies in the camp, and when it was evident that any day might see the shipment of the clean-up, they took to holding up every stage that left Deadwood. The gang obtained some small booty and, for good measure, robbed several incoming stages of currency shipments and such of the passengers' property as appealed to them. Under threat of their activities, however, the bullion was withheld from shipment. Several posses were organized to go after the highwaymen, but these were eluded and hold-ups continued. After all, getting the bullion through was the express company's business, and most of Deadwood felt that chances involved in going against a crowd like Dune Blackburn's might reasonably be left to those whom Wells, Fargo and Company paid for such services.

"In the course of their depredations, Blackburn and his followers killed or wounded a number of stage-drivers and shot-gun messengers, as the armed guardians of express company treasure were called, from the weapons they generally favored for repelling boarders. In a majority of instances, when Dunc stepped into the road -- neither he nor his followers attempted to conceal their identities -- with the command, 'Whoa-up, and throw off the box,' the stage-team was pulled to a halt and the treasure-chest heaved to the roadside. Occasionally some more daring driver had run for it while the messenger cracked down on the highwaymen, efforts that had led to fatal consequences. The climax to the Blackburn series of highway murders came when the outlaw shot Johnny Slaughter, possibly the most famous and most fearless of all Black Hills' drivers.

"Gray, the Wells-Fargo agent at Deadwood, might have organized an escort of gun-fighters to take out the bullion, or have sent to the nearest army post for troops, but two factors deterred him. Wells, Fargo and Company was in business for profit, charges for handling bullion were fixed, and the cost of a special escort would have been excessive. Second, was the loss of prestige which the famous express company would have suffered in abandoning standard practice for a gang of bandits. Of the two, in the frontier West, the latter was by far the more important consideration. The whole structure of Wells, Fargo and Company's business had been founded on the company's reputation -- the proud boast was far from idle -- for the safe-conduct of all commerce with which it might be entrusted, through all the hell or high water that could be raised by human or natural forces.

"When Wyatt Earp went to the stage-office to reserve a seat in the Cheyenne stage -- he had sold his team to a Deadwood resident -- his plan to leave camp furnished the Wells-Fargo agent with the possible solution for a pressing problem. After persuading Wyatt to postpone his departure, Gray posted a bulletin on the door of the Wells-Fargo office:

"NOTICE TO BULLION SHIPPERS

"The Spring Clean-up will leave for Cheyenne on the Regular Stage at 7:00 A.M., next Monday. Wyatt Earp, of Dodge, will ride shotgun.

"On Monday morning, with more than $200,000 in the box and Wyatt in the boot, the Cheyenne stage rolled out of Deadwood as per advertisement.

"'I was a traveling arsenal that morning,' Wyatt recalled. 'On that particular occasion my six-guns were auxiliary weapons. Across my knees, for the first fifty miles, I carried a regulation Wells-Fargo sawed-off shotgun loaded with buckshot, nine to the barrel, and a Winchester rifle. If Blackburn jumped us from the roadside, I would use the shotgun; for anything but short-range surprise, I figured to hold off the outlaws with the rifle while the team ran for it. In case an animal was shot down in a long-distance attack, I believed that, by using the stage as cover, I could pick off the six or eight men in the Blackburn gang before they could get close enough to do much damage.'

"Gray's advertising had the desired effect. Dunc Blackburn's spies carried word of the warning poster and the spring clean-up went through to Cheyenne under Wyatt Earp's escort with no stop other than for team changes. About ten miles out of Deadwood, however, two parties of four horsemen each kept pace with the stage for a time along the base of the hills at either side of the road. Certain that these were Blackburn men, Wyatt fired several rifle-shots at each party. One group stopped abruptly and, as the stage drew ahead, the second bunch rode to join the first.

"'I never heard what happened,' Wyatt said, 'but I always thought I hit a horse. That would account for the sudden stop. When I saw the two parties holding abreast of us, one on either side, I figured they were preparing for a long-range attack, and would close in on us if they could down one or more of the animals. In dealing with such men, I have always found that advantage is gained by taking the initiative, and I figured that if shooting was to be done, I might as well start it. We saw no more of Blackburn's gang. Later, Scott Davis ran Dunc into his hole and wound up his career as a road-agent. We reached Cheyenne about four o'clock Wednesday afternoon with every ounce of dust intact. We had changed drivers during the three-hundred-mile trip, but I was on duty every minute. Wells, Fargo and Company had provided my stage-coach passage, and at the end of the run paid me fifty dollars.'"[1]

Of course either Wyatt Earp or Stuart N. Lake was mistaken about the above described events, but still there may have been something to it.

In examining the Lake collection at the Huntington Library I ran across some penciled hand-written notes that appeared to be in Lake's hand writing. These seem to be tickler notes that one could take to jog his memory while conducting an oral interview. Two notes about Deadwood interested me. They were:

"76, Sept. 9. outfitted went to Deadwood, S.D. hauled Wood.. netted $120 $130 a day."

"77 June, road shotgun-Wells Fargo. $50."

On November 22, 1988 Mr. Robert J. Chandler, historical officer of the Wells-Fargo Bank, San Francisco sent me the following letter in response to my inquiry about Wyatt Earp being a shotgun-guard for Wells Fargo in June of 1877 at Deadwood. His letter was very interesting. He wrote:

"Dear Mr. Erwin: Good to hear from you.   Per your two questions of October 22nd, regarding Wyatt Earp, Agnus Wright Spring's "The Cheyenne and Black Hills Stage and Express Route," (Glendale R.H. Clark Company, 1949), (University of Nebraska Press) describes the Deadwood area stage routes.   Wells Fargo sold its overland coaches in 1870.   We have no explanation for Earp's notation that in June 1877 he rode shotgun for Wells Fargo for $50 for agent Gray.   Our first listed agent for Deadwood is Charles F. Sheldon in 1886.   Perhaps the "Gray" is Isaac Gray whom Spring notes as the agent for Gilmer and Sailsbury's Staging.   Signed, Robert J. Chandler"

An examination of the book The Cheyenne and Black Hills Stage and Express Routes reveals that a company known as the Cheyenne and Black Hills Stage and Express was owned by three partners, Monroe Salisbury, Jack Gilmer and Colonel Mat T. Patrick and that Isaac H. Gray was the company agent at Deadwood. It also reveals that in the spring of 1877 the company was sorely troubled by bandits and holdup men. Example, on March 25, 1877, agent Gray sent the

---

[1]   Wyatt Earp, Frontier Marshal, pp. 160-163.

following telegram to his Superintendent in Cheyenne.

"Deadwood, March 25. Road agents attempted to rob the coach about 2 1/2 miles from here tonight. They killed Johnny Slaughter and wounded Mr. Iler. We start after body now. Notify Johnny's father. Gray."[1]

While it appears untrue that Wyatt rode shotgun for Wells Fargo and that the notoriety of his guarding this spring shipment of bullion frightened away any potential robbers, there does appear to be some basis for the story. In the book, we find the following statement:

"One of the first most important responsibilities for the stage company in 1877, was the transportation of a spring 'clean up' from the hills, which approximated $200,000 in gold. Among the special shotgun messengers who brought the shipment through to Cheyenne without mishap, was the gun-handy ex-marshal, Wyatt B. Earp, who was on his way back to Kansas."[2]

It is difficult to believe Lake's story of Wyatt Earp's amazing feat in scaring away the usual road agents. It is more likely that as stated in the "Cheyenne and Black Hills Stage and Express Routes," Wyatt Earp along with a number of other well known and brave gunmen escorted the shipment through to Cheyenne.

It cannot be said here that the whole story was a figment of Lake's or Wyatt's imagination as there are some facts that can be verified. At least we know that he was in Deadwood and that the country was plagued with bandits. We also know there was a spring clean-up shipment of gold of approximately $200,000 and that the agent for the express company was Isaac H. Gray, approximately the same name Lake gave to the supposed agent for Wells Fargo; and that Wyatt Earp, being on his way back to Kansas, was one of the special shotgun messengers who brought the shipment through to Cheyenne without mishap. These stories could be true, or partially true, and it could easily happen that after the lapse of 50 years Wyatt Earp remembered Gray as being an agent for Wells Fargo or on the other hand, Lake having been so familiar with the activities of Wells Fargo in western history may have just assumed that the express company involved was Wells Fargo. But the known facts dispute the heroic action of Wyatt Earp bravely riding shotgun and scaring away the robbers. It is more likely that he was "among the special shotgun messengers who brought the shipment through to Cheyenne without mishap."

---

[1]   The Cheyenne and Black Hills Stage & Express Routes, p. 186.

[2]   Ibid, p. 188.

CHAPTER X

EARP RETURNS TO DODGE CITY

DID Wyatt Earp really return to the Dodge City Marshal's office in 1877? He may have served briefly, but evidence that he served at all is unavailable.

Stuart N. Lake says: "While idling in Cheyenne, Wyatt received a telegram from Jim Kelley, newly elected mayor of Dodge City, urging him to return to the cowboy capitol to resume his job as marshal at an increase of $100 a month in wages over his pay of the preceding summer.

"In the year of 1877, Dodge was to reach the high mark as the longhorn cattle center of the universe and by June the camp was overrun by Texas cowboys. In the absence of any peace officer of sufficiently forceful attainments to ensure respect for local ordinances -- fat Larry Deger and Joe Mason were supposed to preserve order -- gun-toters were swaggering along Front Street, gun play was an hourly occupance, hurrahing the camp in the roar of six-gun fusillades was once again the favorite relaxation. When mayor Kelley wired to Wyatt Earp at Cheyenne, Dodge, if she was not exactly treed, certainly had been up-ended. Deger had resigned and the peace officer's job had been entrusted to Joe Mason as the only available substitute. Wherefore the town authorities faced Fourth of July festivities with a grave forebearing."[1]

Wyatt Earp reportedly reached Dodge City in the early morning of July 5th and was immediately appointed marshal.[2]

The first thing to check is Lake's statement that Deger had resigned and that the peace officer's job had been entrusted to Joe Mason. The contemporary records at Dodge City do not bear out that statement. The Dodge City Times, on June the 9th, described an attempt by Bat Masterson to interfere with an arrest by Marshal Deger that occurred on June the 6th, 1877.[3]

Deger was certainly Marshal at that time. On June 9, 1877 the Dodge City Times announced that Ed Masterson had been appointed

---

[1] Wyatt Earp, Frontier Marshal, pp. 164-165.

[2] Ibid, p. 166.

[3] Great Gunfighters of the Kansas Cowtowns, p. 202.

Assistant Marshal of the city and on July 3, 1877 the Times reported that he had been appointed Assistant Marshal to serve under Marshal L.E. Deger and over Joe Mason.[1] The paper said that each of them was to receive $75.00 per month.

On December 8, 1877, the Times reported the discharge of Larry Deger as City Marshal at the December 4th meeting of the City counsel - as follows: "On motion of John Newton, the office of City Marshal was declared vacant, the Mayor thereupon appointed Edward J. Masterson to said Marshalship, which appointment the Council confirmed."[2]

On July 7, 1877, the day after Lake had Wyatt Earp appointed Marshal of Dodge City, the Dodge City Times, noted:

"Wyatt Earp, who was on our City police force last summer, is in town again. We hope he will accept a position on the force once more. He had a quiet way of talking the most desperate characters into custody which invariably gave one the impression that the City was able to enforce her mandates and preserve her dignity. It wasn't considered policy to draw a gun on Wyatt unless you got the drop and meant to burn powder without any preliminary talk."[3]

It should be noted that while the Times article expressed the hope that Wyatt would accept the position on the police force, it did not indicate that he had done so. But on July 21 1877 the Times published another story that indicated that as of that date he had not done so. That story was:

". . . Miss Franky Bell, who wears the belt for superiority in point of muscular ability, heaped epithets upon the unoffending head of Mr. Earp to such an extent as to provoke a slap from the ex-officer, besides creating a disturbance of the quiet and dignity of the city for which she received a night's lodging in the dog house and a reception at the police court next morning, the expense of this was about $20.00. Wyatt Earp was assessed the lowest limit of the law, $1.00."[4]

Now that we have established that Wyatt Earp was neither marshal of Dodge City nor assistant marshal, and in fact had no official position whatever in Dodge City during the summer and fall of 1877 and spring of 1878, this leaves Lake with having created a fictitious marshal, an entirely fictitious situation and an opportunity to create a whole bunch of fictitious episodes that marked his man as

---

[1]   Ibid, p. 171.

[2]   Great Gunfighters of the Kansas Cowtowns, p. 175.

[3]   Ibid, p. 86.

[4]   Ibid, p. 86; Dodge City Times, July 7th, 1877 & July 21, 1877.

the greatest law man of all time. Lake must have had a premonition of the appetite of the coming television audiences for the consumption of his stories of the Wild and Wooley West. At any rate, he couldn't have done better had he known that in twenty five years, each one of the episodes that he created for Wyatt Earp in Dodge City would end up being re-created on television for world wide audiences. It has to be admitted that they did make wonderful T.V. programs, but as history, they were worse than nothing, because they were fiction masquerading as history.

Now having his fictitious hero properly installed in the fictitious job as Marshal of Dodge City, Lake proceeds to create his myth with gusto.

The first thing he does is create a mythical fictitious weapon for his mythical fictitious character. To do that, he said:

"Meanwhile the fame of Wyatt Earp was spreading beyond the kin of those for whom he solved problems of law and order and word of his prowess brought Ned Buntline (E.Z.C. Judson) to Dodge. Buntline's prolific pen furnished lurid tales of life on the plains for consumption by an effete world that dwelt east of the Mississippi River and which, in the seventies, demanded that its portraits of Western characters be done in bloody red. Buntline's outstanding literary achievements had been to make William Cody, a buffalo-hunter, into the renowned 'Buffalo Bill,' and from the exploits of Wyatt Earp and his associates he now obtained material for hundreds of frontier yarns, few authentic, but many the basis of fables still current as facts.

"Buntline was so grateful to the Dodge City peace officers for the color they supplied that he set about arming them as befitted their accomplishments. He sent to the Colt's factory for five special forty-five-caliber six-guns of regulation single-action style, but with barrels four inches longer than standard - a foot in length - making them eighteen inches over all. Each gun had a demountable walnut rifle stock, with a thumbscrew arrangement to fit the weapon for a shoulder piece in long-range shooting. A buckskin thong slung the stock to belt or saddle-horn when not in use. The walnut butt of each gun had the word 'Ned' carved deeply in the wood and each was accompanied by a hand-tooled holster modeled for the weapon. The author gave a 'Buntline Special' - as he called the guns - to Wyatt Earp, Charlie Bassett, Bat Masterson, Bill Tilghman, and Neal Brown.

"'There was a lot of talk in Dodge about the specials slowing us on the draw,' Wyatt recalled. 'Bat and Bill Tilghman cut off the barrels to make them standard length, but Bassett, Brown and I kept ours as they came. Mine was my favorite over any other gun. I could jerk it as fast as I could my old one and I carried it on my right hip throughout my career as marshal. . ."[1]

Throughout Lake's book on Wyatt Earp, he made reference to Wyatt using the Buntline Special. It was an intriguing idea, and tended to make the user of it appear ten feet tall.

A number of authors and researchers, this author being one of them, had some doubts about the existence of the Buntline Special. I thought I had some confirmation of the story when reading the biography of E.Z.C. Judson, who wrote wild west novels and magazine articles under the name of Ned Buntline. His biography by Jay Monaghan, entitled, The Great Rascal, repeats Lake's story about the Buntline Special almost verbatim except that he tells of only three of the special guns, those being given to Wyatt Earp, Bat Masterson and Bill Tilghman, but in a footnote the only authority he gave was Stuart N. Lake's, Wyatt Earp, Frontier Marshal, pp. 145-146.[2]

Historian and author, William B. Schillingberg, became so intrigued with the story that he did an in-depth research project on the subject and concluded that the story was purely fiction. He discovered that the Colt Company had been making Peacemakers with 10 inch and 16 inch barrels on special occasions for years, but that the Company had not shipped a 12 inch Peacemaker until August, 1892. After an intensive research job, Schillingberg concluded that:

"The entire story ceased to have any foundation since, contrary to the claim that Wyatt Earp made the Buntline Special famous, no published account of Ned Buntline's presentation can be found that predates Lake's writings."[3]

This author did considerable research on the Buntline Special and failed to find a single reference to it in anything written prior to Lake's writing in 1929. I think that is pretty good evidence that the Buntline Special, like many of Lake's stories, was a figment of his imagination. However, it was a very clever way of making his mythical character more interesting.

Another example of the myth-building technique of Stuart N. Lake is his handling of the case of Tobe Driskill. Lake told the following fanciful story: "Tobe Driskill, a sure-enough cattle king, decided that the time was ripe for him to cut loose on Dodge in whole-hearted Texas fashion.

"In celebrating the sale of his herd, Tobe acquired, with his liquor, delusions of a call to shoot Front Street wide open. A Dodge

---

[1]   Wyatt Earp, Frontier Marshal, pp. 145-146.

[2]   The Great Rascal, pp. 258-259.

[3]   Wyatt Earp and the "Buntline Special" Myth, p. 37.

citizen of anti-Kelley leanings returned Driskill's guns to him from the check-rack of his establishment after Tobe stated his purpose, and with others of like affiliation stood in the doorway of the saloon from which Driskill sallied, to watch the fireworks.

"Momentarily Dodge reverted. With a six-gun smoking in either hand, the Texan bellowed his intent to stand the camp on her ear and invited attempts to stop him, emphasizing his remarks with gunfire too promiscuous for the safety of bystanders.

"As Driskill halted before the Alhambra Saloon and bawled an obscene invitation to Mayor Kelley and his customers to step out and see what was being done to the community, Wyatt Earp ran across the Plaza. Someone called a warning, and Driskill turned, but, before Tobe could collect the poise for a course of action, he was knocked sprawling. Next he knew, his guns had been taken from him, a muscular hand had seized the scruff of his neck, and he was walking-turkey toward the calaboose, into which he was heaved headlong.

"'I would have been justified in shooting Driskill,' Wyatt said after years, 'but there was no need for gunplay. His identity did not influence me. I handled him as I would have any cowboy, but to a man of Driskill's standing and conceit, the mauling I gave him would rankle deeper and longer than any other punishment. He never would live down the fact that I had held him in too small esteem to draw a gun on him. And I wanted every move I made against the Texas men to belittle them as much as possible.'

"Word that Wyatt Earp had thrown Tobe Driskill into jail spread quickly. Numerous persons hastened to Mayor Kelley to demand that the wealthy herd-owner be released.

"'As long as I was marshal of Dodge,' Wyatt recalled with no small satisfaction, 'Jim Kelley backed me to the limit. The Tobe Driskill case was no exception. His only reply to demands for Tobe's release was that I had full authority. When pressure was brought to bear on me, I insisted that Driskill was entitled to less consideration than if he had been some poor, ignorant cow-puncher, and that he'd stay in the calaboose until morning.'

"Tobe Driskill's friends were not to be turned thus easily from retaliation. Frank Warren, at the time a bartender in the Long Branch Saloon, has furnished an eye-witness account of immediately subsequent happenings.

"News of Tobe's predicament was sent to the Driskill outfit with a suggestion for rescue. Presently, Tobe's foreman, a professional fighting man of note, led twenty-five cowboys of like proclivities over the toll bridge into town, yelling like mad, leading a riderless pony which Tobe was to use in his getaway. Several dismounted before the jail and one ran to Tom Nixon's blacksmith shop for a sledgehammer. Others sat their ponies about the door with guns drawn and, in the custom of their kind, bawled their boasts that they were taking Tobe Driskill out of jail and dared Dodge's fighting men to stop them.

"Wyatt Earp reached the calaboose as a cowboy started pounding at the door with the sledgehammer. Frank Warren took cover in a shed beside the jail. Wyatt, he said, walked straight into the group of cowboys, alone and without drawing a weapon.

"'Quit pounding on that lock,' Wyatt ordered. 'You fellows better not start something you can't stop.'

"There followed another of those remarkable tributes to the force of Wyatt Earp's personality.

"'In an instant,' Frank Warren testified, 'it was as quiet as a churchyard around that calaboose. The pounding stopped and the cowboys quit yelling.'

"'Put up your guns,' Wyatt continued, 'and get out of town. Before you go, put that sledgehammer back where you got it.'

"Wyatt had his eye on the gun-fighting foreman, and that individual undoubtedly figured that he was marked for Boot Hill with the first move toward further hostilities. The Marshal afterwards confirmed the accuracy of the foreman's reasoning. The leader of the rescue party wheeled his pony and started out of Dodge, followed by his troop of killers. Wyatt watched the last one cross the toll bridge, then went back to Front Street. Next morning, Tobe Driskill was fined one hundred dollars."[1]

The Dodge City newspapers were alert to any disturbance, and usually printed any story that appeared interesting. A ruckus like the one just described, would certainly have drawn their attention,but not a word about it was published in any of the local newspapers, nor was the story ever written by contemporaries who were present. The name Tobe Driskill appeared in the Ford County Globe of September 24, 1878 as being one of the party of civilians who went in pursuit of the Cheyenne Indians during their outbreak that summer. The paper indicated that he was the brother, or at least closely connected with Bud Driskill in the cattle business.[2] He seems to have been a man of sufficient importance that an event involving him would have drawn the attention of the local press, but not a word about the exciting event appeared.

[1]   Wyatt Earp, Frontier Marshal, pp. 170-172.

[2]   Ford County Globe, September 24, 1878.

CHAPTER XI

THE BOB RACHAL AFFAIR

ANOTHER one of Lake's fictitious stories was the following:

"Hard on the heels of the Driskill affair, Bob Rachal also got drunk enough to defy Dodge City regulations.

"At the evening hour, when Dodge took supper, Wyatt was called from the Delmonico Restaurant by the noise of gunfire. He stepped into Front Street to see an undersized fellow, whom he recognized as a violinist with a traveling theatrical troupe, running toward him.

"'I'm shot! I'm shot!' the musician screamed, and as blood streamed from a wound across his scalp, it was not difficult to believe him. Behind him at some distance, a drunken man made such speed as he might, waving a Colt's in either hand and calling upon the fugitive to stop and be killed, which demand he emphasized with profanity and punctuated with pistol-shots.

"'Get in out of sight,' Wyatt directed, pushing the little man into the Long Branch doorway. The Marshal recognized the pursuer as Bob Rachal, and prepared to deal with him. As Rachal saw his quarry disappear, he, too, started for the doorway. Wyatt stepped out to meet him.

"'Drop those guns, Rachal,' the Marshal ordered.

"'Get to hell out of the way, you blankety-blanked short-horn!' Rachal answered. 'I'll kill that little fiddling son of a so-and-so.'

"Whereupon the twelve-inch barrel of the Buntline Special was laid alongside and just underneath the Rachal hat brim most effectively. The buffaloed cattleman dropped to the walk, unconscious.

"The sound of gunfire had brought Neal Brown on the run, and when Rachal's gunbelts had been removed, Wyatt and his deputy started for the calaboose, lugging their senseless prisoner between them. By the time they were halfway to the lock-up, the cowman's Dodge City friends were intervening. When their suasion failed to turn the marshal from his purpose, they sent for Bob Wright, a founder of Dodge, half owner of the cowcamps' most important business establishment, Ford County, representative in the Kansas Legislature, astute politician, warm friend to numerous Texas men, and by all odds the wealthiest of the local citizenry. Wright reached the calaboose as Wyatt unlocked the door.

"'Here, Earp; you can't lock up Bob Rachal,' Wright said.

"'What makes you think so?' Wyatt asked.

"'Why, his business is worth half a million dollars a year to Dodge.'

"'I know that,' Wyatt admitted, while Neal Brown sloshed water over the cattle king to hasten his return to consciousness. Wright's anger mounted as the marshal answered further protestations by heaving Rachal into jail. Emboldened possibly by the crowd which had gathered, Wright made open threats.

"'You'll let him out if you know what's good for you,' he warned the Marshal. Wyatt locked the calaboose door. Wright seized his arm.

"'You let Rachal out or Dodge'll have a new marshal in twenty-four hours,' he stormed.

"'Take your hand off my arm,' Wyatt said.

"Bob Wright erred. He snatched at the key in Wyatt's hand and grappled with him, mixing with muscular efforts a highly colored prophecy of the marshal's immediate future. Thereupon Wyatt swung open the door of the calaboose and pitched the irate legislator into jail with Rachal, turned the key, and went across the railroad tracks to ascertain the extent of the violinist's injuries.

"Rachal, it appeared, had invited the musician to battle over the way certain tunes had been played by the traveling orchestra. When the violinist demurred, the cowman struck him over the head with a gun-barrel, splitting his skin with the wound which bled so profusely. Rachal started to shoot as the panic-stricken fiddler started to run, and thanks to inebriation the scalp wound was the only one inflicted.

"Jim Kelley, at the Alhambra, was besieged with demands for the release of Rachal and Wright. Kelley heard his marshal's report and refused to interfere. Wyatt, when arguments were turned upon him, declined to discuss the matter. Someone persuaded Bat Masterson to intervene, and Bat never forgot the thinly veiled reproof which met his proposals.

"'After I was all through,' Bat said, 'Wyatt reminded me, of what I knew all along, that he'd never hold the Texas men in line if he played favorites with anyone; and that when Bob Wright tried to run a bluff on him before half of Dodge and a whole crowd of Texans, he left but one course, as Wyatt saw it -- to call Wright's hand. Then it was Wright's move, to make good or crawfish.

"'If I had done anything else,' Wyatt said, 'I'd have to leave town, because I'd have lost whatever edge I've got on these trouble-makers. Now, I've put the play squarely up to Bob Wright and everybody knows it.'"[1]

About this story Drago wrote:

[1]   Wyatt Earp, Frontier Marshal, pp. 172-174.

"We are asked to believe that Wright was in jail overnight. Larry Deger was still city marshal. He certainly had authority over his assistant marshal. Had he permitted this indignity to be suffered by his best friend, Robert Wright? Would Chalk Beeson, George Hoover, Charlie Bassett, and a dozen others, the big men of Dodge, have kept hands off? Bat Masterson can be included. Of Bob Wright he said:

"'Everybody in the state knows Bob Wright. His honesty and integrity have never been questioned.'

"And what about Earp himself? Would he have dared anything so rash? It passes belief. Would the Dodge City Globe, if not the Times, Bob Wright's staunchest supporter, have remained silent? There is only one answer; it never happened. It is a fabrication equalled only by the Ellsworth fiction."[1]

One of the most compelling pieces of evidence against the truth of the story is the fact that within four years, Robert M. Wright's name headed the list of forty-five prominent citizens of Dodge City highly praising Wyatt Earp as a high-minded honorable citizen, ever vigilant in the discharge of his duties, brave and unflinching, etc. that was submitted to the court by the defense in the preliminary hearing of the O.K. Corral affair.[2]

If Wyatt Earp had humiliated Bob Wright by defying him and locking him in the city jail for a night, it seems unlikely that he would have been the first in line to sing his praises when he was in trouble in Tombstone and needed a helping hand.

---

[1]   Wild, Wooly and Wicked, p. 297.

[2]   The O.K. Corral Inquest, p. 168.

CHAPTER XII

WINTER 1877-1878

WHERE was Wyatt Earp in the later part of 1877 and the early part of 1878?

An exhaustive search of public records and newspapers did not turn up a paper trail of Wyatt Earp after the story in the Dodge City Times of July 21, 1877 reporting his encounter with Miss Franky Bell, purportedly a lady of the street. His return to Dodge City on May 8, 1878 was duly reported in the Dodge City times of May 11, 1878.

"Mr. Wyatt Earp, who had during the past served with credit on the police force arrived in this city from Texas last Wednesday. We predict that his services as an officer will again be required this summer."[1]

Although exactly where Wyatt Earp was between those two dates has been a subject of speculation, no one has turned up any contemporary records establishing his whereabouts. It's certain that he was not working as a Marshal in Dodge City.

Dale T. Schoenberg covers the area thusly:

"For the next ten months - from July, 1877, to May 1878 -- Wyatt followed the gambling circuit in Texas; from Sweetwater (later changed to Mobeetie) to Ft. Worth, Jacksboro, Ft. Griffin, Ft. Davis, Ft. Clark, and back to Ft. Worth. Sometime during 1877 Wyatt met Doc Holliday, the professional gambler and dentist, at Fort Griffin."[2]

That event was to have a lot of bearing on Wyatt Earp's future.

Lake recounts the Tobe Driskill affair, the Bob Rachal ruckus and the Clay Allison story at a point in his book that would indicate that they all occurred in 1877. On page 190 he states: "The closing weeks of the cattle shipping season of '77 were fairly quiet." He goes on to describe in some detail the activities that took place in Dodge City during that time, quoting Wyatt as saying:

"As the cattle business fell off, my brother Virgil lost interest in his job under me and started for Prescott, Arizona, then becoming a mining center. I stuck in Dodge for the Fall elections, at which Bat Masterson was elected sheriff over Larry Deger by a two-to-one

---

[1]   Great Gunfighters of the Kansas Cowtowns, p.86.

[2]   The Gunfighters, p. 33.

majority."[1]

Lake was wrong on two counts.

One, Miller and Snell report that Bat Masterson was elected Sheriff on November 6, 1877 by a majority of three votes over his opponent.[2]

Two, I can find no evidence that Virgil Earp ever worked with Wyatt as an officer in Dodge City. Even if he did, the story is still wrong. He says that Virgil lost interest as the cattle business fell off.

Yet it is generally reported that the cattle business in Dodge City started in the spring and ended in the fall.

Although I have very little confidence in anything that Frank Water's wrote in his book, The Earp Brothers of Tombstone, his story of Virgil leaving for Prescott seems to have some validity. According to Waters, Virgil's wife Allie told him of their travels to Prescott, and said that they camped at the summit, that would be Flagstaff, before dropping down into Prescott on July 4, 1877, just four days short of two months after leaving Peace.[3] That would mean that Virgil Earp had to leave Dodge City at least by May 8, 1877, and probably quite some time before.

It doesn't sound right that the cattle business would be falling off by May. The truth of the matter is that Wyatt wasn't in Dodge City that summer and Virgil never worked there.

Continuing with Earp's report of his doings in 1877, he told Lake that:

"Late in November, the Santa Fe Railroad asked me to round up the Dave Rudabaugh-Mike Roark gang of outlaws which was robbing construction camps and pay trains. Rudabaugh was about the most notorious outlaw in the range country, rustler and robber by trade with the added specialty of killing jailers in the breaks for liberty at which he was invariably successful whenever he was arrested. He was the same Rudabaugh who later ran with Billy the Kid, down in the Pecos Country. After a series of hold-ups, word came that Rudabaugh and Roark were in Texas and as I was a Deputy United States Marshal I was offered $10 a day and expenses if I'd go get them. I left after promising Kelly that I'd come back to Dodge City."[4]

There's something wrong with this story too. Wyatt Earp was not a United States Marshal at that time, nor so far as can be

---

[1]   Wyatt Earp, Frontier Marshal, p. 191.

[2]   Great Gunfighters of the Kansas Cowtowns, p. 207.

[3]   The Earp Brothers of Tombstone, pp. 63-64.

[4]   Wyatt Earp, Frontier Marshal, p. 191.

determined was he ever a United States Marshal during the time that he was at Dodge City.

The only paper trail I have been able to locate for Wyatt Earp during the fall of '77 and spring of '88 is a short statement in the Ford County Globe stating that "Wyatt Earp, our old assistant Marshal, is at Fort Clark, Texas."[1]

It may be that if Earp was not actually employed by the Santa Fe Railroad to capture Rudabaugh he was bounty hunting for reward money and at the same time indulging in his favorite business of following the gambling circuit. If that is true, it was a very unsuccessful venture, for while he was supposedly chasing Rudabaugh in Texas, Rudabaugh had returned to the vicinity of Dodge and committed another train robbery.

The Santa Fe Railroad train was robbed on January 27, 1878 at a station in Kingsley, a small settlement 37 miles up the line from Dodge. The new Sheriff Bat Masterson immediately organized a posse and went in pursuit of the robbers.

The Dodge City Times of February 2, 1878 reported a partial success of the manhunt with the arrest of Ed West, and Dave Rudabaugh, spelled Raddebaugh by the Times.[2]

The Dodge City papers continued to report the activities of Sheriff Masterson and his posse and on March 16, 1878, reported the capture of two more of the robbers, Tom Got, alias Dugan, and one Green.[3]

That means only five days, from January 27 to February 2nd, 1888, elapsed between the robbery and the capture of Dave Rudabaugh right near Dodge City while Earp was running around in Texas in hot pursuit. He went to Ft. Griffin where he met a man by the name of John Shaunassy from whom he learned that Dave Rudabaugh and his gang had left Ft. Griffin. He didn't know whether the outlaws had headed across the stake plains for New Mexico or South toward the Rio Grande. He had recommended to Earp that his best source of information would be a gambler known as Doc Holliday who was at the time hanging out in Ft. Griffin with his live-in girlfriend, a prostitute commonly known as Big Nosed Kate Fisher. Shaunassy introduced Wyatt Earp to Doc Holiday and about this, Earp stated:

"When Shaunassy told Holliday what I wanted, Doc said he'd

---

[1]   Ford County Globe, January 28, 1878; Great Gunfighters of the Kansas Cowtowns, p. 86.

[2]   Great Gunfighters of the Kansas Cowtowns, p. 211.

[3]   Ibid, p. 217.

learn Rudabaugh's whereabouts if I'd give him time. Within the next week or so I saw a great deal of Holiday and I learned, then and later, more than anyone else, in the West knew of his early life and his family."[1]

About Doc Holliday's association with Kate Fisher, Earp said:

"It was in Shaunassy's saloon, I think, that Doc Holliday first met Kate Fisher, a dance hall girl better known as 'Big Nosed Kate.' Doc lived with Kate off and on, over a period of years. She saved his life on one occasion and when memory of this was upper most Doc would refer to Kate as Mrs. Holliday. Their relationship had its temperamental ups and downs, however, and when Kate was riding under Doc's scorn she'd get drunk as well as furious and make Doc more trouble than any shooting-scrape."[2]

In an interview with a San Francisco Examiner reporter, printed on August 2, 1896, Wyatt told a somewhat different story about his meeting with Doc Holliday. In that interview he said:

"It happened in 1877, when I was City Marshal of Dodge City, Kansas. I had followed the trail of some cattle thieves across the border into Texas, and during a short stay in Ft. Griffin, I first met Doc Holliday and the woman who was known variously as 'Big Nose Kate,' Kate Fisher, and on occasions of ceremony, Mrs. Doc Holliday. Holliday asked me a good many questions about Dodge City and seemed inclined to go there, but before he had made up his mind about it, my business called me over to Ft. Clarke. It was while I was on my way back to Ft. Griffin that my new friend and his Kate found it necessary to pull their stakes hurriedly, wherefore, the plain, unvarnished facts were these:

"Doc Holliday was spending the evening in a poker game which was his custom whenever faro bank did not present superior claims to his attention. On his right sat Ed Bailey, who needs no description because he is soon to be dropped out of this narrative. The trouble began, as it was related to me by Ed Bailey monkeying with the deadwood or what people who live in cities call 'discards.' Doc Holliday admonished him once or twice to 'play poker' -- which is your seasoned gamblers method of cautioning a friend to stop cheating - but misguided Bailey persisted in his furtive attentions to the deadwood. Finally, having detected him again, Holliday pulled down a pot without showing his hand, which he had a perfect right to do, thereupon Bailey started to throw his gun around on Holliday as might have been expected. But before he could pull the trigger,

---

[1]   Wyatt Earp, Frontier Marshal, p. 195.

[2]   Ibid, p. 197.

Doc Holliday had jerked a knife out of his breast-pocket and with one sideways sweep had got Bailey just below the brisket.

"Well, that broke up the game, and pretty soon Doc Holliday was sitting cheerfully in the front room of the Hotel, guarded while the gamblers clambered for his blood. You see, he had not lived in Ft. Griffin very long, while Ed Bailey was well liked. It wasn't long before Big Nosed Kate, who had a room downtown, heard about the trouble and went up to take a look at her Doc through a back window. What she saw and heard led her to think that his life wasn't worth ten minutes purchase, and I don't believe it was. There was a shed at the back of the lot, and a horse was stabled in it. She was a kind-hearted girl, was Kate, for she went to the trouble of leading the horse into the alley and tethering it there before she set fire to the shed. She also got a six-shooter from a friend down the street, which, with the one she always carried, made two.

"It all happened just as she had planned it. The shed blazed up and she hammered at the door, yelling 'Fire!' Everybody rushed out, except the Marshal and the Constables and their prisoner. Kate walked in as bold as a lion, threw one of her six-shooters on the Marshal and handed the other to Doc Holliday.

"'Come on, Doc,' she said with a laugh.

"He didn't need any second invitation and the two of them backed out of the Hotel, keeping the officers covered. All that night they hid among the willows down by the creek, and early next morning a friend of Kate's brought them two horses and some of Doc Holliday's clothes from his room. Kate dressed up in a pair of pants, a pair of boots, a shirt and a hat and the pair of them got away safely and rode the 400 miles to Dodge City, where they were installed in great style when I got back home."[1]

His presence in Dodge City is verified by an advertisement in the Dodge City Times offering his professional dental services and a statement that "Where satisfaction is not given, money will be refunded."[2]

There are at least three glaring inconsistencies in this report by Earp. One, his claim to be City Marshal of Dodge when we know that position was then occupied either by Lawrence E. Deger, or by Ed Masterson who was appointed to the position of City Marshal to replace Larry Deger on December 4, 1877.[3]

---

[1]   The San Francisco Examiner, August 2, 1896;
The Earp's Talk, P. 4.

[2]   Dodge City Times, June 8, 1878.

[3]   Great Gunfighters of the Kansas Cowtowns, P. 175.

Two, if Wyatt Earp was City Marshal of Dodge City at that time, what was a City Marshal doing trailing cattle thieves across the boarder into Texas? And three, what about Lake's story that he went to Texas at the request of the Santa Fe Railroad trying to capture Dave Rudabaugh and his gang of robbers?

Going back to Lake's original story, Wyatt claimed to have received information from Doc Holliday that Dave Rudabaugh had gone to Ft. Davis, and following on his trail, he went from Ft. Davis to Ft. Clark and from Ft. Clark to Ft. Concho, then to Ft. Kavett and back to Ft. Griffin which he reached for the second time on January 20th, 1878. On his second arrival at Ft. Griffin, he received word from Dodge City that the Rudabaugh gang had doubled back on their trail and had gone back near Dodge City where they had engaged in the Kingsley holed up and that Rudabaugh had been captured by Bat Masterson. Roark was still on the loose, and Wyatt claims to have gone to San Antonio on his trail and arrived there about 48 hours behind the fugitives only to learn that he was making for his old home near Joplin, Missouri. Wyatt claimed that he went to Joplin, Missouri, arriving ahead of his quarry, and at that time received a message from Mayor Dog Kelley of Dodge City urging him to return at once to Dodge City. One has to wonder how Mayor Kelley knew that Wyatt would receive his telegram at Joplin, Missouri.

On April 9th, 1878 Ed Masterson was killed in a gunfight in Dodge City. He had been appointed Assistant Marshal serving under Marshal L.E. Deger and over Policeman Joe Mason on July 3rd, 1877.[1]

On December 4th, 1877 the Dodge City Council had discharged Larry Deger as City Marshal and appointed Ed Masterson to that position.[2]

The Ford County Globe got out an extra the next day after the shooting of Ed Masterson which account was published in the Topeka Commonwealth on April 12, 1878 as follows:

"DEATH OF MARSHAL MASTERSON.

"The Dodge City Globe Extra, of the 10th has the following about the death of Marshal Masters. At 10 o'clock last night, City Marshal Edward Masterson, discovered that a cowboy who was working for Soburn of Kansas City, named Jack Wagner, was carrying a six-shooter contrary to the city ordinance. Wagner was at the time under the influence of liquor, but quietly gave up the pistol. The Marshal gave it to some one of Wagner's friends for safe keeping and stepped

---

[1]   Ibid, p. 171.

[2]   Ibid, p. 175.

out into the street. No sooner had he done so than Wagner ran out after him pulling another pistol, which the Marshal had not observed. The Marshal saw him coming and turned upon Wagner and grabbed hold of him.

"Wagner shot Marshal Masterson at once through the abdomen, being so close to him that the discharge set the Marshal's clothes on fire.

"Marshal Masterson then shot Wagner.

"About this time a man named Walker got mixed up in the fight. He, it appears, was boss herder for Oburn, and Wagner was working under him. He also got shot once through the left lung and his right arm was twice broken.

"Marshal Masterson walked across the street to (George M.) Hoover's Saloon, where after telling that he was shot, he sank to the floor. He was immediately moved to his room, where in half an hour he expired. Walker and Wagner were nearly all night insensible and none thought that either of them could live through the night. However, morning has come and neither are dead; both are in very precarious condition and their chances of recovery very small.

"The city is mourning; every door is draped with crepe; businesses entirely suspended till after the funeral of Marshal Masterson which will take place at two o'clock p.m. and will be attended by everybody in the city.

"Marshal Masterson will be buried in the Military Cemetery, Ft. Dodge. "[1]

Immediately upon the death of Marshal Edward J. Masterson, Charles E. Bassett, then under Sheriff to Bat Masterson, was appointed Marshal of Dodge City.

The Dodge City Times of April 13, 1878 carried a more detailed story of the killing of Edward J. Masterson as follows:

"THE PISTOL TO MURDER OF EDWARD J. MASTERSON CITY MARSHAL.

"THE ASSAILANTS SHOT - ONE OF THEM DEAD.

"DODGE CITY IN MOURNING."

"On Tuesday evening, about 10 o'clock, Edward J. Masterson, Marshal of Dodge City, was murdered by Jack Wagner and Alph Walker, two cattle drivers from near Haze City. The two cowboys were under the influence of bad whiskey and were carrying revolvers. Early in the evening, Marshal Masterson disarmed Wagner; later Marshal Masterson and Deputy Marshal Nat Haywood tried the second time to disarm Wagner. While in the act, Masterson was shot in the abdomen. Walker in the meantime snapped a pistol in the face

[1]   Great Gunfighters of Kansas Cowtowns, p. 178.

of officer Haywood. Masterson fired four shots one of them striking Wagner in the bowels, Walker was struck three times, and his right arm partially shattered with the other shot.

"The shooting occurred on the South side of the railroad track. Marshal Masterson coolly walked over to the business side of the street, a distance of about 200 yards, and upon reaching the sidewalk, he fell exhausted. He was taken to his room where he died about 40 minutes later.

"Wagner and Walker were removed to Mr. Lane's room, where the former died at about 7 o'clock Wednesday evening. Walker is laying dangerously wounded with no hope of recovery. Some of the flying shots grazed the faces of one of our citizens and a cattleman. The shots were fired almost simultaneously, and the wonder is expressed that more death and destruction did not ensue, as a large crowd surrounded the scene of the shooting.

"The officers were brave and cool though both were at a disadvantage, as neither desired to kill the whisky-crazed assailants. The death of Marshal Masterson caused great feeling in Dodge City. The business houses were draped in mourning, and business on Wednesday generally suspended.

"Elsewhere, we give the expression of sympathy and ceremony following the terrible tragedy."[1]

Contrast this story with the story written by Stewart Lake. He wrote:

"Bat Masterson, who helped Ed in handling local law breakers as his Sheriff's duties allowed, rounded the corner of Second Avenue on the way to his brother's assistance just in time to see Walker and Wagoner down the Marshal. Ham Bell who witnessed the shooting from a window, of the Lone Star, has told me of what followed.

"Bat Masterson, fully 60 feet away as his brother fell, fired 4 shots. The first slug hit Wagner squarely in the pit of the stomach and killed him. Bat came on, shooting at Walker, who was shooting back. Walker was hit three times, once in the lung and twice in the right arm, none of his shots at Bat took effect. With his gun-arm out of commission, the cowboy turned and ran for cover in the Lone Star. 'Catch me!' Walker gasped to Ham Bell as he reeled through the door. 'Catch me! I'm dying.'

"'That corner's as good a place as any,' Ham replied, and as no one in the place offered additional succor, Walker went on out the rear door. He escaped Bat's further vengeance because the Sheriff believed that Walker was mortally wounded and because word that his brother had but a few minutes to live was shouted to him from

[1]   Great Gunfighters of the Kansas Cowtowns, p. 181.

Hoover's Saloon into which place Ed had been carried. Walker got down the trail into Texas, where he died of pneumonia induced by the lung wound."[1]

The story that Bat Masterson with a fast gun avenged the death of his brother by killing both of his attackers has been told for many years, but there is no evidence that it is true. Bat Masterson's best biographer, De Arment, concluded that it was clear from the newspaper accounts of the shooting that it was a gun in the hand of Marshal Ed Masterson who killed both Wagner and Walker.

In remarking on Lake's statement that Ham Bell witnessed the fight from a window of the Lone Star dance hall and saw Bat Masterson cut down Wagner and Walker from a distance of 60 feet, De Arment said that was not true. He said that Ham Bell told George C. Thompson that he was in Peacock's Saloon, and he either could not or would not state definitely who shot the cowboys.[2]

It is quite apparent that Bat Masterson did not kill his brother's murderers and that the Lake's story, like most of his about Dodge City, is not correct.

The killing of Ed Masterson did have some effect on the career of Wyatt Earp, however. Lake says that on the morning of May 12, 1878, Wyatt reached Dodge in response to Mayor Kelly's message.

Schoenberg says that, "On May 8, 1878, Wyatt Earp returned to Dodge City. Mattie Blaylock came with him. The Dodge City Times of May 11th, commented on Earp's return:

"'Mr. Earp, who has during the past, served with credit on the police (force) arrived in this City from Texas last Wednesday. We predict that his services as an officer will again be required this summer.'"[3]

The Ford County Globe on May 14, printed the following story:

"Wyatt Earp, one of the most efficient officers Dodge ever had, has just returned from Ft. Worth, Texas. He was immediately appointed assistant Marshal by our City dads, much to their credit."[4]

Compare that story to Lake's story, and you'll see one glaring difference. Lake quoted the Globe for May 14 as stating:

"Wyatt Earp, *the most efficient officer Dodge ever had,* has just returned from Texas, he was immediately reappointed Marshal by our

1   Wyatt Earp, Frontier Marshal, p. 200.

2   Wyatt Earp, Frontier Marshal, p. 200.

3   The Dodge City Times, May 11, 1878.

4   Great Gunfighters of the Kansas Cowtowns, p. 86.

city dads, much to their credit."[1]

The difference, while very small, is extremely significant for it demonstrates how Lake trimmed the facts to suit his purposes. In this case, he left out a most important two words. Instead of Wyatt Earp, one of the most efficient officers, he left out the words "one of," thus making the paper state that Wyatt Earp was the most efficient officer Dodge ever had, a proposition that would start quite an argument if stated publicly in and around Dodge City, then or now. It is also interesting to note that Lake has Wyatt Earp receiving a telegram at Joplin, Missouri urging his return to Dodge City. The Dodge City Times of May 11th said he had just arrived from Texas and The Globe of the 14th said that he had just returned from Fort Worth, Texas.

Thus, it appears that Wyatt Earp left Dodge City sometime after July 26, 1877 and returned about May 8, 1878. It is interesting to note that when he came back he brought Mattie Blaylock with him and lived with her in Dodge City. Later, he took her with him to Arizona where she lived with him. She went to Colton, California with Virgil Earp and his wife when some of the Earp's left Tombstone after Morgan Earp was murdered.

It is also interesting that nowhere can I find any direct quote or reference by Wyatt Earp himself to the fact that Mattie Blaylock was his wife or any mention of her as a companion. The nearest I can come to that is that at Tombstone, he named one of his mining claims The Mattie Blaylock. The reason that no author quotes Wyatt Earp as mentioning Mattie Blaylock as his wife will be explained later by the actions of his last wife, Josephine Sarah Marcus Earp, and her conduct toward any one that she thought might mention Mattie as being Wyatt's wife.

---

[1]   Wyatt Earp, Frontier Marshal, p. 202.

CHAPTER XIII

THE CLAY ALLISON AFFAIR

WHEN telling of the Clay Allison event, Lake carefully avoided giving it a date. From the chronology of his story, it would seem that he intended that it should have happened in the summer of 1877 when Wyatt Earp returned from the Dakota territory. However, Lake gets conveniently vague about dates, and it is difficult to determine when any of the events that he described are supposed to have taken place.

He gave one clue in the following story:

"On the second day after Rachal's arrest Wyatt Earp was informed that a standing offer of $1,000 had been posted for any gunman who would kill him, in a fair fight or otherwise, and with this went a guarantee against prosecution if the killer could escape Dodge City jurisdiction. The first attempt to collect this bounty was made early one morning, as Wyatt crossed the railroad tracks at First Avenue. Three shots were fired from behind a freight-car, two missing the target entirely, the third cutting a hole through the marshal's sombrero. A few nights later, when Wyatt reached his room on the ground floor of the Dodge house, and stepped quickly to the window for a look outside before he lighted the lamp, the roar of a double-barreled shotgun brought the sash around his head in splinters.

"'The fellow was too anxious,' Wyatt said, 'and shot high. I saw him run for the South Side and went through the window after him. I wanted to get him in talking condition, so I shot him in the leg, and he tumbled.

"'Tom Finnerty and I lugged the fellow to the calaboose and sent for Dr. McCarty. I told my prisoner that if he'd tell me why he tried to kill me and who put him up to it, I wouldn't make any charge against him. He was just an ordinary cowboy, who didn't know anything about the men back of the business. He had lost his year's pay, pony, saddle, and guns, gambling, he said, and a herd-boss had promised him a thousand dollars if he'd kill me, provided a shotgun for the job, and posted him on my habit of looking out of my window, which showed how well the gang had me spotted.'

"When Wyatt Earp next appeared on Front Street, all Dodge knew of the conspiracy against him. 'Dog' Kelley suggested a bodyguard and a number of Dodge's foremost gun-fighters volunteered for regular turns of duty in Wyatt's company. The marshal declined their offers.

"'I told my friends,' Wyatt recalled, 'that I would not give my enemies the satisfaction of seeing me take precautions against them. That was foolish, but where Texas men and their kind were concerned, I've never denied that what I wanted most of all was the personal satisfaction of winning with a lone hand against the whole outfit.'"

"Dodge and her cowboy hang-outs now went agog with excitement.

"'They've sent for Clay Allison to cut down Wyatt Earp,' the news ran; 'Clay Allison of the Washita!'

"Confirmation came with Texas boasts that Clay Allison, a six-gun killer with twenty-one men to his 'credit' -- of whom six were frontier marshals or sheriffs -- was coming over from Las Animas to shake up Dodge in smoke, to go against Wyatt Earp in his own bailiwick.

"'They've sent for Clay Allison, sure enough,' 'Dog' Kelley told Wyatt. 'Clay's made talk in Las Animas that he's been invited to come over here and run you out, or knock you off, and that he's heading for Dodge to fill the order. What do you want me to do?'

"'Nothing,' Wyatt answered. 'I'll decide what to do with Clay when the time comes.'

"Jim Kelley always maintained that Wyatt made no preparation for the reception of the man who was coming to kill him. The rest of Dodge awaited feverishly what it was freely predicted would be the six-gun classic of the century.

"Clay Allison was a Tennessee-born Texan, whose six-gun skill, at the age of twenty-six, had filled graves from Dodge to Santa Fe. He was strikingly handsome, six feet two inches in his socks, weighing about one hundred and eighty pounds, broad-shouldered, slim-hipped, muscularly powerful, lithe, quick as the proverbial cat, with remarkably slender hands and feet of which he was inordinately vain. A profusion of wavy black hair set off his high forehead, dark blue eyes, and aquiline nose; the boldness of his countenance was further enhanced by the black mustache and beard which he wore more neatly an closely trimmed than was currently fashionable. Allison was a fastidious dresser, affecting all the cowboy trappings for horse and man, but holding to a single black-and-white color scheme. He complemented this distinctive attire through ownership of two cow-ponies, each with a thoroughbred cross; one, coal-black; the other, cream-white, and referred to as his 'war-horse.'

"Upon the mountain man's inherent aptitude for firearms Clay grafted the six-shooter tradition of the range-riders. So assiduously did he cultivate the development, that by 1873 the frontier settlements in Texas, Colorado, New Mexico, and Kansas knew and feared him as a killer who would shoot a man to see him kick.

"'Sober,' one of his earlier associates has written, 'Clay Allison could be a mighty good fellow. Throw a couple of drinks into him and he was a hell-bound turned-loose, rarin' to shoot -- in self-defense.'

"Next to out-and-out gunplay, Allison found his chief delight in standing the Western camps on end, and for a number of years he paid scheduled visits to a regular list of communities and hurrahed them to a finish. Christmas and Fourth of July, for example, he regularly devoted to running Las Animas up a tree, although he was not averse to standing that particular town on her ear at such other odd times as the spirit moved him.

"The temper of Clay's celebrant moods is exemplified in his visit to a Las Animas dentist for relief from a toothache. The dentist pulled the wrong tooth, an error which later came painfully to Clay's attention; whereupon Allison returned to the dentists's office, buffaloed the practitioner, and pulled a half-dozen teeth from the dentist's jaws with that gentleman's own forceps.

"On another occasion, Clay treated Canadian, Texas, to a cowboy version of Lady Godiva's Ride. He took his black pony to the edge of camp, stripped to his skin, barring gunbelts and boots, tied his clothing to his saddle and headed down Main Street on a whooping, shooting gallop, standing full length in his stirrups, stark naked above the shins except for his cartridge-carriers. When this exhibition palled, he pulled up in front of a saloon, dismounted, and, without dressing, went inside for a drink. Not all of his celebrations were as harmless.

"Allison once rode into Cimarron, New Mexico, and while in Lambert's saloon, accumulating inspiration for scheduled festivities, met Marshal Pancho, a well-known frontier peace officer. Lambert said that Pancho, while trying to talk Allison out of his contemplated spree in the interests of the community, removed his sombrero and let the hand which held the hat drop to his waist. Clay jerked a gun and shot Pancho dead.

"Allison asserted that the marshal had used his sombrero as a shield behind which he had tried to draw his gun, and that, as the marshal had no warrant for his arrest, he had shot in self-defense.

"Again in Las Animas, Clay shot and killed Marshal Charlie Farber, who had ordered Clay and his brother, John Allison, to check their guns while in a local dance hall. The brothers refused, and Farber left the hall to return with a double-barreled shotgun. He ordered John Allison to throw up his hands. John went for his Colt's and Farber shot him through the gun-arm. Clay Allison, from a far corner of the room, shot the marshal through the chest and killed him. Again, Clay pleaded self-defense, on the ground that Farber had a load in the second barrel of his gun and was after either Allison he could get. After a Las Animas jury cleared him on the strength of that argument, Clay added the courts to his list of playgrounds.

"Allison had himself appointed foreman of a grand jury and kept that august body in a twenty-eight-day-and-night session during which the jurors transacted no business, but did keep hilariously drunk on liquor which Clay purchased with county warrants. Again, when he reached Las Animas to find court in session, Clay rode into the courtroom on his war-horse and ordered the tribunal of justice adjourned to stay that way until he had left town. The judge accommodated him.

"In Clifton, New Mexico, Clay met another killer, one Chunk, who with eleven notches in his gun had announced that he would cut Number 12 for Clay Allison whenever he met him. So highly regarded was Chunk's proficiency on the draw-and-shoot that in the frontier camps the betting was at even money on the outcome of the anticipated battle.

"Clay rode up to the Clifton House to find Chunk there ahead of him, with neither man previously aware that the other was on that trail. To work up to fighting pitch, the men bought drinks for one another, then matched ponies in a race which Chunk won. Next, Chunk invited Clay to dine with him at a restaurant. The men sat at opposite sides of the table and ordered food, but gave their best attention to whiskey. Clay got impatient, reached across the table and slapped Chunk's face. Chunk went for his gun, but Clay beat him to the draw and shot him through the head. As Chunk had advertised his intention of killing Allison, Clay was not held.

"The only killing credited to Clay Allison's account in Dodge had taken place in the early days of that camp, when Wyatt Earp was in Wichita. Clay was eating in a restaurant when a drunken man with whom he had quarreled entered with a gun in his hand and the announcement that he was hunting Allison.

"'Here I am,' Clay called, and while his inebriated enemy was trying to focus his wavering eye and sights, Allison drew a gun and shot him. Legend adds that Clay went on with his meal while someone else dragged his victim to Boot Hill. He strutted in Dodge for several weeks that season, but eventually returned to his Las Animas stamping-ground.

"Wyatt Earp, while marshal of Dodge, was on active duty in the streets until four o'clock each morning and, unless court business called him, slept until noon. Thus it happened that when Clay Allison hit Dodge City one morning, Wyatt was in bed. The marshal's first knowledge of Allison's arrival came with a message from the mayor that the gunman was in town, had been in several saloons buying drinks, and was boasting of the purpose of his visit. Clay was rapidly approaching the stage of intoxication at which he was most dangerous. Wherefor Mayor Kelley and his supporters were anxiously awaiting Wyatt's appearance.

"'I'll be right along,' Wyatt said in response to the summons, then went about the routine of shaving and breakfast.

"'With Clay in town the time for fussing was past,' Wyatt commented. 'Now, it was up to me to leave Dodge by the back alley or go down Front Street and meet Allison.

"'I did not intent to give Clay the satisfaction of thinking he had hurried me. He knew that I'd been sent for before I did, and I knew enough about the average braggart killer to be certain that a lot of Clay's fight would go into all the talk he'd be making while he waited. And the more I could irritate him by tardiness, the less sure of himself he'd be at the showdown.

"'I wore my guns at breakfast on the chance that Clay might bring the fight into the dining room. While I was eating, several men came to ask if they could help any, but beyond asking Bat Masterson and Charlie Bassett to make sure I was not ambushed by Allison's friends, I declined their offers. About ten o'clock I walked down Front Street toward Second Avenue.'

"Accounts of men who witnessed Wyatt Earp's meeting with Clay Allison do not differ in essential details, but few who have told their stories occupied positions as commanding as those of Chalk Beeson and Bill Harris, proprietors of the Long Branch in front of which the marshal met the gunman, and Luke Short who ran the Long Branch gambling concession.

"Between gun-fighter and gunman, one marked similarity was noted in the colors of their clothing. Clay Allison had followed his predilection for black-and-white from the toes of his fancy boots to the tip of his huge sombrero, through his full array of white buck-skin and silver-trimmed accouterments. Wyatt Earp was dressed as for any other mid-summer morning. He wore no coat and his dark trousers were pulled down over the tops of his boots; a gun was belted to either hip; on his soft white shirt was his marshal's badge; for shade, he wore a sombrero as large and as black as Allison's.

"As Wyatt started toward Second Avenue, the north side of Front Street cleared instantly, a few spectators taking vantage-points in stores and saloons, a majority utilizing the hitch beside the railroad. As Wyatt neared the Long Branch, three doors from Second Avenue, Clay Allison came out of Wright and Beverly's door on the corner.

"Wyatt stopped and leaned against the wall of the Long Branch, just west of the doorway. Allison came along the walk, turned, as if to enter the saloon, and halted abruptly.

"'Are you Wyatt Earp?' the killer demanded.

"'I am Wyatt Earp,' the marshal replied.

"'I've been looking for you.'

"'You've found me.'

"'You're the fellow who killed that soldier the other night, aren't you?' Allison continued.

"'What business is it of yours if I am?' Wyatt countered, although the charge implied was without foundation.

"'He was a friend of mine,' Allison retorted.

"As Allison talked, he had stepped close, and was actually leaning against Wyatt, thus shielding his right side and his right hand from the marshal's view.

"'Clay was working for his gun all the time,' Wyatt said, 'trying to get into such a position that I couldn't see him start after it.'

"'I'm making it my business right now,' Allison snarled.

"Wyatt felt the muscles of the body which pressed against him tighten.

"The watchers in the Long Branch said that Clay Allison had his thumb hooked around the hammer of his Colt's and the weapon half-out of the holster when stark amazement replaced the fighting scowl which had distorted his face, he dropped his gun as though the butt had turned red-hot, and jerked both hands, empty, above his waist. Then onlookers saw the reason for the transformation, although none had caught the action which brought it. The muzzle of Wyatt Earp's forty-five was jammed into Allison's left side, just underneath the ribs.

"With his gun against Allison's body, Wyatt waited for the other to move or speak.

"A few seconds of threatening suspense brought the strain to a pitch Clay could not endure. Hesitantly, Allison backed across the walk. With several feet between him and the muzzle of Wyatt's forty-five he found voice.

"'I'm going around the corner,' Clay suggested.

"'Go ahead,' Wyatt told him. 'Don't come back.'

"Allison backed out of sight beyond Wright and Beverly's.

"A moment later, when the marshal peered around the same corner, Second Avenue was empty. From across the road, Bat Masterson called. Armed with a shotgun, the deputy sheriff had taken his stand in a doorway to command three approaches to the Front Street intersection, thus precluding any attempt to gang-up on Wyatt from those quarters. Bat called that Allison had gone into Wright and Beverly's by the side entrance and that there were some twenty other men in the place who would bear watching. Then he pointed across the Plaza to Sheriff Charlie Bassett, guarding against a shot in the back from that direction. Wyatt returned to his post beside the Long Branch door. Allison's war-horse was hitched to the rail before Wright and Beverly's front doorway. Harris, Beeson, and Short could forestall any bush-whacking operations through the saloon. To reach his pony, Allison would have to come into Wyatt's line of vision, and from where he stood the marshal could keep cases until the killer made his next move.

"Allison probably was taking on liquid courage in Wright and Beverly's, and while Wyatt waited, the door of the Long Branch opened behind him and a double-barreled shotgun was thrust within reach of his hand.

"'Take this and give him both barrels,' Chalk Beeson counseled.

"The proffered gun, incidentally, was the same fine English made piece with which Bill Thompson killed Sheriff Whitney in Ellsworth. The gun belonged to Bill's brother Ben, and was his favorite weapon. Early in '77, Ben Thompson went broke in Dodge and posted the shotgun with Chalk Beeson for a loan of seventy-five dollars. Chalk kept the gun back of the bar while waiting for Ben Thompson to redeem it.

"Wyatt Earp, without taking his eye from the Wright and Beverly door, shook his head at Chalk's suggestion. Bill Harris joined his partner.

"'Don't be a fool, Wyatt,' Harris counseled. 'Take the shotgun and use it.'

"'All Clay's got is a pair of six-guns,' Wyatt answered.

"Allison strode out of Wright and Beverly's door; Beeson and Harris ducked back through their own. The gunman, pistols in their holsters, walked straight to his war-horse, swung into the saddle, and sat staring savagely. He turned to the marshal.

"'Come over here, Earp,' he suggested. 'I want to talk to you.'

"'Make your talk,' Wyatt answered. 'I can hear you.'

"'You, Bob Wright!' Allison bellowed, 'Bob Wright!'

"Wright stepped to the walk in front of his store.

"'Now, Clay ----' he began, but Allison cut him short.

"'You're a hell of a fellow,' the gunman shouted so that half of Dodge City heard. 'You made some promises about this morning, and agreed to have some fighting men here, but I haven't seen any signs of them.'

"'What do you mean, Clay?' Bob Wright inquired suavely.

"'You know what I mean,' Allison answered with a string of oaths, 'and so do the fellows you sent to Las Animas after me.'

"With which telling observation, Clay Allison wheeled his war-horse and started for the tollbridge on a run. As he reached the bridgehead, Clay pulled up and turned to face the Plaza. With a wild whoop, he jerked a gun, put spurs and quirt to his mount, and headed back toward Wright and Beverly's.

"'Watch the store, boys,' Wyatt called to Masterson and Bassett, 'I'm going to get him.'

"The marshal walked to the middle of Second Avenue. Clay

came at a gallop, gun in his right hand, quirt flailing in his left, yelling madly. When he was about fifty yards distant, Bat Masterson saw the Buntline Special move slowly from Wyatt's side to a level slightly above his waist. As Bat and the others waited for the roar of gunfire that would relieve the West of a killer or rob it of a peace officer, Clay yanked his war-horse to his haunches, in the sliding stop that only a highly trained cow-pony can achieve, wheeled, and rode breakneck again for the tollbridge. This time he kept on, out of Dodge, toward Las Animas. The showdown had come and gone. Clay Allison had quit the fight.

"Wyatt turned from the roadway to face Bob Wright and several of the legislator's friends who had watched Allison's departing gesture.

"'I thought so,' Wyatt remarked. No one answered."[1]

In a book written by Chuck Parsons in 1983, the author tried to determine the truth of the above story and similar ones and reached the following conclusions:

"Since so far as known no incident describing Allison being run out of town, or making Dodge City officers run for cover, was printed during Allison's lifetime, it is worthy to attempt to determine when the legend and confusion started. Research by this writer suggests that the first version of an Allison - lawman confrontation came from Wyatt Earp himself. In 1896 Earp was interviewed by a reporter for the San Francisco Examiner. One of these interviews appeared in an issue of August 16, 1896 under the title: 'Wyatt Earp's tribute to Bat Masterson, hero of Dobe Walls.'"[2]

The Examiner interview was published in full by Alford E. Turner in his book, The O.K. Corral Inquest. There is only a slight difference in the story told by Wyatt Earp to the San Francisco Examiner and the one told by Lake and quoted above. The difference is the thing that gives us the date that Lake or Wyatt Earp would have us believe the event occurred. In the Examiner Allison is quoted as saying, "You're the man that killed my friend Hoyt." Earp replied, "Yes, I guess I'm the man you're looking for." In Lake's book he changes the words from Hoyt to "You're the fellow who killed that soldier the other night, aren't you?" The significance of the changes is that by inserting the name of Hoyt, he enables us to place a fairly exact date of the alleged occurrence, for on July 26, 1878 approximately a year after Lake would have you believe that Wyatt faced down Clay Allison, the Times wrote a long story about the killing of a young man by the name of George Hoy or Hoyt. This

[1]   Wyatt Earp, Frontier Marshal, pp. 176-184.

[2]   Clay Allison, Portrait of a Shootist, p. 36.

story will be gone into later, but at least for the present, it dates the killing as of July 26, 1878 thus making the date of any confrontation between Wyatt Earp and Clay Allison after that time.

It is highly probably that Clay Allison was in Dodge City in the later part of July, 1878. On August 6, 1878, The Globe noted that, "Clay Allison, one of the Allison bros., from the Cimarron, south of Los Animas, Colorado, stopped off at Dodge last week on his way home from St. Louis. We are glad to say that Clay has about recovered from the effects of the East St. Louis scrimmage."[1]   The St. Louis scrimmage referred to was a fight engaged in by Clay Allison and reported in the St. Louis Republican on July 25, 1878. The article described an encounter between a man by the name of Kessinger and Allison which wound up with this statement:

"With this last remark, the Texan (Clay Allison) made a motion towards his pistol pocket, as if to draw a weapon, and Kessinger, who thought that the Texan who pretended not to know him actually did know him, and that he was about to commence shooting, hauled off and stuck the Texan, who measured about 6'2" in his stocking feet, knocking him down and afterwards pounded him fearfully until he cried for quarter."

Like many other Earp stories, there was probably a modicum of fact to this story. Allison was probably in Dodge, at about the time Wyatt was referring to in his 1896 Examiner interview, but the fact that the Globe reported his presence and remarked about the adverse effects of the St. Louis scrimmage but failed to mention any incident between him and Wyatt Earp is almost proof positive that no such incident occurred.

Not all the exaggerating and fictitious stories were thought up by one side. There is another story about Clay Allison and his activities in Dodge City. That story was written by an old cowboy by the name of Charlie Siringo in a book entitled Reatta and Spurs. His story was this:

"About the first of October, 1800 steers were cut out of my four herds and started for Dodge City Kansas . . . I secured permission to . . . accompany them to Chicago . . .

"A twenty five mile ride brought us to the toughest town on earth, Dodge City. It was now daylight, and the first man on the street was Cape Willingham, who gave us our first news of the great Indian outbreak. He told us of many murders committed by the Reds south of Dodge City the day previous -- one man was killed at Mead City, and two others near the Crooked Creek Store.

"Riding up the main street Ferris and I saw twenty-five mounted

---

[1]   Ibid, p. 40.

cowboys, holding rifles in their hands, and facing one of the half dozen saloons, adjoining each other, on that side of the street. In passing this armed crowd, one of them recognized me. Calling me by name he said, 'Fall in line quick, H--l is going to pop in a few minutes.'

"We jerked our Winchester rifles from the scabbards and fell in line, like most any other fool cowboys would have done. In a moment Clay Allison, the man-killer, came out of one of the saloons holding a pistol in his hand. With him was Mr. McNulty, owner of the large pan handle 'Turkey-Track' cattle outfit. Clay was hunting for some of the town's policemen, or the city marshal, so as to wipe them off the face of the earth. His twenty-five cowboy friends had promised to help him clean up Dodge City.

"After all the saloons had been searched, Mr. McNulty succeeded in getting Clay to bed at the Bob Wright Hotel. Then we all dispersed. Soon after, the city law officers began to crawl out of their hiding places and appear on the streets."[1]

Charles Siringo's story in Reatta and Spurs is the only place that story is recounted by a purported eye-witness. It has been copied and adopted by many writers but the story always came from the same source. While Siringo was not reputed to be a liar or a teller of tall tales, there is no evidence of the truth in his story.

Compare that story with the one he wrote 45 years earlier entitled A Texas Cowboy, published by M. Umberstoc, Inc., Chicago, Illinois in 1885 where he said:

"We arrived there a short while after sun-up next morning; and the first man we met - an old friend by the name of Willingham - informed us of the Indian outbreak. There had been several men killed on Crooked Creek the evening before - hence John and I finding the ranches deserted.

"On riding through the streets that morning, crowds of women, some of them crying, seeing we were just in from the South, flocked around us inquiring for their absent ones, fathers, brothers, lovers and sons, some of whom had already been killed, no doubt; there having been hundreds of men killed in the past few days."[2]

There is no doubt that he was referring to the same time, and place, but a most interesting fact is that not one word was said about the incident of Allison running the law officers of Dodge City into their holes.

The book Reatta and Spurs was published in 1927, forty five

---

[1]   Reatta and Spurs p. 59.

[2]   A Texas Cowboy, p. 171.

years after the book, <u>A Texas Cowboy</u>. One has to wonder if that episode was added to <u>Reatta and Spurs</u> to spice up the sale of the book.

De Arment in his biography of Bat Masterson, appears not to doubt that the episode occurred, but figured out another reason why the Dodge City police never did respond to the conduct of Clay Allison and why the incident was never reported in the Dodge City newspapers. He says that the date that Siringo came into Dodge City, according to Siringo, is in error and fixes the date by the statement in Siringo's own story that upon arriving in Dodge City, Cape Willingham first gave them the news of a great Indian outbreak.

The Great Indian Outbreak occurred on September 9, 1878 when some 300 Northern Cheyennes under Chief Dull Knife broke out of their reservation in the Indian Nations and headed north towards their traditional hunting grounds in the Big Horn Mountains. There was much excitement in Dodge City and it was described in detail in the Dodge City <u>Times</u> of September 21, 1878 as follows:

"There has been great excitement all week over the news brought in almost hourly of murder and depredations by the straggling bands of Northern Cheyenne Indians.

"Wednesday the excitement was at its highest pitch in Dodge City. The frequent arrival of messengers and couriers and messages from off the plains, bringing accounts of the Cheyenne murders and stealing, threw the people of Dodge City into the wildest tremor, when it was reported that the Indians were seen within a few miles of the city. The ringing of the fire bell at 2 o'clock, calling upon the people to assemble at the engine house, added zest to the already highly inflamed patriot heart . . .

"At this time flames were seen issuing from the house of Harrison Berry, on an island four miles west of this city. It was at once rumored the Indians had fired the house.

"A locomotive loaded with civilians was at once dispatched to the scene of configuration . . . P.L. Beatty, Chuck Beason, Wyatt Earp, and S.E. Isaacson were principals in extinguishing the flames.

"A large party from Dodge carried by an engine and car as far as Cimarron, returning in the evening, but no Indians were seen along the line of the road."[1]

De Arment calculated that this was when Charlie Siringo rode into Dodge City and that he struck town in the third week of September, not in October as he had said in his book. He concluded that with the entire town in an uproar over the Indian scare, Clay Allison could have made any kind of a ruckus he chose without fear

---

[1]   <u>The Times</u>, September 21, 1878.

of drawing attention from the local police officers as they would have been, and according to the Times were busy elsewhere.

It is highly likely that at that particular time, Bat Masterson was out of town, since a number of telegrams requesting help from the governor were sent from Dodge City, but none were from Bat Masterson. Wyatt Earp, and probably the rest of the law enforcement officers, were out chasing Indians and extinguishing fires. So it is quite possible that Clay Allison could have put on quite a show in a town without having any officers even know that it had occurred and without the newspapers paying any attention to it, because of the excitement around the town.

I feel certain that the whole story was cooked up by Charlie Siringo when he wrote his second book some 45 years after the event was supposed to have happened. There doesn't appear to be any reports by other eye-witnesses who wrote about the event. Some writers have added considerably to the story, but I believe that his book, Reatta and Spurs, 1927, is the basis of the story in every instance, and that the event was pure fiction.

CHAPTER XIV

THE KILLING OF YOUNG HOY OR HOYT

ON June 1, 1878, Jim Masterson, the young brother of Ed and Bat Masterson was hired as a deputy marshal in Dodge City. So that within two months after the death of Ed Masterson, another Masterson was wearing the badge.

"The Dodge City Police Department in the summer of 1878 consisted of Marshal Charles E. Basset, Assistant Marshal Wyatt Earp, Policeman John Brown, and Policeman, Jim Masterson. The marshal's salary was $100 while all the others earned $75 a month."[1]

During the early part of the shipping season, the Dodge City newspapers did not report very much activity by way of lawlessness in the city. However, that situation changed on July 26, when Dodge had its second fatal shooting within two weeks. Lake would have us believe that the shooting was the result of someone having placed a bounty on the head of Wyatt Earp because of his strict enforcement of the law. That proposition doesn't seem to be born out by the facts, and has never been recorded or reported by anyone other than Lake. However in order to get a good view of how Lake treated a story by comparison to how the newspapers reported it, it is necessary to quote both in full here.

Lake reported the story as follows:

"The first attempt in the season of '78 to collect the bounty on Wyatt's head was made July 26. Eddie Foy and his partner, Jim Thompson, were playing at the Comique Theater, and as Wyatt's duties precluded his presence inside the theater, he stood in the street just outside the thin board stagewall where he could hear the songs and jokes, while keeping an eye and an ear out for trouble.

"Foy had just started his celebrated 'Kalamazoo in Michigan' when Wyatt noticed a horseman pass in the road, turn, and jog by again. A block away he turned once more and came down the road at a gallop. As the pony sped by the point where Wyatt stood, the roar of a forty-five and a flash of flame sent a heavy slug through the plank at the marshal's side, across the stage, and into the opposite wall. A second, then a third bullet followed.

"Inside the theater, Eddie Foy has written, the act terminated suddenly in the scream of lead. The comedian threw himself flat on

---

[1]   Great Gunfighters of the Kansas Cowtowns, p. 186.

the stage and half of his audience dropped from their seats to the floor.

"Outside, Wyatt went into action toward the horseman, jerking his Colts as he jumped.

"The rider had a mount of more spirit than steadiness. At the roar of gunfire the cayuse shied, plunged, and reared. Wyatt grabbed for the pony's tail with his left hand, to throw himself into the animal's hindquarters and hold himself so closely against the pony's legs that he could not be hurt by flying hoofs while his weight would be more effective than hobbles against a speedy getaway. As he lunged, so did the pony, and Wyatt missed the hold. The rider shot at Wyatt again, and missed. The bucking spoiled his aim.

"Wyatt shot in reply, but also missed, as the pony jumped sideways, and was off toward the tollbridge on a dead run. The horseman turned in his saddle and fired once more, flipping the brim of the marshal's sombrero with the slug. Wyatt squatted on his haunches to bring his target into greater relief against the dark sky and shot a second time. The pony's hoofs clattered on the bridge at a decreasing pace, then halted. The rider had fallen from the saddle, and at the south end of the bridge Wyatt found him, unconscious, with a bullet through the small of his back. At the calaboose Dr. McCarty pronounced him mortally wounded.

"Next morning the wounded man was identified as George Hoyt, a Texas cowboy, but, as he recovered consciousness only to go into a delirium, Wyatt was unable to question him. Hoyt was still delirious when Wyatt took leave of absence from his marshal's job."[1]

Now contrast that story with the one printed on July 26, 1878 in The Times:

"BULLETS IN THE AIR.

"MUSIC FROM THE FESTIVE REVOLVER.

"TWENTY SHOTS FIRED AND ONLY ONE MAN WOUNDED.

"Yesterday morning about 3 o'clock this peaceful suburban city was thrown into unusual excitement, and the turmoil was all caused by a cantankerous cowboy who started the mischief ship by too free use of his little revolver.

"In Dodge City, after dark, the report of a revolver generally means business and is an indication that somebody is on the war path, therefore when the noise of this shooting and the yells of excited voices rang out on the midnight breeze, the sleeping community awoke from their slumbers, listened a while to the click of the revolver, wondered who was shot this time, and then went to sleep

---

[1]   Wyatt Earp, Frontier Marshal, pp. 205-207.

again. But in the morning many dreaded to hear the result of the war lest it should be a story of bloodshed and carnage, or of death to some familiar friend. But in this instance there was an abundance of noise and smoke, with no very terrible results.

"It seems that three or four herders were paying their respects to the city and its institutions, and as is usually their custom, remained until about 3 o'clock in the morning, when they prepared to return to their camps. They buckled on their revolvers, which they were not allowed to wear around town, and mounted their horses, when all at once one of them conceived the idea that to finish the night's revelry and give the natives due warning of his departure, he must do some shooting, and forthwith he commenced to bang away, one of the bullets whizzing into a dance hall nearby, causing no little commotion among the participants in the "dreamy waltz" and quadrille. Policemen Earp and [James] Masterson made a raid on the shootist who gave them two or three volleys, but fortunately without effect. The policemen returned the fire and followed the herders with the intention of arresting them. The firing then became general, and some rooster who did not exactly understand the situation, perched himself in the window of the dance hall and indulged in a promiscuous shoot all by himself. The herders rode across the bridge, followed by the officers. A few yards from the bridge one of the herders fell from his horse from weakness caused by a wound in the arm which he had received during the fracas. The other herder made good his escape. The wounded man was properly cared for and his wound, which proved to be a bad one, was dressed by Dr. [T.L.] McCarty. His name is George Hoy, and he is rather an intelligent looking young man."[1]

Lake says that Wyatt Earp then left town to appear as a delegate at the Republican State Convention held in Topeka, Kansas on the second week in August. When he returned from the convention, he learned that Hoy was dying and had given full information concerning the plot against the marshal other than identities of the men who had hired him for the killing. Lake says: "The Globe verified and later published Hoy's story."[2]

Lake's statement that The Globe had verified and published Hoy's story referring to the fact that he had been hired to kill Wyatt Earp is not true. Hoy died on August the 21st, 1878 and on August 27, the Ford County Globe published this story:

"DIED. -- On Wednesday last, George Hoy, the young Texan

---

1   The Dodge City Times, July 26, 1878; Great Gunfighters of the Kansas Cowtowns, p. 87.

2   Wyatt Earp, Frontier Marshal, p. 207.

who was wounded some weeks since in the midnight scrimmage, died from the effects of his wound. George was apparently rather a good young man, having those chivalrous qualities, so common to frontiersmen, well developed. He was, at the time of his death, under a bond of $1,500 for his appearance in Texas on account of some cattle scrape, wherein he was charged with aiding and assisting some other men in 'rounding up' about 1,000 head of cattle which were claimed by other parties. He had many friends and no enemies among Texas men who knew him. George was nothing but a poor cow-boy, but his brother cow-boys permitted him to want for nothing during his illness, and buried him in grand style when dead, which was very creditable to them. We have been informed by those who pretend to know, that the deceased, although under bond for a misdemeanor in Texas, was in no wise a criminal, and would have been released at the next setting of the court if he had not been removed by death from its jurisdiction. Let his faults, if he had any, be hidden in the grave."[1]

You can search the Globe's publication of the story about Hoy in vain to find any indication that Hoy ever confessed that he had been hired to kill Wyatt Earp. Lake's coverage of this incident is decidedly flawed in that it doesn't tell the whole story about the shooting and misstates the story that was printed in the paper for a good measure.

Although Lake gives Wyatt Earp credit for killing young Hoy, and in later life, Wyatt would claim him as one of his victims, a close examination of The Times story reveals that both Wyatt Earp and Jim Masterson as well as some volunteer perched in the window of the dance hall were firing their weapons at him. Without modern ballistics tests it would have been impossible to determine who fired the fatal shot.

Again, Wyatt Earp told a different story to a reporter for the San Francisco Examiner that was published on August 16, 1896. He told the reporter that shortly after the Bob Rachal affair when he had thrown Bob Wright into jail with Rachal, the Texans began to hatch a plot to kill him by foul means or fair. He then went on to say:

"The first attempt fell to the lot of a desperado named Hoyt, who was no 'prentice in the art of assassination. I was standing on the sidewalk outside a saloon one bright moon lit night, talking to Eddie Foy, who was leaning against the door, when Hoyt came riding down the street on a white horse. I noticed that he had his right hand by his side but did not suspect anything until he came within 10 paces of where I was standing. Then he threw the gun over like lightening and took a shot at me. But by the time he was on a level with me, he

---

[1]   Great Gunfighters of the Kansas Cowtowns, p. 88.

had taken another shot but both missed.

"I ran out, intending to pull him off his horse, and failing that I tried to grab his horse's tail as it passed me, and as Hoyt dug in his spurs he wheeled in his saddle and fired at me again. With that I crouched down in the middle of the road for a steady aim and emptied my gun after him as he tore down the rode. I saw him disappear over the bridge that spanned the Arkansas River, and was sure I had missed him. But five minutes later, when I was telling the story to Bat Masterson and a crowd of citizens, the white horse came galloping back, mounted by a boy, who told us that its rider was lying badly shot just beyond the bridge. Half suspecting an ambush, Bat and I took shotguns and went back with the boy. There, sure enough, was Hoyt full of lead and remorse, and moaning most dutifully. Two or three days later he died."[1]

It should be noted that in this version, Earp made no reference whatever to Policeman or Marshal James Masterson and the fact that both he, Earp, and Masterson, as well as some other citizen were all firing at Hoy as he dashed out of town.

Albert Turner writes that:

"Wyatt Earp's version of the killing of George Hoy (Hoyt) was repeated by Bat Masterson on a number of occasions and has found its way into the literature of The Kansas Cowtowns. Contemporary newspapers however provide more precise details to the incident."[2]

In view of the fact that at least three people were firing at young Hoy, it is impossible to say who actually killed him.

---

[1]   San Francisco Examiner, August 16, 1896.

[2]   The Earp's Talk, p. 151.

CHAPTER XV

THE DUTCH HENRY-TOM OWENS STORY

ANOTHER fictional episode that would have, and probably did make a good television program is the Dutch Henry - Tom Owens story. This is the way Lake tells it:

"About a week after Hoyt's death, two shots were fired at Wyatt as he walked along First Avenue. The gunman sat his pony in the shadows of a cross-street and as he fired wheeled, turned, and galloped for the tollbridge. Neither shot hit the marshal and Wyatt commandeered the first cow-pony to hand in a string near by.

"Beyond the south bridgehead, Wyatt could see the rider streaking down the trail which branched toward the camp of the Dutch Henry-Tom Owens gang of rustlers. Chancing a short cut, he reached the outlaws' fire in time to see Tom Owens rip the saddle from a pony and drop down with four or five of his fellows. Dismounting, Wyatt walked straight to Owens.

"'Get up!' he commanded.

"Dutch Henry edged away from the light. He stopped as Wyatt's gun flashed from his holster.

"'On your feet, all of you, hands in the air!' Wyatt ordered. The rustlers obeyed and Wyatt disarmed them.

"'Head for town, Owens,' the marshal continued. 'You're walking, I'm riding behind you.'

"Wyatt slung the collection of confiscated belts and weapons over his saddle-horn.

"'Get going, Owens,' he said 'The rest of you'll find your guns wherever you find Owens in the morning. In the mean time, keep out of Dodge.'

"On the way into town, Wyatt wrung from Owens the admission that the horse-thief had hoped to collect the thousand-dollar bounty on the marshal's head, although Owens swore he had no definite knowledge of who was to pay the money for the killing. Wyatt locked the outlaw in the calaboose for the night, saw him fined one hundred dollars in court the next morning, and started him for his camp on foot, carrying the weapons which had been confiscated from his associates.

"'Don't come into Dodge again, any of you, as long as I'm in town,' Wyatt warned the rustlers.

"Owens was another individual who owed his life to a magnanimity which Bat Masterson criticized sharply, but there may be some justification for Wyatt's attitude in the fact that thereafter, while the Owens-Henry gang operated extensively in Kansas, none of the leaders ever ventured into Wyatt Earp's bailiwick."[1]

Bartholomew notes, in Wyatt Earp, The Untold Story, that there is a very good reason why Tom Owens never returned to Dodge to face the wrath of "Marshal Earp," the reason being that he had been dead for four years.

He quoted a statement by Emanual Dubbs, an early Dodge pioneer, known all over the buffalo ranges, and later a Texas judge, as telling a story of a posse gathered from Dodge City, facing a bunch of horse thieves including Dutch Henry and Thomas Owens:

"We caught up with them in the hills west of Hayes City and after a desperate battle, Dutch Henry was wounded six times, Owens was killed and others of the gang killed and wounded. Twenty men from Hayes had helped the Dodge Posse. Dutch Henry escaped and recovered and for years was well known in Kansas, Nebraska, Texas, Indian Territory, New Mexico and other western slopes and on the western slope of the rockies."[2]

Typical of Bartholomew, he sights no authority and gives no information as to where he got the statement or how it could be checked out to determine its validity.

Miller and Snell in their Great Gunfighters of the Kansas Cowtowns, reproduced most of the newspaper stories of the day relating to the activities of law enforcement in and around Dodge City, and they fail to index any reference to Owens. However, a great deal was written about Dutch Henry. The Dodge City Times, of January 4, 1879 reported that Dutch Henry was under arrest at Trinidad, Colorado but that the Colorado sheriff would not deliver him to Bat Masterson unless he was paid $500.00. Three days later, on January 7, the Ford County Globe, wrote a long story about Dutch Henry and his court proceedings in Trinidad and announced that Bat Masterson had brought him to Dodge for trial. On January 14, 1879 The Globe reported on a preliminary examination of Dutch Henry for horse stealing. They reported that Dutch Henry had waived preliminary examination and had been bound over for his appearance at the next term of the district court in the sum of $600.00 bail and default of which he was committed to jail.

On January 25th, (1879) The Times reported:

"Dutch Henry's trial occupied two days of the time of the court, and Thursday night the jury brought in a verdict of not guilty. The

---

[1]   Wyatt Earp, Frontier Marshal, pp. 208-209.

[2]   Wyatt Earp, the Untold Story, p. 248.

prisoner was charged with horse stealing. Insufficient evidence and barred by the statute of limitations, though the later point was negatively decided by a jury, probably lead to the prisoner's acquittal. Coburn, and Jones conducted the prosecution and H.E. Gryden and Heard for the defense."[1]

Thus is appears that whether Dutch Henry liked it or not, he did eventually come back into Wyatt Earp's bailiwick. The same cannot be said of Tom Owens, since no record of him can be found except the statement by Bartholomew that he was already dead.

The whole story of Wyatt Earp going into the outlaw camp of Dutch Henry and Tom Owens and taking Owens to jail, sounds almost unbelievable and not one shred of evidence has ever been produced to show that it actually happened. It would seem that had it occurred, there would have been some record either in the courts or the newspapers, or perhaps something written by some contemporary that would give some credence to the story. None has been found. It was apparently another one of the factitious episodes created for Wyatt Earp twenty-five years before it was needed for television.

---

[1]   Great Gunfighters of the Kansas Cowtowns, p. 246.

CHAPTER XVI

ANOTHER TOBE DRISKILL
AFFAIR

ANOTHER episode that Lake unintentionally created for television was concocted out of the Indian outbreak already alluded to in the Clay Allison story above. Lake told the story this way:

"On September 16, (1878) word was brought to Dodge that a large band of Northern Cheyenne Indians under Chief Dull Knife had broken out of Indian Territory, and were making for their old home in the Dakotas, pillaging ranches, homesteads, and white settlements. Troops were sent in pursuit, but when the red warriors crossed the Cimarron at the Kansas Line, raided Mead City, a trading-post on Crooked Creek, and pillaged the Chapman and Tuttle Ranch on the Mulberry eighteen miles from the cowtown, Wyatt Earp went out at the head of a force of civilian volunteers to reenforce the cavalry. His part in the chase ended when he returned to town about September 24, with a few Indian prisoners placed in his custody by the military authorities.

"Wyatt barely had locked his prisoners in the Ford County jail when some twenty-five Texas cowmen, under the leadership of his ancient enemies, Tobe Driskill and Ed Morrison whom he had run out of Wichita, rode into Dodge under the impression that Wyatt was still absent, and with the single purpose of hurrahing the camp as they long had felt she must be hurrahed for the satisfaction of Texas.

"There is small doubt that the instigator of the cowboy expedition was Tobe Driskill, nursing his memory of a manhandling by Wyatt Earp, and Ed Morrison, who's grudge against Dodge was in reality one against that same marshal, but dating back to the Shanghai Pearce affair in Wichita. Furthermore, in view of subsequent records made as peace officers, it is of interest to note that two of the Driskill-Morrison trouble-makers on this occasion were none other than Pat Garrett and Smoky Hill Thompson.

"The Driskill-Morrison outfit left their chuck-wagon at Cimarron Crossing, west of Dodge, late in the afternoon. The wagon was to continue southward while the riders were taking Dodge by surprise, shooting up the South Side honky tonks, shaking up sacrosanct Front Street, high-tailing the citizenry, and otherwise disporting themselves in such forty-five-caliber pleasantries as opportunity and a few quick drinks might combine to inspire.

"Driskill and Morrison led their gun-toters into Dodge by way of Front Street to Second Avenue, crossed the railroad, and dismounted in front of a saloon, where they fed and tethered their ponies and from which point they figured to make their getaway once such fighting men as might be left in Dodge gave sign of getting organized. The cowboys ate an early meal at the South Side restaurant, and then, with the streets of Dodge deserted for the supper hour, went into uproarious action.

"To the best recollection of Dodge citizens who saw something of the Driskill-Morrison raid, the cowboys devoted less than five minutes to South Side joints, and headed across the Dead Line, whooping, shooting, and inviting Dodge out to oppose them. Their first stop on the North Side was a saloon at the corner of Front Street and Fourth Avenue, where they ran the bartender and a few hangers-on to cover, helped themselves to liquor, wrecked the interior, and piled out again. Thence they hurrahed Front Street systematically, every light and every pane of glass they saw a target for fifty six-shooters.

"As the Texans proceeded eastward toward the camp's main four-corners, their evident intentions so disorganized Dodge's customary aplomb that, as the cowboys moved, the lights in various establishments ahead of them were doused by frantic merchants and saloon-keepers as they and their patrons took to Tin Can Alley. Front Street was soon in darkness, except for the incessant flares from the roaring six-guns and the glow through the windows of the single place of business which had not completely abandoned camp to the mercy of the gunmen -- the Long Branch Saloon, in which Cockeyed Frank Loving sat dealing faro for a lean, pale-faced, ash-blond gambler who could not be chased from a run of luck by all the gun-throwers in Texas.

"When the cowboys fired their first fusillade, Wyatt Earp was at the northeast edge of town feeding his Indian prisoners. By the time he had his charges locked up for the night, the cowboys had been across the Dead Line for some minutes.

"As Wyatt turned into Front Street, the Texas gang was at Second Avenue, showering lead along that cross-thoroughfare. As the marshal reached First Avenue, the cowboys were in front of Wright and Beverly's. Wyatt noted the light in the Long Branch, and hurried to reach that doorway and one of his shotguns, ahead of the Texans. He was late by the fraction of a second. Driskill and Morrison were at the door discussing in loud voices what they'd do to the Long Branch when Wyatt stepped from the shadow. For a moment, possibly, the cowboys were startled, but liquid courage made them quick to act on their advantage.

"Wyatt's Colts were in their holsters. Each cowboy had a pair of guns in his hands. Furthermore, every Texan was sufficiently flushed with alcohol and success to be at his deadliest.

"'By God,' Driskill roared, 'it's Earp!'

"'You son-of-a-bitch,' Morrison added, 'I've waited five years for this!'

"'I owe him some myself,' Driskill observed, with a string of epithets.

"'We've got him,' Morrison said, 'and, by God, he's going to get it! You're such a fighter, Earp; here's your chance to do some.'

"Morrison called to the crowd behind him.

"'If he makes a move, boys, let him have it.'

"He addressed himself once more to Wyatt.

"'You white-livered Northern this-and-that,' he raged, 'if you've got any praying to do, get at it.'

"That night in Dodge was one of two occasions in Wyatt's career when he figured he was about to go out with his boots on.

"'Those Texans were in an ugly mood,' he recalled. 'They had held the upper hand long enough to make them believe they could maintain it; they had taken on enough liquor to be vicious, but not enough to be unsteady; they were led by men who hated me; they had me at complete disadvantage as far as gunplay went, and a getaway so well arranged as to be almost a certainty. Those last two items always influenced the cowboy attitude.

"While Driskill and Morrison were threatening me, I was trying to get where I could make one jump through the Long Branch door, and the only praying I did was that the door hadn't been locked. There was a chance I could make such a jump, or that I might get so close to Driskill or Morrison that with all the talking they were doing, I could catch one of them off guard long enough to shove a gun into his belly, while he shielded me from the rest. I hadn't much hope that either move would succeed, but I didn't dare jerk a gun until I was ready for one or the other. I had edged almost to the doorway, with my eye on Morrison while he cursed me. Then I saw a look in his eye that made me abandon all ideas but that of taking a few Texans with me to where I knew I was going.

"It all took place in so much less time than is required to tell about it that the speed of the action is hard to make clear. Not more than two minutes elapsed from the time the cowboys first saw me until Morrison told me a second time to hurry with my prayers. Like all Texans of his stripe, he had to do a certain amount of bragging before he got down to shooting. I recall his final threat as vividly as though he made it yesterday.

"'Pray, you son-of-a-bitch,' he said, 'or jerk your gun and ---'

"'Throw 'em up!' challenged a voice at Wyatt's shoulder as the door of the Long Branch burst open and a long, lean, ash-blond individual with a six-gun in either hand leaped into silhouette against the light.

"'Throw 'em up, you blank-dashed so-and-so murdering cow

thieves!'

"'There were times,' Wyatt commented, 'when Doc Holliday swore beautifully, and what I next heard over my shoulder -- I didn't dare look around -- made Morrison's ranting sound like a Sunday-School lesson.'

"The interruption was all I needed. Before Driskill, Morrison, or any of their crowd caught up with their surprise, I had jerked both my guns, and there we stood, Doc and I, with four guns against fifty, but with the break closer to even.

"To understand what had happened, it is necessary to revert to the time at which the cowboys made their move on Front Street and business places were deserted in the path of their roaring progress. Messrs. Beeson, Harris, and Short were absent from the Long Branch at supper; a bartender was in charge, with Cockeyed Frank Loving dealing faro for the benefit of Doc Holliday. When everyone else in the place decamped ahead of the oncoming cowboys, the bartender reported, Loving and Holliday continued their game without comment that he heard before he fled to the alley.

"Frank Loving was a cool, courageous fellow who would have gone quickly to Wyatt's assistance. He said later that, before he could move, Doc Holliday had run to the six-shooter rack at the end of the bar, grabbed his own nickel plated weapon which hung there and another beside it, and jumped through the door.

"Under the guns of Doc Holliday and Wyatt Earp, the temper of the Texas crowd altered instantaneously. Doc was quick to turn their hesitancy to advantage.

"'What'll we do with 'em, Wyatt?' he asked as though the question of ascendancy had been fully determined.

"In reply, Wyatt Earp took a single step toward Ed Morrison and, before that individual or any of his followers sensed what was happening, laid the barrel of his Buntline Special over the cowboy's head. Morrison dropped as though he had been shot instead of buffaloed.

"'Throw 'em up!' Wyatt commanded. 'All the way and empty! You, Driskill! You're next!'

"Six-shooters clattered to the walk as the cowboys' hands went skyward, but in the rear of the crowd, one Texan took a chance.

"'Look out, Wyatt!'

"Quicker than speech, however, Doc cut loose at the cowboy who tried a pot-shot at the marshal. Two reports roared almost as one, but a howl of pain established the accuracy of Holliday's gunfire -- the cowboy was a split-second late and missed.

"'Years afterward it was told that Doc Holliday killed that Texan,' Wyatt said. 'He didn't. He hit him in the shoulder. The result disappointed Doc, but it was all I needed.'

"'With the gang grabbing air, Doc and I herded them across the tracks and into the calaboose. Then we went back and picked up about fifty guns in front of the Long Branch. Next morning Driskill and Morrison were fined one hundred dollars apiece, and each of the others, twenty-five dollars. I put their guns in a couple of gunnysacks and told them not to distribute them until they were well out of town. What's more, they minded me, and the last I saw of that crowd they were riding off to catch their chuck-wagon. I never heard that they painted "Dodge" on the cover, either.

"'One thing I've always believed: if it hadn't been for Doc Holliday, I'd have cashed in that night. There was no real call for Doc to make the play he did; everybody else in camp had high-tailed it, including some of my deputies, and why Doc wasn't knocked off is more than I can tell you. He wasn't, and if anyone ever questions the motive of my loyalty to Doc Holliday, there's my answer. In the old days, neither Doc nor I bothered to make explanations; I never was given to such things and in our case they would have been contrary to Doc's sense of decency. The only way anyone appreciated the feeling I always had for Doc after the Driskill-Morrison business would have been to stood in my boots at the time Doc came through the Long Branch doorway.'"[1]

Of Doc Holliday's relationship with Wyatt Earp while at Dodge City, Dale Schoenberg says that although any record of Doc Holliday's actions at Dodge City are extremely sketchy, there appears to be no record that he was involved in any trouble while there. He notes that at the preliminary hearing in Tombstone Wyatt Earp repeated under oath substantially the same story he told of being rescued by Doc Holliday and suggests that it could possibly be true, saying that Wyatt Earp had no reason to lie about it.[2] Of course that's true, but he had no apparent reason to lie about many of the other things he told either.

For whatever reason, there was a strong bond of friendship and loyalty between Doc Holliday and Wyatt Earp. An analysis of the Tombstone troubles of Wyatt Earp would lead to a conclusion that a lot of, if not most of Wyatt Earp's problems in Tombstone arose from his friendship with, and defense, of Doc Holliday. About the relationship, Bat Masterson said,

"His whole heart and soul were wrapped up in Wyatt Earp and he was always ready to stake his life in defense of any cause in which Wyatt was interested . . . Damond did not more for Pitheous than

[1]   Wyatt Earp, Frontier Marshal, pp. 209-215.

[2]   The Gunfighters, p. 99.

Holliday did for Wyatt Earp."[1]

So that while it is a virtual certainty that the occasion described above did not occur in the way that Lake described it, something certainly must have happened that created a bond between Doc Holliday and Wyatt Earp that lasted for the rest of their lives.

Not only is there no evidence whatever that Tobe Driskill and his cowboys tried to take over Dodge City on September 24th as recounted by Wyatt Earp, but there is a substantial body of evidence that it never did happen.

It is true that on September 16, 1878, the Northern Cheyenne Indians under Chief Dull Knife had broken out of the Indian Territory and were heading north, passing near Dodge City and created havoc in the surrounding country. That Indian outbreak was referred to previously in Chapter 13, The Clay Allison Affair. The activities of everyone connected with that Indian raid were fairly well reported in the Dodge City press. The only time that Wyatt Earp's name appeared in any of the press reports about the Indian outbreak was in the Dodge City Times of Saturday, September 21, 1878 where the newspaper reported that P.L. Beatty, Chalk Beeson, Wyatt Earp and S. E. Isaacson were principals in extinguishing a fire set by the Indians.[2]

While Wyatt Earp was never mentioned again in relation to the Indian uprising, Driskill and almost anyone else that had anything to do with it were mentioned in the newspapers. For instance, the Ford County Globe of Tuesday, September 24, 1878, ran a long story where they detailed the daily activities of those engaged in suppressing the Indian uprising from Monday the 16th through Monday September 23rd. The following is an excerpt of some of the activities reported in the Globe.

"On Monday (September 16) morning a squad ran into Driskill's camp and captured 55 horses. Dave Driskill, however, had the pleasure of running one of the red devils down and killing him; his scalp now hangs in the Driskill camp.

"By Friday morning (September 20) every farmer within 30 miles of Dodge, south and southwest had come into town for safety.

"On Tuesday (September 17) the Driskill boys with Doc and Tony Day and about 20 other cattlemen and cowboys, fell in with Captain Henfield's Company of Calvary, and the combined followed the trail to the head brakes of Sand Creek, one of the feeders of Crooked Creek, and there found 200 Indians encamped. A sharp

---

[1]   Bat Masterson, p. 227.

[2]   The Dodge City Times, Saturday September 21, 1878.

engagement was had which lasted about an hour. One 'Injun' was killed and one Soldier and two Calvary horses were wounded. The Captain deeming it unadvisable to fight any longer against such odds, retreated, the cattlemen arriving in Dodge on Wednesday night, (September 18) and soldiers on Thursday morning.

"On Thursday night (September 19) the same company of Calvary accompanied by 25 cowboys and scouts with provisions and supplies for several days march went west by freight train to Pierceville, 40 miles west of Dodge, where they were joined by a company of Calvary from Ft. Lion, Colorado. The whole Company now numbering about 150 men marched south to find the Indians who, from the accounts brought in by Ervin's outfit, the night previous, were still camped on Sand Creek.

"From cattlemen who arrived at 10 o'clock last night we ascertain that an attack was made on the Indians on Sunday (September 22) the civilians being in the lead with one company of dismounted Calvary supporting them. The cattlemen under Driskill, drove the Indians from the ridge they occupied and were calamerous of a general charge. Captain Raundebrook sent one company to assist them, but retained two companies to guard his camp. A scrimmage of half an hour was kept up with the Indians, who hid and dodged behind the rocks, after which the troops withdrew. The soldiers were anxious for a general fight, while the officers seemed haunted by the ghost of Custard and were evidently afraid to take least risk.

"On Monday (September 23) the Indians, with about 400 captured horses, moved north, while the troops remained all day in the camp.

"The following persons went out in the Driskill party: J.M. Day, W. H. Day, L. Ward, Major Hinkle, A.C. Allen, Dave Crestwell, E. Evans, Jesse, Dal, Tobe and Bud Driskill, Hyrum Caller, Wash Lumpkins, J.A. Von, William Wells, William J. Spaulding, Dud Pannel, Chase Elliot, Felps White and Mr. Bates who left Dodge City Friday at 11 o'clock a.m. went to Cimarron River and joined the Soldiers and the following party of cattlemen following Salt Fork."

And here they named another half dozen or so citizens from Dodge who made up a total number of 52 men. The paper described how the cattlemen had the Indians surrounded on Sunday and said that if they had been properly supported by the army they could have overwhelmed the Indians. But that because they had no support from the army, during the night the Indians left their stronghold and made for the head waters of Crooked Creek. The paper went on to say:

"The stockmen followed up the trail 3 or 4 miles so as to satisfy themselves as to the direction they had taken when they returned to camp and reported to the officers in charge, who, instead of pursuing, pulled up and move camp about 2 miles to a place where they had camped Saturday night. When the cattlemen saw the action of the officers in command they came home utterly disgusted."

From the newspaper account, they, including Tobe and Bud Driskill and their cowboys came back to Dodge City on the 23rd.

In all of the details of the Indian scrimmages, there was never a mention of any Indians being taken prisoner. Lake says that Earp's part in the chase ended when he returned to town about September 24 with a few Indian prisoners, placed in his custody by the military authority.

Doesn't it seem odd that while the paper seems to name almost everyone who was active in the Indian affair, Wyatt Earp's name never shows up and also doesn't it seem peculiar that the military would have placed their prisoners in the custody of Wyatt Earp, who at most, at that time was an Assistant City Marshal, not a Sheriff, not a United States Marshal, not a member of the military.

Further, the Driskill outfit was in the cattle business. They had a large herd of cattle and a camp and must have had a lot of problems with their cattle since the Indians had captured 55 of their horses. According to the paper they returned to Dodge on September 23rd which would have been Monday, and the odds are strong that having been away from their camp for about a week, they would be worrying about the condition of their herd and would immediately take leave of Dodge and head for their camp to straighten out their problems. It is highly unlikely that they would have stayed in Dodge for another day, that is until the 24th, when Wyatt Earp claimed they had tried to tree Dodge City and that he put them all in jail. Further, it appears from the newspaper that almost every move that was made by the Driskill's during this affair was reported in the newspaper and it would be unthinkable that they would be rounded up by Wyatt Earp and placed in the Dodge City jail to remain there during the night of the 24th and to be released by the Court on the Morning of the 25th without a word of it being printed in the local paper. That fact alone is sufficient to convince this author that the event never happened.

CHAPTER XVII

THE DORA HAND KILLING

AROUND the first of October, 1878, Mayor "Dog" Kelley, a joint proprietor of the Alhambra Saloon and gambling house, found it necessary to eject a young cowboy by the name of Jim Kennedy from his establishment and in doing so may have used more force than was necessary. At any rate, Jim Kennedy, the son of Captain Mifflin Kennedy a partner in one of the major Texas cattle ranches, swore vengeance against Mayor Kelley. In finding his revenge Kennedy decided to kill Kelley while he was asleep in his bed. Unknown to Kennedy, Kelley had rented his shack to a couple of women entertainers, one by the name of Dora Hand, also known as Fanny Keenan and the other Fanny Garrettson, frequenters of Dodge City dance halls.

About 3 o'clock on the morning of October 4, 1878, Jim Kennedy rode by what he thought was Mayor "Dog" Kelley's residence and fired two shots into the house aiming at what he thought would be the place where Kelley would be sleeping. Unknown to him, he shot and killed Dora Hand. Without determining the success of his attack, he immediately headed south for his Texas home, hoping to get a good start ahead of any pursuit by law officers.

Lake, as usual, trying to make the big hero of his character, Wyatt Earp, wrote the following:

"Because Wyatt Earp, who held the commission of Deputy United States Marshal jointly with his municipal office could be relied upon to take Jim Kennedy from under the guns of all his father's henchmen, the Mayor ordered Wyatt to lead a posse after the fugitive. Wyatt elected Bat Masterson, Charlie Basset, and Bill Tilghman, and the quartet took the trail a few hours behind their quarry."[1]

The killing of Dora Hand and capture of James Kennedy was fully reported in the local newspapers and their stories are reproduced here. Before setting out the newspaper reports it might be well to examine the truth of Lake's statement.

There is nothing in any record to show that Wyatt Earp was ever a Deputy United States Marshal while he was in Kansas. Wyatt Earp was an Assistant City Marshal and had no jurisdiction outside of Dodge City, but Bat Masterson was a County Sheriff at the time and

---

[1]   <u>Wyatt Earp, Frontier Marshal</u>, p. 218.

had wide jurisdiction. Legally and factually, the job was one for Bat Masterson, not for Wyatt Earp.

The Times first broke the story on October 5, 1878 when it reported the killing of Dora Hand as follows:

"ANOTHER VICTIM.

"THE PISTOL DOES ITS WORK.

"THE KILLING OF DORA HAND.

"ALIAS FANNIE KEENAN.

"At about half past four o'clock this (Friday) morning [October 4], two pistol shots were fired into the building occupied by Dora Hand, alias Fannie Keenan. The person who did the firing stood on horseback at the front door of the little frame [house] south of the railroad track. The house has two rooms, the back room being occupied by Fannie Keenan. A plastered partition wall divides the two rooms. The first shot went through the front door and struck the facing of the partition. The remarkable penetration of a pistol ball was in the second shot. It passed through the door, several thicknesses of bed clothing on the bed in the front room occupied by a female lodger; through the plastered partition wall, and the bed clothing on the second bed, and striking Fannie Keenan on the right side under the arm, killing her instantly. The pistol was of 44 calibre, nearly a half-inch ball.

"The deceased came to Dodge City this summer and was engaged as vocalist in the Varieties and Comique shows. She was a prepossessing woman and her artful winning ways brought many admirers within her smiles and blandishments. If we mistake not, Dora Hand has an eventful history. She had applied for a divorce from Theodore Hand. After a varied life the unexpected death messenger cut her down in the full bloom of gaiety and womanhood. She was the innocent victim.

"The pistol shot was intended for the male occupant of the bed in the front room, but who has been absent for several days. The bed, however, was occupied by a female lodger at the time of the shooting, and narrowly escaped the ball that went through the bed covering. The cause for the shooting is supposed to be for an old grudge. The officers are in pursuit of the supposed murderer, to whom circumstances point very directly."[1]

Three days later, the Ford County Globe printed its version of Dora Hand's death as follows:

"MIDNIGHT ASSASSIN.

"DORA HAND, ALIAS FANNIE KEENAN, FOULLY

---

[1] Great Gunfighters of the Kansas Cowtowns, p. 230; The Dodge City Times, October 5, 1878.

MURDERED WHILE IN BED AND FAST ASLEEP. JAMES KENNEDY, THE SUPPOSED MURDERER, ARRESTED AFTER RECEIVING A DANGEROUS WOUND AT THE HANDS OF THE OFFICERS.

"On Friday morning, about 4 o'clock, two shots were fired in a small frame building, situated south of the railroad track and back of the Western House, occupied by Miss Fannie Garrettson and Miss Fannie Keenan. The building was divided into two rooms by a plastered partition, Miss Keenan occupying the back room. The first shot, after passing through the front door, struck the floor, passed through the carpet and facing of the partition and lodged in the next room. The second shot also passed through the door, but apparently more elevated, striking the first bed, passing over Miss Garrettson, who occupied the bed, through two quilts, through the plastered partition, and after passing through the bed clothing of the second bed, struck Fannie Keenan in the right side, under the arm, killing her instantly.

"The party who committed this cowardly act must have been on horseback and close to the door when the two shots were fired. From what we can learn the shots were intended for another party who has been absent for a week and who formerly occupied the first room. Thus the assassin missed his intended victim and killed another while fast asleep, who never spoke a word after she was shot.

"James Kennedy, who it is supposed did the shooting made good his escape, and the following morning the officers went in pursuit of him, returning Saturday night with their prisoner, whom they met and on refusal to surrender shot him through the shoulder and with another shot killing the horse he was riding, thus capturing him. What evidence the authorities have that Kennedy is the man who did this shooting we are unable to learn. Below we give the verdict of the coroner's inquest:

"STATE OF KANSAS FORD COUNTY, SS.

"An inquisition holding at Dodge City, in said county, on the 4th day of October, A.D. 1878, before me, a justice of the peace for Dodge township, said county (acting as coroner) on the body of Fannie Keenan, there lying dead, by the jurors, whose names are hereunto subscribed. The said jurors, upon their oath, do say: That Fannie Keenan came to her death by a gunshot wound, and that in their opinion the said gunshot wound was produced by a bullet discharged from a gun in the hands of one James Kennedy.

"In testimony whereof, the said jurors have hereunto set their hands the day and year aforesaid.

"P.L. BEATTY, FOREMAN.
"JOHN B. MEANS,
"J. H. CORNELL,

"W. STRAETER,

"THOS. MCINTIRE,

"JOHN LOUGHEED.

"ATTEST: R. G. Cook, justice of the peace, acting coroner, for Dodge township, said county."[1]

The lawmen who chased and captured Jim Kennedy were some of the most famous in the west. The Dodge City Times of October 12, 1878 told of the chase in detail:

"THE CAPTURE OF JIM KENNEDY.

"THE SUPPOSED ASSASSIN OF DORA HAND ALIAS FANNIE KEENAN. THE PRISONER WOUNDED IN THE LEFT SHOULDER.

"In last week's Times we detailed the circumstances of the killing of Dora Hand alias Fannie Keenan, at about half past four o'clock Friday morning. There were few persons up at this unreasonable hour, though all night walkers and loungers are not uncommon in this city, and the somber hours of that morning found one James Kennedy and another person gyrating in the dim shadows of the flickering light of the solitary opened saloon. Four pistol shots awakened the echoes in that dull misty morning, and aroused the police force and others. Pistol shots are of common occurrence, but this firing betokened something fatal. Assistant Marshal [Wyatt] Earp and Officer Jim Masterson were soon at their wits' end, but promptly surmised the upshot of the shooting. Shortly after the firing Kennedy and his companion were seen in the opened saloon. The arrival of the officers and the movements of the two morning loungers threw suspicions in their direction. Kennedy mounted his horse [and] was soon galloping down the road in the direction of the Fort.

"It was believed the other person knew something of the firing though he had no connection with it. He was arrested and placed in jail; in the meantime expressing his belief to the officers that Kennedy did the shooting. There were some other reasons why the officers believed that Kennedy did the shooting, and accordingly a plan for his capture was commenced, though the officers did not start in pursuit until 2 o'clock in the afternoon. The party consisted of Sheriff Masterson, Marshal Bassett, Assistant [Marshal] Wyatt Earp, Deputy [Sheriff] Duffy and Wm. Tilghman, as intrepid a posse as ever that pulled a trigger. They started down the river road, halting at a ranch below the Fort, thence going south, traveling 75 miles that day. A heavy storm Friday night delayed the pursued and pursuers; but Saturday afternoon found the officers at a ranch near Mead City, 35

---

[1] Great Gunfighters of the Kansas Cowtowns, p. 231; The Ford County Globe, October 8, 1878.

miles south west of Dodge City, one hour in advance of Kennedy who said he was delayed by the storm in his proposed hasty exit to his cattle ranch at Tuscosa, Texas. The officers were lying in wait at Mead City, their horses unsaddled and grazing on the plain, the party avoiding the appearance of a Sheriff's posse in full feather, believing that they were in advance of the object of their search, but prepared to catch any stray straggler that exhibited signs of distress.

"Their patient waiting was rewarded about 4 o'clock Saturday afternoon [October 5], when a solitary horseman appeared on the distant plain approaching the camp. The officers had apprised certain parties to give no heed of their presence, and from them it was afterwards learned that Kennedy had made diligent inquiries concerning the whereabouts of supposed horsemen.   To these inquiries Kennedy received negative replies. The cautious manner in which he approached the camp led the officers to believe that he snuffed the danger from every movement forward. He halted when within a few hundred yards of the camp, apparently dreading to proceed further.   Seeing that he would approach no nearer, the officers thrice commanded Kennedy to throw up his hands. He raised his arm as though to strike his horse with a quirt he held in his hand, when several shots were fired by the officers, one shot striking Kennedy in the left shoulder, making a dangerous wound; three shots struck the horse killing him instantly. Kennedy was armed with a carbine, two revolvers and a knife. He was brought in Sunday and placed in jail, where he is receiving medical treatment, though he lies in a low and critical condition.

"A preliminary examination will be had as soon as the prisoner is able to appear in court."[1]

On October 29, 1878 the Globe reported the results of a preliminary examination of Kennedy, who had been charged with murder. The paper reported:

"FREE AS AIR

"Kennedy, the man who was arrested for the murder of Fannie Keenan, was examined last week before Judge [R.G.] Cook, and acquitted. His trial took place in the sheriff's office, which was too small to admit spectators. We do not know what the evidence was, or upon what grounds he was acquitted. But he is free to go on his way rejoicing whenever he gets ready."[2]

---

[1]   Great Gunfighters of the Kansas Cowtowns, pp. 234-235;
      Dodge City Times, October 12, 1878.

[2]   Great Gunfighters of the Kansas Cowtowns, p. 235;
      The Ford County Globe, October 29, 1878.

Later on December 9, 1878 Kennedy's father arrived in Dodge City to take the boy back home and the <u>Globe</u> reported this event on December 10, 1878 and also reported that before being able to travel he would have to undergo a serious surgical operation. On December 17, 1878 the results of that surgical operation were duly reported.[1]

So despite Lake's attempt to make Wyatt Earp the hero of the chase and capture of Jim Kennedy by making him leader of the posse, it is apparent from the newspaper reports that wasn't the case.

This is just another typical instance of either Earp or Lake exaggerating his part in some real or imagined event. In this case however, it was a real event and Wyatt Earp really did have a part in the event of sufficient importance that it wasn't necessary to exaggerate his conduct, or falsely claim that because he was a Deputy United States Marshal, he was put in charge of the posse.

---

[1]   <u>Great Gunfighters of the Kansas Cowtowns</u>, p. 235; The Ford County <u>Globe</u>, December 17, 1878.

CHAPTER XVIII

LAST GUN PLAY AGAINST WYATT EARP IN DODGE CITY

LAKE put together another one of his fanciful tales about the conduct of Wyatt Earp that had he been aware of it, he would have planned as a television program. He describes a confrontation between Wyatt Earp and a young Texan as follows:

"July 3, however, was marked by the arrival in Dodge of an individual who ever since has remained the cowcamp's outstanding mystery. He rode into town alone, astride an excellent and oft-branded cross-bred cow-pony properly caparisoned for warfare, straight to Wright and Beverly's corner, where he dismounted, hitched a pair of six-guns into hand-position at his hips and stepped to the walk. During his very short stay in Dodge, the stranger revealed neither his identity, his antecedents, his home address, nor his destination upon leaving. Beyond hinting that he was from Texas, he went into no conversational details except those pertaining to the purpose of his visit, which he stated promptly and fully.

"'Is Wyatt Earp still marshal of Dodge?' the stranger inquired of a lounger.

"Informed that such was the case, the visitor stepped into the nearest bar, where he bought two or three drinks and asked where Wyatt Earp might be found. He was told to try the Long Branch.

"'Wyatt may drop in here any minute,' the Long Branch bartender, Adam Jackson, informed the stranger, 'but you'd better shed your guns before you meet him. He won't stand for gun-toting.'

"'So I've heard,' the visitor replied, 'and that's the point I intend to argue with him.'

"'Have one on the house,' Jackson suggested. 'What was that you said?'

"Possibly Dodge City liquor was too potent.

"'I said I've come to Dodge to make Wyatt Earp eat his guns.'

"Bystanders caught the drift of the conversation and the stranger was surrounded by those who sensed possibilities. With each drink the mysterious visitor became more emphatic and more expansive in his description of what was about to happen to Wyatt Earp.

"'He's run it over our Texas boys too long,' he explained, with the proper touch of profanity, 'so I've come up to cut him down.'

"'You rate yourself pretty high, don't you?' someone inquired.

"'See that!' The stranger flipped a gun from the holster. 'Twenty credits, and every one a marshal.'

"Chalk Beeson interposed a request that the killing take place in the open air and the visitor led his auditors to the Plaza, where the crowd of listeners was augmented as the visiting gunman discoursed upon the scores his friends had chalked against Wyatt Earp and the method by which he proposed to pay them. He stood with a gun in either hand and was well into a tirade in which Wyatt was mentioned repeatedly in uncomplimentary fashion when the crowd about him melted. A tall, slender, blue-eyed fellow, wearing a black sombrero, with a badge pinned to the breast of his soft white shirt and a pair of guns swung low in his hip-holsters stood before him.

"'I've been listening to your talk for several minutes,' this person observed. 'I gather you're looking for me. I'm marshal of Dodge. My name's Wyatt Earp.'

"With which introduction Wyatt slapped the stranger's face with his open hand, vigorously, first on one side, then on the other. With a downward sweep of both hands the marshal seized the guns for which twenty credits had been boasted. Then, to the equal surprise of the gunman and the onlookers, Wyatt shoved those guns back into the holsters from which they had been drawn for advertising purposes.

"'You can go back and tell your Texas friends,' said the marshal of Dodge, 'that I didn't bother to take your guns or lock you in the calaboose. Or, if you insist on a gunplay, I'll get you a rifle and a shotgun to go with your pistols and you can go down on the river-bank where nobody'll get hurt when you do your shooting. When you send word you're ready, I'll come down and start you for Texas with a boot in the seat of the pants that'll lift you clean into The Nations.'

"As he concluded this offer of an alternative, Wyatt took the stranger's ear-lobe between his thumb and forefinger and led him to the side of his pony, where he hoisted him to the saddle. With a slap of his hand the marshal started the pony toward the tollbridge. Halfway to the bridgehead, the mysterious horseman stopped, turned, and shook his fist at the marshal. Then he rode on toward Texas."[1]

Lake commented that was the last gunplay made against Earp while he was Marshal of Dodge City. Keep in mind that was on July 3rd, and he didn't leave until September 9th, so the city must have been pretty quiet for sometime before he left if that was true. Lake says that: "On September 9, the editor of the Globe reported: 'Wyatt Earp, the most efficient marshal Dodge City ever had, has

---

[1]   Wyatt Earp, Frontier Marshal, pp. 225-227.

resigned and is leaving for Arizona.'"[1]

His report does not square with the one printed by Miller and Snell in <u>Great Gunfighters</u> where they reported:

"The September 9th issue of the <u>Globe</u> reported that: 'Mr. Wyatt Earp, who has been on our police force for several months, resigned his position last week and took his departure for Las Vegas, New Mexico.'"

They went on to say that Wyatt was paid $13.32, for four days service in September by the city council on October 7, 1879. On September 30th, the <u>Globe</u> mentioned that he was still in Las Vegas but by March 30, 1880, he was in Tombstone and said to be a rich man.[2]

Lake gratuitously changed the September 9th story in the <u>Globe</u> to read:

"Wyatt Earp, the most efficient Marshal Dodge City ever had, has resigned and is leaving for Arizona."[3]

It should be noted that not only did Lake misquote The Globe story of September 9th, but he obviously combined it with the Globe's story of May 14, which he materially changed.

One has to wonder about the motive for such misstatements. It's quite obvious that they could not have been accidental because the material is there for everyone to see and if Lake did any research at all, he would certainly have known that he was misstating the facts. It's doubtful that he would have relied on Wyatt's memory for details such as this. It seem that he just couldn't resist the urge to make Wyatt Earp the most efficient officer Dodge ever had.

---

[1]   <u>Ibid</u>, p. 229.

[2]   <u>Great Gunfighters of the Kansas Cowtowns</u>, p. 90.

[3]   <u>Wyatt Earp, Frontier Marshal</u>, p. 229.

CHAPTER XIX

THE EARPS MOVE WEST

ACCORDING to Waters,[1] Nicholas Earp and his bunch, including Virgil and Alley, moved from Dodge in the fall of '76 and wintered in Pease, Kansas with the rest of the wagon train that was heading west. On May 8, 1877 the wagon train pulled out for California,[2] slowly moved across parts of New Mexico and northern Arizona, and eventually reached Prescott some time right after the fourth day of July, 1877.[3] Here Virgil and his wife dropped out of the wagon train, and Nicholas and the rest of the family proceeded on to San Bernardino, where they established a family headquarters in and around San Bernardino, Colton, and Riverside. Nicholas eventually became Justice of the Peace, and an honored citizen of San Bernardino County. The residence of father Earp and his wife were the magnet for the rest of the Earp family, and they always returned there from wherever their wanderings took them.

Virgil Earp and his wife worked on a ranch outside of Prescott for several months to recover their financial status, and then eventually moved into Prescott where Virgil worked in a saw mill and also as a deputy sheriff. In Arizona he naturally heard about the great silver strikes in Tombstone and apparently went down there to take a look. He wrote to Wyatt in Dodge City telling him of the rich strike and the opportunities that would be available to the early-comers in Tombstone and that was what moved Wyatt to quit his job in Dodge City and take off for Arizona.

On September 9, the <u>Globe</u> reported Wyatt's resignation and departure for Las Vegas, New Mexico.

On September the 30th, the <u>Globe</u> mentioned that Wyatt was still in Las Vegas.[4] Travelling by horse and wagon, a slow mode of

---

[1]   <u>The Earp Brother's of Tombstone</u>, p. 45.

[2]   <u>Ibid</u>, p. 46.

[3]   <u>Ibid</u>, p. 63.

[4]   <u>Great Gunfighters of the Kansas Cowtowns</u>, p. 90.

transportation, Wyatt reached Prescott on November 1, 1879,[1] one month and 21 days after leaving Dodge City.

Bartholomew has Wyatt stopping in Las Vegas, New Mexico and engaging in various nefarious money making schemes with numerous persons and people of bad character, but it is doubtful that he had time to do that.[2] It must be noted that it took Nicholas Earp and his bunch, including Virgil, just four days less than two months to make the crossing from the vicinity of Dodge City, Kansas to Prescott, Arizona and that it only took Wyatt Earp traveling by the same route and mode of transportation, one month and 21 days. I suppose that one could assume that traveling conditions had improved between 1877 and 1879 and that Wyatt could have made better time, but even so, there would not have been very much time to linger around Las Vegas and engage in various nefarious money making schemes as implied, but not directly charged by Bartholomew.

When Wyatt reached Prescott, he contacted Virgil Earp and his wife, and they made arrangements to move to Tombstone. Virgil sold his business interest in Prescott, resigned his position as deputy sheriff and joined the wagon train headed from Prescott to Tombstone. On the way, they stopped at Tucson, where, according to Lake:

"At Tucson, Arizona, Wyatt Earp met Charles Shibell, Sheriff of Pima County, a wild and brutal bailiwick covering 28,000 sq. miles of sagebrush, rock, and cactus which included the Tombstone district and for which Tucson was the seat of government.

"'If you're going to Tombstone,' Shibell told Wyatt, 'I'll make you deputy sheriff.'

"'Much obliged,' Wyatt answered, 'But I'm aiming to run a line of stages.'

"'There are two lines running out of Tombstone already,' Shibell countered, 'With mail and express contracted.'

"Even when convinced that no third stage-line could succeed, Wyatt was loath to return to his Kansas calling.

"'You're a democrat and I'm a republican,' he objected further. 'Your organization wouldn't stand for me.'

"'Politics don't count,' the sheriff replied. 'The sheriff is tax and fee collector as well as peace officer. He gets a percentage of collections, plus mileage. We should get ten or twelve thousand dollars a month from Tombstone, but a lot of fellows in there figure they're too tough to pay taxes, and what little is collected never reaches us. I'm after a deputy who's man enough to collect what's

1   Wyatt Earp, Frontier Marshal, p. 230.

2   Wyatt Earp, The Untold Story, pp. 316-317.

due, and honest enough to make certain that the county gets it. I'll guarantee you $500 a month, if you'll take the job.'

"'I understand,' Wyatt observed, as he considered this last inducement, 'that Tombstone sets up to be a pretty tough camp.'

"'There won't be much criminal work,' Shibell asserted. 'Tombstone's going to organize and will appoint a marshal to handle law and order. Get the county's money and you can suit yourself about the gunmen.'

"Wyatt weighed personal disinclination against responsibility. Virgil's prospecting must be financed, while the other Earps lived decently.

"'I'll take your job,' he told the sheriff.

"On December 1, 1879, Wyatt Earp rode into the boom silver camp as a deputy sheriff of Pima County, but not as a deputy United States Marshal, as has been generally recorded. His federal commission came later."[1]

Here was the start of a lot of arguments that could have easily been settled by a careful examination of the records. Frank Waters stated that, "The Earps stopped at Tucson and here Virgil obtained a commission as a Deputy U.S. Marshal for southern Arizona in case he might be needed by the regular deputy being stationed in Tombstone."[2] In a footnote Waters says, "The commission was signed November 27, 1879. Courtesy John Gilchrese. Lake's biography of Wyatt appropriates the commission for Wyatt as a matter of course."[3] It is not true that Lake appropriated the commission for Wyatt as can be seen from the above quote from Lake but neither is it true that, "On December 1, 1879 Wyatt rode into the boom silver camp as deputy sheriff of Pima County."

Wyatt was not appointed a deputy sheriff of Pima County until July 27, 1880.[4]

As far as Vigil Earp's appointment as United States Marshal is concerned, it is impossible to determine by what process he obtained that commission. The U.S. Marshal was C.P. Dake. At that time the territorial capital for Arizona was at Prescott, and the United States Marshal C.P. Dake maintained his headquarters there. What has been described by all authors as a commission as deputy United States

---

[1]   Wyatt Earp, Frontier Marshal, p. 232.

[2]   The Earp Brothers of Tombstone, p. 76.

[3]   Ibid, p. 242.

[4]   Appendix 1, Exhibit 2, for copy of appointment of Wyatt Earp as Deputy Sheriff.

Marshal was actually an oath. If Dake ever signed a commission, it has not turned up in the records. The oath was as follows,

"TERRITORY OF ARIZONA
COUNTY OF ~~YAVAPAI~~
PIMA

"I, V. W. Earp do solemnly swear that I will support the constitution of the United States and the laws of this territory; that I will true faith and diligence bare to the same, and defend them against all enemies whatsoever; and that I will faithfully and impartially discharge the duties of the office of Deputy United States Marshal according to the best of my abilities, so help me God.

"V. W. Earp

"Subscribed and sworn to this 27th day of November, 1879

"Signed, (Illegible)

"U.S. District Court"

The original of that oath is in the Arizona Historical Society files at Tucson, Arizona and a copy of the same is set forth here.[1] It should be noted that apparently the original was prepared in Yavapai County, that's the County where Prescott was the County seat and where Dake had his office. There must have been some documents issued by C.P. Dake to Virgil Earp while he was in Prescott and it would seem that he must have stopped by the U.S. District Court in Tucson and executed the oath. At that time, someone struck out the County of Yavapai and inserted the County of Pima.

While Water's was incorrect in saying that Earp's biographer, Lake, had appropriated the commission of Deputy United States Marshal as a matter of course, it is true that Wyatt himself appropriated the commission unto himself at a later date. In 1896 in San Francisco, when Wyatt Earp submitted to the series of interviews that were published in the San Francisco <u>Examiner</u> on August 2, 1896, he is quoted as saying:

"In 1879 Dodge City was beginning to lose much of its snap which had given it a charm to men of restless blood, and I decided to move to Tombstone which was just building up a reputation. Doc Holliday thought he would move with me. Big Nose Kate had left him long before - they were always a quarrelsome couple - and settled in Las Vegas, New Mexico, he looked her up en route, and, the old tenderness reasserted itself; she resolved to throw in her lot with his in Arizona. As for me, I was tired of the trials of a peace officer's life and wanted no more of it. But as luck would have it, I stopped at Prescott, Arizona to see my brother Virgil and while there I met C.P. Dake, the United States Marshal of the territory. Dake had heard of

---

[1]   Appendix 1, Exhibit 1.

me before, and he begged me so hard to take the deputyship in Tombstone, that I finally consented. It was thus that the real troubles of my life began."[1]

Virgil executed the oath as Deputy United States Marshal in Tucson on November 27. The Earp wagon train then moved east toward Tombstone, where it arrived on November 29, 1879.

[1]   Interview published in San Francisco Examiner, August 2, 1896; The Earps Talk, p. 5.

CHAPTER XX

TOMBSTONE

IN order to understand the conditions that the Earps moved into, a brief history of the founding of Tombstone and the problems of the political organization is necessary.

The discovery that created Tombstone was made by Edward Schieffelin in the summer of 1877. At that time the country thereabout was over-run by hostile Apaches and any white man going into the territory was taking considerable risk of losing his life. While prospecting in the desert alone, Schieffelin encountered a squad of soldiers from nearby Camp Hauchuca. He was discussing his prospects of making a rich strike with the soldiers when one of them told him that all he would find here would be his "Tombstone." This remark evidently made an impression on Schieffelin, for when he made his first discovery of silver, he named the place "Tombstone." The second claim that he found, he named "Graveyard."[1] He recruited his brother and a well-known mining engineer by the name of Richard Gird in the spring of 1878 to help him develop his discovery. Work of the strike soon got out and the area began to swarm with fortune seekers. Other discoveries were made nearby and a small village sprang up on a mesa then known as Goose Flats. It was later renamed Tombstone and that is the place that finally became the permanent city.

Federal law[2] established simple procedure for obtaining title to federal lands for the purpose of establishing a city in a mining district such as Tombstone. The law required that a group of citizens incorporate as a town-site company, and that the company survey the proposed town site and establish a temporary municipal government under state or territorial law. Once the municipal officers were elected, would petition the United States Department of Interior for a patent to the federal land comprising the town-site. After the patent was issued to the city, the mayor could then issue deeds for nominal fees to the occupants already on the ground. The balance of the town lots were to be held in trust by the City for the benefit of future

---

[1]   The Tombstone Discovery, Arizona and The West, (Spring 1979), pp. 44-67.

[2]   14 U.S. Stat at L., Sections 2382, 2387, (1867), pp. 541-542.

purchasers who could purchase the lots from the City for nominal fees and the City was entitled to keep the money.

The first occupants of the town-site of Tombstone just exercised squatters rights and occupied properties without any pretense of legality. Realizing that something had to be done to establish titles and right of occupancy to those properties being built on and occupied, five men organized the Tombstone Town Site Company, March 5, 1879. This step provided the rudimentary elements of an organized village and led to a survey on three hundred and twenty acres of "Goose Flats." Of the five original incorporators, two, Anson P.K. Safford and Thomas J. Bidwell, were men of good reputations and former holders of public trust.

Two of the organizers, James S. Clark and Joseph C. Palmer were opportunistic politicians who had been engaged in many crooked dealings during the gold rush era of San Francisco and in reconstruction in the South after the Civil War.

The company filed a townsite claim, dated April 19, 1879, at the United States Land Office in Florence and recorded it in the Pima County Recorders office three days later[1]

Before the organization progressed very far, Clark, with an associate by the name of Mike Gray, gained control of the Company by buying out Stafford, Calhoun, Bidwell and Palmer and entered upon a conspiracy to fraudulently gain possession of most of the land in the township.

On November 24, 1879 a first election for city offices was held in Tombstone. The voters elected William A. Harwood as Mayor, and four city councilmen. The council appointed Fred White, a 31 year old New Yorker, as Marshal. In January 1880, Mayor Harwood was replaced by councilman Alder Randall, and Mike Gray of the company of Clark and Gray was appointed village clerk. On March 20, 1880, the Town Council, in accordance with United States law, made an application for a patent to lands for a town-site, consisting of 2,394 lots. On May 22, 1880, Mayor Randall, acting his part in the conspiracy between him, Clark and Gray, deeded over to Clark, Gray & Co. 2,168 lots for a consideration of $5.80.[2] This deed was made before any patent was issued by the U.S. Government, and was totally ineffective, but Clark, Gray & Co. chose to rely on the validity of the deed and made claims against all of the occupants of various properties in the township. They would approach the occupants of lots in Tombstone and offer to sell a clear title to the occupant at a

---

[1]   Arizona and the West, Vol. 21, No. 1, pp. 6-7.

[2]   Ibid, p. 8.

price based on the value of the improvements and the lot. If the occupants refused to pay the price demanded, the company would then try to oust them by force or threats of force to be applied by what became known as cowboys, usually Newman H. Clanton, generally referred to as old man Clanton, his sons, Ike Clanton, Phineas Clanton, and Billy Clanton, the McLaury brothers, Tom, and Frank, an outlaw known as Curly Bill Brocius and another well known outlaw by the name of John Ringo.

This crew was tough enough, at least by reputation, to frighten many brave people into paying up. Those that did not pay up were subjected to considerable harassment, some of which will be noted later.

In researching the history of Tombstone, the three most important sources of information are the two Tombstone Newspapers, and the diary of George W. Parsons.

In October 1879 the newspaper, called the Nugget, began publication, first as a weekly, later as a daily newspaper. The Nugget, was reputed to be financed and underwritten by various politicians, and throughout the early troubles of Tombstone, always supported the crooked politicians and what became known as the cowboy element. They were always supportive of Clark, Gray & Company and their fraudulent real estate dealings and of Sheriff John Behan and his crowd.

In opposition to the Nugget was the Tombstone Epitaph. The editor and founder of the Tombstone Epitaph was John P. Clum. Clum had come west in the early '70s, to serve as an Indian Agent at the San Carlos Indian Reservation. His activities and experiences as an Indian Agent would make a book by itself, but for this book it is sufficient to say that he had considerable difficulty with the Federal bureaucracy and finally left the Indian service very dissatisfied and the Bureau of Indian Affairs apparently felt the same way about him. Upon leaving the Indian Agency he went to Tucson where he commenced the publication of a small newspaper called the Tucson Citizen.

The lure of the booming silver town of Tombstone, he could not resist. After a short time he sold the Tuscon Citizen and moved to Tombstone where on May 1, 1880 he published the first edition of the Tombstone Epitaph. It was a weekly newspaper at first, but after a few months it became a daily paper.

Clum's dealings with the bureaucracy in the Indian Service and his observation of the thievery and graft by politicians seemed to have bent his mind towards hatred of petty bureaucracy and petty thievery. He became a crusader for law and order and against those people who would take advantage of their political position to rob or steal from the public.

In early 1880, a young man by the name of George W. Parsons came to Tombstone from San Francisco to engage in the mining business. He was an avid diarist and was one of the few people in and around Tombstone in the 1880s who wrote of events as they occurred. His diary is looked upon as a gold mine of the history of the area at that time. On Wednesday, May 5, 1880 he made an entry in his diary as follows:

"Quite a row in town this a.m. or yesterday. Gray, the justice, endeavored with several armed assistants to eject Hatch from the lot opposite the P.O. on the SW corner. A crowd gathered and sided with Hatch when Gray and partner, after a flourish of pistols, retired. Nice work for a Justice. Gray offered the lot to Milton the day before for $1500. Having no patent for a town-site, he can't give good title to property."[1]

This is a sample of what was going on around Tombstone shortly after the incorporators of the city had made their application for a patent to the land.

The activities on the part of Clark, Gray and Company so upset the citizens that they organized a vigilante committee to protect the occupants of the various city lots against the use of force and violence to illegally eject them from their property.

On September 20, 1880 a patent was issued which recited that: "the Mayor and the Councilmen of Tombstone, in trust for several use and benefit of the inhabitants of the town, have purchased said premises: and the United States conveys and grants to Alder A. Randall Mayor as aforesaid in trust as aforesaid, unto his successors and assigns, in trust as aforesaid subject to all the conditions contained in Section 2387, supra."[2]   Thus the Mayor and his scheming conspirators acquired title after they had already granted many of the lots away.

That the townspeople had become aware of the gigantic fraud being perpetrated upon them is disclosed by the entry in Parson's journal of Sunday, November 7, 1880 as follows:

". . .The Mayor was summoned to a meeting this day at 1 p.m. and after much diligent searching was found. I was present. He gave his solemn promise that he would not deed until the patent was in his hands and not then until meeting of the council was called when he would be guided by their wishes. Jones present with Alder Randall, the Mayor. Another meeting of the committee was held in the "San Jose" parlor later when and where counselman Jones made a

---

[1]   The Private Journal of George W. Parsons, p. 44.

[2]   Clark v. Titus, 2 Ariz. 147, 11 Pacific 312 (1886).

complete expose of the frauds attempted and perpetrated by the Mayor and his crowd. Bribery and corruption of the worst sort had been practiced. It would take too much time and space to narrate the interview. Suffice it to say that such bare faced fraud and villainy has seldom - if ever - been before practiced in any community. One instance of the Mayor's acts will illustrate. Attachment issued against him of nearly $1,000 and his saloon property was seized. He claimed it wasn't his, and defrauded his creditors or has thus far. He deeded the property to Clark, Gray & Co. as Mayor who in turn deeded to a friend of Randall's who is to re-deed to the Mayor when the right time comes. The Mayor's own words to Jones were, 'There is more sugar in the other crowd,' meaning Clark, Gray & Co. Randall was to make $2,500 and Jones $500. The fact of the latter complicity will operate against his acting for the people now, in all probability. Jones desires to aid the people now and in proof, telegraphed on his way to Tucson tonight, that the Mayor was in-route so after all, he has become scared, afraid of hemp, and left. Determined action is now necessary."[1]

If the citizenry at the meeting were convinced by Mayor Randall's "solemn promise that he would not deed until the patent was in his hands and not then until meeting of the council was called when he would be, "guided by our wishes," they certainly were fooled. For the patent was issued on September 20, 1880, and was undoubtedly in the hands of the mayor at the time he made his solemn promise. Furthermore, as Parson indicates, he was on his way to Tucson, and that he reached there the next day is attested by the fact that on November 8, 1880, he duly executed a new deed as Mayor whereby he again granted and conveyed to Clark, Gray & Co title to most of the lots in the Tombstone township.

In the Tombstone Epitaph of November 9, 1880, Clum wrote of the nefarious dealings of Mayor Randall and his recording on November 8th of the deed to Clark, Gray & Co., "Tombstone has been handed over to the scheming speculators."[2]

Clark and Gray were evidently so brazen that they seemed to think that they could without any legal justification, impose their will upon the citizens of Tombstone. On November the 9th, 1880 the Epitaph reported a statement by Clark and Gray that:

"We intend collecting rents from all tenants on our lots from the first of December, 1880 and call on all tenants to make arrangements to pay."

---

[1]   The Private Journal of George Parsons, p. 99.

[2]   Tombstone Epitaph, November 9, 1880.

Immediately thereafter, the citizen's safety committee headed by John Clum filed a suit in the District Court in Pima County alleging fraud by the Mayor and Clark, Gray & Company, and Judge French issued a temporary injunction prohibiting the defendants from making further deeds or transfer of Tombstone property until the case was resolved.[1]

On the same day that the Epitaph wrote the story about the filing of the lawsuit, Clark & Gray were continuing their assault upon the citizens of Tombstone. On Sunday, December 5, 1880, George Parsons made the following entry in his diary:

"Up early. Great activity this a.m. in the corner house, moving out, and a general report that C.G. & Co. [Clark & Gray] would attempt to move the corner house in the rear of R's [Reilly's] and thus prevent the latter's being moved back to place. Vickers and I had a consultation and then set off to get men to move house back before the other idea was consummated. We didn't have much trouble in raising a crowd and at the word, we all made a rush and in a very few minutes had the house back where it belonged. There was much enthusiasm. Clark was present at the commencement, speedily left and with Gray kept away - a very prudent idea. We used joists - same things the first party used. Eccleston, Clum and others prominent in business took a hand. Few words and quick action. Was among the first and did my share. Was called Trojan. Well, that's over and the citizens won. Redfern said that at the theater last night there were ten men who had shotguns loaded and ready in case the signal for help came and that they had brought some rope to stretch C. and G.'s necks with in case they were not shot, so at last it would look as though the people would assert their rights --"[2]

While the injunction issued by the court effectively prevented the granting of any more deeds to lots, essentially the whole town had already been deeded before the injunction was received, and Clark and Gray proceeded on their merry way to try to enforce their claim to title to most of the town.

If the original Tombstone township organization that appointed Marshal White as their first City Marshal expected him to side with Clark, Gray & Co. and against the business people, they were disappointed. White took the position that he would maintain those people who were in possession in status-quo until their titles had been decided by a court.

On October 28, 1880, White was killed by an outlaw by the name

[1] Tombstone Epitaph, December 5, 1880.

[2] The Private Journal of George W. Parsons, p. 106.

Derry Public Library

of Curly Bill Brocius, the complete story of which will be covered in detail later, and Virgil Earp was appointed temporary Marshal to take his place. Virgil Earp continued the policy of Marshal White and defended those people in possession of lots against the lot jumpers.

It has been hinted by some people that Marshal White was killed because he failed to cooperate with Clark, Gray & Co. but no evidence of that has ever been found.

On January the 4th, 1881, Tombstone held its first election for a permanent government, and elected John Clum (editor of the Tombstone Epitaph) as its third Mayor. Virgil Earp ran for the position of City Marshal, but was defeated in that election by Ben Sippy. Sippy was more friendly towards Clark, Gray & Co. and less inclined to support the rights of people in possession.

Here is another one of those mysteries that I haven't been able to solve.

Virgil Earp was defeated for the office of Town Marshal on January 4, 1881 by Ben Sippy. Sippy served in that office until June of 1881 when he took a leave of absence and never returned. Virgil Earp was appointed to replace him by the Council.

The mystery arises from this: At the Huntington Library I discovered what appears to be an original of the Tombstone City Charter. Article VIII of the charter provides:

"General election shall be held in said city on the first Tuesday of next January, 1882 and every two years thereafter. The Mayor, Councilmen, Treasurer, City Assessor and other officers elected at the last Municipal Election held January 1881 and by said Common Council shall continue to hold their respective offices until the first general Municipal Election to be held on the first Tuesday of January, 1882;

"To take effect immediately.
"Approved - February 21, 1881.
"(Signed) J.C. Fremont, Gov. of T. of A."

The document then sets out a list of City officers elected at the election held in January 1881. It makes no mention of Ben Sippy, but lists the Chief of Police as Virgil Earp. No amount of research has revealed how this came about.

In February of 1881, Pima County was divided into two counties. The eastern portion was named Cochise County, and Tombstone was designated the County Seat. With a court in Tombstone, the citizens no longer had to journey to Tucson to file a lawsuit in a court of general jurisdiction. Immediately, a number of lawsuits were filed by citizens to quiet title to their property against Clark, Gray & Company. While the citizens lawsuits were pending and undecided, a citizen named Robert J. Winders filed criminal charges against the ex-mayor, alleging that Randall's deed to Clark & Gray constituted felony malfeasance in office.   The case came before Justice Spicer, who, although he had no love for Clark & Gray and had represented clients who's interests were adverse to Randall and his relations with the City Property, nevertheless found Randall not guilty for the reason that he could find no laws on the books of the Territory of Arizona that made the conduct of the mayor a crime.

In June of 1881, immediately following Randall's release by Judge Spicer, Ben Sippy, the City Marshal, asked for and was granted a leave of absence by the Council. He never returned to Tombstone, and Virgil Earp was appointed by the Council to succeed him.

Virgil Earp and his brothers Wyatt, Morgan and Warren were thus in place when they were needed to counteract the actions of Clark, Gray & Company, who again attempted to forcibly take possession of most of the city.

This happened on June 22, 1881 when a devastating fire destroyed a major portion of Tombstone's business district. Clark & Gray, who insisted on referring to the Tombstone occupants as their lessee's, placed armed men on the burned out lots hoping thereby to establish possession and enforce their claim to ownership of the property.

In everybody's story of early Tombstone, Fred Dodge appears always to be around the edges of law enforcement, although he was not a law enforcement officer. His apparent occupation was that of gambler and saloon keeper. He always seemed to show up to assist Wyatt Earp or any other law enforcement officer, but it wasn't learned until many years later that unknown to the Earps or anyone else in Tombstone, he was an undercover agent for Wells, Fargo. Lake envisioned writing a biography of Fred Dodge that he hoped would be as successful as the one he wrote on Wyatt Earp, and Dodge cooperated with him by supplying him with a great deal of information in the form of letters and documents.

However, Fred Dodge died in 1938 before he was able to complete the information he was sending to Lake, and Lake never wrote the book, but kept all the files and information locked in a Wells, Fargo box. After his death in 1964, his wife and daughter opened the Wells, Fargo box and found the Dodge information. By that time, Lake's daughter, Carolyn, had become an adult and an accomplished writer. She undertook to edit the papers of Fred Dodge and they were published in a book entitled Under Cover for Wells Fargo in 1969. In view of the position of Fred Dodge at the time he was in Tombstone, except for the passage of time between the events, and his recording them on paper, it would seem that he would be one of the most reliable reporters of the events that occurred during the years that he was there.

Dodge was, of course, a witness to the fire and the events that followed. He said that on the morning following the fire, lot-jumpers, working for Clark, Gray and Company were much in evidence and were squatting on many of the good business lots. These were the lots to which title was in dispute and the final determination of ownership was awaiting the results of court proceedings. He said that Virgil Earp and Wyatt Earp talked with several of the leading businessmen and the head of the Safety Committee and concluded that whoever was in possession at the time of the fire should remain in possession until the controversies over the title were settled by the court.

As a result of this determination, Virgil Earp, who at that time was the chief of police, organized a posse of men of which Fred Dodge was one, and proceeded down Allen Street on one side and up the other side, and where ever they encountered a lot jumper, took him off the lot and put the man who had been in possession before the fire back on the lot. He said that by the time they were through with Allen Street, the lot jumpers were quitting the lots on the other streets in town.

He told about the lot jumpers at the end of Sixth Street to Seventh Street where the sporting houses were, and said that the lot jumpers on those lots had put up little round tents and were going to sleep in their tents. But that night a selected number of horsemen rode around and dropped a lasso rope over the tent pole and then galloped away, jerking the tent free from its holdings and leaving the lot jumper lying there in the open. A cry went up from some of the Committee, "Lot jumpers, you git," and they did, according to Dodge.[1]

The Tombstone Epitaph, for June 23, 1881 reported that Virgil Earp had announced his intention to maintain the same order of things that existed before the fire and up to such time as the Courts settled the question of titles. That of course placed him and his brothers in a camp opposite the Clark, Gray & Co. cohorts which included the cowboys heretofore named who were afterward to become very friendly and cooperative with Johnny Behan when he was appointed sheriff of the newly formed Cochise County.

Although this seems to have put an end to the attempts to forcibly take possession of the townsite, it created some strong animosities between the defenders of the lots and those supporting the claim jumpers, and probably contributed to the feud that culminated in the shoot out at the O.K. Corral, the disabling of Virgil Earp and the murder of his brother Morgan.

Thereafter, rather than force, resort was had to the Courts to

---

[1]   Undercover For Wells Fargo, p. 34-35.

determine title and right to possession of the various lots in Tombstone.

Clark & Gray filed many lawsuits, and a number of them were settled out of court for unknown sums. It seemed that whenever anyone chose to spend the money to contest their lawsuit the occupant of the lot would always win so that there was no way of getting a definitive appellate court decision that would settle the matter once and for all. The winner can't appeal. Finally, Clark sued Benjamin Titus, and in that case tried without a jury Clark won a verdict, thus making it possible to appeal and get a decision from a higher court. The case was appealed to the Territorial Supreme Court and on July 8, 1886, that court rendered its decision.

In deciding the case, the court completely ignored the first set of deeds issued by Mayor Randall prior to the issuance of the patent, and based its decision entirely on the validity of the deeds made after September 20, 1880 when the patent was issued.

In summing up the case, the Court said in part: "The rights of the plaintiffs in this whole case hang on the validity of the deed from Randall, (to) . . . J.S. Clark, M.E. Clark, M. Gray, and . . . J.D. Rouse, (whereby) in consideration of . . . $5.80, (he) granted, . . . 2,168 lots out of the total of 2,394, comprising the whole town-site, to (Clark, Gray and Rouse) . . .

"The deed by Randall, on its face, was a violation of the trust imposed on him by law. Out of 2,394 lots he deeded 2,168 to four persons, not in severalty as occupants, but to them as tenants in common. The findings of the court show that at the time said deed was made three-fourths of the lots were vacant, including the lot sued for. The Mayor held the title to these lots in trust for the occupants. He had no power to convey the title to anyone but to occupants . . . If any profit was to accrue from the sale of such lots, it was carefully guarded for the benefit of the inhabitants of the town. Here was a bold attempt to transfer substantially this whole town-site to four persons which would enable them to speculate off of the present and future inhabitants of the town. It was a legal and actual fraud which ought not to be countenanced for a moment. The deed conveyed to the parties no other title than Randall had and so the title remained in whoever held the legal title in trust for the several 'use and benefit of the occupants' of said town."[1]

So it took until 1886 for the Court to vindicate the correctness of the position of Mayor Clum, Virgil Earp and his brothers in defending the rights of the occupants of the lots.

Of course by that time, the whole situation of Tombstone had

[1]   Clark v. Titus, 2 Arizona 147, 11 Pacific 312 (1886).

changed. The mines had shut down, the Earps and almost everyone else had left Tombstone, and the outlaws were mostly gone. Tombstone had settled into a period of decline that never ended until Lake published his book about Wyatt Earp and the Television Industry created Wyatt Earp, the great hero in the Battle of the O.K. Corral. This activity made the town a popular and interesting place for tourists to gather and investigate, and they're still doing it.

CHAPTER XXI

EARLY BEGINNINGS
IN TOMBSTONE

THE Earp party that entered Tombstone on December 1, 1879 consisted of Wyatt and his purported wife, Mattie, brothers James and his wife Bessy and her 16 year old daughter Hattie and Virgil Earp and his wife Allie.

Doc Holliday and his paramour, Kate Fisher, had remained in Prescott because Doc had run into a winning streak at cards. He would join them later.[1] How much later is a matter of speculation.

Lake says that, "Morgan Earp reached Tombstone early in January (1880) followed closely by Doc Holliday."[2] The next time he mentioned Doc Holliday was after John Behan had been appointed Sheriff of Cochise county in January of 1881 when Doc took a hand in some gun play in the Oriental gambling establishment.[3]

Fred Dodge's first mention of Doc Holliday was to note his presence with the officers protecting Johnny-Behind-the-Deuce from a mob.[4] That event took place on January 14, 1881.[5]

Everyone seems to assume that Doc Holliday came to Tombstone shortly after the Earps arrived, but that is not the case, for on June 2, 1880, the U.S. Census taker listed him as a resident of Prescott.

It is interesting, and could be the subject of some speculation, that he was listed as the member of a household at which also lived one John J. Gosper, age 39, occupation, miner and stock raiser.

Although the Census did not say so, Gosper at that time was also Secretary of State of the Arizona Territory. Under the laws of that territory, and under present state law, the Secretary of State becomes the acting Governor when the Governor is out of the state or unable to serve. Thus, as we will see later on, during the worst of the

---

[1]   Wyatt Earp, Frontier Marshal, p. 230; The Earp Brothers of Tombstone, p. 75.

[2]   Wyatt Earp, Frontier Marshal, p. 238.

[3]   Ibid, p. 254.

[4]   Under Cover for Wells Fargo, p. 12.

[5]   Tombstone's Epitaph, p. 57.

Tombstone troubles, John J. Gosper was the acting governor. Whether he was particularly friendly with Doc Holliday after sharing the same household with him for some time, and whether that friendship translated into a friendly attitude toward Doc's friends, the Earps, makes interesting speculation.

With Doc Holliday being in Prescott on June 2, 1880, it is very doubtful that he arrived in Tombstone before the month of September, 1880.

Prescott was then and is now a beautiful place situated in the high country nestled in a pine forest, a most comfortable place to spend the summer. A summer retreat where the people of southern Arizona, Phoenix, Tucson and Tombstone went to escape the summer heat if they could. No one in his right mind would think of traveling across the burning desert where the thermometer regularly reaches as high as 120° by means of the transportation available in those days during the months of June, July and August.

Based on that fact alone, it can safely be assumed that Doc Holliday didn't reach Tombstone any earlier than September, 1880.

According to what Virgil Earp's wife supposedly told Frank Waters, the Earp's beginnings in Tombstone were rather bleak. She described it this way:

"Tombstone when we got there was still a big booming camp. Every house was taken and as fast as men could haul in lumber from the Huachucas and build another one, there was people campin' on the spot in wagons or a tent waitin' to move in.

"We happened on a one-room adobe on Allen Street, that some Mexicans had just left. It didn't even have a floor - just hard packed dirt but it cost $40 a month. We fixed up the roof, drove the wagons up on each side, and took the wagon sheets off the boughs to stretch out for more room. We cooked in the fireplace and used boxes for chairs.

". . . Our trouble wasn't lack of water. It was money. We run plum out and the men couldn't find anything to do somehow. I could see right off none of them had come to Tombstone to do any prospectin'."[1]

She went on to describe their progress in Tombstone as follows:

"But that big canvas tent with its double rows of stitching changed our luck. Jim got a job dealin' then he and Bessy and Hattie moved off to themselves. Pretty soon Wyatt got a job as shotgun messenger for Wells, Fargo, so he and Mattie moved into a house of their own to. Then Virgie picked up a couple of odd jobs so's he

---

[1]   The Earp Brothers of Tombstone, p. 90.

could get along, and we moved into another house ourselves."¹

It's hard to tell what period of time was covered by the above quotes. It couldn't have been very long.

The records of the Tombstone Mining District list the holdings of the Earps in 1879 and 1880 as follows:

"DATE	LOCATORS	NAME OF CLAIM
12-6-1879	V.W.,W.S.,J.C. EARP & ROBERT WINDERS	1st NORTH EXT. MTN. MAID
12-10-1879	SAME AS ABOVE	EARP
1-14-1880	SAME AS ABOVE AND A.S. NEFF	GRASSHOPPER
2-8-1880	V.W.,W.S.,J.C. EARP	DODGE
2-16-1880	SAME AS ABOVE	MATTIE BLAYLOCK
2-16-1880	WYATT EARP, A.S. NEFF	COMSTOCK
2-21-1880	W.S.,V.W.,J.C. EARP AND A.S. NEFF	ROCKY RIDGE
4-20-1880	WYATT EARP	LONG BRANCH
11-4-1880	C. BILLICKE, W. EARP, ALBERT STEINFIELD	OLE BULL
UNKNOWN	VIRGIL EARP	RED STAR"

It hardly seems that the Earps were as hard up for money as Allie and Frank Waters would lead us to believe. They had only been in town for about six days before they filed their first mining claim.

In addition to their dealing in mining claims, at least ten lots held by the Earps were listed on the 1881 tax roles for Tombstone.

"On August 27, 1880 the Earp brothers leased two of their mining claims, Comstock and the Grasshopper to R.F. Pixley, a San Francisco investor, for a total of $6,000, which was a handsome sum in 1880."²

Allie says that when their financial status improved they moved to separate houses, she and Virgil to a house on the [southwest] corner of First and Fremont, and Wyatt and Mattie on the North East corner of First and Fremont. Jim and Bessie's house was just west on the south side of Fremont. That story tallies rather well with Lake's statement that,

"Wyatt invested heavily in Tombstone real estate including land on the southwest corner of First and Fremont streets where he erected two houses; Virgil Earp moved into one, James into another.

---

¹   Ibid, p. 92.

²   Bonds, Book I, Cochise County, transcribed from Pima County Records.

erected two houses; Virgil Earp moved into one, James into another. At times Wyatt and Morgan boarded with their brothers, although for the most part they batched, at first in the adobe cabin with Fred Dodge near the calaboose[1] on Allen Street, later at the Cosmopolitan Hotel owned by Albert C. (Chris) Billicke."[2]

An interesting fact to note is that here Lake says that Wyatt batched with his brother and Fred Dodge, whereas his sister-in-law says that Wyatt and Mattie moved into a house of their own on the northeast corner of First and Fremont Streets. Here Wyatt had an opportunity to tell Lake about his purported wife, Mattie, but he apparently never mentioned her to Lake. However, before the publication of his book, Lake became acutely aware of her and of the relationship between Josephine Sarah Marcus and Wyatt Earp. According to correspondence between Stuart N. Lake and his publisher, Houghton Mifflin Company, on file in the Harvard University Library, Mrs. Earp was very adamant that Lake not reveal the existence of Wyatt Earp's wife, Mattie Blaylock, or of Josephine's relationship with John Behan. She became very disagreeable about the subject, even threatening to sue. Therefore, in order to avoid trouble, Lake and his publisher agreed not to mention Mattie Blaylock in his book. Her name never appears in Lake's book.

In order to keep her out of the story, Wyatt or Lake had to have him batching with his brother and Fred Dodge. There was no covering up the fact that the mining claim that Wyatt filed on February 16, 1880 was named Mattie Blaylock.

At any rate, it seems to be agreed by all authors that Wyatt's first job in Tombstone was as shotgun messenger for the Wells-Fargo Company. Lake says that the bullion shipments from Tombstone were being robbed in increasing numbers and that because of the Wells-Fargo robberies, Jim Hume, Chief of Wells-Fargo Officers, visited Tombstone. He said:

"Hume engaged Wyatt Earp to guard treasure shipments between Tombstone and Tucson, later shifting the run to Benson. Wyatt deputized Morgan as assistant in the Sheriff's office and went to riding shotgun. For six months thereafter when a bullion shipment left Tombstone or currency came in under Wells-Fargo auspices, Wyatt Earp rode with it. When the Sheriff's business demanded Wyatt's time he sent Morgan out as messenger.

"It is notable that coincidentally with Wyatt Earp's first trip in the

---

[1]   The Dodge cabin was behind what is now known as The Birdcage Theater.

[2]   Wyatt Earp, Frontier Marshal, p. 238.

when an Earp was riding shotgun was any stage so much as threatened by any outlaws."[1]

There's a lot of things wrong with that statement. Keep in mind that Wyatt Earp was appointed Deputy Sheriff on July 27, 1880. The Tombstone Epitaph in commenting on Wyatt's appointment as Deputy Sheriff said:

"Wyatt has filled various positions in which bravery and determination were requisites, and in every instance proved himself the right man in the right place. He is at present filling the position of shotgun messenger for Wells, Fargo & Co., which he will resign to accept the latter appointment.

"Morgan Earp succeeds his brother as shotgun messenger for Wells, Fargo & Co."[2]

So Wyatt did not ride shotgun for Wells Fargo while he was deputy sheriff.

It is doubtful that he had the authority to deputize his brother Morgan as an assistant in the Sheriff's office while he was riding shotgun even if he had wanted to.

I researched the files in the Wells Fargo & Co. corporate archives at the Wells Fargo Bank in San Francisco. Unfortunately, they did not have a complete record of the payments made between January and July 1880, but their records show that in August 1880 they made two payments listed under general salary to Wyatt Earp. One for $125 and the other for $95.82. Since Wyatt's appointment became effective on July 27, 1880, it seems probable that these payments were for services rendered in the month of July of 1880. Thereafter, a record of payments made through December of 1880 do not show that Wyatt Earp rendered any services or was paid any money. The records do show that in September Morgan Earp was paid $35.83, in October $25, in November, December and January $125, each month, and the last record of Morgan Earp receiving a salary was in February 1881, when he was paid the sum of $95.80.

This covers the period between July 27, 1880 and November 9, 1880, during which Wyatt Earp was a Deputy to Sheriff Shibell of Pima County.

Lake continued with this statement:

"Crowley P. Dake, United States Marshal for Arizona, now appointed Wyatt United States Marshal for the Tombstone District, and Wyatt told the bandits bluntly just what they could expect from him. Wyatt's cowtown experience had acquainted him with a majority

[1]   Wyatt Earp, Frontier Marshal, p. 239.

[2]   Tombstone's Epitaph, p. 169.

of the bad men now terrorizing Arizona and identities of Old Man Clanton's followers were such common knowledge that he stopped individual outlaws in the Tombstone streets to deliver his ukase. Stage robberies ceased, but close on the heels of these warnings Wyatt's favorite horse was stolen. For months Wyatt got no trace of the animal."[1]

Lake is very fuzzy on his dates. Wyatt Earp was not appointed Deputy United States Marshal until late December of 1881, or early January 1882.[2]

So it would appear that from the time Wyatt Earp reached Tombstone in December of 1879 until July of 1880 he had no position as a law enforcement officer, but was employed some of the time as a guard for the Wells, Fargo shipments on the local stage coaches. Thereafter, from July 27, 1880 until November 9, 1880, he served as Deputy Sheriff and it was probably during that period of time that he generated the undying hatred of the outlaw element that will be described more fully in a chapter headed, "The Cowboys."

---

[1]   Wyatt Earp, Frontier Marshal, pp. 239-240.

[2]   U.S. Marshals of New Mexico and Arizona Territory, p. 123.

CHAPTER XXII

THE KILLING OF
MARSHAL WHITE

IN the fall of 1880, Tombstone's first City Marshal, Fred White, was shot and killed by one of the local cowboy outlaws known as William "Curly Bill Brocius." It seems that a number of the cowboy element were in town throwing a drunken celebration. Several of them started firing off their pistols, creating a disturbance that was against the law, and Marshal Fred White determined to put a stop to it. He accosted Curly Bill, placed him under arrest and attempted to disarm him. In the succeeding scuffle, Curly Bill's gun was discharged, striking the Marshal in the groin and inflicting a grievous wound from which he died. Curly Bill was struck on the head and rendered hors d'combat by someone, depending upon whom you believe, and landed in jail. Afterwards, he was transferred to Tucson where he supposedly stood trial for the murder of Marshal White and was acquitted.

This case is an excellent example of how difficult it is to get the truth about any event in which Wyatt Earp was involved. The event has been chronicled by numerous authors, some of whom seem to have been fairly competent researchers, yet their stories are so totally different that one sometimes has to wonder if they are deliberately misstating the facts, and certainly who is stating the true facts.

The first written report of the shooting appeared in the Tombstone Epitaph on October 28, 1880 as follows:

"About 12:30 last night, a series of pistol shots startled the late goers on the streets, and visions of funerals, etc. flitted through the brain of the EPITAPH local and the results proved that his surmises were correct. The result in a few words is as follows: A lot of Texas cowboys, as they are called, began firing at the moon and stars on Allen Street, near Sixth. City Marshal White, who happened to be in the immediate neighborhood, interfered to prevent violation of City ordinance, and was ruthlessly shot by one of the number. Deputy Sheriff Earp, who is ever to the front when duty calls, arrived just in the nick of time. Seeing the Marshal fall, he promptly knocked his assailant down with a six shooter, and as promptly locked him up, and with the assistance of his brothers, Virgil and Morgan, went in pursuit of the others. That he found them, an inventory of the roster of the City Prison this morning will testify. Marshal White was shot in the left groin, the ball passing nearly through, and being cut from the buttock by Dr. Matthew. The wound is serious though not a fatal one. Too much praise cannot be given to the Marshal for his gallant attempt to arrest the violators of the ordinance, nor to Deputy Sheriff Earp and his brothers for the energy displayed in bringing the murderers to arrest. At last accounts, 9 a.m., Marshal White was sleeping, and strong hopes of his ultimate recovery were expected."[1]

On the following day, October 29th, the Epitaph reported further:

"The party who shot Marshal White Tuesday night [sic. Thursday morning, October 28th] was brought before Judge Gray yesterday morning on a warrant charging him with assault to murder. The complaint was made by Deputy Sheriff Earp. The prisoner asked until 10 o'clock to enable him to secure counsel. At 10 o'clock the prisoner reappeared in company with his counsel, Judge Haynes, of Tucson, and waiving examination, was committed to jail to await the next meeting of the Grand Jury. He gave the name of William Rosciotis, and claimed to hail from San Simon County. Rumor at the time being rife that Marshal White would not live until sundown, and that a Vigilance committee was organizing to hang the prisoner, it was deemed best to take him to Tucson. A buggy was at hand and Deputy Sheriff Earp, accompanied by George Collins, started. They were guarded for several miles out of town by Messrs. Virgil and Morgan Earp, and others."[2]

Marshal White died on Saturday, October 30, 1880, but before doing so, is reported to have made a death bed statement in which he absolved Curly Bill of intent to kill him saying that he had attempted to jerk the outlaw's gun out of his hand and the weapon discharged accidentally. That statement is said to have ultimately resulted in the discharge of Curly Bill on the murder charge.

The Epitaph's story seems rather straightforward and uncomplicated, but that is without figuring the genius of anything connected with Wyatt Earp to create controversy.

One of the first authors to put Tombstone on the map as the wildest town in the West, "The Town Too Tough to Die," was Walter Noble Burns -- a wonderful story teller; not too great a historian. In his book, Tombstone, first published in 1927, he makes no reference to any newspaper reports or to any other reliable source for his story about the killing of Marshal White. Quite obviously he did not have access to the files of the Tombstone Epitaph for according to Douglas D. Martin, author of a book entitled Tombstone's Epitaph, published in 1951, the files of the Epitaph for the years 1880, 1881 and 1882

1   Tombstone Epitaph, October 28, 1880.

2   Tombstone Epitaph, October 29, 1880.

were thought to have been destroyed in a fire and were missing for sixty years or more until discovered by him in the University of California Library at Berkeley, California and in the Arizona Pioneer Historical Society Library at Tucson, Arizona.[1]

Burn's version is a slightly romanticized version of the Epitaph report of the killing, with no basic conflicts, but he contributed to the general confusion by making the following statement:

"After a preliminary hearing before Justice Gray, Curly Bill, who gave his name as William Brocius, as appeared by the official records, though old timers who knew him say it was William Graham, was removed to Tucson where he stood trial before Justice Neugass. Curly Bill testified that Marshal White had caused his own death by the violence with which he had seized the outlaw's six-shooter. This view of the fatality was sustained by Wyatt Earp on the witness stand and by a dying statement under oath by Marshal White and submitted to the Court. Thus exonerated by the two officers concerned in the affair, Curly Bill was acquitted, Justice Neugass holding the tragedy a 'misadventure.'"[2]

Burn's contribution to the confusion arises from this. He states that there was a preliminary hearing before Judge Gray. This is not true. There was no preliminary hearing before Judge Gray. There was only an arraignment before Judge Gray in Tombstone, at which time Curly Bill was advised of the charges and bail was set. Then he says that Curly Bill stood trial before Justice Neugass. That statement caused this author to spend a great deal of time hunting for the record without success, before finally determining that there was no trial before Justice Neugass. Justice Neugass was a Justice of the Peace and the proceeding held before him was a preliminary hearing, the only purpose of which was to determine if there was probable cause to hold the defendant for appearance before a grand jury.

That is the reason that all of the research failed to turn up any court record of the proceedings had in Tucson. A justice court is not a court of record and no permanent record would be made of a preliminary hearing if the prisoner was discharged. It not being a trial in the court of general jurisdiction, there would never had been any record in the County Clerk's office in Tucson, and there was none.

As can be expected, Stuart N. Lake told the story a little differently. He says that on October 27, 1880, when Wyatt returned to Tombstone from Tucson, he found the camp in an uproar and the

---

[1]   Ibid, pp. 2-3.

[2]   Tombstone, p. 78.

cowboys in possession of Allen Street. He goes on to say that Marshal White told Wyatt that the outlaws had been carousing in the town for two days and had made several gun-plays, and that when he had appealed to Deputy Sheriff Behan for help, Behan had refused to help him arrest them. He had Wyatt directing the operation, saying to Marshal White: "You go in from this side, and I'll come in from the other," and from that point on his story of the killing is substantially the same as that of the Tombstone Epitaph and Walter Noble Burns.[1]

One glaring error in Lake's or Wyatt's story is the statement that White told Wyatt that when he appealed for help to Sheriff Behan, he had refused to help arrest the cowboys. Remember that Wyatt Earp was Deputy Sheriff until he submitted his resignation to Sheriff Charles Shibell on November 9, 1880, and that John Behan was appointed to fill the vacancy created by Wyatt's resignation. So, on October 27, 1880, John Behan was not a Deputy Sheriff in Tombstone.

It hardly seems this erroneous statement could have been accidental. It must have been made intentionally in order to cast a bad reflection on Behan.

Lake also quoted a letter from Fred Dodge who was present and participated in the incident as follows:

"Wyatt's coolness and nerve never showed to better advantage than they did that night, Fred Dodge wrote me recently. 'When Morgan and I reached him, Wyatt was squatted on his heels beside Curly Bill and Fred White.

"Curly Bill's friends were pot-shooting at him in the dark. The shooting was lively and slugs were hitting the chimney and cabin. All of us squatted. In all that racket, Wyatt's voice was as even and quiet as usual. 'Put out the fire in Fred's clothes,' he said. White had been shot at such close range that his coat was burning."[2]

Fred Dodge was a witness to the killing. His story was not very much at odds with the story told by Stuart N. Lake or reported in the Tombstone Epitaph, but he adds some details that were not otherwise reported. He says that the killing took place right at the rear end, close by the chimney of a cabin occupied by Morgan Earp and himself and sometimes by Wyatt. The cabin was on a lot right behind where the Birdcage Theater was afterward built. After Wyatt had arrested Curly Bill, he helped take him to the lock-up, which was close by, and he and Morgan were left to guard the lock-up while Wyatt and Virgil and several others started around the town to roundup the rest of the

---

[1]   Wyatt Earp, Frontier Marshal, pp. 243-244.

[2]   Ibid, p. 244.

rustlers. He said they kept bringing men to the lock-up until it could not hold any more. In this respect, his story backs up the story printed in the <u>Tombstone Epitaph</u>.[1]

Some interesting questions are raised from an analysis of the above and some succeeding stories about the shooting of Fred White.

The Tombstone <u>Epitaph</u> story said that Wyatt Earp, with the assistance of his brothers, Virgil and Morgan (it didn't mention Fred Dodge) "went in pursuit of the others. That he found them, an inventory of the roster of the City Prison this morning will testify."[2]

Burns does not mention the fact that anyone other than Curly Bill was arrested. That tends to substantiate the suspicion that he had no access to the Tombstone <u>Epitaph</u> at the time he was writing.

Lake states that they arrested Frank Patterson, the two McLaurys, Billy Clanton, and Pony Deal. He could have gotten this information from Fred Dodge or from Wyatt Earp himself. Lake said that Wyatt Earp walked up to each of the people that he arrested, buffaloed them with his six-shooter and hauled them off to jail. He quotes Wyatt Earp as saying:

"They remembered their sore heads longer than they did the Judge's warning. They never forgave the manhandling. If I do say so myself, I was thorough."[3]

William M. Breakenridge was a young man who was one of the first deputies appointed by Sheriff Behan after he was made Sheriff of Cochise County in 1881. Some have said that he was only a civil deputy but any student of Tombstone history would have to conclude that he was at times involved in law enforcement. From his position as a Deputy Sheriff for Behan, one could certainly see reasons for his prejudice against the Earps. Yet, in the main an examination of his biography fails to reveal any very strong animosity against the Earps. At any rate, although he does not claim to have been a witness, he was in and about Tombstone at the time of the killing of Fred White and his story is worth recording.

In his book, <u>Helldorado</u>, published in 1928, he described the killing of Fred White substantially the way it had been described by the Tombstone <u>Epitaph</u> and Stuart N. Lake with one notable and very important exception. He says that when the cowboys scattered, Curly Bill ran into an alley where he was caught by Marshal White and Virgil Earp, whom the Marshal had summoned to assist him in making the arrest. And he says that it was Virgil Earp, not Wyatt

---

[1]   <u>Undercover For Wells Fargo</u>, p. 9-10.

[2]   <u>Tombstone's Epitaph</u>, p. 170.

[3]   <u>Wyatt Earp, Frontier Marshal</u>, p. 244.

Earp, who grasped Curly Bill from behind around his arms as White took hold of the gun that went off and killed him. He also says that Curly Bill gave himself up to Virgil Earp and was taken to Tucson for trial.

"He was held in jail there for a month. At his trial Virgil Earp testified that, when White told Curly to give up his gun, he (Earp) grasped Curly Bill from behind around the waist, that White jerked the gun out of Curly's hand, and that it was an accidental shot. He said that he (Virgil) examined the gun at the time and there were still five loads left in it, showing that Curly had not been a party to shooting up the town and disturbing the peace. Curly was acquitted."[1]

There are at least three things wrong with Breakenridge's story. First, he says that Fred White was elected on January 6, 1880. The election was held on January 4, 1880. Then he says that the shooting of Marshal White occurred on November 6, 1880. It was reported in the Tombstone Epitaph on October 28, 1880 and that is the date that I believe it occurred. I note that Fred Dodge also stated it occurred on November 6, and I think that Breakenridge may have gotten the date from Dodge or visa versa. At any rate, they were wrong. The most important error in Breakenridge's story is that he says that Virgil Earp is the one who grasped Curly Bill from behind around his arms and that it was Virgil Earp who was present and arrested Curly Bill.

It is also interesting to note that he said that Curly Bill was taken to Tucson, the County seat, for trial and that he was held there for a month. If he was in jail for a month in Tucson, he would not have been in Charleston to have a conversation with Wyatt Earp that is reported hereafter about the Pima County election where Sheriff Shibell contested the election returns from San Simon precinct that will be detailed later.

Frank Waters, who purportedly got most of his information from "Aunt Allie," Virgil Earp's widow, adds a few details, but in general agrees with the story told by Breakenridge. He says that Marshal White deputized Virgil Earp to help him arrest the cowboys and that it was Virgil Earp who arrested Curly Bill, and that Curly Bill was taken to Tucson for trial and acquitted. Waters does not say who testified at the hearing in Tombstone, but the implication is that it was Virgil.[2]

Waters' account sounds suspiciously like the story told by

---

[1]   Helldorado, pp. 101-102.

[2]   Earp Brothers of Tombstone, p. 106.

Breakenridge. In it he refers to Deputy Sheriff Billy Breakenridge, although at the time of the shooting, Breakenridge was not a Deputy Sheriff, and in his own account of the shooting, Breakenridge gives no source for his information, nor does he state that he was a witness to any of the events.

John Myers wrote two books dealing with Tombstone, one entitled, The Last Chance, published in 1950 and the other entitled Doc Holliday, published in 1955. At first blush, both of his books appear to be based upon substantial research and have a ring of authenticity about them, but upon close scrutiny it is apparent that he got his information from Walter Noble Burns and Stuart N. Lake. In The Last Chance, his account of the killing of Fred White is copied almost word for word from Lake without mentioning where he got it. Of more interest however, is his description of the event in his biography of Doc Holliday.

In that book he wrote:

"When Curly Bill led his crew into town, with intent to hurrah it, White did not hold back, as he could have been pardoned for doing in the absence of backing from his superiors. Having no deputies, he appealed to the Earps - including Doc - for help in rounding up the raiders.

"In the course of the fracas that followed Fred White was slain by Curly, and it was Doc - as he himself remarked to an interviewing newspaperman - who incurred the wrath of the outlaw leader by putting him under arrest. For some decades Western Chroniclers have differed as to whether the exploit of jailing Bill should be credited to Virgil Earp or Wyatt. It was not Doc's practice to deny anything, including his own life, to one, in particular, of this pair of brothers, but at the time he could hardly have foreseen that their parisians - writing decades later - would stake out claims for them to this undertaking. Doc's personal claim dated from 1882, and he plainly saw nothing to get excited about. Far from trying to dramatize it or play it up into a major feat of arms, he treated the matter with causal brevity.

"'Trouble first arose with them,' he said in the course of describing his difficulties with the cowboys of southern Arizona to a Denver reporter, 'by the killing of Marshal White by Curly Bill. Marshal White fell into my arms when he was shot and I arrested Curly Bill.'"[1]

If Myers' story is true, it is peculiar that no other writer of the events of early Tombstone has made such a report, and it is also suspicious that he cites not a single source, not even the name of the

---

[1]   Doc Holliday. p. 132.

newspaper reporter to whom Doc purportedly told the story, by which his story could be even partially verified.

These various stories raise some interesting questions. Number one: When did it happen?

That is easier to answer if one knows that October 28, 1880 was a Thursday. The Tombstone Epitaph reported the incident in it's October 28th edition and started its story with the statement:

"About 12:30 last night a series of pistol shots startled the late goers on the Street --."

Quite obviously what the paper should have said was "about 12:30 this morning," for at the end of the story it says:

"At last reports, 8 a.m., Marshal White was sleeping." The paper for Friday, October 29th stated:

"The party who shot Marshal White Tuesday night [sic. Thursday morning] was brought before Judge Gray yesterday morning on a warrant --"

On October 29th, a Friday, yesterday morning would have been Thursday, October 28th. So it is obvious that the shooting occurred at about 12:30 a.m. on Thursday, October 28th, and that the arraignment before Judge Gray occurred later on the same day.

It is interesting that both Fred Dodge and Billy Breakenridge reported the date of the event to be November 6th. They were in communication with each other in the late 1920's and it's a good guess that one of them got the date from the other. In any event, they were both wrong.

Number two: Was it an accident?

All the reports seem to agree that the weapon was a single action Colt six-shooter. If it was single action, in good working condition and not defective, it could only be fired after the hammer was intentionally pulled back cocking the gun. If Curly Bill took his gun from the holster for the purpose of handing it to Fred White it would not have discharged even if White had grabbed the barrel and jerked it, or if either Wyatt or Virgil Earp had wrapped his arms around Curly Bill, and in some way jerked the pistol. Keeping in mind that this all occurred in the darkness, it is quite possible that Curly Bill either had his gun already cocked in his hand at the time he was apprehended by Fred White, or that he cocked it as he drew it, intending to shoot Fred White.

Number three: Who arrested Curly Bill, Wyatt Earp, Virgil Earp, or Doc Holliday?

None of the writers, some of whom have done a great deal of research, seem to have gone to the one source that would settle the argument. That is the Court Records of the trial or hearing of the murder charges filed against Curly Bill at Tucson, or newspaper reports of the ensuing Court proceedings. That was the state of my knowledge on the subject until the spring of 1989.

That spring I took a trip to Arizona for the purpose of researching some of the problems related to Wyatt Earp. I found, just as I had suspected, that there were no court records available. Either there never was any or they are missing. The Count Clerk reported that there are no court records in Tucson prior to 1882, and that the State Archives have been unable to produce any. Further, if as I suspected, the Court proceeding had been a preliminary hearing, and not a jury trial, they would have been held in a Justice Court. A Justice Court is not now, and was not then, a court of record, and if the prisoner were discharged without being bound over for appearance before the Grand Jury, no permanent record would have ever been made.

I researched the files of the Tombstone Epitaph and the Tombstone Nugget for December 1880 and January 1881 and found no reports about either the killing of Marshal White nor the trial of Bill Brocius. The primary reason I believe is that no complete copies of either paper are available for that period. After almost giving up, I finally got lucky and found the answer. It appeared on the front page of the Arizona Weekly Citizen dated Saturday, January 1, 1881 and read as follows:

"'CURLY BILL' his examination concluded before Justice Neugass -- important testimony for the Defense -- The Justice's Decision.

"The examination of William Brocius alias Curly Bill, charged with murder in the killing of Marshal White, of Tombstone, was concluded Monday morning before Justice of the Peace Neugass. All the testimony is clear and decidedly to the point. Wyatt Earp was called for the Territory, testified. On the 27th of last October was Deputy Sheriff; resided at Tombstone; saw defendant that night at the time Marshal White was shot; was present at the time the fatal shot was fired; saw Mr. Johnson there at the time; my brother came up immediately after; this affair occurred in back of a building in a vacant lot between Allen and Tough Nut Streets; I was in Billy Owens' saloon and heard three or four shots fired; upon hearing the first shot I ran out in the street and I saw the flash of a pistol up the Street about a block from where I was; several shots were fired in quick succession; ran up as quick as I could, and when I got there I met my brother, Morgan Earp, and a man by the name of Dodge; I asked my brother who it was that did the shooting and he said he didn't know - some fellows who ran behind that building; I asked him for his six-shooter and he sent me to Dodge; after I got the pistol I ran around the building and as I turned the corner I ran past this man Johnson, who was standing near the corner of the building; I ran between him and the corner of the building, but before I got there I heard White say: 'I am an officer, give me your pistol,' and just as I was almost there I saw the defendant pull his pistol out of his scabbard and Marshal White grabbed hold of the barrel of it; the parties were not more (than) two feet apart facing each other; both had hold of the pistol, and just then I threw my arms around the defendant to see if he held any other weapons, and looked over his shoulder, and White saw me and said: 'Now you G--- D--- --- of a B----, give up that pistol;' and he gave a quick jerk and the pistol went off; White had it in his hands; and when he fell to the ground, shot, the pistol dropped and I picked it up; as he fell, he said, 'I am shot.' The defendant stood still from the time I first saw him until the pistol went off; when I took the defendant in charge he said, 'What have I done? I have not done anything to be arrested for.' When the pistol exploded, I knocked the defendant down with my six-shooter; he did not get up until I stepped over and picked up the pistol, which had fallen out of White's hands as he fell; I then walked up to the defendant, caught him by the collar and told him to get up. I did not notice that he was drunk; if he was, I did not notice it. When I turned the corner he was in the act of taking the pistol out of his scabbard. I examine the pistol afterwards and found only one cartridge discharged, five remaining. The pistol was a Colt's 45 caliber."[1]

His testimony at the hearing was corroborated by the testimony of James K. Johnson who was the person that Wyatt said he passed by as he ran to the scene, and by his brother Morgan. The name of Virgil Earp does not appear in the newspaper account of the hearing, so it appears that both Breakenridge and Waters were either intentionally or accidentally misstating the facts when they attributed the arrest of Curly Bill to Virgil.

A most important witness was one Jacob Gruber, gunsmith, who testified that he had examined the pistol of Curly Bill and that it was defective so that it could be discharged at half cock.

I believe that it was this testimony together with the testimony of Wyatt Earp that resulted in the discharge of Curly Bill without trial. The testimony of Wyatt, Morgan and Johnson established that the shooting was probably an accident, and the testimony of Jacob Gruber established that the condition of the gun would not preclude an accidental shooting.

This should settle the argument among the authors and researchers about who arrested Curly Bill Brocius. It was Wyatt. Nor Virgil Earp. Not Doc Holliday.

A close examination of the reported testimony of Wyatt Earp at

---

[1]   Arizona Weekly Citizen, January 1, 1881.

the preliminary hearing raises some other interesting questions about the story as told by Lake.

Lake has Wyatt returning home from Tucson to find the cowboys in possession of Allen Street, and he has Marshal White sending for Wyatt to help him subdue them. He has Earp and White conferring on strategy before attempting to arrest Curly Bill.

In his testimony, Earp never mentioned being summoned by Marshal White, but said he was in Billy Owens' Saloon when he heard three or four shots being fired. He ran out in the Street and saw the flash of a pistol up the Street about a block. If this was true, he certainly did not confer on strategy with Marshal White.

Another interesting fact that appears from Wyatt Earp's testimony is that he, then being Deputy Sheriff in a town as tough as Tombstone, was apparently unarmed. He had to borrow a gun from Fred Dodge.

If this was true, at least at that time, Wyatt Earp must have felt perfectly safe in the town without a firearm.

CHAPTER XXIII

THE CONTESTED ELECTION OF
SHERIFF SHIBELL

A general county election was scheduled for November 2, 1880 and one of the contested offices was that of Charles Shibell, the Sheriff of Pima County for whom Wyatt was serving as a Deputy. Lake says that the Law and Order Party selected Bob Paul of Tucson, a Deputy United States Marshal and shotgun messenger for Wells, Fargo to run against Shibell. He quotes Earp as saying: "I'm supporting Bob Paul." Thereupon, he resigned as Shibell's Deputy.

Lake then proceeds to get his dates all mixed up and it becomes rather important. Note the following.

"Shibell moved to offset opposition by appointing Johnny Behan to succeed Wyatt Earp as Deputy Sheriff and to repair political fences. One result was the prompt renewal of rustler activities. A second was the return of the Clanton - Curly Bill crowd, to hurrah, Tombstone."

He then proceeds to describe the killing of Marshal White, an event that occurred on October 28th, 1880.[1]

According to the sequence of events described by Lake, Wyatt Earp was not a Deputy Sheriff at the time that Marshal White was killed, although the Tombstone Epitaph referred to him as a Deputy Sheriff. According to Lake's story, the Deputy Sheriff for Tombstone at that time was Johnny Behan, for he had Wyatt saying that when White appealed to Deputy Sheriff Behan for help, Behan had refused to help arrest Curly Bill and his bunch of rowdies.[2]

Lake goes on to say: "On the Tuesday following White's death, Pima County went to the polls. When the votes were counted, Shibell apparently had been re-elected by a majority of 47. Wyatt noted that the San Simon Precinct, an outlaw stronghold, voting at Galeyville, showed 104 cast, 103 for Shibell, and one for Bob Paul.

"'There aren't fifty votes in the precinct,' Wyatt declared. 'You demand a recount,' he told Bob. 'and if I can make Curly Bill talk, you'll be Sheriff.'

"Wyatt rode to Charleston and told Curly Bill flatly that he could reveal what had happened in the San Simon precinct on election day

---

[1]   Wyatt Earp, Frontier Marshal, p. 243.

[2]   Ibid, p. 243.

or be hanged for the murder of Marshal White.

"'Come through about the Galeyville votes,' Wyatt told the outlaw. 'and I won't dispute White's dying statement. Otherwise, I'll swear you shot White as he reached for your gun. If the law doesn't hang you on that, Fred White's friends will.'

"Wyatt's bluff stood up. Curly Bill agreed to get affidavits from the man who had stuffed the San Simon ballot box . . .

"In December, on the strength of affidavits which Wyatt obtained through Curly Bill, the Board of Elections threw out the San Simon ballots and declared Bob Paul's election. Shibell appealed to the courts and held office pending decision. Curly Bill was arraigned for the death of Fred White and discharged on the strength of White's ante-mortem statement."[1]

The entire statement deserves close scrutiny for it does not appear to square with the facts.

Let's look first at the statement that: "Wyatt rode to Charleston and told Curly Bill flatly that he could reveal what had happened in the San Simon Precinct on Election Day or be hanged for the Murder of Marshal White."

Wyatt Earp could not have ridden to Charleston and told Curly Bill anything because after his arraignment on October 29 before Judge Gray, he waved examination (that would have been preliminary examination) and was committed to jail to await the next meeting of the Grand Jury.[2] On that same day, Wyatt Earp and George Collins started for Tucson where they lodged him in jail to await further proceedings, and he remained there until a completion of his hearing on December 27th, 1880 when he was discharged from custody.

At Tucson, Curly Bill's lawyer, J.C. Perry, filed a motion to vacate the waiver of the preliminary hearing before Justice Neugass. The motion was granted and the preliminary hearing was set for December 22nd. The witnesses not being readily available on that date, the matter was continued to December 27, when after hearing the evidence outlined in the chapter on "The Killing of Marshal White," the Justice held that the evidence was insufficient to hold Curly Bill for trial and discharged him from custody.[3]

Nor does there appear to be any truth to the statement that, "Curly Bill agreed to get affidavits from the man who had stuffed the

---

[1]   Wyatt Earp, Frontier Marshal, p. 245.

[2]   Tombstone's Epitaph, p. 170.

[3]   Tucson Citizen, December 28, 1880; Tucson Star, December 28, 1880.

San Simon ballot box." In the lengthy court proceedings that were had in the trial of the contested election, no affidavits were submitted, and all of the testimony was taken in court from eye witnesses.

Lake's statement quoting Earp as saying: "I'm supporting Bob Paul," thereupon resigning as Shibell's deputy intimates, if it doesn't directly say, that Earp resigned as Shibell's deputy before the election. The facts are that he resigned on November 9th, a week after the election. Although Earp may have been supporting Bob Paul, he did so as a deputy to Sheriff Shibell. After the election, Earp did play a large part in aiding and assisting Bob Paul in his legal contest of the election results. Earp was active in securing witnesses, serving subpoenas, etc., that eventually resulted in Bob Paul reversing the results of the election and gaining the office of sheriff of Pima County.

There were numerous allegations of fraud in the election, but the principal one was in the San Simon voting precinct. In that precinct, the election judges had certified 103 votes for Shibell, and one for Bob Paul. A look at the people who ran the election in the San Simon voting precinct would immediately raise suspicion that something crooked had gone on. The San Simon polling place was originally scheduled to be at Joe Hill's house, with Ike Clanton designated as the election inspector and John Ringo and H.A. Thompson as election judges. The election results were certified to the County Election Board by someone named "Henry Johnson." Nobody seemed to know who Henry Johnson was, but Wyatt Earp finally smoked out the fact that Henry Johnson, who certified the election results from the San Simon precinct, was the same person as James K. Johnson who was present when Marshal White was killed and who testified at Curly Bill's preliminary hearing. Johnson was one of the members of Curly Bill's gang of rustlers.

The Pima County Board met on November 15th, 1880 and tallied the returns from all of the precincts. They declared Shibell elected Sheriff. Thereafter, on November 19th, Bob Paul started proceedings to contest the election. The legal proceedings were very interesting, but they would almost make another book. It is sufficient to say that the case was transferred to the district court in Tucson, and after much legal maneuvering and a continuance, the trial finally began on January 17, 1881. The evidence of fraud was overwhelming. The Arizona Weekly Star for January 20, 1881 reporting on the trial said:

"Some very singular evidence was brought out yesterday in the hearing of the above case before the district court. There is evidently 'something very rotten in Denmark,' or in plain language there has been some big cheating somewhere, and by some persons. The evidence is very straight forward and to the point and unless an earth, or some other kind of quake, occurs to upset the testimony given yesterday, why it looks to us like a very plain case, that out of 104 votes cast at San Simon, about 100 were fraudulent. We shall watch the further proceedings with great interest and trust that the whole matter will be sifted to bed-rock and hope that if fraud is proven, that fraud will meet its just reward. Of course the end has not been reached, the other side has to be heard, but if no more is made in the different evidence from the defendant, than was made yesterday in the cross-examination of the plaintiff's witnesses, why a case appears about divided, so far as the results of the election depends upon the returns for San Simon. We regret that such appears to be the fact --- that there is the possibility of fraud having been committed -- and we cannot but wish for the honor of the County and all concerned, that something may be developed whereby the honesty of the election to the Sheriff and other County Officers will be established, but we have fears that our wishes will not be realized."[1]

On January 29, 1881, Judge French filed his written decision in the case. He declared the entire vote cast for Shibell at San Simon invalid. Ultimately ruling that of 3,312 legal votes cast, Paul had received 1,684 and Shibell 1,628 and declared that Robert H. Paul was duly elected Sheriff.[2]

It is interesting to note that the Arizona Weekly Star for January 27, 1881 reported the conclusion of the case two days before Judge French filed his written decision on January 29th. They miscalculated the Judges ruling and misstated the results. The paper made the following report:

"THE CLOSE

"The end of the contest has been reached. The evidence we believe is now all before the court, save that of one witness, and rebuttal, and the result may be summed up as follows: throwing out the 92 votes in San Simon, which were clearly illegal, and omitting the Tres Alimos vote, which gives Paul 12 votes, and adopting the Tombstone count, which was made in court, which gives Paul 48 majority in that precinct, Shibell comes out with 4 majority on the whole count.

"What has the evidence in the case shown? Clearly that there has been reckless counting in Tombstone, fraud at San Simon, and carelessness on the part of the election board at Tres Alimos. It shows more, be it said to the honor of Mr. Shibell, that neither directly nor

---

[1] Arizona Weekly Star, January 20, 1881, (Special Collections Section, University of Arizona Library).

[2] Opinion of Judge C.G.W. French, January 29, 1881. Case #479, Pima County Clerk, Tucson, Arizona.

indirectly has he been connected with the irregularity or fraud which may have been committed.

"It shows conclusively that after all fraud, mistakes and irregularities have been eliminated Mr. Shibell, although by small majority, has been elected to the office of sheriff of Pima County by the people."[1]

It's hard to understand why the paper would have declared Shibell to be elected by a small majority before the judges decision was announced. Apparently this paper was extremely partisan and just hated to face the reality of their protege losing the election, or perhaps printed the story before the Judge's opinion was filed in the hopes that it might influence his final decision. At any rate, they were wrong, and the final decision gave the office to Bob Paul.

One might think that the court decision would settle the matter, but it did not, for Shibell's lawyers immediately filed an appeal to the Arizona Supreme Court. The appeal automatically stayed the judgement of the court, and left Shibell in office until the appeal was decided about two and a half months later.

On April 12, 1881, the Supreme Court of the Territory made an order dismissing the appeal, thus finally making Bob Paul the Sheriff of Pima County.[2]

Between the date of the election and the decision by the Supreme Court that gave the election to Bob Paul, the Territorial Legislature passed an enabling act effective February 1, 1881, establishing Cochise County out of the Eastern part of Pima County so that by the time Bob Paul took office, Tombstone was no longer under his jurisdiction.

As we shall see later, the election of Bob Paul, Wyatt Earp's friend, as Sheriff of Pima County would have considerable effect on Wyatt's future. He would later be accused of having committed murder in Pima County and leaving the state to avoid arrest. Extradition proceedings against Wyatt Earp and Doc Holliday in the State of Colorado were unsuccessfully handled by Bob Paul. Neither Earp nor Holliday were ever returned to Arizona to answer the murder charges.

The extradition proceedings have been reported by numerous authors, all of which agree that extradition was denied by Governor Pitkin of Colorado. Although most of the writers refer to reports of

---

[1] Arizona Weekly Star, January 27, 1881. Special Collections Section, University of Arizona Library.

[2] Order of the Supreme Court, April 12, 1881, In Case of Shibell, Paul, Case #479.

the proceedings in various newspapers, none that I have found cite the Governor's extradition files. In the summer of 1991, I found a good reason for this.

The Governor's extradition files are kept in the State Archives, and are filed in date order. A thorough search of all the files for the year 1882 fails to reveal any extradition file on Wyatt Earp or his associates. Like so many other files pertaining to the Earps, the file is missing.

CHAPTER XXIV

JOHNNY BEHAN

IN order to understand the circumstances surrounding the Earp-Behan vendetta that was one of the things behind all of the blood letting that occurred in and about Tombstone and ultimately resulted in the Battle of the O.K. Corral and the departure of the Earps from Arizona, it is necessary to take an in-depth look at Johnny Behan, his antecedents and his political connections.

Johnny Behan was about three years older than Wyatt Earp, having been born on October 23, 1845 at Westport, now a part of Kansas City, Missouri. His antecedents are very interesting, but not particularly relevant to the subject under investigation. Suffice to say that in order to avoid being forced into either the Union Army or the Confederate Army during the Civil War, he left Missouri and went to California. He eventually turned up in Northern Arizona where he apparently established a ranch in the vicinity of Prescott and, on October 8, 1866 he was appointed Deputy Sheriff of Yavapai County of which Prescott was the County seat. By October of 1867, he had become under-sheriff to Sheriff Burke and subsequently occupied the same position under Sheriff Moore. His work as a deputy sheriff and under-sheriff were always commented on favorably by the local newspaper, the Miner.

His resignation as under-sheriff was reported in the Miner for March 21, 1868. He resigned in order to run for the office of County Recorder. The Miner reported on June 20, 1868 that he had been elected to that office, one of the most important elective offices in the County.

Behan was elected Sheriff of Yavapai County in 1871. His wife sued him for divorce on May 22, 1875. A divorce decree was issued on June 2, 1875. Custody of his young son, Albert, age 4, was awarded to the mother, and Behan was ordered to pay support in the magnificent sum of $16.66 a month.

The divorce file reveals what later became apparent in Tombstone, that is, that John Behan was a first class womanizer, and apparently not too discreet about it.

In the divorce complaint, Victoria Behan alleged that: "The said defendant--has within two years last past at diverse times and places openly and notoriously visited houses of prostitution . . . and that he did cohabit with the inmates of said houses of prostitution." She

named places, dates, times and the name of one woman.
There's something unusual about the proceedings. That came
in the timing. The complaint was filed on May 22nd. Ordinarily a
defendant has ten days to answer a complaint, but Behan's answer
was filed four days later on the 26th. His answer was what is known
as a general denial, which denies the plaintiff's allegations and puts
them on their proof.

Ordinarily after an answer is filed, it takes considerable time to
get a hearing date, but in this case, on the day the answer was filed
the Judge made an order appointing his clerk referee to take
testimony and proof and report the same to the court.

Thereafter, on June 1st, William Wilkerson, the clerk, took
depositions of Mrs. Behan and two men witnesses who proved by their
own knowledge that allegations that John Behan regularly patronized
houses of prostitution were true.

No evidence was offered on behalf of the defendant. The next
day Judge Charles Atwood issued his judgement granting the divorce.

So, it was only ten days from the filing of the divorce action to
the date of judgement. A rather unusual procedure it seems. One
can't help wondering what the hurry was, and how Behan got away
with paying no support for his spouse and only $16.66 per month for
child support.

Behan was elected to represent Yavapai County in the Seventh
State Legislative Assembly that met in 1873. Afterwards, when there
was a big mining boom at Signal, Arizona in Mojave County, Behan
moved there and ran for Sheriff. He was defeated but later
successfully ran for the territorial Legislature and was elected to
represent Mojave County in the Tenth Legislative Assembly which
met in 1879. It was while a member of the Legislative Assembly that
he made connections with politicians who later founded a powerful
alliance to use the county government of Cochise County for their
own purposes. One of these people was Artemus Emmett Fay, editor
of the Tucson Star. Glenn G. Boyer says that, "The meeting between
Fay and Behan at the 10th Assembly during the governorship of John
C. Fremont laid the cornerstone for what was to be known as the
County Ring at Tombstone. The political machine that they created
was to be at the root of much, if not all, of the violence to take place
there - by omission if not by commission."[1]

Others who would be important to Behan's political career were
Harry Martyn Woods, who would be editor of the Tombstone Nugget
for Artemus Fay and who would also fill the position of under-sheriff
to Behan; Don Dunbar, the man who introduced the Cochise County
enabling act in the Legislative Assembly; and his brother, John

[1]   John Behan Assistant Folk Hero, Real West, April 1981.

Dunbar, who would be Behan's partner in the livery stable business at Tombstone and County Treasurer. A cozy little arrangement.

Boyer says that the Dunbars had acquired considerable political influence by their acquaintances back in Maine with James G. Blaine, U.S. Secretary of State and a real power in national Republican politics.

In October of 1879, an incident occurred that would in the future have an important affect on the relationship between Wyatt Earp and Johnny Behan. Behan was acting as a Deputy Sheriff out of Gilette, a small town between Prescott and Phoenix when, in pursuit of Mexican stage robbers, the posse he was with encountered a group of entertainers riding in rented stages from Tucson to Prescott. One of the members of that group of entertainers was 18 year old Josephine Sarah Marcus, a runaway from what has sometimes been referred to as a prominent and wealthy San Francisco family. Behan met Josephine, and immediately began courting her. He returned to Prescott with the entertainment troupe and persuaded her to marry him. However, before this could be accomplished, her family caught up with her and got her to return to San Francisco. He had been planning to move to Tombstone, which at that time was getting a lot of publicity as a booming silver town, and they agreed that as soon as he was able to establish himself in Tombstone, he would send for her and she would come to Tombstone and marry him.

Following this plan, in the early part of 1880 -- I have not been able to establish the exact date -- Johnny Behan moved to Tombstone where he obtained employment as a bartender at the Grand hotel and started a livery stable known as The Dexter Corral in partnership with John O. Dunbar. Later that same year, Josephine Marcus arrived in Tombstone on the stage coach. The exact date, again, is hard to establish, but it must have been after July 27, when Wyatt Earp was appointed Deputy Sheriff and his job as guard for the Wells Fargo stage was taken over by his brother Morgan, for on the stage ride to Tombstone Josephine met Morgan Earp who was riding shotgun.[1]

The details are not clear as Josephine was never really honest about her relationship with Johnny Behan. She told her story to Mabel Earp Carson and Vanola Earp Ackerman from which Boyer got the information to write the book entitled, I Married Wyatt Earp, but it is apparent that she set up housekeeping with Johnny Behan in the absence of a marriage license and took care of Johnny Behan's son, Albert, who, although legally in his mother's custody, was

---

[1]   I Married Wyatt Earp, p. 21.

temporarily staying with his father. She apparently lived with Behan for more than one year, and probably with money that she received from her parents, purchased a house that was put in Behan's name and which he eventually beat her out of.

At any rate, the relationship between Johnny Behan and Josephine was not all together satisfactory as she discovered that, true to form, he was also paying court to another woman at the same time. He apparently was quite a lady's man and took his loving where he could get it.

At the same time, Wyatt Earp was living with Mattie Blaylock, his purported wife. Researchers have been unable to find any evidence that a marriage ceremony between them was performed, but under the laws that existed at that time, their relationship would probably have constituted a legal, common law, marriage. At any rate, Wyatt Earp began paying court to Josephine Marcus, and somewhere along the line she dumped Johnny Behan in favor of Wyatt Earp. This probably happened about the time Behan was appointed sheriff of the newly formed Cochise County, as will appear from Behan's testimony at the O.K. Corral murder hearing.

So, in addition to his connections with the politicians who established Cochise County, his relationship with the town-lot company and his friendship with the cowboy element, Johnny Behan had reasons for personal animosity against Wyatt Earp, for what he probably considered stealing his girlfriend.

The political friends that Behan made while in the Territorial Legislature joined together to engineer an enabling act that created a new county from part of Pima County. The new County was named for the Apache Chief, Cochise. Dunbar introduced the bill and has been known as the father of Cochise County.[1]

George W. Parson's, our diarist, may also have had something to do with getting the bill creating the county passed. The entry in his diary on February 2, 1881 certainly indicates that he had more than a passing interest, both in getting the county created and in who was going to get the political appointments. His entry read:

". . . a bill has finally passed and been signed by the governor creating Cochise County - making us pay perhaps $10,000. Now the fight begins for offices. Some of the Tucsonites are here for offices and their names are in - sent in by the governor. Much cheek. Went to prayer meeting tonight and afterwards saw some ladies home. Some wrestling this afternoon. Fellows made me tie one arm to my

---

[1]   Johnny Behan Assistant Folk Hero, <u>Real West</u>, April 1981.

side and tackle Van three times. Finally threw him."[1]

On February 3, 1881, he wrote:

"Much kicking in counsel on account of Tucsonites appointed. Much telegraphing between Mark Hayne and me. I got some private telegrams off from leading men to Governor for his benefit. All out of my pocket. Fellows got back for Sonora this evening thoroughly and entirely disgusted with the Country and each other, though they wouldn't let on at first."[2]

Apparently, Parson's had some rather high connections himself, for on February 7, 1881 he wrote:

"Some more petition business today. Eccleston came for me this a.m. before I was dressed, at banker Hudson's request for me to work for him as County Treasurer, so I pitched in and soon fixed matters, sending a long telegram to governor Fremont and General Rollins - also Mark Hayne - to the latter in Redfern's interest too, as recorder. We sent long letter to R's father to get Blaine, Cameron and Sherman to fix things with Fremont. He responded. So we're in a little now. R. and I to run office together should he get it . . ."[3]

Obviously there was a general scramble for public offices when the legislation creating the new County was adopted. Wyatt Earp, having served as a deputy sheriff for Pima County, and being a Republican, felt that he had the inside track for the appointment. He obviously was not fully aware of the connections of the other most prominent applicant for the job, Johnny Behan, who really had the inside track, even though he was a Democrat. Both being applicants for the position of sheriff, it was obvious that one of them would have to lose. Wyatt Earp, in order to hedge his bets, talked to Johnny Behan about it, and Behan agreed that if Wyatt would withdraw his candidacy for the office of sheriff, Behan would appoint him as under Sheriff, if he got the appointment.

At the preliminary hearing on the O.K. Corral murder case, Behan came near to admitting that something came between them (that something being Josephine Sarah Marcus). Try reading between the lines of Behan's testimony and see what you make of it. Behan was asked the following question:

"Q.: Were not you and Wyatt Earp applicants to Governor Fremont for the appointment of Sheriff of Cochise County, and did not he, (Wyatt) withdraw his application upon your promise to divide the profits of the office, and did you not subsequently refuse to comply

---

1   Private Journal of George W. Parsons, p. 122.

2   Ibid, p. 132.

3   Ibid, p. 123.

with your part of the contract?

"A.: We were both applicants for the office, that is, I was and I understood Earp was. I became satisfied I would get the appointment and then went to Mr. Earp and told him I knew that I would get the appointment, and that I would like to have him in the office with me. I also told him I did not wish him to cease his efforts to get it if he could; that I was sure I would get the appointment and if I did would take him in with me; that in case he got the office, I did not want anything to do with it. He said that was very kind of me. If he got the office, he had brothers to provide for and he could not return the compliment. I said I asked nothing but in case I got it I would like to have him in the office with me. Something later transpired so that I did not employ him in the office."[1]

Behan made no explanation of what transpired, but a good guess is that this is about the time Earp beat Behan out for the affections of Josephine Sarah Marcus.

Behan was a political hack, well entrenched with the most powerful politicians who were intent on making as much money as possible out of the creation and operation of the County Government of Cochise County.   This background sets the stage for future troubles.

---

[1]   The O.K. Corral Inquest, p. 142; Document 94, The Wells Spicer Hearing, County Clerk, Cochise County.

CHAPTER XXV

THE COWBOYS

ORDINARILY the term Cowboy was used to describe a person engaged in raising, herding, and tending cattle; but in southeastern Arizona, because the newspapers almost always referred to the outlaw element of that part of the country as the cowboys, it became a term describing robbers, outlaws and cattle rustlers. There were plenty of them in southeastern Arizona. By the early 1880s, law enforcement in the Western part of the United States was beginning to close in on the outlaw element. The Younger James bank robbery gang were practically wiped out in the Northfield, Minnesota bank robbery in September of 1876. Only Jesse and Frank James escaped from that fiasco. Later, on April 3, 1882 Jesse James was murdered by one of the members of his gang who did it in order to collect the reward offered by the state of Missouri.

In late 1880, in New Mexico, Billy the Kid was captured, tried, and sentenced to be hanged. He escaped and after a diligent manhunt by Sheriff Pat Garrett, he was killed on July 14, 1881. Outlaws from all over the west were on the run. One place they considered safe was eastern and southeastern Arizona which was sparsely populated and without adequate law enforcement.

Outlaws who were on the run elsewhere were attracted like moths to candles; they moved in and quickly set up shop.

The people who have written about the Tombstone epic seem to agree that Newman H. Clanton, commonly known as 'Old Man Clanton' was the head of the outlaw faction in Cochise County. Almost all the authors are very short on real information about Old Man Clanton and the origin of the Clanton clan, as will appear from the following recitations of various authors trying to report on him, his family, and his activities.

Lake says: "The field forces of Arizona's organized outlawry are typified in Old Man Clanton and his following. Clanton was a tough old Texas renegade who had gone to California in '49, then chased out by vigilantes, drifted to Arizona, where he took up a ranch near Ft. Thomas, and existed for some years through his ability to out-Apache the Apaches. With the Tombstone strike, Clanton, his initials were N. H., but even in the court records he was designated as Old Man - moved to Lewis Springs, just up the San Pedro from Charleston, where ore was turned into bullion and booty.

"With Old Man Clanton rode his sons, Joseph Isaac, the notorious Ike; Phineas, called Phin; and William, Billy; all three born and raised in outlawry. Curly Bill Brocius, John Ringo, Frank and Tom McLaury, Joel Hill, Jim Hughes, Pony Deal, Frank Stilwell, and Pete Spence were other lieutenants. Under them, three hundred outcasts of frontier society dominated the human rights and life in southern and eastern Arizona.

"Clanton followers, in the guise of ranchers, squatted on every desert water hole from old Mexico to the Mogollon, and from the Hauchucas to Los Animas."[1]

Glen Boyer obviously did considerably more research on the matter than Lake did. He says that the full name of Old Man Clanton was Newman Haynes Clanton. That his son Ike indicated his place of birth as Missouri on the 1881 Cochise County Great Register and listed his age at that time as 34. According to him, we can safely conclude that the Clantons must have been Missourians in 1847; that they probably migrated to Texas by 1858 and that he had confirmed their residence in California by a letter from a William H. Frink, "the old time Martinez Ranch."[2]

Paula Mitchell Marks, who seldom gives a very good source for her material but is usually pretty reliable, has the Clantons ranging from Missouri to Texas, Texas to California, and then to Arizona, and has them as old Arizona settlers. She mistakenly has Newman (Old Man) Clanton establishing his brood, including five sons and three daughters, on the Gila River in southwestern Arizona in 1868 or 1869, and states that he claimed a desert waterhole on the trail between Yuma and Phoenix, a site still known as Clanton Well to this day. She then has him move his ranching and farming activities near to the U.S. Army's Camp Thomas in 1873.[3]

In this, Paula Mitchell Marks was mistaken. The Clanton for whom the Clanton Wells and nearby hill are named was not Newman Haynes Clanton, but was one Thomas Newton Clanton who came to Southern Arizona in 1877. He may have had five sons and three daughters, but Newman Haynes had only two daughters and three sons. Thomas later moved to Phoenix where he lived for many years.[4]

---

[1]   _Wyatt Earp, Frontier Marshal_, p. 234.

[2]   _I Married Wyatt Earp_, Note 12, p. 40.

[3]   _And Die in the West_, p. 26.

[4]   _Arizona Place Names_, p. 371.

While all of the authors quoted seem to have the general idea of where the Clantons came from and who they were, none of them had the details correct.

This author has been able to trace the Clantons back a little further. The U.S. Census for the year 1870 for Santa Barbara County, San Buena Ventura Township Number 1 on the 16th day of June, records the following:

"Clanton, Newman H. age 52, male, white, farmer, born in Tennessee 1818. Value of Real Estate, $1,600, personal $750.

"Mary E. Clanton, age 19, white, female, housekeeper born in Illinois, 1851.

"Joseph Jr. (this would be Ike) Clanton, age 22, white male, day laborer, born in Missouri 1848.

"Ester Clanton, age 15, white female, at home, born in Texas 1855.

"William C. Clanton, age 8, male white, at home, born in Texas 1862."

That pretty well takes care of the 1868 date given by Paula Mitchell Marks for the establishment of the Clanton brood on the Gila River in Southwestern Arizona. They were definitely in California in 1870. But Newman H. Clanton was not in California in 1849 as stated by Lake.[1]

It is interesting to note that the Census fails to mention Peter Alonso, born in 1858 according to Paula Mitchell Marks, but does mention two daughters who were age 15 and 19 in 1870 that seem not to have been mentioned by anyone. Possibly Peter Alonso was the son of Thomas Newton Clanton and perhaps by the time the N.H. Clantons moved from California the daughters would have been married and remained in California. The Census also fails to mention Phineas Clanton who Paula Mitchell Marks says was born in 1855, who would have been about 25 years old on the date of the 1870 Census. Perhaps at his age, he had left the family residence and was not at that time living in the house with Newman H. Clanton. Neither was there any mention of a wife in the Census. Walter Noble Burns quotes Melvin Jones of Tucson as saying, "Old Man Clanton's wife was dead when I first knew the family in 1875."[2] It's a pretty good guess that she was dead before the 1870 Census.

So we know that the Clantons were living in San Buena Ventura township, which was part of Santa Barbara County in 1870. That they were still there in 1873 is attested by W. H. Hutchinson, biographer of Thomas Robert Bard. Thomas Bard was a land baron

[1]   Wyatt Earp, Frontier Marshal, p. 234.

[2]   Tombstone, p. 124.

of what eventually became Ventura County, encompassing the area of Oxnard, Port Hueneme, and nearby environs. He had acquired much of his land through purchase of Mexican land grants most of which were based on questionable titles. Because of the questionable titles, numerous squatters moved in and occupied portions of the land, and this resulted in what was by some called the Hueneme War. While it was not really a war, and most of it was fought in the Courts, it had all the ingredients of a war with various parties threatening to use deadly force to settle the right to possession. Hutchinson says:

"Claiming that the lands adjacent to Hueneme were properly a part of the sacred public domain, open to entry by any freeborn American under the Pre-emption and Homestead Laws of the Republic, squatters had hacked out claims amidst the towering mustard and sown their crops. Among them were a truculent, drifting, quasi-farmer from New York, Newman Haynes (Old Man) Clanton, and his waspish brood, the self same Clanton Tribe that later gained a conditional immortality through their contentions with the brothers Earp in Arizona Territory."[1]

That the Clantons used somewhat the same tactics in California that they later would use in Arizona is shown by the following statement:

"Isaac Clanton once stopped Johnny Stow (a surveyor for Thomas Bard) from surveying under pain of death and was called from his shack next morning to gaze squarely into the muzzle of Bard's bear rifle while he was admonished not to molest Stow again."[2]

Bard was an unusually astute business man, and rather than engaging in a violent fight about possession of the lands pending the determination of title in court, he settled with the squatters by an agreement that whoever won the lawsuit would sell to the occupants at a reasonable price and on reasonable terms. He still maintained the right to possession and entered into leases with the squatters. In a letter that he wrote on November 25, 1872 describing the way he was conducting his business, he said:

"Am making headquarters pretty much at Hueneme nowadays and finding it keeps me busy to arrange with these squatters . . . a beggarly conscienceless and ungrateful lot, but I have surprised myself with the patience I have shown in dealing with them. I go to every man on the property, ascertain what he wants to do, what he has got, and if possible convince him, that I have 'malice for none,' and we get along well enough I suppose. I have leased to the best of them, and

---

[1]   Oil, Land and Politics, , p. 5.

[2]   Ibid, p. 176.

intend to arrange with all in some way or another . . ."¹

Bard's lease book shows the following entry during the Autumn of 1872:

"I.C. Barron leases N. Clanton tract, 160 acres for 1/5 crop delivered at Hueneme corn, barley and beans."²

Thus, it is quite apparent that he was or had been doing business with N. Clanton. It would appear that at least as late as the fall of 1872, the Clanton clan were headquartered in and around Hueneme, California.

All of the writers seem to agree in general, but not in detail, that Old Man Clanton established his ranch on the San Pedro River, about 12 miles from Tombstone, and that he was more or less the head of an outlaw community that included not only those named by Lake, but many others. No one ever mentioned the number three hundred as Lake did, most of the writers about that period indicate the number at around fifty. Anyway, it is known that the outlaws, known as cowboys, were engaging in cattle rustling in the United States. They would steal the cattle in Southern Arizona, and drive them into Mexico where they would sell them at bargain prices. Then they would round up a bunch of Mexican cattle and drive them back into the United States where they would again sell them at bargain rates. Old Man Clanton seemed to be the organizer of much of this illicit business. Many of the stolen herds were reputedly handled by the McLaurys at a nearby ranch. The McLaurys association with the Clanton's and Curly Bill will be detailed later, but there is little doubt that they were members of the rustling cowboy faction.

The two most important outlaws associated with the Clanton Gang were Curly Bill Brocius and John Ringo, neither of whom anyone seems to know very much about. Their exploits in and around Tombstone and Cochise County have been written up by numerous writers, but few of them cite any reliable authority for the statements that they make, and although all of them seem to confirm the fact that they were engaged in cattle rustling and lawless activities involving forays into Mexico, none of them tell exactly the same story and it's difficult to know just what the conditions were.

Let's let someone who was there describe the conditions as he saw them at that time. In a letter to John J. Gosper, acting Governor of Arizona Territory, Joseph Bowyer, a resident of Galeyville, described the conditions. His letter was as follows:

"September 17, 1881

---

¹   Ibid, p. 178.

²   Ibid, p. 179.

"Galeyville, A.T.

"His Excellency the Honorable John J. Gosper

"Acting Governor, Arizona Territory

"Dear Sir,

"In reply to your inquiry yesterday concerning the 'cowboys' who are reported to have been and still are raiding along the line of Sonora, and Arizona, I will say --

"The gang who are known as 'cowboys' are engaged in stock raising in the valleys of San Simon and Cloverdale, in the Southeastern portion of Arizona, and from good authority, I learned that the cattle, horses, and sheep now controlled by said cowboys had been stolen from the citizens of Sonora and Arizona, and New Mexico; they are reported to have had about 300 head of cattle at or near Granite Gap, in New Mexico, and close to the line of Arizona. It is a well known fact that they are in the habit of making raids along the border. Until recently, it has been a custom to steal cattle and horses in Arizona and drive them into Sonora for sale, and on the return trip, steal stock in Sonora, and drive them into Arizona and New Mexico for sale; consequently, quite a traffic was kept up. This practice has abated somewhat lately, on account of the killing of four cowboys at Fronteras, in I think, June last.

"The circumstance, as near as can be determined is this - last spring George Turner and Mr. McAlister, two well known cow-boys, obtained the contract at Ft. Bowie for furnishing beef to the commissary, they and two assistants went to Sonora to either buy or steal beef - cattle; they succeeded in driving a large herd as far as Fronteras, when they were attacked by the Mexican citizens. They (the cowboys) were all killed and one Mexican citizen was killed. Upon the bodies of Turner and McAlister, was found the money which they ostensibly took to purchase cattle; which amount coupled with what they were known to have started from here with, proved that the cattle they were driving had not been paid for.

"This affair has caused bad blood between the cow-boys and the citizens of Sonora, each party taking revenge upon the other whenever opportunity occurs. Consequently it is unsafe for any person to travel across the border.

"About a month ago, the 'cow-boys' went across the border into Sonora and seeing a good sized pack train in charge of Mexicans laid an ambush, and at the word of command made a dash and succeeded in capturing the whole outfit consisting of about $4,000 dollars in Mexican coin, silver bullion, mescal, horses, and cattle. One of the cow-boys in relating to me the circumstances said that it was the d--st lot of truck he ever saw; he showed me a piece of bullion, I should judge it looked 1/2 gold. Upon my telling him that trouble would likely arise from this he replied that it was a smuggling train and they would not dare say much. There were 8 Mexicans killed in the affray.

"A notorious cow-boy known as John R.[1] offered to sell all the mutton the town can consume at the rate of $1 per head. No secrecy is observed in this kind of transaction.

"As regards the local officers of the law, I cannot do better than to refer to you to the <u>Arizona Star</u> of September 10th, 1881 which is hereto attached. (Here, rather than attaching a copy, I believe the writer copied the news story which was as follows):

"'Dog berry.

"'How Justice is Sometimes Defeated on the Border.

"'Editor Star: Permit me to give you a brief history of the trial before the Border Justice of the Peace, known as G.M. Ellingwood.

"'David Estis was one of the men who robbed a game of about $400 in cash at the midnight hour in the town of Galeyville, as follows: Estis entered the front door of the saloon in which the game was being played, armed with a Winchester and six-shooter, his "pal" passing in at the rear of the house armed in a similar manner. They ordered the players to throw up their hands and surrender all their cash. This accomplished, Estis proceeded to the corral of Babcock & Co. and extracted and confiscated a valuable horse, making the total cleanup about $500.

"'Estis was subsequently arrested by Deputy Sheriff Goodman and tried before said Ellingwood and discharged. His honor ruled in the examination of the witnesses that they could not testify to the taking of the money (ordered by the bandits to be left on the table) unless they of their own knowledge knew to whom a particular parcel of money belonged. This could not be proven as all the occupants of the room were commanded to (word illegible) instantly, leaving Estis and his "pard" to take and divide. Thus you see a single pair in Galeyville wins $500. Under the ruling of the astute and noble Judge, no evidence was admitted necessary to conviction.

"'Sheriff Goodman asked to be sworn to testify that the prisoner offered him $500 to cast loose his shackles and let him at liberty. This testimony was ruled out by the court as being irrelevant and not material to the issue.

"'While the trial was in progress, the Judge stated to Quartz Johnson that the prisoner could not be convicted, and subsequently that he (the Judge) would now stand with the cow-boys respectfully, Clipper.'

---

[1]   He must surely have been referring to John Ringo.

"I will also state another case. 'Billy the Kid'[1] a stripling belonging to the profession was arrested for stealing horses. Upon his examination the court ruled that the affidavit upon which he was arrested charged him with the crime of theft while the statute showed no such crime, but should have been larceny. Also, the person from whom the horses had been stolen voluntarily stated to the Court that he did not want the boy prosecuted as he agreed to return the horses. The same person, told me afterward that if he prosecuted the boy, the other cow-boys would steal every head of stock he had, which he being a poor man, could not afford to stand.

"The cow-boys frequently visit our town and often salute us with an indiscriminate discharge of fire arms, and after indulging in a few drinks at the saloons, practice shooting at the lamps, bottles, glasses etc., sometimes going to the length of shooting the cigar out of one's mouth; this of course produces a nervous feeling among visitors especially.

"The situation at this writing is not materially changed from the above. The cow-boys as a class are not over brave, though there are some among them who have gone through so much difficulty that they have become desperate and will take desperate chances.

"As regards to my standing and position I will state that at present I am the acting manager of the Texas Consolidated Mining and Smelting Co. and refer you to the Honorable William Springer of Illinois, as to the general facts stated above, who probably remembers the situation as it appeared to him at the time of his visit here during the early part of the season.

"As to my character for truth and veracity I take pleasure in referring you to Honorable George Aisulie, delegate to Congress from Idaho.

"And now in conclusion I will state at any time you feel I can give any information in which will assist you, I will upon receipt of inquiry forward you all of the facts I may be in possession of. I have the honor to be your very obedient servant.

Joseph Bowyer."[2]

---

[1]   This was probably Billy Claiborne later killed by Buckskin Frank Leslie on November 14, 1882 outside the Oriental Saloon in Tombstone.

[2]   Joseph Bowyer, Letter to John J. Gosper, September 17, 1881; Original letter in Arizona Historical Society Files.

CHAPTER XXVI

THE MASSACRE AT
SKELETON CANYON

THE incident related by Joseph Bowyer in his letter of September 17, 1881 in which a Mexican pack train was waylaid by a bunch of cowboys and according to him, eight Mexicans killed and loot including about $4,000 in Mexican coins, silver bullion, mescal, horses and cattle were taken, eventually became known as the Skeleton Canyon Massacre. This occurrence has been widely written about by various authors and the only reason that one can tell that they are writing about the same event is the fact that it happened in Skeleton Canyon. The number of Mexicans killed is anywhere from 4 to 19, depends on the author. A large amount of silver bullion was recovered, anywhere from $4,000 recorded by Mr. Bowyer to millions of dollars supposedly still buried in Skeleton Canyon and the object of a search by a great many treasure hunters.[1]

It took a lot of research to determine the date that the event occurred, and after finally concluding that the event Joseph Bowyer was recounting was the same as that reported as the Skeleton Canyon Massacre, and noting that Mr. Bowyer in telling of the ambush and robbery on September 17, 1881 fixed the time at about a month ago, I have concluded that it must have happened in late July or early August of 1881. Paula Marks says that it occurred early in August but fails to say in what year.[2]

Myers quotes Breakenridge in his book Helldorado, as saying: "The Clantons made cattle forays into Mexico and preyed upon smugglers operating between the two nations. A well attested illustration is the fact that Old Man Clanton personally led the band which ambushed a train of silver-laden mules in Skeleton Canyon near the Mexican Border in the Guadalupes. The rustlers killed 19 mule drivers and guards in the course of their exploit, which netted them $75,000."[3]

Walter Noble Burns also reported the death toll of the Mexicans

---

[1]   Tombstone, p. 96.

[2]   And Die in the West, p. 170.

[3]   Last Chance, p. 119.

as 19 and the take in bullion as $75,000. This is probably where Myers got his information. Two other interesting things mentioned by Walter Noble Burns were that:

"Skeleton Canyon has, too, a tradition of buried outlaw treasure that drips with romance and rivals the wild tales of Cocos Island and the Spanish Main; and all up and down the canyon are the holes dug by treasure hunters who have come with high hopes and have gone away empty handed."[1]

That Burns was right about the affair at Skeleton Canyon starting a tradition of buried treasure, is proved by the inclusion in the book, Lost Mines and Treasure of the Southwest, by R. W. McAlister, published by the Thomas Brothers in Los Angeles, which outlines a total of 219 lost mines and treasures.

The story told there, about the robbery of the pack train in Skeleton Canyon illustrates how difficult it is to ascertain the true facts of any of these reported depredations.

The book headlines the story as 'BURIED PLUNDER' 1884-Arizona.

"Robberies in old Mexico net at about 3 million dollars consisting of a cigar box filled with diamonds worth about 1 million; thirty-nine bars of gold were $600,000; and $90,000 in silver coins; gold statuary figures and stacks of gold coins. Curly Bill Brocius, a robber baron who operated near Tombstone, Arizona, was aware of mule teams bringing smuggled riches into Arizona from old Mexico. Several of these pack teams were attacked by Brocius and his gang in the San Simon Valley, murdering the smugglers. Jim Hughes, a member of the gang, could speak Spanish, so was sent to Sonora, where, posing as a Spaniard, learned about the departure of the pack train which would pass through Skeleton Canyon and San Simon Valley. Reporting back, Hughes found his Chief away, so he decided to engineer the job himself. The smuggler's pack train consisted of 15 men and 30 mules. They entered Skeleton Canyon and posted guards when they hauled in their Devil's Kitchen for lunch and a siesta. Rifle fire from the canyon walls cut the guards down quickly, the others regained their mounts, but four were shot out of their saddles. The remaining Mexican's fled leaving the treasure behind. The loaded mules scattered, but were shot down one by one until all the richly laden packs were recovered. The loot was assembled in one pile so high they didn't have horses enough to carry it, so decided on a temporary place of burial.

"In recent years, coins scattered by the frightened mules, have been found. The job of removing the treasure to its more secure resting place was assigned to two trusted helpers, Zwig Hunt and

---

[1]   Tombstone, p. 96.

Hunt had received proved his undoing, but before he died, he told an Uncle of the buried treasure. Prior to the raid in which Hughes participated, Grounds and Hunt had robbed smugglers.

"This loot, together with the last haul, was removed by them with the aid of a Mexican teamster who was killed to seal his lips. Hunt's map to his uncle set down Davis Mountain, Silver Springs, a rock with two crosses and a spot near the San Simon. Nearby, a waterfall in the canyon affords a good place to bathe. Hunt's mountain is possibly only a mound where one of their pals named Davis was buried with $500 in his pockets. Hunt's uncle, Ground's brother, the Chief of Police of Tombstone, Porter McDonald, and many others have searched in vain for the treasure."[1]

Burns fixes the date of the Skeleton Canyon Robbery as July, 1881, and names some of the cowboys who participated as Old Man Clanton, Ike and Billy Clanton, Tom and Frank McLaury, John Ringo, Joe Hill, Jim Hughes, Rattlesnake Bill, Jake Gauze, Charlie Thomas, and Charlie Snow.[2]

That Burns may have been correct in giving July as the date of the Skeleton Canyon affair is supported by George Parsons in his entry of August 17, 1881 where he told of the killing of several people by the Mexicans in retaliation for killing of several of them and the robbery by cowboys recently. Two people that he named were Dick Gray and the notorious Crane, obviously referring to the notorious Jim Crane.[3]

Old Man Clanton was killed at the same time as Dick Gray and Jim Crane along with a number of others and since Parsons fixes the date of that killing before August 17th, and Burns says that the Skeleton Canyon Affair took place about a month before his death, it would figure that the Skeleton Canyon Robbery might have occurred about the middle of July.

A short time after the Skeleton Canyon incident, a party of American cowboys were accompanying rancher Bill Lang, who was driving 100 head of beef cattle from his New Mexico ranch to a market in Tombstone, among whom was Old Man Clanton who was driving the wagon and acting as cook for the party. Also among the party was outlaw Jim Crane, who at the time was wanted for stage robbery.

Paula Mitchell Marks says:

---

[1]   Lost Mines and Treasures of the Southwest, p. 76.

[2]   Tombstone, p. 106.

[3]   The Private Journal of George Parsons, p. 170.

"The presence of seven men so close to the border with known rustler Clanton among them has naturally led some to conclude that the group was not moving cattle legally owned by Lang."[1]

At any rate, early in the morning, the party was attacked by an unknown number of Mexicans. Old Man Clanton and Charlie Snow were immediately shot down and Dick Gray, son of the Gray involved in the land grab in Tombstone, and Jim Crane were shot and killed while in their sleeping bags. One of the survivors, Bill Byers, told a Tucson newspaper that when they first fired and killed Charlie Snow, he thought the boys were firing at a bear. As soon as he saw what was up, he looked for his rifle and not seeing it, grabbed a revolver and seeing them shooting at them from all sides, started to run but had only gone about 40 feet when he was shot across the body. He didn't fall but in a few more steps he was hit in the arm and the pistol was knocked out of his hand and he fell down. He saw Earnshaw and Lang run by him and saw Lang fall, shot through the legs. The attackers turned out to be Mexican soldiers directed by three commanders on one of the hills. Soon after that he saw some of the attackers coming from the direction Will and Harry had run wearing their hats. He played dead and was not bothered further.[2]

Earnshaw escaped and walked about fifteen miles to the Gray ranch where he gathered some help and with 25 miners returned to the scene of the massacre.

They found Bill Byers about five miles away, walking around, dazed and completely out of his head with a serious bullet wound in his abdomen. They dressed Byers' wounds and buried Charlie Snow where they found him, about half a mile from the others. His body was too badly mangled to move.

The other bodies and the wounded cowhand were loaded into a wagon and taken to the Gray Ranch, where Dick Gray, Old Man Clanton, Jim Crane, and Bill Lang were buried.[3]

This has to be the encounter that was noted in Parson's Journal on August 17, 1881, even though he did not mention Old Man Clanton.

That is a rather important date, for it divides the history of Cochise County from the time when the outlawry was led by Old Man Clanton and the time thereafter when it was probably led by Curly Bill Brocius. It was not a very strong leadership. The Clantons,

---

[1]   And Die In The West, p. 171.

[2]   Ibid, p. 172.

[3]   Ibid, p. 172.

McLaurys, Curly Bill, and John Ringo all worked as a loosely knit group of outlaws, all willing to help each other, but not specifically tied together as they had been under the Old Man Clanton.

CHAPTER XXVII

THE MC LAURYS

THE McLaury brothers, Frank and Tom, were young men who were operating a ranch in the Sulphur Springs Valley about fifteen miles east of Tombstone. No writers have given very good details about their background. According to the 1880 census, they were born in New York, Frank in 1849, Tom in 1853. They apparently came to Arizona by way of Illinois and Texas and had a brother by the name of Will or William who was a practicing attorney in Ft. Worth, Texas, and who later came to Tombstone to assist in the prosecution of the Earps and Doc Holliday for the murder of Frank and Tom McLaury.

The first written record that I have been able to locate is the 1880 Census, at which time they were living near the Patterson Ranch in an area on the Babacomari River about fifteen miles west of Tombstone. Several months after the 1880 Census, they must have moved to their ranch in the Sulphur Springs Valley.

Al Turner says that late in 1880 the McLaurys moved to Sulphur Springs Valley on White River [sic. Whitewater River], four miles south of Soldiers Hole.[1]

By the accounts of some, they were two young, honest, hardworking ranchers and were not in any way involved in the outlawry that pervaded that part of Arizona in the early 1880s. However, the evidence is overwhelming that they were closely associated with the outlaws, and probably acted as middle men for them in the sale and disposition of their ill gotten gains.

Breakenridge, who was a Deputy Sheriff under John Behan at Tombstone in the 1880-81 gives conflicting reports about the McLaurys. At one place he says:

"As long as I was in the Sheriff's office, I never knew of any warrant being issued for any of the McLaurys or Clantons. If there had been, I would certainly have known it, as I served most of the warrants outside of Tombstone. The McLaurys and Clantons were in Tombstone frequently."[2]

---

[1]   The O.K. Corral Inquest, p. 171.

[2]   Helldorado, p. 141.

In another place in his book he says:

"The Clantons looked after the rustlers' interests on the San Pedro, as a lot of stolen stock was brought from Mexico down the river, and there was no one watching the line for smugglers. The McLaurys looked after the stock brought up from Mexico through Aqua Prieta, where Douglas now stands, and to Sulphur Springs Valley."[1]

He tells another story about recovering a stolen horse that reveals more than one would think he would have told about his, and his boss's, connection with and attitude towards the cattle rustlers and outlaws. A horse that belonged to E.B. Gage, general manager of the Contention mine, had been stolen and he was very anxious to get it back. Breakenridge tells the following story:

"One afternoon Ike Clanton met me on the street and told me that if I wanted the Contention horse to get to McLaury's Ranch before dark, and I should find him there. Ike passed on with no further information. I had just come in from a hard trip and my horse was as tired, so, going to a livery stable, I hired a pony to make the trip.

"I did not arrive at the Ranch until after dark, as the pony was very slow and lazy.

"As I rode up, I saw that there was a large crowd of cowboys there, and the place in front of the house was covered with water from an irrigation ditch. Not wanting to come on them unawares, I hollered and asked if it was safe to drive through the water. Frank McLaury came to the door. When I told him who I was, he asked me in, and on entering I found Curly Bill and some ten or twelve rustlers that were there with him. They were all strangers to me. I went out with Frank to put up my horse in the corral, and told him what I was there for. I said: 'Frank, I am not the only one who knows that horse is here. Half of Tombstone knows it. You are posing here as an honest ranchman. It is well known that you are harboring rustlers and outlaws and dealing in stolen cattle, and you dare not let me go back without the horse. You are under suspicion, and if I go back without the horse and tell that you would not give it up, you will have to quit ranching here and turn out with the rest of the rustlers.'

"He thought it over and said the horse was not there at the time, but would be there before morning; he would not tell me who stole it. He asked me to remain overnight and we entered the house. It was crowded and Curly and some of the others divided blankets with me and I slept on the floor with them all night. I was up at daylight and the horse was in the corral. Several parties came in during the

---

[1]   Ibid, p. 105.

night, but I did not know who they were."[1]

Wyatt Earp's first encounter with the McLaurys occurred about July 15, 1880 and was recounted by Lake in the following story:

"Curly Bill, Frank and Tom McLaury, Frank Patterson, and Billy Clanton ran off a bunch of Government Mules from Camp Rucker. Captain Hurst, with four troopers, rode to Tombstone to ask the Marshal's aid in recovering the animals. Wyatt, Virgil, and Morgan took the trail with Hurst and tracked the mules to the McLaury's Ranch near Soldier's Holes in the Sulphur Springs Valley, where they found six of the stolen animals.[2]

"Captain Hurst held parley with Frank Patterson and reported that the outlaws would give up all Government animals they had if the Earps went back to Tombstone, but that he must be satisfied with six if he kept the Earps in his posse.

"'You say the word,' Wyatt told Hurst, 'and I'll bring out every mule in the place. This is a trick to get us out of the way. If we leave, you won't get a mule.'

"The army officer insisted that eight men would be no match for the fifteen or twenty rustlers at the ranch, and that his first duty was to recover stolen property not fight outlaws.

"'Virg, Morg, and I will attend to the fighting,' Wyatt assured him, but Hurst preferred the compromise.

"A few days later, Captain Hurst rode into Tombstone without any mules, but with a message for Wyatt.

"'The McLaurys sent word that if you or your brothers interfered with them again, they'd shoot you on sight.'

"'Tell 'em they'll have their chance,' Wyatt answered.

"Three weeks later, Wyatt met Frank and Tom McLaury in the Street at Charleston.

"'That army officer gave you our message?' Tom McLaury asked.

"'He did,' Wyatt replied, 'but in case you didn't get my answer, I'll repeat it.'

"The McLaury's wanted no gun-play that morning.

"'If you ever follow us again,' Frank McLaury promised, as he and his brothers walked away, 'Your friends'll find what the coyotes leave of you in the sage brush.'"[3]

Paula Mitchell Marks says that this event occurred on July 25,

---

[1]   Ibid, p. 142.

[2]   Lake is mistaken. At that time the McLaury Ranch was on the Babacomari River.

[3]   Wyatt Earp Frontier Marshal, p. 240.

1880.[1] Wyatt Earp was not a law enforcement officer at the time, for he did not become a Deputy Sheriff until July 27th. However, Virgil was a Deputy U.S. Marshal and had a duty to protect U.S. Government property.

Lt. Hurst, having returned to Tombstone empty handed, angrily published a notice in the Tombstone Epitaph offering rewards for the "arrest, trial and conviction" of the thieves and for the return of the animals. He stated:

"It is known that the stolen animals were secreted at or in the vicinity of the McLaury Brothers Ranch on the Babacomari River on July 15, 1880; and it is also believed that they were there branded on the left shoulder over the government brand U.S., by the letter and figure D8.

"The notice identified the thieves as 'Pony Diehl, A. T. Hasbrough, and McMasters' and charged that Patterson and Frank 'McLaury' were among those who helped them hide the cattle."[2] [sic. Mules]

Frank McLaury apparently became enraged by the fact that Hurst had identified him along with the mule thieves as being an accomplice to the theft.

"On August 5, in the pages of the Weekly Nugget, the rancher charged that Hurst was a 'coward, a vagabond, a rascal and a malicious liar' who had possibly stolen the mules himself. 'My name is well known in Arizona,' McLaury wrote, 'and thank God this is the first time in my life that the name of dishonesty was ever attached to me . . . I'm willing to let the people of Arizona decide who was right.'"[3]

This was the beginning of the ill will that existed between the Earps and the McLaurys. The McLaurys evidently did not recognize the fact that when the Earps appeared at their ranch with Lt. J. H. Hurst and his squad of soldiers, at least Virgil Earp was acting within the scope of his duties as a Deputy United States Marshal with jurisdiction to investigate and arrest people for the theft of United States Government property.   Virgil could have appointed his brothers as special officers as the need arose in attempting to recover the stolen government property.

That the McLaurys were engaged in nefarious dealings with the outlaws and cattle thieves, I think will be more apparent when we

[1]   And Die in the West, p. 90.

[2]   Tombstone Epitaph, July 30, 1880.

[3]   Tombstone Weekly Nugget, August 5, 1880.

examine the evidence taken at the preliminary examination held on the murder charges against Wyatt Earp, Virgil Earp, Morgan Earp and Doc Holliday.

CHAPTER XXVIII

JOHNNY RINGO

JOHN Ringo was one of the most mysterious characters of the Old West. Although many writers have tried to tell his story, almost all that they have written is based on hearsay and speculation. Much of it can be proved to be false.

The only biography I have been able to locate on John Ringo was written by Jack Burrows entitled, "John Ringo, The Gunfighter Who Never Was." Burrows attempted to trace Ringo's background and antecedents and succeeded in doing so in a manner that was apparently even unsatisfactory to himself. He was able to find very little if any documentary evidence to support or validate such information that he was able to put together on Ringo.

The same is true of Stuart N. Lake. Lake's notes in the Huntington Library indicate that John Slaughter, one of the best known ranchers around Tombstone, a deadly enemy of cattle rustlers, cow thieves and outlaws, and eventually the Sheriff of Cochise County who completed the job started by the Earps of cleaning out the outlaws, moved his herd of cattle from Texas to southwestern Arizona in the late 1870s. When making that drive, he inadvertently imported some of the worst bandits to appear in Arizona. Among them it is alleged were John Ringo, Curly Bill Brocius, Frank Stilwell, and Billy Claiborne. The date of this trek from Texas to Arizona I have been unable to establish, but it must have happened after August 25, 1877 when John Ringo's name appeared in the Galveston News, as being one of the occupants of Travis county jail along with John Wesley Hardin and several other notorious criminals. Jack Burrows says that in "Arizona Ringo was described as a handsome, well educated, morose, loner known by some as the 'fastest' and 'deadliest' gunfighter in Southeastern Arizona. 'Amazing dexterity with Colt and Winchester' completed the embodiment of the 'balanced,' 'temperamental' and 'mechanical' qualities of the classic gunfighter."[1]

Burrows says that Cunningham in his book, Triggernomotry blew the Ringo myth all out of proportion and upon demanding from Mr. Cunningham the source of his information, he was referred back to Breakenridge's, Helldorado.

I will quote freely from Breakenridge's Helldorado, but it does

---

[1] John Ringo, p. 26.

not substantiate the description of the super gunman and bad man described by Cunningham in Triggernomotry.

Breakenridge's description of Johnny Ringo not only gives an insight into Ringo's character, but, probably unintentionally, discloses as much as anything the close connection between Sheriff John Behan, the politicians running Cochise County and the outlaw element.

Breakenridge tells the following story about John Ringo that I think illustrates the point:

"John Ringo and Curly Bill were the big chiefs among the rustlers in and around Galeyville. Ringo was a very mysterious man. He had a college education, but was reserved and morose. He drank heavily as if to drown his troubles; he was a perfect gentleman when sober, but inclined to be quarrelsome when drinking. He was a good shot and afraid of nothing and had great authority with the rustling element. Although he was the leader on their trips to Mexico after cattle and in their raids against the smugglers, he generally kept by himself after they returned to Galeyville. He read a great deal and had a small collection of standard books in his cabin.

"One night while drinking, he got into a poker game with some miners in a Galeyville saloon and lost about $100. He asked for an advance of $100 on his watch and chain, but as he was drinking, they were afraid of him, and told him they were about to close the game as it was late, and to come around the next morning and they would give him revenge. He left the saloon and getting his horse came back. On entering the saloon where there were two poker games still going on, with 10 or 12 players, he drew down on them with his gun and held them up. They were playing with money and had no chips.

"He remarked, 'You fellows held the top hand all the evening, I hold it now,' and took all the money on both tables, then left and went to Joe Hill's place in the San Simon Cienaga.

"By the time he reached there he was sober and told Joe what he had done. He said that if he had not been drunk he would not have done it, as they were all friends of his, and asked Joe to take the money back and turn it into the saloon. The players all got their money back and were satisfied, as they all liked Ringo.

"Some dissatisfied person came to Tombstone several months later, and went before the Grand Jury. As a consequence, Ringo was indicted for highway robbery and a warrant was issued and given to me to serve.

"I had met Ringo frequently on my trips to Galeyville and was very well acquainted with him, and we had many pleasant visits. I was advised to take a posse with me, as they thought he was sure to resist arrest, but I said that if I could not get him alone, it would take a troop of soldiers to get him as he had some fifty or sixty followers who would stay with him, and I was satisfied that I could arrest him alone. I refused to go if they wanted me to take a posse.

"Mounting my saddle horse, I got to Prue's Ranch that night, and the next morning I started over the mountain for Galeyville. I reached there before Ringo was up, and on going to his room, knocked. He came to the door with his six-shooter in his hand. He invited me in, and I told him I had a warrant for him for holding up the poker game.

"'What,' he said, 'Are you going to arrest me for that? Why, that was all settled.'

"He dressed and we went to breakfast together and he asked me not to say anything about it, as he did not want any of the boys to know that he was under arrest. He said that he would have to wait until Turner, their banker, came in that afternoon to get some money and if I would go back to Prue's Ranch, he would meet me there in the morning. I considered his word as good as a bond, so I went back to the Ranch, and next morning Ringo was there for breakfast. He had come in the night and rather than disturb anyone, he had slept in a haystack.

"We rode into Tombstone that day, and Ringo told me enough about his family for me to know that they were not aware that he was an outlaw. We were both heavily armed, for the Indians were out and we had to be on the alert all the time. On reaching the town, we put up our horses, and as it was about dark we first got supper at a restaurant and then went to the jail. I asked the jailer, who I knew had an extra room, to let Ringo keep his arms and sleep in his house across the street from the jail, and I would be down early next morning and help him get his bond. Ringo waived examination and his bond was fixed and John Dunbar, County Treasurer, Al Jones, County Recorder, and a gambler friend of Ringo's were ready to sign it.

"There was a law and order committee formed in Tombstone that stood in with the gang that was opposed to the Sheriff, and it was reported that some of them had gone toward Charleston to arrest Curly Bill and a lot of the cowboys and bring them to Tombstone. Ringo was anxious to get down there and be with his friends. While waiting for Judge Stilwell to approve the bond, Ringo's attorney came to the Sheriff's office and said, 'All right, Johnny, the bond is approved,' and Ringo got on his horse, which I had brought to the office for him and went to Charleston. He got there before the law and order party did: In fact they never got there.

"That evening the Judge met Sheriff Behan and remarked that he would look into the matter of Ringo's bond in the morning and to have him in court. Behan told him that Ringo's attorney had said that the bond had been approved, and that he had turned him loose.

The Judge replied that he had not approved it and that he held Behan responsible for the prisoner. The Judge then issued a warrant for Ringo and gave it to two of the so-called law and order committee to serve."[1]

Although Breakenridge did not give a date for this occurrence, Parsons supplied that date in his diary entry of January 25, 1882, when he recorded, "Was routed out of bed night before last to help get a horse for posse which left at 4:00 a.m. for Charleston to rearrest Ringo."[2]

Breakenridge continues,

"They proceeded to Charleston that night to arrest Ringo. On their arrival, they were held up at the bridge going into town by a bunch of cowboys who were guarding it, as they were expecting some of the law and order gang and were watching for them. The cowboys disarmed them and took them to the saloon while they woke Ringo and told him what was up, and that the men were there with a warrant for him. He told them there were not enough of them to arrest him and it looked like a put-up job on the sheriff, and to hold them there until he got across the bridge. Mounting his horse he ran them back to Tombstone came to my room and told me what they had tried to do. As it was nearly morning, I took him to the Sheriff's office and made him a bed on the lounge and informed the Sheriff regarding it.

"The law and order posse in the meantime remained in Charleston until the next day and did not return until afternoon. Next morning when court opened, the Judge told Sheriff Behan to bring Ringo into court and he would look into the bail matter. He did not know at that time that Ringo was in custody. Behan told me to bring him in, and I called him from the office, and as the bonds men were perfectly good, the Judge had to approve the bond, and Ringo returned to his friends. At this time, the Republican officials were making a strong fight against Sheriff Behan. The case of highway robbery against Ringo was dismissed, as they could find no witnesses to appear against him. This was the only warrant that was ever issued against him as far as I could learn, and he came and went whenever and wherever he wanted to."[3]

If Breakenridge can be believed in anything, this is the most outright admission of cooperation and collusion between the sheriff, the county officers, and the outlaws that can be imagined. If there

---

[1] Helldorado, p. 137.

[2] Private Journal of George W. Parsons, p 208.

[3] Helldorado, p. 138.

ever was a question about whose side the sheriff was on, that is the law and order party or the rustlers and outlaws, this statement of Deputy Sheriff Breakenridge should settle that matter. It is almost ludicrous to think that a Deputy Sheriff would go so far as to leave him in possession of his arms and secure a place for him to sleep with a friend. And the fact that his bond was signed by John Dunbar, County Treasurer, and Al Jones, County Recorder should alert anyone to the possibility that the higher-ups in county government were also aligned with the outlaws.

It's hard to believe anything that has been written about John Ringo because everyone seemed to want to make him into a mythical western cowboy fast-gun artist and killer. Lake fell into the same trap. He says:

"John Ringo was tall, slender, auburn-haired, and handsome. Though he robbed, killed, and caroused with his fellows, he was of a solemn temperament and periodically so vicious that even his friends avoided him.

"Ringo, a week after Wyatt reached Tombstone, invited a chance acquaintance in a saloon, one Lewis Hancock, to have a drink, and shot his guest through the throat when Hancock ordered beer, as Ringo took Whiskey."[1]

It would seem that if a man had a reputation of being a vicious killer, someone else would be able to give the name of one or two or a dozen of the victims of their six-gun proficiency. Lake names one, Lewis Hancock, and although he doesn't say so, the implication is that he was killed by Ringo in a saloon in Tombstone. Like many of the other things that Lake wrote, the only thing right about it is the name.

Jack Burrows, Ringo's biographer, is extremely critical of Lake's story of the Hancock shooting. He points out that Lake offers no source for his description of Ringo and suggests that it probably came from Wyatt Earp. He calls attention to the fact that Lake fails to mention the name of the saloon or the town in which the shooting of Hancock occurred and whether or not Hancock was killed. He points out that the Tucson Star and the Arizona Miner, both of which covered the story explicitly in their December 14, 1879 issues, described the shooting as having taken place in Safford, Arizona and Hancock as being only superficially wounded. Like many of my own criticisms of Lake, Burrows says that Lake had to have access to these accounts, but apparently ignored them, hoping that the reader would believe that the shooting took place in Tombstone and that Hancock was killed, thus making John Ringo a more formidable opponent than

---

[1]   Wyatt Earp Frontier Marshal, p. 235.

he actually was.[1]

The truth is that if John Ringo ever killed anyone, no one has ever written about any specific incident. No one knows the name of any of his victims, and the probabilities are good that there never were any.

It's probably true that Johnny Ringo had a reputation as a dangerous gunman and a killer. And like so many of the famous gun fighters of the west, the reputation was unjustified.

It is this writer's belief that the reputation of being a dangerous gun-fighter and killer was fostered and promoted by the alleged gun fighters themselves as a means of self protection. One way they fostered the reputation was to always be, or at least appear to be ready, willing and able to draw a pistol and fire. That kept any reasonable person from inviting such conduct.

Look at some of the alleged great gunfighters. Bat Masterson may have killed one man - surely no more.

Wyatt Earp never killed anyone before the O.K. Corral Shoot Out and never after he left Tombstone, yet all of his life he was believed to be a gunfighter. The same is true of most of the West's bad men and gunfighters.

---

[1]   John Ringo, p. 33.

CHAPTER XXIX

CURLY BILL BROCIUS

CURLY Bill Brocius, sometimes known as Graham, was another of the southeastern Arizona cowboys who came to Arizona with John Slaughter. His antecedents are even less known than those of John Ringo. Although Lake says that Wyatt Earp had run across him in Dodge City, I don't find any statement about him during Wyatt Earp's tenure in Dodge City that would support that, but it well could have been that Curly Bill was involved in trailing herds from Texas to Dodge City in the late 1870s.

Curly Bill Brocius was described by Lake as "a swart and muscular six-footer, with a heavy shock of kinky black hair, and course, ugly features. In leisure hours he could be a good-natured, open-handed fellow. On business bent, he was a brutal thug to whom murder was routine."[1]

Josephine Sarah Marcus who was living with Johnny Behan at that time and claimed to be his housekeeper and baby sitter for his son, Albert, said in her memoirs that Johnny Behan at various times entertained all of the rustlers except Old Man Clanton at the house that she and Johnny occupied. She claimed that the entertaining was done for political motives and that he was always having a little poker get-together with the boys, that after their business became widely known, the rustler crowd was no longer invited to come to their house.

Josephine evaluated the rustler crowd in an interesting way from a woman's point of view. She said that Curly Bill was the most likable one of the bunch, and she felt that he might have amounted to something had he had a chance. He always brought Johnny Behan's son, Albert, something to play with, such as an old unserviceable six-shooter, and she stated that he always treated her like a lady and that she would not have been afraid to be in his company alone, "which is more than can be said for some of the others, Billy Clanton, for example."[2]

The evidence seems to support her statement that Curly Bill was a very pleasant man and easy to get along with on some occasions.

---

[1] _Wyatt Earp, Frontier Marshal_, p. 235.

[2] _I Married Wyatt Earp_, p. 66

The best picture of him was drawn by William Breakenridge in his book, <u>Helldorado</u>. His story not only tells a lot about Curly Bill, but also about the political situation and the cooperation between the law enforcement, the county ring and the outlaws. He tells of being assigned to collect taxes for Cochise County. Apparently with some trepidation, he approached the hang-out of the outlaws but speaks with pride of the success that he had there. He says:

"I had already made my plans, and as soon as I reached Galeyville I hunted up a Mr. Turner, the Banker for the rustlers, and asked him to introduce me to Curly Bill. He took me to Babcock's Saloon and corral where Curly was, then Turner called him out and introduced me to him. I told him who I was and what I was and said I wanted to hire him to go with me as a Deputy assessor and help me collect the taxes, as I was afraid I might be held up and my tax money taken from me if I went alone.

"The idea of my asking the Chief of all the cattle rustlers in that part of the country to help me collect taxes from them, struck him as a good joke. He thought it over for a few moments and then laughing said,

"'Yes, and we will make everyone of those blank blank cow-thieves pay his tax.'

"Next day we started and he lead me into a lot of blind canyons and hiding places where the rustlers had a lot of stolen Mexican cattle, and introduced me something like this:

"'Boys, this is the County Assessor, and I am his Deputy. We are all good, law-abiding citizens here, and we cannot run the County without we pay our taxes.'

". . . I was treated fine by all of them, I never want to travel with a better companion than Curly was on that trip. He was a remarkable shot with a pistol and hit a rabbit every time when it was running 30 or 40 yards away . . .

"I learned one thing with him, and that was that he would not lie to me. What he told me he believed, and his word to me was better than the oaths of some of whom were known as good citizens.

"After assessing the town of Galeyville, I left there with nearly $1,000 tax money, with which I arrived safely in Tombstone, and was much relieved when I did so. But I should never have done it if I had tried to assess the rustlers alone."[1]

As in most other cases, Breakenridge failed to give a date, but we can fairly well calculate it. He says that Johnny Behan was appointed Sheriff of the new Cochise County in January, 1881 and that Harry Woods was appointed under-sheriff and he was appointed Deputy

---

[1]   <u>Helldorado</u>, p. 131-133.

Sheriff.[1]

In May of 1881, Curly Bill was shot and wounded in the neck in a drunken brawl with one of his good friends, Jim Wallace. Deputy Sheriff Breakenridge took Wallace before Justice of the Peace G.W. Ellingwood, but when no witnesses appeared he was discharged. Breakenridge says that he loaned Jim ten dollars and let him go his own way. He later heard that he was killed in a fight near Roswell, New Mexico.

"Curly Bill was laid up only about two weeks and was well as ever."[2]

---

[1]   That must have been in January, 1881.

[2]   Helldorado, p. 168.

CHAPTER XXX

BUCKSKIN FRANK LESLIE AND LAWLESS TOMBSTONE

ALTHOUGH the activities of Buckskin Frank Leslie had very little bearing on the life of Wyatt Earp while at Tombstone, it would be impossible to ignore his presence there. He is a part of the lore of Tombstone and his story must be included in any story of the early days of that town.

Not very much seems to be known about his antecedents, although it is supposed that he was once an army scout. It is known that he was a trick shooter and an exhibitionist. He dressed as a fancy Dan wearing buckskin shirts with fringes, thus acquiring the name of Buckskin Frank Leslie. Over his life time it appears that he was not only a fancy Dan, but was very attractive to women. While in Tombstone, he worked as a Bartender, and Dealer. He was reputed to be an excellent tracker, and his name shows up frequently as a member of various posses, sometimes John Behan's and occasionally with Wyatt Earp trying to capture stage robbers. Wyatt Earp paid him the supreme compliment when he said that the only man he ever regarded as anywhere near the equal of Doc Holliday on the draw was Buckskin Frank Leslie.[1]

Martin, in his Tombstone's Epitaph, says that Frank Leslie killed two men and one woman in the nine years he spent in the mining camp. He says the first man he killed was Mike Killeen on June 22, 1880 in a gunfight over Killeen's wife.[2]

Martin says that the copy of the Epitaph for June 22, 1880 is missing and therefore he cannot give the original report of the killing but summarizes the first proceeding this way:

"Buckskin Frank and George Perine, a companion, had been arrested after the gunfight and held until Killeen died. Taken before the court on murder charges, Leslie claimed he fired the fatal shot in self-defense and the court believed him. There was no evidence introduced which implicated Perine, so both men were discharged."[3]

It seems that Killeen had made a death bed statement stating

---

[1]   Wyatt Earp, Frontier Marshal, p. 196.

[2]   Tombstone's Epitaph, p. 79.

[3]   Ibid, p. 79.

216   Buckskin Frank Leslie and Lawless Tombstone

that he had been shot by Perine not by Leslie, and when the facts of that death bed statement became public, the prosecution filed murder charges against George Perine, and a new preliminary examination was held. At the hearing, which was some two months after the killing, Killeen's statement was introduced as evidence and reported in full in the Tombstone <u>Epitaph</u>. It was as follows:

"At the ball I wanted to see my wife. I heard that she had gone home with Leslie, and when I was told she had gone home I went down to the hotel with the expectation of finding both of them in Leslie's room, but they were not there; meanwhile, I started toward the porch, having heard voices, and I thought it might be them; I got to the door of the porch and satisfied myself, she and Leslie were sitting side by side, his arm around her waist; that settled it; I thought I would go off now, started back again; Perine came along pistol in hand and knowing him to be a particular friend of Leslie I looked for trouble as in the early part of the evening he went into Tasker's and Hoke's and bought a box of cartridges and filled all the chambers of his pistol and deposited the remainder of the box with me; I started away from the porch when Perine came along and yelled out 'Look out Frank, there is Mike.' With that Leslie rose from his chair in a half standing position, pulling his pistol; he fired the pistol at me and I fired one shot at him; I saw I was in for it and I made a jump and caught the pistol and beat him over the head with mine, which I had in my hand at the time; I happened to look and saw Perine standing in the door with his pistol leveled at me; he pulled the trigger, which he repeated twice, firing in all three shots; by this time I had used up Leslie pretty well; then turned and jumped and caught Perine's pistol, and did the same to him; by this time people commenced to congregate and I dropped this man not thinking of my own wounds; all I knew was I was shot in the nose somewhere. I fired two shots myself intentionally and every time I would strike the pistol went off accidentally; fired at Perine when he fired at me; one shot was at Perine and one was at Leslie; fired at Leslie when he pulled his revolver first and stood in a half stooping position; this was right after he first fired at me.

Signed,
M.D. Killeen"[1]

Perine took the stand and testified in his own behalf. He denied that he fired any shot or that he was armed with any weapon except a pocket knife. He said that he believed that Leslie fired a shot at Killeen and rushed down the hall in the direction of Killeen.

---

[1]   Tombstone <u>Epitaph</u>, August 24, 1880;
<u>Tombstone's Epitaph</u> p. 81.

Buckskin Frank Leslie took the witness stand to testify on behalf of his friend Perine. He described the beating over the head with a pistol by Killeen very much as Killeen had done in his dying statement. But in addition, stated that the second shot that Killeen had fired had struck him on top of the head.[1]

At the end of the hearing, Judge Riley, the Justice of the Peace, made an order holding the prisoner to await the action of the County Grand Jury on the charge of manslaughter and fixed bail in the sum of $5,000. Being unable to furnish that amount of bail, Perine was taken to Tucson by Deputy Sheriff Wyatt Earp and held in the Tucson jail pending action of the Grand Jury.

Killeen's widow testified at the hearing, but she was not a ex-Mrs. Killeen at that time for by August 25, the date she testified, she had married Frank Leslie and was then his wife. She testified that she was there and described the events somewhat the same as Perine and Buckskin Frank Leslie had described them except that she said that she never did see Perine there at all and that if he had been there she would have seen him.[2]

He was held in the Tucson jail for about two months until a grand jury met. The jury returned a number of true bills against various offenders, but not against Perine. It apparently did not agree with the findings of the Tombstone Judge and Perine was freed and Buckskin Leslie's claim was made good.

Each of the other two killings by Frank Leslie that took place in Tombstone make very good stories. They both occurred after the Earps had left Tombstone and, therefore, will not be covered in this book.

Just to summarize the lawlessness of the area in and about Tombstone, let me quote a couple of letters printed in the Tombstone Epitaph that described conditions.

"DISTRICT ATTORNEY

"Hugh Farley, Democratic candidate for District Attorney, is the present incumbent in that office and has held the position since the first of January, 1879. During his term of office there had been more than thirty homicides committed and crimes of all classes had been of frequent occurrence in Pima County. The use of the six-shooter has become so common as to be scarcely remarked and soon forgotten except by the unfortunate person against whom the argument was decided.

"From the first of October of 1879 to the opening of the present

---

[1]   Ibid, p. 85.

[2]   Ibid, p. 86.

term of court, not less than twenty five homicides have been committed in this county and 15 persons have been confined in the Tucson jail awaiting investigation on a charge of murder. (Note: Tucson was then and is now the county seat of Pima County.) Of this number not one has been convicted and but one has been tried . . .

"Quite a number of cattle thieves have been bound over to appear before the grand jury, and they have not appeared, and the grand jury left in ignorance of the evidence against them. These are cases where inditements have been made against cattle thieves, and receivers of stolen cattle, and the indicted persons have not been assigned and inditements left to slumber and in the pigeon holes of the clerk's office until time and dust have hidden them from view. These facts are all of record. The records are open to the public, and any person who doubts or denies them may be convinced of the truth by examination.

"Signed,

"Republican County Committee

"(October 20, 1880)"[1]

Some months later, the Epitaph printed the following letter to the editor.

"Editor Epitaph:

"I am not a growler or a chronic grumbler, but I own stock, am a butcher and supply my immediate neighborhood beef, and to do so must keep cattle on hand, and do try and could do so always if I had not to divide with unknown and irresponsible partners. Viz: 'Cowboys,' or some other cattle thieves. Since my advent into the territory and more particularly on the San Pedro River, I have lost 50 head of cattle by cattle thieves. I am not the only one who has suffered from these robbers and cattle thieves on the San Pedro within the last six months. Aside from 50 head of good beef that I have been robbed of Judge Blair has lost his entire heard. P. McMinnimen has lost all of his fine steers (oxen). Dunbar at Tres Alamos has lost a number of head. Burton of Huachuca, lost almost his entire heard, and others - and in fact all engaged in the stock business - have lost heavily from cattle thieves. And not always do these thieves confine themselves to cattle; horses and mules are gobbled up by these robbers as well as cattle. Is there no way to stop this wholesale stealing of stock in this vicinity or in this county?

"T. W. Ayles, Cattle Dealer

"March 18, 1881"[2]

Thus life in and around Tombstone appears to have been pretty precarious during the years of 1881 and 1882.

---

1   Ibid, p. 140.

2   Ibid, p. 141.

CHAPTER XXXI

JOHNNY-BEHIND-THE-DEUCE
(JOHN O'ROURKE)

ON January 14, 1881 in the city of Tombstone and nearby Charleston, an event occurred that reminds the reader of Wyatt Earp's episodes in Ellsworth, Wichita, and Dodge City, Kansas where he claimed to have confronted and overwhelmed large numbers of irate men. Keep in mind that on January 14, 1881, neither Virgil or Wyatt or any of the Earps held any position of authority either in the City of Tombstone or County of Pima, although Virgil held the position of Deputy United States Marshal. In order to analyze this story, once again it will be necessary to quote the whole story from Lake's book. The story is as follows:

"On January 12, Virgil Earp gave way to Ben Sippy. Three days later, in the Tombstone streets, a mob of five hundred of the toughest citizens that Tombstone and Charleston could muster made wild and woolly Arizona's first real play against this Wyatt Earp, who, the more desperate characters had been insisting, was overly feared and greatly overrated.

"Johnny-Behind-the-Deuce (John O'Rourke) was a tinhorn gambler. Aside from his predilection for playing the two-spot open when in funds to buck a faro bank and through which he gained his frontier sobriquet, there was nothing notable about him. He was an insignificant runt who hung around Charleston gambling-houses, figured himself as one of the outlaw gang, but never stacked high enough to enjoy serious consideration until he got his 'man for breakfast' one morning.

"After an all-night poker session at Charleston, in which Henry Schneider,[1] burly chief engineer of the Tombstone Mining and Milling Corporation, was a heavy loser, the tinhorn passed some comment on the engineer as a gambler. Words led to violence, and as Schneider drew a knife, Johnny-Behind-the-Deuce jerked a six-gun and killed him.

"George McKelvey, Charleston constable, heard that a bunch of Curly Bill's rustlers had suggested to a crowd of Schneider's employees that there'd be a morning's entertainment in trying and hanging the tinhorn and that the lynching party was organizing in

---

[1] The man's name was Phillip Schneider, not Henry. See 1880 U.S. Census for Charleston, A.T.

Quinn's Saloon. McKelvey hitched a pair of mules to a buckboard and started his prisoner for Tombstone.

"Halfway up the San Pedro slope, McKelvey looked back to see a mob of horsemen hot after him, and poured leather. Three miles out of Tombstone, the riders opened fire at long range on the buckboard. Half a mile ahead was Jack McCann's adobe, 'The Last Chance Saloon.' McKelvey took the final ounce from his team to reach this dubious haven three hundred yards ahead of his pursuers.

"At this point legendary accounts of the episode differ from contemporary records. Yarn-spinners have sent Jack McCann to the constable's aid on his race-mare, Molly McCarthy. The horseman who met McKelvey by chance was Virgil Earp, riding Dick Naylor, a thoroughbred animal belonging to Wyatt.

"'That gang's aiming to lynch this fellow,' McKelvey shouted to Virgil. 'These mules are done.'

"Virgil, who did not know Johnny-Behind-the-Deuce from Adam, worked Dick Naylor close to the buckboard.

"'Jump on behind,' he yelled. The tinhorn obeyed, and Dick Naylor started for Tombstone.

"The powerful thoroughbred, carrying double, easily distanced the cow-ponies which had come ten miles upgrade on a dead run. At Tombstone, Virgil found Wyatt and Morgan at the Wells-Fargo office. Johnny-Behind-the-Deuce got out enough of his story to let Wyatt know that John Ringo and other cowboys were leading his pursuers before Jim Earp ran over with word that the Charleston mob had ridden up Tough Nut Street and dismounted to mix with the 'graveyard shift' of miners from Dick Gird's property on the hill. They had recruited about three hundred Tombstone men employed by this company for which Schneider had worked, were getting rifles and shotguns from the mine arsenal, and planned to storm the calaboose to which they assumed Johnny would be taken.

"Wyatt picked up a double-barreled, sawed-off shotgun. Across Allen Street was Jim Vogan's bowling-alley, a long, narrow, solid, adobe building, walls sealed on either side by adjoining structures, a small door and high windows at the rear, double-doors fronting Allen Street.

"'Take him into Vogan's,' Wyatt told Virgil and Morgan. 'If they try for the back, you can pick 'em off faster than they can crowd in. If they get by me in front, give this fellow a gun and let him help you.'

"Five hundred blood-lusting frontiersmen poured into Allen Street as Virgil and Morgan got Johnny-Behind-the-Deuce into the bowling-alley. Wyatt stood alone at the curbline, his shotgun in the crook of his right arm. The mob was to the east. To the west, Allen Street had cleared of traffic with ominous celerity.

"'Where is he?' the mob clamored.

"'Over in Vogan's,' someone shouted.   The five hundred executed a surging flank movement that filled Allen Street from curb to curb, faced the United States Marshal, and halted abruptly.

"'Go in and drag him out!' the jamming rear ranks called.

"Again folklore departs from history. Wyatt's version of what followed is borne out by Jack Archer, old-time stage driver, who stood that morning in the Wells-Fargo doorway.

"'Wyatt didn't swear, or call names,' Archer insists. 'He didn't have to raise his voice. The mob wasn't thirty feet from him.'

"'Most accounts have me cursing that crowd plenty' Wyatt commented, 'but that was no time for hot language.

"'Boys,' I said, 'don't you make any fool play here; that little tinhorn isn't worth it.'

"The lynchers were not to be turned this readily from their blood-letting.

"'Go in after him!' those in the rear kept yelling. 'Earp can't stop you!'

"Under pressure the front rank edged forward. The surging movement shifted to the rhythmic stamp of an Indian war dance. This was no mob of the cities. Half of the men in the crowd had fought Apaches. The rest were highwaymen, rustlers, cowboys, and boom-camp miners on a rampage. Shouts and cat-calls merged in the whooping staccato of the red man's war-cry.

"Wyatt threw his shotgun before him, left hand on the fore-end, right on grip and triggers.

"In the crowd every man had a shotgun, rifle, or six-gun, ready to pour lead into the lone peace officer. At the rear, those who could not see the marshal's eye, waved and fired their guns in the air, their rage increasing as those in front bore back from the threat of Wyatt's weapon.

"'Yi-yi-yi-yi-yi-! Ya-a-a-hoo!'

"Tapping his mouth with his hand, an old-timer screeched an Apache death-yell. The mob took up the familiar signal.

"'Rush him!' someone called. 'He'll quit! If he doesn't, let him have it! Get that tinhorn strung up and get this over!'

"Wyatt swung the twin muzzles slowly back and forth across the crowded street.

"'Don't fool yourselves,' he cautioned the front ranks.

"'That tinhorn's my prisoner, and I'm not bluffing.'[1]

"His eye traveled swiftly over the maddened faces.

---

[1] By what authority was he Wyatt Earp's prisoner? He held no official position in law enforcement at that time.

"'The most dangerous mob in the world,' he observed fifty years afterward, 'is a leaderless one, for the reason that there's no one on whom you can pin anything.   The crowd that wanted to lynch Johnny-Behind-the-Deuce had shown no leader, so I picked one for them, and gave him a few assistants.   There in the front row, with a rifle in his hand was Dick Gird, multi-millionaire, employer of half of the men at his back, as popular a fellow as there was in the camp and one of the best friends I had in Tombstone.   He told me afterwards he never knew how he went crazy enough to get there.'

"Again the rear ranks tried to force action.

"'Cut him down!   Turn loose on him!   You'll get him!'

"The front rank surged to within twenty feet of the marshal.

"'Stop where you are,' Wyatt ordered. 'Sure you can get me. But I'll take eight or ten of you along.   There's eighteen buckshot in this gun and the wads are slit.   Once step more, and you get it.'

"Jack Archer and two others who saw the play have said that Wyatt paled beneath his tan until he looked as though he had jaundice.

"'Nice mob you've got, Mr. Gird,' Wyatt remarked in a casual tone, fixing leadership as he had determined. 'I didn't know you trailed with such company.

"He swung his gun-muzzle on the mine-owner's belly.

"'If I have to get anyone, Mr. Gird,' the marshal continued, 'you're first.   Three or four will go down with you.' He named the men at Gird's right and left in the same matter-of-fact fashion. 'Your friends may get me, but there'll be my brothers.   It'll cost good men to lynch that tinhorn, and Number One'll be Dick Gird.'

"The rear ranks pressed forward.   Those in front bore back from the step into eternity.   One man against five hundred.   This was a showdown.

"Wyatt sensed the high point.

"'Don't be a fool, Dick,' he suggested.

"Gird grinned sheepishly, turned and shouldered through the crowd.   One by one, others followed.   The front rank grew raged, broke up.   The Tombstone residents edged to the far sidewalk and the rear, leaving forty or fifty Charlestonians, mostly of the Clanton crowd, to face the marshal.   Wyatt dropped his shotgun into the crook of his elbow, and eyed his professional enemies scornfully.

"While Wyatt Earp held the lynch-mob at bay, Deputy Sheriff Johnny Behan, two of his deputies, and Ben Sippy the Tombstone marshal, stood across Allen Street from the bowling-alley and made no move to assist Wyatt."[1]

---

[1]   <u>Wyatt Earp Frontier Marshal</u>, pp. 246-250.

Compare that story with the stories published in the Tombstone Epitaph.

"SLAUGHTERED
"Brutal Murder of an Upright Citizen at Charleston
by a Desperado

"Again, the bloody hand of a murderer has been raised against a peaceable citizen; again the law is scoffed at and Justice derided. Yesterday's sun rose bright and cheerful over our neighboring village of Charleston, mellowing the crisp night air with its rays. Once more her toilers began their daily avocations with renewed energy, little dreaming of the damnable deed that, in the glowing light of noonday, was to await one of their number.

"Sometime since the cabin of Mr. W.P. Schneider, chief engineer of the Corbin Mill, was entered and robbed of several articles including some clothing. Circumstances pointed very strongly to two parties, one of whom is so well known by the cognomen of 'Johnny-Behind-the-Deuce' that we were unable last night to obtain his real name, but direct proof not being sufficient, no arrest was made. Yesterday at noon Mr. Schneider left his duties and went to a restaurant where he was accustomed to take his meals, and on entering approached the stove and, noticing a friend standing by, entered into conversation. Having just left the heated engine room the air without felt cool which brought from Mr. S. a remark to that effect. 'Johnny-Behind-the-Deuce' who was also in the room, then said, 'I thought you never got cold.' Not desiring to have anything to do with one of his character, Mr. Schneider turned and said, 'I was not talking to you, sir.' This raised the lurking devil in the diminutive heart of 'J-B-the-D,' who blurted out, 'G-d d--n you I'll shoot you when you come out,' and left the room. After eating his dinner Mr. Schneider passed out the door, and was proceeding to the mill, when, true to his promise, the lurking fiend, who had desecrated himself with hell in his heart and death in his mind, drew deadly aim and dropped his victim dead in his tracks.

"Immediately after the shooting the following telegrams were sent to Mr. Richard Gird, the superintendent, who was in the mine here at the time:

"'Charleston, Jan. 14, 1:30 p.m.

"'To Richard Gird; Schneider has just been killed by a gambler; no provocation. Cow boys are preparing to take him out of custody. We need fifty well armed men.'

"'Charleston, Jan. 14, 1:35 p.m.

"'To Richard Gird; Prisoner has just gone to Tombstone. Try and head him off and bring him back.'

"'Charleston, Jan. 14, 1:50 p.m.

"'To Richard Gird; Burnett has telegraphed to the officers who have the murderer in charge to bring him back to appear at inquest. See that he is brought back.'

"Considerable delay occurred in getting these dispatches to Mr. Gird, who at the time was in the mine, and just where was not known; but as soon as he received it, prompt action was taken, and a number of the miners were ordered to report to the officers, to resist any attempted rescue of the prisoner. Owing to some delay in delivery at the office of the company, and subsequent loss time in finding Mr. Gird, over a hour elapsed, we are informed, after transmission before the dispatches were opened and during this time the murderer was flying over the road toward the city, reaching the corner of Fifth and Allen a few minutes after the dispatches had been read. It is asserted that the officers, fearing pursuit, sent the murderer, who was on horseback, on ahead. However, this may be, it is certain that he came in ahead, his horse reeking with sweat, and, dismounting in front of Vogan's saloon asked for protection, acknowledging that he had killed his man. In a few minutes Allen Street was jammed with an excited crowd, rapidly augmented by scores from all direction. By this time Marshal Sippy, realizing the situation at once, in the light of the repeated murders that have been committed and the ultimate liberty of the offenders, had secured a well armed posse of over a score of men to prevent any attempt on the part of the crowd to lynch the prisoner; but feeling that no guard would be strong enough to resist a justly enraged public long, procured a light wagon in which the prisoner was placed, guarded by himself, Virgil Earp and Deputy Sheriff Behan, assisted by a strong posse well armed. Moving down the street, closely followed by the throng, a halt was made and rifles leveled on the advancing citizens, several of whom were armed with rifles and shotguns. At this juncture a well known individual with more avoirdupois than brains, called to the officers to turn loose and fire in the crowd. But Marshall Sippy's sound judgement prevented any such outbreak as would have been the certain result, and cool as an iceberg he held the crowd in check. No one who was a witness of yesterday's proceedings can validate that but for his presence, blood would have flown freely. The posse following would not have been considered; but, bowing to the majesty of the law, the crowd subsided and the wagon proceeded on its way to Benson with the prisoner, who by daylight this morning was lodged in the Tucson jail.

"Scarcely had the outfit got out of sight until stories of all description regarding the killing and attending circumstances grew rife. One was to the effect that Schneider had chased 'Johnny-Behind-the-Deuce' out of the restaurant with a drawn knife. This grew and brought forth a revolver in the other hand. Then it was reported that Mr. Gird had turned his mine loose for the purpose of lynching the prisoner. Again it was said by some of the pals of "Johnny-Behind-the-Deuce," that he was an honorable citizen, etc. etc. With regard to the knife story the facts given by an eye-witness and borne out by the character of the deceased, prove them to be false. Concerning the charge that the miners were turned out to defeat the law, we have it from Mr. Gird himself that they were ordered to report to the officers, in keeping with the tenor of the dispatches received by him, to sustain the law. In view of the diabolical and unprovoked crime committed, it is not to be wondered at that some of them should have joined the crowd that followed, desiring vengeance. As to the honorable character of the martyred kid who sails under the banner of 'Johnny-Behind-the-Deuce,' it is a well known fact that he was driven out of Tiger District by the best element of that camp, about a year ago, and tonight he will repose at the county expense in a jail on whose walls are inscribed horrid mockery of justice blamed in the names of other murderers who have partaken of county refreshment to be turned loose again to fasten themselves on the Tombstone public, a living curse. Today the clouds will fall over his victim, silent in his last long sleep, no more to be a staff to parents who having assessed the summit of life's divide with whitened locks already stand beneath the descending scythe of Time. Mails will come and go, anxious hearts with eager beat will note perhaps the postman's knock. No news from day to day until at last the sad tidings will cross the threshold, and bending under the weight of woe two or more souls will gladly welcome death . . . (Jan. 17, 1881.)"[1]

One can look in vain through the newspaper reports for the name of Wyatt Earp. The name of Virgil Earp does appear, and since he was no longer Marshal of Tombstone and had been replaced by Marshal Sippy, one had to wonder what he was doing helping out Deputy Sheriff Behan and Marshal Sippy, it could be supposed that as Deputy United States Marshal he felt it his duty to help out.

Since the newspaper states that Virgil Earp and Deputy Sheriff Behan, assisted by a strong posse well armed, it is possible, and even probable, that Wyatt Earp was a member of that posse. If he took a prominent part in the activities of the posse, the newspaper reporters failed to notice it.

George W. Parsons, our favorite diarist, happened to be in the vicinity when the occurrence in Tombstone took place. A part of his entry of Friday, January 14, 1881 read as follows:

"A gambler called, 'Johnny-Behind-the-Deuce' his favorite way

---

[1]   Tombstone's Epitaph, pp. 57-60.

at faro rode into town followed by mounted men who chased him from Charleston, he having shot and killed Schneider, engineer of T.M. & M Co. The officers sought to protect him and swore in deputies themselves, gambling men (the deputies that is) to help. Many of the miners armed themselves and tried to get at the murderer. Several times, yes a number of times, rushes were made and rifles leveled, causing Mr. Stanley and me to get behind the most available shelter. Terrible excitement, but the officers got through finally and out of town with their man bound for Tucson. This man should have been killed in his tracks. Too much of this kind of business is going on. I believe in killing such men as one would a wild animal. The law must be carried out by the citizens or should be when it fails in its performance as it has lately done . . ."[1]

You will note that Parsons failed to mention Wyatt Earp, but his memory seems to have changed considerably in the next fifty years. On November 6, 1928 he wrote a letter to Stuart N. Lake citing some incidents that occurred in Tombstone and commenting on some other stories and in the letter he said:

"About the episode in Tombstone 'Johnny-Behind-the-Deuces' raced up to the City from Charleston on a fast horse to seek refuge from his pursuers, I will say that I happened to be in the street as he entered the town and placed himself under the protection of the officers. A crowd soon gathered and the outlook was very stormy for the safety of the murderer, he having just killed the Engineer of the Works at the Charleston. It was deemed proper to take him out of town, the excitement was growing so great. So the officers surrounded the store and he was taken to a wagon in the street, made to lie down, and during this time Wyatt was present on guard to prevent any rescue or violence. So when things were ready they mounted their horses and Wyatt, I could see him now as his team went down the street, he backed his horse down the street fronting the mob and lowered his rifle every now and then on them when a rush was attempted. Several others were with him and kept the crowd back from the would-be lynching. It was not long before they were out of town and on the road to Tucson, 75 miles away where this murderer was finally landed and the officers returned. It was a very nervy proposition, particularly on the part of Wyatt. This story is related in the book called Tombstone by a writer named Burns, I think, which it might be well for you to see."[2]

Myers in his book, The Last Chance, repeats almost verbatim the

---

[1]   The Private Journal of George W. Parsons, p. 116.

[2]   Letter from George W. Parsons to Stuart N. Lake, dated November 6, 1928.

story told by Walter Noble Burns in his book Tombstone. He repeats
the story that Richard Gird, the Superintendent of a mine in
Tombstone, was picked out by Wyatt Earp to center his threats upon
knowing that Gird was the leader of the crowd of miners who had
gathered. None of the people who support Earp's story seem to take
into consideration the telegrams recounted in the Tombstone Epitaph
of January 17, however. Richard Gird had been warned by telegram
that the gamblers and cowboys were preparing to take Johnny-
Behind-the-Deuce from the custody of the officers, with the
implication that they were intending to hang him. The first telegram
ended, "we need fifty well-armed men." These men were not
requested for the purpose of lynching Johnny-Behind-the-Deuce, but
were requested to prevent such a lynching. In all probability that is
the reason that Richard Gird showed up with his group of miners
who, rather than threatening to lynch Johnny-Behind-the-Deuce,
were there to prevent any such thing happening. Therefore, the story
that Wyatt Earp picked out Dick Gird to threaten and back down
doesn't hold water.

William M. Breakenridge wrote the story of Johnny-Behind-the-
Deuce, and his story raised a number of questions. He told the story
this way:

"The Smelter men to the number of twenty-five or thirty
followed and were overhauling him when he met a man exercising a
race mare, and got him to take the prisoner on behind him and make
a run for Tombstone as the mules had given out. Here the prisoner
was turned over to Wyatt Earp, who was a Deputy United States
Marshal. When the mob, increased by about an equal number of
miners from the hill, came up to take 'Johnny-Behind-the-Deuce'
away to hang him, Earp stood them off with a shotgun, and dared
them to come and get him. It didn't look good to the mob, and Earp
took him to Tucson which at that time was the County Seat. 'Johnny'
was bound over to the Grand Jury, but before he was indicted, he
escaped on May 17, 1881 after laying in jail nearly a year."[1]

There are several things wrong with this story. Wyatt Earp was
not a Deputy U.S. Marshal at that time, and if Breakenridge was
telling the story from his own knowledge, he should have known that.
The event did not occur in 1880. According to the Tombstone
Epitaph it occurred on January 14, 1881, and this date is corroborated
by the Parsons diary.[2]. His statement that Johnny was bound over
to the grand jury but before he was indicted he escaped on May 17,

[1]   Helldorado, pp. 211-212.

[2]   The Private Journal of George W. Parsons, p. 116.

1881 after lying in jail for nearly a year could not be true. Generally in those days, as well as now, when a person had been bound over for appearance before the Grand Jury he was indicted within a very short period of time. Ordinarily not more than 30 days.

I doubt seriously that Breakenridge knew anything about the event or was there. His book was written in 1928; I suspect that he got the story from Walter Noble Burns book, Tombstone, which was written in 1927. At least both authors had Wyatt Earp backing down the mob with a shotgun, and it is almost certain that didn't happen.

CHAPTER XXXII

LIFE IN TOMBSTONE

ALTHOUGH Lake fails to give dates, the events that he talks about must have occurred at about the end of 1880, or the first part of 1881 just before Cochise County was created. He describes the Oriental Building, which housed the Oriental saloon and gambling place as being owned by Jim Vizina and rented as a restaurant and bar to Mike Joyce.[1] Joyce sublet his gambling interest to Lou Rickabaugh and his associates, who included William H. Harris, formerly partner with Chalk Beeson in the Long Branch Saloon in Dodge City, and Dick Clark of San Francisco who had a long career in Tombstone and environs in the gambling business.

Harris when a part owner of the Long Branch saloon in Dodge City had sublet his gambling activities to Luke Short, and on occasion had employed Bat Masterson. When he got to Arizona he sent for Luke Short and Bat Masterson to come from Dodge City to deal and work with him in the gambling facility at the Oriental Saloon. Bat left Dodge City February 8, 1881[2] and arrived about the middle of February, joining his friends dealing cards at the Oriental.[3]

Lake says that: "Other gamblers, envious of the Oriental's popularity hired a core of professional fighting men under John Tyler to hurrah the Rickabaugh place so consistently as to scare away patronage."[4]

Rickabaugh went to Wyatt Earp and offered him one quarter interest in the gambling concession if he would work as a dealer, guard and a bouncer at the place.

Wyatt accepted Rickabaugh's offer, and one can be quite certain that he was glad to be re-associated with his old friends Luke Short and Bat Masterson from Dodge City. About his experience as guard

---

[1]   Joyce's correct name was Milton E. Joyce. Lake mistakenly called him Mike and most other authors followed his lead. See Records of Tombstone County.

[2]   Great Gunfighters of Kansas Cowtowns, p. 281.

[3]   And Die in the West, p. 130.

[4]   Wyatt Earp, Frontier Marshal, p. 253.

in the Oriental Saloon, Lake tells the following story:
"Opposition gunmen had been usurping the Oriental bar and gambling-tables during hours which should have been the most profitable, and driving customers out by gunplay and other violence. The first evening of Wyatt's partnership, Johnny Tyler led a dozen followers in to continue the intimidation. Wyatt sat in a chair against the rear wall of the gambling room.

"While his companions lingered at the bar, Tyler walked to a faro layout where Rickabaugh was dealing and changed in one hundred dollars. After a steady run of bickering and abuse of Rickabaugh, Tyler jerked a six-gun to shove his stack of chips across the layout to the queen. 'Deal 'em, you big-so-and-so,' he challenged. 'and if the queen loses, I'll blow that stack into your bank!'

"Rickabaugh filled the dealers slot to overflowing and a shot that scattered the stack of chips would send the forty-five caliber slug tearing through his body. Lou looked the gambler in the eye, and made a turn. The queen did not show.

"Johnny Tyler screamed with pain. A muscular thumb and forefinger was hoisting him from his seat by his ear-lobe. If he had an idea of gunplay, he abandoned it when he saw who had him.

"'I didn't know you had an interest in this place,' Tyler exclaimed. 'I have,' Wyatt assured him, 'and you can tell your friends it's a fighting interest.'

"Using the ear as a lever, Wyatt propelled Tyler to the door. With a shove and a boot he sent the gunman sprawling to Allen Street. As he turned back into the Oriental, Wyatt saw Tyler's followers lined up at the bar hands in the air and looking into Doc Holliday's nickel-plated six-gun.

"'Much obliged, Doc,' Wyatt said. 'Herd 'm outside with their friend.'"[1]

Lake states that the gambling partnership was forced to purchase the Oriental Saloon soon after, when Milt Joyce was appointed to the Cochise County's newly formed Board of Supervisors and threw in politically with their enemies.

This must have happened about the time Bat Masterson arrived in Tombstone, as Cochise County was created on February 1, 1881 and it took a while to make all of the political appointments including that of member of the Board of Supervisors.

That Wyatt Earp was fairly friendly with Behan and his friends seems to be evidenced by a Court document in the Justice court of the village of Tombstone dated October 11th and 12th, 1880. It is the record of a case in which Doc Holliday was charged with assault with

---

1   Wyatt Earp, Frontier Marshal, p. 253.

a deadly weapon with intent to kill. The first entry in the proceedings dated October 11, 1880 is as follows:

"On this day M.E. Joyce appeared in court and on oath accused J.H. Holliday of an assault with a deadly weapon with intent to kill. Warrant issued to Fred White, Village Marshal."

The next entry on the docket is to the effect that subpoenas had been issued for M.E. Joyce, John H. Behan, _____ Woods, and _____ Fuller, as prosecution witnesses. (The Woods was probably Harry Woods, the Editor of the Daily Nugget, and the Fuller was probably Wes or Wesley Fuller, who would later appear as a witness against Wyatt Earp in the O.K. Corral battle case). The record shows that on October 12th, Doc Holliday entered a plea of guilty to the crime of assault and battery, a misdemeanor, and the charge of assault with a deadly weapon with intent to kill was dismissed. Doc Holliday was fined $20 and costs.

The story of what happened on that occasion has been told by numerous authors, very few of them agreeing on the details, and all of them being erroneous on the date.

For instance, Myers in his book on Doc Holliday, tells of an instance when Milt Joyce, owner of the Oriental, and one day to be a member of the Board of Supervisors of Cochise County collaborated with John Behan to get Big Nosed Kate drunk and get from her a statement incriminating Doc Holliday in the Benson Stage Holdup that occurred on March 15, 1881, which will be recounted in Chapter XXXIII. Doc Holliday was in the Oriental Saloon that was owned and operated by Milt Joyce.

According to John Myers: "While Doc was giving the Supervisors his views on the matter his enemies got near enough to make him the meat of their sandwich. Trying to make sure he wouldn't get a chance to draw, they suddenly jumped him from two directions. Frail as Doc was, this rough and tumble was no contest; yet his attackers hardly had things their own way. Joyce was getting ready to shoot the man whom he and his partner had borne to the floor, but by the time other inmates of the Saloon had hastened to break it up, Doc Holliday had already shot. Somehow, as he went down, he had managed to draw, pull the trigger and score twice. For a souvenir of the engagement, Joyce had a hole in his left hand, while the other fellow got a bullet through the foot. Behan and Wyatt acting for once in unison, later saved Joyce's life. Grieved about his sore fist, the supervisor accosted Earp and Holliday, when the latter was in shape to handle himself. The Sheriff dragged Mike [sic Milt] away and Wyatt talked Doc into staying put. This was in all likelihood one of the occasions which led Bat Masterson - who had not yet left Tombstone then - to make one of his dicta about John Henry Holliday. Remarking on his affection for Wyatt Earp, Bat Masterson went on:

"'The depth of his sentiment was shown not only by Doc's demonstrated willingness to stake his life for Wyatt without a second thought; it was even more clearly established by the fact, despite his almost uncontrollable temper and his manacle love of fight, Doc Holliday could avoid trouble when there was a possibility that some encounter might prove embarrassing to Wyatt.'"[1]

The trouble with this story and most of the others written about the event is that none of them seem to pay any attention to dates. He talks about Joyce being a supervisor, and that was probably an error since Cochise County was not formed until January 1881, and had no Supervisors on October 11, 1880. Bat Masterson didn't arrive in Tombstone until the middle of February, 1881.[2] He left in about two months.[3] Big Nosed Kate must have made her written statement incriminating Doc Holliday about the first week of July, for Sheriff Behan arrested him on a murder charge July 6, 1881.[4] By that time Bat Masterson had been long gone.

The incident that they got Big Nosed Kate to make an incriminating statement about Doc Holliday occurred on March 15, 1881 and the shooting of Milt Joyce by Doc Holliday occurred on October 11, 1880.

Myers also refers to John Behan as being the Sheriff of Cochise County when in fact at the time that the incident occurred on October 11, 1880 Wyatt Earp was Deputy Sheriff of Pima County of which Tombstone was a part.

It's interesting to note, that on the date that Doc Holliday shot Milt Joyce, both Wyatt Earp and John Behan were present in the Oriental Saloon along with Harry M. Woods, who would later be appointed Deputy to John Behan and who was Editor of the Daily Nugget and also Wes Fuller who was no friend of the Earps and would be a witness against Wyatt Earp in the O.K. Corral battle case.

This event occurred at a time when Wyatt Earp had an interest in the Oriental Saloon, was a Deputy Sheriff of Pima County and was on fairly good terms with both Milt Joyce and John Behan. Unless there were two such incidents, this also occurred before Bat Masterson arrived from Dodge City.

That there could have been two or even three confrontations

---

[1]   Doc Holliday, p. 156.

[2]   Great Gunfighters of Kansas Cowtowns, p. 281.

[3]   Bat Masterson, p. 203.

[4]   Helldorado, p. 124.

between Doc Holliday and Milt Joyce is not an impossibility.

Dale Schoenberg says: "Holliday's first encounter with Joyce came between April 13 and May 30, 1881, when Doc shot Joyce in the hand at the Oriental Saloon. Holliday also shot one of Joyce's bartenders in the foot during the melee. Doc was indicted by the grand jury on May 30, but nothing came of it."[1]

As authority for the statement, Schoenberg cites the Tombstone Epitaph for May 30, 1881.

I could find no such story in the May 30th, 1881 Epitaph, but did find about a 4 line statement on page 4 of the May 29th edition that simply stated that Doc Holliday had been indicted by the grand jury.

None of the dates fit. The dates that we are fairly sure of are: Doc Holliday was charged with assault with intent to kill in the Justice Court on October 11, 1880. The stage coach robbery for which Doc Holliday was arrested on the basis of Big Nose Kate's statement supposedly made to Milt Joyce and Sheriff Behan in July, 1881,[2] occurred on March 15, 1881. Doc couldn't have been quarreling with Milt Joyce over his helping Behan get the statement from Kate Fisher until after March 15, 1881.

If there were either two or three confrontations between Doc Holliday and Milt Joyce, no one has described them in detail, giving a date that would permit a researcher to verify them.

Al Turner has named William Crownover Parker, Jr., as the other victim of the shooting, he having been shot in the foot. , but it is not certain that such was the case, since no other person was named in the court proceedings in which Holliday was charged with assault with a deadly weapon with intent to kill Milt Joyce.

It's hard to determine just how long Wyatt Earp retained an interest in the Oriental Gambling House. Lake says that early in January, 1882, Lou Rickabaugh, Dick Clark, and Bill Harris decided to sell the Oriental back to Milt Joyce, the first owner.

He says the arrangement was that Joyce was to take over the place on January 5, 1882. Joyce had said that he had a partner to run the gambling, but would not identify him.[3]

It turned out later that his gambling partner was none other than John Behan.[4]

One can't help noticing that at the time Wyatt Earp was supposed

---

[1]   The Gunfighters, p. 108.

[2]   Helldorado, p. 124.

[3]   Wyatt Earp, Frontier Marshal, p. 309.

[4]   Ibid, p. 312.

to have gained a one fourth interest in the Oriental Gambling concession, he was Deputy Sheriff, and that later, after he resigned as Deputy Sheriff, and Behan was appointed Sheriff of Cochise County, Behan became a partner in the gambling house. Could it be that neither Earp nor Behan purchased an interest in the gambling place, but were given the interest in lieu of protection?

There were other incidents in the Oriental that became a part of the lore of Tombstone. One of them was a killing of a gambler by the name of Charlie Storms.

Charlie Storms was a member of the gambling fraternity and was well-known throughout the west. Bat Masterson encountered him in Cheyenne, Wyoming in 1876.[1] And Wyatt Earp mentions him as being in Deadwood, Dakota Territory in the Fall and Winter of 1876-77.[2]

Charlie Storms had evidently followed the pattern of going to mining boom towns to engage in gambling, and was pursuing that occupation in Tombstone when on February 25, 1881 he got into an altercation with Luke Short and lost his life. We have two eye-witness accounts of what occurred. Bat Masterson who was then working at the Oriental with Luke Short told the story this way:

"One morning I went into the Oriental Gambling House where Luke (Short) was working, just in time to keep him from killing a gambler named Charlie Storms. . . Charlie Storms was one of the best-known gamblers in the entire west and had, on several occasions successfully defended himself in pistol fights with Western 'gunfighters.'

"Charlie Storms and I were very close friends -- as much so as Short and I were -- and for that reason I didn't care to see him get into what I knew would be a very serious difficulty. Storms didn't know Short, and . . . had sized him up as an insignificant-looking fellow, whom he could slap in the face without expecting a return. Both men were about to pull their pistols when I jumped between them and grabbed Storms, at the same time requesting Luke not to shoot - a request I knew he would respect if it was possible without endangering his own life too much. I had no trouble in getting Storms out of the house, as he knew me to be his friend. When Storms and I reached the Street, I advised him to go to his room and take a sleep, for I then learned for the first time that he had been up all night, and had been quarreling with other persons."

Bat took Storms to his room and tried to quiet him. Leaving

---

[1]   <u>Bat Masterson</u>, p. 75.

[2]   <u>Wyatt Earp Frontier Marshal</u>, p. 158.

him at his Hotel, he hurried back to the Oriental to talk to Short but found the little gambler standing outside the Allen Street entrance to the Saloon. Bat urged Luke to let the matter pass, without further trouble and was attempting to make excuses for Storms' behavior when Storms suddenly appeared to plead his own case. Wrote Bat:

"I was just explaining to Luke that Storms was a very decent sort of man when, low and behold!   There he stood before us. Without saying a word, he took hold of Luke's arm and pulled him off the sidewalk where he had been standing, at the same time pulling his pistol, a Colt's cut-off 45 caliber, single action; but . . . he was too slow, although he succeeded in getting his pistol out. Luke stuck the muzzle of his own pistol against Storms' heart and pulled the trigger. The bullet tore the heart asunder, and as he was falling, Luke shot him again. Storms was dead when he hit the ground."[1]

The other reported eye-witness was our trusted diarist, George W. Parsons who wrote in his diary for February 25, 1881 the following:

"Quite peaceable times lately, but today the monotony was broken by the shooting of Charles Storms by Luke Short on corner of Oriental. Shots - the first two were so deliberate I didn't think anything much was out of the way, but at next shot I seized my hat and ran into the street just in time to see Storms die, shot through the heart. Both gamblers, L.S. [Luke Short] running game at Oriental. Trouble brewing during night and morning and S. (Storms) was probably aggressor, though very drunk. He was game to the last and after being shot through the heart, by a desperate effort steadying revolver with both hands fired - four shots in all I believe.   Dr. Goodfellow brought bullet into my room and showed it to me. 45 caliber and slightly flattened. Also showed a bloody handkerchief, part of which was carried into wound by pistol.   Short, very unconcerned after shooting - probably a case of kill or be killed . . ."[2]

As in all eye-witness testimony there is a difference between the stories of each. I suspect the testimony of Bat Masterson is the most accurate, since I doubt seriously that if Charlie Storms were shot in the heart as everyone including the Dr. seemed to agree, he would be able to pull his weapon and get off four shots before dying.

On July 25, 1880, just two days before Wyatt Earp was appointed Deputy Sheriff for Pima County, Tombstone Epitaph reported on the killing of one J.T. Waters by E.L. Bradshaw. The newspaper report recounted that Bradshaw and Waters were very good friends and had

---

[1]   W.B. Masterson "Luke Short," Human Life (April 1907).

[2]   The Private Journal of George W. Parsons, p. 128.

prospected together and that when Waters first came to Tombstone he lived in Bradshaw's cabin. The paper went on to report:

"Yesterday morning Water's purchased a blue and black plaid shirt, little dreaming that the faded garment would hurl his soul into eternity before the sun had set. It so happened that several good natured remarks were made about the new shirt during the day until Waters had taken sufficient liquor to make the joking obnoxious to him, and he began to show an ugly resentment and was very abusive, concluding with, 'now if anyone don't like what I've said, let him get up, G-D D-M him. I'm chief. I'm boss. I'll knock the first S- of B- down that says anything about my shirt again.' This happened in the back room at Corrigan Saloon and as Water's stepped into the front room Bradshaw happened in and seeing the new shirt his friend was wearing made some pleasant remark about it whereupon Waters, without a word, struck Bradshaw a powerful blow over the left eye which sent him senseless to the floor. Waters then walked over to Vogan's and Flynn's, to see, as he said, 'If any S- of a B- there don't like his shirt.' He had just entered the street when Ed Farris made some remark about the new shirt, which Waters promptly resented in his pugilistic style. After some more rowing Waters went back to Corrigan's Saloon. As soon as Bradshaw recovered from the knock-down he went into the back room, washed off the blood, went down to his cabin, put a bandage on his eye and his pistol in his pocket. He then came up to Allen Street and took his seat in front of Vogan's and Flynn's Saloon. Seeing Waters in Corrigan's door, Bradshaw crossed towards the Eagle Brewery, and walking down the sidewalk until within a few feet of Waters, said, 'Why did you do that?' Waters said something whereupon Bradshaw drew his pistol and fired four shots, all taking effect, one under the left arm probably pierced the heart, two entered about the center of his back between his shoulders, and one in the top of the head which would probably have resulted fatally. Water's fell at the second shot and soon expired. Bradshaw was promptly arrested and an examination will be had in the morning before Justice Gray."[1]

Many years later (1926) when Wyatt Earp was giving a deposition in the Crabtree Estate Case in Boston, he was asked about violence in Tombstone, and the above case was one of only four that he mentioned. Of course, by that time, he was trying to play down the violence in Tombstone during the time when he was there.[2]

---

[1]   Tombstone's Epitaph, p. 61.

[2]   The Triumphs and Trials of Lotta Crabtree, p. 280.

CHAPTER XXXIII

STAGE COACH ROBBERIES, KEY TO O.K. CORRAL SHOOTOUT

IN the Spring and Summer of 1881 there were a number of stagecoach robberies. Two of them involved the Earps deeply and the conduct of all of the parties involved led either directly or indirectly to the shootout at the O.K. Corral.

While Bob Paul was awaiting the decision of the Supreme Court in his appeal involving the Sheriff's election in November of 1880, he continued to ride as a guard for the Wells Fargo company on the Kinnear & Co.'s coach. Here it should be noted, as it has never been mentioned before, that while most people believe that the coaches were Wells, Fargo and Company coaches, they were not. The one running between Tombstone and Benson was owned by Kinnear & Co., and the Wells, Fargo & Co. had a contract with them to haul their freight which included money and bullion. The stage coach company did not hire guards, but the Wells, Fargo & Co. did and it was their guards who rode shot-gun on the stages when they were carrying large amounts of money.

On March 15, 1881 Bob Paul was the Wells, Fargo & Co. guard on the Kinnear & Co. coach from Tombstone to Benson. For some reason variously explained as his being ill or his hands being very cold, Bob Paul had exchanged seats with Bud Philpot, the driver of the outfit just before they were accosted by some armed men. The Tombstone Epitaph told the story this way:

"As the stage was going up a small incline about 200 yards this side of Drew station and about a mile the other side of Contention City, a man stepped into the road from the east side and called out 'Hold.' At the same moment a number of men--believed to have been eight--made their appearance and a shot was fired from the same side of the road instantly followed by another. One of those shots struck 'Bud' Philpot, the driver, who fell heavily forward between the wheels carrying the reins with him. The horses immediately sprang into a dead run. Meanwhile, Bob Paul, Wells Fargo & Co.'s messenger, one of the bravest and coolest men who ever sat on a box seat, was ready with his gun and answered back shot for shot before the frightened horses had whirled the coach out of range. It was fully a mile before the team could be brought to a stand, where it was discovered that one of the shots had mortally wounded a passenger on the coach named Roerig. As soon as the coach could be stopped, Paul secured the reins and drove rapidly to Benson and immediately started back

for the scene of the murder. At Benson a telegram was sent to the
Epitaph office stating that Roerig could not possibly live. There were
eight passengers on the coach and they all unite in praise of Mr.
Paul's bravery and presence of mind."[1]

The simple statement by the Epitaph of the facts of the robbery
were not very much in dispute, but the aftermath became the subject
of heated disputes and, as will appear hereafter, the stories about it
were substantially different when told by various people who claimed
to know the facts.

Except for making Wyatt Earp a Deputy United States Marshal
and putting him in charge of the posse, Lake's description of what
occurred seems to be more accurate than does the description written
by William M. Breakenridge in Helldorado although by comparing
the two and reading some of the newspaper reports, it's not difficult
to figure out who was telling the truth.

It will be necessary to quote substantially from Lake's book in
order to lay out the story as told by Wyatt and compare it to the one
told by Breakenridge. Lake said: "Wyatt deputized Virgil and
Morgan Earp, Bat Masterson and Marshall Williams as his posse, and
started for Drew's Ranch. Wyatt Earp suspected that Bill Leonard,
Jim Crane, Harry Head, and Luther King, of the Clanton Outfit, who
had been camping for a week in an abandoned adobe on the
Contention Road, were the Benson-Stage bandits, a suspicion speedily
confirmed after his posse reached Drew's and was joined by Sheriff
Behan and his Deputy, Breakenridge. Bob Paul and passengers who
had ridden through the attack gave details of the attempted hold-up."

The details did not differ substantially from those printed in the
Tombstone Epitaph. Lake continued on thusly:

"At daylight, Wyatt found seventeen empty rifle-shells in the road
where the highwaymen had stood pumping lead after the vanishing
bullion."[2]

"Earp said that 'Sheriff Behan sought to discourage pursuit of the
bandits by picturing the hopelessness of a desert trail that was twelve
hours old.' Marshal Earp, however, had confidence in his ability to
pick up signs. Then Behan protested that Wyatt would have no
authority to take prisoners if he caught up with them, and stated that,
as Sheriff, he would make no arrests on suspicion. Wyatt replied that
the stage had carried mail, and took up the trail. Behan and
Breakenridge followed."[3]

---

[1]   Tombstone's Epitaph, p. 172.

[2]   Wyatt Earp, Frontier Marshal, p. 254-256.

[3]   Ibid, p. 257.

The Earp party continued to trail the suspects and early on the morning of March 19th, they rode into Wheaton's abandoned ranch and found a badly used up horse that Luther King had ridden into Tombstone a week earlier.

Apparently the rider had obtained a fresh mount and headed for the ranch owned by Hank Redfield. They trailed him to there, and Morgan Earp ran him down hiding near the ranch and arrested him.

King disclaimed any knowledge of the hold-up at first, but under questioning by Wyatt and Bob Paul, he admitted that the hold up men had been Bill Leonard, Harry Head, Jim Crane and himself and protested that the only part that he had taken in the hold-up was to hold the horses. He denied doing any shooting. Later, in the presence of Bob Paul, Virgil and Morgan Earp, Marshall Williams, Sheriff Behan and Deputy Sheriff Breakenridge, Luther King repeated the full story of the attempted robbery and admitted that the horse found at Wheaton's was his.

At about that point, Behan claimed King as his prisoner, declaring that he was arresting him for murder and that was a County offense, not Federal. As Behan and Breakenridge were going to return to Tombstone with the prisoner, Marshall Williams, the Wells Fargo agent decided to go with them. Wyatt and the rest of his posse continued after Leonard, Head and Crane.

Lake describes the chase. "For more than three hundred miles over the most desolate sections of Arizona, Wyatt tracked his quarry after leaving Redfield's, north and west along the Tangue Verde, Rincon, and Santa Catalina Mountains, through the Oracles and Canada del Oro, east through the Santa Cruz, across the San Pedro and back to the Dragoons. At Helm's Ranch in the Dragoons, Behan and Breakenridge rejoined the posse bringing with them Buckskin Frank Leslie ostensibly because of Leslie's great skill as a trailer."[1]

Meanwhile, before Behan and Breakenridge returned to join up with Earp's posse at the Helm's Ranch, Luther King escaped. The story of his escape was told by The Daily Nugget of March 19, 1881 as follows:

"Luther King, the man arrested at Redfield's ranch charged with being implicated in the Bud Philpot murder, escaped from the Sheriff's office by quietly stepping out the back door while Harry Jones, esq. was drawing up a bill of sale for a horse the prisoner was disposing of to John Dunbar. Under Sheriff Harry Woods and Dunbar were present. He had been absent but a few seconds before he was missed. A confederate on the outside had a horse in readiness for him. It was a well planned job by outsiders to get him away. He

---

[1]   Ibid, p. 259.

was an important witness against Holliday. He, it was, that gave the names of the three that were being followed at the time he was arrested. There names were Bill Leonard, Jim Crane and Harry Head."[1]

When Sheriff Behan, Bill Breakenridge and Frank Leslie met up with Wyatt Earp and his posse at the Helm's Ranch, Behan failed to mention the fact that Luther King had escaped to Wyatt Earp. He didn't learn that until the posse was overtaken by Jim Hume, the Chief Special Officer for Wells Fargo & Co. When accosted by Wyatt Earp as to why he had not mentioned the fact that King had escaped, Behan replied that he didn't consider that it was any of his business.[2]

The escape story smells. It appears that while Harry Jones was drawing up a bill of sale to transfer possession of the horse to John Dunbar, who was County Treasurer and Behan's partner in the Dexter Corral and Livery Stable at Tombstone and while both Dunbar and Under-sheriff Harry Wood, who was also editor of the Daily Nugget was present, the prisoner just stepped out of the door and disappeared.

The Sheriff and his gang were trying to blame the robbery on the Earps by implicating Doc Holliday and used this unlikely story to try to show that the Earps may have had something to do with helping Luther King escape so he could not be a witness against Holliday. They must have taken the Tombstone public to be a real bunch of dummies to think that they would swallow such a far-fetched story. Nobody, not even Breakenridge ever said that Luther King had implicated Holliday, although they tried to imply that he could have if he wanted to. The only persons they ever quote him as naming as participants in the hold-up were Bill Leonard, Jim Crane, and Harry Head.

Next, the Nugget, trying to make a case for Holliday's participation in the hold-up, published the following story:

"On the afternoon of the attempted robbery, he (Holliday) engaged a horse at Tombstone Livery, stating that he might be gone for seven or eight days or might return that night. He left town about 4 o'clock armed with an Henry rifle and a six-shooter. He started for Charleston, and about a mile below Tombstone cut across to Contention. When next seen it was between 10 and 1 o'clock at night, riding back into the Livery at Tombstone, his horse fagged out. He at once called for another horse which he hitched in the street for some hours, but he did not again leave town. Statements attributed

---

[1]   Helldorado, p. 123.

[2]   Wyatt Earp, Frontier Marshal, p. 260.

to him, if true, look very bad, and if proved, are most conclusive as to his guilt either as a principal or as an accessory after the fact."[1]

It should be noted that the statements attributed to him were nonexistent. The Nugget did not quote any of them at all.

Back to the posse. The posse continued to trail the robbers and without proper supplies of food or water travelled several hundred miles. Eventually, the horses began to give out and the posse had to double up on the remaining animals. At one time two horses had been without water or food for 48 hours when they reached a desert waterhole at the edge of San Simon Valley. Lake says that: "Certain that the Marshal's men had abandoned the pursuit of the outlaws, the Sheriff's party left them. Riding at night, the Behan party reached Joe Hill's Ranch, forty miles distance about daylight. Hill was a Clanton follower, and a friend of Behan's. No help for the Marshal's men was sent from his place. Late the next night, Behan and his two Deputies reached the San Simon Ranch where they reported the plight of the Earp posse. The rancher immediately sent cowboys to the rescue with provisions and fresh ponies. When succor reached them, Virgil, Morgan, and Bob Paul had been without food for five days. However, they immediately started across country and made Tombstone but a few hours after Behan."[2]

William Breakenridge tells quite a different story, although the general outline is somewhat the same. After describing the hold-up and the killing of Bud Philpot in substantially the same way that Lake did, he proceeds as follows:

"Jim Crane, Harry Head, and Bill Leonard were accused of the crime and were searched for diligently but their trail was lost. A short time afterward it was reported that they were at Cloverdale in New Mexico, near the Mexican line. This was a cattle ranch and an outlaw rendezvous. Sheriff Behan started with Frank Leslie and myself to hunt them. Wyatt Earp, a Deputy United States Marshal, sent out his brothers Virgil and Morgan Earp and another man whose name I have forgotten as a posse to hunt for the stage robbers.

"As none of us had ever been in that part of the country before, we had to inquire the way to Cloverdale, and were directed wrongly as we ought to have expected. Next morning, taking a lunch with us we started on the trail we were directed to take, and that night reached a deserted ranch house known as the double 'dobe. This was forty miles from the Cienega. The following day we started out early, and passing through a gap in a mountain, found ourselves on a wide

---

[1]   Ibid, p. 263.

[2]   Ibid, p. 262.

open plain with no trees or water in sight. We made a dry camp that night and next morning found the stakes of the Atchison Topeka and Santa Fe Railroad Line that was being surveyed toward Benson. We followed them and about noon came in sight of the double 'dobe where we had stayed the first night out. We went there for water for ourselves and horses.

"We had seen no one since we left Joe Hill's; we had no provisions, having eaten the last of our lunch the night before, so we let our horses graze and rest until evening. Although both posses camped together at night we did not travel together, as our party was better mounted and we were more used to the saddle. We reached the water sometime before the others. Our horses were tired and we did not know the way or whether there was a ranch in which we could get aid, and after a consultation, I decided that my horse was able to carry me back to San Simon Cienaga that night as he would be in the morning. Behan and Leslie thought the same, but the Marshal's posse decided to wait until morning. We saddled up and struck out after dark and reached Joe Hill's Ranch about daylight. We got Hill's people up and hired a man to take some provisions back to the Marshal's party. He met them on the way and they were glad to see him. We lay at Hill's ranch one day, then returned to Tombstone.

"The stage hold-ups, Crane, Head and Leonard were in hiding in New Mexico and that summer they were all three killed at Hachita, New Mexico by some cowboys who were after the reward."[1]

There are several things about this story that bears some scrutiny. In the first place, he refers to Wyatt Earp as Deputy United States Marshal. At this point, I have never, and probably never will be able to understand why Wyatt Earp was always referred to as a Deputy United States Marshal, both by Breakenridge, who should have known better, and by Fred Dodge, who also should have known that he either was, or was not a United States Marshal.

De Arment also referred to Wyatt Earp as then being the Deputy United States Marshal and supplied the name of at least one of the posse that Breakenridge could not remember. He stated that the posse consisted of Wyatt, his brothers Morgan and Virgil, Marshall Williams a Wells Fargo agent, and Bat Masterson.[2]

It's hard to tell from his description whether or not Bob Paul was a member of the posse, but I think it can be implied from his statement that he was. So, Breakenridge apparently only named

---

[1]   Helldorado, pp. 121-123.

[2]   Bat Masterson, p. 200.

about half of Wyatt Earp's posse.

Here's a good place to raise another problem that continues to bother me.

Wyatt Earp's resignation as Deputy Sheriff of Pima County was filed on November 9, 1880.[1] The records that I have been able to locate indicate that Wyatt Earp received no money from Wells Fargo after about the first of July, 1880. After November 9, what official position did Wyatt Earp hold in law enforcement, and why was he out with a posse seeking to arrest the stage robbers? No matter who you believe . . . Lake, Earp, De Arment or Breakenridge, there's no doubt that both posses underwent a strenuous time and traveled somewhere between 300 and 400 miles in the dry Southern Arizona desert in an attempt to capture the stage robbers. The hardships of such a trip would be hard for a modern day traveler to imagine. They had no chuck wagon, pack mule, tents, or bedrolls and very little food and water. Although they were Westerners, none of them were used to the hardships of say a Texas cowboy on a drive from Texas to Dodge City or the old trappers in the early days. It must have been a gruesome, miserable trip, and the only motivation for the expenditure of the effort that I can think of is that either Wyatt Earp was someway or another commissioned as a Deputy United States Marshal, or he was hired by the Wells Fargo detective, James Hume.

Although no one else ever mentioned it, and it seems to have been overlooked by all writers and researchers, Wyatt Earp testified at the O.K. Corral hearings that at that time he was working as a detective for Wells, Fargo & Company (see page 319).

It just doesn't seem logical that Wyatt Earp or Bat Masterson, or Wyatt's brothers for that matter, would put themselves through so much misery in an attempt to capture the robbers unless they were officially backed by someone.

The reports could be all wrong in naming Wyatt Earp as leading the posse, since the only person who really had any legal authority, as far as I can determine, to form a posse and chase the bandits with any hope of being reimbursed by any government agency was Deputy U.S. Marshal Virgil Earp. This creates a mystery that becomes even deeper when we describe the efforts by Wyatt and Morgan Earp to capture and arrest the robbers in the Bisbee Stage Robbery that occurred on September 13, 1881 in which Virgil took no part.

I have recently discovered that the Wells Fargo History Department has more records than I was aware of. Unfortunately, there must have been many more destroyed in the 1906 San Francisco earthquake and fire. It appears that my conclusions, based

---

[1]   See Appendix I, Exhibit 3.

on circumstances, were not too far from the true facts.

Wells Fargo has now supplied a record of some of the payments bearing on the subject as follows:

"<u>March 1881</u>
Loss and damages: Tombstone
Expenses for search for stage robbers.

Garrison & Spangle	$5.00
Team hire	$19.50
B.H. Paul, team	$47.00

<u>June 1881</u>
Loss & damages: Tombstone
Expenses for search of stage robbers.

V. Earp	$32.00
W. Earp	$72.00
M. Earp	$72.00

(This must have been payment for services rendered in March and April.)

<u>July 1881</u>
Loss & damages: Tombstone
Expenses for search of stage robbers.

W.B. Masterson	$32.00

<u>October 1881</u>
Loss & damages: Tombstone
Expenses in prosecuting robbers of Bisbee Stage and for search and pursuit of robbers.

W. Earp	$12.00
M. Earp	$12.00
F. Dodge	$12.00
Reward posters	$4.00

GENERAL SALARY
<u>May 1881</u>

W. Earp	$4.75

<u>June 1881</u>

M. Earp	$16.65

<u>August 1881</u>
Tombstone

W. Earp	$100.00
W. Earp	$16.60

<u>September 1881</u>
Tombstone

W. Earp	$95.82"

This is all the records of payments made to the Earps that are currently available. That does not mean that there were not more and the efforts made by the Earps in attempting to capture the robbers of Wells Fargo shipments convinces me that there were more.

Behan's explanation of how Luther King escaped, as reprinted here from the Arizona Weekly Star of March 24, 1881 was heartily contradicted by James Hume, the Chief Detective for Wells Fargo. According to Lake the Wells Fargo officer said:

"When Behan, Breakenridge, and Marshall Williams rode into Tombstone with King, Behan announced that he would not put King in the calaboose, but would take him to the lodging-house at the edge of town run by the wife of Under-Sheriff Woods. Marshall Williams objected, but Behan persisted and assigned a single Deputy, Lance Perkins, to watch King. During the night, King walked out of the room which he shared with Perkins, mounted a horse waiting at the rear of the house, and rode off, taking with him a pair of guns and ammunition-belts which were property of the Sheriff's office. Later, the truth of Hume's story was incontestably established."[1]

I have been unable to find anywhere or anything that incontestably established the truth of Hume's story, although the way things were operating in Tombstone, it is not unlikely that it happened just that way.

After the search for the robbers was abandoned, rumors continued that Doc Holliday had taken part in the holdup as representative of the Earps and had fired the shot that killed Bud Philpot. Lake says: "Gossip connecting Doc Holliday with the Philpot murder was dying out when Doc quarreled with Big-Nosed Kate. Kate went on a spree during which several of Wyatt's enemies persuaded her to sign an affidavit charging Doc with participation in the attempted hold up. On the strength of this, Sheriff Behan arrested Holliday for the murder of Bud Philpot and Pete Roerig.

"Wyatt promptly posted $5,000 cash bail for Doc's release, and Virgil Earp locked Big-Nosed Kate in a hotel room to get her sober. At the hearing, Kate disappointed Johnny Behan woefully. She had signed some paper she said, while drunk with Behan, Mike [sic Milt] Joyce, and some of their friends, but what it was or had in it she could not remember."[2]

Big-Nosed Kate's testimony referred to above had to be at a preliminary hearing and in that hearing, Doc Holliday testified, admitting that he had ridden to Charleston and engaged in a big poker game and had returned to Tombstone about 6 o'clock, had supper and played for the rest of the night. He produced several alibi witnesses who stated that they had been in the game with him.[3]

---

[1]   Wyatt Earp, Frontier Marshal, p. 261.

[2]   Wyatt Earp, Frontier Marshal, p. 264.

[3]   Ibid., p. 265.

Breakenridge tells the story a little more simply, but not too much differently. He says that: "On July 6, 1881, Sheriff Behan arrested Doc Holliday on a warrant sworn out by Kate Elder, Holliday's mistress, for killing Bud Philpot. He was released on a bail bond for $5,000 given by Wyatt Earp and two other men. The next day Virgil Earp arrested Kate Elder on a charge of being drunk, and she was fined $12.50 - her punishment for having Holliday arrested. At his hearing before the Justice of the Peace, Holliday was discharged on account of insufficient evidence."[1]

On July 10, 1881, the Daily Nugget reporting on the court proceedings said: "The case of Territory vs. John Holliday was called for hearing yesterday morning at 10 o'clock. The District Attorney addressing the court said that he had examined all of the witnesses summoned for the prosecution and from their statements he was satisfied that there was not the slightest evidence to show the guilt of the defendant; therefore, he asked that the complaint in the case be withdrawn and that the case be dismissed. The court thereupon dismissed the case and discharged the defendant, and thus ended what - at the time was supposed to be - an important trial."[2]

After Doc Holliday was discharged from custody, Lake quotes him as saying to Wyatt: "'You say the word and I'll leave Tombstone,' and Earp replying, 'You send the fool woman away and I'll be satisfied.'. . . That evening Big-Nosed Kate left Tombstone, and as far as Wyatt Earp ever knew, she and Doc Holliday parted company forever."[3]

Both Lake's and Breakenridge's story have always left a researcher wondering what Big-Nosed Kate really said about Doc Holliday's participation in the robbery and if it was true. Fortunately we have part of that answer.

In 1935, Dr. A. W. Bork was a graduate student at the University of Arizona in Tucson. From a friend in Prescott he received a letter describing an acquaintance of hers by the name of Mary Cummings who was then a resident of the Pioneer Home in Prescott. She was believed to be Big-Nosed Kate Fisher. He made arrangements to visit the Pioneer Home, and in the company of Mrs. Martin, interviewed Mrs. Cummings on Thanksgiving Day in 1935. From the interview, he determined that Mrs. Cummings was in fact the person known as

---

[1]   Helldorado, p. 124.

[2]   Daily Nugget, July 10, 1881. The newspaper report was certainly at variance with either Lake or Breakenridge. Take your pick.

[3]   Wyatt Earp, Frontier Marshal, p. 265.

Big-Nosed Kate. Her maiden name was Mary Catherine Horney. And she claimed to have married Doc Holliday in Valdosta, Georgia, on May 25, 1876. She told a very interesting story which was recorded by Mr. Bork, and later an article was written and published in the magazine, Arizona and the West, entitled the "O.K. Corral Fight at Tombstone, a footnote by Kate Elder," edited by A. W. Bork and Glen G. Boyer.[1]

In the interview they touched on many subjects and incidents in the life and times of Doc Holliday that were of interest. Unfortunately, her memory for dates, particularly for years was atrocious. She was about 85 years old at the time of the interview, and although she could recount events rather well, her recollection of the dates was like many people of her age, highly unreliable.

Contrary to what Wyatt Earp apparently told Lake, Big-Nosed Kate, if she'd left Tombstone after Doc was discharged on the robbery case, had not parted company with him forever.

According to her story, she did not go to Tombstone with Doc Holliday when he first went there from Prescott. She left Prescott with him and traveled with him as far as Gillette; there they split up and she went to Globe and he went to Tombstone. Thereafter, she visited him at Tombstone on several occasions. She happened to be there on March 15, 1881, the date that the stage was held up and Bud Philpot was killed. She was also there, and was a witness to the fight at the O.K. Corral. About Doc Holliday being involved in the robbery, she said this:

"Now, after all these years, I see it in print that it was the Earps and Doc Holliday and that Doc Holliday was the one that killed Bud Philpot. Although Doc did not come to his room until late that night, that does not mean that the Earps and Holliday were in that hold-up. There were plenty of people in Tombstone who knew where the Earps and Holliday were that night. There was no arrest made, nothing was done about it, there could not be. The cry was all over the camp that the hunters were hunting themselves."[2]

Of course her memory was wrong when she said that no arrest was made and nothing was done about it. Unfortunately the interviewer never did ask her if she had made a statement implicating Doc Holliday, and she said nothing about it.

In the summer of 1881 Wyatt Earp was making plans to run for Sheriff against John Behan at the next election. He intended to use it against Sheriff Behan that he had been unable to solve the Bisbee

[1]   Arizona and the West, Vol 19, No 1, Spring 1977.

[2]   Ibid, p. 77-78.

Stage Coach robbery and capture the robbers, and he wanted to show himself up as the super law man by capturing them himself.

In order to do this, he concluded that he would have to have the cooperation of some of the gang who knew the robbers. Lake told the story of how Wyatt Earp went about implementing this project.

He said: "In the afternoon of June 2nd, 1881 Wyatt met Ike Clanton alone in front of the Eagle Brewery Saloon. (This is the same place that afterwards was named the Crystal Palace).

"'Ike,' the Marshal asked without prelude, 'how'd you'd like to make $6,000?'

"'What d'ya mean?' Clanton countered.

"'Meet me out back of the Saloon in ten minutes and I'll tell you,' Wyatt answered.

"At the appointed time, Wyatt found Ike Clanton waiting and knew he had judged his man correctly.

"'Ike,' Wyatt said, 'you help me catch Leonard, Head, and Crane and you can have every cent of the Wells-Fargo reward.'

"Ike displayed no resentment at the inference, and for half an hour Marshal and outlaw discussed means whereby Leonard, Head and Crane might be captured after which Ike left for Sulphur Springs Valley to get the help of Joe Hill and the McLaurys. On June 6, he returned to Tombstone with Hill and Frank McLowery [sic].

"'Any strings on your offer?' Joe Hill asked the Marshal.

"'None,' Wyatt answered.

"'We can use the money,' Frank McLaury said, 'but if the rest of the crowd ever learns who turned up these fellows, we won't live twenty four hours.'

"'I won't give you away,' Wyatt assured the trio. 'You get Leonard, Head and Crane where I can grab them, then I'll collect the reward and turn it over to you in cash. You won't appear in the business.'

"'You'll never take them alive,' McLaury said, which led Ike Clanton to another question.

"'How about that?' he asked. 'The reward is offered for their arrest. Does that go, dead or alive?'

"From this point the rustlers refused to proceed without official assurance that the blood-money would be paid regardless of condition in which the highway men were taken. Wyatt asked Marshall Williams to telegraph the necessary query to San Francisco. The reply came next morning, but as the conspirators would not take Wyatt's word for its content he was forced to ask Marshall Williams for the message. Williams saw Wyatt show the telegram to Hill, Clanton and McLaury.

"The whole fabric of the later Clanton-Behan conspiracy against Wyatt Earp was woven around Ike Clanton's denial that there had been any such telegram as Wyatt received. So much has been made of the doubt that the message existed, even in official histories of Arizona, that it appears advisable to quote the much-discussed telegram exactly as copied from the original found in the long mislaid court records of Cochise County. The message read:

"'SAN FRANCISCO CALIFORNIA JUNE 7, 1881
"'Marshall Williams Tombstone, Arizona
"'Yes, we will pay rewards for them dead or alive.
"'L.F. Rowell.'

"Rowell was assistant in San Francisco to John J. Valentine, President of Wells, Fargo & Co."[1]

The rustlers agreed to cooperate with Earp and Clanton and they proceeded to set the trap for their victims. On July 4, 1881 Clanton, Hill and McLaury came into Tombstone and reported to Earp that Head and Crane were camping near Eureka, and that they planned to lure them to Rabbit Springs on the Bisbee Road for the pretended purpose of holding up a stage carrying the Copper Queen payroll. Earp was to take over from that point and make his arrest.

It is interesting to note that Lake explained why the setting of the trap for Leonard, Head and Crane was delayed, stating that:

"Setting the trap was again delayed while the conspirators rode with Old Man Clanton, John Ringo, Jim Hughes, Rattle Snake Bill Johnson, Jake Dauze, and Charlie Snow to the massacre of Skeleton Canyon. A mule train carrying $75,000 in silver bullion was ambushed and 19 muleteers slaughtered."[2]

This date figures closely with the date heretofore given as the probable time of the Skeleton Canyon Massacre. After the money was distributed to the outlaws, they went on a big binge and bragged about the massacre, but no arrests were made. It took a couple of weeks for the outlaws to spend their ill-gotten loot and recover from their hangovers.

It was shortly afterward that the Mexicans caught a group of cowboys with a herd of stolen cattle on the way through Guadalupe Canyon. The cattle thieves were ambushed, and Old Man Clanton and four of his men were killed. A couple of days later, Joe Hill rode into Tombstone and told Wyatt Earp that Jim Crane had been killed along with Old Man Clanton at Guadalupe Canyon. Wyatt Earp urged Joe Hill to keep after Leonard and Head, and Hill started for their New Mexico hideout.

When he got there he found that Leonard and Harry Head had

[1]   Wyatt Earp, Frontier Marshal, pp. 269-270.

[2]   Ibid, p. 271.

been killed by Ike and Billy Haslett, brothers who ran a small store which the outlaws had attempted to rob. Lake said that Wyatt sent Morgan out to verify the story and that Morgan learned that Leonard had lived some hours after being shot and while dying made a statement that identified Luther King, Jim Crane and Harry Head as his only associates in the hold up.

"Crane, he declared, had fired the shot which killed Bud Philpot. Who had killed Roerig he could not say as Crane, Head, and he had stood in the road and shot at the back of the stage."[1]

Marshall Williams, Wells Fargo agent in Tombstone, was quite a heavy drinker and gambler. He was also quite shrewd, and when he saw Wyatt Earp show the telegram guaranteeing the reward money dead or alive, he correctly figured that something was going on between Wyatt Earp and Ike Clanton. While intoxicated, he broached the subject to Ike Clanton, who, not realizing that Williams really didn't know what he was talking about, opened his big mouth and told Williams all about it. Later, Ike Clanton accused Wyatt Earp of having told of the plot to betray Leonard, Head and Crane and swore that he'd be killed as soon as the news reached his fellow outlaws. Wyatt truthfully denied that he had mentioned the conspiracy to anyone, but Clanton would have no part of it. He felt sure that Earp had double crossed him. This was one of the major factors in creating the atmosphere that lead to the O.K. Corral shootout.

Another thing that lead to the shootout was the hold-up of the Tombstone-Bisbee stage on September 8, 1881.

We have the stories of three participants in the search for and arrest of the robbers in that case and they're all so different, that each one has to be examined in order for the reader to determine what he thinks may have happened.

Lake-Earp tell the story this way: "On September 8, at 11 o'clock at night, the Tombstone - Bisbee stage was held up near Hereford and robbed of twenty-five hundred dollars in the Wells-Fargo box and a mail sack. Jewelry and $750 in currency were taken from four passengers. There was no shotgun messenger on the stage, and Levy McDaniels, the driver, offered no resistance when two masked men, one with a shotgun, the other with a Colt stepped into the road with the order to halt and throw off the box. McDaniels recognized the bandit who relieved the passengers of their cash and jewelry as Pete Spence, and the second as Sheriff's Behan's Deputy, Frank Stilwell. Off in the chaparral McDaniels saw two other men whom he could not identify. Wyatt Earp joined McDaniels at Hereford to take the

[1]   Ibid, p. 272.

trail at daylight. Morgan Earp, Marshall Williams and Fred Dodge were with him. Sheriff Behan sent out his deputies, Breakenridge and Neagle. There had been rain and in the damp sand beside the road Wyatt Earp noted a number of prints from the narrow, high heels of a cow-puncher's boots, each track showing the imprint of four nail heads in pattern. Again, in the chaparral where the mail sack had been slit and rifled, similar tracks had been found. From this spot the trail of the four horsemen led into the hills.

"In Hereford, Wyatt had learned that Frank Stilwell, Curly Bill, and Pony Deal had been together all afternoon and evening, until just before the robbery they were joined by Spence, when the four rode out the Bisbee Road. Wyatt believed this quartet had left the sign he noted until the fugitives separated and he chose to follow the trail of a single horseman into Bisbee.[1]

"As the posse rode through town, Frank Stilwell stepped into a saloon just ahead of them. Wyatt's eye caught the broad, flat heels on Stilwell's boots, such an anomaly in that country that Wyatt wheeled to the hitching rail, dismounted, and went into a boot shop.

"'Frank Stilwell been here?' Wyatt asked Beaver, the Shoemaker.

"'He just went out,' Beaver answered.

"'Have the heels changed on his boots?'

"'Yes, I made him some new boots the other day and he came in and had me put on low heels in place of high ones.'

"'Got the heels you took off?'

"Beaver handed over the pair of narrow heels with four nail heads in each one forming a pattern that every man in the posse recognized.

"Wyatt announced that he intended to arrest Stilwell for the stage-robbery.

"'I'm going to get something to eat,' Breakenridge remarked.

"'Don't let us catch you eating with Stilwell,' Morgan Earp called after him.

"Wyatt went into the saloon where Stilwell submitted to arrest with the boast that he'd be turned loose after he saw Johnny Behan.

"Fred Dodge and Marshall Williams started Stilwell for Tombstone while Wyatt and Morgan headed for Charleston on the chance of finding Pete Spence. They overtook Spence on the trail and had him in Tombstone soon after Stilwell's arrival.

"Sheriff Behan tried to hold jurisdiction of Stilwell and Spence, but Wyatt swore out federal warrants and took them into Tucson, where they were bound over for robbing the mails, with bail at

---

[1]   The trail of a single horseman into Bisbee doesn't fit anyone's story of the event, as you shall see.

$5,000."[1]

Although Fred Dodge was always friendly with Wyatt Earp, and many of his statements tend to confirm the statements made by Earp, he told a somewhat different story of this event.

He described being a member of the posse with the same people that Wyatt Earp had named and said that shortly after they arrived at the scene William Breakenridge and Dave Neagle, deputy sheriffs who had been sent out by Sheriff Behan, arrived. He said that the posse started trailing the two men who had left the scene of the robbery toward Tombstone. They soon lost the trail because a bunch of cattle had been driven across it.

At that point Breakenridge and Neagle left them and headed down the road that led to Bisbee. He and Wyatt Earp being experienced trailers split up and rode off quite a distance that put them to the outside of where the cattle had obscured the trail, and he took one side and Wyatt took the other to make a circle. Before they met, Dodge had found a trail and it soon turned toward Bisbee through the Mule Mountains. He said that both he and Wyatt were off their horses and trailing on foot. When nearing the summit of the mountain they found a boot heel. It was one like all cowboys and men who were in the saddle very much used.

It seemed that the boot heel would be extremely important evidence, so they decided to follow the trail carefully to be sure they caught up with the person who had lost the boot heel which carried a mark similar to that which had been found near the scene of the robbery. Therefore, they stayed on the trail all night and the next morning, following it right into Bisbee. Wyatt Earp went to the shoemaker and Fred Dodge went down to the corral to look around and see if he could find any new heels on a pair of boots. He did find one and it was on the boot of Frank Stilwell.

In the meantime, Wyatt had discovered from the shoemaker that he had put new heels on the boots of Frank Stilwell and that Pete Spence was with Stilwell when they were at his shop.

Apparently, Breakenridge and Neagle had spent the night in Bisbee and they came in contact with Wyatt Earp and Fred Dodge and were told about the evidence of the boot heel and that they were going to arrest Frank Stilwell and Pete Spence. Dodge said they got a John Doe warrant and he and Wyatt arrested Frank Stilwell and Morgan Earp and Dave Neagle arrested Pete Spence. The whole posse got together again, including Morgan Earp, Dave Neagle, William Breakenridge, Wyatt Earp and Fred Dodge, and started for Tombstone with the prisoners.

---

[1]   Wyatt Earp, Frontier Marshal, pp. 273-274.

When they got to Tombstone, the prisoners were taken before the magistrate and admitted to bond on the state charge. They also made a separate bond before the United States Commissioner on the federal charge of robbing the mails.[1]

Fred Dodge said nothing about Stilwell and Spence being taken to Tucson for arraignment, but I think they must have been. I don't believe that there was a U.S. Commissioner in Tombstone who had the authority to issue a warrant for arrest or to set and receive a bond in Federal Court. Most other reports of this incident seem to have Wyatt or Virgil taking the two prisoners to Tucson for arraignment before the United States Commissioner.

Breakenridge told still a different story. He said that: "In September, 1881, the stage running between Tombstone and Bisbee via Hereford was held up by two masked men. The passengers were robbed and the mail and express taken. Sheriff Behan sent Dave Neagle and me out to do what we could toward tracking down the highway men. We went to the place where they had held up the stage, and were able to get a good view of the tracks of both men on horses. We had no difficulty in following the horses tracks towards Bisbee until they were obliterated by a drove of cattle passing over them. On our arrival in Bisbee, where we spent the night, we interviewed several of the passengers. They told us that the smaller of the two robbers did most of the talking, and asked each one if he had any sugar. This was a well-known expression of Frank Stilwell's, who always called money 'sugar.' We learned also that Stilwell had his high heels taken from his boots and low heels put on in place of them. A shoemaker gave us the ones he had taken off and they fitted the tracks at the scene of the hold-up. Pete Spence and Frank Stilwell had come into Bisbee together and were still there. After we had gathered what evidence we could, we were of the opinion that Stilwell and Spence were the guilty parties. Wyatt Earp, Morgan Earp, Marshall Williams a Wells-Fargo agent at Tombstone, and Fred Dodge, a gambler, as a United States Marshal's posse, left Tombstone sometime after we did. They came direct to Bisbee where we met them and told them what evidence we had and wanted Williams to swear out a warrant for Spence and Stilwell. He refused at first to do so and fearing the men might leave town before we arrested them, I went to the corral where we were stopping and put them under arrest while Neagle went before the Justice and got a warrant for them.

"When the Earp party saw that we had arrested the men, they prevailed upon Williams to swear out a federal warrant for them for robbing the mail and express, and we all went to Tombstone together

[1]   Under Cover for Wells Fargo, p. 13.

over the trail on horse back with the prisoners.

"Stilwell and Spence were taken before Justice Spicer and bound over in two thousand dollars' bond, which they gave. They were at once re-arrested by Wyatt Earp as Deputy United States Marshal, charged with robbing the mail, and were bound over to the grand jury to the sum of five thousand dollars which they also secured and were given their liberty."[1]

Here are some of the differences in the stories that should be noted. Earp had two gunmen rob the stage and two others who he named as Curly Bill and Pony Deal nearby and apparently were in the group that was tracked by the Earp party. From his story, it would seem that Wyatt Earp and his posse joined McDaniels when the stage coach driver was at Hereford to take the trail at daylight. That would have been on September 9th. Wyatt Earp said that Sheriff Behan sent out his Deputies, Breakenridge and Neagle but does not mention them further until they arrive in Bisbee, but from the thread of his story it would appear that they all traveled to Bisbee together, for when Wyatt announced that he intended to arrest Stilwell for the stage-robbery, Breakenridge announced that "I'm going to get something to eat," and Morgan Earp said, "Don't let us catch you eating with Stilwell," thus indicating that at that time the party was all together.

Fred Dodge said that there were only two horses to trail. That they lost the trail by reason of a cattle crossing and that Breakenridge and Neagle left them at that point. This fits better with Breakenridge's story that he and Neagle headed straight for Bisbee and spent the night there, while Wyatt Earp, Fred Dodge, and his group spent the night in the open trailing the robbers. The important difference is that Dodge said that while trailing the horses on foot, "I found a boot heel---it was a long heel and one like all cowboys and men who were much in the saddle used."[2] And then when they got into Bisbee, Wyatt Earp went to the shoemaker and he (Dodge) went down to the corral to look around to see if he could find a new heel on a pair of boots. So, according to Dodge's story, it would not have been Breakenridge who recovered the heels from the shoemaker as he had claimed. Wyatt's story was still different, for he said that he recovered a pair of heels from the shoemaker.[3]

Another difference in their stories is that according to Breakenridge, Pete Spence and Frank Stilwell had come into Bisbee

---

Helldorado, p.139-140.

Undercover for Wells Fargo, p. 13

Wyatt Earp, Frontier Marshal, p. 274

together, and were still there, and were arrested there. But according to Wyatt Earp, Stilwell was arrested there and Fred Dodge and Marshall Williams started with Stilwell for Tombstone while Wyatt and Morgan headed for Charleston on the chance of finding Pete Spence and did in fact overtake Spence on the trail, arrested him and had him in Tombstone, shortly after Stilwell's arrival. Fred Dodge still told it differently. He said that, "Wyatt Earp and I arrested Frank Stilwell and Morgan Earp and Dave Neagle arrested Pete Spence."

So, with all of these stories differing in minor details, it's hard to determine exactly what did happen. The Tombstone _Epitaph_ didn't help very much when it wrote up the story on September 13, 1881 as follows:

"IMPORTANT CAPTURE
"Wyatt and Morgan Earp, Marshall Williams and Deputy Sheriff Breakenridge who went to Bisbee to arrest the stage robbers on Sunday evening brought in Deputy Sheriff T.C. Stilwell and P. Spence, whom the evidence strongly points out as the robbers. They were examined before Wells Spicer, Esq. yesterday, and admitted to bail in the sum of $7,000 each - $5,000 for robbing the mail, and $2,000 for robbing D.B. Rea. The evidence against Deputy Sheriff Stilwell is circumstantial, and rests principally upon the tracks made by his boot heels in the mud, which corresponded with those he had removed by a shoemaker upon his return to Bisbee. The _Epitaph_ has no desire to prejudge the case, but if it turns out as now anticipated, that the officers of the law are implicated in this nefarious business, it would seem to be in order for Sheriff Behan to appoint another Deputy. (September 13, 1881)"[1]

No mention was made of Fred Dodge's participation by the Tombstone _Epitaph_.

The charge of robbing the U.S. mails was a federal offense. The Federal Court for that District was in Tucson, not in Tombstone. Whether Stilwell and Spence posted $5,000 bail each with a Federal Commissioner in Tombstone or in Tucson, the bail was to secure their appearance in the U.S. District Court in Tucson for a preliminary examination.

Most non-lawyer authors fail to distinguish between a preliminary examination and a trial. A preliminary examination is not a trial. It is a hearing to determine if there is sufficient evidence to hold an accused to appear before a grand jury.

Paula Mitchell Marks didn't quite understand the distinction. In one place she said ". . . when the trial of Frank Stilwell and Pete Spence began in Tucson, Virgil and Wyatt re-apprehended the two on

---

[1]   Tombstone's Epitaph, p. 175.

the thirteenth, (October, 1881), with Virgil accompanying them to Tucson."[1]

In another place she outlined the evidence presented at the "Judicial Proceedings" and said that the Cochise County Sheriff, (Behan) and the Tombstone City Marshal did not stay for the full examination, but returned home on the 21st.[2]

Neither she, nor any other author states that Stilwell and Spence were bound over for appearance before the Grand Jury, but they must have been because the Tombstone Epitaph in reporting the death of Frank Stilwell in Tucson at the hands of Wyatt Earp on March 21st, 1882 stated that: "Stilwell arrived here Sunday (March 19, 1882) to appear before the Grand Jury on a charge of stage robbery near Bisbee last November."[3]

Here the Tombstone Epitaph made a mistake, for the robbery of the stage near Bisbee occurred on September 8, 1881 and the capture of the robbers is reported in the Epitaph on September 13, 1881.[4]

The arrest of Spence and Stilwell resulted in more ill will between the Earps and the Clantons and McLaurys.

Lake says that: "While Wyatt was at Tucson, (presumably taking Stilwell and Spence for arraignment in Federal Court), Ike and Billy Clanton, Frank and Tom McLaury, John Ringo, Milt Hicks, and Joe Hill rode in to Tombstone. They met Morgan Earp on foot in Allen Street, and circled around him.

"'I'm telling you Earps something,' Frank McLaury began in the hearing of Ed Byrns and Charlie Smith who were loafing nearby.

"'You may have arrested Pete Spence and Frank Stilwell, but don't get it in your heads you can arrest me. If you ever lay hands on a McLaury, I'll kill you.'

"Morgan was alone and unarmed.

"'If the Earps ever have occasion to come after you, they'll get you,' Morgan replied and walked away."[5]

Breakenridge supplied some evidence that the conversation probably took place. He said:

"The feud between the two gangs was growing very bitter. A short time after Neagle and I arrested Spence and Stilwell, Virgil

---

[1]   And Die in the West, p. 188.

[2]   Ibid, p. 189.

[3]   Tombstone's Epitaph, p. 209.

[4]   Ibid, p. 175.

[5]   Wyatt Earp, Frontier Marshal, p. 275.

Earp told me that the McLaurys had threatened to kill every one who had a hand in arresting Stilwell and Spence and advised me to shoot either or both of them the first time I met them or they would get me sure. I laughed at him, as I knew about the feud between them."[1]

---

[1]   Helldorado, p. 241.

CHAPTER XXXIV

FIGHT AT THE O.K. CORRAL

THE fight at the O.K. Corral was a misnomer. The O.K. Corral was on Allen Street. The fight actually took place through the block from the O.K. Corral on a vacant lot next to Fly's Photo Gallery on Fremont street. However, folklore has designated the fight or shootout as the fight at the O.K. Corral; and while it didn't happen there, I shall continue to refer to it in that manner. Everybody knows what is meant and it is easier that way.

The ill will felt by the Clantons and McLaurys toward the Earps was building to a show down. Wyatt had traveled to Tucson to attend the preliminary examination of Frank Stilwell and Pete Spence for the robbery of the Bisbee Stage. That was about the 15th of October, 1881. While he, and possibly Virgil were there, the incident related by Breakenridge when the youngest brother, Morgan Earp was surrounded by Ike and Billy Clanton, Frank and Tom McLaury, John Ringo, Milt Hicks, and Joe Hill in Tombstone and threatened by Frank McLaury occurred.[1]

Lake says that Wyatt returned home on October 17, 1881 and was told by Old Man Fuller, the father of Wess Fuller who would later testify at the O.K. Corral hearings, that the McLaurys, Ringo, Hicks, and Hill had all openly boasted around the saloons that they'd kill the Earps and Doc Holliday.[2]

Immediately after his return from Tucson, he had another confrontation with Ike Clanton. Clanton threatened Doc Holliday and the Earps. Lake tells it this way: "Three days later, fear stricken Ike again sought Wyatt and accused him of having told Doc Holliday of the proposed betrayal. When Ike insisted that this was true, Wyatt said, 'Doc's been out of town for ten days. I don't see how he could have spread much around. He's coming back on the 6 o'clock stage. We'll see what he says.'

"Wyatt and Ike were at the Wells-Fargo office when Doc climbed out of the stage.

"'Doc,' Wyatt asked bluntly, 'Did I ever tell you that Ike Clanton and I were in any deal together?'

---

[1]   Wyatt Earp, Frontier Marshal, p. 275.

[2]   Ibid

"'No,' Doc replied.

"'Ike says I did. Ike's a liar.'

"Clanton insisted that his secret had been divulged. Doc inquired ingeniously what the secret might be, and Ike in hearing of numerous bystanders burst into full account of the deal he said he was accused of having made, thus giving first public knowledge of the outlaws agreement to betray their fellows."[1]

After that Doc Holliday and Ike Clanton got into a loud profane argument with Doc berating Ike Clanton vigorously and profanely. When he finished he turned and walked away, while Ike shouted after him threats to kill the very next man who coupled his name with that of Wyatt Earp.

After the confrontation of Wyatt Earp and Doc Holliday with Ike Clanton, Wyatt supposedly took possession of his Faro bank money, met Holliday on the street between the Oriental and the Alhambra and walked with him westward onto Allen Street with Doc going to his room for the night and Wyatt to his house.

A most unlikely event occurred shortly after that, on the night of October 25, 1881 when Ike Clanton entered the Occidental and engaged in an all-night poker game. The other participants were Tom McLaury, Virgil Earp, Johnny Behan, and some unknown person. Ike Clanton complained that Virgil Earp had spent the evening playing poker with his gun on his lap.[2] Virgil evidently went home rather late in the morning and went to sleep. He was awakened on two different occasions by people coming in and warning him that the Clantons were making the brag around town that they were going to kill him and his brothers.[3] The story of the events that occurred after that are so confusing that this author cannot guarantee the truth of any of them. It seems that the better way to tell the story is to take it from the people who were there and claimed to know. We can get all kinds of stories and conflicting statements, but I believe that by studying the testimony of the various witnesses involved the reader can arrive at a rather accurate assessment of the truth.

Martin, in his Tombstone's Epitaph, set the stage for the battle of the O.K. Corral in the following statement:

"The town knew the showdown was coming. The cowboys had been bragging for 24 hours that they were after the Earps. Virgil Earp had pistol whipped Ike Clanton early that afternoon when he

---

[1]   Ibid, p. 277.

[2]   The O.K. Corral Inquest, p 33.

[3]   Ibid, p 192.

caught him with a Winchester and a six-gun. Wyatt had done the same to Tom McLaury who had threatened him on the street. With a courage which should have shaken the nerve of the group, he backed up the play by following three of his enemies to a gun shop, where they were filling their cartridge belts, and finding Frank McLaury's horse standing on the sidewalk with its head in the gun shop door, seized the animal by the bridal, and backed it into the street. As a Deputy City Marshal he was acting within his authority but it must have taken cold chilled nerve to perform the significant act in the face of three armed foes.

"The last act came within a few minutes. The point at issue was whether the McLaurys and Clantons were to be disarmed. Behan, scuttling back and forth between the two groups, promised to get the cowboys guns but failed to do so. As City Marshal, Virgil called his brothers and Holliday and started for the corral to do the job. For all they knew they were striding to their death and they would probably have been surprised to learn that they were going to immortality. Here is the complete Epitaph story in which Clum first gives the background of the battle and then proceeds to report it chronologically.

"'YESTERDAY'S TRAGEDY
"'THREE MEN HURLED INTO ETERNITY INTO THE
"'DURATION OF A MOMENT
"'THE CAUSES THAT LED TO THE SAD AFFAIR.

"'Stormy as were the early days of Tombstone, nothing ever occurred equal to the event of yesterday. Since the retirement of Ben Sippy as Marshal and the appointment of V.W. Earp to fill the vacancy, the town has been noted for its quietness and good order. The fractious and much dreaded cow-boys when they came to town were upon their good behavior and no unseemly brawls were indulged in, and it was hoped by our citizens that no more such deeds would occur as led to the killing of Marshal White one year ago. It seems that this quiet state of affairs was but the calm that precedes the storm that burst in all its fury yesterday, with this difference in results, that the lightning bolts struck in a different quarter from the one that fell a year ago. This time it struck with its full and awful force upon those who, heretofore, have made the good name of this county a byword and a reproach, instead of some officer in the discharge of his duty or a peaceable and unoffending citizen.

"'THE PROXIMATE CAUSE

"'Since the arrest of Stilwell and Spence for the robbery of the Bisbee stage, there have been oft repeated threats conveyed to the Earp brothers -- Virgil, Morgan and Wyatt --that the friends of the accused, or in other words the cow-boys, would get even with them for the part they had taken in the pursuit and arrest of Stilwell and

Spence. The active part of the Earps in going after stage robbers, beginning with the one last spring where Bud Philpot lost his life, and the more recent one near Contention, has made them exceedingly obnoxious to the bad element of this county and put their lives in jeopardy every month.

"'Sometime Tuesday October 25th Ike Clanton came into town and during the evening had some little talk with Doc Holliday and Marshal Earp but nothing to cause either to suspect, further than their general knowledge of the man and the threats that had previously been conveyed to the Marshal, that the gang intended to clean out the Earps, that he was thirsting for blood at this time with one exception and that was that Clanton told the Marshal, in answer to a question, that the McLaurys were in Sonora.

"'Shortly after this occurrence someone came to the Marshal and told him that the McLaurys had been seen a short time before just below town. Marshal Earp, now knowing what might happen and feeling his responsibility for the peace and order of the city, stayed on duty all night and added to the police force his brother Morgan and Holliday. The night passed without any disturbance whatever and at sunrise he went home and retired to rest and sleep. A short time afterwards one of his brothers came to his house and told him that Clanton was hunting him with threats of shooting him on sight. He discredited the report and did not get out of bed. It was not long before another of his brothers came down, and told him the same thing, whereupon he got up, dressed and went with his brother Morgan uptown. They walked up Allen Street to Fifth, crossed over to Fremont and down to Fourth, where, upon turning up Fourth toward Allen, they came upon Clanton with a Winchester rifle in his hand and a revolver on his hip. The Marshal walked up to him, grabbed the rifle and hit him a blow on the head at the same time, stunning him so that he was able to disarm him without further trouble. He marched Clanton off to the police court where he entered a complaint against him for carrying deadly weapons, and the court fined Clanton $25 and costs, making $27.50 altogether. This occurrence must have been about 1 o'clock in the afternoon.

"'The After-Occurrence

"'Close upon the heels of this came the finale, which is best told in the words of R.F. Coleman who was an eye-witness from the beginning to the end. Mr. Coleman says: I was in the O.K. Corral at 2:30 p.m., when I saw the two Clantons (Ike and Bill) and the two McLaurys (Frank and Tom) in an earnest conversation across the street in Dunbar's corral. I went up the street and notified Sheriff Behan and told him it was my opinion they meant trouble, and it was his duty, as sheriff, to go and disarm them. I told him they had gone to the West End Corral. I then went and saw Marshal Virgil Earp and notified him to the same effect. I then met Billy Allen and we walked through the O.K. Corral, about fifty yards behind the sheriff. On reaching Fremont street I saw Virgil Earp, Wyatt Earp, Morgan Earp and Doc Holliday, in the center of the street, all armed. I had reached Bauer's meat market. Johnny Behan had just left the cowboys, after having a conversation with them. I went along to Fly's photograph gallery, when I heard Virg Earp say, "Give up your arms or throw up your arms." There was some reply made by Frank McLaury, when firing became general, over thirty shots being fired. Tom McLaury fell first, but raised and fired again before he died. Bill Clanton fell next, and raised to fire again when Mr. Fly took his revolver from him. Frank McLaury ran a few rods and fell. Morgan Earp was shot through and fell. Doc Holliday was hit in the left hip but kept on firing. Virgil Earp was hit in the third or fourth fire, in the leg which staggered him but he kept up his effective work. Wyatt Earp stood up and fired in rapid succession, as cool as a cucumber, and was not hit. Doc Holliday was as calm as though at target practice and fired rapidly. After the firing was over, Sheriff Behan went up to Wyatt Earp and said, "I'll have to arrest you." Wyatt replied, "I won't be arrested today. I am right here and am not going away. You have deceived me. You told me these men were disarmed; I went to disarm them.'"

"'This ends Mr. Coleman's story which in the most essential particulars has been confirmed by others. Marshal Virgil Earp says that he and his party met the Clantons and the McLaurys in the alleyway by the McDonald [sic. Harwood] place; he called to them to throw up their hands, that he had come to disarm them.

"'Instantaneously Bill Clanton and one of the McLaurys fired, and then it became general. Mr. Earp says it was the first shot from Frank McLaury that hit him. In other particulars his statement does not materially differ from the statement above given. Ike Clanton was not armed and ran across to Allen street and took refuge in the dance hall there. The two McLaurys and Bill Clanton all died within a few minutes after being shot. The Marshal was shot through the calf of the right leg, the ball going clear through. His brother, Morgan, was shot through the shoulders, the ball entering the point of the right shoulder blade, following across the back, shattering off a piece of one vertebrae and passing out the left shoulder in about the same position that it entered the right. This wound is dangerous but not necessarily fatal, and Virgil's is far more painful than dangerous.. Doc Holliday was hit upon the scabbard of his pistol, the leather breaking the force of the ball so that no material damage was done other than to make him limp a little in his walk.

"'Dr. Matthews impaneled a coroner's jury, who went and viewed the bodies as they lay in the cabin in the rear of Dunbar's stables on

Fifth street, and then adjourned until 10 o'clock this morning.
"'The Alarm Given
"'The moment the word of the shooting reached the Vizina and Tough Nut mines the whistles blew a shrill signal, and the miners came to the surface, armed themselves, and poured into the town like an invading army. A few moments served to bring out all the better portions of the citizens, thoroughly armed and ready for any emergency. Precautions were immediately taken to preserve law and order, even if they had to fight for it. A guard of ten men were stationed around the county jail, and extra policeman put on for the night.[1]
"'THE EARP BROTHERS JUSTIFIED
"'The feeling among the best class of our citizens is that the Marshal was entirely justified in his efforts to disarm these men, and that being fired upon they had to defend themselves, which they did most bravely. So long as our peace officers make effort to preserve the peace and put down highway robbery--which the Earp brothers have done, having engaged in the pursuit and capture, where captures have been made of every gang of stage robbers in the county--they will have the support of all good citizens. If the present lesson is not sufficient to teach the cow-boy element that they cannot come into the streets of Tombstone, in broad daylight, armed with six-shooters and Henry rifles to hunt down their victims, then the citizens will most assuredly take such steps to preserve the peace as will be forever a bar to further raids.'"[2]

The Daily Nugget, the newspaper that ordinarily supported Behan and his political henchmen, published their version of the fight on October 27, 1881. Since the Nugget, edited by Harry Woods, Under-sheriff, was pro-Behan and anti-Earp, it is doubtful that they got the information for their story from the Earps. It is more likely that it came from Behan and that he told the truth before he had an opportunity to compare notes and cook up a story with his cow-boy friends.

Having that in mind, it seems worthwhile to print the Nugget story in its entirety.

This is how the Nugget initially report Tombstone's most famous story:

"The 26th of October, 1881, will always be marked as one of the

---

[1]   John P. Clum, at page 17 of his book, It Happened in Tombstone, says that a detachment of the Citizens' Safety Committee, armed and marching in twos, reported to him within ten minutes after the fight bent on keeping the peace.

[2] Tombstone's Epitaph, p. 177-181.

crimson days in the annals of Tombstone, a day when blood flowed as water, and human life was held as a shuttlecock, a day always to be remembered as witnessing the bloodiest and deadliest street fight that has ever occurred in this place, or probably in the Territory.

"The origin of the trouble dates back to the first arrest of Stillwell [sic] and Spence, for the robbery of the Bisbee stage. The co-operation of the Earps and the Sheriff and his deputies in the arrest caused a number of the cowboys to, it is said, threaten the lives of all interested in the capture. Still, nothing occurred to indicate that any such threats would be carried into execution. But Tuesday night Ike Clanton and Doc Holliday had some difficulty in the Alhambra saloon. Hard words passed between them, and when they parted it was generally understood that the feeling between the two men was that of intense hatred. Yesterday morning Clanton came on the street armed with a rifle and revolver, but was almost immediately arrested by Marshal Earp, disarmed and fined by Justice Wallace for carrying concealed weapons. While in the courtroom Wyatt Earp told him that as he had made threats against his life, he wanted him to make his fight, to say how, when and where he would fight, and to get his crowd, and he (Wyatt) would be on hand.

"In reply, Clanton said: 'Four feet of ground is enough for me to fight on, and I'll be there.' A short time after this Billy Clanton and Frank McLowry [sic] came in town, and as Tom McLowrey [sic] was already here the feeling soon became general that a fight would ensue before the day was over, and cords of expectant men stood on the corner of Allen and Fourth Streets awaiting the coming conflict.

"It was now about two o'clock, and at this time Sheriff Behan appeared upon the scene and told Marshal Earp that if he disarmed his posse, composed of Morgan and Wyatt Earp, and Doc Holliday, he would go down to the O.K. Corral, where Ike and Billy Clanton and Frank and Tom McLowry [sic] were and disarm them. The Marshal did not desire to do this until assured that there was no danger of an attack from the other party. The Sheriff went to the corral and told the cowboys that they must put their arms away and not have any trouble. Ike Clanton and Tom McLowry [sic] said they were not armed, and Frank McLowry [sic] said he would not lay his aside. In the meantime the Marshal had concluded to go and, if possible, end the matter by disarming them, and as he and his posse came down Fremont Street toward the corral, the Sheriff stepped out and said: 'Hold up boys, don't go down there or there will be trouble; I have been down there to disarm them.' But they passed on, and when within a few feet of them Marshal said to the Clantons and McLowreys [sic]: 'Throw up your hands boys, I intend to disarm you.'

"As he spoke Frank McLowry [sic] made a motion to draw his revolver, when Wyatt Earp pulled his and shot him, the ball striking on the right side of his abdomen. About the same time Doc Holliday shot Tom McLowry [sic] in the right side, using a short shotgun, such as is carried by Well-Fargo & Co.'s messengers. In the meantime Billy Clanton had shot at Morgan Earp, the ball passing through the left shoulder blade across his back, just grazing the backbone and coming out at the shoulder, the ball remaining inside of his shirt. He fell to the ground but in an instant gathered himself, and raising in a sitting position fired at Frank McLowry [sic] as he crossed Fremont Street, and at the same instant Doc Holliday shot at him, both balls taking effect, either of which would have proved fatal, as one struck him in the right temple and the other in the left breast. As he started across the street, however, he pulled his gun down on Holliday saying, 'I've got you now.' 'Blaze away! You're a daisy if you have,' replied Doc. This shot of McLowrey's [sic] passed through Holliday's pistol pocket, just grazing the skin.

"While this was going on Billy Clanton had shot Virgil Earp in the right leg, the ball passing through the calf, inflicting a severe flesh wound. In turn he had been shot by Morgan Earp in the right side of the abdomen, and twice by Virgil Earp, once in the right wrist and once in the left breast. Soon after the shooting commenced Ike Clanton ran through the O.K. Corral, across Allen Street into Kellogg's Saloon, and thence into Tough Nut Street, where he was arrested and taken to the county jail. The firing altogether didn't occupy more than twenty-five seconds, during which time thirty shots were fired. After the fight was over Billy Clanton, who, with wonderful vitality, survived his wounds for fully an hour, was carried by the editor and foremen of the Nugget into a house where he lay, and everything possible done to make his last moments easy. He was 'game' to the last, never uttering a word of complaint, and just before breathing his last he said, 'Goodby boys; go away and let me die.'

"The wounded were taken to their houses, and at three o'clock next morning were resting comfortably. The dead bodies were taken in charge by the Coroner and an inquest held. Upon the person of Tom McLowry [sic] was found between $300 and $400, and checks and certificates of deposit to the amount of nearly $3000.

"During the shooting Sheriff Behan was standing near by commanding the contestants to cease firing but was powerless to prevent it. Several parties who were in the vicinity of the shooting had narrow escapes from being shot. One man who had lately arrived from the East had a ball pass through his pants. He left for home this morning. A person called 'The Kid,' who shot Hicks at Charleston recently, was also grazed by a ball. When the mine whistle gave the signal that there was a conflict between the officers and the cowboys, the mines on the hill shut down and the miners were brought to the surface. From the Contention mine a number of men, fully armed, were sent to town in a four-horse carriage. At the request of the Sheriff the 'Vigilantes,' or Committee of Safety, were called from the streets by a few sharp toots from the whistle. During the early part of the evening there was rumor that a mob would attempt to take Ike Clanton from jail and lynch him, and to prevent any such unlawful proceedings a strong guard of deputies was placed around the building.

"That evening Finn [sic] Clanton, brother of Billy and Ike, came to town, and placing himself under the guard of the Sheriff, visited the morgue to see the remains of his brother, and then passed the night in jail in company with the other brother.

"Shortly after the shooting ceased the whistle sounded a few short toots, and almost simultaneously a large number of citizens appeared on the streets, armed with rifles and a belt of cartridges around their waists. These men formed in line and offered their services to the peace officers to preserve order in case any attempt at disturbance was made, or any interference offered to the authorities of the law. However, no hostile move was made by anyone, and quiet and order was fully restored, and in a short time the excitement died away.

"At the morgue the bodies of the three slain cowboys lay side by side, covered with a sheet. Very little blood appeared on their clothing, and only on the face of young Billy Clanton was there any distortion of the features or evidence of pain in dying. The features of the two McLowry [sic] boys looked as calm and placid in death as if they had died peaceably. No unkind remarks were made by anyone, but a feeling of unusual sorrow seemed to prevail. Of the McLowry [sic] brothers we could learn nothing of their previous history before coming to Arizona. The two brothers owned quite an extensive ranch on the lower San Pedro, some seventy or eighty miles from the city, to which they had removed their cattle since the recent Mexican and Indian troubles. They did not bear the reputation of being of a quarrelsome disposition, but were known as fighting men, and had generally conducted themselves in a quiet and orderly manner when in Tombstone."[1]

The Nugget story sheds some new light on the events that were not revealed either in the Epitaph story, the testimony at the subsequent court hearings or Lake or any other author that I am aware of. The story is the first notice this author had that soon after the fight, Ike Clanton was arrested and taken to the County Jail.

The Tombstone Epitaph story said that a "guard of 10 men were stationed around the county jail," but there was no hint that it was

---

[1]   The Daily Nugget, October 27, 1881, reprinted in the Tucson Citizen.

placed there to protect Ike Clanton from the possibility that a lynch mob might attempt to take him from the jail and lynch him, or that brother Phin Clanton came to town and placed himself under the protection of the Sheriff.

The Nugget story agrees well with the testimony of Wyatt Earp at the hearing, when he testified that "the first two shots were fired by Billy Clanton and myself, he shooting at me and I shooting at Frank McLaury."

The killing of the McLaurys and Billy Clanton caused great excitement in the town and plans were made for a gigantic funeral. The Tombstone Epitaph reported on the funeral as follows:

"THE FUNERAL

"The funeral of the McLaury brothers and Clanton yesterday was numerically one of the largest ever witnessed in Tombstone. It took place at 3:30 from the undertaking rooms of Messrs. Ritter and Ream. The procession headed by the Tombstone brass band, moved down Allen Street and thence to the cemetery. The sidewalks were densely packed for three or four blocks. The body of Clanton was in the first hearse and those of the two McLaury brothers in the second, side by side, and were interred in the same grave. It was a most impressive and saddening sight and such a one as it is to be hoped may never occur again in this community. --(Oct 28, 1881.)"[1]

Shortly after the gunfight, Cochise County's coroner H.M. Matthews impaneled a jury of citizens to hold an inquest into the deaths of Billy Clanton and Tom and Frank McLaury. Nine witnesses were called and statements were taken from eight of them.

The Tombstone Epitaph reported on the action of the coroner's jury as follows:

"CORONER'S VERDICT

"The coroner's jury, after deliberating for two hours in regard to the late killing of William Clanton, Frank and Thomas McLaury, brought in a verdict that the men named came to their deaths in the town of Tombstone on October 26, 1881, from the effect of pistol and gunshot wounds inflicted by Virgil Earp, Morgan Earp, Wyatt Earp and one Holliday commonly called "Doc" Holliday. The verdict does not seem to meet with general approval, as it does not state whether the cowboys were killed by the marshal and his party in the discharge of their duty, or whether the killing was justifiable."[2]

---

[1]   Tombstone's Epitaph, p. 182.

[2]   The testimony taken at the Coroner's inquest was recorded and filed in the County Clerk's office as Document No. 48. It was reprinted verbatim by Alford E. Turner in his book, The O.K. Corral Inquest.

CHAPTER XXXV

THE COURT PROCEEDINGS

"ON Saturday warrants for the arrest of Wyatt, Virgil and Morgan Earp and J.H. (Doc) Holliday were placed in the hands of the sheriff but as Morgan and Virgil Earp were confined to their beds through wounds received in the late street fight, the warrants were not in their cases served and only Wyatt Earp and Holliday were placed under arrest. When these persons were taken before Justice Spicer he at first denied bail, but upon showing of the facts by affidavits bail was granted and fixed in the sum of $10,000 each, being justified in the sum of $20,000 each for each of the defendants, which amount was furnished.

"Today Holliday and Wyatt Earp were before Justice Spicer to answer to the charge. The investigation was conducted with closed doors. No one, except the officers of the court, and the witness whose testimony was being taken up, were allowed inside. The investigation is not yet concluded and will probably occupy the court for several days. -- (Oct 31, 1881.)"[1]

The hearing was brought on when Ike Clanton filed a complaint charging Virgil, Wyatt and Morgan and Doc Holliday with the murder of Billy Clanton and the two McLaury brothers. Judge Wells Spicer, a Justice of the Peace in Tombstone, did not have jurisdiction to try a murder case, and this proceeding became the subject of the same misconception that I have spoken about before and that is that a preliminary hearing is not a trial. What Judge Spicer did was to conduct a preliminary examination for the sole purpose of determining if there was sufficient evidence to hold the defendants to answer before a grand jury to the charge of murder.

If the Judge thought he could hold a hearing behind closed doors, barred to the public, he soon found out that the public would not stand for it. The newspapers put up such a howl that he very quickly opened the court room to anyone who could get in. The hearings began on November 2nd, 1881, and ended on November 29, 1881, after 30 witnesses had been sworn and testified, and numerous documents entered into evidence. Unlike most preliminary hearings, the testimony of the witnesses at this hearing was reduced to writing in the form of depositions by a court stenographer by the name of

---

[1] Tombstone's Epitaph, p. 182-183.

Fred W. Craig. I have never read anything about his qualifications, whether or not he was able to record the testimony of the witnesses verbatim, or whether he reduced it to writing and then had the witnesses read and sign the documents. Unfortunately, the original document is missing. Stuart Lake says that he discovered the records of the hearing on the dusty shelves of the Cochise County Court House.

He doesn't give the date, but that must have been sometime around 1929. Afterwards, in the depth of the depression of the 30s, the Federal Writers' Project undertook the job of restoring the testimony that was taken at the hearing, and under the tutelage of one "Howell Pat Hayhurst" a transcript of the original testimony was made.

Alford E. Turner says that: "Sometime during the early 1930s the hand written documents were reduced to a type script by Howell A. Hayhurst, a part-time newspaper reporter who was working for the Federal Writers' Project of Works Projects Association [Sic. Works Progress Administration W.P.A.], after which the originals were lost, stolen, or destroyed.[1] Mr. Hayhurst's transcript, on which this work is based, was not complete. He deleted some of the material, apparently because he thought it was unnecessary or couldn't make out the handwriting. He also was thoroughly anti-Earp in his viewpoint and footnoted his work accordingly. However, even with its shortcomings, it remains the best and most accurate chronicle of the gunfight that I know about."[2]

I have read the record of other early proceedings such as preliminary examinations and coroner's inquests where witnesses were examined and deposed and found that the questions and answers were written by a clerk. Most frequently the questions were omitted all together and only the answers to the questions written down and then the witness was asked to read what was written and to sign it. Some of the testimony in the Hayhurst type script appears to have been done in that manner, although some of it appears to have been done by a regular court reporter; it is difficult to know.

At the time of the hearing there was an excellent professional shorthand court reporter who was also a reporter for the Daily Nugget, and who recorded and transcribed all of the testimony. That

---

[1]   I doubt that Mr. Hayhurst should receive credit for the disappearance of the hand written record of the hearing, because F. Water's says (on p. 175 of The Earp Brothers of Tombstone), that he examined the document in the County Clerk's Office at Bisbee in 1937.

[2]   The O.K. Corral Inquest, p. 16.

testimony was published daily in the Nugget. His transcript of the hearing appears in some places to be more complete than the Hayhurst document. In addition, he records some of the court proceedings such as the admission of William McLaury as assistant prosecutor, the remanding of Wyatt Earp and Doc Holliday to custody without bail, and their subsequent release on bail that are not covered in the Hayhurst document.

For many years Earp researchers were under the impression that the copies of the Daily Nugget for the period covered by the O.K. Corral hearing were missing. Walter Noble Burns makes reference to bound volumes of the Nugget on the shelves of the Arizona Pioneer Historical Society in 1927 in his "sources," but makes no further reference to them in his book. He evidently did not realize their value.

Frank Waters makes reference to the fact that the Nugget published a day by day account of the hearings,[1] and he seems to have been aware of the value of the publication, but no other author including Alford E. Turner seems to have been aware of or had access to the Nugget's accounts of the hearings.

I have located a friend by the name of Carl Chafin who more than 25 years ago, obtained photocopies of the Daily Nugget editions that reported the trial. He kept these photocopies in a locker in El Paso, Texas and I finally persuaded him to go down there and find them. He gave me copies of the Nugget stories of the Coroner's Inquest published on October 29th, and 30th and the issues of November 3rd through December 1, 1881, encompassing the whole hearing, except the testimony of Virgil Earp. I have recently learned that The Arizona Historical Society has a complete microfilm copy of the same, although no one produced it for me when I was there.

For some unknown reason, all of the researchers that I have studied, except Frank Waters, have overlooked this valuable source of documentation, and even Waters didn't make any use of it.

The course of the hearing was influenced a lot by the arrival on November 4 in Tombstone of one William R. McLaury, a brother of the two dead McLaurys, and a highly competent attorney from Fort Worth, Texas. From the reading of his correspondence, I think it could be said that he arrived with blood in his eye and a malignant heart with every intent in the world of avenging the death of his brothers. He made a motion to be permitted to join the district attorney's team of prosecutors, and having been permitted to do so, his first move was to make a motion to remand Wyatt Earp and Doc Holliday to custody without bail. He made this motion on November

---

[1]   The Earp Brothers of Tombstone, p. 166.

5, 1881, and by that date, Justice of the Peace Wells Spicer had heard enough evidence to convince him that there was a strong possibility that a murder charge could be proved. He therefore granted the motion and made an order directing the Sheriff to take Wyatt Earp and Doc Holliday into custody and detain them until further order of court or until they were legally discharged.[1]

On the same date, the defense attorneys filed a petition for a writ of habeas corpus which read as follows:

"We command you that you have the bodies of Wyatt Earp and J. H. Holliday, by you imprisoned and detained, as it is said, together with the time and cause of such imprisonment and detention before me at my office, room 1, Mining Exchange Building, in the city of Tombstone in said county forthwith to do and receive what shall then and there be considered concerning the said Wyatt Earp and the said John H. Holliday and have you then and there this writ.

"Attested J.A. Lucas, Probate Judge

"Dated Tombstone, November 7, 1881."[2]

Again, unfortunately, the record is not clear as to what happened upon the hearing of this writ of habeas corpus.

Paula Mitchell Marks says that "on the evening of the 7th, various attorneys wrangled over the writ with McLaury, pressing to keep his work from being undone.

"Nonetheless, McLaury won the battle; after argument the writ was dismissed and Earp and Holliday were remanded into custody of the Sheriff."[3]

I'm not sure where Paula Mitchell Marks got her information. I think she relied on the letters of William R. McLaury. Fortunately the proceedings were alluded to in the November 6th issue of The Nugget as follows:

"Motion was made by attorney for the prosecution (this must have been William McLaury, although his name was not mentioned) that the defendants be remanded to the custody of the Sheriff without bail.

"After considerable argument by council, the motion was granted and "the prisoners were remanded to the custody of the Sheriff until

---

[1]   The Daily Nugget, (November 6, 1881). The O.K. Corral Inquest, p. 227. Note: the copy of the order of commitment, p. 227, is dated November 7, 1881, whereas the Nugget story reporting it was printed November 6, 1881 reporting the event to have occurred on November 5th.

[2]   And Die in the West, p. 268.

[3]   Ibid.

further order of Court."[1]

Apparently Wyatt Earp and Doc Holliday went to jail on November 5th and remained in custody until bail was again set by Judge Spicer, this time the sum of $20,000 each on November 23, 1881.[2]

It seems odd that the fact that Wyatt Earp and Doc Holliday spent 23 or 24 days in the custody of John Behan was never mentioned by Lake, Burns, Breakenridge, or any of the other well-known historians or writers.

That Will McLaury firmly believed that his brothers had been murdered and that he fully intended to wreak vengeance on the Earps and Holliday through means either legal or illegal is demonstrated by a letter he wrote to a friend in Forth Worth, Texas on November the 8th, 1881. The letter is set forth as follows:

"Tombstone.A.T. Nov. 8th 1881

"S.P. Green Wynn

"Fort Worth, Tex.

"Dear Captain:

"Up to this time I have not heard from you, nor received any news from home, and I am anxious about my family. I wish Mr. Billingsly or his wife would send me a Post Card at least every two days if they only say how my child seems and this will do. I will cause but little trouble. I have sent you some papers that give the evidence of witness present at the time my brothers and the boy, young Clanton, were murdered. As to the perpetration of the crime I can only say it was as bloody and foul a murder as has been recorded. My brothers had no quarrel nor interest in any quarrel with those men. My brother and young Clanton who was killed had been with other parties gathering stock for several weeks and had come to this town on business and had been here about fifteen minutes, had transacted their business and were ready to mount their horses and leave. Brother Tom and Isaac Clanton were going out in wagon their team being about ready. Brother Tom and I. Clanton had been in town from the morning of the day previous and were unarmed. Frank and William Clanton were armed but were completely surprised. After Frank was mortally wounded, he shot Holliday, Morgan & Virgil Earp, wounding Morgan and Virgil seriously.

"When I arrived here on the 4th, those who were able to be out were out on Bail and the people were many of them in dread of these men. They came into the Court House heavily armed. The District

---

[1]   <u>The Daily Nugget</u>, (November 6, 1881), reporting the proceedings of November 5th.

[2]   <u>Ibid</u>, November 24, 1881.

Attorney was completely 'cowed' and after promising me on the 4th to move the court to commit these men without bail he would not do it and after agreeing in the presence of all our attorneys to do so would not do it and none of our attorneys would do so and would not permit me to do so, and said they did not want to get me killed and to prevent me from making the motion refused to appear in court with me. I did not think they, the defendants, would make a move and did not fear them. The fact is I only hoped they would, as I could kill them both before they could get a start. On yesterday I told our folk I would make the motion. I had consulted the court and knew he would grant it and told them to do as they pleased. I made the motion. They were as quiet as could be, only looked a little scared. It was granted after some discussions. They then got a writ of Habeas Corpus and we fought over that last night. The petition was dismissed. People were afraid to talk. Our witnesses were running away. No one but their witnesses and (illegible) dared come forward to give any information unless brought into court by attachment.

"Now I consider Defendants are in Jail and in bed. But my Dear Captain this don't bring back my dead brothers. If Dr. George wants to know where Hades is I can inform him. Last night after it was known the murderers were in Jail the Hotel was a perfect jam until early morning. Everybody wanted to see me and shake my hand. I will remain here during this term of court which will be in session Monday next. We are going on with the examination of witnesses before examining court for we fear some of our most important witnesses will be killed by friends of these brutes.

"There are two Earp brothers who were not engaged in the murders.

"As soon as any disposition is made of this case I will come home. But if it is continued I shall come back to the trial. I think I can hang them. The people are in sympathy with the prosecution generally. There is a few Gamblers and sneaks who are not. And I think now that will change around. I think I could put an end to this thing in around five hours. And I cannot afford to do it now Dear Captain. But this thing has a tendency to arouse all the devil there is in me. It will not bring my brothers back to prosecute these men but I regard it as my duty to my self and family to see that these brutes do not go unwhipped of Justice. Exercise your own Judgement as to our business and as to my affairs do the same. I think Mr. Billingsly and wife will go on tonight. Called the rules promptly. You had best get some of the young men to do it. In the O.P. Ashworth Cal. I had called $10.00 treat. I do not remember to have accounted for nor paid over to Mrs. Clark.

"When you see my son John tell him for me not to forget his

promise to obey Mr. and Mrs. B. That I will try to bring him and the girls something nice.

"Send me some of our cards. Remember me to my friends, Mrs. Hoyaitt and Dr. George in particular.

"I am truly yours,

"W.R. McLaury"[1]

Alford Turner in commenting on the activities of Will McLaury said: "There is little doubt that Will McLowry financed the prosecution's case against the Earps, and many others believed that he had also paid for the shooting that was directed at them later. In a letter to his father, April 13, 1884, he wrote: 'my experience out there (Tombstone) has been very unfortunate as to my health and badly injured me as to money matters - and none of the results have been satisfactory. The only result is the death of Morgan and crippling of Virgil Earp and death of McMasters . . .'[2] There can be little doubt that Will McLaury played an important role in the Earp/Clanton feud, if not that of trigger man, at least as instigator of much of the action."[3]

The Coroner's Inquest was commenced on October 28, 1881, and was reported verbatim in the Daily Nugget on October 29th and October 30th. Ten witnesses were called, sworn and testified. Most of these same witnesses were called and testified at the preliminary hearing in more detail, and therefore their testimony at the Coroner's Inquest is not repeated here.

---

[1]   Earp Collection, Arizona Historical Society.

[2]   I have been unable to find anything that reveals how, when or where McMasters died.

[3]   The O.K. Corral Inquest, p. 51

CHAPTER XXXVI

JOHN BEHAN TESTIFIES

ON Thursday, November 3rd, 1881, the Daily Nugget printed its first report of the hearing. It headed its column:
"THE EARP EXAMINATION.
"TESTIMONY OF SHERIFF JOHN H. BEHAN AN EYEWITNESS TO THE TRAGEDY.
"The examination of the Earp brothers and J.H. (Doc) Holliday was continued yesterday before Judge Wells Spicer. When the court convened the Hon. Thos. Fitch rose and, addressing his honor, said that as it appeared impossible to curtail the enterprise of the press, he hoped the order against the publication of the testimony would be revoked; that the Nugget had so far furnished its readers with a full account of the trial, and had published all of the testimony taken on Tuesday. His Honor therewith revoked the order. The morning session was consumed in the argument of a point raised by one of the attorney's for the defendant, who contended that a Justice of the Peace sitting as an examining court was entirely without any judicial function; that he was merely administerial officer, and as such had no power to pass on the relevancy or materiality of any evidence offered. Or, in other words, he was only a clerk who's only duty was to write down such evidence as was offered, and when an objection or exception was taken, to note the same on a deposition. The court decided that in an examining trial the Justice acted as a court, and in consequence had power to pass on the admissability of any evidence offered. If any other position had been taken by the magistrate the trial might have consumed just as much time as council saw proper to devote to it; and, indeed, the evidence under such a ruling need not apply to the case at all in order to be given in full on the depositions.
"JOHN H. BEHAN'S TESTIMONY
"John H. Behan, being sworn says; I am Sheriff, and reside in Tombstone, Cochise County, Arizona; I know the defendants Wyatt Earp, and John H. Holliday; I know Virg and Morg Earp; I knew Thomas McLaury, Frank McLaury, and William Clanton; I was in Tombstone October 26, when a difficulty, or shooting affray took place between the parties named. The first I knew that there was likely to be any trouble, I was sitting in a chair getting shaved in a barber shop; it was about half past one or two, it may have been later, but not much; saw a crowd gathering on the corner of Fourth and

Allen Streets; someone in the shop said there was liable to be trouble between Clanton and the Earps; there was considerable said about it in the shop and I asked the barber to hurry up and get through, as I intended to go out and disarm and arrest the parties; after I had finished in the barber shop I crossed over to Hafford's corner; saw Marshal Earp standing there and asked him what was the excitement; Marshal Earp is Virgil Earp; he said there were a lot of s-s of b-s in town looking for a fight; he did not mention any names; I said to Earp you had better disarm the crowd; he said he would not, he would give them a chance to make the fight; I said to him: It is your duty as a Peace Officer to disarm them rather than encourage the fight; don't remember what reply he gave me, but I said I was going down TO DISARM THE BOYS.

"I meant any parties connected with the cowboys who had arms; Marshal Earp at that time was standing in Hafford's door; several people were around him; I don't know who; Morgan Earp and Doc Holliday were then standing out near the middle of the street, at or near the intersection of Allen and Fourth Streets; I saw none other of the defendants there; Virgil Earp had a shotgun; with the muzzle touching the door-sill, down at his side; I did not see any arms on the others at the time; I then went down Fourth Street to the corner of Fremont, and I met there Frank McLaury holding a horse and talking to somebody; I greeted him; I said to him: (defendants here object to any conversation between witness and Frank McLaury, court overrules the objection at this time) I told McLaury that I would have to disarm him, as there was likely to be trouble in town and I propose to disarm everybody in town that had arms. He said he would not give up his arms as he did not intend to have any trouble; I told him that he would have to give up his pistol, all the same; I may have said gun, as gun and pistol are synonymous terms; about that time I saw Ike Clanton and Tom McLaury down the street below Fly's Photography Gallery; I said to Frank, 'Come with me;' we went down to where Ike Clanton and Tom were standing; I said to the boys, 'You must give up your arms!' Billy Clanton was there; when I got down to where Ike was I found Tom McLowry, William Clanton, and Will Claiborne; I said to them, 'Boys you have got to give up your arms.' Frank McLaury demurred; I don't know his exact language; he did not seem inclined, at first, to give up his arms. Ike told me he DID NOT HAVE ANY ARMS.

"I put my arm around his waist to see if he was armed, and found he was not; Tom McLaury showed me by pulling his coat open, that he was not armed, I saw five standing there and asked them how many there were of them; they said four of us; this young man, Claiborne said he was not one on the party; he wanted them to leave town; I said boys you must go up to the Sheriff's office and take off your arms and stay there until I get back; I told them I was going to disarm the other party; at that time I saw the Earps and Holliday coming down the sidewalk, on the south side of Fremont Street; they were a little below the post office; Virgil, Morgan and Wyatt Earp and Doc Holliday were the ones; I said to the Clantons wait there for awhile, I see them coming down, I will go up and stop them; I walked up the Street twenty-two or twenty-three steps and met them at Bauer's Butcher Shop, under the awning, in front, and told them not to go any farther, that I was down there for the purpose of arresting and disarming the McLaury's and Clantons; they did not heed me and I threw up my hands and said go back, I'm the Sheriff of this county and am not going to allow any trouble if I can help it; they brushed past me and I turned and went with them, or followed them two steps or so in the rear as they went down the street, expostulating with them all the time; when they arrived within a very few feet of the Clantons and McLaurys I heard one of them say - I THINK IT WAS WYATT EARP -

"'You s- of b-s you have been looking for a fight and now you can have it;' about that time I heard a voice say 'Throw up your hands;' during this time I saw a nickel-plated pistol pointed at one of the Clanton parties - I think Billy Clanton - my impression at the time was that Holliday had the nickel-plated pistol; I will not say for certain that Holliday had it; these pistols I speak of were in the hands of the Earp party; when the order was given, 'Throw up your hands,' I heard Billy Clanton say, 'Don't shoot me, I don't want to fight;' Tom McLaury at the same time threw open his coat and said, 'I have nothing,' or 'I am not armed;' he made the same remark and the same gesture that he made to me when he first told me he was not armed; I can't tell the position of Billy Clanton's hands at the time he said, 'I don't want to fight;' my attention was directed just at that moment to the nickel-plated pistol; the nickel-plated pistol was the first to fire, and another followed instantly; these two shots were not from the same pistol, they were too nearly instantaneous to be fired from the same pistol; the nickel-plated pistol was fired by the second man from the right; the second shot came from the third man from the right. The fight became general.

"Two of the three fired shots were very rapid after the first shot; by whom I do not know; the first two shots were fired by the Earp party; I could not say by whom; the next three shots I thought at the time came from the Earp party; this was my impression at the time from being on the ground and seeing them; after the party said, 'Throw up your hands;' the nickel-plated pistol went off immediately; I think V.W. Earp said, 'Throw up your hands;' there was a good deal of fighting and shouting going on. I saw Frank McLaury staggering on the street with one hand on his belly and his pistol in his right

[hand]; I saw him shoot at Morgan Earp, and from the direction of his pistol should judge that the shot went in the ground; he shot twice there in towards Fly's Building at Morg Earp, and he started across the street; heard a couple of shots from that direction; did not see him after he got about half way across the street; then heard a couple of shots from his direction; looked and saw McLaury running and a shot was fired and he fell on his head; heard Morg say, 'I got him;' there might have been a couple of shots afterwards, but that was about the end of the fight; I can't say I knew the effect of the first two shots; the only parties I saw fall were Morg Earp and Frank McLaury. My impression was that the nickel-plated pistol was pointed at Billy Clanton; the first man that I was certain that was hit was Frank McLaury, as I saw him staggering and bewildered and knew he was hit; this shortly after the first five shots; I never saw any arms in the hands of any of the McLaury party except Frank McLaury and Billy Clanton; saw Frank McLaury on the sidewalk, within a very few feet of the inside line of the street; did not see a pistol in the hands of any of the McLaury party until 8 or 10 shots had been fired; Frank was the first of the party in whose hands I saw a pistol; Ike Clanton broke and ran after the first few shots were fired; Ike, I think, went through Fly's Building; the last I saw of him he was running through the back of Fly's Building towards Allen Street.

"At the conclusion of the above testimony the court adjourned until 9 o'clock this morning."[1]

On November the 4th, the Daily Nugget continued reporting the testimony of John Behan as follows:

"SHERIFF BEHAN'S TESTIMONY RESUMED.

"I could not tell exactly where Ike was going; he was trying to get out of the way; I saw him at the corner of Fly's and he ran from them; never saw him after he passed the corner of the Gallery; I saw a shotgun before the fight commence; Doc Holliday had it as he passed down the street; he had it under his coat; when I walked up to meet him he pulled his coat farther over the gun; did not see the gun go off, but I knew afterwards that the shotgun had been fired; did not distinguish the shotgun report; did not see the gun after the fight commence; don't know what became of the gun afterwards; saw the bodies of the boys after the shooting; Clanton was not then dead; I said nothing to Clanton; heard him say when removed to the house, 'Get away from me and let me die;' I saw him lying on the side of the street and saw him shoot once while lying down; there was quite a number in the room where Clanton was carried, but cannot say whom; saw Dr. Gilberson, I remember in the crowd around;

---

[1]   The Daily Nugget, November 3, 1881.

Gilberson said, 'There is no use in giving him any thing, he is dying;' I was not in the house when Billy Clanton died; he was gasping when I left; Tom McLaury and Bill Clanton were carried into the same house; Billy Clanton's feet were towards the door; don't remember the position of Tom McLaury."[1] [2]

The cross-examination of Behan commenced on November 3rd, and was published in the November 4th edition. The Nugget continued to report his testimony by printing only the answers, and not the questions; whereas, on cross examination, the official court reporter included both the questions and the answers.

Therefore, for the cross examination of John Behan, we will go to the official court reports as worked over by Mr. Hayhurst and reprinted in the O.K. Corral Inquest commencing at page 140.

"[COURT ADJOURNED UNTIL TOMORROW MORNING AT 9 O'CLOCK]

"[THURSDAY, NOVEMBER 13, 1881-EXAMINATION OF JOHN H. BEHAN RESUMED] (This actually occurred on November 3rd.)[3]

"I couldn't tell where he [Ike Clanton] was going to. I found him on Tough Nut Street, at Judge Lucas' old office. I saw him at the corner of the Photograph Gallery. I never saw him after he passed the corner of the gallery. He seemed to be trying to get away. I should judge he went through the house. I saw a shotgun before the fight commenced. Doc Holliday had it. He had it under his coat. I do not know of my knowledge that it was fired, as I did not see it go off. I could not distinguish it from the other shots. I did not notice it afterward. I do not know what became of it.

"I saw the bodies of the deceased after they were dead. Clanton was not quite dead. I saw Clanton lying on the sidewalk. I heard him say, 'Go away and let me die.' He said it after being taken in the

---

[1] The Daily Nugget, November 4, 1881

[2] [Author's note: You will note to this point, very few questions were recorded. Most of the reported testimony of Behan consisted of his answers to questions, but the reader has to guess at the question. That is also true of the Hayhurst version of the same testimony. Alfred E. Turner mistakenly has John H. Behan's testimony being given to the court on the 13th day of November 1881, and then on the following day which he also designated as November 13th, 1881 he resumed his testimony. Both of these dates are in error, because the Daily Nugget published the testimony of Behan on November 3rd, 4th and 5th.]

[3] The Daily Nugget, November 4 1881.

house. I saw him lying on the sidewalk, and I saw him when he shot at Morgan Earp, while lying down. Quite a number was in the room. I do not know who they were. I saw Dr. Gilberson in the room. He said nothing would do him, Clanton, any good he was dying. I was not in the house when he died. I left before he died. Tom McLaury was in the same room. Clanton's feet were toward the door. I do not remember McLaury's position.

"CROSS-EXAMINATION

"(Q) Did you receive the first information of the anticipated difficulty between the Earp party and the Clanton party at the barber shop, of which you have spoken?

"(A) My recollection is that I heard of it first in the barber shop.

"(Q) Had you previous to that time heard of a difficulty between Wyatt Earp and Tom McLaury in the neighborhood of Wallace's office?

"(A) I had not.

"(Q) You being in town and assumedly mingling with the people, if those difficulties were a matter of common comment, how did it happen that a report of it did not reach your?

"[Objected to by Prosecution. Sustained.]

"(Q) Were you not in Hafford's Saloon some 15 or 20 minutes before the fight?

"(A) I was in Hafford's Saloon some 10 or 15 minutes before the fight.

"(Q) Did you not cross the street in company with one Shibell?

"(A) I did, with Charles A. Shibell.

"(Q) Did you see Virgil Earp?

"(A) I do not remember whether I did or not.

"(Q) Did you not say to Virgil Earp at the time, 'We are going to take a drink. Won't you join us?'

"(A) I do not remember whether he took a drink or not.

"(Q) Do you not remember that while the parties were drinking, that Captain Murray came in and called Virgil Earp to the lower end of the counter?

"(A) I do not remember.

"(Q) Do you remember that when Virgil Earp came back from Murray's to where you were standing, you said to him: 'What does that son-of-a-bitch strangler want?'

"(A) I do not remember, and I do not think such words passed my lips as Captain Murray and I are on the best of terms.

"(Q) Do you remember that you then asked Virgil Earp what he was going to do?

"(A) No, I do not.

"(Q) Do you recollect Virgil Earp replying: 'I am going to disarm them.'

"(A) No.

"(Q) Do you recollect replying to that remark: 'Don't undertake to do that,' or: 'They will kill you' --referring to the Clanton crowd. 'They were just down in my corral having a gun talk against you and threatening your life.'

"(A) No such conversation happened. I made no such reply. I had not been down in my corral.

"(Q) Do you recollect further saying: 'I will go down where they are; they won't hurt me, and I will get them to lay off their arms' -- this was said to Virgil Earp?

"(A) This conversation did not take place at that time.

"(Q) Did you, subsequent to the fight, somewhere in the city of Tombstone, and upon the day of the fight and speaking of the fight between the Earp crowd and the Clanton crowd, say to Charles Shibell that it was a dead square fight and the you could not tell who shot first?

"(A) No sir.

"(Q) Did you not make that remark, or [one] of similar import to Wyatt Earp after the fight, on the corner of Fremont and Fourth Streets, and upon the day of the fight?

"(A) No sir.

"(Q) If anything, how much have you contributed or have promised to contribute to the associated attorneys who are now prosecuting this case?

"(A) I have not contributed a cent, nor have I promised to.

"(Q) Were not you and Wyatt Earp applicants to General Fremont for the appointment of Sheriff of Cochise County, and did not Wyatt Earp withdraw his application upon your promise to divide the profits of the office and did not you subsequently refuse to comply with your part of the contract?

"[Objected to by the Prosecution. Overruled.]

"(A) In the first place we were both applicants for the office. I was, and I understood Mr. Earp was. When I became satisfied that I would get the appointment, I went to Mr. Earp and told him that I knew I would get the appointment of Sheriff, and that I would like to have him in the office with me. I also told him that I did not want him to cease his efforts to get the office if he could. I told him I was sure I could get it and that if I did, I would take him in, that in case he got the office, I did not want anything to do with it. He said it was very kind of me, that if he got the office he had his brothers to provide for, and could not return the compliment if he got it. I said I asked nothing if he got it, but in case I got it, and I was certain of it, I would like to have him in the office with me. I said, 'Let this talk make no difference with you in your efforts to get the office.' Something afterwards transpired that I did not take him into the office.[1]

"(Q) Up to the time of this difficulty under consideration, have you not regarded Wyatt Earp as an aspirant for the office of Sheriff of Cochise County?

"(A) I have not.

"(Q) [Question not written.]

"(A) I did not see anyone take a pistol from William Clanton.

"(Q) After the fight was over, how soon did you leave the battleground and where did you go?

"(A) I cannot say how long, probably four or five minutes. I came up Fremont Street, thence to Hafford's Corner.

"(Q) Did you meet Wyatt Earp at the corner of Fremont and Fourth Streets?

"(A) I did.

"(Q) Did you have any conversation with him?

"(A) We had some conversation.

"(Q) After the fight, were you upon the stoop in the passageway between the lodging house and the photograph gallery, and how long?

"(A) I was on the stoop a very [few] seconds after the fight.

"(Q) Did you not at the time suppose that you were [the] only, or about the only witness, outside of the parties concerned in the difficulty, who witnessed the difficulty?

"[Objected to on the ground that it is irrelevant and immaterial. Objection sustained.]

"(Q) Did you not, at the time and place, say to one of the Flys: 'I'm about the only witness to that fight, am I not?'

"(A) I don't remember. I told him I saw it all. He was trying to get Claiborne out of the house. I told him to let him stay, as he was not to blame and might get killed.

"(Q) After you followed or accompanied the Earps from under the awning of the butcher shop, and the fight commenced, did you occupy one position until the shooting ceased?

"(A) No sir, I did not stand still. I moved around pretty lively.

"(Q) When you heard the expression: 'You sons-of-bitches, etc., hold up your hands, etc.' locate on this diagram [diagram shown] the exact position of the Clanton crowds.

"(A) [Here witness makes use of diagram marked "Exhibit A," and the witness indicates the position of the parties as follows: 1.Frank McLaury; 2.Billy Clanton; 3.Thomas McLaury; 4.Ike Clanton.] Claiborne was standing back of them, farther into the lot. I cannot

---

[1]   What transpired was that Wyatt beat out Sheriff Behan for the affections of his live-in girlfriend, Josephine Sarah Marcus.

state exactly where. The four numbered were not standing in as straight a row as the figures on the diagram. [Here witness corrects the positions.]

"(Q) How long was it after the expressions of, 'You sons-of-bitches, etc.,' and 'throw up your hands!' was it that the firing commenced?

"(A) I don't think it was more than a second interval.

"(Q) What interval of time between the expression, 'You sons-of-bitches,' and 'Throw up your hands?'

"(A)   One expression followed the other--it was almost simultaneous.

"(Q) At the time of those two expressions, I understand you to say you had your eye on a nickel-plated pistol.   Did you see the nickel-plated pistol before you heard the expressions?

"(A)   I saw the nickel-plated pistol at the same time the expressions were made.

"(Q) Did you see it in any interval before the expressions were made

"(A) I saw it at the same time.

"(Q) Was it pointed, the first time you saw it?

"(A) Yes, it was pointed at Billy Clanton.

"(Q) Was it the commencement of the expressions, 'You sons-of-bitches, etc.,' that diverted your attention from the Clanton crowd and concentrated it upon the Earp crowd?

"(A) My attention was on the Earp crowd.

"(Q) How long had your attention been especially on the Earp crowd?

"(A) From the time I turned to go with them.

"(Q) Did you see a shotgun in the hands of the Earp party, and if so, which one of them?

"(A) The last time I saw the shotgun [it] was in the hands of Doc Holliday--he had it under his coat.

"(Q) Did you see the shotgun employed in that difficulty?

"(A) I did not.

"(Q) Holliday having a shotgun just preceding the difficulty, and on the way to the difficulty, and your attention being especially directed to the Earp party, how does it happen that you do not know what became of the shotgun?

"(A) I do not know--it might have been used and I not know of it.

"(Q) Locate Holliday at the time, as you say, you think he discharged the nickel-plated pistol.

"(A) [Witness marks on the diagram marked "Exhibit A", by the figure 5, the position occupied by Holliday at the time he thinks Holliday fired the shot.]

"(Q) And at what distance from the nearest of the Clanton Party?

"(A) About five and a half or six feet, I should judge.

"(Q) Do you still insist that the first shot was fired from the nickel-plated pistol?

"(A) Yes.

"(Q) Is it not a fact that at the time of the firing of the first shot, Holliday was in the street, at least 25 feet from where you have located the Clanton crowd?

"(A) No, it is not.

"(Q) Is it not a fact that the first shot fired by Holliday was from a shotgun; that he then threw the shotgun down and drew the nickel-plated pistol from his person and then discharged the nickel-plated pistol: Presuming Holliday to be number 5 on the diagram, is it not a fact that he fired the shotgun first?

"(A) [Question not answered.]

"[COURT HERE RECESSES UNTIL 1 O'CLOCK]

"[HEARING RESUMED]

"(Q) Had not the Clanton party, meaning the parties named as engaged in the conflict, a reputation for courage and determination? [Objection by the Prosecution. Overruled.]

"(A) They have that reputation. That is Frank McLaury and Ike Clanton--I never heard the reputation of the other two discussed.

"(Q) Have not the Earp party the same reputation as to courage and determination?

"(A) They have.

"(Q) With your knowledge of the character of the two parties, were you not satisfied after the first hostile demonstration that the contact would proceed to a bitter end, and beyond the power of ordinary or extraordinary interference?

"[Question objected to. Question overruled on the ground that it is mere opinion of the witness, upon the acts, that he has already related, and as being such opinion, is immaterial and irrelevant.]

"(Q) With Allen fleeing into an alleyway, Claiborne, or the Kid, hiding in the photograph gallery, [and] Ike Clanton running away, why did you hover around there, exposing your person and life?

"[Question overruled in its present form.]

"(Q) What was the exterior dress of Doc Holliday at the time you saw him with a shotgun?

"(A) He had on a heavy overcoat of gray color which came below his knees.

"(Q) Did he change the overcoat from the time you first saw him until you think he discharged the nickel-plated pistol?

"(A) I don't think he changed it. He did not have time.

"(Q) Did any other of the Earp party have a similar garment on?

"(A) I think not.

"(Q) What space of time was occupied between the first and last shot?

"(A) I don't think the fight lasted over 20 or 30 seconds.

"(Q) Were you satisfied when you put your arm around the waist of Ike Clanton, Tom McLaury threw the lapels of his coat aside, and Billy Clanton said he did not want to fight, that these parties had no arms?

"(A) When I left the Clanton party to meet the Earps, I was satisfied that Ike Clanton and Tom McLaury had no arms on them.

"(Q) Could they not have had arms and you not know it?

"(A) Ike Clanton could not without my knowing it.   Tom McLaury might have had a pistol and I not know it.

"(Q) As you examined him simply around the waist, could he not have had a pistol in his pocket?

"(A) He could not have had a pistol in his pocket, as I examined him very closely with my eye.

"(Q) Did you see a horse in that neighborhood?

"(A) Yes sir.

"(Q) Where exactly--noted on the diagram.

"(A) I cannot designate precisely on the diagram where the horse was.

"(Q) At what time connected with the hostilities did you see Frank McLaury hold that horse?

"(A) He had hold of the horse when the Earp party first went down there.

"(Q) What became of the horse when Frank McLaury occupied the position designated on the diagram as Figure 17?

"(A) As long as I saw him occupy that position, he was holding the horse.

"(Q) Then was the horse inside or outside the vacant lot?

"(A) Inside the vacant lot.

"(Q) How long before the difficulty did you see the horse in that position?

"(A) They were occupying that position when I left to meet the Earp party and walked 21 or 22 steps and back, and the party all seemed to be in the same position.

"(Q) Where was the horse immediately previous to and during the shooting?

"(A) At the beginning of the shooting he was occupying that position.

"(Q) Did the horse intervene between the Clanton party and Doc Holliday?

"(A) I think not. It is possible that Frank McLaury may have stepped back behind the horse.

"(Q) Did you see Tom McLaury discharge one or more pistol

shots toward the Earp party--or, in other words, did you see Tom McLaury shoot over the horse's back?

"(A) No sir.

"(Q) Did you see or hear any evidence of a shot proceeding from the alleyway between Fly's house and the building east of it?

"(A) No.

"(Q) Have you ever heard any threats within the last few months on the part of the Clantons and McLaurys against the defendants in this prosecution?

"(A) I never heard any threats at any time.

"(Q) Once or twice in your direct examination, you spoke of cowboys. What is a cowboy?

"(A) My idea of a cowboy is men who deal in cattle--stockmen.

"(Q) Do you regard the Clantons and McLaurys as cowboys? [Question overruled on the ground that it is eliciting the opinion of the witness and is immaterial and irrelevant.]

"(Q) Do you know the reputation of the Clantons and McLaurys in the section of the county in which they live and roam for turbulence? [Objected to on the ground that it is not (proper) cross-examination and is immaterial. Answer delayed. Objection sustained on the ground that it is not (proper) cross-examination and is immaterial.]

"(Q) Have not the disturbance and main difficulties, breaches of the peace, and killings in this city and county been, in your opinion and knowledge, or either, connected with Clantons or their confederates? [Prosecution objects on the same grounds as above. Overruled.]

"(A) I never knew the McLaurys to be in any trouble or rows. Ike Clanton I have seen in one row here, and Billy Clanton I know nothing about.

"(Q) Do you know William Allen?

"(A) Yes sir.

"(Q) Did you see him that day at or near the difficulty or shooting, at or near the time of said shooting?

"(A) I don't remember seeing him there.

"(Q) Were you, during the time of the shooting, in the alleyway between Fly's Gallery and the building on the east?

"(A) I was not in any alleyway during the progress of the fight.

"(Q) When you left the Clanton party, as you stated, and ascended Fremont Street to meet the Earps, did you not say, addressing Wyatt Earp and Morgan Earp: 'I have got them disarmed.' Or words to that effect?

"(A) No sir.

"(Q) Did not the Earp party, after some remark made by you to them, put their pistols farther back in their pants and did not Holliday pull his coat over his gun?

"(A) No sir. Holliday pulled his coat over his gun before I spoke to him.

"(Q) Have you, since the difficulty, had any interview with William Allen, to compare your recollections with him in regard to the difficulty?

"(A) I had no interview with Allen about the matter; have met him and talked about it on the street. [Verbatim as in original.]

"(Q) During the progress of the fight, did you see Ike Clanton take hold of Wyatt Earps left arm and hear Wyatt Earp say to him, 'This fight has commenced, either fight or get away!'

"(A) No sir.

"(Q) Indicate on the diagram the position of the Earp party at the time of the firing of the first shot.

"(A) I can locate the party but cannot give the position of each particular one [here witness marks on diagram "a"]. [The figures] 6, 7, and 8 represent three of the Earp party, and number 5 represents the one with the nickel-plated pistol. The Earp party were facing the Clanton party.

"(Q) To the best of your belief, how far apart were the two parties?

"(A) About five and a half or six feet; very close together.

"(Q) Which represents [number] 8, to the best of your knowledge?

"(A) I can't tell exactly; my impression is that number 8 represents Virgil Earp.

"(Q) What party is number 7, to the best of your knowledge?

"(A) I don't know.

"(Q) Mark the position of the horse as number 9.

"(A) Number 1, Frank McLaury was holding the horse. I cannot designate on the diagram the position of the horse, for I have forgotten; there may have been two horses there for all I know.

"(Q) If one or two horses, were they inside of the vacant lot?

"(A) They were inside of the vacant lot.

"RE-DIRECT EXAMINATION

"(Q) When you first saw the Clanton and McLaurys on the day of the difficulty, were they, or either of them, making any noise or disturbance?

"(A) No sir. They were not.

"(Q) When you saw the Earp party going down Fremont Street towards the Clanton party, what noise or disturbance were they making, if any?

"(A) They were making no noise or disturbance.

"(Q) Did you personally know Billy Clanton, and if so, how long, and about how old was he, if you knew him?

"(A) I knew him, have known him about three or four months. He was a boy, I should not take him to be of age.

"(Q) During the time you knew him, did you know or hear of his being in any difficulty?

"(A) I never knew or heard of his being in any rows. I knew very little about him.

"(Q) In your cross-examination you state that Isaac Clanton had been in some difficulties. Please state the number, with whom, and where, and when.

"(A) The only difficulty that I know of his being in, was with Danny McCann, in Tombstone, about a month or two ago.

"(Q) In your cross-examination you were asked if you know of Isaac Clanton being in any difficulties, please state if you heard of his being in any difficulties; if so, with whom, and where?

"(A) I heard he had a difficulty with the Deputy Sheriff at Charleston some months ago, and then again I heard he had some trouble with Holliday the night before the shooting. I can't call to mind any other.

"(Q) Did you hear of any difficulty on the morning of the 26th of October?

"(A) I heard of a difficulty on the morning of the 26th, with Morgan and Virgil Earp.

"[COURT ADJOURNED UNTIL FRIDAY, NOVEMBER 14, 1881, AT 9 O'CLOCK A.M.] (This actually occurred on November 4th.) [1]

"[FRIDAY, NOVEMBER 14, 1881, EXAMINATION RESUMED]

"[All answers of witness Behan touching [the] character of the deceased were stricken out, on the ground that they were not proper matters of cross-examination.] [The following question [was] asked witness Behan by the defense, by consent.]

"(Q) Did you visit Virgil Earp at his residence the evening after the fight?

"(A) I did.

"(Q) Did not some discussion ensue between you and Virgil Earp about the fight?

"(A) There was some.

"(Q) Did you not make use of this language: 'I went to see the Clanton crowd and told them to disarm. They would not do it. I went back and met you and spoke to you and you did not stop. I heard you say, "Boys throw up your hands, I have come to disarm you." When one of the McLaury boys said, "We will," and drew his gun, and the shooting commenced. I am your friend, and you did

---

[1]   The Daily Nugget, November 5, 1881.

perfectly right.' --or language of such substance or like import?

"(A) I went down that evening and when I got in the house, Virgil Earp said, 'You better go slow, Behan, and not push this matter too far.' I told him I did not come there to have any words--that I intended to do my duty as an officer. Then he said he heard I tried to get the vigilance committee to hang them. I told him I did nothing of the kind, that I never called for them. He said about the same thing that Wyatt Earp did, about me deceiving them or throwing them off. Then is when I explained to him about stopping him and telling them to stop. In the conversation he told me he was my friend. I told him I had always been his friend. That seemed to settle the matter about the vigilance committee. I suppose I told him that I heard him say, 'Throw up your hands!' I never told him I heard McLaury say anything or that I saw him draw a pistol.

"RE-EXAMINATION

"(Q) On your cross-examination you stated that you promised Wyatt Earp a position in your office, and that something subsequently occurred that caused you to do it. Please state what that something was.

"(A) It was this: Shortly after I had the conversation with Wyatt Earp, I received a telegram from Charles A. Shibell, Sheriff of Pima County to subpoena Ike Clanton. I was Deputy Sheriff [in Tombstone, before Cochise County was formed] under Shibell. I didn't know where Clanton lived at the time. I went to Virgil Earp and asked him. He told me where [Ike] lived. I hitched up a team and started to Charleston. I had gotten about halfway to Charleston, and a man dashed by me on horseback, on the run; and about five minutes afterwards another passed me on the run. I got to Charleston and found a man going to Clanton's place. I gave him the dispatch and told him to hand it to Ike Clanton, and stayed around Charleston an hour or so, and met Wyatt Earp and Doc Holliday. I think I asked them what they were doing or what they were on. Wyatt Earp told me he was down after a horse that had been stolen from him sometime before.

"Nothing more was said, and I returned to Tombstone. I went over to Tucson a few days afterwards and was told by Clanton that I came near getting myself in a hell of a scrape--[Defense counsel objects to the witness testifying to verbal statements of Clanton not connected [with] or a part of the circumstances of the homicide. Objection overruled and objected to.] He, Ike, said Earp sent him word that I had taken a posse of nine men down there to arrest him and send him to Tucson, and then he told me he had armed his crowd and was not going to stand it, and they got out [a word here is illegible] guns and was not going to Tucson.

"(Q) Who was the first and the second man that passed you on the [Charleston] road of whom you spoke?

"(A) It was dark, and my impression was that it was Virgil Earp, I did not know, but thought it his form, and the next [man] I thought was Holliday. When I got to Charleston, I saw Wyatt Earp instead of Virgil, and concluded I had made a mistake.

"(Q) Who was with you, if any person?

"(A) Les Blackburn and a man named Lawrence Geary.

"(Q) Who did you send the dispatch by, from Charleston to Ike Clanton?

"(A) I think by a man named Oates.

"(Q) Can you tell anywhere near about the time of month it was, or what case the subpoena was in?

"(A) No, I cannot tell the time; [it was] in [the] case of Paul vs. Shibell.

"(Q) Was there any conversation between you and Wyatt Earp immediately after the difficulty as to your deceiving him about the McLaurys and Clantons being armed, and if so, what was the conversation?

"(A)   There was a conversation on Fremont Street near the Butcher Shop on the sidewalk. Wyatt Earp said, 'Behan, you deceived me,' or, 'threw me off. You said you had disarmed them.' I told him he was mistaken, I did not say anything of the kind. Then I related to him what I had said. I said, 'Earp, I told you I was there for the purpose of arresting and disarming them.' He said he thought I had said I had disarmed them.

"(Q) What was the distance you were from the Clanton and McLaury party, and how near the Earp party when you told the Earps to stop, and that you were there for the purpose of disarming and arresting the Clanton party?

"(A)   I was within 9 or 10 feet of the Earp party when I commanded them to stop, and about 19 or 20 yards from the Clantons and McLaurys.

"(Q) Where did this difficulty occur?

"(A) In Tombstone, Cochise County, Arizona Territory.

"(Q) [No written question appears.]

"(A) The [man] named, spoken of as Captain Murray is known as Billy Murray and is a partner of F.A. Tritle.

"(Q) At the time you demanded [his arms] of Frank McLaury, at the corner of Fremont and Fourth Streets, and he demurred to giving them up, was the demurrer a conditional one or an absolute refusal?

"(A) He did not want to give up his arms unless the other party was disarmed.

"[The defendants reserved the right to further cross-examine the witness after they opened their case for the defense.]

[signed] John H. Behan"

A number of other witnesses were sworn in and testified, but none of them added anything very new or contradictory to what is contained in the testimony of John Behan, Ike Clanton, Wyatt and Virgil Earp. Therefore, their testimony will be set forth here in full with excerpts from other witnesses testimony that might shed some light on some of the controversial points.

CHAPTER XXXVII

IKE CLANTON TESTIFIES

ON November 9th, Ike Clanton took the witness stand and testified. His testimony, including questions and answers seemed to have been fully reported in both the court records and in the Tombstone Nugget. I have examined them both very carefully and find almost no difference and am therefore setting forth here the testimony taken from the court reporter as reworked by Hayhurst rather than the testimony reported in the Nugget of November 10th, for the simple reason that the photocopies that I have of the Nugget are extremely difficult to read.

The testimony of Ike Clanton was as follows:

"My name is Joseph I. Clanton. I reside four miles above Charleston, on the San Pedro River. My occupation is stock raising and cattle dealer."

"(Q) Where were you on the 26th [of] October, 1881?

"(A) I was here in Tombstone.

"(Q) Do you know Virgil Earp, Morgan Earp, Wyatt Earp, and J.H. Holliday.

"(A) I do.

"(Q) Did you know Frank and Tom McLaury and Billy Clanton?

"(A) Yes sir.

"(Q) Are they living or dead, and if so, when did they die?

"(A) They are dead. They died on the 26th of October, 1881, on Fremont Street, between Third and Fourth Streets, in Tombstone, Cochise County, Arizona Territory.

"(Q) Did they die a natural death or a violent death?

"(A) A violent death, they were killed.

"(Q) Were you present at the time they were killed?

"(A) I was.

"(Q) Who else was present at the time, that you saw?

"(A) There was Holliday, Morgan, Virgil and Wyatt Earp, Sheriff Behan, and William Claiborne. No [one] else, that I can remember, at the time they were killed.

"(Q) Who was engaged in the killing of these parties?

"(A) Wyatt, Morgan and Virgil Earp, and Holliday.

"(Q) Now you begin at the commencement of the difficulty and tell all you saw about. [As written in the original.]

"(A) Well, I and the McLaury brothers and William Clanton, and a young fellow named Billy Claiborne were standing in a vacant space talking, west of the photograph gallery on Fremont Street--between that and the building next to it and the Sheriff Johnny Behan came down and told us he would have to arrest us and disarm us.

"[The defense moves that the witness be instructed not to detail conversation without the hearing of the defendants. Objection overruled. Counsel for the defense then asks that the Court give the ground for his ruling, which the Court refuses to do, because the law does not require it, and it would be objectionable to encumber the deposition of the witnesses with the opinion of the Court.]

"(A) I asked the Sheriff, 'What for?' The Sheriff told me, 'To preserve the peace.' I told him I had no arms. Then William Clanton told him he was just leaving town. The Sheriff then said, if he was leaving town, 'all right.' He then told Frank and Tom McLaury he would have to take their arms. Tom McLaury told him he had none. Frank McLaury said he would go out of town, but did not want to give his arms up until after the party that hit his brother was disarmed. The Sheriff told him that he should do it, and take his arms to his, the sheriff's office, and lay them off. Then Frank McLaury said he had business in town that he would like to attend to, but he said he would not lay off his arms and attend to his business unless the Earps were disarmed. The Sheriff then put his arms around me and felt if I was armed. Tom McLaury remarked to the Sheriff, 'I am not armed, either,' and opened his coat by taking hold of the lapels and throwing it open, this way [witness shows how]. The Sheriff looked up Fremont Street, and ordered us to stay there 'till he came back.

"[Defense moves that the entire conversation above be stricken out on the ground that it forms no part of the "res gestae"--that it did not transpire in the presence of the defendants or in their hearing and that it is making testimony for the prosecution. Objected to by the prosecution. Objection sustained on the ground that such conversations are hearsay, and not strictly "res gestae," and all conversations in the foregoing testimony shown as included in brackets are stricken out. Prosecution objects to the ruling of striking out the testimony.]

"(A) And started up that way. Just as he started up the street, the Earp party and Holliday appeared on the sidewalk and were coming down.[1]

"(Q) When the Sheriff started up the street from where the McLaurys and the Clantons were standing, did you remain there, and

---

[1]   Both Ike Clanton and Johnny Behan had the Earp party coming down the sidewalk. Other witnesses said they were in the street.

if so, why did you remain?

"[Defense objects to witness giving reason for doing an act or refraining from doing an act. Objection overruled, and defense asks for the grounds of the ruling.]

"(A) We all remained there because the Sheriff had ordered us to. [Defense moves to have the answer stricken out because the prosecution has obtained indirectly, what the court refused directly. Motion overruled by the Court.]

"(Q) When Mr. Behan went up the street, who did he meet coming down, and what did he do or say?

"(A) He met Virgil Earp, Morgan Earp, Wyatt Earp, and Holliday coming down Fremont Street. He held up his hands and told them to stop, that he had our party in charge.

"(Q) State what they did, whether they stopped, and if they did not, what did they do?

"(A) They did not stop, but passed by him and came down where we were.

"(Q) How far was it from where you were standing to the point where Sheriff Behan met the Earps and Holliday?

"(A) I should judge it to be about twenty paces.

"(Q) You say the Earps and Holliday came on down to where you were--what did they do when they got here, and what did they say?

"(A) They pulled their pistols as they got there, and Wyatt Earp and Virgil Earp said, 'You sons-of-bitches, you have been looking for a fight!' and at the same time ordered us to throw up our hands. And they said, 'You have been looking for a fight!' and commenced shooting.[1]

"(Q) Who commenced shooting?

"(A) The first two shots were fired by Holliday and Morgan Earp. Wyatt Earp and Virgil Earp fired the next shots, immediately afterward. Virgil Earp shot before Wyatt did.

"(Q) How close together were the two first shots that were fired by Holliday and Morgan Earp?

"(A) They were fired so close together I could not tell which one shot first.

"(Q) How long after that was it that Virgil Earp fired?

"(A) It was almost immediately, perhaps a couple of seconds afterwards.

"(Q) State, if you know, at whom Mr. Holliday and Morgan Earp

---

[1]   A good defense attorney would never have let them get away with "they said," he would insist that the witness testify who said. It's unlikely that both Wyatt and Virgil said the same thing.

fired?

"(A) Morgan Earp shot William Clanton, and I don't know which one of the McLaury Holliday shot at. He shot at one of them.

"(Q) How do you know that Morgan Earp shot Billy Clanton?

"(A) Because I seen his pistol pointed within two or three feet of his bosom, saw him fire and saw William Clanton stagger and fall up against the house and put his hands onto his breast.

"(Q) In what position were Billy Clanton's hands at the time Morgan Earp fired at him, and you saw him stagger and fall up against the house?

"(A) His hands were thrown up about even with the level of his head--his hands in front of him.

"(Q) When those first shots were fired, in what position were the hand of Frank and Tom McLaury and yourself?

"(A) Frank McLaury had his hands up [witness shows how he held up his hands, by holding his hands up, with the palms open, his fingers about level with the top of his head]. I was holding my hands the same way, and Tom McLaury took hold of the lapels of his coat, threw them open, and showed that he had no arms on.

"(Q) Were you or not at any time during the shooting, armed; and if not, where were your arms, if you know?

"(A) I was not at any time during the shooting armed. I understood Virgil Earp had taken my arms a short time before that and left them behind the Grand Hotel bar.

"(Q) What sort of arms did Virgil Earp take from you, and leave behind the bar?

"(A) A Colt .45 caliber pistol, and a Winchester carbine.

"(Q) State, if you know, whether at any time during the shooting, Tom McLaury was armed?

"(A) I never saw him with any arms during the shooting.[1]

"(Q) Do you know where his arms were, or any of them at the time of the shooting?

"(A) His Winchester was in the stable on Fremont Street below where the shooting occurred [West End Corral]. I don't know where his other arms were.

"(Q) Did you come into town with Tom McLaury, and if so, how long before the shooting?

"(A) Yes sir, I came into town with him on the day previous to the shooting; it was about 11 o'clock in the forenoon. We came in a spring wagon.

---

[1]   Note that he never testified that Tom McLaury was not armed. He only said that he didn't see him with any arms. Sheriff Behan had said that: "Tom McLaury might have had a pistol and I not know it."

"(Q) Now state, if you know, how many arms he brought in with him, and what kind they were?

"(A) He brought in with him, a Winchester carbine and a six-shooter. [Here, Andrew J. Mehan, who has formerly testified, produces the pistol he had in court at the time of his examination, which pistol is handed to the witness, who says, 'This is the same pistol that Tom McLaury brought into town the day before the shooting. I know it by the guard being sprung and by its general appearance.']

"(Q) State, if you please, now, whether or not the Winchester carbine of Tom McLaury's that you say he brought in with him the day before, was the same one that was at the stable on the day of the shooting.

"(A) It was.

"(Q) At the time the Earp party and Holliday came up to where you and the McLaurys and Bill Clanton were standing, what if anything, did Wyatt Earp do?

"(A) He shoved his pistol up against my belly and told me to throw up my hands. He said, 'You-son-of-a-bitch, you can have a fight!' I turned on my heel, taking Wyatt Earp's hand and pistol with my left hand and grabbed him around the shoulder with my right hand and held him for a few seconds. While I was holding him he shot. I pushed him around the corner of the photograph gallery and then I jumped into the door. I went right on through the hall and out of the back way. I then went on across Allen Street and into the dance hall on that street. As I jumped into the door of the photograph gallery, I heard some bullets pass my head. As I went by an opening, I heard some more bullets pass by me.

"(Q) In passing from Fly's photograph gallery towards Allen Street, state whether or not you passed by a house to the right of the Fly's photograph gallery, and if so, state whether or not you heard any shots strike it.

"(A) I heard some bullets strike the building ahead of me.

"(Q) How many shots were fired by the Earp party before you left the ground where the shooting occurred?

"(A) To the best of my belief, there were four or five. There were four, and I think five.

"(Q) Up to that time, had there been any shots fired by either of the Clantons or the McLaurys?

"(A) There had not.

"(Q) Up to that time, did you see any weapon of any kind drawn by or in the hands of either of the Clantons or McLaurys?

"(A) No sir. They all had their hands up, up to that time. Tom

McLaury had his hands up, holding his coat open.[1]

"(Q) Did you see any weapons in the hands of Frank or Tom McLaury or Billy Clanton while you remained on the ground?

"(A) No sir, I did not.

"(Q) Did you or not, at any time during the shooting, see a horse or horses on the ground where the shooting occurred? If so, state who, if anybody, had them.

"(A) Yes sir, there were two horses there. Frank McLaury was holding a horse; Billy Clanton had a horse also, and standing right by him.

"(Q) What became of those horses, while you remained there, as far as you could see?

"(A) I never noticed the horses after the shooting commenced.

"(Q) Were there or not, any arms on those horses, and if so, what kind were they?

"(A) Yes sir, there were arms on them. They were Winchester carbines. There was on each horse, in the gun scabbards.

"(Q) State whether or not those arms were drawn from their scabbards while you stayed there.

"(A) No sir, they were not, while I stayed there.

"(Q) How come you and Billy Clanton and the McLaurys to be there? [Objected to on the ground that reasons permitted to be entered into would exonerate all persons charged with crime. Objection overruled.]

"(A) My reason for going there was to get mine and Tom McLaury's team. By mutual understanding Billy Clanton and Frank McLaury had given orders to have our team hitched up. [Defense Counsel moves to strike out the foregoing answer. Motion overruled.]

"(Q) At the time the Earp party approached the Clantons and McLaurys on Fremont Street, at the place where the shooting occurred, was the latter party making any noise or disturbance, or were they peaceable and quiet? [Question objected to on the ground that inference and deductions of acts are called for instead of the acts themselves. Objection overruled.]

"(A) They were making no disturbance or noise and they were peaceable and quiet.

"(Q) State if there was any previous difficulty between you and the defendants or either of them; and if yes, when and where?

"(A) Yes sir, there was a difficulty between Holliday and Morgan Earp and I, the night before at a lunch stand in this town near the Eagle Brewery Saloon, on the north side of Allen Street. As well as

---

[1]   It would seem rather difficult for him to have his hands up and be holding his coat open at the same time.

I remember, it was about 1 o'clock in the morning. I went in there to get a lunch. While sitting down at the table, Doc Holliday came in and commenced cursing me and said I was, 'A son-of-a-bitch of a cowboy,' and told me to get my gun out and get to work. I told him I had no gun. He said I was a damned liar and had threatened the Earps. I told him I had not, to bring whoever said so to me and I would convince him that I had not. He told me again to pull out my gun and if there was any grit in me, to go to fighting. All the time he was talking, he had his hand in his bosom and I supposed on his pistol. I looked behind me and saw Morgan Earp with his feet over the lunch counter. He has his hand in his bosom also, looking at me. I then got up and went out on the sidewalk. Doc Holliday said, as I walked out, 'You-son-of-a-bitch, if you ain't heeled, go and heel yourself.' Just as I stepped out, Morgan Earp stepped up and said, 'Yes, you son-of-a-bitch, you can have all the fight you want now!' I thanked him and told him I did not want any of it now, I was not heeled. Virgil Earp stood off about 10 or 15 feet from us on the sidewalk. Just about this time, or perhaps a minute later, Wyatt Earp came up where I was. Wyatt did not say anything. Morgan Earp told me if I was not heeled, when I came back on the street to be heeled. I walked off and asked them not to shoot me in the back.

"[COURT HERE ADJOURNED UNTIL THURSDAY, NOVEMBER 10, 1881, AT 9 O'CLOCK A.M.]

"[THURSDAY, NOVEMBER 10, 1881, EXAMINATION OF JOSEPH I. CLANTON RESUMED]

"I did not see Morgan Earp or Doc Holliday any more to speak to them that night. A half hour after that, I presume, I came back to the next saloon on the west, called the Occidental. I sat down in this saloon and played poker all night, until daylight. Tom Corrigan was tending bar there in that saloon. Virgil Earp and Tom McLaury and another gentleman, I don't know his name, and Johnny Behan, were playing the game. While the row was going on, on the sidewalk, just as I walked away, Virgil Earp told Morgan Earp and Holliday to let me alone while Jim was there.

"(Q) To whom did Virgil Earp refer when he told Morgan Earp and Holliday to let you alone while Jim was there?

"(A) Jim Flynn the policeman, the only person that I know there by that name. When the poker game broke up in the morning at daylight, I saw Virgil take his six-shooter out of his lap and stick it in his pants. I got up and followed him out of doors on the sidewalk. He was going down Allen Street towards the Cosmopolitan Hotel. I walked up to him and told him in regard to what he said to the policeman the night before and playing poker with a six-shooter in his lap, that I thought he stood in with those parties that tried to murder me the night before. I told him if that was so, that I was in town. He said he was going to bed. I went back and passed my chips into the poker game and had no more talk with Virgil that morning. I think it was about half-past one o'clock (P.M.), as I was walking up on Fourth Street from Fremont to Allen Street, Virgil and Morgan Earp came up behind--don't know where they came from. Virgil Earp struck me on the side [of] the head behind the ear with a six-shooter and knocked me up against the wall. Morgan Earp cocked his pistol and stuck it at me. Virgil Earp took my six-shooter and Winchester from me. I did not know who struck me until after I recovered from my fall against the house. They pulled me along and said, 'You damned son-of-a-bitch, we'll take you up here to Judge Wallace's.'

"When I got there and was put behind the railing, Wyatt Earp came in and told me I could have all the shooting I wanted, and cursed me. I did not see Doc Holliday there. He called me a thief and son-of-bitch, and told me I could have all the shooting I wanted, to name my style of fighting, or something like that. Virgil Earp spoke up and told me he would pay my fine if I would fight them. I told him that I would. Wyatt Earp offered me my rifle, told me to take it. He handed it to me muzzle first, the muzzle pointed down as he presented it. I saw Virgil Earp put his hand in his bosom, this way, [shows the motion]. Morgan Earp stood over me and behind me on the bench in the rear. Wyatt Earp stood to the right and in front of me, and then I told them I did not want any of it, that way. Wyatt Earp asked me where I wanted to fight and as well as I remember, I told him I would fight him anywhere or any way. This conversation occurred in the Courthouse while I was a prisoner. I am not positive whether Judge Wallace was present or not. I don't think he was, as we waited there sometime for something or other before he imposed the fine. There were others there. The front of the building was full. I was fined and paid it and was released. This occurred about one o'clock, I think or just before. This all occurred on the day of the killing, I should judge about an hour and a half, as well as I can calculate the time.

"(Q) At the time you were released, who if anybody had your arms?

"(A) Virgil took them in charge when I was arrested and I hadn't got them.

"(Q) When, after that time, and where did you get your arms?

"(A) I got them a couple of days after that from William Soule, the jailer.

"(Q) Had you, at the time you state that Doc Holliday charged you with having threatened the Earps ever in fact threatened the Earps or Doc Holliday?

"(A) No sir. I never threatened the Earps or Doc Holliday.

"[HERE THE EXAMINATION OF WITNESS WAS

SUSPENDED UNTIL SATURDAY, NOVEMBER 12, 1881 AT 10
O'CLOCK A.M.]
    "[SATURDAY, NOVEMBER 12, 1881, EXAMINATION OF
JOSEPH I. CLANTON RESUMED]
    "CROSS EXAMINATION
    "(Q) On what day and at what time of day did you arrive in
Tombstone from your ranch prior to the 26th of October, 1881?
    "(A) I came in town on the 25th [day] [of] October. I think it
was about between 10 or 11 o'clock in the morning. I did not come
from my ranch. I came from Sulphur Spring Valley. I left my ranch
three days before that.
    "(Q) Who went with you from your ranch to Sulphur Spring
Valley?
    "(A) I went by myself, alone.
    "(Q) Who came in with you from Sulphur Spring Valley?
    "(A) Tom McLaury.
    "(Q) Did you or did Tom McLaury, to your knowledge, on the
night of the 25th, or at any time during the 25th or 26th [of] October,
send, or cause to be sent, a telegraphic dispatch from the office here
to Charleston or any other point, to William Clanton or Frank
McLaury or to any person or persons, directing Frank McLaury or
William Clanton to come to Tombstone?
    "(A) I did not, and I know that Tom did not, for we had taken
breakfast with Frank McLaury and William Clanton the day we came
into town, at Jack Chandler's milk ranch, which is ten miles from
here, at the foot of the Dragoon Mountains.
    "(Q) Do you know a man by the name of Neil Boyle, the saloon
keeper at the Oriental?
    "(A) I know a man named Ned Boyle.
    "(Q) Were you in the Oriental Saloon about 8 o'clock the
morning of the day of the difficulty?
    "(A) I don't remember being there.
    "(Q) Did you not say, in the presence of this Boyle at about that
time, in the Oriental Saloon, that as soon as the Earps came on the
street, they had to fight?
    "(A) I don't remember seeing Ned Boyle that day.
    "(Q) Were you in Kelley's Saloon at or about the hour of 10
A.M. on the morning of the day of the difficulty?
    "(A) I was.
    "(Q) Did you not make the remark in Kelley's Saloon in [the]
presence of Joe Stump and Kelley, and in answer to the question of
Kelley to you: 'What was the matter?' [that] the Earp crowd had
insulted you the night before when you were unarmed, --'I have
fixed,' or 'heeled' myself now and they have got a fight on sight, or
language of like import?

"(A) I remember that there was very near that conversation in Kelley's Saloon. It was about 10 A.M., I think.[1]

"(Q) Did not Kelly say to you, you meant to shoot if you said so? [Objected to by prosecution on the ground that it is not "res gestae." Objection sustained.]

"(Q) Did you not at the time, have a Winchester rifle in your hand, and a six-shooter in your belt?

"(A) I had no belt on. I had a Winchester and a six-shooter, which I had for self-defense.

"(Q) Do you not know William Daly, commonly known as Farmer Daly?

"(A) Yes sir, I know him.

"(Q) Do you remember, about four weeks ago, that you and Frank McLaury rode up in front of Hafford's Saloon in this city and that you or Frank McLaury called Daly out of the saloon and that either you or Frank McLaury said, 'We understand they have formed a Vigilance Committee against us?' That Daly said there was some talk about the matter, but he did not know much about the matter. One of you said--you or Frank McLaury-- 'Can you deny but that man in there [meaning Morgan Earp, who was in the saloon] belongs to the committee?' Daly said, 'He does not belong to it.' One of you said, 'We don't believe it. Even if it were so, it don't make any difference, they [meaning the Earps] are in our way, anyway, and will have to be got out.' Did not that conversation ensue between you and Frank McLaury and Daly at or about the time indicated, at the place specified, and under the circumstances, or conversation of similar import, and was not Morgan Earp in Hafford's Saloon and within your vision?

"[Objected to by [the] prosecution. Objection sustained, on the ground that it assumes facts that have not been stated or proven by the witness or relates conversation of persons who were not the defendants or the persons injured.]

"(Q) Do you not remember ever riding up with Frank McLaury about four weeks ago to Hafford's Saloon in company with Frank McLaury?

"(A) I don't remember ever riding up to that saloon in company with Frank McLaury.

"(Q) Do you, or do you not, recollect the conversation detailed in the previous question, transpiring between you and Daly or between Frank McLaury and Daly, within the hearing of you three,

---

[1]   Here we have an admission under oath that Ike Clanton intended to start a fight with the Earps as soon as he saw them. The judge evidently relied heavily on this admission.

at the time and place specified in that question? [Question objected to by prosecution. Objection sustained on same grounds given above.]

"(Q) Did you ever, at any time or place in this city, within the last two months, and prior to October 26, 1881, say to any person whatever, 'They [meaning the Earp brothers] are in our way, anyway, and will have to be got out,' or language of similar import? [Objected to by prosecution upon the ground that the person is not named in the question to whom the remark, if made, was made. Defense does not press the question.]

"(Q) You made, did you not, the sworn complaint in this case?

"(A) I did.

"(Q) Have you not, employed counsel to prosecute in this case?

"(A) Yes sir.

"(Q) Where, precisely, is your ranch and the McLaury ranch?

"(A) My ranch is about 14 miles from Tombstone, about four miles from Charleston, on the San Pedro River, and McLaury's ranch is about 30 miles from mine, in Sulphur Spring Valley. It is located 25 miles from this place.

"(Q) Did you ever see this telegram before? [Here witness is presented with a paper purporting to be a telegram, reading as follows 'San Francisco, June 7, 1881. Received at [blank] June 7, 1881, 4 o'clock P.M., To Marshall Williams. Yes we will pay rewards for them dead or alive. L. F. Rowell.']¹

"(A) I never saw it before.

"(Q) The night of the difficulty or controversy between you and Doc Holliday, in what language did Doc Holliday first approach you?

"(A) He first said I had been using his name. He did not say in what way.

"(Q) To what did he refer to in making use of that language?

"(A) He said I had threatened the Earps.

"(Q) Was that all?

"(A) I told him I had not threatened the Earps or had not used his name. I did not know what he referred to about using his name.

"(Q) Were you, up to that time, friendly with the Earps?

"(A) Yes sir.

"(Q) Did you know Billy Leonard, Harry Head and Jim Crane?

"(A) I knew Billy Leonard and Jim Crane, and had seen Harry Head a few times, but was not acquainted with him.

"(Q) Did not these persons often stop at your ranch?

"(A) They sometimes stopped at a ranch I had over in New

---

¹   Researchers seem to have searched in vain for the telegram that was received in evidence as Exhibit "A." It must have long ago disappeared from the files.

Mexico, and Billy Leonard often had stopped at my ranch four miles above Charleston before this trouble of killing Bud Philpot.

"(Q) Were these parties supposed to be connected with the attempt to rob the stage and the killing of Bud Philpot?

"(A) I don't know anything, only what Doc Holliday, Wyatt, Virgil, and Morgan Earp, and others told me about it. [Objected to. Objection overruled subjected to a reserved ruling as to whether they shall be stricken out for failure to show their relevancy and materiality.]

"(Q) Did not Wyatt Earp approach you, Frank McLaury and Joe Hill for the purpose of getting you three parties to give Leonard, Head and Crane away--in the Arizona parlance--so that he, Wyatt Earp, could capture them?

"(A) Wyatt Earp approached me, but I do not [know] that he ever approached Frank McLaury or Joe Hill. I met him in the Eagle Brewery Saloon one night and he asked me to take a drink with him, and while they were mixing our drinks, he told me that he wanted a long private talk with me. After we had drank, he stepped out into the middle of the street with me. He then told me he would put me on a scheme to make six thousand dollars. I asked him what it was. He told me he would not tell me unless I would promise to do it, or if I would not promise to do it, not to mention our conversation to any one else. He then made me promise on my honor as a gentleman not to repeat the conversation if I did not like the proposition. I asked him what it was. He told me it was a legitimate transaction. He then made me promise the second time that I would not mention it any more. He told me he wanted me to help put up a job to kill Crane, Leonard and Head. He said there was between four and five thousand reward for them, and he said he would make the balance of the six thousand dollars up out of his own pocket. I then asked him why he was anxious to capture these fellows. He said that his business was such that he could not afford to capture them. He would have to kill them or else leave the country. He said he and his brother, Morgan, had piped off to Doc Holliday and William Leonard, the money that was going off on the stage, and he said he could not afford to capture them, and he would have to kill them or leave the country, for they [were] stopping around the country so damned long that he was afraid some of them would be caught and would squeal on him. I then told him I would see him again before I left town. I never talked to Wyatt Earp any more about it.[1]

---

[1] Alford E. Turner described this testimony as "a ludicrous tale that is impossible to believe," because the highway-men didn't even succeed in stopping the stage. The O.K. Corral Inquest, Page 121.

"(Q) Where were you born sir?

"(A) I was born in Missouri.

"(Q) At what time of the day of the shooting did Frank McLaury and Billy Clanton arrive in town?

"(A) They arrived in town about half an hour before they were killed.

"(Q) Where did they come from?

"(A) They came from Antelope Springs. They are east of here and about 13 miles from town.

"(Q) Did you have four or five conversations with Wyatt Earp in the yard connected with the Oriental Saloon in reference to the arrest of Leonard, Head, and Crane?   "[Question objected to by the Prosecution. Objection sustained on the ground that no limit of time is mentioned.]

"(Q) Did he not tell you in some of these conversations he had with you, or in some other conversation, that he expected to run for sheriff at the next election; that he would like to capture these men if he could; that he would give you and your party all the reward that had been offered if, Wyatt, could catch them; [that] he, Wyatt, would rather have the glory than the money; and that you and Frank McLaury and Joe Hill agreed to give up, or capture those parties, or to lead them to a place where Wyatt could capture them, provided the reward was paid dead or alive; and did not this conversation take place in the yard connected with the Oriental Saloon, in this city, between Wyatt, yourself, and some one or more of the parties I have indicated, -- Virgil Earp, Wyatt Earp, yourself, Frank McLaury, and Joe Hill -- about six weeks after the Philpot killing?

"(A) I had never any conversation with him in company with Joe Hill or Frank McLaury or Virgil Earp, in the yard of the Oriental Saloon. I never heard him say anything about running for sheriff and I never heard him say that he wanted to capture them.

"(Q) Did you not have a conversation or conversations of the like import and about the time and at the place mentioned in the proceeding interrogatory, with Wyatt Earp?

"(A) I never had no conversation with Wyatt Earp in regard to that in the Oriental yard.

"(Q) Did you say in such conversation that these parties would make a fight, and that Wells Fargo & Company were not in the habit of paying rewards except upon conviction, and that you would not consent to ambuscade them unless Wells Fargo & Company would pay the reward dead or alive? [Objection made by prosecution and withdrawn.]

"(A) I never had but one conversation with Wyatt Earp upon that subject, and did not talk anything about Wells Fargo's business, only that he said that Wells Fargo would give between four and five thousand dollars.

"(A)   And did not Wyatt Earp, either upon his own or your suggestion, upon some one of the conversations, tell you that he would have Wells Fargo & Company telegraph if they would pay the reward dead or alive?

"(A) I never heard anything about the telegram to Wells Fargo before today, and I made no suggestion in the conversation and had only one conversation with Wyatt Earp on that subject.

"(Q) Did not Wyatt Earp, during these conversations, show you that document, in front of the Alhambra, four or five days after he had the first conversation? [Shows witness the telegram.] [Here, after argument, the paper shown to the witness and called a copy of the telegram, is hereto attached and marked, "Exhibit A."]

"(A) I never heard of, or saw that telegram before, and do not know what conversation is alluded to, as I never had but one.

"(Q) Did you not, in some one of these conversations, tell Wyatt Earp that you knew where Leonard, Head and Crane were concealed?

"(A) I did not, in the conversation I had with him, for I did not know where they were concealed.

"(Q) Did not these three parties frequent, about the time of these conversations, your or your father's cattle ranch?

"(A) What conversations do you mean?

"(Q) The conversations about which I have interrogated you.

"(A) I had no conversations. I had but one conversation, at the time of that conversation with Wyatt Earp, I don't know, as I was not there.

"(Q) Were not these parties, up to that time, frequent visitors at your and McLaury's ranches?

"(A) As regards McLaury's ranch, I don't know. They sometimes came to my place before I had this talk with Wyatt Earp.

"(Q) Did you not, in concert or agreement with Wyatt Earp, dispatch Joe Hill, from Tombstone, to bring these parties to McLaury's ranch for the purpose of having them arrested by Wyatt Earp?

"(A) I never had no talk with Joe Hill about this business and, consequently, never dispatched Joe and had no arrangement with Wyatt Earp and Joe Hill to act in concert about.

"(Q) And were you not present when Joe Hill deposited his watch and money with Virgil Earp, before departing on this expedition?

"[In protection to the witness, question is overruled by [the] court on its own motion, on the ground that it is assuming certain facts that have not been proved or testified to by witness.]

"(Q) Have you not frequently, you and Frank McLaury, charged

Wyatt Earp, Virgil and Morgan Earp, with having given you two away to Marshall Williams and Doc Holliday, in making them confidant in your effort at surrendering Leonard, Head, and Crane to justice--your particular friends and associates?

   "[Counsel for the prosecution object to the words, "Your particular friends and associates," as being an assumption of facts not established or testified to by witness. Objection sustained on the ground the words objected to assume a state of facts not testified to by the witness.]

   "(Q) Omitting [the] words in the last question, 'your particular friends and associates,' answer the question.

   "(A) In regard to Frank McLaury, I don't know whether he ever charged anything of the kind or not, and as to my part, I had nothing to do with bringing them to justice, consequently I could not charge the Earp brothers with giving me away to anybody.

   "(Q) Did you not so state to several parties, and if so, to whom, and at what time?

   "[Objected to on the ground that it is not proper cross-examination, that it does not state the time, place, and persons to whom the statement was made, if made at all. Question not pressed.]

   "(Q) What were the first words addressed to you by Doctor Holliday on the first intercourse, of which you have spoken on the night of the day preceding the difficulty in which these parties were killed? Did he not say to you, 'I understand that you say the Earp brothers have given you away to me and that you have been talking about me.'

   "(A) I don't recollect exactly what were his first words--they were not those, though. He said to me that I had been using his name and had threatened the Earp brothers.

   "(Q) Did you not, sometime during the day of the difficulty and preceding the difficulty, telegraph to Charleston for William and Phin Clanton to come to Tombstone?

   "(A) No sir.

   "(Q) In what position upon your person were the Winchester rifle and pistol at the time you encountered Virgil and Morgan Earp--I mean, at the time you were disarmed, on the day of the difficulty?

   "(A) My pistol was stuck in the waistband of my pants. The handle was exposed to view, but under my coat; I was packing the Winchester in my hand.

   "(Q) Where, precisely, did they encounter you?

   "(A) On Fourth Street, between Fremont Street and Allen, on the left-hand sidewalk, going from Fremont to Allen. I was just leaving the Capitol Saloon--Moses and Mehan keeps it--I was going to the Pima County Bank. I had those weapons about my person for self-defense.

"(Q) In the conversation that transpired between you and the Earp boys in Wallace's Court Room, is it not a fact that Virgil Earp did not participate herein, but that he was absent in pursuit of Justice Wallace?

"(A) In the commencement of the abuse by Morg and Wyatt Earp, I do not think that Virgil Earp was there. He was there in the later part of the time they were cursing me, and remarked that they would 'give it to me now!' or something to that effect.

"(Q) Did you see William, or Billy Clanton as he is called, with a pistol in his hands during the fight?

"(A) No sir.

"(Q) Are you aware, from any source, that he did have a pistol during the fight, and what is your source of information?

"(A) I never saw him have any pistol at that time, and don't know that he had any, only from hearsay.

"(Q) Do you know where he got the weapon?

"[Question objected to on the ground that it assumed he had a weapon. Objection sustained on the ground that the witness has already answered that he did not know that Billy Clanton had a weapon, and the question assumes that he did. The question is still pressed by the defense and refused by the court.]

"(Q) How long after you retreated, as you have stated, from the scene of the firing, and how long after the shooting ceased, did you return to the scene of the firing, if you returned at all?

"(A) I did not return at all to the scene of the firing, only I passed by there eight or ten days after it was done, and then was back there two or three days ago.

"(Q) Was Billy Clanton a brother of yours?

"(A) He was.

"(Q) During the lifetime of Frank McLaury, were you not with them in close business and friendly relations?

"(A) I was.

"(Q) How many cattle have you sold during the past year, or about how many, if any, and how many of those cattle had you procured by legitimate means?

"[Objected to by [the] prosecution. Objection withdrawn.]

"(A) To the best of my recollection in the neighborhood of 700 head. I raised and purchased in connection with the McLaury boys, about 700 head. I got them honestly by raising and purchasing them.

"(Q) When you took hold of Wyatt Earp's arm at some stage of the shooting, as you say, did he not say to you, 'This fight has commenced, and you must either fight or get away!'

"(A) No sir, he made no such remark. The only thing he said was to, 'throw up your hands!' and stuck his pistol against my belly.

"(Q) How many shots had been fired at the time he made that observation to you?

"(A) There had not been any fired.

"(Q) Is Charleston directly upon the route between your ranch and Tombstone, or is that the route, or do you generally take Charleston in your route?

"(A) There is a nearer road to my ranch than going by the way of Charleston, I sometimes take Charleston in my route and sometimes take the nearer road.

"(Q) Do you know Ned Boyle, who keeps bar at the Oriental Saloon?

"(A) Yes sir.

"(Q) Did you not, about the hour of 8 A.M. on the day of the shooting somewhere in Tombstone, say to Ned Boyle, that as soon as the Earps showed themselves on the street, they had to fight--having at the same time, a pistol in your hand? If so, state the precise point where this remark was made.

"[Objected to as not being sufficiently definite as to place. Objection overruled.]

"(A) I don't remember speaking to Ned Boyle about it. I think I saw him, but don't remember saying anything to him about it. I don't think I said the Earps had to fight when they came on the street. There were three of them that I never had an unpleasant word with in my life, up to that time. I don't remember having any pistol in my hand.

"(Q) How long preceding the shooting were you and Tom McLaury and Billy Clanton and Frank McLaury in the gun shop on Fourth Street? [Question withdrawn]

"(Q) Were you, William Clanton, Frank and Tom McLaury in the gun shop on Fourth Street during the day of the shooting, and if so, how long before the shooting commenced?

"(A) I was in the gun shop. William Clanton came there after me. I don't know whether he came in the shop or not. I am very sure that Tom McLaury was not there; Frank McLaury came in the shop and asked where Tom was.

"(Q) Is it not a fact that Billy Clanton and Tom and Frank McLaury were there and that you came there subsequently as the fourth party?

"(A) I was the first party that was there.

"(Q) Do you remember Wyatt Earp moving a horse belonging to one of your party from the pavement into the street, and that at that time you seized hold of a gun in the gun shop?

"[Objected to on the ground that it assumed that he had or took hold of a gun, without such fact being proved, and that it assumed that there was a horse on the pavement and removed into the street by Wyatt Earp, and no such fact has been proved. Objection sustained on the ground that the question assumed facts to exist that have not been proven or testified to by the witness. Counsel for [the] Defense presses the question, and the Court refuses.][1]

"(Q) Did not Virgil Earp tell you where he had deposited your Winchester and pistol sometime after he had taken them from you?

"(A) He did not, in Wallace's Court Room. He told me where he would leave them at, while under arrest. He said he would leave them at the Grand Hotel Bar.

"(Q) At what period of the shooting did you run?

"(A) There had been four or five shots fired.

"(Q) Knowing, as you say, that those shots proceeded from the Earp party, was not your attention directed entirely upon the Earp party?

"(A) No sir, not entirely upon the Earp party. I was looking at my brother and the McLaury brothers too.

"(Q) How much time was consumed from the expression, 'Hold up your hands!', and the first four shots?

"(A) It was done as quick as it could be done. I suppose in five, or six, or ten seconds.

"(Q) Did you run into the door of the photograph gallery facing Fremont Street?

"(A) I did.

"(Q) Where was Claiborne, or the Kid, at the time you commenced running?

"(A) I don't know where he was when I commenced running.

"(Q) Where were you precisely, in reference to the corner of the photograph gallery when Wyatt Earp thrust, as you say, his pistol against your belly, and made use of the remark, 'Hold up your hands?'

"(A) I was standing almost at the northwest corner of the photograph gallery. Wyatt Earp was standing north of the northwest corner, and I was standing west of the same corner. Doc Holliday was standing near the outer edge of the sidewalk, and about opposite the corner. I cannot locate exactly, where Virgil Earp was, but I think he was to the left of Doc Holliday, on the sidewalk. Frank McLaury was standing in front of the vacant lot and tolerable close to the corner of the building west of the photograph gallery, as well as I can judge, he was about four feet east of the corner, and four feet in front of it. Tom McLaury was standing just to the left of Frank on the sidewalk, right behind him almost. Billy Clanton was standing in the vacant lot, about four [feet] east of the building, and about two

---

[1]   Here, if counsel had reframed his question into about four separate questions he could have got them all answered.

feet in from the sidewalk, as well as I can judge the distance.

"(Q) Were you frightened at all sir?

"(A) Well sir, I cannot say that I was frightened when they first came there, because I had no idea they intended to murder the boys and me. But when I came to see them shooting the boys with their hands up, and knew I was disarmed, and while Wyatt Earp was trying to murder me, I knew I would be killed if I did not get away.

"(Q) Where did you retreat from? State the course of your retreat.

"(A) I ran through the front door of Fly's lodging house, through the hall to the open space between the lodging house and the daguerrean gallery, thence into the open space west of the daguerrean gallery, thence southerly to Allen Street - going past the door of a house standing southwest of the daguerrean gallery, I don't think I entered the O.K. Corral in going to Allen Street, I don't remember exactly how the buildings are located there.

"(Q) Did you not, before you reached Allen Street, draw from your person and throw on the ground, a loaded pistol that you had procured from the gun shop on Fourth Street?

"(A) No sir. I had procured no pistol from the gun shop or no other place after I was disarmed by Virgil Earp.

"(Q) Who started to run first, you or Claiborne?

"(A) I never noticed Claiborne after the shooting commenced, and don't know.

"(Q) If you know, state where Billy Clanton procured the pistol he used during the melee.

"[Objected to because it assumed that Billy Clanton had a pistol, and used it at the shooting, when such fact has not been proven by this witness. Objection sustained on the ground that it assumed facts to exist not proven nor testified to by the witness. Question pressed by the Defense and the Court refuses to have the same put.]

"RE-DIRECT EXAMINATION

"(Q) Who was with you when you were knocked up against the building and disarmed on Fourth Street, between Fremont and Allen, on the day of the shooting, if any person.

"[Question objected to as the subject matter was entered into by the prosecution and should have been exhausted by the prosecution and is not a legitimate subject of rebuttal. Objection overruled.]

"(A) There was a gentleman with me by the name of William Stilwell.

"(Q) At the time stated in the question propounded to you in your cross-examination about a conversation with Ned Boyle, state if Thomas McLaury, Frank McLaury, or Billy Clanton or either of them were with you at 8 o'clock of that day?

"(A) I don't remember of any conversation with Ned Boyle at 8 o'clock of that day, or about that time. Tom and Frank McLaury and Billy Clanton were not with me.

"(Q) What were you doing in the gun shop on Fourth Street, between Fremont and Allen on the day of the shooting, and before the shooting, and what was your physical condition at that time?

"(A) I often frequent the gun shop everyday that I am in town, almost. I went there and asked for a pistol. The gentleman that runs the shop remarked that my head was bleeding, that I had been in trouble, and he would not let me have it. My physical condition was that from the blow I received from Virgil Earp, I felt very sick. The blow was just over the ear, on the side of my head.

"[Counsel for defense moves that the answer on his physical condition be stricken out, as it was a matter entered into by the prosecution, fully explained, and is not a subject of re-examination for the prosecution. Objection overruled. The defense asked the Court [to] give its reasons for its ruling. Court rules that the defense has no right to ask it on a question of this kind.]

"(Q) You were asked, in you cross-examination, if Billy Leonard, Jim Crane, and Harry Head were supposed to be connected with the attempt to rob the stage at the killing of Bud Philpot and to which you answered, 'I don't know anything about it but what Virgil Earp, Morgan Earp, Wyatt Earp and Doc Holliday and others told.' Please state what Doc Holliday told you upon the subject, and when you have answered as to him, state what Morgan Earp told you, then sate what Virgil Earp told you, then state what Wyatt Earp told you.

"[Objected to by defense on the ground that the question by the defense was generic in character, and neither sought nor asked source of his information, if he had any; never enquired of any conversation between him and other parties , and therefore, such unsolicited conversations are not subject to extra-action by the prosecution in rebuttal. Objection overruled.]

"(A) To the best of my recollection, what Doc Holliday told me was this: I came into town a few days after Bud Philpot was killed, Doc Holliday asked me if I had seen William Leonard and his party. I told him I had, I had seen them the day before and they told me to tell Doc Holliday they were going to the San Jose Mountains. He asked me if I had a talk with them. I told him only for a moment or two. He told me then that he would see me later in the evening. This was in front of the Cosmopolitan Hotel. Later I met him at Jim Vogan's place, and after talking with him a while, he asked me if Leonard told me how he came to kill Bud Philpot. I told him that Leonard told me nothing about it. He, Doc Holliday, then told me that Bob Paul, the messenger, had the line, and that Bud Philpot had the shotgun, and that Philpot made a fight and got left. About that time, someone came along and our conversation ended. I told Doc

Holliday not to take me into his confidence, as I did not want to know anything more about it. Doc Holliday told me he was there at the killing of Bud Philpot--at the time he told me Bud Philpot made a fight and got left, he told me that he, Doc Holliday, shot him through the heart. [Witness says, "Scratch that out and put it down just as Doc Holliday said."] He said he saw, 'Bud Philpot, the damned son-of-a-bitch, tumble off the cart!' That was the last conversation concerning that affair I had with Doc Holliday. He has often told me that if I saw Bill Leonard, Crane and Harry, to tell them that he was all right.

"Sometime in June I came in here, as well as I remember, I met Wyatt Earp in the Eagle Brewery Saloon. He asked me to take a drink with him, and while the barkeeper was mixing our drinks, he told me he wanted a long private talk with me. After our drink, he stepped out into the middle of the street. He told me then he could put me on a scheme to make six thousand dollars. I asked him what it was. He told me he would not tell me unless I would either promise to do it, or to promise not to mention our conversation again. He then told me it was legitimate, and we then had the same conversation I have heretofore related on my cross-examination.

"The morning after my conversation with Wyatt Earp, I met Morg Earp in the Alhambra Saloon and he asked me what conclusion I had come to in regard to my conversation with Wyatt. I told him I would let him know before I left town. He approached me again on the same subject about four or five days afterwards and we had considerable talk about it at that time, and I only remember that he told me that 10 or 12 days before Bud Philpot was killed, that he piped off $1400 to Doc Holliday and Bill Leonard, and that his brother Wyatt, had given away a number of dollars to Doc Holliday and Bill Leonard that was going away on the stage the night Bud Philpot was killed. We talked a while longer, but I don't know what was said, only that I told him I was not going to have anything to do with helping to kill Bill Leonard, Crane and Harry Head.

"[At the time of stating the above sentence, the witness first said, 'capture,' and then corrected it to 'kill.' of which correction and change, Counsel for Defense asked a memorandum be made, which is here done. [signed] Wells Spicer, Justice of the Peace.][1]

"Virgil told me to tell Bill Leonard at one time, not to think he was trying to catch him when they were running him, and told me to tell Billy that he [had] thrown Paul and the posse that was after him off of his track, the time he left Helm's ranch at the foot of the

---

[1]   This is important. Note that Clanton first used the term "capture," which comports with Wyatt Earp's testimony, and then insisted on changing the word to "kill."

Dragoon Mountains, and that he had taken them on to a trail that went down into New Mexico, and that he had done all he could for him, and that he wanted them to get those other fellows that were with him--Crane and Head--out of the country, for he was afraid that one of them might get captured and get all of his friends into trouble. In that conversation he said they had quit their trail of three horses and taken a trail of fifteen horses. He was sending this to assure Billy Leonard that he was not trying to catch him and was not going back on him. He stated that Leonard, Head of Crane's trail had gone south toward [the] San Jose Mountains. He said they followed the other trail that led into New Mexico.

"(Q) Why have you not told what Doc Holliday, Wyatt Earp, Virgil Earp, and Morgan Earp said about the attempted stage robbery and the killing of Bud Philpot before you have told it in his examination.

"(A) Before they told me, I made a sacred promise not to tell it, and never would have told it, had I not been on the stand. And another reason is, I found out by Wyatt Earp's conversation that he was offering money to kill men that were in the attempted stage robbery, his confederates, for fear that Bill Leonard, Crane and Head would be captured and tell on him, and I knew that after Leonard, Crane and Head was killed that some of them would murder me for what they had told me.

"RE-CROSS EXAMINATION

"(Q) Did you relate these conversations or the substance of these conversations with Doc Holliday, Virgil Earp, or Morgan Earp, to any of the counsel for the prosecution, or any person, before coming upon the stand this afternoon?

"(A) I did not communicate this to my counsel until after I was put on the stand. Yes, I did relate it prior to this afternoon. I did not relate it to any person prior to being put on the stand.

"[COURT TOOK RECESS UNTIL TUESDAY, NOVEMBER 15, 1881, AT 9 O'CLOCK A.M.]

"[TUESDAY, NOVEMBER 15, 1881, 9 O'CLOCK A.M.]

"[CROSS-EXAMINATION OF JOSEPH I. CLANTON RESUMED:]

"(Q) Did you not, on Sunday last, in this city, in the presence of County Recorder Jones and his Deputy, repeat the substance of what you have testified to here concerning the alleged disclosures to you by the Earps and Holliday, concerning the killing of Bud Philpot and attempted robbery of the stage?

"(A) I did.

"(Q) Is the gentleman named Stilwell, to use your language, who you say was with you when you were disarmed on the day of the shooting, the same gentleman recently committed at Tucson on a charge of robbing the Bisbee stage?

"(A) No sir. It was William Stilwell.[1]

"(Q) Where and when did you meet Leonard, Head and Crane, at the time they told you to tell Holliday they were going to the San Jose Mountains?

"(A) I don't remember exactly, what day it was, I only remember it was a few days after Bud Philpot was killed--it was close to Hereford on the San Pedro River.

"(Q) Did Leonard, Head, and Crane, then or at any time, tell you that Holliday was with them when Bud Philpot was killed?

"(A) He did not tell me then that Doc Holliday was with them. But he, Leonard, afterwards told me that if Doc Holliday had not been there, and drunk, that Philpot would not have been killed.

"(Q) How many days after Bud Philpot was killed, was it before you had the interview with Holliday at the Cosmopolitan Hotel?

"(A) I don't remember exactly how many days it was--to the best of my recollection, I think it was five or six days.

"(Q) Did Holliday give you any reason why he told you that he was the man that fired the shot that killed Philpot?

"(A) He did not give me any reason why he told me, only afterwards in his conversation he told me he knew Bill Leonard had told me about it.

"(Q) Did he put you under any pledge of secrecy?

"(A) Yes, I promised him I would never say anything about it-- the promise was exacted by Holliday.

"(Q) Did you have any conversation with Wyatt Earp upon the subject of giving away Leonard, Head and Crane, except the one you have testified to?

"(A) I never had but the one conversation with him in regard to killing them, Leonard, Head and Crane.

"(Q) Did you ever have any conversation with Wyatt Earp in the yard of the Oriental Saloon?

"[Objected to by prosecution. Objection sustained on the ground that the question is too general and sweeping, irrelevant and not admissible as cross examination at this time.]

"(Q) Where did you hold the first conversation with Morgan Earp, to which you have testified?

"(A) In the Alhambra Saloon.

"(Q) Where the second?

"(A) In the Alhambra Saloon.

"(Q) Where did Morgan tell you that Holliday shot Philpot?

---

[1]   Turner says that William Stilwell was Judge of the District Court. The O.K. Corral Inquest, Page 122 Note 16

"[Objection by the prosecution. Objection sustained on the ground that the question assumed facts to exist not proven or testified to by the witness. Question reiterated by defense. The court refuses to put the question.][1]

"(Q) When and where did you hold the conversation with Virgil Earp you have testified to?

"(A) I don't remember--it was in one of the saloons on the right-hand side of Allen Street between Fourth and Fifth Streets.

"(Q) Was I correct in my understanding that you stated on your redirect examination that one reason why you did not tell before this, of what Doc Holliday, Wyatt Earp, Virgil Earp, or Morgan Earp said or either of them said about the attempted stage robbery and the killing of Philpot, was that you feared for your own life if you did so?

"[Objected to by prosecution for the reason that the witness is asked to testify as to the correctness of counsel and not as to his own understanding and correctness. Objection sustained on the ground that the witness is not asked to relate facts or circumstances, but [is] interrogated as to the understanding of counsel. Question pressed and refused by the Court.]

"(Q) About what time did you hear of the killing of Philpot and Holliday's participation in it?

"(A) I heard of it the night it was done, [but] I did not hear of Doc Holliday's being implicated in it until several days afterwards.

"(Q) Did you rely upon the information which you received in reference to Doc Holliday's participation in said killing?

"(A) I said that after Leonard, Crane and Head were killed, I was afraid I would be murdered.

"(Q) Do you still entertain that fear?

"(A) Well, after the attempt to murder me the other day, I do.

"(Q) Did anybody else beside Doc Holliday, Wyatt Earp, Virgil Earp, and Morgan Earp, or anyone of them , confess to you that they were confederates in stopping the stage and murdering Bud Philpot?

"[Question objected to on the ground that it is immaterial.]

"(Q) Did not Marshall Williams, the agent of the Express company at Tombstone, state to you, and if at Tombstone, and if so, where, that he was personally concerned in the attempted stage robbery and the murder of Philpot?

"[Question objected to by prosecution.]

"(Q) Did not James Earp, a brother of Virgil, Morgan and Wyatt, also confess to you that he was [a] murderer and stage robber?

"[Objected to by prosecution, objection sustained on the ground

---

[1]   Here, if counsel had reframed the question leaving out the word "where" he would have got his answer.

that it is immaterial and irrelevant.]"[1]
Author's comments on Ike Clanton's testimony.
It should be remembered that almost all derogatory statements made about the Earps and their conduct while in Tombstone can be traced directly or indirectly to the testimony of Ike Clanton at the O.K. Corral hearings. Almost none of it can be corroborated by independent sources. Therefore, it is almost mandatory that his testimony be carefully and critically examined.

The prosecution's case was based on the premise that the Earps entered into the affair with the intent to kill Ike Clanton, Billy Clanton and the McLaurys. Clanton make this clear when, in answer to the question, "Were you frightened at all Sir?" he answered: "Well sir, I cannot say that I was frightened when they first came there, because I had no idea they intended to murder the boys and me. But when I came to see them shooting the boys with their hands up, and knew I was disarmed, and while Wyatt Earp was trying to murder me, I knew I would be killed if I did not get away."

If Wyatt really intended to kill Ike Clanton, according to his own testimony he certainly had every opportunity to do it. (see supra, p 235).

Earlier, he had been asked:
"(Q) When you took hold of Wyatt Earps' arm at some stage in the shooting, as you say, did he not say to you, 'This fight has commenced, and you either fight or get away?'
"(A) No Sir, he made no such remark. The only thing he said was to 'throw up my hands!' and stuck his pistol against my belly.[2]
"(Q) How many shots had been fired at the time he made that observation?
"(A) None had been fired then."
Something is wrong with Clanton's testimony. Picture from his testimony, Wyatt Earp standing in front of Ike Clanton with his pistol cocked and stuck against Clanton's belly.

Now Consider his answer to this Question: (supra p. 238)
"(Q) At what period of the shooting did you run?
"(A) There had been four or five shots fired."
This testimony should leave no doubt that Wyatt Earp could have

[1]   The O.K. Corral Inquest, Pages 91-119, reprint of Document 94, Records of the County Clerk, Cochise County. Also Arizona State Archives.

[2]   The Daily Nugget of November 13, 1881 quotes Clanton as testifying that Earp said "throw up your hands!" and cocked his pistol and stuck it in my belly. This would have given him more of a chance to kill Clanton if he wanted to.

killed Ike Clanton if he wanted to.

What is sometimes factitiously ridiculed as the Code of the West, "Never shoot an unarmed man," seems to have had a very powerful deterrent influence in Tombstone. Reading through the testimony at the hearing you will find numerous instances where an unarmed man would quarrel with an armed one and then turn his back and walk away apparently relying on the Code of the West to assure that he would not be shot in the back.

Ike's testimony that Wyatt Earp had confessed to him that he and his brother, Morgan, had piped off to Doc Holliday and William Leonard the money that was going off on the stage when Bud Philpot was killed is questionable on two grounds.

First, what circumstance would impel a reasonable intelligent person as Wyatt Earp gave every appearance of being, to confess to a crime that would ruin his career and that of his brother to someone he considered to be a cow thief and outlaw. No explanation for that has ever been attempted even by the most avid Earp bashers.[1]

Second, and most important is the fact that no money was taken, it was on the stage, and remained there until it reached its destination.

---

[1]   See Ike Clanton's testimony, supra, P 217.

CHAPTER XXXVIII

WYATT EARP TESTIFIES

ON the 16th day of November, 1881, Wyatt S. Earp took the witness stand to testify in his own behalf. To the surprise of everyone, he showed up in court with a written statement which, over the objection of the prosecution he insisted on reading to the court as his direct testimony.

The following version is that of the official court transcript as reworked by Hayhurst. I have checked the testimony of Wyatt Earp as recorded in the Hayhurst manuscript against that reported in the Daily Nugget of November 17, 1881 and find that the official court report as reworked by Hayhurst, appears to be the most complete. The record of the court proceedings and the testimony of Wyatt S. Earp is as follows:

"On this sixteenth day of November, 1881, upon the hearing of the above entitled action, on the examination of Wyatt Earp and J. H. Holliday, the prosecution having closed their evidence in chief, and the defendants, Wyatt Earp and J. H. Holliday, having first been informed of his rights to make a statement as provided in Section 133, page 22 of the laws of Arizona, approved February 12, 1881, and the said Wyatt Earp having chosen to make a statement under oath and having been personally sworn, makes such statement under oath in answer to interrogators as follows:

"(Q) What is you name and age?

"(A) My name is Wyatt Earp: 32[1] years old last March the 19th.

"(Q) Where were you born?

"(A) In Monmouth, Warren County, Illinois.

"(Q) Where do you reside and how long have you resided there?

"(A) I reside in Tombstone, Cochise County Arizona: since December 1, 1879.

"(Q) What is your business and profession?

"(A) Saloon keeper at present. Also have been Deputy Sheriff and also a detective.

"(Q) Give any explanations you may think proper of the circumstances appearing in the testimony against you, and state any facts which you think will tend to your exculpation.

"(A) The difficulty which resulted in the death of William

---

[1]   Wyatt was, in fact, 33 years old on March 19, 1881.

Clanton and Frank McLaury originated last spring, [Objection made by prosecution against the defendant, Wyatt Earp, in making his statement, of using a manuscript from which to make such statement, and object to the said defendant being allowed to make statement without limit as to its relevancy. Objection overruled.] and at a little over a year ago, I followed Tom and Frank McLaury and two other parties who had stolen six government mules from Camp Rucker. Myself, Virgil Earp, and Morgan Earp, and Marshall Williams, Captain Hurst and four soldiers; we traced those mules to McLaury's ranch. [Prosecution moved to strike out the foregoing statement as irrelevant. Objection overruled.]

"While at Charleston I met a man by the name of Dave Estis. He told me I would find the mules at McLaury's ranch. He said he had seen them there the day before. He said they were branding the mules 'D S'" making the 'D S' out [of] 'U S' We tracked the mules right up to the ranch. Also found the branding iron 'D S' Afterwards, some of those mules were found with the same brand.

"After we arrived at McLaury's ranch, there was a man by the name of Frank Patterson. He made some kind of a compromise with Captain Hurst. Captain Hurst come to us boys and told us he had made this compromise, and by so doing, he would get his mules back. We insisted on following them up. Hurst prevailed on us to go back to Tombstone, and so we came back. Hurst told us two or three weeks afterward, that they would not give up the mules to him after we left, saying that they only wanted to get us away, that they could stand the soldiers off. Captain Hurst cautioned me and my brothers, Virgil and Morgan, to look out for those men, as they had made some threats against our lives.

"About one month after we had followed up those mules. I met Frank and Tom McLaury in Charleston. They tried to pick a fuss out of me down there, and told me if I ever followed them up again as close as I did before, they would kill me. Shortly after the time Bud Philpot was killed by the men who tried to rob the Benson stage, as a detective [working for Wells, Fargo & Co.] I helped trace the matter up, and I was satisfied that three men, named Billy Leonard, Harry Head, and James Crane were in that robbery. I knew that Leonard, Head and Crane were friends and associates of the Clantons and McLaurys and often stopped at their ranches.

"It was generally understood among officers and those who have information about criminals, that Ike Clanton was sort of chief among the cowboys, that the Clantons and McLaurys were cattle thieves and generally in the secret of the stage robbery, and that the Clanton and McLaury ranches were meeting places and places of shelter for the gang.

"I had an ambition to be Sheriff of this County at the next

election, and I thought it would be a great help to me with the people and businessmen if I could capture the men who killed Philpot. There were rewards offered of about $1,200 each for the capture of the robbers. Altogether there was about $3,600 offered for their capture. I thought this sum might tempt Ike Clanton and Frank McLaury to give away Leonard, Head, and Crane, so I went to Ike Clanton, Frank McLaury, and Joe Hill when they came to town. I had an interview with them in the back yard of the Oriental Saloon. I told them what I wanted. I told them I wanted the glory of capturing Leonard, Head and Crane and if I could do it, it would help me make the race for Sheriff at the next election. I told them if they would put me on the track of Leonard, Head and Crane, and tell me where those men were hid, I would give them all the reward and would never let anyone know where I got the information.

"Ike Clanton said he would like to see them captured. He said that Leonard claimed a ranch that he claimed, and that if he could get him out of the way, he would have no opposition in regard to the ranch. Clanton said that Leonard, Head, and Crane would make a fight, that they would never be taken alive, and that I must find out if the reward would be paid for the capture of the robbers dead or alive. I then went to Marshall Williams, the agent of Wells, Fargo & Co., in this town and at my request, he telegraphed to the agent, or superintendent, in San Francisco to find out if the reward would be paid for the robbers dead or alive. He received, in June, 1881, a telegram, which he showed me, promising the reward would be paid dead or alive.

"The next day I met Ike Clanton and Joe Hill on Allen Street in front of a little cigar store next to the Alhambra. I told them that the dispatch had come. I went to Marshall Williams and told him I wanted to see the dispatch for a few minutes. He went to look for it and could not find it, but went over to the telegraph office and got a copy of it, and he came back and gave it to me. I went and showed it to Ike Clanton and Joe Hill and returned it to Marshall Williams, and afterwards told Frank McLaury of its contents.

"It was then agreed between us that they were to have all the $3,600 reward, outside of necessary expenses for horse hire in going after them, and that Joe Hill should go to where Leonard, Head, and Crane were hid, over near Yreka, in New Mexico, and lure them in near Frank and Tom McLaury's ranch near Soldier's Holes, 30 miles from here, and I would be on hand with a posse and capture them.

"I asked Joe Hill, Ike Clanton, and Frank McLaury what tale they would tell them to get them over here. They said they had agreed upon a plan to tell them there would be a paymaster going from Tombstone to Bisbee, to pay off the miners, and they wanted them to come in and take him in. Ike Clanton then sent Joe Hill to bring them in. Before starting, Joe Hill took off his watch and chain and between two and three hundred dollars in money , and gave it to Virgil Earp to keep for him until he got back. He was gone about ten days and returned with the word that he got here a day too late; that Leonard and Harry Head had been killed the day before he got there by horse thieves. I learned afterward that the thieves had been killed subsequently by members of the Clanton and McLaury gang.

"After that, Ike Clanton and Frank McLaury claimed that I had given them away to Marshall Williams and Doc Holliday, and when they came in town, they shunned us, and Morgan, Virgil Earp, Doc Holliday and myself began to hear their threats against us.

"I am a friend of Doc Holliday because when I was city marshal of Dodge City, Kansas, he came to my rescue and saved my life when I was surrounded by desperadoes.

"About a month or more ago [October 1881], Morgan Earp and myself assisted to arrest Stilwell and Spence on the charge of robbing the Bisbee stage. The McLaurys and Clantons were always friendly with Spence and Stilwell, and they laid the whole blame of their arrest on us, though the fact is, we only went as a sheriff's posse.[1] After we got in town with Spence and Stilwell, Ike Clanton and Frank McLaury came in.

"Frank McLaury took Morgan Earp into the street in front of the Alhambra, where John Ringo, Ike Clanton, and the two Hicks boys were also standing. Frank McLaury commenced to abuse Morgan Earp for going after Spence and Stilwell. Frank McLaury said he would never speak to Spence again for being arrested by us.

"He said to Morgan, 'If you ever come after me, you will never take me.' Morgan replied that if he ever had occasion to go after him, he would arrest him. Frank McLaury then said to Morgan Earp, 'I have threatened you boys' lives, and a few days later I had taken it back, but since this arrest, it now goes.' Morgan made no reply and walked off.

"Before this and after this, Marshall Williams, Farmer Daly, Ed Barnes, Old Man Urrides, Charley Smith and three or four others had told us at different times of threats to kill us, by Ike Clanton, Frank McLaury, Tom McLaury, Joe Hill, and John Ringo. I knew all these men were desperate and dangerous men, that they were connected with outlaws, cattle thieves, robbers and murderers. I knew of the McLaurys stealing six government mules, and also cattle, and when the owners went after them finding his stock on the

---

[1]   Wyatt Earp never claimed that he was operating as a Sheriff's posse any other time. He and Morgan were working with Marshall Williams and Fred Dodge, both Wells Fargo employees. The sheriffs posse was William Breakenridge and Dave Neagle.

McLaury's ranch; that he was drove off and told that if he ever said anything about it, he would be killed, and he kept his mouth shut until several days ago, for fear of being killed.

"I heard of John Ringo shooting a man down in cold blood near Camp Thomas.[1] I was satisfied that Frank and Tom McLaury killed and robbed Mexicans in Skeleton Canyon, about three or four months ago, and I naturally kept my eyes open and did not intend that any of the gang should get the drop on me if I could help it.

"Ike Clanton met me at the Alhambra five or six weeks ago and told me I had told Holliday about this transaction, concerning the capture of Head, Leonard, and Crane. I told him I had never told Holliday anything. I told him when Holliday came up from Tucson I would prove it. Ike said that Holliday had told him so. When Holliday came back I asked him if he said so.

"On the night of the 25th of October, Holliday met Ike Clanton in the Alhambra Saloon and asked him about it. Clanton denied it. They quarreled for three or four minutes. Holliday told Clanton he was a damned liar, if he said so. I was sitting eating lunch at the lunch counter. Morgan Earp was standing at the Alhambra bar talking with the bartender. I called him over to where I was sitting, knowing that he was an officer and told him that Holliday and Clanton were quarreling in the lunch room and for him to go in and stop it. He climbed over the lunch room counter from the Alhambra bar and went into the room, took Holliday by the arm and led him into the street. Ike Clanton in a few seconds followed them out. I got through eating and walked out of the bar. As I stopped at the door of the bar, they were still quarreling.

"Just then Virgil Earp came up, I think out of the Occidental, and told them, Holliday and Clanton, if they didn't stop their quarreling he would have to arrest them. They all separated at that time, Morgan Earp going down the street to the Oriental Saloon, Ike going across the street to the Grand Hotel. I walked in the Eagle Brewery where I had a faro game which I had not closed. I stayed in there for a few minutes and walked out to the street and there met Ike Clanton. He asked me if I would take a walk with him, that he wanted to talk to me. I told him I would if he did not go too far, as I was waiting for my game in the Brewery to close, and I would have to take care of the money. We walked about halfway down the brewery building, going down Fifth Street and stopped.

"He told me when Holliday approached him in the Alhambra that he wasn't fixed just right. He said that in the morning he would have man-for-man, that this fighting talk had been going on for a

---

[1]   According to Ringo's biographer it never happened.

long time, and he guessed it was about time to fetch it to a close. I told him I would not fight no one if I could get away from it, because there was no money in it. He walked off and left me saying, 'I will be ready for you in the morning.'

"I walked over to the Oriental. He followed me in and took a drink, having his six-shooter in plain sight. He says, 'You must not think I won't be after you all in the morning.' He said he would like to make a fight with Holliday now. I told him Holliday did not want to fight, but only to satisfy him that this talk had not been made. About that time the man that is dealing my game closed it and brought the money to me. I locked it in the safe and started home. I met Holliday on the street between the Oriental and Alhambra. Myself and Holliday walked down Allen Street, he going to his room, and I to my house, going to bed.

"I got up the next day, October 26, about noon. Before I got up, Ned Boyle came to me and told me that he met Ike Clanton on Allen Street near the telegraph office, that Ike was armed, that he said, 'as soon as those damned Earps make their appearance on the street today the ball will open, we are here to make a fight. We are looking for the sons-of-bitches!' I laid in bed some little time after that, and got up and went down to the Oriental Saloon.

"Harry Jones came to me after I got up and said, 'What does all this mean?' I asked him what he meant. He says, 'Ike Clanton is hunting you boys with a Winchester rifle and six-shooter.' I said, 'I will go down and find him and see what he wants.' I went out and on the corner of Fifth and Allen I met Virgil Earp, the marshal. He told me how he heard Ike Clanton was hunting us. I went down Allen Street and Virgil went down Fifth Street and then Fremont Street. Virgil found Ike Clanton on Fourth Street near Fremont Street, in the mouth of an alleyway.

"I walked up to him and said, 'I hear you are hunting for some of us.' I was coming down Fourth Street at the time. Ike Clanton then threw his Winchester rifle around toward Virgil. Virgil grabbed it and hit Ike Clanton with his six-shooter and knocked him down. Clanton had his rifle and his six-shooter was in his pants. By that time I came up. Virgil and Morgan Earp took his rifle and six-shooter and took them to the Grand Hotel after examination, and I took Ike Clanton before Justice Wallace.

"Before the investigation, Morgan Earp had Ike Clanton in charge, as Virgil Earp was out at the time. After I went into Wallace's Court and sat down on a bench, Ike Clanton looked over to me and said, 'I will get even with all of you for this. If I had a six-shooter now I would make a fight with all of you.' Morgan Earp then said to him, 'If you want to make a fight right bad, I will give you this one!', at the same time offering Ike Clanton his own six-shooter.

"Ike Clanton started to get up and take it, when Campbell, the deputy sheriff, pushed him back in his seat, saying he would not allow any fuss. I never had Ike Clanton's arms at any time, as he stated.

"I would like to describe the positions we occupied in the courtroom. Ike Clanton sat on a bench with his face fronting to the north wall of the building. I myself sat down on a bench that ran against and along the north wall in front of where Ike sat. Morgan Earp stood up on his feet with his back against the wall and to the right of where I sat, and two or three feet from me.

"Morgan Earp had Ike Clanton's Winchester in his hand, like this, with one end on the floor, with Clanton's six-shooter in his right hand. We had them all the time. Virgil Earp was not in the courtroom during any of this time and came there after I had walked out. He was out, he told me, hunting for Judge Wallace.

"I was tired of being threatened by Ike Clanton and his gang and believe from what he said to me and others, and from their movements that they intended to assassinate me the first chance they had, and I thought that if I had to fight for my life with them I had better make them face me in an open fight. So I said to Ike Clanton, who was then sitting about eight feet away from me. 'You damned dirty cow thief, you have been threatening our lives and I know it. I think I would be justified in shooting you down any place I should meet you, but if you are anxious to make a fight, I will go anywhere on earth to make a fight with you, even over the San Simon among your crowd!'

"He replied, 'I will see you after I get through here. I only want four feet of ground to fight on!'

"I walked out and then just outside of the courtroom near the Justice's Office, I met Tom McLaury. He came up to me and said to me, 'If you want to make a fight I will make a fight with you anywhere.' I supposed at the time that he had heard what had just transpired between Ike Clanton and myself. I knew of his having threatened me, and I felt just as I did about Ike Clanton and if the fight had to come, I had better have it come when I had an even show to defend myself. So I said to him, 'All right, make a fight right here!' And at the same time slapped him in the face with my left hand and drew my pistol with my right. He had a pistol in plain sight on his right hip in his pants, but made no move to draw it. I said to him, 'Jerk your gun and use it!' He made no reply and I hit him on the head with my six-shooter and walked away, down to Hafford's Corner. I went into Hafford's and got a cigar and came out and stood by the door.

"Pretty soon after I saw Tom McLaury, Frank McLaury, and William Clanton pass me and went down Fourth Street to the gunsmith shop. I followed them to see what they were going to do.

When I got there, Frank McLaury's horse was standing on the sidewalk with his head in the door of the gun shop. I took the horse by the bit, as I was deputy city marshal, and commenced to back him off the sidewalk. Tom and Frank and Billy Clanton came to the door. Billy Clanton laid his hand on his six-shooter. Frank McLaury took hold of the horse's bridle and I said, 'You will have to get this horse off the sidewalk.' He backed him off into the street. Ike Clanton came up about this time and they all walked into the gun shop. I saw them in the gun shop changing cartridges into their belts. They came out of the shop and walked along Fourth Street to the corner of Allen Street. I followed them as far as the corner of Fourth and Allen Streets. They went down Allen Street and over to Dunbar's Corral. [Dunbar and Behan.]

"Virgil Earp was then City Marshal; Morgan Earp was a special policeman for six weeks or two months, wore a badge and drew pay. I had been sworn in, in Virgil's place, to act for him while Virgil was gone to Tucson on Spence's and Stilwell's trial. Virgil had been back several days but I was still acting and I knew it was Virgil's duty to disarm those men. I expected he would have trouble in doing so, and I followed up to give assistance if necessary, especially as they had been threatening us, as I have already stated.

"About ten minutes afterwards, and while Virgil, Morgan, Doc Holliday and myself were standing on the corner of Fourth and Allen Streets, several people said, 'There is going to be trouble with those fellows,' and one man named Coleman said to Virgil Earp, 'They mean trouble. They have just gone from Dunbar's Corral into the O.K. Corral, all armed, and I think you had better go and disarm them.' Virgil turned around to Doc Holliday, Morgan Earp and myself and told us to come and assist him in disarming them.

"Morgan Earp said to me, 'They have horses, had we not better get some horses ourselves, so that if they make a running fight we can catch them?' I said, 'No, if they try to make a running fight we can kill their horses and then capture them.'

"We four started through Fourth to Fremont Street. When we turned the corner of Fourth and Fremont we could see them standing near or about the vacant space between Fly's photograph gallery and the next building west. I first saw Frank McLaury, Tom McLaury, Billy Clanton and Sheriff Behan standing there. We went down the left-hand side of Fremont Street.

"When we got within about 150 feet of them I saw Ike Clanton and Billy Clanton and another party. We had walked a few steps further and I saw Behan leave the party and come toward us. Every few steps he would look back as if he apprehended danger. I heard him say to Virgil Earp, 'For God's sake, don't go down there, you will get murdered!' Virgil Earp replied, 'I am going to disarm them,' he,

Virgil, being in the lead. When I and Morgan came up to Behan he said, 'I have disarmed them.' When he said this, I took my pistol, which I had in my hand, under my coat, and put it in my overcoat pocket. Behan then passed up the street, and we walked on down.

"We came up on them close; Frank McLaury, Tom McLaury, and Billy Clanton standing in a row against the east side of the building on the opposite side of the vacant space west of Fly's photograph gallery. Ike Clanton and Billy Claiborne and a man I don't know were standing in the vacant space about halfway between the photograph gallery and the next building west.

"I saw that Billy Clanton and Frank and Tom McLaury had their hands by their sides, Frank McLaury and Billy Clanton's six-shooters were in plain sight. Virgil said, 'Throw up your hands, I have come to disarm you!' Billy Clanton and Frank McLaury laid their hands on their six-shooters. Virgil said, 'Hold, I don't mean that! I have come to disarm you!' Then Billy Clanton and Frank McLaury commenced to draw their pistols. At the same time, Tom McLaury threw his hand to his right hip, throwing his coat open like this, [showing how] and jumped behind his horse. [Actually it was Billy Clanton's horse.]

"I had my pistol in my overcoat pocket, where I had put it when Behan told us he had disarmed the other parties. When I saw Billy Clanton and Frank McLaury draw their pistols, I drew my pistol. Billy Clanton leveled his pistol at me, but I did not aim at him. I knew that Frank McLaury had the reputation of being a good shot and a dangerous man, and I aimed at Frank McLaury. The first two shots were fired by Billy Clanton and myself, he shooting at me, and I shooting at Frank McLaury. I don't know which was fired first. We fired almost together. The fight then became general.

"After about four shots were fired, Ike Clanton ran up and grabbed my left arm. I could see no weapon in his hand, and thought at the time he had none, and so I said to him, 'The fight had commenced. Go to fighting or get away,' at the same time pushing him off with my left hand, like this. He started and ran down the side of the building and disappeared between the lodging house and photograph gallery.

"My first shot struck Frank McLaury in the belly. He staggered off on the sidewalk but fired one shot at me. When we told them to throw up their hands Claiborne threw up his left hand and broke and ran. I never saw him afterwards until late in the afternoon, after the fight. I never drew my pistol or made a motion to shoot until after Billy Clanton and Frank McLaury drew their pistols. If Tom McLaury was unarmed, I did not know it, I believe he was armed and fired two shots at our party before Holliday, who had the shotgun, fired and killed him. If he was unarmed, there was nothing in the circumstances or in what had been communicated to me, or in his acts

or threats, that would have led me even to suspect his being unarmed.
"I never fired at Ike Clanton, even after the shooting
commenced, because I thought he was unarmed. I believed then, and
believe now, from the acts I have stated and the threats I have related
and the other threats communicated to me by other persons as having
been made by Tom McLaury, Frank McLaury, and Ike Clanton, that
these men last named had formed a conspiracy to murder my
brothers, Morgan and Virgil, Doc Holliday and myself. I believe I
would have been legally and morally justified in shooting any of them
on sight, but I did not do so, nor attempt to do so. I sought no
advantage when I went as deputy marshal [city marshal] to help
disarm them and arrest them. I went as a part of my duty and under
the direction of my brother, the marshal, I did not intend to fight
unless it became necessary in self-defense and in the performance of
official duty. When Billy Clanton and Frank McLaury drew their
pistols, I knew it was a fight for life, and I drew in defense of my own
life and the lives of my brothers and Doc Holliday.

"I have been in Tombstone since December 1, 1879. I came
here directly from Dodge City, Kansas. Against the protest of
businessmen and officials, I resigned the office of City Marshal, which
I held from 1876.[1] I came to Dodge City from Wichita, Kansas. I
was on the police force in Wichita from 1874 until I went to Dodge
City.[2]

"The testimony of Isaac Clanton that I ever said to him that I
had anything to do with any stage robbery or giving information to
Morgan Earp going on the stage, or any improper communication
whatever with any criminal enterprise is a tissue of lies from
beginning to end.

"Sheriff Behan made me an offer in his office on Allen Street in
the back room of a cigar store, where he, Behan, had his office, that
if I would withdraw and not try to get appointed sheriff of Cochise
County, that he would hire a clerk and divide the profits. I done so,
and he never said another word about it afterwards, but claimed in
his statement and gave his reason for not complying with his contract,
which is false in every particular.

"Myself and Doc Holliday happened to go to Charleston the night
that Behan went down there to subpoena Ike Clanton. We went
there for the purpose to get a horse that I had stolen from me a few

---

[1]   Here he is stretching things a bit. He was never City
      Marshall, only a deputy Marshal and Assistant Marshal and he
      was not there continuously from 1876.

[2]   He was appointed to the Wichita police force on April 21,
      1875, Great Gunfighters of Kansas Cowtowns, p. 80.

days after I came to Tombstone. I had heard several times that the Clantons had him. When I got there that night, I was told by a friend of mine that the man that carried the dispatch from Charleston to Ike Clanton's ranch had rode my horse. At this time I did not know where Ike Clanton's ranch was.

"A short time afterwards I was in the Hauchucas locating some water rights. I had started home to Tombstone. I had got within 12 or 15 miles of Charleston when I met a man named McMasters. He told me if I would hurry up, I would find my horse in Charleston. I drove into Charleston and saw my horse going through the streets toward the corral. I put up for the night in another corral. I went to Burnett's office to get papers for the recovery of the horse. He was not at home having gone down to Sonora to some coal fields that had been discovered. I telegraphed to Tombstone to James Earp and told him to have papers made out and sent to me. He went to Judge Wallace and Mr. Street. They made the papers out and sent them to Charleston by my youngest brother, Warren Earp, that night. While I was waiting for the papers, Billy Clanton found out that I was in town and went and tried to take the horse out of the corral. I told him that he could not take him out, that it was my horse. After the papers came, he gave the horse up without the papers being served, and asked me if I had any more horses to lose. I told him I would keep them in the stable after this, and give him no chance to steal them.

"I give here, as part of the statement, document sent me from Dodge City since my arrest on this charge, which I wish attached to this statement and marked "Exhibit A."

"[Here counsel for the Prosecution objects to this paper being introduced or used for, or attached as an exhibit as a part of this statement, on the ground that the paper is not on its face, a statement of the defendant, but a statement of other persons made long after the alleged commission of this crime. Counsel for the Defense objects to any objections interpolated by counsel for the prosecution in a statutory statement made by the party charged with crime, for the reason that the law contemplates such statement shall not be interrupted by the court, the counsel for the prosecution, or the counsel for the defense, or for the further reason that it is perfect evidence of character lacking only the absurd formality. Objection of counsel for prosecution overruled and the paper ordered to be filed as part of this statement.]

"In relation to the conversation that I had with Ike Clanton, Frank McLaury, and Joe Hill was four or five different times, and they were all held in the backyard of the Oriental Saloon.

"I told Ike Clanton in one of those conversations that there were some parties here in town that were trying to give Doc Holliday the worst of it by their talk, that there was some suspicion that he knew something about the attempted robbery and killing of Bud Philpot, and if I could catch Leonard, Head, and Crane, I could prove to the citizens that he knew nothing of it.

"In following the trail of Leonard, Head, and Crane, we struck it at the scene of the attempted robbery, and never lost the trail or hardly a footprint from the time we started from Drew's ranch on the San Pedro, until we got to Helm's ranch in the Dragoons. After following about 80 miles down the San Pedro River and capturing one of the men named King that was supposed to be with them, we then crossed the Catalina Mountains within 15 miles of Tucson following their trail around the foot of the mountain to Tres Alamos on the San Pedro River, thence to the Dragoons to Helm's ranch.

"We then started out from Helm's ranch and got on their trail. They had stolen 15 or 20 head of stock, so as to cover their trail. Virgil Earp and Morgan Earp, Robert H. Paul, Breakenridge the deputy sheriff, Johnny Behan the sheriff and one or two others still followed their trail to New Mexico.

"Their trail never led south from Helm's ranch as Ike Clanton has stated. We used every effort we could to capture those men or robbers. I was out ten days. Virgil and Morgan Earp were out sixteen days, and [we] all done all we could to catch those men, and I safely say if it had not been for myself and Morgan Earp they would not have got King as he started to run when we rode up to his hiding place and was making for a big patch of brush on the river and would have got in it, if [it] had not been for us two.

"[signed] Wyatt S. Earp[1]

"DEFENSE EXHIBIT 'A'

"To All Whom It May Concern, Greetings:

"We, the undersigned citizens of Dodge City, Ford County, Kansas, and vicinity do by these presents certify that we are personally acquainted with Wyatt Earp, late of this city; that he came here in the

---

[1]   The O.K. Corral Inquest, p 155-168, reprint of Document 94, Records of the County Clerk, Cochise County. Although some of Wyatt Earp's statements appear to be in answer to unrecorded questions, apparently they were not. His testimony was published in the November 17th issue of the Daily Nugget. It does not show any questions and no material variation from the court record. The record does not show that he was subjected to cross examination, or that he was asked any questions by his own lawyer, although a careful examination of the record would lead one to conclude that at some point his testimony must have been in answer to questions propounded by someone. Unfortunately the questions, and the name of the questioner were not recorded.

year 1876; that during the years of 1877, 1878, and 1879, he was Marshal of our city; that he left our place in the fall of 1879; that during his whole stay here he occupied a place of high social position and was regarded and looked upon as a high-minded, honorable citizen; that as Marshal of our city he was ever vigilant in the discharge of his duties, and while kind and courteous to all, he was brave, unflinching, and on all occasions proved himself the right man in the right place.

"Hearing that he is now under arrest, charged with complicity in the killing of those men termed 'Cow Boys,' from our knowledge of him we do not believe that he would wantonly take the life of his fellow man, and that if he was implicated, he only took life in the discharge of his sacred trust to the people; and earnestly appeal to the citizens of Tombstone, Arizona, to use all means to secure him a fair and impartial trial, fully confident that when tried he will be fully vindicated and exonerated of any crime."

"R.M. Wright, Representative, Ford County
"Lloyd Shinn, Probate Judge, Ford County, Kansas
"M.W. Sutton, County Attorney, Ford County
"George F. Hinkle, Sheriff, Ford County, Kansas
"G.M. Homer, Chairman, County Board
"J.W. Liellow, Ford County Commissioner
"F.C. Zimmerman, Ford County,Treasurer
        and Tax Collector
"G.W. Potter Clerk of Ford County
"Thomas S. Jones, Police Judge and Attorney at Law
"A.B. Webster, Mayor, Dodge City, Kansas
"C.M. Beeson, City Council, Dodge City, Kansas
"Geo. Emerson, City Council, Dodge City, Kansas
"P.F. Sughrue, City Council, Dodge City, Kansas
"A.H. Boyd, City Council, Dodge City, Kansas
"J.H. Philips, Deputy County Treasurer, Ford County
"R.G. Cook, U.S. Commissioner
"Wright, Beverly & Co., Dodge City Merchants
"Herman F. Fringey, Postmaster, Dodge City, Kansas
"O.W. Wright, Pastor, Presbyterian Church
"Marsh and Son, Merchants
"H.P. Weiss, Shoemaker
"Fred T.M. Wenir, Notary Public and Insurance Agent
"R.C. Burns, Attorney
"H.M. Bell, Deputy United State Marshal
"T.L. McCarty, M.D.
"D.E. Frost, ex-Police Judge
"Beeson and Harris, Liquor Dealers
"W.F. Petillon, Register of Deeds, Ford County

"J. Ormond, Bookkeeper
"N.B. Klaine, Editor, [Dodge City] Times,
     City Treasurer, School Director,
     and Notary Public
"Walter Straeter, _____?
"J.H. Kelley, ex-Mayor, Dodge City
"Jim Anderson, Livery Man
"J. McGinnis, R.R.. Agent, & Agent,
     Wells Fargo & Co. Express
"D.C. Kane, Mgr. Western Union Tel. Co.
"P.G. Reynolds and Son, _____?
"Tom Bugg, Deputy Sheriff
"Coe and Boyd, Props., Dodge House
"Oscar Tsevalle, Boots and Shoes
"B.C. Vanderburg, City Marshal
"T. Coller, Merchant
"Ed. Cooley, Constable and Dep. Sheriff
"R.E. McAnulty, Cattle Dealer
"Bond and Nizon, Liquor Dealers
"John Mueleer, Cattle Dealer
"H.F. Wray, _____?
"Jon. T. Lytle, Cattle Dealer
"R.W. Evans
[And 13 others on paper]
"Notarized or acknowledged by; H.P. Myton, Clerk of the District
Court, Ford County, Kansas. [With Seal]
                    "DEFENSE EXHIBIT 'B'
"STATE OF KANSAS   }
                                    }   ss
"COUNTY OF SEDGEWICK   }
     "We, the undersigned citizens of Wichita in the County and State
aforesaid are well acquainted with Mr. Wyatt S. Earp and that we
were intimately acquainted with him while he was on the Police force
of this city, in the years A.D. 1874, 1875 and part of the year 1876.
We further certify that the said Wyatt S. Earp was a good and efficient
officer, and was well known for his honesty, and integrity, that his
character while here was of the best, and that no fault was ever found
with him as an officer, or as a man.
               "Geo. E. Harris, Mayor in 1875
               "M. Zimmerly, Councilman in 1875
               "C.M. Garrison, Councilman in 1875
               "R.C. Ogdell, ex-City Marshal
               "J.M. True, ex-City Treasurer
               "Fred Sclattner, City Clerk
               "James Cairns, City Marshal

"Sworn and subscribed to and before me this fourth day of November A.D. 1881."

"CHARLES HATTON, NOTARY PUBLIC

Next Mr. Hatton adds a statement of his own:

"I hereby certify that I knew personally Wyatt S. Earp during his residence in the city of Wichita. That I served four years as city attorney of said city and have known personally all of the officers of said city for the past ten years. I take great pleasure in saying that Wyatt S. Earp was one of the most efficient officers that Wichita ever had and I can safely testify that Mr. Earp is in every sense reliable and a trustworthy gentleman.

[signed] Chas. Hatton"[1]

---

[1]   No reference was made by Wyatt Earp in his testimony to Exhibit "B" but it was nevertheless made a part of the court record. The Exhibits were not published in the Nugget along with Wyatt Earps testimony on November 17th but were published in full the next day with a statement that they had not been available on the previous day.

CHAPTER XXXIX

VIRGIL EARP TESTIFIES

NEITHER Virgil nor Morgan Earp were arrested and brought before the court for the hearing, for the reason that both were at home suffering from rather severe wounds inflicted in the battle.

Virgil Earp, however, left his bed to come to the court hearings and testify. His testimony as recorded by the court reporter and reworked by Hayhurst is set forth in the O.K. Corral Inquest at page 190. My copies of the Daily Nugget do not include the testimony of Virgil Earp although I believe that they did report it in full.

The testimony of Virgil Earp was as follows:

"On this nineteenth day of November, 1881, on the hearing of the above entitled cause on the examination of Wyatt Earp and J.H. Holliday; Virgil W. Earp, a witness of lawful age, being produced and sworn, deposes and says as follows:

"My name is Virgil W. Earp, I reside in Tombstone, Cochise County, Arizona Territory. My occupation: Chief of Police of Tombstone and Deputy U.S. Marshal.

"(Q) State what official position, if any, you occupied on the 25th and 26th of October last.

"(A) Chief of Police of Tombstone and Deputy United States Marshal, and was acting as such on those days.

"(Q) State what official or other position, if any, with respect to the police department of Tombstone, was occupied on the 25th and 26th of October last by Morgan Earp.

"(A) He was sworn in as Special Policeman and wore a badge with 'Special Police' engraved on it, and he had been sworn and acted as a 'Special' for about a month.

"(Q) State what official or other position, if any, with respect to the police department of Tombstone, was occupied on the 25th and 26th of October last by Wyatt Earp.

"(A) Wyatt Earp had been sworn in to act in my place while I was in Tucson, and on my return his saloon [Oriental] was opened and I appointed him a 'Special,' to keep the peace, with power to make arrest, and also called on him on the 26th, to assist me in disarming those parties: Ike Clanton and Billy Clanton, Frank McLaury, and Tom McLaury.

"(Q) State what position or deputization, if any, with respect to assisting you as Chief of Police, was occupied on the 26th of October last, or anytime during that day by John H. Holliday.

last, or anytime during that day by John H. Holliday.

"(A) I called on him that day for assistance to help disarm the Clantons and McLaurys.

"(Q) State fully all the circumstances of and attendant upon the difficulty which resulted in the death of Frank McLaury, Thomas McLaury, and Billy Clanton, commencing on the day of the difficulty and confining your answers for the present entirely to what occurred within your sight and hearing on the day of the difficulty, on the 26th of October.

"(A) On the morning of the 26th, somewhere about six or seven o'clock, I started to go home, and Ike Clanton stopped me and wanted to know if I would carry a message from him to Doc Holliday. I asked him what it was. He said, 'The damned son of a bitch has got to fight.' I said, 'Ike, I am an officer and I don't want to hear you talking that way at all. I am going down home now, to go to bed, I don't want you to raise any disturbance while I am in bed.'

"I started to go home, and when I got ten feet from him he said, 'You won't carry the message?' I said, 'No, of course I won't.' I made four or five steps more. He said, 'You may have to fight before you know it.' [Here, counsel for the prosecution reserves the right to strike out at the close, any portion of the answer]. I made no reply to him and went home and went to bed. I don't know how long I had been in bed. It must have been between 9 and 10 o'clock when one of the policeman came and told me to get up, as there was liable to be hell.

"I did not get up right away, but in about half an hour I got up. I cannot tell exactly what time it was. Along about 11 or 12 o'clock I came up on the street and met a man by the name of Lynch. I found Ike Clanton on Fourth Street between Fremont and Allen with a Winchester rifle in his hand and a six-shooter stuck down in his breeches. I walked up and grabbed the rifle in my left hand. He let loose and started to draw his six-shooter. I hit him over the head with mine and knocked him to his knees and took his six-shooter from him. I asked him if he was hunting for me. He said he was, and if he had seen me a second sooner he would have killed me. I arrested Ike for carrying firearms, I believe was the charge, inside the city limits.

"When I took him to the courtroom, Judge Wallace was not there. I left him in charge of Special Officer Morgan Earp while I went out to look for the Judge. After the examination I asked him where he wanted his arms left, and he said, 'Anywhere I can get them, for you hit me over the head with your six-shooter.' I told him I would leave them at the Grand Hotel bar, and done so. I did not hear, at that time, any quarrel between Wyatt Earp and Ike Clanton. The next I saw them, they were, all four; Ike Clanton, Billy Clanton,

Frank McLaury, and Tom McLaury in the gun shop on Fourth Street. I saw Wyatt Earp shooing a horse off the sidewalk and went down and saw them all in the gun shop, filling up their belts with cartridges and looking at the pistols and guns.

"There was a committee waiting on me there and called me away to one side. I turned to Wyatt Earp and told him to keep peace and order until I came back and to move the crowd off the sidewalk and not let them obstruct it. When I saw them again, all four of them were going in Dunbar's Coral. They did not remain long there. They came out and went into the O.K. Corral.

"I called on Johnny Behan who refused to go with me, to go help disarm these parties. He said if he went along with me, there would be a fight sure; that they would not give up their arms to me. He said, 'They won't hurt me,' and, 'I will go down alone and see if I can disarm them.' I told him that was all I wanted them to do; to lay off their arms while they were in town. Shortly after he left I was notified that they were on Fremont Street, and I called on Wyatt and Morgan Earp, and Doc Holliday to go and help me disarm the Clantons and McLaurys. We started down Fourth Street to Fremont, turned down Fremont west, towards Fly's lodging house. When we got about somewhere by Baurer's butcher shop, I saw the parties before we got there, in a vacant lot between the photograph gallery and the house west of it. The parties were Ike and Billy Clanton, Tom and Frank McLaury, Johnny Behan, and the Kid.

"Johnny Behan seen myself and party coming down towards them. He left the Clanton and McLaury party and came on a fast walk towards us, and once in a while he would look behind at the party he left, as though expecting danger of some kind. He met us somewhere close to the butcher shop. He threw up both hands, like this [illustrating] and said, 'For God's sake, don't go there or they will murder you!'

"I said, 'Johnny, I am going down to disarm them.' By this time I had passed him a step and heard him say, 'I have disarmed them all.' When he said that, I had a walking stick in my left hand, and my right hand was on my six-shooter in my waist pants [verbatim], and when he said he had disarmed them, I shoved it clean around to my left hip and changed my walking stick to my right hand.

"As soon as Behan left them, they moved in between the two buildings, out of sight of me. We could not see them. All we could [see] was about half a horse. They were all standing in a row. Billy Clanton and Frank McLaury had their hands on their six-shooters. I don't hardly know how Ike Clanton was standing, but I think he had his hands in an attitude where I supposed he had a gun. Tom McLaury had his hand on a Winchester rifle on a horse.

"As soon as I saw them, I said, 'Boys, throw up your hands, I want your guns,' or 'arms.' With that, Frank McLaury and Billy Clanton drew their six-shooters and commenced to cock them, and [I] heard them go "click-click." Ike Clanton threw his hand in his breast, this way [illustrates]. At that, I said, throwing both hands up, with the cane in my right hand, 'Hold on, I don't want that!' As I said that, Billy Clanton threw his six-shooter down, full cocked. I was standing to the left of my party, and he was standing on the right of Frank and Tom McLaury. He was not aiming at me, but his pistol was kind of past me. Two shots went off right together. Billy Clanton's was one of them. At that time I changed my cane to my left hand, and went to shooting; it was general then, and everybody went to fighting.

"At the crack of the first two pistols, the horse jumped to one side, and Tom McLaury failed to get the Winchester. He threw his hand back this way [shows the motion]. He followed the movement of the horse around, making him a kind of breastwork, and fired once, if not twice, over the horse's back."

"[COURT ADJOURNED TO MEET TUESDAY, NOVEMBER 22, 1881]

"[TUESDAY, NOVEMBER 22, 1881, EXAMINATION RESUMED]

"(Q) When you met Lynch on the morning, or noon, of October 26th, what did he tell you?

"(A) He told me to look out for Ike Clanton, that he was hunting me, and vowed to kill me on sight.

"(Q) State what threats, if any, were made by Isaac Clanton, William Clanton, Thomas McLaury, or Frank McLaury, to you, or in your presence, and what threats if any, by either of the aforementioned persons were communicated to you as having been made in the presence of others, giving the name of the persons making the communications to you, in detail.

"(A) The first man who spoke to me about any threats was Officer Bronk. I was down home in bed when he called. He came down after [a] commitment I had for a party that was in jail. It was about 9 o'clock I should think, on the 26th of October. While he was getting the commitment, he said, 'You had better get up. There is liable to be hell!' He said, 'Ike Clanton has threatened to kill Holliday as soon as he gets up.' And he said, 'He's counting you fellows in too,' meaning me and my brothers. I told him I would get up after a while, and he went off.

"The next man was Lynch; I've stated what he said. The next I met, was Morgan and James Earp. One of them asked me if I had seen Ike Clanton. I told them I had not. One of them said, 'He has got a Winchester rifle and six-shooter on, and threatens to kill us on sight.' I asked Morgan if he had any idea where we could find him. He said he did not. I told him then to come and go with me, and we could go and arrest him, and disarm him.

"Several men came on Allen Street between Fourth and Fifth; miners whose names I do not know. This was after Ike Clanton's arrest and before the fight. There was one man in particular who came and said, 'Ain't you liable to have trouble?' I told him I didn't know, it looks kind of that way, but couldn't tell. He said, 'I seen two more of them just rode in,' and he said, 'Ike walked up to them and was telling them about you hitting him over the head with a six-shooter.' He said that one of them rode in on a horse [and] said, 'Now is our time to make a fight.'

"This was after the arms of Ike Clanton were returned to the Grand Hotel.

"Just about the time the man was telling me this, Bob Hatch came and beckoned to me, as though he wanted to speak to me, and said, 'For God's sake, hurry down there to the gun shop, for they are all down there, and Wyatt is alone!' He said, 'They are liable to kill him before you get there!' The other man told me to be careful, and not turn my back on them or I would be killed, that they meant mischief. Lynch remarked--[paragraph not completed.]

"There was a man named W.B. Murray and a man named J.L. Fonck came at separate times and said, 'I know you are going to have trouble, and we have got plenty of men and arms to assist you.' Murray was the first man to approach me, on the afternoon of the 26th. I was talking to Behan at the time in Hafford's Saloon, trying to get him to go down and help me disarm them. Murray took me to one side and said, 'I have been looking into this matter and know you are going to have trouble. I can get 25 armed men at a minutes notice.' He said, 'If you want them, say so.' I told him, as long as they stayed in the corral, the O.K. Corral, I would not go down to disarm them; if they came out on the street, I would take their arms off and arrest them. He said, 'You can count on me if there is any danger.'

"I walked from the corner of Fourth and Allen Streets, west, just across the street. J.L. Fonck met me there, and he said, 'The cowboys are making threats against you.' And he said, 'If you want any help, I can furnish ten men to assist.' I told him I would not bother them as long as they were in the corral; if they showed up on the street, I would disarm them. 'Why,' he said, 'they are all down on Fremont street there now.' Then I called on Wyatt and Morgan Earp, and Doc Holliday to go with me and help disarm them.

"Frank McLaury made a threat to me one day on the street. It must have been about a month before the shooting and it might have been a week after the notice in the paper of the formation of a vigilance committee. Frank McLaury stepped up to me in the street between the Express Office and the Grand Hotel. He said, 'I understand you are raising a vigilance committee to hang us boys.'

I said, 'You boys?' He said, 'Yes, us and [the] Clantons, Hicks, Ringo, and all us cowboys.' I said to him, 'Frank, do [you] remember the time Curly Bill killed White?' He said, 'Yes.' I said, 'Who guarded him that night and run him to Tucson next morning to keep the vigilance committee from hanging him?' He said, 'You boys, now do you believe we belong to it? I can't help but believe the man who told me you do.' I said, 'Who told you?' He said, 'Johnny Behan.' 'Now,' he says, 'I'll tell you, it makes no difference what I do, I never will surrender my arms to you.' He said, 'I'd rather die fighting than be strangled.' I made some remark to him, 'Alright,' or something - and then left him.

"[Counsel for the Prosecution moves to strike out all the proceeding conversation with Frank McLaury on the ground that it is irrelevant and contains no threats against this defendant. Objection taken under advisement.]

"(Q)   State any conversation had by you, if any, with Isaac Clanton or Frank McLaury in this town with respect to obtaining information from them, or either of them, that should lead to the capture or killing of the parties suspected to have been engaged in the killing of Bud Philpot and the attempt to rob the Benson Stage.

"[Objected to by Prosecution on the ground that the question is too broad and enquiries into conversations with Frank McLaury which are more hearsay and irrelevant and for which no foundation had been laid. Objection sustained as to Frank McLaury, but overruled as to Ike Clanton and admitted to contradict his statement.]

"(A)   About last June, in Tombstone, Ike Clanton asked me where we could go to have a long talk, where nobody could hear us excepting those who were along at the time. We turned around the corner of Allen and Fifth Streets, alongside of Danner and Owen's Saloon. He said, 'I've had a long talk with Wyatt in regard to Leonard, Head, and Crane,' and he said, 'I believe I can trust you.' He said, 'I am going to put up a job for you boys to catch them.'

"I said, 'How can I know you are in earnest and can trust you?' 'Well,' he said, 'now I'll tell you all about it.' He said that Leonard had a fine ranch over in the Cloverdale County [New Mexico]. He said, 'As soon as I heard of him robbing the stage, I rounded up my cattle on the San Pedro here, and run them over and jumped his ranch.' And he said, 'Shortly after you boys gave up the chase who should come riding up but Leonard, Head, and Crane.' And he said, 'By God, they have been stopping around there ever since, and it looks as though they are going to stay.' He said, 'They have already told me that I would either have to buy the ranch or get off of it. I told them that I supposed after what they had done, they would not dare to stay in the country and I suppose you would rather your friends would get your ranch than anybody else.' He said, 'But if they were going to stay in the country he would either get off or buy the ranch. Now you can see why I want these men either captured or killed, and I would rather have them killed.' I said, 'There are three of you and there is only three of them. Why don't you capture or kill them, and I would see that you get the reward?' He says, 'Jesus Christ? I would not last longer than a snowball in hell if I should do that!' He says, 'The rest of the gang would think we killed them for the reward and they would kill us. But,' he says, 'we have agreed with Wyatt to bring them to a certain spot, where you boys can capture them.' And he said, 'As soon as Wyatt gets a telegram he is going to send for, in regard to the reward dead or alive, and they will give it, dead or alive, we'll start right after them, to bring them over.' I said, 'Where will you bring them to?' He said, 'Either to McLaury's ranch or Willow Springs.'

"'Now,' he said, 'I want you never to give us away or say a word about it, except [to] the party you take along.' There were some few more remarks made - I don't remember what they were - and we broke up for that time. This is about 3 o'clock in the morning after [the] conversation Ike Clanton had with Wyatt Earp. I had another conversation with him when he said Wyatt showed him the dispatch saying that the Wells, Fargo would pay the reward dead or alive.

"(Q) In reference to the statement made by Isaac Clanton in his testimony, I ask you: Did you ever, at an time, tell Isaac Clanton to tell Billy Leonard not to think that you were trying to catch him when you were running him, or to tell Billy Leonard that you had thrown Paul and the posse off Leonard's track when he left Helm's ranch at the foot of the Dragoon Mountains, or to tell Billy Leonard that you [had] taken the posse in pursuit of him on to a trail in New Mexico, or to tell Billy Leonard you had done all you could for him, or to tell Billy Leonard that you wanted him to get Crane and Head and get them out of the country, because you were afraid one of them might get captured and get all his friends into trouble?

"(A) I never did.

"(Q) State now, Mr. Earp, any threats communicated to you that you have omitted to state heretofore.

"(A) There was a man met me on the corner of Fourth and Allen Streets about 2 o'clock in the afternoon of the day of the shooting. He said, 'I just passed the O.K. Corral,' and he said, he saw four or five men all armed and heard one of them say, 'Be sure to get Earp, the Marshal.' Another replied and said, 'We will kill them all!' When he met me on the corner he said, 'Is you name Earp?' and I told him it was. He said, 'Are you the Marshal?' and I told him I was. I did not know the man. I have ascertained who he was since. His name is Sills, I believe.

"CROSS-EXAMINATION

"(Q) Where does Sills live, and what is his business?

"(A) I never met him until that day. I do not know what his business is, I don't know where he resides.

"(Q) At what house in Tombstone does he live?

"(A) I don't know, only by say-so.

"(Q) Can you give us any information as to where he lives?

"(A) I understand he is stopping at the hospital.

"(Q) When did you last see him?

"(A) Yesterday. I saw him here.

"(Q) Who, if anybody, was present when he made that communication to you, on the corner of Fourth and Allen Streets?

"(A) I don't think anybody was close enough to hear the conversation.

"(Q) How long did that conversation take place, before you started for Fremont street?

"(A) Somewhere in the neighborhood of a quarter or half an hour -- not over half an hour; it might not have been that long.

"(Q) Was it before or after Behan left Hafford's Saloon?

"(A) To the best of my recollection, it was just after.

"(Q) At the time you took Isaac Clanton's rifle and pistol from him, did you approach in front or behind him?

"(A) Behind him.

"(Q) Did you speak to him before you seized his rifle?

"(A) I think not.

"(Q) With which hand did you take his rifle?

"(A) With my left hand.

"(Q) Where was your pistol when you seized his rifle?

"(A) In my right hand.

"(Q) Was he facing you, or was his back towards you when you struck him?

"(A) He was turned about halfway around. I don't know whether his body was turned; his head was.

"(Q) Which of the Clantons or McLaurys did you see putting cartridges in their belts at the gun shop on the occasion you have spoken of in your direct examination?

"(A) William Clanton, Frank McLaury was standing right beside him. I don't think I saw any of the others putting cartridges in their belt. It looked like Frank McLaury was helping Billy Clanton.

"(Q) Where was Tom McLaury at the time, and what was he doing?

"(A) I can't say. They were all in a bunch, and I could not see what each was doing.

"(Q) Were Isaac Clanton and Frank McLaury in the gun shop at that time?

"(A) I am positive that Billy Clanton, Ike Clanton and Frank McLaury were in there, and am under the impression that Tom was there.

"(Q) Where was Wyatt Earp at the time?

"(A) He was standing on the edge of the sidewalk when I first discovered him in front of the gun shop.

"(Q) Was that during the time that Billy Clanton and the other persons you have named were in the gun shop?

"(A) It was. I first saw Wyatt Earp as I turned the corner of Allen and Fourth Streets, in front of the gun shop, on the edge of the sidewalk. I noticed him step into the crowd and take hold of a horse and "shoo" him off the sidewalk.

"(Q) What crowd do you allude [to]?

"(A) There was a dozen or more on the sidewalk, gathered in a knot. I can't call to mind who they were.

"(Q) Where were Morgan Earp and Holliday at this time?

"(A) I don't remember seeing him at that time. I saw them on the corner of Allen and Fourth Streets about five or ten minutes before that. I can't say whether Holliday was armed at that time. Morgan Earp was.

"(Q) At the time spoken of, when you were in Hafford's Saloon, did you have a shotgun or rifle?

"(A) I had a shotgun and six-shooter.

"(Q) When and where did you get that shotgun?

"(A) [Verbatim as in original document] Got it in the Express Office of Wells Fargo, on Allen Street, at the time they were down at the gun shop. It had been at my service for six months. No one handed it to me at the time. I got it myself.

"(Q) What did you do with it?

"(A) When I called Morgan Earp, Wyatt Earp, and Doc Holliday to go and help me disarm the McLaurys and Clantons, Holliday had a large overcoat on, and I told him to let me have his cane, and he take the shotgun, that I did not want to create any excitement going down the street with a shotgun in my hand. When we made the exchange, I said, 'Come along,' and we all went along.

"(Q) You speak of a committee that called on you when you were in front of the gun shop. Who composed that committee?

"(A) I don't know their names. They were miners, I should judge.

"(Q) At the time when Behan met you on Fremont Street and said, 'For God's sake, don't go down there or they will murder you!' where were Wyatt and Morgan Earp?

"(A) They were right behind me.

"(Q) Where was Holliday?

"(A) We were all in a bunch. I think he was also right behind me.

"(Q) You say at the commencement of the affray, two shots went off close together, and that Billy Clanton's was one of them. Who fired the other shot?

"(A) Well, I'm inclined to think it was Wyatt Earp that fired it.

"(Q) How many shots did you fire, and at whom?

"(A) I fired four shots. Once at Frank McLaury, and I believe the other three were at Billy Clanton. I am pretty positive one was at Frank McLaury and three at Billy Clanton.

"(Q) What is Lynch's first name, and place of residence?

"(A) I don't know his first name. After the fight he was put on the police force.

[signed] Virgil W. Earp"[1]

---

[1]   The O.K. Corral Inquest, P 190-201, reprint of Document 94, Records of the County Clerk, Cochise County and Arizona State Archives.

CHAPTER XL

MOST DISPUTED ISSUES

TWO of the most disputed issues during the course of the hearing were: Was Billy Clanton shot while he had his hand up and was Tom McLaury armed?

The evidence produced at the hearing on those two points is set out and discussed here.

William Claiborne, a friend of the Clantons - testified on the 8th day of November concerning both the fact that the Clanton party had their hands in the air when the fighting started and that Tom McLaury was not armed when the shooting commenced. That portion of his testimony was as follows:

"Something was said by Behan. I think it was, 'Hold on boys, don't go down there!' The Earps made no reply that I heard. They brushed right on by and did not stop. They came within 10 feet of where we were standing (note that Claiborne was standing with the Clantons and McLaurys). When they got to the corner of Fly's building, they had their six-shooters in their hands and Marshal Earp said, 'You sons-of-bitches, you've been looking for a fight, and you can have it!' and then said 'throw up your hands.'

"Billy Clanton threw up his hands; Ike Clanton threw up his, and Tom McLaury threw open his coat and said, 'I haven't got anything, boys, I am disarmed.' [Showing action of Tom McLaury and throwing open his coat][1] Then the shooting commenced right then, in an instant, by Doc Holliday and Morgan Earp - the two shots were fired so close together it was hard to distinguish them. I could not, I saw them shoot. Doc Holliday shot at Tom McLaury and Morgan Earp shot at Billy Clanton when Doc Holliday fired that shot, Tom McLaury staggered backwards and Billy Clanton fell up against the corner of the window and laid himself down on the ground. Frank McLaury had hold of a horse, about the corner of a post. Ike Clanton was dodging when I saw him and trying to get away."[2]

---

[1]   Turner says that Tom McLaury was not wearing a coat. He doesn't give the source of his information. The O.K. Corral Inquest, Note 3, p 202.

[2]   The O.K. Corral Inquest, p. 76-77, reprint of Document 94, Records of the County Clerk, Cochise County.

He was asked, "Did you or not, at any time during the shooting, see Tom McLaury with any weapon in his hands, and if so, what kind of arms or weapons?" and he answered, "I did not see any at all."[1]

On the question of whether or not the Clantons had their hand in the air at the time the fight started, Ike Clanton's testimony was quite positive. He was asked:

"(Q) In what position were Billy Clanton's hands at the time Morgan Earp fired at him, and you saw him stagger and fall up against the house?

"(A) His hands were thrown up about even with the level of his head -- his hands in front of him."[2]

Thomas Keefe testified on the tenth day of November, 1881 he was at the scene of the killing after the killing was done and tells of unbuttoning Tom's clothing,

"And as soon as Dr. Matthews came, we searched the body and did not find any arms on him. We examined him close enough to see if there were any arms on him, and there were none on him; we only found money on him."[3]

Al Turner says that, "Thomas McLaury was a frontier banker, often making loans to cowboys, ranchers, and other frontier persons. He had recently sold a herd of cattle and had $2,923.45 on his person when he was killed."[4]

Thomas Keefe who was sworn and began testifying on November 10th continued his testimony on November 12th. With regard to fire arms and the question of whether or not Tom McLaury had his hands in the air when he was shot, his testimony was as follows:

"(Q) You say at the time you ran up Third Street to where Tom McLaury was lying that there were three or four men around him; state if you can, when they came there?

"(A) We all got there together; some of them were three or four steps ahead of me; I first raised his head up.

"(Q) I asked you at the time you got to where Tom McLaury was laying whether there was any weapons, or if you saw any on the ground, or on him, or on his person, or any belt on his person?

"(A) There was no belt or firearms or ammunition around him

Ibid, p 78.

[2]   The O.K. Corral Inquest, p 52, reprint of Document 94, Records of the County Clerk, Cochise County and Arizona State Archives.

[3]   Ibid, p. 128.

[4]   Ibid, Note 2, p. 133.

or on his person.

"(Q) When you took him into the house who was there?

"(A) Wes Fuller, Mr. Noble, Cantwell, Clerk of the Board of Supervisors, and a gentleman who used to stop at Vogan's, don't know his name, think he stops there yet.

"(Q) Did you examine Billy Clanton?

"(A) Yes sir.

"(Q) State where and how he was wounded.

"(A) Shot through the arm, and right wrist; he was shot on the right side of the belly, he was shot below the left nipple, and the lung was oozing out of the wound; he was shot through the pants of the right leg.

"(Q) How do you know he was shot through the right wrist?

"(A) Because I examined it closely, and put my finger in the wound to the bone.

"(Q) Did the ball go through the arm?

"(A) Right through, the wound passed about 2 inches from the knuckle, through the wrist, I mean the knuckle-joint of the wrist."

"About the wound on cross-examination he said:

"(Q) Do I understand you that the wound on Billy Clanton's wrist was from the inside to the outside? I mean that the ball entered on the inside and emerged on the outside?

"(A) I mean that the ball went from the inside to the outside.

"(Q) How much farther up the arm towards the elbow was the outside wound than the inside wound?

"(A) About equal, in a diagonal way across the wrist.

"[Here witness illustrates upon the arm of Mr. Fitch, the manner in which the ball passed through the wrist of William Clanton by showing that the ball entered the wrist nearly in line with the base of the thumb and emerged on the back of the wrist, nearly in line with the base of the third finger, passing through the wrist diagonally.]

"(Q) Which was the largest orifice, the one on the inside or the one on the outside of the wrist?

"(A) The one on the outside."[1]

More evidence on the question of whether or not Billy Clanton had his hands up when the shooting began was supplied by Robert S. Hatch. He testified on November 17th.

"As I turned to go I saw Billy Clanton standing near the corner of the building below Fly's house, with a pistol in his hand, in the act of shooting; probably there had been three or four shots fired at that

---

[1]   Daily Nugget (November 12, 1881).

time . . ."[1]

One of the most interesting, and certainly a controversial witness was one Addie Bourland. On the twenty-eight day of November, she testified at the hearing, and since the Judge apparently relied quite heavily on her testimony, with respect to whether or not the parties had their hands in the air at the time the shooting commenced, I feel her testimony should be set forth here in full. It was as follows:

"ADDIE BOURLAND

"(Q) [No written question.]

"(A) I live on the opposite side of Fremont Street from the entrance to Fly's lodging house.

"(Q) Questioned on the difficulty.

"(A) I saw first five men opposite my house, leaning against a small house [the Harwood house] west of Fly's Gallery and one man was holding a horse [Frank McLaury], standing a little out from the house. I supposed them to be cowboys, and saw four men [the Earps and Doc Holliday] coming down the street towards them, and a man with a long coat on [Doc Holliday] walked up to the man holding the horse and put a pistol to his stomach and then he, the man with the long coat on, stepped back two or three feet, and then the firing seemed to be general. That is all I saw.

"(Q) Where were you at the time you saw this?

"(A) I was in my house at the window.

"(Q) How long after the two parties met, did the firing commence?

"(A) It was very shortly, only a few seconds.

"(Q) Which party fired first?

"(A) I don't know.

"(Q) Were you looking at both parties when the firing commenced?

"(A) I was looking at them, but not at anyone in particular. I did not know there was going to be a difficulty.

"(Q) Did you know, or do you know now, the man with the long coat on?

"(A) I did not know him then. I recognize Doctor Holliday, the man sitting there writing, as the man to the best of my judgement.

"(Q) Did you notice the character of weapon Doc Holliday had in his hand?

"(A) It was a very large pistol.

"(Q) Did you notice the color of the pistol?

---

[1]   The O.K. Corral Inquest, p. 176, reprint of Document 94, Records of the County Clerk, Cochise County and Arizona State Archives.

"(A) It was dark bronze.

"(Q) Was it or was it not, a nickle-plated pistol?

"(A) It was not a nickel-plated pistol.[1]

"(Q) Did you see at the time of the approach of the party descending Fremont Street, any of the party you thought were cowboys, throw up their hands?

"(A) I did not.

"(Q) Did you hear any conversation or exclamation between the two parties after they met, and before the firing commenced?

"(A) I did not, for my door was closed.

"(Q) How long did you continue to look at the parties after they met?

"(A) Until they commenced to fire, and I got up then and went into my back room.

"(Q) What did these men that you speak of as cowboys first do when the other party approached them?

"(A) They came out to meet them from the side of the house, and this man with the long coat on stepped up and put his pistol to the stomach of the man who was holding the horse, and stepped back two or three feet and the firing seemed to be general.

"(Q) About how many shots were fired before you left the window?

"(A) I could not tell; all was confusion, and I could not tell.

"(Q) Were all the parties shooting at each other at the time you were looking at them?

"(A) It looked to me like it.

"(Q) Had any of the parties fallen at the time you left the window?

"(A) I saw no parties fall.

[signed] Addie Bourland"[2]

"ADDIE BOURLAND IS RECALLED BY THE COURT

"[Inserted loose part of page reads: "The prosecution objects to the further examination of the witness Addie Bourland after she has been examined by the defense, and cross-examined by the prosecution, her testimony read to her and signed by her and not brought before the court as the solicitation of counsel on either side. The court voluntarily states that after recess, and the witness had

---

[1] All other witness seem to agree that Doc Holliday's pistol was nickel-plated. Most of them agree that his first shot was fired by a shot gun.

[2] The O.K. Corral Inquest, p 207, reprint of Document 94, Records of the County Clerk, Cochise County and Arizona State Archives.

retired, he went to see the witness at her house and talked with her about what she might further know about the case, and that he, of his own motion, says that he believed she knew more than she had testified to on her examination, now introduces her upon the stand for the purpose of further examination without the solicitation of either the prosecution or defense.]

"[Objection overruled, and questions asked of witness by the court as follows:]

"(Q) You say in your examination in chief, that you were looking at parties engaged in [the] fatal affray in Tombstone on the 26th of October last, at the time the firing commenced. Please state the position in which the party called the cowboys held their hands at the time the firing commenced; that is, were they holding up their hands, or were they firing back at the other party. State the facts as particularly as may be. [Counsel for the prosecution objects to court questioning witness after he admits he had talked with the witness, etc., crossed out.]

"(A) I didn't see anyone holding up their hands; they all seemed to be firing in general, on both sides. They were firing on both sides, at each other; I mean by this at the time the firing commenced.

"RE-CROSS EXAMINATION

"(Q) Did you say this morning, that you did not see who fired the first shot?

"(A) I did say so.

"(Q) Did you say this morning, there were two shots fired close together?

"(A) I did not.

"(Q) Did you say there were any shots fired at all?

"(A) I did.

"(Q) Did you say this morning, that when the first two or four shots were fired, you were excited and confused, and got up from the window and went into the back room?

"(A) I didn't say how many shots were fired, for I didn't know when I went into the other room.

"(A) What conversation did you have with Judge Spicer, if any with reference to your testimony to be given here since you signed your testimony this morning?

"(A) He asked me one or two questions in regard to seeing the difficulty, and if I saw any men throw up their hands, whether I would have seen it, and I told him I thought I would have seen it.

"(Q) Did you not testify this morning that those men did not throw up their hands, that you saw?

"(A) Yes sir, I did.

[signed] Addie Bourland"[1]
It's rather puzzling to understand why the judge recalled her because at her first testimony the question, "Did you see at the time of the approach of the party descending Fremont Street, any of the party you thought were cowboys, throw up their hands?" She answered, "I did not."

It seems that the judge was not satisfied that her testimony indicated that she actually was in a position to see what transpired, but at any rate after being recalled she restated her testimony by saying, "I didn't see anyone holding up their hands; they all seemed to be firing in general on both sides. They were firing on both sides at each other; I mean by this at the time the firing commenced."[2]

On the question of whether or not Tom McLaury was armed, Virgil Earp shed some light. In his testimony he said:

"We were all standing in a row, Billy Clanton and Frank McLaury had their hands on their six-shooters. I don't hardly know how Ike Clanton was standing, but I think he had his hands in an attitude where I supposed he had a gun. Tom McLaury had his hand on a Winchester Rifle on a horse . . ."

"At the crack of the first two pistols, the horse jumped to one side, and Tom McLaury failed to get the Winchester. He threw his hand back this way [showing the motion]. He followed the movement of the horse around, making him a kind of breastwork and fired once, if not twice, over the horse's back."[3]

Although he was not called as a witness in the Spicer hearing, H. Fellehy testified at the coroner's inquest and supplied some evidence that was overlooked by the Earp defense team and has evidently been overlooked ever since by all the researchers on the subject. In his testimony before the coroner's inquest he said:

"After the shooting commenced, I see Doc Holliday in the middle of the street, and the youngest one of the Earp brothers [that would be Morgan Earp], I judge three feet from the sidewalk. The younger one of the Earps was firing at a man behind the horse. Holliday was also firing at the same man behind the horse, and firing at a man who had run by him to the opposite side of the street. [By all accounts the man running would have been Frank McLaury.] Then I see the man who had the horse [that would have been Tom McLaury] let go of the reigns of the bridle and kept staggering all the time until he fell on

---

1   The O.K. Corral Inquest, p 207-209, reprint of the records of the County Clerk, Cochise County and Arizona State Archives.

2   The O.K. Corral Inquest, p 210.

3   Ibid, p. 193.

his back near a horse. He still held his pistol in his hand, but did not see it go off after he had fell."[1]

Another witness who testified at the coroners inquest but did not testify at the hearing was R.F. Coleman. Perhaps, that was because his testimony was not clear, but that could have been cleared up with a few well directed questions. About Tom McLaury he said. "Tom McLaury, after the first two shots were fired, ran down Fremont Street and fell.[2] Compare that with his reported statement to the Tombstone Epitaph, "I heard Virgil Earp say give up your arms or throw up your arms". There was some reply make by Frank McLowry, when the firing became general, over thirty shots were fired, Tom McLaury fell first, but raised and fired again before he died."[3]

Another witness who thought that Tom McLaury was armed at the time of the fight was Albert Bilicke. Turner says that Albert Bilicke was a prominent Tombstone business man and was a good friend of the Earps and other old time residents. Interestingly, after he left Tombstone he went to Los Angeles, California where he operated hotels and built the Alexandria Hotel, one of Los Angeles' finest for many years. It's in that hotel that Wyatt Earp was arrested in 1911 in the company with Death Valley Scottie and was charged with an illegal gambling scam that will be detailed in a later chapter.

The record of the hearing shows that Bilicke's testimony was as follows:

"Albert Billickie [sic.], Cosmopolitan Hotel, 409 Allen Street, Tombstone, Arizona, hotel keeper.

"In response to questions:

"[I] knew Tom McLaury by sight, and saw him on October 26th last, "walking down the south side of Allen Street and enter Everhardy's butcher shop, and very shortly come out again, walk down the street a few steps further, cross Allen Street obliquely to the corner of Fourth Street. This was probably about 2 o'clock."

"(Q) State if you observed what change if any occurred between the time of his going into the butcher shop and the time of his coming out, with respect to his possession of any arms.

"(A) I saw no arms on him, neither when he went into the butcher shop nor when he came out.

"(Q) What was his appearance when he went in, and what was

---

[1]   Ibid, p. 38.

[2]   Ibid, p 30. reprint of Document 94, Records of the County Clerk, Cochise County and Arizona State Archives.

[3]   Tombstone's Epitaph, p 180.

his appearance when he came out; with respect to the possession of concealed arms?

"(A) When he went into the butcher shop his right-hand pants pocket was flat and appeared as if nothing was in it. When he came out, his pants pocket protruded, as if there was a revolver therein.

"CROSS-EXAMINATION

"(Q) You say in your examination in chief, that you only knew Tom McLaury by sight and had no personal acquaintance with him,. How did it happen that you watched him so closely the different places he went and the exact position of his right-hand pants pocket when he went into the butcher shop and the exact form of a revolver in the same right-hand pocket when he came out?

"(A) Every good citizen in this city was watching all those cowboys very closely on the day the affray occurred, and as he was walking down the street my attention was called to this McLaury by a friend and so it happened that I watched him very closely.

"(Q) Do you know every good citizen in Tombstone, or did you on that day?

"(A) I know not all of them, but a great many.

"(Q) Do you know what the opinions of all good citizens of Tombstone were on that day by conversation or conversations with them about watching Thomas McLaury in this city, and if so, tell us who they were. [Question crossed, without comment.]

"(Q) About how long did he stay in the butcher shop, and was he in your sight while in there?

"(A) He was in the butcher shop but a few moments and was out of my sight from the time he entered until he again appeared. He then walked a few feet down Allen Street and crossed to the corner of Fourth and Allen and walked down Fourth Street. I did not see him alive anymore that day. Everhardy's butcher shop is directly opposite the Cosmopolitan Hotel, and I was standing on the sidewalk in front of the hotel when I saw what I have related.

[signed] Albert Billickie"[sic.][1]

J.B.W. Gardiner testified as a witness and to some degree collaborated the testimony of Albert Bilicke. He said that:

"He, [Tom McLaury] entered the butcher shop and on coming out I observed to one Albert Billickie [sic.] that I saw no pistol but supposed at the time on seeing the right hand pocket of his pants

---

[1]   The O.K. Corral Inquest, p 211, reprint of Document 94, Records of the County Clerk, Cochise County and Arizona State Archives.

extending outwards, that he had gotten a pistol."[1]

There was one other person who could have shed some light on the event, but she never testified at the hearing. She was the wife of one Ed Colyer, and they spent some time in Tombstone in the fall of 1881. They happened to be there on October 26, and she witnessed the fight. She was interviewed by a reporter for the Kansas City Star, and the interview was published. Later, on December 30, 1881, the story was re-published by the Tombstone Epitaph.

The only copy of the story I was able to get was a very poor reproduction. It was almost illegible, but I reprint here my best interpretation of her statement. The following article, apparently copied from the Kansas City Star was printed in the Tombstone Epitaph on December 30, 1881.

"BLOODY DEEDS

A GRAPHIC PICTURE OF LIFE IN TOMBSTONE, ARIZONA

(The first four lines I can't read, but they appear to indicate that Mrs. Colyer was interviewed by the press as she passed through Kansas City.)

From the Kansas City Star.

"Mr. Ed Colyer and his wife, accompanied by their two children arrived here this morning over the Santa Fe road in route from Tombstone, Arizona to their former home near Indianapolis. They passed through here last August, westward bound and since that time have seen ten men die with their boots on. Mrs. Colyer stated:

"I was a witness to one of the bloodiest fights that has taken place in Tombstone for some time. It was October 26. We were visiting at my brother in law's at Iketon Mill. My sister and I drove into the town with their children. All the way in the children kept talking about the Cow Boys and asking what we'd do if we saw any of them. As we drove around the corner near the Post Office,[2] we saw five cow boys standing in the middle of the road. We stopped at the post office and my sister went in while I sat in the wagon with the children. We were not fifty yards from the cow boys. Presently the Chief of Police, Virgil Earp, came around the corner accompanied by his brothers, Wyatt and Morgan Earp and another man. They were all armed TO THE TEETH. The Sheriff met them and said: 'For god sakes boys don't go down there or there'l [sic.] be war. ' The Chief of Police told him he must go, that it was his duty to disarm the cow boys who had been making threats against the officers. They approached the cow

---

[1]   Ibid, p. 213, reprint of Document 94, Records of the County Clerk, Cochise County and Arizona State Archives.

[2]   The post office at that time was located on the southeast corner of Fourth and Fremont.

boys and told them to hold up their hands. The cow boys opened fire on them and you never saw such shooting as followed. Three seriously injured. One of the cow boys after he had been shot three times raised himself on his elbow and shot one of the officers, and fell back dead. <u>Another used his horse as barricade and shot under this neck.</u> (Ed. Note: This would have been Tom McLaury.) You see their chief had been disarmed that morning by the police and handled pretty roughly and they were bent on revenge. The cow boys swore out warrants for the officers and they had a trial on THE CHARGE OF MURDER which lasted three weeks. They were acquitted. The cow boys are bitter against the Earps and will make trouble yet. The Earps own the Oriental Saloon and gambling room in which every night from --- to --- people congregate. The night before we left the cow boys had organized a raid on this saloon. Fifteen or twenty cow boys, heavily armed were in the saloon. Just on the edge of town were about thirty more and others were scattered around town ready to jump into the fight at the signal. A fire broke out and so. . .them that gave up for that time. You see we became intimately acquainted with a gentleman who boarded at the same hotel that we did and who is in sympathy with the cow boys and is acquainted with all their plans. He told us about this and being in contemplation and said that this was the second time they had been all prepared to make a. . ."

(Unreadable from there on. There are only three or four more lines on this column and no indication as to where it is continued. It seems to end in the middle of a sentence. It isn't continued elsewhere on the same page.)[1]

The prosecution produced a witness to counteract the testimony of Albert Bilicke and Dr. Gardiner. The witness was Earnest Storm who testified on the twenty-ninth day of November, 1881. He stated that he was a butcher and kept the Eagle Market, opposite the Cosmopolitan Hotel and that he knew Thomas McLaury in his lifetime. To the question, "Did you see Thomas McLaury on the 26th day of October in your butcher shop in this city; and if so, about what time of day? When you saw him there, did you see him have any arms upon his person, or did he not procure any arms in the butcher shop while there, if you know?" He replied, "I saw Tom coming in about 2 or 3 o'clock. He stayed there about five minutes. He was bleeding on the side of the head when he came in. He stayed there about five or ten minutes and then he went out. He had no arms on

[1]   Tombstone <u>Epitaph</u>, December 30, 1881.

his person and did not get any in there that I saw."[1]
"(Q) Was there anything said in there about arms for McLaury?
"(A) No Sir."[2]
Although authors and researchers have argued for years about whether or not Tom McLaury was in fact armed, the best evidence seems to be that he was.

Alford E. Turner, after years of research, reached the same conclusion. He said, "I believe that Tom McLaury was armed with a pistol when the fight started; but his weapon was never found. Someone, possibly Sheriff John H. Behan, picked it up during the confusion that followed the shooting. The Sheriff admitted that he had not searched Tom's person thoroughly, and said that he might have had a pistol concealed in the waistband of his pants covered by his long blouse and vest. Tom McLaury was not wearing a coat."[3]

---

[1]   The O.K. Corral Inquest, p. 217, reprint Document 94, Records of the County Clerk, Cochise County and Arizona State Archives.

[2]   Ibid, p 216, reprint, Document 94, Records of the County Clerk, Cochise County and Arizona State Archives.

[3]   The O.K. Corral Inquest, Note 3, p 202.

CHAPTER XLI

THE JUDGE'S DECISION

THE taking of testimony was completed on November 29th. Judge Wells Spicer then took the matter under submission and wrote a long decision. The decision was published in the Daily Nugget on December 1, 1881, which means that they must have got it on November 30th, the day after the testimony was finished and the case was taken under submission.

This meant that either Judge Spicer had prepared much of his opinion before hearing the last witnesses or that he was an extremely fast and competent writer. An examination of his opinion indicates that he listened to and considered all of the evidence in the case and addressed all of the questions of facts and law that had been presented to him.

His opinion was also printed as part of Document 94, in the record of the hearing, and is as follows:

"TERRITORY OF ARIZONA   }
                                        }

         vs.   }   Judge Wells
                                          }   Spicer's
                                          }   Decision

"MORGAN EARP, et al DEFENDANTS   }

"Defendants Wyatt Earp and John Holliday, two of the defendants named in the above entitled action, were arrested upon a warrant issued by me on the 29th day of October, on a charge of murder. The complaint filed, upon which this warrant was issued, accuses said defendants of the murder of William Clanton, Frank McLaury, and Thomas McLaury on the 26th day of last month, at Tombstone, in this County.

"This case has now been on hearing for the past thirty days, during which time a volume of testimony has been taken and eminent legal talent employed on both sides.

"The great importance of the case, as well as the great interest taken in it by the entire community, demand that I should be full and explicit in my findings and conclusions and should give ample reasons for what I do.

"From the mass of evidence before--much of which is upon collateral matter -- I have found it necessary for the purposes of this decision to consider only those facts which are conceded by both sides or are established by a large preponderance of testimony.

"Viewing it in this manner, I find that on the morning of the 26th day of October, 1881, and up to noon of that day, Joseph I. Clanton or Isaac Clanton, the prosecuting witness in this case, was about the streets and in several saloons of Tombstone, armed with revolver and Winchester rifle, declaring publicly that the Earp brothers and Holliday had insulted him the night before when he was unarmed, and now he was armed and intended to shoot them or fight them on sight. These threats were communicated to defendants, Virgil Earp and Wyatt Earp.

"Virgil Earp was at this time the chief of police of Tombstone and charged as such officer by the city ordinance with the duty of preserving the peace, and arresting, with or without warrant, all persons engaged in any disorderly act, whereby a breach of the peace might be occasioned, and to arrest and disarm all persons violating the city ordinance which declares it to be unlawful to carry on the person any deadly weapon within the city limits, without obtaining a permit in writing.

"Shortly after noon of October 26th, defendant Virgil Earp, as chief of police, assisted by Morgan Earp, who was also at the time a special policeman in the pay of the city and wearing a badge, arrested and disarmed said Isaac Clanton, and in such arrest and disarmament, inflicted upon the side of his head a blow from a pistol - whether this blow was necessary is not material here to determine.

"Isaac Clanton was then taken to Justice or Recorder Wallace, where he was fined and his arms, consisting of a revolver and Winchester rifle, taken from him and deposited at the Grand Hotel, subject to his orders.

"While at Justice Wallace's court and awaiting the coming of Judge Wallace, some hot words passed between Isaac Clanton and Wyatt Earp. Earp accused Clanton of having previously threatened to take his life, and then proposed to make a fight with him anywhere, to which Isaac Clanton assented, and then declared that 'Fight was his racket,' and that when he was arrested and disarmed, if Earp had been a second later, 'there would have been a coroner's inquest in town.'

"Immediately subsequent to this, a difficulty occurred in front of Judge Wallace's courtroom, between Wyatt Earp and the deceased Thomas McLaury, in which the latter was struck by the former with a pistol and knocked down.

"In view of these controversies between Wyatt Earp and Isaac Clanton and Thomas McLaury, and in further view of this quarrel the night before between Isaac Clanton and J.H. Holliday, I am of the opinion that the defendant, Virgil Earp, as chief of police, subsequently calling upon Wyatt Earp, and J.H. Holliday to assist him in arresting and disarming the Clantons and McLaurys - committed an injudicious and censurable act, and although in this he acted incautiously and without due circumspection, yet when we consider the conditions of affairs incident to a frontier country; the lawlessness and disregard for human life; the existence of a law-defying element in [our] midst; the fear and feeling of insecurity that has existed; the supposed prevalence of bad, desperate and reckless men who have been a terror to the country and kept away capital and enterprise; and considering the many threats that have been made against the Earps, I can attach no criminality to his unwise act. In fact, as the result plainly proves, he needed the assistance and support of staunch and true friends, upon whose courage, coolness and fidelity he could depend, in case of an emergency.

"Soon after the conclusion of proceedings at Judge Wallace's court, Isaac Clanton and Thomas McLaury were joined by William Clanton and Frank McLaury, who had arrived in town. In the afternoon these parties went to [the] gunshop, where they were seen loading their guns and obtaining cartridges. These proceedings were seen by Wyatt Earp, who reported the same to Virgil Earp, chief of police, said Wyatt Earp at the time being a sworn policeman.

"After this, the Clantons and McLaurys went to the Dexter Stables, on Allen Street, and shortly after, crossed the street to the O.K. Corral and passed through to Fremont Street. With what purpose they crossed through to Fremont Street will probably never be known.[1] It is claimed by the prosecution that their purpose was to leave town. It is asserted by the defendants that their purpose was to make an attack upon them or at least to feloniously resist any attempt to arrest or disarm them that might be made by the chief of police and his assistants.

"Whatever their purpose may have been, it is clear to my mind that Virgil Earp, the chief of police, honestly believed [and from information of threats that day given him, his belief was reasonable], that their purpose was, if not to attempt the deaths of himself and brothers, at least to resist with force and arms any attempt on his part

---

[1]   It is thought by some that they went there searching for Doc Holliday. Kate Elder told Dr. A.W. Bork in 1935 that she was staying in a room over the Photo Gallery with Doc Holliday and that about a half hour before the fight started, Ike Clanton came to the Photo Gallery with a rifle looking for Doc Holliday. At that time he was still in bed. She went to the room and said: "Doc, Ike Clanton was here looking for you and had a rifle with him." Doc said: " If God will let me live long enough, he will see me." With that he got up and dressed and went out. Arizona and the West, Vol. 19, No. 1, Spring 1977.

to perform his duty as a peace officer by arresting and disarming them.

"At this time Virgil Earp was informed by one H.F. Sills, an engineer from the A.T.& S.F.R.R., then absent from duty, on a lay-off furlough, and who had arrived in town only the day before and totally unacquainted [with] any person in town, or the state of affairs existing here. Sills had overheard armed parties just then passing through the O.K. Corral say, in effect, that they would make sure to kill Earp, the marshal, and would kill all the Earps.

"At the same time, several citizens and a committee of citizens came to Virgil Earp, the chief of police, and insisted that he should perform his duty as such officer and arrest and disarm the cowboys, as they termed the Clantons and McLaurys.

"Was it for Virgil Earp as chief of police to abandon his clear duty as an officer because its performance was likely to be fraught with danger? Or was it not his duty that as such officer he owed to the peaceable and law-abiding citizens of the city, who looked to him to preserve peace and order, and their protection and security, to at once call to his aid sufficient assistance and persons to arrest and disarm these men?

"There can be but one answer to these questions, and that answer is such as will divest the subsequent approach of the defendants toward the decreased of all presumption of malice or of illegality.

"When, therefore, the defendants, regularly or specially appointed officers, marched down Fremont Street to the scene of the subsequent homicide, they were going where it was their right and duty to go; and they were doing what it was their right and duty to do; and they were armed, as it was their right and duty to be armed, when approaching men they believed to be armed and contemplating resistance.

"The legal character of the homicide must therefore be determined by what occurred at the time and not by the precedent facts. To constitute the crime of murder there must be proven not only the killing, but also the felonious intent. In this case, the *corpus delicti* or fact of killing, is in fact admitted as well as clearly proven. The felonious intent is as much a fact to be proven as the *corpus delicti*, and in looking over this mass of testimony for evidence upon this point, I find that it is anything but clear.

"Witnesses of credibility testify that each of the deceased or at least two of them yielded to a demand to surrender. Other witnesses of equal credibility testify that William Clanton and Frank McLaury met the demand for surrender by drawing their pistols, and that the discharge of firearms from both sides was almost instantaneous.

"There is a dispute as to whether Thomas McLaury was armed

at all, except with a Winchester rifle that was on the horse beside him. I will not consider this question, because it is not of controlling importance. Certain it is that the Clantons and McLaurys had among them at least two six-shooters in their hands, and two Winchester rifles on their horses. Therefore, if Thomas McLaury was one of the party who were thus armed and were making felonious resistance to an arrest, and in the melee that followed was shot, the fact of his being unarmed, if it be a fact, could not of itself criminate the defendants, if they were not otherwise criminated.

"It is beyond doubt that William Clanton and Frank McLaury were armed, and made such quick and effective use of their arms as to seriously wound Morgan Earp and Virgil Earp.

"In determining the important question of whether the deceased offered to surrender before resisting, I must give as much weight to the testimony of persons unacquainted with the deceased or the defendants, as to the testimony of persons who were companions and acquaintances, if not partisans of the deceased. And I am of [the] opinion that those who observed the conflict from a short distance and from points of observation that gave them a good view of the scene, to say the least, were quite as likely to be accurate in their observation as those mingled up in or fleeing from the melee.

"Witnesses for the prosecution state unequivocally that William Clanton fell or was shot at the first fire and Claiborne says he was shot when the pistol was only about a foot from his belly. Yet it is clear that there were no powder burns nor marks on his clothes. And Judge Lucas says he saw him fire or in the act of firing several times before he was shot, and he thinks two shots afterwards.

"Addie Bourland, who saw distinctly the approach of the Earps and the beginning of the affray, from a point across the street, where she could correctly observe all their movements, says she cannot tell which fired first - that the firing commenced at once, from both sides, on the approach of the Earps, and that no hands were held up; that she could have seen them if there had been. Sills asserted that the firing was almost simultaneous. I could not tell which side fired first.

"Considering all the testimony together, I am of the opinion that the weight of evidence sustains and corroborates the testimony of Wyatt Earp, that their demand for surrender was met by William Clanton and Frank McLaury drawing or making motions to draw their pistols. Upon this hypothesis my duty is clear. The defendants were officers charged with the duty of arresting and disarming armed and determined men who were expert in the use of firearms, as quick as thought and as certain as death and who had previously declared their intention not to be arrested nor disarmed. Under the statutes [Sec. 32, page 74 of Comp. Laws], as well as the common law, they have a right to repel force with force.

"In coming to this conclusion, I give great weight to several particular circumstances connected with [the] affray. It is claimed by the prosecution that the deceased were shot while holding up their hands in obedience of the command of the chief of police, and on the other hand the defense claims that William Clanton and Frank McLaury at once drew their pistols and began firing simultaneously with [the] defendants. William Clanton was wounded on the wrists of the right hand on the first fire and thereafter used his pistol with his left. This wound is such as could not have been received with his hands thrown up, and the wound received by Thomas McLaury was such as could not have been received with his hands on his coat lapels. These circumstances being indubital [indubitable] facts, throw great doubt upon the correctness of the statement of witnesses to the contrary.

"The testimony of Isaac Clanton, that this tragedy was the result of a scheme on the part of the Earps to assassinate him and thereby bury in oblivion the confessions the Earps had made to him about 'piping' away the shipment of coin by Wells Fargo & Co. falls short of being a sound theory, [on] account of the great fact, most prominent in this matter, to-wit: that Isaac Clanton was not injured at all, and could have been killed first and easiest, if it was the object of the attack to kill him. He would have been the first to fall; but, as it was, he was known or believed to be unarmed, and was suffered and, as Wyatt Earp testified, told to go away, and was not harmed.

"I also give great weight in this matter to the testimony of Sheriff Behan, who said that on one occasion a short time ago Isaac Clanton told Behan that he, Clanton, had been informed that the sheriff was coming to arrest him and that he, Clanton, armed his crowd with guns and was determined not to be arrested by the sheriff-or words to that effect. And Sheriff Behan further testified that a few minutes before the Earps came to them, that he as Sheriff had demanded of the Clantons and McLaurys that they give up their arms, and that they 'demurred,' as he said, and did not do it, and that Frank McLaury refused and gave as a reason that he was not ready to leave town just then and would not give up his arms unless the Earps were disarmed - that is, that the chief of police and his assistants should be disarmed.

"In view of the past history of the county and the generally believed existence at this time of desperate, reckless and lawless men in our midst, banded together for mutual support and living by felonious and predatory pursuits, regarding neither life nor property in their career, and at the same time for men to parade the street armed with repeating rifles and six-shooters and demand that the chief of police and his assistants should be disarmed is a proposition both monstrous and startling! This was said by one of the deceased only a few minutes before the arrival of the Earps.

"Another fact that rises up preeminent in the consideration of this said affair is the leading fact that the deceased, from the very first inception of the encounter, were standing their ground and fighting back, giving and taking death with unflinching bravery. It does not appear to have been a wanton slaughter of unresisting and unarmed innocents, who were yielding graceful submission to the officers of the law, or surrendering to, or fleeing from their assailants; but armed and defiant men, accepting their wager of battle and succumbing only in death.

"The prosecution claims much upon the point, as they allege, that the Earp party acted with criminal haste - that they precipitated the triple homicide by a felonious intent then and there to kill and murder the deceased, and that they made use of their official characters as a pretext. I cannot believe this theory, and cannot resist the firm conviction that the Earps acted wisely, discretely [sic.] and prudentially, to secure their own self-preservation. They saw at once the dire necessity of giving the first shots, to save themselves from certain death! They acted. Their shots were effective, and this alone saved the Earp party from being slain.

"In view of all the facts and circumstances of the case, considering the threats made, the character and positions of the parties, and the tragical results accomplished in manner and form as they were, with all surrounding influences bearing upon resgestae of the affair, I cannot resist the conclusion that the defendants were fully justified in committing these homicides - that it is a necessary act, done in the discharge of an official duty.

"It is the duty of an examining and committing magistrate in this territory to issue a warrant of arrest in the first place, whenever from the depositions given there is reasonable ground to believe that the defendant has committed a public offense [Sec. 87, page 111 of Comp. Laws].

"After hearing evidence, however, the statute changes the rule, and he is then required to commit the defendant only when there is 'Sufficient cause to believe' him guilty. [Sec 143, page 111 of Comp. Laws].

"My interpretation is that the rule which should govern an examination magistrate is the same as that which should govern the conclusions of a Grand Jury. That such as prescribed by statute [Sec. 188, page 121 of Comp. Laws] is: 'The Grand Jury ought to find an indictment when all the evidence before them, taken together, is such as in their judgement will, if unexplained or uncontradicted, warrant a conviction by the trial jury.'

"The evidence taken before me in this case, would not, in my judgement, warrant a conviction of the defendants by trial jury of any offense whatever. I do not believe that any trial jury that could be got together in this territory, would, on all the evidence taken before me, with the rule of law applicable thereto given them by the court, find the defendants guilty of any offense.

"It may be that my judgement is erroneous, and my view of the law incorrect, yet it is my own judgement and my own understanding of the law as I find it laid down, and upon this I must act and decide, and not upon those of any other persons. I have given over four weeks of patient attention to the hearing of evidence in this case, and at least four-fifths of my waking hours have been devoted, at this time, to an earnest study of the evidence before me, and such is the conclusion to which I am forced to arrive.

"I have the less reluctance in announcing this conclusion because the Grand Jury of this county is now in session, and it is quite within the power of that body, if dissatisfied with my decision, to call witnesses before them or use the depositions taken before me, and which I shall return to the district court, as by law required, and to thereupon disregard my findings, and find an indictment against the defendants, if they think the evidence sufficient to warrant a conviction.

"I conclude the performance of this duty imposed upon me by saying in the language of the Statute: 'There being no sufficient cause to believe the within named Wyatt S. Earp and John H. Holliday guilty of the offense mentioned within. I order them to be released.'

[signed] Wells Spicer, Magistrate"

Note: On the back of this opinion and decision is: "Filed January 3, 1882. No. 94. Territory of Arizona vs. Morgan Earp, Virgil W. Earp, Wyatt S. Earp and John H. Holliday. Testimony on examination of Wyatt S. Earp and John H. Holliday."[1]

This raises once again the interesting question I raised before to-wit, were Wyatt Earp and Doc Holliday confined to the custody of John Behan during the last weeks of the hearing. The last order of the Judge would seem to indicate that they were. "I order them to be released." Ordinarily at the end of a preliminary hearing if a defendant is on bail the Court will make a statement, "there being no sufficient evidence to believe the within named defendants guilty of the offence charged, I hereby order them discharged, bail exonerated." If the person is not on bail but is in custody, then the order is that they be released.

I will leave it up to some future researcher to answer that question for sure, but I think they were in custody.

---

[1]   The O.K. Corral Inquest, p 217-226, reprint, Document 94, Records of the County Clerk, Cochise County and Arizona State Archives.

CHAPTER XLII

THE AFTERMATH

THE shoot out, and the hearing before Judge Spicer received nationwide publicity. It was carried almost daily in the San Francisco, Dodge City, and New York newspapers.

After it was over, the attention of the nation was focused on Tombstone and its outlawry and efforts were made to cool the situation down.

On November 28th, the day before the hearings ended, John J. Gosper, acting governor, wrote a long letter to C.P. Dake, the United States Marshal, commenting on the problems of the Tombstone area and making some suggestions. His letter is set forth in full as follows:

"Office of the Executive

"Prescott A.T., November 28th, 1881

"The Hon. C.P. Dake

"U.S. Marshal

"Dear Sir:

"In reply to your communication of this date, asking me to give you my opinion of the causes of the frequent disturbances of the public peace at Tombstone and vicinity in this territory, with such suggestions as might occur to me looking to a remedy for the unfortunate occurrences, based upon facts obtained by me on my recent - visit to that section, permit me to say, that the underlying causes of all the disturbance of the peace, and the taking of property unlawfully, is the fact that all men of every shade of character in that new and rapidly developed section of mineral wealth, in their mad career after money, have grossly neglected local self-government, until the more lazy and lawless elements of society have undertaken to pray upon the more industrious and honorable classes for their substance and gains. The Civil offices of the County of Cochise and City of Tombstone, partaking of the general reckless spirit of rapid accumulation of money and property, is another of public disturbances, in as much as they have sinned to "wink at crime" and to have neglected a prompt discharge of duty, for the hope and sake of gain.

"The thoroughly abandoned class of men called Highway Robbers and Cattle thieves called "Cow Boys" cunningly taking advantage of the favorable state of affairs for themselves, have robbed from the wealthier class of citizens and when apprehended or detected by the officers of the law have in many cases, no doubt, purchased their liberty, or have paid well to be left unmolested.

"The peaceful and law abiding citizens of the section of the Territory above named are very generally of the opinion that the officers of the law are often themselves in league with the "Cow Boy" element to obtain illegal gains.

"Another cause of the troubles alluded to is the fact that the present Sheriff of Cochise county and one of the Earp brothers, not your Deputy - but a brother to the latter being in some manner connected with the police force for the City of Tombstone are candidates or aspirants for the Sheriffship at the polls another season; the rivalry between them having extended into a strife to secure influence and aid from all quarters, has led them and the particular friends of each to sins of commission and omission greatly at the cost of peace and property.

"The two newspapers published in Tombstone, are also censorable for the course they have pursued in relation to public and private matters.

"In the strife and jealousies between the Sheriff and his Deputies of the County and the City Marshal, the two papers have taken sides very largely through selfish motives of gain - the County patronage being given to one of the papers for its hearty support - and the City patronage to the other for its support.

"Still another cause for the general lawlessness prevailing in that section of our Territory is the fact that many citizens are dealing dishonestly with one hand secretly behind them, handling the stolen property of the "Cow Boys," while with the other hand opening before them they are disposing of the stolen property (mostly beef, Cattle) to the honest citizens, afterwards dividing with the regular thieves.

"This class of criminal is the most difficult to reach and bring to justice. Hotels, saloons, restaurants, etc., where the rough "Cow Boy" element spend their money freely, are both weak and wicked in their sympathy for, & protection of this lawless class.

"From my last visit to Tombstone and vicinity since the killing of the McLaury boys and Clanton in the streets of Tombstone by the Earps I gather the above, and many other facts and beliefs.

"Now as to the remedy to be applied. I would suggest that the Department of Justice in which you are serving be requested to furnish you with funds sufficient to enable you to employ a man of well-known courage and character of cool sound judgement, which your good judgement can secure, who with a suitable posse of men, can first fully comprehend the true nature of the situation, and then with proper discretion and courage, go forward with a firm and steady hand bringing as rapidly as possible the leading spirits of this lawless class to a severe and speedy punishment.

"It might be a wise and successful measure for the Executive of the Territory to cause the removal from office of the Sheriff while yourself as U.S. Marshal, act likewise in securing Deputies to the end that men possessing the confidence of the public and who would work in harmony with each other in enforcing the law and keeping the peace, could be appointed.

"At present however, I do not think it would be prudent for me as acting governor to resort to measures of that character.

"Simply as acting governor, I am not assured the time it would require to inaugurate and carry through the extreme or radical measures the situation certainly requires.

"Having the knowledge and suggestions given above, may become available to you in the matter of bringing about a better state of affairs, and pledging you all the aid and support possible to be given from this department;

"I am most respectfully
"your obedient servant,
"John J. Gosper
"Acting Governor"[1]

From the governor's letter it is obvious that he didn't think very much of Sheriff Behan and seemed to be rather convinced that Behan was in cahoots with the cowboys. He didn't seem to be overly enamored with the Earps either as he seemed critical of the fact that Wyatt Earp was attempting to gain election to Sheriff and blamed part of the problems on the friction between Wyatt Earp and the Sheriff over the coming election.

I was not able to locate Dake's answer to the governor, but did locate a letter written a few days later by Marshal Dake to F.S. Phillips, the Acting Attorney General of the United States.

In this letter, Dake seems to be very supportive of the Earps, and of particular note is the fact that he seems to refer to Wyatt Earp as one of his deputies on a number of occasions.   This I have commented on before, and I cannot fully explain.

The letter was as follows:
"Prescott, Arizona, December 3, 1881
"Hon.: S.F. Phillips Acting Att. General,
"Washington D.C.
"Sir:
"In reply to your favor of the seventeenth Ultimo, with enclosure from Secretary Blaine, I have the honor to report as follows:
"I do not know of any rivalry between the United States officers and the County officials of Tombstone or elsewhere that in any way interferes or retards my deputies from bringing to justice outlaws or

---

[1]   Original in the files of The Arizona Historical Society.

"cowboys" so called.

"It is true, the Sheriff of Cochise County (bordering on Sonora) in which Tombstone is situated, attempted to interfere with the messrs. Earp and their assistants - but - the attempt has completely failed. The Earps have rid Tombstone and neighborhood of the presence of this outlaw element. They killed several in Tombstone recently - and the Sheriff's faction had my deputies arrested - and after a trial my deputies were vindicated and publicly complemented for their bravery and driving this outlaw element from this part of our territory. The magistrate discharged my deputies on the ground that when they killed Clanton and the McLaury's they were in the legitimate discharge of their duties as my officers. Hereafter my deputies will not be interfered with in hunting down stage robbers, mail robbers, train robbers, cattle thieves, and all that class of murdering bandits on the border. I am proud to report that I have some of the best and bravest men in my employee in this hazardous business - men who are trusty and tried and who strike fear into the hearts of these outlaws.

"In conclusion I beg leave to state that I am fully able to grapple with this outlaw element having this force of deputies at my command.

"Yet, the expense you must doubtless perceive is great. Therefore, if you will make a special appropriation for this purpose only for such an amount (as you may deem fit the premises considered) I will put this element out of the way and drive them from our borders as was done with the revolutionists under Marquez.

"The existing fees allowed by law are insufficient to induce men to risk their lives in this business. They must be allowed living fees, such as are allowed by our territorial Laws to Sheriff's for such services and mileage. I will promptly send on the vouchers for your approval as they accrue and will keep close attention to the expense list, and will be as economical in this matter as I possibly can.

"I enclose herewith clippings, to show how the press support my deputies, also a letter from Governor Gosper who has recently returned from the border.

"Very appreciatively,
"your obedient servant,
"C.P. Dake, U.S. Marshal"[1]

Apparently Dake and some very important politicians really got the attention of the Attorney General, and also the President of the United States. On December 6, 1881, President Chester A. Arthur in his first annual message to Congress mentioned the situation. In the

---

[1]   Original in the files of The Arizona Historical Society.

following statement:

"The acting Attorney General also calls attention to the disturbance of the public tranquility during the past year in the Territory of Arizona.   A band of armed desperados known as "cowboys," probably numbering from 50 to 100 men, have been engaged for months in committing acts of lawlessness and brutality which the local authorities have been unable to repress.   The depredations of these "cowboys" have also extended into Mexico, which the murderers reach from the Arizona frontier.   With every disposition to meet the exigencies of the case I am embarrassed by lack of authority to deal with them effectively.   The punishment of crimes committed within Arizona should ordinarily, of course, be left to the Territorial authorities; but it is worth consideration whether acts which necessarily tend to embroil the United States with neighboring governments should not be declared crimes against the United States."[1]

The President went on to urge new legislation, and a repeal of the statute prohibiting the army from acting as a posse comitatus, stating:

"From sparseness of population and other circumstances, it is often quite impracticable to summon a civil posse in places where officers of justice require assistance and where a military force is within easy reach."[2]

Territorial officers had for many years promoted the idea of permitting armed forces stationed within the territories to act as posse comitatus, but the law was never changed, and is in effect to this day.

Neither the battle of the O.K. Corral nor the one month's hearing followed by the written decision by Judge Spicer settled the problems that existed in and around Tombstone.   Ill will was apparent, and people took sides either with the Earps or with the sheriff and the cowboys.   While the politicians were writing letters and trying to figure out a way to stop the lawlessness, things seemed to proceed almost as usual.

On December 14, 1881, John Clum, the Mayor and Editor of the Tombstone Epitaph started on a trip to Washington D.C. to see his parents.   Martin's Tombstone's Epitaph reported that:

"The Epitaph's attack on banditry and its support of the Earps were not overlooked by the cowboys.   They may not be able to get Governor Gosper but they apparently intended to kill John P. Clum, Editor and Mayor.   At least that was the view the Epitaph and Clum

---

[1]   Letters and Papers of the Presidents, pp. 4640-4641.

[2]   Ibid, pp. 4640-4641.

took of the attempted hold up of a stage on which Clum was riding."[1]

The December 15th issue of the Epitaph carried the following story:

"HOLD UP

"As we go to press this morning, we learn through the kindness of Mr. Samdom, one of Sandy Bob's drivers, that an attempt was made to stop the stage last night about three and one-half miles out of town. Simultaneously with the command to stop the coach came a volley of shots evidently aimed at the horses for the purpose of disabling them and thus stopping the coach.

"It could not be discovered in the darkness from whence the shots came or how many men were engaged in the assault. The horses were frightened at the firing and started off at a dead run, continuing their flight for about half a mile, when one of the lead horses fell dead having been wounded by the Highwaymen, and the coach proceeded on without him. The robbers did not overtake the coach and nothing more was heard of them. The only casualties to the passengers was a slight wound on the leg received by 'Whistling Dick,' and the disappearance of Mayor Clum, who was on his way to Tucson.

"As near as could be ascertained, Mr. Clum was on the outside and either fell or jumped off during the shooting as nothing has been heard of him at the present writing - 2:30 a.m. -- the gravest apprehensions are felt concerning his safety as unless he has been killed or wounded by the fusillade, it would seem that he must have reported himself by this time . . . this information was obtained by Sandy Bob's driver when he met Kinnear's coach on his way in last night.

"Arrangements are now being made to send out a party in quest of the missing Mayor."[2]

On the next day, the Epitaph reported further that the Mayor was safe in the following story:

"MAYOR CLUM SAFE

"The announcement in yesterday's Epitaph on the attack of the coach night before last, threw the City into the wildest excitement and the gravest apprehensions for Mayor Clum. As before stated upon receipt of the news, a party started out about 3:00 a.m. to obtain some tidings of the missing Mayor, among whom were Sheriff Behan and C.D. Reppy. (Note: Reppy was Clum's business partner). The Sheriff and Mr. Reppy started first and arrived in Contention between 4 and

[1]   Tombstone's Epitaph, p. 148.

[2]   Ibid, p. 149.

5 o'clock where they learned from Mr. Dunham, of Philadelphia who was on the stage, the first particulars of the affair. The six horse-coach driven by Jimmy Harrington and the bullion wagon driven by 'Whistling Dick' had just left Malcom's water station, which is the last house on the road to Contention, and only about four miles from Tombstone and were bowling along at a rapid gate when the order to 'halt' was given from the roadside and almost simultaneously a volley was fired into them. The offleader of the coach was struck in the neck and all the horses became unmanageable. Dick was hit in the calf of the leg and received a painful flesh wound but kept his seat and his wagon right side up. The horses ran about half a mile when the wounded one weakened and fell from loss of blood. Mr. Clum, with the assistance of other passengers, cut the leaders loose and on they went, it being the general impression that all the passengers were aboard. Mr. Clum had been riding on the inside and he was missed but it was supposed by his fellow passengers that he had taken a seat on the outside, consequently his absence was not detected until the arrival of the coach at Contention.

"Upon learning of this Messrs's Behan and Reppy started from Tombstone and upon arriving at the place where the attack was made examined the locality carefully but no trace of the missing man could be found. In the meantime, the second party which had left Tombstone about 4:00 a.m., upon arriving at Malcom's station learned that two teamsters in the camp with their wagons, at that point, had not only heard the noise of the shooting but could distinctly see the flashes, the attack having been made about the apex of the first rise beyond . . . The party proceeded onto Contention where from Mr. Dunham it was learned that after assisting and releasing the wounded leader, it was supposed by the passengers that Mr. Clum had either taken a seat with the driver or on the bullion wagon, while it was rationally presumed by the driver that he was inside and his absence was not ascertained until arrival at Contention. Just after leaving Mr. Dunham, it was stated that Mr. Clum had been heard of at the Grand Central mill, whither the party proceeded, and learned that the Mayor had taken the ore road to the mill from whence after resting, he had gone by saddle to Benson arriving between 7 and 8 o'clock."[1]

Many years later, John P. Clum wrote about the events of that night in a small book entitled, It All Happened in Tombstone. In the book he explained that when the stage coach caught up with the wagon driven by Whistling Dick it stopped also and at that time they discovered that one of Dick's lead horses had been shot. At that point, before the stage and wagon started moving again, Clum stepped from

---

[1]   Tombstone's Epitaph, p. 150.

the stage coach into the brush alongside, and walked to the Grand Central Quartz Mill where he was able to borrow a horse and complete his journey to Benson.[1]

On December 16, 1881, that is after Clum had left Tombstone and was on his way to Washington, D.C. to visit his parents, an editorial appeared in the paper that pretty well outlined the situation existing in Tombstone at that time, as well as a fair prediction of what might happen in the future.

The editorial was as follows:

"THE LAST OUTRAGE

"The assault upon the Benson stage by would-be assassins Wednesday night, within four miles of the town is the greatest outrage ever perpetuated upon the traveling public of Arizona and is an event calculated to do more harm to the business interests of Tombstone than all other causes operating against us put together. It is a well-known fact that the night stages do not carry either treasure or the mail; therefore the ordinary excuse for plunder cannot be alleged as an incentive to the deed. Since the late unfortunate affair [Note: the famous fight at the O.K. Corral between the Earps and the Cowboys] rumors have been rife of the intended assassination of not only the Earp brothers and Holliday, but Marshall Williams, Mayor Clum, Judge Spicer and Thomas Fitch. Why the feeling of deadly hatred should exist in relation to the Earps and Holliday everyone here can understand; but as against the others it is one of those inscrutable mysteries that none but the most depraved can possibly assign a reason for. That the affair of Wednesday night was intended for the murder of John P. Clum, we are fully satisfied. The threats of the last few days have been too well authenticated to leave any doubt on that point. That the damnable deed miscarried does not rob the event of one jot or tittle of its enormity. The killings and attempted killings heretofore recorded as occurring in Tombstone and the surrounding country have been the outgrowth of drunkenness, wrongs, or fancied wrongs suffered at the hands of one or the other parties to the difficulties. This last has neither the one nor the other to plead in extenuation of the crime. As affairs now stand there seems to be no remedy for our evils other than for the general government to step in and declare military law and keep a sufficient forces here to maintain law and order. It is evident that the civil authorities are unable to put down the lawless element. This remedy is one that we exceedingly dislike to see applied, but where all other remedies fail, we must accept the only remaining one, for life and property must be made as safe in Tombstone as elsewhere in the union or else all good

---

[1]   It All Happened In Tombstone, pp. 21-30.

men will abandon the place."[1]

About this occurrence, Lake said:

"On December 14, Frank Stilwell, Ike Clanton and John Ringo were recognized in a gang of twenty which attempted to assassinate Mayor Clum as he rode from Tombstone to Benson in the stage. Sheriff Behan refused to send a posse after the attackers."[2]

From reading the newspaper articles it is apparent that Lake was gilding the lily, no evidence was ever produced that showed that Frank Stilwell, Ike Clanton and John Ringo were recognized as those who attacked the Benson Stage, nor did anyone ever state that the attackers numbered as many as twenty. The statement that Behan refused to send out a posse after the attackers, was also untrue, since it was recounted in the newspapers that he personally went out with others in an attempt to capture the attackers.

To show that Lake was very careless about his dates and times, he follows his story about the attempted assassination of Mayor Clum by the statement:

"Shortly after this, Doc Holliday and John Ringo had their famous encounter on Allen Street."[3]

Again, Lake was only about half right. That encounter occurred about a month later, January 17, 1882, and will be recounted in the chronological order of its occurrence.

About this time Judge Spicer received a very threatening letter dated December 13, 1881. It was published in the Tombstone Epitaph on December 16, or possibly on December 17th, as follows:

"Tombstone, A.T. December 13, 1881.

"To Wells Spicer - Sir, if you will take my advice you will take your Departure for a more congenial clime as I don't think this One Healthy for you much longer. As you are liable to get a hole through your coat at any moment. If such Sons of Bitches as you are Allowed to dispense justice in this Territory the Sooner you depart from us the better for yourself And the community at large. You may make light of this but it is only a matter of time you will get it sooner or later So with those few gentle hints I will Conclude for the first and Last time.

A Miner"[4]

The Judge wrote a long answer to these threats which was published in full in the Tombstone Epitaph of December 18, 1881.

---

[1]   Tombstone's Epitaph, p. 151.

[2]   Wyatt Earp Frontier Marshal, p. 306.

[3]   Ibid, p. 306.

[4]   Tombstone's Epitaph, p. 152.

The conclusion of his letter was as follows:

"There is a rabble in our City who would like to be thugs if they had the courage; would be proud to be called cow-boys, if people would give them that distinction; but as they can be neither, they do the best they can to show how vile they are, and slander, abuse and threaten everybody they dare to. Of all such I say, that whenever they are denouncing me they are lying from a low, wicked and villainous heart; and that when they threaten me they are low-bred arrant cowards and know that 'fight is not my racket' - if it was they would not dare to do it."[1]

The forebodings of violence expressed in the editorial of the Epitaph were soon to materialize. On December 28, 1881, Virgil Earp was ambushed and severely injured. The story of the shooting was published in the Tombstone Epitaph as follows:

"MIDNIGHT ASSASSINS
"U.S. DEPUTY MARSHAL VIRGIL W. EARP
"SHOT IN THE BACK
"THE FACTS AS FAR AS LEARNED

"About 11:30 o'clock last night U.S. Marshal Virgil Earp was proceeding from the Oriental Saloon from the northeast corner of Allen and Fifth Streets to his room at the Cosmopolitan Hotel, and when he was about the middle of the crossing of Fifth Street, five shots were fired in rapid succession by unknown men who were standing in the old Palace Saloon that is being rebuilt next door above Trasker & Pridham's Store, on the southwest corner of the same street. Immediately after the firing the assassins ran rapidly down Fifth past the Combination Shaft and disappeared in the darkness beyond Tough Nut Street.

"Two of the shots took effect on Mr. Earp, one badly shattering his left arm, and the other entering his left side, producing a wound, the nature of which has not been ascertained at the present writing. Three of the shots went through one of the windows of the Eagle Brewery Saloon on the northeast corner in range of which Mr. Earp happened to be at the time of the firing. The holes in the windows were about at the height of four, six, and seven feet respectively above the sidewalk, but fortunately none of the inmates of the saloon were injured, the shots impinging harmlessly about the opposite wall of the room.

"LATER PARTICULARS

"Since the above was written it has been learned that immediately after the shooting three men ran past the Ice House on Tough Nut Street and sung out to the man in attendance who had his door open

---

[1]   Ibid, p. 152.

at the time, "lock your door." The same three men were seen by a miner a few minutes later making down into the gulch below the Vizina hoisting works. The shots were evidently fired from double-barreled shotguns loaded with buck shot, and there must have been three men as five shots were fired in rapid succession. It's simply a miracle that Mr. Earp was not instantly killed, as in the darkness, with the simple aid of a bit of lighted paper the marks of nineteen shots were found on the east side of the Eagle Brewery and in the awning post, three of them passing through a window on the side of the house.

"Mr. Earp walked into the Oriental and told his brother Wyatt, that he was shot. His friends escorted him to his room at the Cosmopolitan Hotel and Drs. Matthews and Goodfellow were immediately called to attend upon him. It was learned before going to press that his left arm received the principle damage, the shot taking effect just above the elbow, producing a longitudinal fracture of the bone between the shoulder and elbow. So far as could be learned the wound in his back is not necessarily dangerous, though painful. This further proves that there is a band of assassins in our midst, who having threatened the lives of Judge Spicer, Mayor Clum, Mr. Williams, the Earp brothers and Holliday have attempted upon two occasions to carry their threats into execution, first upon Mayor Clum and second upon Virgil Earp. The question naturally arises, who will be the next subject? and a further question, How long will our people stand for this sort of thing? It is no fault of these damned assassins that several persons were not killed in their dastardly attempt to murder a United States Officer last night; for there were many people in the Eagle Brewery, over the heads of whom the passing shots flew on their course. A few inches lower and there would have been corpses prostate upon the floor in place of frightened people wondering what had happened to cause this bombardment."[1]

Lake, in describing the investigation by Wyatt Earp, and it is believable that he got this directly from him, stated that:

"While the surgeon was working over Virgil, Wyatt went to the building where the assassins had hidden. There he picked up a sombrero with Ike Clanton's name in it. A few minutes later, a watchman at an Ice-house on Tough Nut Street told him that Ike Clanton, Frank Stilwell, and Hank Swilling, all carrying shotguns had run by. A trio was seen a few minutes later by a miner, mounting horses tethered in Tombstone Gulch and started towards Charleston on the gallop. John Ringo had been recognized as one of the two

---

[1]   Tombstone's Epitaph, p. 204.

gunman that had run down Allen Street. Who the fifth man was, no one appeared to know. Meanwhile, Dr. Goodfellow was removing four inches of shattered bone from Virgil's left upper arm, and twenty odd buckshots from his body. The surgeon told Wyatt that his brother's recovery was doubtful."[1]

Our faithful diarist, George W. Parsons was almost a witness to the event, and he recorded it in his diary in the following statement: "Wednesday December 28, 1881

"Tonight about 11:30 Doc G. (Goodfellow) had just left and I thought couldn't have crossed the street - when four shots were fired in quick succession from very heavily charged guns, making a terrible noise and I thought were fired under my window, under which I quickly dropped, keeping the adobe wall between me and the outside till the fusillade was over. I immediately thought Doc had been shot and fired in return, remembering a late episode and knowing how pronounced he was on the Earp - Cow-boy question. He had crossed through and passed Virgil Earp who crossed to West side of Fifth and was fired upon when in range of my window, by men two or three concealed in the timbers of the new two story adobe going up for the Huachuca Water Company. He did not fall, but recrossed to the Oriental and was taken from there to the Cosmopolitan being hit with buckshot and badly wounded in left arm with flesh wound above left thigh. Cries of "there they go," and "head them off" were heard but the cowardly, apathetic, guardians of the peace were not inclined to risk themselves and the other brave men all more or less armed did nothing. Doc had a close shave. Van and I went to hospital for Doc and got various things. Hotel well guarded, so much so that I had hard trouble to get to Earp's room. He was easy. Told him I was sorry for him. "It's hell isn't it?" said he. His wife was troubled. "Never mind, I've got one arm to hug you with," said he. . . "[2]

Although one reads Frank Waters book, The Earp Brothers of Tombstone, with considerable reservation, and particularly any quotes of Allie, who was obviously extremely biased, and frequently mistaken about dates and times, it is interesting to note that in the Earp biography, she quoted Virgil in exactly the same words that Parson's did. I doubt that she had access to Parson's diary, and therefore it would appear that both people were there when Virgil said to her, "Never mind, I've got one arm left to hug you with."[3]

My friend Carl Chafin suggests another possibility. He says that

[1]   Wyatt Earp, Frontier Marshal, p. 310.

[2]   The Private Journal of George W. Parsons, p. 202.

[3]   The Earp Brothers of Tombstone, p. 185.

Frank Waters could have read a copy of Parsons' diary at the Arizona Pioneer Historical Society and put the words in Allie's mouth.

Larry D. Ball in his book, The United States Marshals of New Mexico and Arizona Territories, 1846-1912 analyzed the political and outlaw situation in Tombstone at that time as follows:

"While the federal lawman groped for aid against the outlaws, the Earp-cowboy vendetta erupted into more violence. On November 8, even before Dake's letter to Washington, Deputy Marshal Virgil Earp telegraphed General Orlando B. Wilcox for military protection for himself and his brothers during the hearing over the deceased outlaws. The General was bound by the restrictions of the Posse Comitatus Act and referred the matter to Acting Governor Gosper. The territorial executive was not alarmed since he was aware of the existence of the committee of public safety (vigilantes) in Tombstone. Sheriff Behan also notified Gosper that, in spite of Deputy Marshal Earp's fears, the village was quiet.

"Virgil Earp had cause for alarm, although Governor Gosper could not have known the reason. On the night of December 28, several assassins attempted to kill him. He miraculously survived the blast of shotguns, but permanently lost the use of one arm. Wyatt Earp telegraphed Marshal Dake the following day:

"'Virgil Earp was shot by concealed assassin last night. The wound is considered fatal. Telegraph me appointment (as a Deputy Marshal) with power to appoint deputies. Local authorities have done nothing. Lives of our citizens have been threatened (by the cowboys).'

"Although Marshal Dake evidently complied with Wyatt Earp's request, the exact date and nature of this commission is unclear, Deputy Marshal Wyatt Earp was noted in the field soon after against robbers who held up a coach on January 6, 1882."[1]

No author or researcher to date has produced a copy of the telegram that Dake supposedly sent to Wyatt appointing him as Deputy Marshal. The Miner published the telegram from Wyatt Earp set out above but did not publish or comment on a reply. In addition to the telegram, The Miner story said:

"For some time past, the Earps, Doc. Holliday, Tom Fitch and others who upheld and defended the Earps in their late trial, have received almost daily, anonymous letters, warning them to leave town or suffer death, supposed to have been written by friends of the Clanton and McLaury boys, three of whom the Earps and Holliday killed, and little attention was paid to them, as they were believed to be idle boasts, but the shooting of Virgil Earp last night shows that the

---

[1]   United States Marshals of New Mexico and Arizona Territories, p. 123.

men were in earnest.

"Virgil Earp formerly lived in Prescott, and at one time was night-watchman. He left during the Tombstone excitement and has since been a resident of that town."[1]

An election of City officers was scheduled for January 3, 1882, just six days after Virgil Earp was shot.

Fred Dodge says that:

"Virgil Earp was on the citizen's ticket for Marshal against the Behan clique ticket, and when Virgil was shot it precluded any further service as a peace officer-at least for some time-and Dave Neagle was named on the ticket in place of Virgil Earp. And at the elections January 3, 1882, Dave Neagle was elected City Marshal - first set back in an Election for the Sheriff's clique."[2]

Lake says that:

"Sheriff Behan deputized one hundred Curly Bill-Clanton followers 'to keep order at the polls' and on election day rustlers with six-guns and rifles paraded the Tombstone streets. Their campaign of intimidation was cut short when two armed vigilantes took posts beside each of the cowboy deputies. Carr (candidate for Mayor) and Neagle (candidate for Chief of Police) were elected by large majorities.

"On the following day, Johnny Behan billed Cochise county for $2,000, as pay for his election day posse."[3]

I have searched the records of Cochise County for January, 1882 and have been unable to locate any record of John Behan having billed the County for $2,000 to pay for his election day posse.

---

[1]   The Miner, (Prescott, Ariz.), December 30, 1881.

[2]   Undercover for Wells Fargo, p. 39.

[3]   Wyatt Earp, Frontier Marshal, p. 312. Author's Note: I could find no newspaper or documentary evidence to substantiate this statement.

CHAPTER XLIII

A NEW SERIES OF ROBBERIES

LAKE reports that:

"Late in the afternoon of Friday, January 6, the Tombstone - Bisbee stage was held up in the Mule Mountains by five bandits and robbed of an eighty-five-hundred dollar payroll for the Copper Queen Mine. The handkerchief mask dropped from the face of one bandit, revealing the familiar countenance of Sheriff Behan's Deputy, Frank Stilwell. Two of his companions laughed and pulled off their masks - Pony Deal and Curly Bill. Billy Waite, the driver and Charles Bartholomew, shotgun messenger, identified the others as Pete Spence and Ike Clanton. Pony Deal cut out a stage horse to lead away; Curly Bill took Bartholomew's shotgun with the remark that he'd take his next Wells-Fargo box at the muzzle of the express companies own weapon.

"At daylight the next morning as Wyatt Earp, now presumably Deputy U.S. Marshal, took up the trail of the payroll bandits, he got word that the Tombstone-Benson Stage had also been held up near Contention, and robbed of mail and express worth twenty-five hundred dollars. At the scene of the second hold-up Wyatt found J.B. Hume, the Wells-Fargo officer, who had been asleep inside the coach when it was stopped. There had been no shotgun messenger on this stage.

"Pony Deal and Curly Bill had pulled off the second robbery without assistance; neither had worn a mask and both had talked with the driver and Hume freely. Curly Bill took from Jim Hume a pair of ivory handled, gold mounted six-guns, and joked about his growing collection of Wells Fargo weapons. Hume had recognized the shotgun which Curly Bill threw down on him as express company property and the driver had spotted Pony Deal's mount as one of Waite's horses.

"Wyatt Earp, with Sherman McMasters and Jack Johnson, who was Turkey Creek Jack of Deadwood fame, followed the trail of Curly Bill and Pony Deal to Hank Redfern's Ranch found fagged horses which the bandits had traded for fresh animals, and picked up signs which indicated that the robbers were heading back towards Charleston."[1]

---

[1]   Wyatt, Earp Frontier Marshal, p. 314.

It was while Wyatt Earp was out hunting the bandits in the Bisbee Stage Copper Queen payroll robbery that he got word that the Tombstone-Benson stage, on which J.B. Hume, was a passenger, had been held up near Contention and robbed of mail and express worth twenty-five thousand dollars.

You'd hardly recognize it as the same robbery when the incident was described by Fred Dodge. He said that James Hume, Chief Detective for Wells Fargo, was on a trip to Tombstone and left the railroad at Benson and took the stage for Tombstone. Hume was in the back seat of the stage, and it being very hot and him getting along in years, was tired and had fallen asleep, when he was awakened by the command, "throw up your hands," and found two guns levelled on him. The robbers disarmed him, taking a pair of pistols and a short, double barrelled shotgun from him. He said that when Hume finally got to Tombstone he looked Dodge up right away and asked him to locate Wyatt Earp.

Dodge sent for Wyatt, who came at once, and Hume took them into a back room and gave them such an accurate description of the robbers, stating that there were four in number, that Dodge said he could name the men in the robbery since he knew them all. He said that these men always hung out at Charleston, where J.B. Ayers, another under cover Wells Fargo agent operated a saloon.

He told how Wyatt and Morgan Earp, Charlie Smith and himself started out to track down the robbers. They spent the night, and the next day about two o'clock they rode into Charleston where they went to J.B. Ayers' Saloon. To their surprise they found that Jim Hume was in the saloon and so were two of the men that they were looking for. He said that J.B. Ayers tipped him off as to who the robbers were.

Hume had armed himself again and that morning had got a team and driven down to Charleston alone and was at Ayers' Saloon when the two robbers rode up. Although Hume was apparently satisfied that the two men were the ones who had held him up, he told Dodge that he thought the evidence would be insufficient because, "all four of the robbers were masked."[1]

Dodge said that quite awhile afterwards he recovered Hume's pistols and returned them to him, but he never did get the shotgun, although he said he knew who had it. The pistols were the same ones worn by Curly Bill in the fight at Iron Springs in which Curly Bill was killed by Wyatt Earp. "While Wyatt was chasing the highway

---

[1]   Under Cover for Wells Fargo, pp. 17-19. Note that Earp/Lake said that the robbers who took Hume's guns were Pony Deal and Curly Bill and that neither of them wore masks.

men, John Ringo was arrested by Billy Breakenridge on a Grand Jury Indictment for robbery of a Galeyville card game and taken to Tombstone for arraignment before the Magistrate (this is the same incident related by Breakenridge in Chapter XXVIII on Ringo).[1]

"Soon afterwards, a vigilante messenger brought warning that twenty rustlers were in ambush at the Charleston Bridge awaiting Wyatt Earp's attempt to arrest Curly Bill and Pony Deal.   Ten vigilantes under John H. Jackson were sent to ride with Wyatt into the outlaw stronghold.

"Johnny Behan promptly turned John Ringo loose, sending him to Charleston to warn and help his friends.   Ringo, armed with a rifle, was one of the three rustlers on watch in the Charleston street when Wyatt started into town.   Impatience betrayed the presence of the posse and the outlaws vanished.   Curly Bill and Pony Deal had fled when Wyatt at last reached their hangout."[2]

That makes a good story, but it never happened.   I think that both Wyatt Earp and Bill Breakenridge mixed up the two events, that is, the robbery when Hume lost his pistols and the time that a posse went to Charleston to re-arrest Ringo.   The first occurred on January 6th or 7th, 1882.   The posse went out to re-arrest Ringo on January 23, 1882.[3]

Breakenridge partially corroborated Earp's story when he said:

"There was a law and order committee formed in Tombstone that stood in with the gang that was opposed to the Sheriff, and it was reported that some of them had gone towards Charleston to arrest Curly Bill and a lot of cowboys and bring them to Tombstone."[4]

Breakenridge said that Ringo was mistakenly turned loose under the impression that his bond had been posted and that Ringo was furnished a horse by Breakenridge and went to Charleston.   He got there before the law and order party did; in fact they never got there.[5]

It's hard to determine exactly what did happen because here we have three different stories again, all about the same event.   Wyatt Earp's story parallels Fred Dodge's story of tracking the bandits and their circling around and going back to Charleston.   However, here

---

[1]   Helldorado, p. 138.

[2]   Wyatt Earp, Frontier Marshal, pp. 314-315.

[3]   The Private Journal of George W. Parsons, January 25, 1882.

[4]   Helldorado, p. 137.

[5]   Ibid, p. 137.

their stories diverge since Earp said that the presence of the posse had been betrayed and Curly Bill and Pony Deal had fled when the Earp party reached their hangout. Another significant difference in their two stories aside from the fact that Wyatt Earp never mentioned that Fred Dodge was a member of the posse, is that according to Earp it was a two-man job, Pony Deal and Curly Bill, who were not masked, whereas Fred Dodge said that it was four men and they were masked. Although Fred Dodge claimed to know who the bandits were, he did not name them so we cannot be sure that they're talking about the same robbery.

CHAPTER XLIV

THE POT CONTINUES TO BOIL

THINGS were happening in the Earp camp. In January, Mike Joyce, who was still a County Supervisor, resumed control of the Oriental Saloon from Lou Rickabaugh, and shut Wyatt out of the gambling operation. The Daily Nugget of January 8, 1882, reported that:

"Wyatt Earp has sold his interest in the Oriental Saloon (gambling concession) to Rickabaugh & Clark. The Oriental Saloon was reopened last evening under the auspices of M.E. Joyce, who is to be congratulated upon bringing the Oriental back to its old-time popularity."

Paula Mitchell Marks says that:

"By one account, Wyatt simply moved his formal gambling operation to the Bank Exchange Saloon."[1]

On January 17th, George Parson recorded in his private journal the following:

"Snow yesterday. Light fall. Much blood in the air this afternoon. Ringo and Doc Holliday came nearly having it with pistols and Ben Maynard and Rickabaugh later tried to kick each other's lungs out. Bad time expected with the cowboy leader and D. H. (Doc Holliday). I passed both not knowing blood was up. One with hand in breast pocket and the other probably ready. Earps just beyond. Crowded street and looked like another battle. Police vigilant for once and both disarmed. . ."[2]

From such a laconic entry, it's hard to believe the fabulous stories that were spun about the event. An illustration is the stories told by Lake, Breakenridge, and Marks.

Lake, without giving a date, but indicating that the event occurred somewhat earlier than January 17th as he inserts it in his book shortly after telling the story of the attempt to murder Mayor Clum, which occurred on December 14th, and stating that shortly after this Doc Holliday and John Ringo had their famous encounter at Allen Street. He tells the story this way:

"On the afternoon in question, Doc Holliday walked up Allen

---

[1]   And Die in the West, p. 326.

[2]   Private Journal of George W. Parsons, p. 206.

Street to find John Ringo awaiting him in front of the Cosmopolitan. Ringo wore a heavy ulster with slit-pockets in which he kept his hands.

"'I understand you've possibly been talking about me, Holliday,' Ringo snarled.

"'I have,' Doc replied pleasantly. 'I have said, and I repeat, I'm sorry to see a first-class cow-thief like yourself fall in with a bunch of cheap bushwackers.'

"Doc's nickel plated six-gun was swung underneath the skirt of his square-cut coat. In each of his slit pockets John Ringo had a thumb on the hammer of a Colt's forty-five, as Doc well knew. Ringo began to berate Holliday in a style of which the gun-fighting Dentist need not have been ashamed, demanding that Doc retract publicly all that he had said about the rustler. He was trying to goad Holliday into moving for his gun. But Doc could be exasperating even-tempered when he chose. He stepped close to the outlaw leader; George Parson heard what he said.

"'Let's move into the road where no one else'll get hurt.' Holliday suggested.

"'What I said about you goes, and if you get what I'm driving at, all I want of you is ten feet out here in the road.'

"Doc turned his back on Ringo and started off the walk. Before Ringo could follow he was seized from behind by a husky young fellow named Flynn, who had been appointed to the police force by Virgil Earp. 'Turn him loose, Flynn,' Doc Holliday called.

"'And you Ringo, when you start, start shooting.'

"Flynn held Ringo in a bear-like grip and Holliday was urging the officer to let go when Wyatt Earp stepped into the street. Wyatt's eye caught one factor in a possible battle which Holliday had overlooked.

"'Quit this foolishness, Doc' Wyatt said, nodding to a shuttered window in the Grand Hotel from which the muzzle of a rifle was withdrawn as Wyatt spoke. 'That fellow would have dropped you at your first move for a gun.'

"In each of Ringo's holster pockets Flynn found a loaded Colt. He took the rustler and his weapons to the calaboose, where, according to the statement of one of Behan's Deputies, who related the incident with great gusto to show what a good fellow he was, Sheriff Behan got Ringo into his office, placed the outlaws guns in plain view on his desk, then walked out. A few minutes later, Ringo was back at the Grand Hotel, with his six-guns in his pocket again."[1]

Although it's a little difficult to recognize it as the same event, it

[1]   <u>Wyatt Earp, Frontier Marshal</u>, pp. 307-308.

surely must have been, as there has only been recorded one such confrontation between Holliday and Ringo.

Breakenridge told the story this way:

"After the killing of Billy Clanton and the McLaurys, the Earp party made their headquarters at Bob Hatch's Saloon on Allen Street, and whenever a bunch of cowboys came to town, their headquarters were at the Grand Hotel opposite Hatch's Saloon. One day [note the author fails to give the date] John Ringo was standing in front of the hotel alone. Seeing the Earp party coming down the street to their headquarters, he crossed to where they were, and accosting Wyatt Earp said:

"'Wyatt, let's end this now. It has gone on long enough, let Holliday get out here in the middle of the street and shoot it out. If you get me, the cowboys will go home and consider the feud ended. If I am the winner, you agree to do the same and it will be all over.' And turning on his heel he started for the middle of the street.

"This arrangement, however, was not acceptable to the Earp party, and they all went into the saloon.

"Someone came to the Sheriff's office and told him that Ringo was uptown trying to start a fight, and I was told to go and bring him to the office. When I got to Allen Street, the only man in sight was Ringo. He was walking up and down in front of the hotel with his hands in his side pockets of his coat. I told him that Behan wanted him, and asked him what he was up to. He said he was trying to end the feud, but the others were not game to meet him man to man and face to face, that they would rather wait for a chance to shoot him in the back.

"When he got to the office, Behan told him he would have to give up his arms, as it was against the law to carry arms in town. Ringo handed him two pistols from his pockets, and Behan put them in a drawer in the desk and walked out of the office.

"'What are you going to do with me?' asked Ringo. 'Am I under arrest?' I told him he could go whenever he pleased.

"'But John took my guns, and if I go uptown without them, and they (the Earps) find it out, I won't last longer than a snowball in hell. I was about ready to leave town when you came after me.'

"'I told him I could not help his being disarmed and, when he was ready to leave, no doubt the Sheriff would return his pistols. I walked over to the drawer and pulled it out to see if the guns were still there, and forgetting to close it, I walked out also. On my return,

Ringo and his guns were gone, and he left town right away.'"[1]

Paula Mitchell Marks turned up another description of the affair written by John Pleasant Gray in his memoirs. She quotes him as follows:

"Ringo on horseback was riding uptown when he saw three of the Earps together in front of the Crystal Palace Saloon.[2] Ringo, who rode up and dismounted near them and called out to Wyatt that they had just as well have it out there and then. Ringo pulled from his neck, his big red silk handkerchief, flipping it in the air towards Wyatt, told him to take the other end and say when. Of course, Wyatt Earp was too wise to be caught in such a trap . . ."

Analyzing the various stories, Marks said:

"The Gray and Breakenridge accounts may describe other related encounters or maybe variations on the one legendary confrontation. Police court records show that in the January 17th incident, Ringo, Holliday, and Wyatt Earp were all charged with carrying concealed weapons. The charge against Wyatt was dismissed because of his United States Deputy Marshal appointment, while Holliday and Ringo were fined $30 each."[3]

The reader of course, must make his choice of which of the stories to believe; this author chooses to rely on Parson's, who it is believed, generally tried to record the truth in his diary, having no particular axe to grind when committing what he considered to be facts to his diary.

Shortly after Marshal Dake had sent Wyatt Earp a telegram appointing him as Deputy United States Marshal, an urgent telegram from the former governor, Anson Stafford, persuaded Marshal Dake to meet with Acting Governor Gosper in Tombstone to investigate the situation and take the necessary steps to protect the life and property of the mining village.

According to Larry D. Ball, Dake and Gosper arrived in Tombstone on the night of January 26, 1882. He was wrong; it had

---

[1]   Helldorado, pp. 157-158. Note: One possible explanation of Behan's friendship with Ringo was the fact that they may have been roommates. The 1882 Arizona Territorial Census for Tombstone shows them both to be living in the same house in Tombstone.

[2]   At that time there was no Crystal Palace Saloon. It came later. The Saloon he is referring to was the Golden Eagle Brewery.

[3]   And Die in The West, p. 328. Memoirs of John Pleasant Grey, Arizona Historical Society.

to be January 23 or January 24th.¹ He says that Dake had somehow acquired some funds and deposited $3,000 to the account of Deputy Marshal Earp to finance a posse to be used against the cowboys. Just as this author does, he doubts that Governor Gosper superseded Sheriff John Behan as a peace officer and invested Wyatt Earp with complete powers of law enforcement as described by Lake. He was also critical of the men that Earp deputized, stating that they were hardly savory characters. Two were suspected of stage coach robbery and the remaining men were gambling friends of Wyatt Earp.²

Lake tells the story of Governor Gosper and Marshal Dake's visit to Tombstone a little differently. He says:

"Governor Gosper invested Marshal Wyatt Earp with complete powers of law enforcement and appointed under him seven Deputies named by the vigilantes: Morgan and Warren Earp, Doc Holliday, Sherman McMasters, Texas Jack Vermillion, and Turkey Creek Jack Johnson. He authorized Wyatt to appoint other Deputies and placed $5,000 to Wyatt's credit in the local banks. Wells, Fargo & Co. and the Southern Pacific railroad matched this sum, and the citizens of Cochise County subscribed another $5,000. With this cash, Wyatt was to arm and equip his posse's payrolls and traveling expenses. Preliminaries arranged, Governor Gosper issued final orders.

"'Judge Stilwell will give you the warrants you need,' the Governor told Wyatt. 'Now go out and clean up this County.'

"As Judge Stilwell handed over a sheaf of warrants, he offered some advise which Wyatt also carried in his memory. 'If I were serving these warrants, Wyatt,' Judge Stilwell suggested, 'I'd leave my prisoners in the mesquite where alibies don't count.'"³

There are a number of things wrong with the way Lake tells the story. In the first place Governor Gosper had no authority to invest Marshal Wyatt Earp with complete powers of law enforcement, or authorize him to appoint other deputies. It's doubtful that the governor had the authority to suspend the duly appointed Sheriff, John Behan, and in any event he did not do so. Lake raised the funds provided by U.S. Marshal Dake from the $3,000 noted by Ball

¹ The Private Journal of George W. Parsons, January 25th, 1882, p. 208 and proclamation of Mayor John Carr, January 24, 1882, published in the Tombstone Epitaph.

² The U.S. Marshals of New Mexico & Arizona Territory, p. 124. Note: It should be remembered that gambling was considered to be an honorable profession. Many public officials were professional gamblers.

³ Wyatt Earp, Frontier Marshal, p. 315-316.

and added another $10,000 supposedly contributed by Wells Fargo, the Southern Pacific Railroad Co., and the citizens of Cochise County. The source and disposition of the money used by Marshal Dake caused no end of trouble, and was never settled very satisfactorily. Ball, who had access to correspondence between Attorney General Brewster and Marshal Dake during the period of time from 1882 to 1886 made a valiant effort to determine exactly what happened. I'm not sure he got it right, but he must have got pretty close.

According to him, Dake borrowed $3,000 from the Wells Fargo Company in San Francisco to finance his attempt to run the outlaws out of southeastern Arizona. He assured the Wells Fargo people that he would return the money as soon as he could get reimbursed by the Attorney General's office. The promise and transaction was alleged to be fraudulent, but it may not have been. He was always underfunded and was very conscientious about running down the outlaws. At any rate, the Wells Fargo officials gave him $3,000 and on January 20, 1882 he deposited $2,985 with Hudson and Company for the use of Wyatt Earp in tracking down the stage robbers. Paula Mitchell Marks[1] quotes Earp as reporting that Dake had provided him with $2,985 in the Hudson and Company account, minus $340, which Dake had spent while drunk, and that Wyatt used the remaining $2,645 in outfitting and maintaining his posse.

The Attorney General's office kept hounding Dake for several years to account for the expenditure of the funds, which Dake never did satisfactorily. He always claimed that his deputies had been run out of the country and that he was unable to get from them the vouchers and necessary documentation to prove what happened to the money. The Attorney General appointed a special examiner to audit Dake's records and much of the information obtained by both Paula Mitchell Marks and Larry C. Ball, was gleaned from the correspondence between the examiner and the Attorney General.

According to Marks, the special examiner would find that Wyatt drew only $536.65 of the amount that Dake had deposited to his account. Dake himself drew out the rest by February 7. She also quotes a posse member, Charles Smith, who was with Earp all during the time, as testifying that to his knowledge, Wyatt Earp only received about $500 from Dake.[2]

Ball quotes a special examiner, Leigh Chalmers, as stating that the $3,000 that Dake borrowed from the Wells Fargo agent was obtained under "false and fraudulent representations." He says Earp

---

[1]   And Die in the West, p. 329.

[2]   Ibid, p. 329.

evidently spent most of the money in the pursuit of the cowboys, but that Dake spent some $300 of the sum in a drunken celebration with the posse in the sporting houses of Tombstone.[1]

Paula Mitchell Marks correctly states that "the confusion was only heightened by the existence of a citizens' fund raised by law-and-order businessmen and placed at least in part at Wyatt's disposal." . . . Lawyer and Citizens' Safety Committee member William Herring of Tombstone would also identify a citizens' fund held by George Parson's friend Milton B. Clapp and would state that Wells Fargo contributed to this fund with all or most of the money collected, "placed at the disposal of Earp."[2]

Although some authors have concluded that Dake never did get his account squared with the Attorney General's office, Ball says that he did. Stating "the case dragged on into 1886, when in June, Dake entered in a demurer, and the Prescott Miner reported that a settlement of his account was underway in Washington."[3] The settlement was undoubtedly based on the report of an examiner recommended by Jas. A. Zabraskie to Benjamin Harris Brewster, U.S. District Attorney in his letter of January 22, 1885. Portions of the letter were as follows:

"January 22, 1885

"Hon. Benjamin Harris Brewster,

"Attorney General,

"Washington, D.C.

"Sir:

"The important case of the United States versus C.P. Dake, late Marshal of the Territory of Arizona, was commenced by me while at Prescott.

"The most of the bondsmen are scattered over the entire country and the only two that are solvent are in Prescott, this Territory.

"The defendant Dake claims, and I believe with a great deal of truth, that the money for which his accounts are short was disbursed by Deputy Marshal Earp during the great excitement which prevailed in southern Arizona, over the "cow-boy" raids, and depredations at the incipiency of Governor Tritle's administration. The country was almost in a state of revolution, and a reign of terror existed at the time. Deputy Marshal Earp was very active in his efforts to suppress

---

[1]   United States Marshals of New Mexico and Arizona Territories, Pg 132.

[2]   And Die in the West, p 329.

[3]   United States Marshals of New Mexico and Arizona Territories, Pg 132.

this "quasi" insurrection and prevent the violation of United States laws, and the contest became so bitter and violent that, as you remember, President Arthur, at the request of Governor Tritle, placed the Territory under Martial law.

"Deputy Marshal Earp and his band killed quite a number of these cow-boys, and a regular vendetta war ensued between the Marshal and his posse, and the combined force of the cow-boy element throughout the southern portion of the Territory. Mr. Earp finally resigned and left the Territory, and subsequently these discordant elements were suppressed, after great exertion, chiefly by the United States Authorities. Marshal Dake came down from Prescott to the scene of the disorders in this part of the country, near the close of the struggle, and gave matters his personal attention; Earp and his party being then in the mountains, pursuing and pursued. Dake did not see Earp again, as he did not return to Tombstone, but went into New Mexico and subsequently Colorado, where he disappeared for the time being.

"Now, Marshal Dake, claims that he has never been able to settle with the Government, because he has been unable to see Deputy Earp since, and obtain from him vouchers for all of the expenses, as Earp was really driven out of the country by the enemies of the Government, and sent his resignation to Marshal Dake, by mail.

"The defendant, Dake, has assured me repeatedly, and so have many of his friends and bondsmen, that every dollar of this deficiency can be accounted for as honestly expended during this period, if he could only obtain these vouchers or a statement of the facts from Deputy Marshal Earp; but until recently the whereabouts of Mr. Earp was not known to Mr. Dake or to his friends, and now, when Dake is confined to his bed by what is feared to be a fatal illness, Mr. Earp says it is impossible for him to come to Arizona to see Mr. Dake and attend to this business, on account of the disturbed relations he left here.

"In view of the fact that Mr. Dake is at present very ill at Prescott, from the breaking out of old wounds received during the war, and his life is almost despaired of; and inasmuch as the defense will be based upon the facts that heretofore stated, (which are notorious throughout the Territory), and because of the deep sympathy that is felt for Mr. Dake in his present condition, (he being regarded more the victim of untoward circumstances than an intentional wrong-doer), it would be very difficult to obtain a judgement against him for any amount, unless the Government first determines what credits, if any, are due him on account of advances made, under proper authority to suppress the "cow-boy" war.

"I would therefore, most earnestly recommend that an Examiner be detailed to investigate this case, and ascertain if possible, what

amount of money Mr. Dake gave this deputy and others, if advances
were made to others, and what amount was expended by him or them
in the service of process; and what amount can be accounted for upon
a just and satisfactory basis to the Government. . .
   "As this case is set for trial at the next Prescott term, I would
respectfully request that an Examiner be sent as soon as practicable.
          "Very respectfully,
          "Your obedient servant,
          "[signed Jas. A. Zabraskie]
          "U.S. District Attorney"[1]
   I think it is a fair conclusion to say without giving exact details
and amounts that Wells Fargo, Marshal Dake, and the Citizens' Safety
Committee all contributed funds to cover the expense of Wyatt Earp
and his posse and that eventually Earp left the territory without ever
accounting for the expenditure of the funds. Whether or not he
profited from that transaction is difficult to tell. No one that I know
of has ever charged that he stole or misused the money.
   Lake says that,
   "After the Denver (Extradition) hearing, Wyatt went to Trinidad,
where Bat Masterson had a gambling house, and there he and the
men who had accompanied him from Arizona parted company. Wyatt
had about two thousand dollars in cash. He split this six ways, giving
a full share to each of the others, keeping only one share for Warren
and himself."[2]
   The Mayor of Tombstone was well aware that warrants had been
placed in the hands of Wyatt Earp for execution.
   On January 24, 1882, the new Mayor, John Carr, issued the
proclamation which was printed in the Tombstone Epitaph as follows:
          "PROCLAMATION
   "To The Citizens of the City of Tombstone:
   "I am informed by his Honor, William H. Stilwell, Judge of the
District Court of the First Judicial District, that Wyatt Earp, who left
this city yesterday with a posse, was entrusted with warrants for the
arrest of diverse persons charged with criminal offenses. I request the
public to abstain from any interference with the execution of said
warrants.
          "Dated: January 24, 1882
          "John Carr, Mayor"[3]
   Lake says that pursuant to his instructions:

---

[1]   Letter in files of Arizona Historical Society.

[2]   Wyatt Earp, Frontier Marshal, p. 356.

[3]   Tombstone's Epitaph, p 215.

"For two weeks Wyatt Earp and his posse rounded up Curly Bill's followers and sent them into Tombstone or ran them into old Mexico. Purposely they were throwing the fear of death and disaster into the souls of the rank and file, which would simplify the final campaign against the leaders."[1]

Wyatt Earp and his posse may have been harassing and trying to throw the fear of death and disaster into the rank and file of the outlaws, but if he made any arrest and sent them to Tombstone, no one ever recorded the name of the men arrested, and no publicity was ever seen that described who was arrested, what they were charged with and the disposition of their cases. It is very doubtful that they arrested any of the outlaws, but they most certainly had shook them up.

Even if Wyatt Earp and his posse made no arrests, it is probably true that he threw a scare into the rank and file of the cowboy rustler gang. The cowboy gang evidently decided that the best defense was a good offense. Following that plan, Ike Clanton went before Justice of the Peace, J.B. Smith at Contention on February 9, 1882 and filed a complaint charging Wyatt Earp, Morgan Earp, Virgil Earp, and Doc Holliday with the murder of William Clanton and the McLaury brothers in the city of Tombstone on the 26th day of October, 1881.

The legal reasoning behind this complaint was that as stated before, the Earps and Doc Holliday had not been subjected to a trial, but only to a preliminary examination and such an examination is not res adjudicata, does not place the parties in jeopardy and is not a bar to a refiling and re-examination of the same charges. However, it is extremely unusual for a case to be reheard after a judge has once heard the evidence at a preliminary examination and has discharged the defendant. About the only time that this might occur would be if there were newly discovered evidence. In the complaint filed by Ike Clanton with the Justice of the Peace in Contention, there were no new allegations, nor any allegation of newly discovered evidence.

Nevertheless, the Justice of the Peace issued a warrant for the arrest of the Earps and Doc Holliday. The Earps heard about the warrant, and in order to avoid being arrested by Sheriff Behan, Wyatt sent word to the Sheriff that Morgan, Doc Holliday and he would answer the murder charges at Contention on February 14.

Lake says that:

"On the morning set, Wyatt, Morgan, and Doc Holliday rode up to Behan's office, each armed and wearing his Federal badge. Sheriff Behan, Under-Sheriff Woods, Deputy Breakenridge, and Special Deputy Ike Clanton were awaiting them, mounted, but with a buck-

---

[1]   Wyatt Earp, Frontier Marshal, p. 317.

board for their prisoners.

"'You men are under arrest,' Behan said. 'Give me your guns and get into the buck-board. One of you'll drive. We'll ride behind you.'

"'And herd us down the road where your friends can shoot us in the back?' Wyatt observed. 'Not much. Get going, and ride ahead.'

"As Behan argued, a posse of heavily armed vigilantes led by Colonel William Herring, the attorney, rode out of a side street to join the Contention party. Behan abandoned his buck-board idea and the rustlers stationed along the road to assassinate the Earps and Holliday took to the brush when the cavalcade rolled into sight."[1]

George W. Parsons corroborates Lake's statement about the posse in his entry of Wednesday, February 15, 1882, in which he said:

". . . yesterday Earps were taken to Contention to be tried for killing of Clanton. Quite a posse went out. Many of Earps friends accompanied armed to the teeth. They came back later in the day, the good people below beseeching them to leave and try case here. A bad time is expected again in town at any time. Earps on one side of the street with their friends and Ike Clanton and Ringo with theirs on the other side -- watching each other. Blood will surely come. Hope no innocents will be killed."[2]

When the Earps and Doc Holliday appeared in Court for arraignment, Colonel Herring, their attorney made a motion that the matter be transferred to Tombstone, and Judge Smith probably was very relieved and happy to grant the motion. The case was thereupon transferred to Tombstone for further proceedings before the Justice of the Peace.

Before the matter could be heard in that Court, a petition for a Writ of Habeas Corpus was filed on behalf of Doc Holliday and the Earps before the Honorable J.H. Lucas, Probate Judge, he being the only Judge with jurisdiction to issue a Writ of Habeas Corpus available in the County at the time. In the petition for a Writ of Habeas Corpus, the petitioners alleged that the same accusations had been made before the Honorable Wells Spicer, Justice of the Peace of the city of Tombstone on the 29th day of October, 1881 by the same J.I. Clanton that signed the complaint in this case and that after full inquiry into the accusation, the petitioners were discharged on the 20th [sic. 30th] day of November, 1881. They further alleged on information and belief that during the last term of the district court, a grand jury had been duly summoned and had made inquiry into the

[1]   Wyatt Earp Frontier Marshal, p 317-318.

[2]   The Private Journal of George W. Parsons, February 15, 1882, p 213.

offenses committed and charged in the County and that the charges were passed upon by the grand jury and the grand jury voted by ballot and refused to find an indictment on the charges and that the District Court had not made any order since the adjournment of the grand jury directing another grand jury to consider the charges.[1]

In other words, they set up the prior preliminary hearing and grand jury investigation as a bar to any further prosecution of the case.

Ike Clanton filed another declaration against the Earps and Holliday in Judge Lucas' Court. Alford E. Turner in The O.K. Corral Inquest misinterpreted this third declaration by Ike Clanton to mean that he was making a third attempt at prosecuting the Earps. This was not true. The third declaration was merely an appendage to and a part of his second attempt at prosecution of the Earps.[2] If they had xerox machines in those days they would have filed a xerox copy of the declaration that Ike Clanton had filed with the Justice of the Peace at Contention.[3]

Judge Lucas considered all of the documents presented to him and the arguments of counsel and then ordered that the Writ of

---

[1]   The O.K. Corral Inquest, p 232-233.

[2]   Ibid, Note 5, p 246.

[3]   The files of the Tombstone newspapers, both the Epitaph and the Nugget are incomplete and I was unable to find any stories about this event published in either paper. Also it is interesting to note that Martin, in his book Tombstone's Epitaph, failed to refer to any newspaper stories about the second filing of murder charges against the Earps. Perhaps by the time he got around to his research the newspaper files had already been pilfered.

After spending many days research using the current newspapers of Tucson and Tombstone, I have come to the conclusion that someone has gone through the files and deliberately removed most of the materials relating to the Earp-Clanton feud. Later I will refer to some of the stories that were printed in the Sacramento newspaper that whoever was cleaning out the files around Tombstone and Tucson failed to find. It is my belief that someone has in their possession a vast amount of documentary materials relating to the Earps, not only including newspaper stories, but also many of the court files that appear to have been stripped. Whether or not they were stripped and destroyed, or they were stripped and are now in someone else's possession, I cannot say, but they are very likely in someone's possession and will some day be turned up by some ambitious researcher.

Habeas Corpus be granted that, "the realtors, the said Wyatt Earp, Morgan Earp and J.H. Holliday be and they hereby are discharged from custody of said sheriff."[1]

Lake continues to describe the activities of Wyatt Earp and his posse as follows: "Wyatt's round-up of the small fry was producing results. Ranchers in the outlying districts found courage to lynch several rustlers who fell into their hands while separated from their gangs, and sent information which enabled Wyatt to catch Frank Stilwell and Pete Spence. The pair gave bond to appear before the federal grand jury in Tucson on the morning of Tuesday, March 21."[2]

If Wyatt Earp ever rounded up any small fry, no one seemed to know anything about it, and if the ranchers in the outlying districts found courage to lynch several rustlers, no one ever wrote anything about that either. There was nothing in the Tombstone newspapers indicting that any such lynching occurred. As far as someone sending information which enabled Wyatt to catch Frank Stilwell and Pete Spence and take them to a federal court where they gave bond to appear before the federal grand jury in Tucson on Tuesday, March 21, according to his own story that didn't happen either. Lake must have forgotten about his story describing the capture of Frank Stilwell and Pete Spence by Wyatt Earp, Morgan Earp, Frank Dodge and Billy Breakenridge for the September 8th robbery of the Bisbee Stage. In that case, they were taken to Tombstone after their arrest where they posted bail, and by one account, were both taken to Tucson where they posted bail in the federal court. That was the case that was still pending and that they were to appear in on March 21, when Frank Stilwell was killed in Tucson.[3]

Lake says that the safety committee swore out warrants charging Ike Clanton, Frank Stilwell and Hank Swilling with attempted murder of Virgil Earp. That the three surrendered to Sheriff Behan and that at their preliminary examination, a dozen cowboys testified that the three rustlers had been miles away from Tombstone. They were not bound over for hearing before the Grand Jury, and no further action was ever taken, to solve the crime or prosecute the perpetrators.[4]

Lake does not give a date of the preliminary examination or any of the details about the hearing. He states that the cowboys left court with renewed confidence in their immunity from the law, and implies

---

[1]   The O.K. Corral Inquest, p 245.

[2]   Wyatt Earp Frontier Marshal, p 318-319.

[3]   Ibid, p 274.

[4]   Ibid, p 312.

that this feeling of immunity contributed to later robbery attempts against the local stages. Parsons, probably referring to Ike Clanton, Frank Stilwell and Hank Swilling had them surrendering in Tombstone on or before January 30, 1882.[1] On that date he made this entry in his diary:

"Met the Earp posse on the outskirts of Charleston returning to town, their parties having surrendered at Tombstone. Came in and delivered up. Charleston looked almost like a deserted village and as though having undergone a siege. . ."[2]

The parties who had already surrendered at Tombstone were apparently Ike Clanton, Phin Clanton, Frank Stilwell, Hank Swilling and Pony Deal.

Paula Mitchell Marks says that, "When Wyatt brought his Posse back to town on January 30, Ike, Phin and Pony Deal were already appearing in Court on the attempted murder charge."[3]

Turner is the only one who gives any authority for his statement about the event, which is probably the most accurate. He says, citing the Tombstone Nugget of January 31, 1882, which I cannot locate, that:

"The would-be assassins who attempted to kill Deputy U.S. Marshal Virgil Earp were never brought to justice. After successfully evading U.S. Marshal Wyatt Earp's posse for almost a month, Ike and Phineas Clanton became tired of hiding and came into Tombstone and surrendered to Sheriff Behan. Sheriff Behan has thoughtfully provided the two cowboys with 'protection from the Earps' by appointing a large posse to guard them which was headed by Charley Bartholomew and Peter Spencer [Pete Spence]. The Sheriff and Clantons were under the impression that the cowboys were wanted for 'robbing the U.S. Mail,' and had several of their friends ready to swear to a false alibi. They were charged with attempted murder, the specific offense being the shooting of Virgil Earp. The charge did not stick, however, because the defense attorneys, Alexander Campbell and Ben Goodrich, pointed out the technicality that the warrant had been served by John H. Jackson, who was not a legally constituted officer and did not have the power to arrest and hold anyone. Since Sheriff Behan and the Courts were 'protecting' the cowboys where possible, the case was dropped."[4]

---

[1]   The Private Journal of George W. Parsons, Jan 30, 1882, p. 208.

[2]   The Private Journal of George W. Parsons, January 30, 1882, p 208.

[3]   And Die in the West, p. 333.

[4]   The Earps Talk, Note 19, p. 31.

CHAPTER XLV

THE MURDER OF MORGAN EARP AND ITS AFTERMATH

APPARENTLY, the Earps continued with their usual routine in Tombstone; that is, making a living by gambling, and as a sideline attempting to serve some of the warrants that had been given to Wyatt by Judge Stilwell earlier. No further activity was recorded, either in the newspapers or by George Parsons until March 18, 1882, when there was an attempt to kill both Wyatt and Morgan as they were engaged in playing billiards in a local pool hall. The account as published in the Tombstone Epitaph was as follows:

"THE DEADLY BULLET

"The Assassin at Last Successful in His Devilish Mission

"Morgan Earp Shot Down and Killed While Playing

"Billiards

"At 10:50 Saturday night while engaging in playing a game of billiards in Campbell & Hatch's billiard parlor, on Allen street between Fourth and Fifth, Morgan Earp was shot through the body by an unknown assassin. At the time the shot was fired he was playing a game of billiards with Bob Hatch, one of the proprietors of the house and was standing with his back to the glass door in the rear of the room that opens out upon the alley that leads straight through the block along the west side of A.D. Otis & Co.'s store to Fremont street. This door is the ordinary glass door with four panes in the top in place of panels. The two lower panes are painted, the upper ones being clear. Anyone standing outside can look over the painted glass and see anything going on in the room just as well as though standing in the open door. At the time the shot was fired the deceased must have been standing within ten feet of the door, and the assassin standing near enough to see his position, took aim for about the middle of his person, shooting through the upper portion of the whitened glass. The bullet entered the right side of the abdomen, passing through the spinal column, completely shattering it, emerging on the left side, passing the length of the room and lodging in the thigh of Geo. A.B. Berry, who was standing by the stove, inflicting a painful flesh wound. Instantly after the first shot a second was fired through the top of the upper glass which passed across the room and lodged in the wall near the ceiling over the head of Wyatt Earp, who was sitting a spectator of the game. Morgan fell instantly upon the first fire and lived only about one hour. His brother Wyatt, Tipton, and McMasters rushed to the side of the wounded man and tenderly picked him up and moved him some ten feet away near the door of the card room, where Drs. Matthews, Goodfellow and Miller, who were called, examined him and, after a brief consultation, pronounced the wound mortal. He was then moved into the card room and placed on the lounge where in a few brief moments he breathed his last, surrounded by his brothers Wyatt, Virgil, James and Warren with the wives of Virgil and James and a few of his most intimate friends. Notwithstanding the intensity of his mortal agony, not a word of complaint escaped his lips, and all that were heard, except those whispered into the ears of his brother and known only to him were, 'Don't, I can't stand it. This is the last game of pool I'll ever play.' The first part of the sentence being wrung from him by an attempt to place him on his feet.

"His body was placed in a casket and sent to his parents at Colton, Cal., for burial, being guarded to Contention by his brothers and two or three of his most intimate friends. The funeral cortege started away for the Cosmopolitan hotel about 12:30 yesterday with the fire bell tolling out its solemn peals of 'Earth to earth, dust to dust.' (March 20, 1882.)"[1]

A coroner's jury was impanelled and an inquest was held. Wyatt Earp testified at the inquest, but he had no direct evidence to present. The most damaging testimony at the inquest was given by the wife of Pete Spence who had some direct knowledge of what had occurred. Her testimony, as reported in the Tombstone Epitaph, was as follows:

"Marietta D. Spence, being sworn, testifies as follows: Reside in Tombstone and am the wife of Peter Spence; on last Saturday, the 18th of March, was in my home on Fremont street; for two days my husband was not home, but in Charleston, but came home about 12 o'clock p.m. Saturday. He came with two parties, one named Freis, a German; I don't know the other's name but he lives in the house of Manuel Acusto. Then they entered the front room and began to converse with Frank Stilwell. When they had finished, Frank Stilwell went out and Spence went to bed. This all happened that night. Spence remained in bed until 9 o'clock a.m. Sunday. Freis slept there. The other man went to his house on Friday and stayed all day; went out Friday night but returned in a short time to sleep. Saturday he was out all day and up to 12 o'clock at night, when Spence came in. There was an Indian with Stilwell called Charley. He was armed with a pistol and a carbine. He left Saturday morning with Stilwell and came back with him at 12 o'clock at night. Both Charley and

---

[1]   Tombstone's Epitaph, p 208.

Stilwell were armed with pistols and carbines when they returned to the house Saturday night. The conversation between Spence and Stilwell and the others was carried on in a low tone. They appeared to be talking some secret. When they came in I got out of bed to receive them and noticed they were excited, why I don't know. Stilwell came into the house about an hour before Spence and the other two. Stilwell brought me a dispatch from Spence, saying he would be up from Charleston that night, Saturday; (received it about two o'clock in the day). Think Spence left last night, the 20th, for Sonora. Don't know positively that he went. On Sunday morning Spence told me to get breakfast about six o'clock -- which I did, after we had a quarrel during which he struck me and my mother and during which he threatened to shoot me, when my mother told him he would have to shoot her too. His expression said that if I said a word about something I knew that he would kill me; that he was going to Sonora and would leave my dead body behind him. Spence didn't tell me so but I know he killed Morgan Earp; I think he did it because he arrived at the house all of a tremble, and both the others who came with him. Spence's teeth were chattering when he came in. I asked him if he wanted something to eat and he said he did not. Myself and mother heard the shots and it was a little after when Stilwell and the Indian, Charley, came in, and from one-half to three-quarters of an hour after Spence and the other two men came. I think that Spence and the other two men, although they might have arrived during the night, had left their horses outside of town, and after the shooting had gone and got them. I judged they had been doing wrong from the condition, white and trembling, in which they arrived. Spence and the two men had been for several days in the habit of leaving home in the middle of the day and returning in the middle of the night, but they never returned in the same condition as they did on that night, and after hearing the next morning of Earp's death, I came to the conclusion that Spence and the others had done the deed. Have not seen the Indian, Charley, since that night; do not know where he is. Four days ago while mother and myself were standing at Spence's house, talking with Spence and the Indian, Morgan Earp passed by, when Spence nudged the Indian and said 'That's him; that's him.' The Indian then started down the street so as to get ahead of him and get a good look at him. Freis is a German who works for Acusto as a teamster. Think he was with Spence, Saturday night and assisted in killing Earp, also Stilwell and Indian Charley."[1]

The coroner's jury found that Morgan Earp came to his death

---

[1]   Tombstone's Epitaph, p 211-212.

"By reason of a gunshot wound inflicted at the hands of Pete Spence, Frank Stilwell, a party by the name of Freis and two Indian half-breeds, one whose name is Charley, but the name of the other not ascertained."[1]

The Earp family decided to ship Morgan Earp's body to Colton for burial by his father. At the same time, they concluded that Virgil and their wives would not be safe in Tombstone and would probably interfere with the job that Wyatt felt he had to do. Therefore, along with the body of Morgan Earp went Virgil Earp and his wife, and Wyatt's wife, Mattie.

Lake says that, "Wyatt also went before the Cochise County grand jury to testify regarding Morgan's death and left the jury room to start Virgil for the railroad. . .

"At Contention, Wyatt left Warren Earp, McMasters, Johnson, and Texas Jack with the horses while Doc Holliday and he went on to Tucson with Virgil."[2]

That statement does not square with the newspaper reports or the grand jury indictments that were returned by a Tucson Grand Jury. The Tucson Daily Record on March 21, 1882, wrote,

"Two of the Earp brothers and Doc Holliday arrived here last night from Tombstone. Virgil Earp passed on to Colton with the remains of his brother, Morgan, who was assassinated Saturday night at Tombstone. A body of fifteen armed men accompanied the brothers from Tombstone to Contention and six on to this place. There is no danger of their being molested here."

It was while the train was stopped at Tucson that Wyatt Earp and his friends left the train, and it was during that stop that Wyatt Earp killed Frank Stilwell. As is usual in anything connected with the Earps, you can get three or four different stories. Lake's story is the most important, since it purports to be Wyatt's own version of what happened, and since there were no other eye witnesses to the killing, who is to say it was not true. Lake's story was this:

"Dusk was falling as the train reached the Tucson station. Wyatt and Doc guarded Virgil and his wife while they ate supper and then helped Virgil into his car.[3]   The eastbound train, which Wyatt

---

[1]   Tombstone Epitaph, March 20, 1882.

[2]   Wyatt Earp Frontier Marshal, p 324.

[3]   Note here that Wyatt said nothing about his wife, Mattie, being aboard the train, but other sources indicate that she was and her name was never mentioned again by Wyatt Earp. This may have been the last time that Wyatt Earp ever saw her.

expected to take back to Benson, would leave soon, and Wyatt sent
Holliday to the eating-house to order a meal which they could eat
hurriedly, once Virgil was under way. A few minutes before the
California train was to start, Wyatt took leave of his brother. It was
almost dark now.

"'Good-bye, Virgil,' Wyatt said, 'I'll be seeing you soon.'

"Virgil understood the cryptic promise.

"'I'll be seeing you soon,' he answered. 'Take care of yourself
Wyatt.'

"Wyatt hurried through the car, in the windowless vestibule he
halted, then worked his way to peer from the platform around the
corner and alongside of the car away from the station. On the
adjoining track, parallel to the train, was a string of flat cars. Two
cars ahead, the lights from the train window glinted on two rifle-
barrels resting on the far edge of a flat car, and in the shadows Wyatt
made out three or four figures crouched.

"Wyatt raised his sawed-off shotgun toward his shoulder. Loaded
with nine buckshot to the barrel, and with the wad split, that weapon
would sweep eighteen slugs across the flat car. That ought to get
every man back of it. The gun would not come to a firing position.
Wyatt suddenly realized that he was trying to raise it to his left
shoulder, necessary if he was to keep the shelter of the car-corner,
with his hands placed for right shoulder shooting. In shifting his grip,
the gun hit a handrail, and as steel clanked against iron, the figures
behind the flat car were off on a run. Wyatt jumped from the car and
ran forward along the station side of the train, figuring the men
would cross the tracks toward town. From this point on, no one who
lived but Wyatt Earp could tell what happened that night in the
railroad yard at Tucson. Until he gave the story be set down here,
Wyatt Earp kept his own lips sealed. Certain evidence of certain
happenings was found; for the rest all has been pure surmise. . .

"Twenty yards ahead, a man hurried across the tracks in the
glare of the engine headlight. Wyatt ran after him. Two rifle shots
sounded at his left and two bullets swept through the darkness. Wyatt
kept on.

"'Halt,' he shouted, 'Or you'll get it in the back.' The man
stopped and turned. This was better. If he was one of the outlaws,
at least he intended to make his fight. Less than thirty feet separated
the two men when Wyatt recognized Sheriff Behan's Deputy, Frank
Stilwell.

"When Marshal and outlaw were about fifteen feet apart, Stilwell
halted.

"'His guns were in plain sight, and I figured he'd jerk them,'
Wyatt said. 'As I got closer, his right hand started down, but quit half
way and he stood as if he was paralyzed. I never said a word. About

3 feet from Stilwell I stopped and looked at him, then he lunged for me. Stilwell caught the barrel of my Wells Fargo gun with both hands, his left hand uppermost, almost covering the muzzle, and the right well down. I've never forgotten the look in Frank Stilwell's eyes, or the expression that came over his face as he struggled for the gun.

"'I forced the gun down until the muzzle of the right barrel was just underneath Stilwell's heart. I had not spoken to him, and did not at any time. But Stilwell found his voice. You'd guess a million times wrong, without guessing what he said. I'll tell you and you can make what you care to out of it.

"'Morg! he said, and then a second time, Morg! I've often wondered what made him say that.'

"For some moments Wyatt's narrative was suspended. The interlude of retrospection was broken by the questions that would not be denied.

"'What happened then,' I asked.

"'I let him have it,' Wyatt answered simply. 'The muzzle of one barrel, as I told you, was just underneath his heart, he got the second before he hit the ground.'"[1]

Lake's statement that Wyatt left Warren Earp, McMasters, Johnson and Texas Jack with the horses at Contention while Wyatt and Doc Holliday went on to Tucson with Virgil seems to be in error. While much of the story of the Earps is missing from the Tombstone and Tucson papers, other papers in the country reprinted the local paper's reports and I discovered a number of them in Sacramento in the Daily Record Union. On March 21, 1882, that paper reported under "Items from Tombstone" the same story that was printed in the Tucson Daily Record on March 21, 1882 stating that six men accompanied Wyatt and Doc Holliday to Tucson.

On March 22, 1882, the San Francisco Chronicle printed a story, dateline Tucson, March 21 and told the story of the shooting this way,

"Last night another crime was added to the many which have occurred during the last few months, arising out of the well-known trouble in Cochise County between cowboys and the Earp brothers. A young man, about 20 years of age, named Frank Stilwell came to his death from gunshot wounds inflicted, it is supposed, by four men belonging to the Earp party. Just as the western-bound passenger train was pulling out of the depot at seven o'clock, several shots were heard, but they attracted no attention, being attributed to the excessive enthusiasm of some citizens on account of the illumination of the town by gaslight. Daylight this morning, however, revealed the dead body of Stilwell lying a short distance west of Porter's Hotel,

---

[1]   Wyatt Earp Frontier Marshal, p 325-327.

near the railroad track, riddled with bullets and buckshot, six shots having taken effect. One load of seven buckshot had entered the left breast, passed downward and out through the back. His left hand and coat were burned and blackened by powder, showing that the gun, when discharged, was in close proximity to him. His right leg was badly mutilated. He had no doubt, been taken unawares, as a pistol with all the loads intact was found on his person. When discovered, the body was stripped of all valuables, including a watch and chain. A part of the latter was found attached to the vest.

"AT THE RAILROAD STATION

"Last night, when the west bound passenger train arrived, it brought the remains of Morgan Earp, who had been killed Saturday night at Tombstone, and his three brothers, accompanied by Sherman McMasters, Doc Holliday and a man known as Johnson, all heavily armed with shotguns and revolvers. A few moments before the train started Stilwell and Ike Clanton, brother of the Clanton who was killed in Tombstone by the Earps, went to the depot to meet a man by the name of McDowell, who was to have come in as a witness before the grand jury. On their arrival at the depot, they saw the Earp party walking on the platform. Stilwell advised Clanton to leave at once, saying that they wanted to kill him. Clanton left, and a few moments later, Stilwell was seen walking down the track in the direction where his body was found. Four of the armed men who were on the platform soon followed. One was described as a slender, light complexioned man, wearing a light hat.

"ESCAPE OF THE MURDERERS

"The murder is thought to have been done by the Earp party. It is supposed that they continued on the train for a short distance, got off, waited for the east bound freight, flagged it and returned to Tombstone. This afternoon a warrant was issued for their arrest and the Sheriff at that place was instructed to arrest Wyatt and Warren Earp, Sherman McMasters and a man named Johnson, but they resisted with an armed force of eight or ten men, and are all at large.

"STILWELL'S BAD RECORD

"Stilwell has been known of late years as a hard character. He was for a short time Deputy Sheriff of Cochise County, but was removed because of a discrepancy in his accounts. He was afterwards implicated in the ritual killing of an old man named Horton, whose brains were beaten out with stones at the Brokow Mine, south of Tombstone. He escaped though due to some technicalities in the law. He next came into notoriety in connection with the Bisbee Stage robbery last October, by which Wells Fargo and Company lost $25,000. He was in town at the time of his death to stand trial on those charges. He was 27 years old, was a native of Texas, and a brother of the Texas scout Jack Stilwell. He was buried this afternoon, the coffin being conveyed to the grave on a wagon unfollowed by a single mourner."[1]

This story differs from Lake's story in the number of people involved, in the number of shots that took effect on the body of Frank Stilwell, and in the fact that in no place does it mention the name of Doc Holliday. Otherwise it seems to more or less confirm the story told by Lake.

On the same day that the body was discovered, March 21, 1882, a coroner's inquest was held. It was reported in the Daily Record Union in Sacramento, California on March 23, 1882, as follows:

"Tucson, March 22 -- the coroner's jury who were impanelled in the case of the assassination of Frank Stilwell returned a verdict that he came to his death from shots fired by Wyatt and Warren Earp, Doc Holliday, Texas Jack, alias Johnson, and McMasters.

"Intelligence received tonight says that the Earp party are at Benson. It is thought by many that they will arrive here tonight, either to surrender to the authorities or make way with Ike Clanton. It is now definitely known that after they killed Stilwell they searched for Clanton for some time before leaving Tucson.

"This morning about eight o'clock eight mounted men, heavily armed, all wearing grey slouch hats, were seen on the outskirts of this city. Their animals were jaded, having apparently travelled a long distance. They were supposed to be friends of Stilwell from Tombstone, a party of whom left that place last night.

"The last account says that Sheriffs Paul and Behan are out with an organized force to take the parties. A strong posse of armed men are organized here to enforce the law. The indignation of the citizens of Tucson is growing more and more intense. A case of assassination is now before the grand jury, which is in session."[2]

The grand jury did in fact issue an indictment on March 25, 1882, naming Doc Holliday, Wyatt Earp, Warren Earp, Sherman McMasters and John Johnson as parties defendant. Like many of the files and newspaper articles concerning the Earps, the file in this case has been stripped. After extensive research in the County Clerk's Office in Tucson, I located a file that was supposed to contain the indictment, but all it actually contained was the face sheet of the indictment, giving the names of the parties and the date the indictment was filed.

After killing Frank Stilwell, the Earp party spent a couple of hours searching for Ike Clanton without success. They then took the

---

[1]   San Francisco Chronicle, March 22, 1882.

[2]   The Daily Record Union, Sacramento, March 22, 1882.

train to Contention where they got their horses and returned to
Tombstone. According to Lake they were met by a posse of 50 armed
vigilantes, but this sounds like some of Lake's usual exaggeration. It
is unlikely that the 50 men would have been waiting for them to
return without any previous knowledge of when they would get there.
At any rate, sometime after arriving in Tombstone a telegraph was
sent from Tucson requesting the Sheriff to arrest Wyatt Earp and his
men. When Sheriff Behan tried to do so, Wyatt refused to be arrested
and he and his men left the town, ostensibly to continue their work
of rounding up rustlers and outlaws, but probably in truth for the
purpose of seeking the murderers of his brother and dealing with
them in what they considered to be the appropriate manner.

The Tombstone Nugget carried a sensational story the next day
in which it charged that Sheriff Behan had attempted to arrest Wyatt
Earp, and had been immediately confronted by six-shooters.
According to Martin, the Epitaph reported the story in a much calmer
and more truthful manner. This is the Epitaph's story.

"DOES MISREPRESENTATION PAY?

"The mission of a journal is to give news in a plain, intelligent
manner, devoid of distortion and misrepresentation. In deviating
from such a course it ceases to be a newspaper and becomes a
medium for the communication of personal malice and doing grave
public injustice. The Nugget this morning was guilty of a gross mis-
statement in reporting a matter of news that the public were entitled
to have in all its nakedness and truth. It states in the most positive
terms that the sheriff made an attempt to arrest the Earp party at the
Cosmopolitan Hotel and was instantly confronted by a six-shooter in
the hands of each one of the six men composing the party. Now the
facts of the case are, as derived from eye-witnesses and as good and
reliable men as there are in Tombstone, that all that passed between
the sheriff and the Earp party was this; Sheriff Behan was standing in
the office of the Cosmopolitan Hotel, when Wyatt Earp and the others
composing the party came into the office from the rear entrance, each
one having a rifle in his hands, in the ordinary manner of carrying a
gun, and passed through the room to the street. As Wyatt advanced
to the front and approached Sheriff Behan, the sheriff said to him,
'Wyatt, I want to see you.' Wyatt replied, 'You can't see me; you have
seen me once too often,' or words to that effect. He passed out into
the street and turned around and said, 'I will see Paul,' [Note: Sheriff
Paul of Tucson] and then the party passed on down the street. These
gentlemen say that no word was spoken by the sheriff that implied a
demand for an arrest and that no weapons were drawn or pointed at
the sheriff. Furthermore, one of these gentlemen says that he
considers the sheriff did well in not attempting to make the arrest last
night, under the circumstances; that he expects the Earp party will

surrender themselves to Sheriff Paul, of Pima County, when he arrives. These are the plain, unvarnished facts, that can be substantiated, as before said, by some of the best men in Tombstone. -- (March 22, 1882.)"[1]

A story in the San Francisco Chronicle more or less corroborated the story in the Tombstone Epitaph. In that paper it was stated: "There is intense excitement in town this evening. The Earp party, consisting of Wyatt Earp, (Doc) Holliday, McMasters and man named Johnson, all supposed to have been engaged in the assassination of Frank Stilwell at Tucson last night came in town today about noon. About 1:00 p.m. Sheriff Behan received a telegram from Tucson to arrest them for the murder of Frank Stilwell. The party refused to be arrested and, heavily armed, left the Cosmopolitan Hotel, walked down Allen Street, mounted their horses and left town. The streets are crowded with excited people. The Sheriff raised a posse of armed men who will start on the trail at 5 a.m. tomorrow. The impression prevails that the Earp party have gone to Tucson to give themselves up."[2]

The posse raised by Sheriff Behan and sworn in as his deputies included many of the tough characters that he knew were Earp's deadliest enemies. Among them were Ike Clanton, Johnny Ringo, and Curly Bill.[3]

The next day Wyatt Earp and his posse showed up at Pete Spence's wood camp[4] looking for Pete Spence or anyone else that he might have a warrant for or who might be under suspicion for the killing of his brother Morgan. He located a Mexican by the name of Florentine Cruz, who was also known as Indian Charlie. According to Lake, Florentine Cruz did a lot of talking. He named Ike Clanton, Frank Stilwell, Curly Bill, John Ringo, Billy Claiborne, Hank Swilling, and Phin Clanton as parties who attempted to assassinate Mayor Clum. He also told Wyatt that Curly Bill, Ike Clanton, John Ringo and Frank Stilwell had plotted to kill Wyatt and Morgan Earp and that Frank Stilwell, Pete Spence, Frank Swilling, Curly Bill and John Ringo had all been in Tombstone and were all implicated in the killing of Morgan Earp. He stated that he had stood guard at the end of an alley at the time that Morgan Earp was shot and that he had been paid $25 for doing that.

---

[1]   Tombstone's Epitaph, p 213.

[2]   San Francisco Chronicle, March 22, 1882.

[3]   Tombstone's Epitaph, p 214.

[4]   I have never found a description of exactly where that was.

Wyatt Earp told Lake he gave Florentine Cruz a chance to draw on him by a count of three, but that Cruz was too slow and that he pulled his six-shooter and shot him.[1] Whether or not that's the way it happened has been the subject of argument for many years. The Epitaph told the story this way.

"STILL ANOTHER KILLING
"A Mexican Found Dead This Morning
"The Act Supposed to be the Work of the Earps

"This afternoon Theodore D. Judah came in from Pete Spence's wood camp in the South Pass of the Dragoons and gave an Epitaph reporter the following information: Yesterday morning, about 11 o'clock, Wyatt and Warren Earp, Doc Holliday, McMasters, Texas Jack and Johnson, came into the camp and inquired for Pete Spence and Indian Charley; also as to the number of men there and their whereabouts. Judah informed them that Spence was in Tombstone and that a Mexican named Florentine was looking for some stock which had strayed away. Judah indicated the direction taken by the Mexican and the party immediately left as directed, passing over a hill which hid them from view.

"A few minutes later ten or twelve shots were heard. Florentine not returning, this morning Judah proceeded in search of him and found the body not far from camp, riddled with bullets. Judah immediately came to town with the news. He states that had the sheriff's posse come a mile further they would have had all the information they wanted. (March 20, 1882.)"[2]

The same story was published on March 24 in the Daily Record Union in Sacramento, California.

Lake says that Sheriff Bob Paul, who it will be remembered was the Sheriff of Pima County, and a friend of Wyatt Earp, warned that Sheriff Behan was proceeding against Wyatt Earp without sanction from Pima County, and that the character of Behan's posse was evidence of his purpose to use Stilwell's death as justification for killing Wyatt Earp and Doc Holliday in cold blood.[3]

Near confirmation for that statement will be found in the Daily Record Union of Sacramento on March 28, 1882, when the paper printed an article stating: "Sheriff Paul has returned from Tombstone. He says that he did not join in pursuit of the Earps, because the posse selected by Sheriff Behan, of Tombstone, were mostly hostile to the Earps, and that a meeting meant blood without any probability of

---

[1]   Wyatt Earp, Frontier Marshal, p 333-337.

[2]   Tombstone's Epitaph, p 214.

[3]   Wyatt Earp Frontier Marshall, p 338.

arrest. Sheriff Paul says the Earps will come to Tucson and surrender to the authorities. The reported fight at Burleigh Springs is not credited and up to the present lacks confirmation."[1]

The fight at Burleigh Springs referred to by the Sacramento Daily Record Union was a fight in which Wyatt Earp shot and killed Curly Bill Brocius. It did not occur at Burleigh Springs, but has been referred to by that name because it was so reported in the Epitaph in order to confuse the opposition as to the exact location where the fight took place. The place was actually known as Iron Springs and on later maps is designated as Mescal Springs. Lake tells the story of Wyatt and his posse, Doc Holliday, Sherman McMasters, Turkey Creek Jack Johnson, and Texas Jack Vermillion riding up to Iron Springs this way.

"Fifty feet from the Springs, intuition brought Wyatt Earp up short. He swung out of the saddle, looped his reins in his left hand, and with a shotgun in his right hand, walked forward. Texas Jack and Sherman McMasters, still mounted, were behind him. Holliday and Johnson were much farther in the rear. In the sand their advance made no sound. Another step gave Wyatt full view of the hollow. As he took it, two men jumped to their feet less than ten yards away. One yanked a sawed off shotgun to his shoulder and the other breaking for the cottonwoods.

"'Curly Bill!' Sherman McMasters yelled in astonishment, wheeled his horse and ran. Texas Jack followed instantaneous suit. Curly Bill's shotgun roared, and a double charge of buckshot tore through the skirt of Wyatt's coat where it flared out and hung down over the butt of the six-gun at this right hip.

"The outlaw leader threw his hands above his head, hurled the weapons which he had stolen from Bartholomew in the Bisbee Stage holdup against the bank almost at Wyatt's feet, screamed once in awful agony, and fell dead. Eighteen buckshot, a double load from Wyatt's Wells Fargo gun as the Marshal pressed both triggers, had struck Curly Bill squarely in the abdomen, just below the chest wall, well nigh cutting his body in two.

"Pony Deal, who had been Curly Bill's companion, was almost to the cottonwoods. The flimsy shack threatened to burst as seven other rustlers fought in panic to be first through the narrow door into the timber.

"'From the instant I laid eyes on Curly Bill,' Wyatt said in after years, 'I was seeing and thinking clearly. Nothing that went on in that gully escaped me, although what happened in a very few seconds

---

[1]   The Daily Record Union, Sacramento, California, March 28, 1882.

takes much longer to tell.

"'I can see Curly Bill's left eye squinting shut and his right eye sighting over that shotgun to this day, and I remember thinking, as I felt my coat jerk with his fire, "he missed me; I can't miss him, but I'll give him both barrels to make sure."

"'I saw the Wells Fargo plate on the gun Curly Bill was using and I saw the ivory butts of Jim Hume's pet six-guns and Hume's fancy holsters at Curly Bill's waist as clearly as could be. I recognized Pony Deal and, as seven others broke for the cottonwoods, I named each one as he ran, saying to myself, I've got a warrant for him.

"'Johnny Barnes, Ed and Johnny Lyle, Milt Hicks, Rattlesnake Bill Johnson, Bill Hicks, and Frank Patterson, were legging it across the little clearing to join Pony Deal.

"'I knew Curly Bill was cut in two and I threw the loop of my shotgun over my saddlehorn and grabbed for my rifle. My horse was a high strung fellow and I started him off by shooting Curly Bill right across his nose. He reared and I missed the rifle.'

"Pony Deal and his friends chose this moment to open up on Wyatt from the cottonwoods. The rustlers had been too frantic to remember their rifles, were restricted to the six-guns they wore, and were highly excited. Wyatt got behind his horse, but could not calm the animal sufficiently to get his Winchester from the boot. Holding the reins in his left hand, he dropped his right hand to jerk his own six-shooter. The Buntline Special wasn't there. He finally located the weapon hanging well down on his leg, and at the back. The loose belt had let it slide out of place.

"In the meantime, Wyatt had been mystified at the absence of support from his posse, and as he ducked back of his horse he glanced over his shoulder. Holliday, McMasters and Johnson were riding for the rocky shoulder at the other side of the open flat, and just about making it. Halfway between was Texas Jack, struggling to get free of his horse which had been killed by the rustler's fire. Wyatt turned his six-gun loose at the cottonwoods and was rewarded by yells of pain. He had scored two hits he knew, and possibly a third. In the lull he tried to swing into the saddle, but his gun belt had slipped down on his side and he could not spread his legs to mount. He put two more slugs into the cottonwoods to gain a moment's time in which to manage to hitch the belt to his waistline and shove his empty six-gun into the right holster and jerk the one from the left hip. With this in his right hand and with the hand holding his ammunition belt in place, he snubbed the reins in his left hand with which he grabbed the saddle horn and endeavored to pull himself astride. The outlaws cut loose again.

"'If you get my position,' Wyatt explained, 'You'll understand that my nose was almost touching the tip of the saddlehorn. I thought someone had struck a match on the end of it -- my nose -- I mean, and I smelled a very rotten egg.'

"A forty-five slug from the outlaw's gun had creased the leather point of the pommel.

"As his horse quieted, the Marshal got astride and his right hand free to put five shots into the timber. Outlaw firing ceased abruptly, and Wyatt jerked his Winchester, his horse now back steady while Wyatt kept the cottonwoods covered with his rifle. . . Wyatt put two rifle shots into the grove as a silencer, wheeled his horse, and made for cover. A volley of pistol shots followed him and his left leg went numb.

"Beyond the shoulder of rock, his four companions waited, their panic had passed.

"'What a great fight you made, Wyatt,' Doc Holliday said. 'How bad are you hit?'

"'Just my left leg, I guess.'

"Wyatt swung off to inspect the damages. The saddlehorn had been splintered, his coat hung in shreds, there were three holes through the leg of his trousers, five holes through the crown of his sombrero and three through the brim. Despite the numbness of his left leg, he could find no wound. He lifted his boot for a closer inspection and found a bullet imbedded in the high heel. As far as his body was concerned, he had come out of that hail of lead unscratched. His horse had been nicked in three spots by slugs which barely gouged out the hair."[1]

This rather fanciful story told by Lake deserves some examination. In the first place, Lake has Wyatt reaching for his six-shooter, the Buntline Special and finding it wasn't there. There may have been some gun there, but it wasn't the Buntline Special, for no Buntline Special ever existed. That was a total figment of Lake's imagination. Second, he stated that Wyatt shoved his empty six-gun into the right holster and jerked the one from his left hip. This is another obvious attempt of Lake to fictionalize or romanticize the conduct of Wyatt Earp. I can find nothing to indicate that Wyatt Earp ever wore two guns.

It seems to me that his conduct was sufficiently brave and heroic that it didn't need to be pumped up by adding unnecessary and untrue facts.

He went on to guild the lily by adding that, "his coat hung in shreds, there were three holes through the legs of his trousers, five holes through the crown of his sombrero, and three through the brim." Even for a rabid Earp fan, those statements are a little hard

---

[1]   <u>Wyatt Earp Frontier Marshall</u>, p 339-342.

to believe. It seems that if they were true, they would have been commented upon by numerous authors and researchers, and certainly by the newspapers who reported the incident, but no one has ever mentioned any of those facts except Lake in his story of the shoot out. There is little doubt that Wyatt Earp killed Curly Bill Brocius, but it was strenuously denied by the cowboy element and the Tombstone Nugget. On April 14, 1882, the Tombstone Epitaph ran a reprint of a series of stories that had previously appeared in the Epitaph and in the Nugget in an attempt to show that the Nugget was an organ of the cowboys and outlaws and that the Epitaph was a upholder of law and order and printed nothing but the truth. About the killing of Curly Bill, the Epitaph wrote the following: "The Epitaph was the first paper to obtain the news of the attack of the Earp party by nine cowboys and the death of Curly Bill, which facts the Nugget most strenuously denied, as did all the cowboy element. The Nugget went so far as to publish a challenge for the payment of a $100 reward for conclusive evidence of the death of Curly Bill, but upon demand that the money be placed in escrow subject to payment upon proof being adduced, it backed down.   The Epitaph offered to pay $2,000 to any worthy charity provided that Curly Bill would put in an appearance alive and well.   Up to the present time he does not materialize to claim the forfeiture of the reward, nor will he, as his friends have been reluctantly forced to concede the fact of his death in the battle of Burleigh, so called."[1]

More evidence that Wyatt killed Curly Bill was obtained through Fred Dodge, who was present in Tombstone and aware of what was going on. In a letter dated October 8, 1928 to Stuart N. Lake, Dodge stated that immediately after this fight, he interested himself in ascertaining the true facts about the death of Curly Bill. He stated that J.B. Ayers, who you will remember was the under cover Wells Fargo agent who kept a saloon at Charleston where the outlaws and rustlers hung out, told him that the men who were in the fight had stated that Wyatt Earp killed Curly Bill and that his body was buried on the Patterson ranch on the Babacomari. He also said that Johnny Barnes, who was also in the fight and received a gunshot wound that eventually resulted in his death, told him personally that Wyatt Earp had killed Curly Bill. He also said that Ike Clanton had personally told him that Wyatt Earp killed Curly Bill.[2] There doesn't seem to be any question at all that Wyatt Earp did kill Curly Bill, despite the fact that the rustlers and Sheriff Behan and his gang always denied it.

---

[1]   Tombstone Epitaph, April 14, 1882.

[2]   Under Cover for Wells Fargo, p. 234-235.

The reason for their denial is hard to figure. I think they just didn't want to give him the satisfaction of acknowledging that he put an end to the life of one of their leaders.

Nothing was heard from the Earp party for several days and then on the fifth of April, the Tombstone Epitaph printed a letter it had received along with an editor's note as follows:

"THE EARP PARTY

"Journal of Their Adventures and Wanderings

"The following letter was received today written upon detached leaves from an account book, and post-marked Wilcox. It may be genuine and may not be; each reader may judge for himself.

"In Camp, April 4, 1882

"Editor Epitaph:-- In reply to the article in the Nugget of March 31, relating to the Earp party and some of the citizens of Graham and Cochise counties I would like to give you the facts in this case concerning our trip in Cochise and Graham counties. Leaving Tombstone Saturday evening, March 25.

"We Went Into Camp

six miles north of town. Next morning we were overtaken by six prospectors on their way from Tombstone to Winchester district who asked us to partake of their frugal meal, which we ate with relish, after which we travelled in company with them on the main road to Summit station, where we had dinner and awaited the arrival of the passenger train from the west, expecting

"A Friendly Messenger.

"From here we continued our journey on the wagon road to Henderson's ranch where we had refreshments for ourselves and horses. Here we were informed that a gentlemanly deputy sheriff of Cochise county, Mr. Frank Hereford (for whom we have the greatest respect as a gentleman and officer) was at the ranch at the time of our arrival and departure and have since learned the reason for not presenting himself was fears for his safety, which we assure him were groundless. Leaving this ranch we went into camp in good grass one mile north. At seven next morning we saddled and went north to

"Mr. H.C. Hooker's Ranch

in Graham county where we met Mr. Hooker and asked for refreshments for ourselves and stock, which he kindly granted us with the same hospitality that was tendered us by the ranchers of Cochise County. As regards to Mr. Hooker outfitting us with supplies and fresh horses as was mentioned in the Nugget, it is false and without foundation, as we are riding the same horses we left Tombstone on, with the exception of Texas Jack's horse, which was killed in the

"Fight With Curly Bill

and posse, which we replaced by hiring a horse on the San Pedro river. In regard to the reward paid by Stock Association which the

Nugget claims Mr. Hooker paid to Wyatt Earp for the killing of Curly Bill, it is also false as no reward has been asked for or tendered.

"Leaving Hooker's ranch on the evening of that day we journeyed north to within five miles of Eureka Springs. There we camped with a freighter and was cheerfully offered the best his camp afforded. Next morning, not being in a hurry to break camp, our stay was long enough to notice the

"Movements of Sheriff Behan

and his posse of honest ranchers, with whom, if they had possessed the trailing abilities of an average Arizona ranchman, we might have had trouble, which we are not seeking. Neither are we avoiding these honest ranchers as we thoroughly understand their designs.

"At Cottonwood we remained overnight and here picked up the trail of the

"Lost Charley Ross

'and a hot one.' We are confident that our trailing abilities will soon enable us to turn over to the "gentlemen" the fruits of our efforts so that they may not again return to Tombstone empty-handed. Yours respectfully,

One of them."[1]

There has always been considerable controversy over what occurred when the Earp party went to Hooker's ranch on March 27, and what occurred the next morning, March 28, when Sheriff Behan and his posse rode up to the house of Mr. Hooker. About those occurrences, the Tombstone Epitaph printed the following story,

"FACTS OF HISTORY

'Truth Crushed to Earth Shall Rise Again.'

"Fortunately for the facts of history the Epitaph has a correspondent at the Sierra Bonita ranch, who vouches for the truth of the following narrative of what did occur there during the visits of both the Earp and Sheriff parties.

"The Earp party reached Hooker's ranch Monday afternoon, March 27th, where they asked for refreshments for themselves and their horses, which was cheerfully granted them by the proprietor. About seven o'clock in the evening they left the ranch without giving any indication as to what direction they were going that night or in the future. The next morning the sheriff and his posse rode up to the house of Mr. Hooker and DEMANDED refreshments for themselves and beasts which was freely granted them.

"After Occurrences

"The following is a brief digest of the occurrences at the ranch: Sheriff Behan asked Mr. Hooker if he knew the whereabouts of the

---

[1]   Tombstone's Epitaph, p 219-220.

Earp party. Mr. Hooker replied that he did not know and that if he did he would not tell him. Sheriff Behan then said, 'You must be upholding murderers and outlaws, then.' Hooker said, 'No sir, I am not; I know the Earps and I know you and I know they have always treated me like a gentlemen; damn such laws and damn you, and damn your posse; they are a set of horse thieves and outlaws.' At this one of the 'honest farms' (?) of the posse spoke up and said, 'Damn the son of a b----, he knows where they are and let us make him tell.' At this Hooker's hostler stepped away for a moment and returned with a Winchester and drawing a bead on the honest granger said, 'You can't come here into a gentleman's yard and call him a son of a b----! now you skin it back! skin it back! If you are looking for a fight and come here to talk that way you can get it before you find the Earps; you can get it right here.'

"Mr. Hooker then turned to Sheriff Behan and said, 'These are a pretty set of fellows you have got with you; a set of horse thieves and cut-throats.' Behan and Woods both spoke up and said, 'They are not our associates, they are only here on this occasion with us.' Hooker then replied, 'Well, if they are not your associates I will set an extra table for you and set them by themselves,' which he did.

"That Diamond Stud

"After breakfast Sheriff Behan went out to the stable and spoke to the hostler saying, 'Don't say anything about this,' at the same time taking a diamond stud from his shirt bosom and presenting it to the hostler, saying as he did so, 'Take this, it cost a hundred dollars, but don't say anything about what occurred here.' He then turned to Mr. Hooker and remarked, 'If I can catch the Earp party it will help me in the next election.'

"Leaving the ranch, they started off on the trail and crossed the valley to the foot of the mountains and then took up the valley and around to Fort Grant, where they tried to get Indian scouts. Behan offered $500 for the services of the scouts to Col. Bidwell, and during the negotiations remarked that he wanted them to hunt down the Earp party, saying, 'I have just come from Hooker's ranch and I asked Mr. Hooker if he knew where the Earps were, and he said, "No and I would not tell you if I did." Col. Bidwell, stroking his beard with this left hand, looked straight at the sheriff and said, 'Hooker said he didn't know, and would not tell you if he did? Hooker said that, did he? Well if he did

"You Can't Get Any Scouts Here.'

"This ended the interview.

"It will be seen by a comparison of the foregoing with the Nugget report that there is the traditional grain of truth in that garbled statement; just enough, in fact, to swear by. Anyone doubting the truth of the Epitaph correspondent's report of what occurred at Mr.

Hooker's are referred to Mr. Lou Cooley, who will supply all the evidence needed to convince the most skeptical. . ."[1]

The slight discrepancy between the story published in the Tombstone Epitaph and the way it was published in Lake's Wyatt Earp Frontier Marshal, was that the Epitaph did not name the "honest farmer," who just spoke up and said, "Damn the Son of a B---, he knows where they are and let's make him tell." Lake named that person as Ike Clanton. There is no indication where Lake got his information, and it's quite possible that he supplied the missing name himself.

Lake also supplied some other narrative from General Hooker that he gives no authority for. He could have gotten this information from Wyatt Earp, but he doesn't say so; or he could have invented it. At any rate, he says:

"Back at Hooker's, Behan reported his failure to get the scout.

"'I'll tell you where they are, since you can't find him,' General Hooker offered. 'They're over there on top of Reilly Hill. Wyatt Earp, Doc Holliday, Texas Jack, Turkey Creek Jack Johnson, Sherman McMasters and young Warren Earp and Dan Tipton. Seven of 'em. There are twenty-one of you. Why don't you go arrest 'em?

"'We hear they're heavily armed,' Behan countered.

"'Just the way you are,' Hooker replied. 'Six-guns, rifles, and shotguns. Go on over. Wyatt told me to send you.'"[2]

Lake says that Behan and his men had a conference and then rode away, heading for Tombstone, which they reached in safety. He also says that Johnny Behan filed an expense account for his posse and that his friend and business associate the County Treasurer, promptly honored the warrant in the sum of $13,000. I have been unable to find any confirmation of that statement.

---

[1]   Tombstone's Epitaph, p 221-222.

[2]   Wyatt Earp Frontier Marshall, p 351.

CHAPTER XLVI

END OF TOMBSTONE EPISODE

ACCORDING to Martin,[1] the April 14th story in which the Epitaph offered to pay $2,000 to any worthy charity provided Curly Bill would put in an appearance alive and well was the last story published in the Epitaph of the whereabouts of Wyatt Earp and his posse. He says that the Nugget continued to carry wild tales of desperate battles on the desert and capped them with a story that Wyatt himself had been killed.

Lake says that for almost a month Wyatt and his posse ranged the Cochise County desert harassing the outlaws and that late in April they returned to the Tombstone powderhouse for a conference with the vigilantes and after conference with one of their attorneys, they decided to leave Arizona and let Governor Trittle file extradition proceedings on the Tucson warrant, which would give them a chance to contest the worth of the charges before an unprejudiced court.[2]

Paula Mitchell Marks disputes Lake's statement that they hung around harassing outlaws for almost a month or that they returned to Tombstone late in April. She says that the Earp band, consisting of eight men, pushed on toward Silver City, New Mexico, the San Simon Valley and over the mountains to the territorial line. They arrived on Saturday evening, April 8, 1882, and took the Atchison Topeka and Santa Fe rail line to the east.[3]

Unfortunately, Ms. Marks fails to cite any authority for her statement, but her statements, when possible to check out, are generally quite accurate and she probably got the information from a reliable source. I have been told that it was reported in the newspaper at Albuquerque, but was unable to find it.[4]

At any rate, it is agreed by all authors and researchers that Wyatt Earp and his posse did go to Colorado, where eventually extradition

---

[1]   Tombstone's Epitaph, p 223.

[2]   Wyatt Earp, Frontier Marshal, p 355.

[3]   And Die in the West, p. 374.

[4]   Carl Chafin says, "I found this in a Silver City, New Mexico newspaper and passed it on to Al Turner.

proceedings were started by the Governor of Arizona and after numerous and sundry legal maneuvers, Governor Pitkin of Colorado denied extradition. That is a whole other story that has been and is being well covered by several excellent authors and historians, among whom are Robert K. De Arment in his book, <u>Bat Masterson, the Man and the Legend</u>.

When Wyatt Earp left Tombstone, he was 34 years of age. He had been in Tombstone about 2 years and 4 months. That was a very small portion of his life since he lived another 47 years. Despite the assertions of some authors, it was the notoriety of the O.K. Corral gun battle, the killing of his brother Morgan and the subsequent feud that resulted in the killing of Frank Stilwell, Indian Charlie and Curly Bill that gave Wyatt so much national notoriety and in effect, made him into a living legend. Never, during his remaining 47 years was he able to get out from under the shadow of the Tombstone feud. Wherever he or his family went after that, they were covered by newspaper reporters and the news stories always referred back to the battle of the O.K. Corral and the gun fights in which Wyatt Earp was prominently involved; sometimes re-telling the story from the viewpoint of Behan and the cowboys.

He had a very interesting career after Tombstone. But it is not this author's intention to follow his career in detail beyond that point because this book is long enough and it has been well covered by other authors. The best and most complete work was done by Glenn G. Boyer in his book, <u>I Married Wyatt Earp</u>. Based on a manuscript prepared by his wife, Josephine Marcus Earp, this book gives a fairly accurate story of Wyatt Earp's activities from the time he rejoined her in Colorado shortly after leaving Tombstone until the time of his death.

He spent the next two years or so on the gambling circuit with Bat Masterson in Colorado.

In 1883, he joined with Bat Masterson and a number of their friends to form what was known by the newspapers as the "Dodge City Peace Commission." They went there to uphold the rights of Luke Short, who had returned to Dodge City, to be treated equal in the operation of his Alamo Saloon when he was being rousted by the politicians. The story is told quite accurately by Robert K. De Arment in his biography of Bat Masterson, <u>Bat Masterson, the Man and the Legend</u>. Copies of newspaper reports of the affair are set out in the Wyatt Earp and Bat Masterson sections of <u>Great Gunfighters of the Kansas Cowtowns</u>. If the reader wishes more detail of Wyatt's activities while in Colorado for the next two years, he is referred to a small book entitled, <u>Doc Holliday, Bat Masterson, and Wyatt Earp: Their Colorado Careers</u> by E. Richard Churchill, printed by Timberline Books, Leadville, Colorado 80461.

In 1884, he joined the gold rush to Coeur d'Alene, Idaho, and in the usual Wyatt Earp fashion, there was considerable squabbling between him and other people in the town. He opened up a bar and gambling place, was involved in a possible shoot out, and was reported in at least one newspaper to be acting as Deputy Sheriff.[1]

Later that year he went to El Paso, Texas, where he was involved in an encounter with a man named Bill Raynor, which received a lot of publicity and makes a very interesting story.

In 1885, Wyatt and his brother Virgil opened operations in San Diego, where they owned and operated two bars and gambling establishments. Some authors have stated that Wyatt Earp was in the real estate business in San Diego, but my research indicates otherwise. It has also been stated that he acquired a string of thoroughbred race horses which occupied him for a number of years.

In the 1890s, Wyatt was in San Francisco and lived there for about three years. During his stay there, in the fall of 1896, he was involved in a dispute about the outcome of a prize fight between Bob Fitzsimmons and Tom Sharkey that he refereed. The story of that controversy, like all of the others involving Wyatt Earp, had protagonists on both sides, one group claiming that he was a crook and the other group that he was an honest referee. His involvement in the Tombstone affair got thoroughly reviewed in the press at that time.

Outside of the Tombstone affair, his refereeing fiasco in San Francisco gained him more publicity, both good and bad, than any other event in his life. It was constantly in the papers and the argument resulted in a law suit that was fully covered by the press.

One of the most interesting facts developed by the law suit was that Wyatt Earp had been misrepresenting himself as the big shot owner of a string of race horses, when in fact, as he admitted under oath on the witness stand, he had no ownership interest in the horses and they were owned by a Mrs. Orchell of Santa Rosa, and that he merely managed them on a commission.[2]

The whole story, and a very interesting one, is told by Jack DeMattos in his book, The Earp Decision, taken almost entirely from the newspapers published at the time.

Wyatt joined the gold rush to Alaska in 1898 and his activities there are extremely interesting. For once he seemed to get along for a couple of years without any extreme controversy. However, Earp bashers couldn't let it rest at that. Someone published a totally

---

[1]   Information supplied by Judge Richard G. Magnuson of Wallace, Idaho.

[2]   The Earp Decision, p. 153.

fictitious story about his having been disarmed, belittled and embarrassed by a young Canadian Mountie at Dawson in the Yukon. The story was re-published many times and found its way in to the Earp folklore. The best evidence that it was fictitious is the fact that although Wyatt attempted to get to Dawson, he never made it. He went to Nome where he opened a very successful bar and gambling place instead.

He sold out his saloon in Nome, Alaska in 1901 and returned to the States with a substantial fortune. In 1902 and 1903, Wyatt joined the mining boom in Tonopah and Goldfield, Nevada. He established a saloon and gambling establishment in Tonopah, which he called the Great Northern. For some reason, he didn't stay there very long and sold out to one of his partners. After leaving the Nevada boomtowns in the early 1900s, he spent the rest of his life prospecting and travelling about between the California/Arizona desert in the winters, spending summers in Los Angeles and San Francisco, always accompanied by his wife, Josephine.

Researchers have not done a very complete job tracing his movements from that time on. Public records are available to establish where he was and what he did, and there are several good researchers presently engaged in tracking down the story.

CHAPTER XLVII

EPILOGUE

WHEN I started writing this book, it was my intention to tell "The Truth About Wyatt Earp." I'm not sure that I have been successful, but I have tried. I have tried to compare the stories of different authors, writers and historians and examine existing records and old newspaper files to arrive at the truth where possible. Where not possible, I have left it up to the reader to draw his own conclusion about what happened. I have been highly critical of Lake's book because he was obviously biased in favor of Wyatt Earp and attempted to create a fictional hero when the facts that were available were of sufficient interest that it was not necessary to fabricate in order to make a fascinating story.

At the start of the book, I categorized some authors as Earp bashers. Most of these I have examined and compared their stories to other researchers' stories and to original documents and newspapers. One of them, and the most critical of the Earp bashers, I did not examine with respect to every incident related in the life of Wyatt Earp, and that is Frank Waters' book, The Earp Brothers of Tombstone. That book deserves special treatment, as it is widely credited as being one of the best biographies of Wyatt Earp and is quoted as authority for numerous misstatements of fact about Wyatt Earp and relied on as history as no other book is. I therefore feel that book deserves a critical examination in light of other facts that have turned up in the course of my investigation. An examination of the book will reveal that not only were there deliberate misstatements of fact, but numerous innuendos that were intended to disparage the character of Wyatt Earp without making direct accusations.

The primary reason for Frank Waters' prejudice against Wyatt Earp is probably told in the introduction to his book, The Earp Brothers of Tombstone, when he relates the following story:

"In order to substantiate her account with adequate historical records, I went to Arizona. When I came back, I learned that Mrs. Josephine Sarah Marcus Earp had called on my mother and sister, threatening to bring tort action against me if I published Aunt Allie's story, which had grown into book length."[1]

And then he continued, "Despite the threatened suit, I sent out

---

[1]   The Earp Brothers of Tombstone, p. 8.

the book, but no one was then interested in the lurid happenings of more than fifty years ago. A few years later both Mrs. Josephine Sarah Marcus Earp and Aunt Allie died, and I presented the manuscript to the Arizona Pioneer Historical Society in Tombstone merely as a valuable record for its files."[1]

Glenn G. Boyer adds to Waters' story the fact that Mrs. Waters, who had a weak heart, had a seizure as a result of the disturbance created by Mrs. Earp, and remarked that, "not surprisingly, under the circumstances, Frank's book turned out to be highly critical of Wyatt, but he unwisely also included Virgil in his overdone condemnation of the Earps. Allie, who had adored her husband, repudiated the manuscript as a bunch of lies and threatened to sue if Waters published. Significantly, Waters' book did not appear until thirteen years after Allie had died and sixteen years after Josey had passed away."[2]

I can well believe that the incident actually happened, since Stuart N. Lake had a similar experience that resulted in his removing the name of Mattie Blaylock, Wyatt's second wife, entirely from his book.

Correspondence in the Houghton Mifflin collection at the Harvard University Library between Lake and his publisher indicates that Earp's wife had extracted a similar promise from Breakenridge before the publication of his book, Helldorado, which promise he kept and Mattie Blaylock's name does not appear in Breakenridge's book either.

The following are examples of the lengths that Waters went to in trying to blacken the character and name of Wyatt Earp. Writing about some of Wyatt's exploits in Wichita, and describing a ruckus with Melvin A. King, a hard drinking, hard fighting corporal on furlough from Troop H, Fourth United States Calvary who had roared into town, he stated:

"The previously mentioned Ben Thompson witnessed the incident and related later what actually happened to Franklin Reynolds, former U.S. Marshal and fingerprint specialist. Covered by two men standing with shotguns behind him, Wyatt walked up to King, 'slapped him across the head with the barrel of his six-shooter four or five times and King was as bloody as a stabbed hog.' Then Earp and the others carried him down the street to Jewett's office (Ed Jewett, Justice of the Peace). They closed the door and pulled some shades across the windows. Then they almost beat the defenseless

---

[1]   Ibid, p. 9.

[2]   I Married Wyatt Earp, p. 253-254.

man to death. Pretending to fine him, they went through his pockets and robbed him of everything he had."[1]

The source Waters give as his authority for this story as disclosed by footnote 8, page 241, was "The King Incident, as related in detail in the Novel Magazine of March, 1934." I'm sure that the Novel Magazine would not be considered a reliable source of history. Without the phony footnote, the story would be unbelievable. With it, it is even more so. This was the same Melvin King, Corporal of Troop H, Fourth United States Calvary, who was killed by Bat Masterson at Sweetwater, Texas, on January 24, 1876.[2]

He relates a matter reported in the Wichita Beacon of April 5, 1876, as follows:

"On last Sunday night, a difficulty occurred between policemen Erp [sic] and Wm. Smith, candidate for City Marshal. Erp [sic] was arrested for violation of the peace and order of the city and was fined on Monday afternoon by His Honor, Judge Atwood, $30 and costs, and was relieved from the police force . . . "[3]

A part of the Beacon story of April 5, 1876 was laudatory of Earp, but Frank Waters did not see fit to print that portion of the story. The part that Waters omitted was this: "The good order of the city was properly vindicated in the fining and dismissal of Erp [sic]. It is but justice to Erp [sic] to say he has made an excellent officer, and heretofore, his conduct has been unexceptionable."[4] This is a good illustration that wherever Frank Waters could find something derogatory about Earp, he printed it, but if it was complimentary, he left it out.

In many places in Waters' book, he refers sneeringly to Wyatt Earp as being a church deacon, implying that he was a fraud and a phony. Lake tells the story about Earp being a deacon as follows,

"After several abortive attempts at founding a church on the part of overly zealous ministers whose dogmatic tendencies the Cowboys resented, the Reverend O.W. Wright had come to town with a tolerant, broad-gauge brand of religion, appealing strongly to Dodge through the common quality of his creed and the humanism of its preacher. When the Reverend Mr. Wright observed that he needed a church, the Front Street gambling-houses, in two days of play, 'kittied' out enough money to build one for him, and that with rough

---

[1]   Earp Brothers of Tombstone, p 38.

[2]   Bat Masterson, p. 52, 58.; And Die in the West, p. 80.

[3]   The Earp Brothers of Tombstone, p 39.

[4]   Great Gunfighters of The Kansas Cowtowns, p 84.

lumber at $50 a thousand. Further evidence of the Reverend Mr. Wright's standing in Dodge is to be found in the record that Marshal Wyatt Earp and Sheriff Bat Masterson were chosen as his deacons, thereby solving in advance any problems of congregational deportment."[1]

About this incident Waters wrote, quoting Allie, Virgil's wife: "One Sunday we went into church and I was mixed up even more. It was the Union Church, established by Dodge's first minister, Reverend O.W. Wright, and there was Wyatt sanctimonious and God-fearin' as all get out, acting as a church deacon! In fact, the law firm of Sutton and Colburn presented him with a bible on whose inside leaf was inscribed,

'To Wyatt S. Earp as a slight recognition of his many Christian virtues and steady following in the footsteps of the meek and the lowly Jesus. Sutton and Colburn.'"[2]

An illustration of how he tried to imply some devious conduct by Wyatt Earp is the following quote, "She was still confused by the three contradictory roles Wyatt was playing out his strange repertoire: that of card sharp and shady character; the sanctimonious church deacon; and of a fictitious frontier marshal heroically taming one hell popping cow-town after another for the benefit of future movie and TV audiences."[3]

Neither she nor Waters gives any indication of what kind of a shady character Wyatt Earp was or what was sanctimonious about his having served as a church deacon, nor do either of them give any illustration of how he, at that time, was posing as a heroic frontier marshal taming one cowtown after another. At that time he had only worked in two cowtowns.

This is just some additional slime served up by Waters to cast a bad reflection on the character of Wyatt Earp.

Referring to Wyatt Earp's movements in Tombstone, Waters concocted another story to discredit Wyatt Earp. He said, "Wyatt now made his first bid for prominence. Engaging an influential citizen in a poker game, he got the man deeply indebted to him and compromised the debt by asking the man to secure him an appointment as Deputy Sheriff."[4] As authority for this statement he cites Franklin Reynolds' correspondence with the author between

---

[1]   Wyatt Earp Frontier Marshal, p 220.

[2]   The Earp Brothers of Tombstone, p 41.

[3]   Ibid, p 45.

[4]   Ibid, p 102.

December 17, 1937 and January 25, 1938.

That is about the flimsiest citation of authority that one could imagine. If Frank Reynolds wrote such a statement himself, one would naturally ask him where he got his information unless he happened to be present, and the answer, if there was one, would be interesting. But certainly the statement made by Waters cannot be relied on. With many other authors and purported historians looking for material derogatory of the Earps, it is surprising to say the least, that not a single one of them ever came up with such a story. Waters could at least have given the name of the influential citizen that got him appointed as deputy sheriff.

Waters was not only intentionally deceptive, but was extremely careless of his facts. At one point he wrote, "another dealer in the Oriental was Luke Short, from Dodge City, whose Long Branch Saloon Wyatt had protected from unjust competition by organizing the 'Peace Commission.' Luke had not been housebroken yet of his impatient tactics. Getting into an argument over a game of cards, he shot and killed Charlie Storms."[1]

The trouble with this quote is that Charlie Storm was killed on February 25, 1881 in Tombstone. Wyatt Earp and Bat Masterson organized the notorious "Peace Commission" that went to Dodge City to obtain justice for their friend Luke Short in 1883, after Bat Masterson, Wyatt Earp and Luke Short had all left Tombstone.[2]

In order to make Earp look bad, Waters deliberately misquotes Stuart Lake when he says, "Wyatt's biographer claims for his party an exhaustive search during which Wyatt and his companions were in the saddle for seventeen days. Virgil's horse dropped dead under him; they were without food and water once for forty-eight hours and again without food for five days."[3]

What Lake said was, "In ten days and nights of trailing, the posse covered more than four hundred miles, for the greater part over endless wastes of rock and cactus, where for a hundred miles at a stretch there was no sign of human habitation, and, as their horses slowed down with fatigue it might be forty-eight hours between water holes. . . Bat Masterson's horse gave out, and Bat returned to

---

1   Ibid, p 103.

2   Great Gunfighters of The Kansas Cowtowns, p. 387.; The Kansas City (Mo.) Journal, May 15, 1883.

     See Photograph of Famous Peace Commission on the following page.

3   The Earp Brothers of Tombstone, p 132.

PEACE COMMISSIONERS OF DODGE CITY, KANSAS, IN EARLY EIGHTIES

W. H. Harris	Luke Short	Bat Masterson	
Charley Bassett	Wyatt Earp	L. McLean	Neal Brown

WYATT EARP with his Famous Peace Commission
at Dodge City, Kansas in the year 1883
(Courtesy of Arizona Historical Society Library)

Tombstone with a passing teamster. . ."[1]   There was never any statement that Wyatt and his companions were in the saddle for seventeen days, or of Virgil's horse dropping dead.

Waters accuses the Earps of being in cahoots with highway robbers and actually conspiring to kill Bob Paul. His statements are equally fictitious as he accuses Lake of writing about Wyatt Earp in northwest Kansas. About the subject of highway robberies, Waters said:

"It was further known that Doc Holliday and Bill Leonard, one of the three other highway men and a jeweler were good friends and saw each other often. Indeed it was common talk throughout town that the Earps were clearly implicated. States Robert A. Lewis, a prominent mining engineer: 'Wyatt Earp and Doc Holliday were at head of a gang with Ike Clanton and a bunch of cowboys to do stage holdups just below the town of Contention whenever they were tipped off that the valuables would be thrown out and nobody hurt. Wells Fargo was sure of all this and sent down from California a trusty agent, Robert Paul, to put this business out of existence. So it seems the Clanton crowd got tipped off to shoot up the stage one night and Bob Paul.

"'But it being a cold, sleety night, the stage driver, Bud Philpot (a good lad), exchanged seats with Bob Paul to warm his hands, so when the hold up came, Bud Philpot was killed instead of Paul. This started the war between the Earp crowd and the Clanton Crowd.'"[2]

As authority for that statement, he cites "Arizona Pioneers' Historical Society Files." Without being more specific, that's like citing "New York Public Library." It's no citation at all and doesn't give a clue to where the statement came from. If the statement were true and he did any kind of job of research, he should have been able to come up with more support for it than a general reference to Arizona's Pioneer Historical Society Files. What files?

Further, Waters overlooks the fact that Wyatt Earp was a friend and supporter of Bob Paul and assisted him in his successful election contest, and that Virgil Earp, as Deputy U.S. Marshal was very active in running down suspected Wells Fargo robbers. If Wells Fargo were so suspicious of the Earps that they sent Bob Paul out from California to put a stop to their depredations, it seems highly unlikely that they would have presented Virgil Earp with a gold five star police badge engraved "Marshal of Tombstone" on the front and Virgil's initials,

---

[1]   Wyatt Earp Frontier Marshal, p 260.

[2]   The Earp Brothers of Tombstone, p 134. Recently discovered records in Wells Fargo Archives reveal that Robert H. Paul was on the Wells Fargo payroll in the Tombstone-Tucson area from September, 1878. (Added to 1993 edition.)

V.W.E., on the inside,[1] or another handsome gold Marshal's badge when he was Marshal of Colton, California.

According to San Bernardino <u>Daily Times</u> of July 14, 1887, the badge was presented to Virgil Earp by Wells Fargo and Company, "In appreciation of services rendered at Tombstone, Arizona Territory many years ago."

Waters took every opportunity to imply without outright declaring that Wyatt Earp and his brothers were engaged in stage robberies. He never produced one whit of evidence to substantiate his statements. Of the robberies, he said: "More stages were being robbed, money was coming in, and the Earps were quietly getting hold of town lots and mining claims. Everything was going nicely as planned . . . "[2]

He went on to say, "Allie also heard the prevalent opinion about town that the Earp gang was responsible for half the robberies that were taking place." As authority for that statement, he cited Frederick O. Becholdt, author of <u>When the West Was Young</u>, which cited in support of that statement a history written by Major McClintock, who was definitely unfriendly to the Earps and relied as authority for his statements on the testimony of Ike Clanton at the hearing on the O.K. Corral killings.

Another illustration of how Waters implied without offering any evidence or direct statement that the Earps were engaged in robberies was this statement supposedly made by Allie, Virgil's wife,

". . . So one night I said right off to Vergie, 'Vergie, it's about your turn to go to Colton. Let's both go and never come back!'

"The reason I said that was because all spring and summer one or another of the Earp boys would traipse off to Colton, California every so often to visit old Nicholas Porter and Grandma Earp. Just why these big grown men couldn't let a month go by without seein' their mother and father seemed mighty silly. And every time they went, they carried suitcases so heavy you could hardly lift them. They were packed so full, it looked like they was going away for good. Wyatt, Morgan, Jim, even Warren had a turn going. All but Vergie. That's why I mentioned it to Vergie as an excuse for us to get away from Tombstone."[3]

Now this is about as broad an implication of unlawful activities on the part of the Earp brothers as one could find without saying anything.

---

[1]   <u>Ibid</u>, p. 141.

[2]   <u>Ibid</u>, p 146.

[3]   <u>Ibid</u>, p 151.

The statement makes no sense. You look a little farther where he said, "Also on October 29, just three days after the fight, Wyatt and Marshall Williams gave notes to H.S. Crocker and Company of San Francisco for loans of $370.74 and $600.00 respectively. . . Neither his nor Wyatt's notes were paid as late as December 9, 1896, when action was taken for judgement against Wyatt in San Francisco."[1]

Neither does it make sense that while the Earps were travelling with loaded suitcases, supposedly stuffed full of loot from stagecoach holdups, Wyatt would be forced to borrow $370.74 from the H.S. Crocker Company.

I can't find out what the $370.74 loan was about. I feel quite certain that at that time Wyatt was not so financially strapped that he needed it for living expenses, but if he needed it for any purpose, it doesn't seem that he would have borrowed if he had available such huge sums of money from stagecoach robberies as implied by Frank Waters.

It certainly doesn't square with Waters' subsequent statement which was as follows,

"There was no doubt about it. The game was up for the Earp gang. Immediately after the street murders in front of the O.K. Corral they began making preparations to clear out of Tombstone. For there is now brought to light here for the first time, evidence of money behind them in a number of financial transactions.

"Wyatt and Doc Holliday had been arrested on October 29; bail was granted and fixed in the sum of $10,000 each, none being required for Virgil and Morgan, as they were confined to bed with their wounds. Immediately a large group of bondsmen rushed in, putting up a total of $42,500 for them both. Of this amount, Jim Earp put up $2,500 apiece for Wyatt and Doc. Wyatt put up $7,000 for Doc. The rest of the bondsmen included several businessmen in town."[2]

Waters cites as authority for that statement the "Minutes Book of Common Council, Village of Tombstone." Of course, the Village of Tombstone had regular meetings and kept regular Minute books and I have a copy of all of them of that period, and I can't find anything that would substantiate this statement. If he was going to quote some authority, he should have given the name of the people who put up the money, or if he was quoting the Minute Book of the Common Counsel, he should have given either the date or the page that the action took place and was recorded. Actually, the Common Council

---

[1]   Ibid, p 180.

[2]   Ibid, p 182.

had nothing whatever to do with bonds to secure appearance in court.

By Waters' own statements, the Earps were far from penniless. He states that,

"Within a few months, still more mining property was transferred by the Earps as grantors to other grantees:

"W.S. Earp, et al to P.T. Colby, et al and also to the

"Intervener Mining Company, December 30, 1881;

"W.S. Earp to N.P. Earp, his father, April 14, 1882;

"James C. Earp to T.S. Harris, April 29, 1882;

"Virgil Earp to W.W. Woodman, August 14, 1883"[1]

The inconsistency of Waters' statement that the Earps had periodically gone to Colton with bags full of loot never appeared more apparent than in this statement, "All three Earp family were now in such desperate straits -- with Virgil maimed and fighting for his life, Morgan still nursing his wounded shoulder and out of a job, and Wyatt mortgaging his and Mattie's house for a few hundred dollars -- that it is rather pathetic to read in fiction his grandiloquent plans now to sweep all Arizona free of outlaws."[2]

Waters was so anxious to disparage the name of Wyatt Earp, and to show that the cowboys were really the good guys that he forgot what he wrote in other parts of his book. For instance, on page 197, he wrote, "It will be remembered that no one had seen Stilwell in Tombstone on the night of Morgan's assassination, but that he had been seen in Tucson the following morning. The dispatch went on to report that Stilwell was in Tucson to appear before the grand jury on a charge of robbing the stage near Bisbee last November . . ."[3] Compare this to what he wrote on page 191, where he said, "A little earlier that same Sunday evening, on March 18, her former neighbor on the corner of First and Fremont, Mrs. Marietta Spencer, was sitting at home when her husband Pete entered. With him were Frank Stilwell, Florentine Cruz, a half-breed commonly known as Indian Charlie who worked in Spence's wood camp, and a German by the name of Freis. The men ate some supper and went out again shortly before ten o'clock."[4]

He must also have forgotten what he wrote on page 193, where he said, "At the coroner's inquest Mrs. Marietta Spence testified that Frank Stilwell and Indian Charlie had returned to her house about

---

1   Ibid, p 183.

2   Ibid, p 187.

3   Ibid, p 197.

4   Ibid, p 191.

midnight, (on the night Morgan was killed), followed soon after by her husband, Pete, Fries, and another man."

Frank Waters never passed up an opportunity to belittle Wyatt Earp by printing every derogatory story he ever heard without checking the facts, and always failing to give the other side of the story if there was one.

Quoting from an article in the Brewery Gulch Gazette, Bisbee, Arizona, dated April 29, 1932, he says: "After Wyatt struck Alaska one night he started to show the boys up there how they used to pull a little show down in Arizona way. U.S. Marshal Albert Lowe took his gun away, slapped his face, and told him to go home and go to bed or he would run him in."[1]

In another story, he quotes a story from the Arizona Daily Citizen of Tucson, dated May 22, 1900.

"Wyat [sic] Earp, the well known gunfighter who made his reputation in Tombstone in its wild and wooly days, was knocked out in San Francisco a few days ago by Tom Mulqueen, a well known horseman. Earp attempted to do the horseman, but the latter put it all over him and knocked him glassy-eyed in the first round."

In a footnote, Waters says: "This was evidently not a boxing match, but a private squabble at the race track as Mulqueen was a well-known professional boxer, who would never have been matched with an amateur like Wyatt Earp."

It is doubtful if the event ever occurred. It was reported on May 22, 1900 to have happened a few days earlier in San Francisco. Twenty-three days after the report, on June 14, 1900, Wyatt was counted by the U.S. census taker aboard the ship Alliance anchored offshore from Nome, Alaska.

Even if it did happen, it doesn't make any negative reflection on Wyatt Earp, who was fifty-two years old at the time and could not be expected to whip a well-known professional boxer in a fist fight.

Once again, never missing an opportunity to disparage and belittle Wyatt Earp, Waters felt called upon to give a misleading report of an incident that happened in Los Angeles in 1911. He said:

"Even in 1911, when Wyatt was sixty-three years old, he was evidently still pursuing his trade in Los Angeles as a confidence man as attested by this report in the Arizona Star of July 26, 1911:

"'Wyatt Earp, Walter Scott and Edward Dean were arraigned a second time today, charged with a conspiracy to fleece J.Y. Patterson out of $25,000 on an alleged bunco game. All were released on a thousand dollars bail.

"Trial on a conspiracy charge was set for July 27. There is also

---

[1]   Ibid, p. 218.

a charge of vagrancy against Earp, but it is likely to be dropped in order to prosecute the conspiracy charge.'"[1]

What Waters fails to report is that the Los Angeles Court records disclose that all of the charges against Wyatt Earp were dismissed. I can't resist the urge to state that the court that Wyatt Earp originally appeared in and had bail set was presided over by Judge Joseph Chambers, who was still sitting as a Municipal Court Judge and before whom I appeared many times in the 1940s and early 1950s. He was born in 1862 and continued to sit on the Municipal Court bench in Los Angeles until he was in his 90s.

I don't fault Waters for reporting the arrest, but I do for not examining the records and telling the whole story. There was more of interest if he wanted to look it up.

For instance, the conspiracy to defraud was reportedly cooked up in the Alexandria Hotel in downtown Los Angeles, a hotel built and operated by Albert Bilicke, one of the witnesses for the defense in the O.K. Corral hearing and a good friend of Wyatt. He later lost his life in the sinking of the Lusitania off the coast of Ireland on May 7, 1915.

The man arrested with him was a well-known desert rat, Death Valley Scottie, whose shenanigans were the subject of much newspaper publicity into the late 1930s, and whose name is attached to one of the most popular attractions in Death Valley known as Scottie's Castle.

---

[1]   Ibid, p. 219.

SUMMARY

WYATT Earp led an interesting and exciting life during one of the most exciting periods of American history. While it was very controversial, a fact contributed to by many careless authors and would-be historians, the true facts are not wholly obscure. I hope I have unearthed some of them.

On January 13, 1929, George W. Parsons, by then a highly respected retired Los Angeles business man, made this entry in his diary:

"Dined at John Clum's who said Wyatt Earp, our old Tombstone friend, died 8:00 a.m. today. Surely a turbulent life. We always stood for him."[1]

His funeral was held at Los Angeles on January 16th and was attended by numerous friends of long standing. Honorary pall bearers were John Clum, William S. Hart, Tom Mix, Wilson Mizner, Charlie Welsh, George W. Parsons, and W.J. Hunsaker, who had been Wyatt's attorney in Tombstone.[2]

Wyatt Earp was not the man painted and created by Stuart N. Lake. If he had been, he would not have needed a funeral. He would have just ascended to heaven on his own power. On the other hand, he was not the villain and scoundrel portrayed by many of his detractors. If he had been, his funeral would not have been attended by numerous friends of many years standing. Like it was reported about Frank Stilwell, "His coffin would have been conveyed to the grave on a wagon unfollowed by a single mourner."

Wyatt Earp was a product of his times. He was a gambler when gambling was a respectable occupation. When it became illegal, he probably continued that activity anyway. He was not a great man, but nevertheless an outstanding man whose exploits epitomized an interesting age in history that has captured and held the interest and imagination of the American people like no other.

---

[1]   The Private Journal of George Whitwell Parsons, January 13, 1929. Courtesy Carl Chafin.

[2]   Los Angeles Herald, January 16, 1929.

APPENDIX 1, Exhibit 1

OATH OF OFFICE OF DEPUTY UNITED STATES MARSHAL
Signed by V.W. Earp

APPENDIX 1, Exhibit 2

APPOINTMENT AND OATH OF OFFICE OF WYATT EARP AS DEPUTY SHERIFF OF PIMA COUNTY, Dated July 27, 1880.

APPENDIX 1, Exhibit 3

RESIGNATION OF THE OFFICE OF DEPUTY SHERIFF OF PIMA COUNTY, Dated November 9th, 1880.

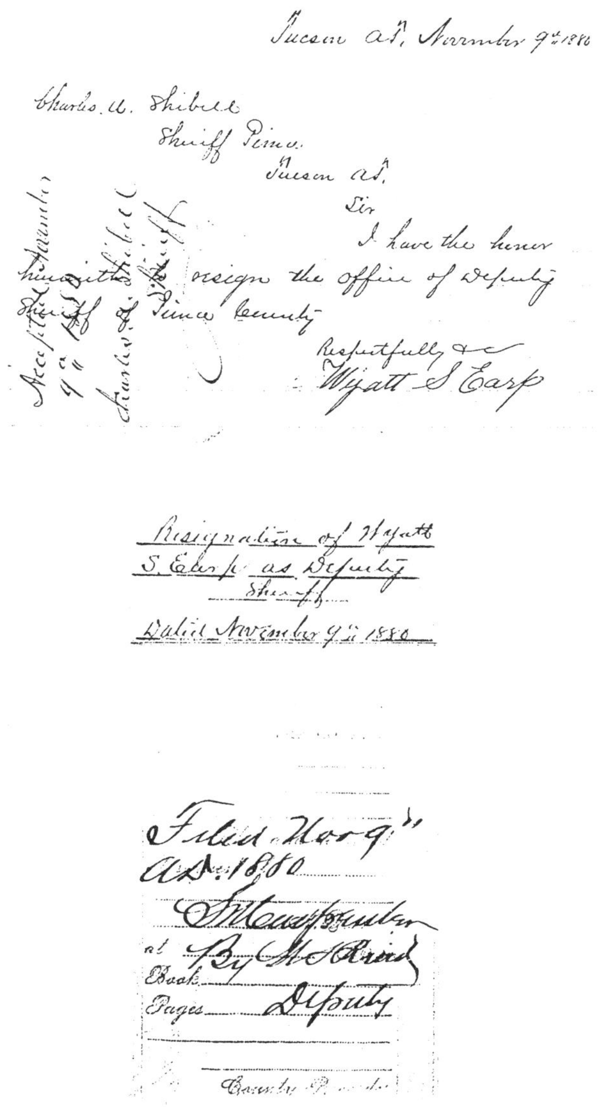

[Handwritten document]

BIBLIOGRAPHY

BOOKS

Adams, Ramon F. Six-guns and Saddle Leather, University of Oklahoma Press, 1954.

Ball, Larry D. The United States Marshals of New Mexico and Arizona Territories, 1846-1912, University of New Mexico Press, 1978.

Barns, Will C. Arizona Place Names, University of Arizona Press, Tucson, Arizona, 1960

Bartholomew, Ed. Wyatt Earp the Man and the Myth, The Frontier Book Company, Toyahvale, Texas, 1964

----, Wyatt Earp: The Untold Story, Frontier Book Company, Toyahvale, Texas, 1963.

Boyer, Glenn G., ed. I Married Wyatt Earp: The Recollections of Josephine Sarah Marcus Earp, University of Arizona, Press, Tucson, Arizona, 1976.

----, The Suppressed Murder of Wyatt Earp, The Naylor Company, San Antonio, Texas, 1967.

Breakenridge, William. Helldorado, Houghton Mifflin Company, Boston, Massachusetts, 1928.

Burns, Walter Noble. Tombstone: An Iliad of the Southwest, Doubleday, Page & Company, New York, New York, 1927.

Burroughs, Jack. The Gunfighter Who Never Was, University of Arizona Press, Tucson, Arizona, 1987.

Churchill, Richard E. Doc Holliday, Bat Masterson and Wyatt Earp. Their Colorado Careers, Timberline Books, Leadville, Colorado, 1974.

Clum, John P. It All Happened in Tombstone, The Northland Press, Flagstaff, Arizona, 1965.

Cox, William R. Luke Short and His Era, Doubleday & Company, New York, New York, 1948.

Calhoun, Frederick S. The Law Men, Smithsonian Institution Press, 1989.

Cunningham, Eugene. Triggernometry, Press of the Pioneers, New York, New York, 1989.

Dempsey, David and Baldwin, Raymond P. The Triumphs and Trials of Lotta Crabtree, William Morrow & Company, Inc., New York, New York, 1968.

DeMattos, Jack. The Earp Decision, Creative Publishing Company, College Station, Texas, 1989.

Drago, Harry Sinclair. Wild Wooly and Wicked, Clarkson N. Potter, New York, New York, 1960.

Flood, John Henry, Jr. Wyatt Earp, OK Bookshop, Taipei, Taiwan, 1980.

Ganzhorn, Jack. I've Killed Men, The Devin-Adair Company, New York, New York, 1959.

Glasscock, Carl Burgess. Lucky Baldwin, Bobs Merril, Indianapolis, Indiana, 1933.

Hallon, W. Eugene. Frontier Violence, Oxford University Press, 1974.

Hunter, J. Marvin, and Rose, Noah H.   The Album of Gunfighters, Bandera, Texas, 1951.

Hutchinson, W.H.   Oil, Land and Politics, University of Oklahoma Press, 1965.

Jahns, Pat.   The Frontier World of Doc Holliday, Hastings House, New York, New York, 1957.

Lake, Stuart N.   Wyatt Earp, Frontier Marshal, Houghton Mifflin Company, Boston, Massachusetts, 1931.

Lowther, Charles G.   Dodge City, Kansas, Dorrance & Company, Philadelphia, Pennsylvania, 1940.

Martin, Douglas D.   Tombstone's Epitaph, University of New Mexico, Albuquerque, New Mexico, 1951.

----, The Earps of Tombstone, The Tombstone Epitaph, Tombstone, Arizona, 1959.

Marks, Paula Mitchell.   And Die in the West, William Morrow and Company, Inc., New York, New York, 1989.

McAllister, R.W.   Lost Mines of California and the Southwest, Thomas Brothers, Los Angeles, California, 1953.

McCool, Grace.   Gunsmoke - The True Story of Old Tombstone, Treasure Chest Publications, Tucson, Arizona, 1954.

McCullough, Harrell.   Selden Lindsey, U.S. Deputy Marshal, Paragon Publishing, Oklahoma City, 1990.

Miller, Nyle H. and Snell, Joseph W.   Great Gunfighters of the Kansas Cowtowns, 1867-1886, University of Nebraska Press, 1963.

Miller, Nyle H.   Kansas in Newspapers, Kansas State Historical Society, Topeka, Kansas, 1963.

Miller, Rick.   Bounty Hunter, Creative Publishing Company, College Station, Texas, 1941.

Monaghan, Jay, The Great Rascal, Little, Brown and Company, Boston, Massachusetts, 1952.

Myers, John. Doc Holliday, Little, Brown and Company, Boston Massachusetts, 1955.

----. The Last Chance, E.P. Dutton Company, New York, 1950.

O'Connor, Richard.   Bat Masterson, Doubleday & Company, New York, 1957.

Parsons, Chuck.   Clay Allison, Portrait of a Shootist, Pioneer Book Publishers, Seagraves, Texas. 1983.

Parsons, George W. The Private Journal of George W. Parsons, Tombstone Epitaph, Tombstone, 1972.

Raine, William MacLeod. Famous Sheriffs and Western Outlaws, Doubleday, Droan and Company, Garden City, New York, 1929.

Richardson, James D.   Messages and Papers of the Presidents, Bureau of National Literature, 1897.

Rosa, Joseph G. They Called Him Wild Bill, University of Oklahoma Press, 1957.

Rosa, Joseph G. and Koop, Waldo E. Rowdy Joe Lowe, Gambler with a Gun, University of Oklahoma Press, 1989.

Samuels, Charles. The Magnificent Rube: The Life and Times of Tex Rickard, McGraw Hill, New York, New York, 1957.

Schillingberg, William B. Wyatt Earp and the "Buntline Special" Myth, Blaine Publishing Company, Tucson, Arizona, 1976.

Schmidt, Jo Ann, Fighting Editors, The Naylor Company, San Antonio, Texas.

Schoenberger, Dale T. The Gunfighters, The Caxton Printers, Caldwell, Idaho, 1971.

Shringo, Charles A. Riata and Spurs, Houghton Mifflin Company, Boston, Massachusetts, 1927.

----. A Texas Cowboy, M. Umbdenstock & Company, Chicago, Illinois, 1885.

Spring, Anges Wright. The Cheyenne and Black Hills Stage and Express Routes, Arthur H. Clark Company, Glendale, California, 1949.

Shirley, Glenn. Law West of Fort Smith, Henry Holt and Company, New York, New York, 1957.

Sonnichsen, C.L. Billy King's Tombstone, University of Arizona Press, Tucson, Arizona, 1972.

Streeter, Floyd B. Ben Thompson, Man With a Gun, Frederick Fell, New York, 1957.

Theobald, John and Lillian. Wells Fargo in Arizona Territory, Arizona Historical Foundation, 1978.

The Gunfighters, Time-Life Book, 1974.

Tilgham, Zoe A. Marshal of the Last Frontier, Arthur H. Clark Company, Glendale, California, 1949.

----. Sportlight: Bat Masterson and Wyatt Earp as U.S. Deputy Marshals, Naylor Company, San Antonio, Texas, 1960.

Turner, Alford E. The OK Corral Inquest, Creative Publishing Company, College Station, Texas, 1981.

----. The Earps Talk, Creative Publishing Company, College Station, Texas, 1980.

Under Cover For Wells Fargo, Houghton Mifflin Co., Boston, Massachusetts, 1969.

Vestal, Stanley. Dodge City, Queen of Cowtowns, Harper & Brothers, New York, New York, 1951.

Walton, William M. Life and Adventures of Ben Thompson, Frontier Press of Texas, Houston, Texas, 1954.

Waters, Frank. The Earp Brothers of Tombstone, Clarkson N. Potter, New York, New York, 1960.

Wright, Robert M. Dodge City, the Cowboy Capital, and the Great Southwest, Wichita Eagle Press, 1913.

BIBLIOGRAPHY

NEWSPAPER ARTICLES

Arizona Weekly Star, Tucson, Arizona

January 20, 1991   January 27, 1881

Dodge City Times, Dodge City, Kansas

December 8, 1877	June 9, 1877	June 6, 1877
July 7, 1877	July 21, 1877	September 21, 1878
July 27, 1878	January 25, 1878	October 5, 1878
October 12, 1878	January 4, 1879	

Ford County Globe, Dodge City, Kansas

September 24, 1878	January 28, 1878	January 14, 1879
October 8, 1878	October 29, 1878	September 9, 1879
February 15, 1881	January 7, 1879	September 16, 1878

Los Angeles Herald, Los Angeles, California

January 16, 1929

Sacramento Daily Record Union, Sacramento, California

March 21, 1882	March 22, 1882	March 23, 1882
March 24, 1882	March 27, 1882	May 17, 1882

San Francisco Call Bulletin, San Francisco, California

April 30, 1990

San Francisco Chronicle, San Francisco, California

March 22, 1882

San Francisco Examiner, San Francisco, California

August 2, 1896

St. Louis Daily Journal, St. Louis, Missouri

October 11, 1878

Tombstone Daily Nugget, Tombstone, Arizona

November 4, 1881	November 5, 1881	November 13, 1881
November 17, 1881	July 10, 1881	October 27, 1881
November 3, 1881	November 6, 1881	November 24, 1881

Tombstone Epitaph, Tombstone, Arizona

October 25, 1880	October 28, 1880	October 29, 1880
November 9, 1880	July 25, 1880	December 5, 1880
January 17, 1881	May 29, 1881	September 13, 1881
October 25, 1881	October 28, 1881	October 31, 1881
November 17, 1881	December 1, 1881	December 9, 1881
December 15, 1881	December 16, 1881	December 18, 1881
December 19, 1881	December 26, 1881	December 30, 1881
December 30, 1881	January 4, 1882	January 9, 1881
January 24, 1882	February 13, 1882	February 20, 1882
March 20, 1882	March 22, 1882	March 22, 1882
March 25, 1882	April 4, 1882	April 4, 1882
April 14, 1882		

Tombstone Weekly Nugget, Tombstone, Arizona

October 30, 1880	November 6, 1880	December 4, 1880

Tucson Star, Tucson, Arizona

December 28, 1880

Tucson Weekly Arizona Citizen, Tucson, Arizona

December 28, 1880	January 1, 1881	October 30, 1881
November 13, 1881	December 11, 1881	January 1, 1882
January 29, 1882	February 12, 1882	February 19, 1882
March 26, 1882	April 2, 1882	April 9, 1882
April 16, 1882	April 23, 1882	

Wichita Beacon, Wichita, Kansas

April 28, 1875	January 12, 1876	April 5, 1876
May 24, 1876		

Wichita Eagle, Wichita, Kansas

December 18, 1873	October 29, 1874

BIBLIOGRAPHY

ARTICLES

Bork, A. W. and Boyer, Glenn G. "The O.K. Corral Fight at Tombstone, a Footnote by Katie Elder," <u>Arizona and the West</u>, Vol 19, No 1.

Boyer, Glenn G. "Johnny Behan of Tombstone," <u>Frontier Times</u>, July 1976.

----. "Trailing an American Myth," <u>Real West</u>, April 1981.

----. "Johnny Behan, Assistant Folk Hero," <u>Real West</u>, April 1981.

----. "Those Marrying Earp Men," <u>True West</u>, April 1976.

----. "Morgan Earp, Brother in the Shadow," <u>Old West</u>, Winter 1983.

----. "Postscripts to Historical Fiction About Wyatt Earp in Tombstone," <u>Arizona and the West, Quarterly Journal of History</u>, Vol 18, No 1, 1976.

Walker, Henry P. "Arizona Land Fraud: Model 1880. The Tombstone Townsite Company," <u>Arizona and the West</u>, Vol 21, No 1, 1979.

Underhill, Lonnie E. "The Tombstone Directory," <u>Arizona and the West</u>, Vol 21, No 1, 1979.

Parker, Marjorie Clum, "John P. Clum," <u>The American West</u>, Vol 9, No 1, January 1972.

BIBLIOGRAPHY

OFFICIAL RECORDS

Proceedings of the Governing Body of Wichita, Kansas, Journal B.

Opinion of Judge C.G.W. French, January 20, 1881. Case No. 479, Pima County Clerk, Tucson, Arizona.

Opinion of the Supreme Court of the Territory of Arizona in Case of Clark v. Titus, 2 Arizona 147, 11 Pacific 313. (1886).

1880 Census for Pima County, Arizona Territory. Compiled, corrected and analyzed by Carl Chafin. Published by Cochise Classics, P.O. Box 8, Tombstone, Arizona 85638.

Minutes of Tombstone Common Council, September 9, 1880 to January 16, 1882. Compiled and edited by Carl Chafin. Published by Cochise Classics, P.O. Box 8, Tombstone, Arizona 85638.

The 1882 Arizona Territorial Census of Cochise County. Complied by Carl Chafin. Published by Cochise Classics, P.O. Box 8, Tombstone, Arizona 85638.

INDEX

ABOUT THE AUTHOR

RICHARD E. ERWIN spent more than forty-five years as a Criminal Defense Lawyer, defending thousands of criminal cases of every kind imaginable. He once took the case of a client, about to be sentenced to death in the gas chamber, to the California Supreme Court and not only saved his client's life, but succeeded in getting the California death penalty law as it then existed (1976), declared to be unconstitutional, thus saving the lives of more than sixty men then on death row.[1]

He retired from the law in 1984, and with the help of his wife, Lyla, a constant companion of more than fifty years, took up the task of ferreting out the true facts surrounding the life and times of Wyatt Earp and attempting to separate the facts from the myths.

He presents here solid evidence, based on old newspaper accounts, public records, documents buried in museums, state and national archives and libraries and reports of other researchers, to substantiate his view of what he believes to be the TRUTH ABOUT WYATT EARP.

---

[1] Rockwell v. Superior Court 18 Cal 3rd 420, 134 Cal.Rptr. 650

DATE DUE

GAYLORD M